W9-BMF-658

(continued on back)

ADULT PSYCHOPATHOLOGY
AND DIAGNOSIS

Adult Psychopathology and Diagnosis

Second Edition

Edited by

Michel Hersen
Samuel M. Turner

A WILEY-INTERSCIENCE PUBLICATION

JOHN WILEY & SONS, INC.

New York • Chichester • Brisbane • Toronto • Singapore

Library of Congress Cataloging-in-Publication Data

Adult psychopathology and diagnosis / edited by Michel Hersen, Samuel
    M. Turner. — 2nd ed.
        p.   cm. — (Wiley series on personality processes)
    "A Wiley-Interscience publication."
    Includes bibliographical references.
    Includes indexes.
    ISBN 0-471-62050-5 (cloth : alk. paper)
    1. Psychology, Pathological.   2. Mental illness—Diagnosis.
I. Hersen, Michel. II. Turner, Samuel M., 1944–   . III. Series.
    [DNLM: 1. Mental Disorders—diagnosis.   2. Mental Disorders—in
adulthood.   WM 141 A244]
    RC454.A324   1991
    616.89—dc20
    DNLM/DLC
    for Library of Congress   90-13025

Printed in the United States of America

91 92 10 9 8 7 6 5 4

Contributors

H. E. Barbaree, Ph.D., Professor of Psychology, Queens University, Kingston, Ontario

Deborah C. Beidel, Ph.D., Assistant Professor of Psychiatry, Western Psychiatric Institute and Clinic, University of Pittsburgh School of Medicine, Pittsburgh, Pennsylvania

Roger K. Blashfield, Ph.D., Professor of Psychiatry, University of Florida, Gainesville, Florida

D. P. Devanand, M.D., Assistant Professor of Clinical Psychiatry, New York State Psychiatric Institute and the College of Physicians and Surgeons, Columbia University, New York, New York

Harold M. Erickson, M.D., Director, Child and Adolescent Division, Department of Psychiatry, Kansas University Medical Center, Kansas City, Kansas

Gerald Goldstein, Ph.D., Director, Neuropsychology Research Program, Veterans Administration Medical Center, Pittsburgh, Pennsylvania

Donald W. Goodwin, M.D., Professor and Chairman, Department of Psychiatry, Kansas University Medical Center, Kansas City, Kansas

Kenneth Urial Gutsch, Ph.D., Professor of Counseling Psychology, University of Southern Mississippi, Hattiesburg, Mississippi

Constance L. Hammen, Ph.D., Professor of Psychology and Psychiatry, University of California, Los Angeles, California

Michel Hersen, Ph.D., Professor of Psychiatry and Psychology, Western Psychiatric Institute and Clinic, University of Pittsburgh School of Medicine, Pittsburgh, Pennsylvania

Bill N. Kinder, Ph.D., Professor of Psychology, University of South Florida, Tampa, Florida

Gloria I. Leo, M.A., Senior Research Assistant, Addiction Research Foundation, Toronto, Ontario, Canada

W. L. Marshall, Ph.D., Professor of Psychology, Queens University, Kingston, Ontario

Nathaniel McConaghy, M.D., Associate Professor of Psychiatry, University of New South Wales, Prince Henry Hospital, Little Bay, New South Wales

Jesse B. Milby, Ph.D., Chief, Psychology Service, Veterans Administration Medical Center, Birmingham, Alabama

Randall L. Morrison, Ph.D., Scientist, Department of Mental Health, American Medical Association, Chicago, Illinois

Sheldon H. Preskorn, M.D., Professor of Psychiatry, University of Kansas Medical Center, Wichita, Kansas

Harold A. Sackeim, Ph.D., Associate Professor of Clinical Psychology in Psychiatry, New York State Psychiatric Institute and the College of Physicians and Surgeons, Columbia University, New York, New York

Shawn Shea, M.D., Director of Continuous Treatment Team, Monadnock Family Services, Keene, New Hampshire

Robert E. Smith, M.D., Clinical Assistant Professor of Psychiatry, The University of Iowa College of Medicine, Des Moines, Iowa

Linda C. Sobell, Ph.D., Professor of Psychology, University of Toronto, Toronto, Ontario, Canada

Mark B. Sobell, Ph.D., Professor of Psychology, University of Toronto, Toronto, Ontario, Canada

Robert D. Stainback, Ph.D., Chief, Alcohol Dependency Treatment Program, Veterans Administration Medical Center, Birmingham, Alabama

Tony Toneatto, Ph.D., Psychologist, Addiction Research Foundation, Toronto, Ontario, Canada

Warren W. Tryon, Ph.D., Professor of Psychology, Fordham University, Bronx, New York

Samuel M. Turner, Ph.D., Professor of Psychiatry, Western Psychiatric Institute and Clinic, University of Pittsburgh School of Medicine, Pittsburgh, Pennsylvania

George Winokur, Ph.D., Professor and Head, Department of Psychiatry, The University of Iowa College of Medicine, Iowa City, Iowa

Series Preface

This series of books is addressed to behavioral scientists interested in the nature of human personality. Its scope should prove pertinent to personality theorists and researchers, as well as to clinicians concerned with applying an understanding of personality processes to the amelioration of emotional difficulties in living. To this end, the series provides a scholarly integration of theoretical formulations, empirical data, and practical recommendations.

Six major aspects of studying and learning about human personality can be designated: personality theory, personality structure and dynamics, personality development, personality assessment, personality change, and personality adjustment. In exploring these aspects of personality, the books in the series discuss a number of distinct but related subject areas: the nature and implications of various theories of personality; personality characteristics that account for consistencies and variations in human behavior; the emergence of personality processes in children and adolescents; the use of interviewing and testing procedures to evaluate individual differences in personality; efforts to modify personality styles through psychotherapy, counseling, behavior therapy, and other methods of influence; and patterns of abnormal personality functioning that impair individual competence.

IRVING B. WEINER

University of South Florida
Tampa, Florida

Preface

Since publication of the first edition of *Adult Psychopathology and Diagnosis* in 1984, DSM-III-R has appeared, DSM-IV is anticipated, data have been adduced in support of existing diagnostic categories, and new semistructured and structured interview schedules have been developed that enhance the reliability and validity of the diagnostic enterprise. Thus, it was clear to us that a revision was timely and warranted.

Like the first edition, the present textbook is designed to present discussion of the major diagnostic categories of adult psychiatric disorders using DSM nomenclature (now DSM-III-R). We believe it is imperative that graduate students and professionals in psychology and other mental health disciplines familiarize themselves with the DSM-III-R diagnostic system. Arranging the chapters in Part Two according to major recognized syndromes allows the student to integrate study of DSM-III-R criteria with those empirical data of a specific clinical syndrome. Each chapter is designed to present the clinical picture for the disorder, crucial diagnostic criteria, major theories of etiology, and techniques of assessing and measuring behavior comprising the syndrome. Treatment is discussed only insofar as it contributes to understanding the psychopathology of a specific condition.

In this second edition, we have included 17 chapters, of which 10 are totally new and 7 are considerably revised to reflect the developments in the field. Part One (Overview) has chapters entitled "Models of Psychiatric Classification" and "Practical Use of DSM-III-R." Part Two (Specific Disorders) represents the bulk of the book and is concerned with detailed discussions of specific syndromes. In Part Three (Special Topics), chapters are entitled "Motor Activity and DSM-III-R," "DSM-III-R and Psychotherapy," "DSM-III, DSM-III-R, and Behavior Therapy," and "DSM-III-R and Pharmacotherapy." The objective in Part Three is to better understand not only the relationship of diagnosis to treatment, but the influence that DSM-III-R has had on the three most prominent schools of therapeutic intervention.

Many individuals have kindly contributed their time and effort to the development of this multiauthored textbook. First, and foremost, we thank our authors for articulating their thoughts about the diagnostic process. Second, we appreciate the technical assistance provided by Mary Newell, Mary

Anne Frederick, and Sandra Gray. Finally, we are most grateful to Herb Reich, our editor at John Wiley & Sons, for his consistent encouragement and support over the years we have known him.

MICHEL HERSEN
SAMUEL M. TURNER

Pittsburgh, Pennsylvania
April 1991

Contents

ADULT PSYCHOPATHOLOGY
AND DIAGNOSIS

PART ONE
Overview

CHAPTER 1

Models of Psychiatric Classification

ROGER K. BLASHFIELD

> Finally, I just let it all out. I said, "I am the Messiah. I need to deal with why people are starving." I began speaking of the second coming of Christ, and I was in the hospital that afternoon. The diagnosis was schizophrenia, thought-voices.
>
> They began to talk to me as if I were a child. They took my clothes and I had to put everything into a locked box. From my huge position of the Messiah, I was degraded to being less than a person.
>
> The medicine cut off the voices immediately. I was impressed. But I was still the Messiah. I've had too many profound experiences to not believe I am the Messiah.
>
> The voices are gone. I have a good job now. But if they say it is bad to think you are the Messiah then they haven't cured me. I can't lose God's message that I am on the right path.
>
> *(Shavelson, 1986, p. 34)*

INTRODUCTION

Mental disorders have long been recognized as part of the human condition. Psalm 102, for instance, contains an excellent first-person presentation of being depressed. The Greeks who wrote in the Hippocratic tradition discussed five forms of mental disorder that are still recognized today: epilepsy, hysteria, melancholia, mania, and paranoia. Despite this long-term awareness of mental disorders, relatively little is known about psychopathology. Knowledge in the neurosciences and in genetics has been growing rapidly, helping us to understand more, but we do not understand why some people develop certain psychopathologies. Even though we now have more effective treatment modalities at our disposal, many of those treatments were discovered serendipitously. Psychopathology is still struggling to develop as a science.

Fundamental to any science is the classification system, which contains the basic concepts from which theories in the science develop as well as the terms used in the language of that science. The classification of psychopathology has undergone a major resurgence in the last 20 years (Millon & Klerman, 1986). Much of this revival in interest has been associated with the powerful effect on both the clinical and the scientific approaches to psychopathology of the American Psychiatric Association's (APA's) *Diagnostic and Statistical Manual of Mental Disorders,* third edition (DSM-III; 1980).

This chapter contains two sections. The first provides a brief history of psychiatric classification. The second discusses the implicit model of classification associated with DSM-III, as well as other models (prototype, categorical, and dimensional) that can be used to form classificatory systems.

SECTION I: BRIEF HISTORY OF PSYCHIATRIC CLASSIFICATION

Early Twentieth Century Approaches to Classification

Emil Kraepelin is the person whose name is usually associated with descriptive psychopathology and classification (Berrios & Hauser, 1988). Kraepelin was a German psychiatrist who was born in 1856, the same year as another famous middle-European psychiatrist, Sigmund Freud. Kraepelin was the product of two disparate forces (Berrios & Hauser, 1988; Kahn, 1959). First, German medicine at the time was growing rapidly as a science, and many important technological advances regarding bacteriology occurred in nineteenth-century Germany. As scientific medicine flourished, the German approach to neurology and psychiatry was to interpret all mental disorders as diseases of the brain (Menninger, 1963). Thus, the dominant view of German medicine was that psychiatry eventually would be reduced to neurology. German psychiatrists were devoted to effecting this reduction. Kraepelin, like his contemporaries, believed that mental disorders ultimately would be explained in terms of brain pathology.

Second, Kraepelin was behavioral in his approach to understanding mental disorders. At the end of his medical training, Kraepelin had spent a year working in the laboratory of a famous German psychologist, Wilhelm Wundt (Kahn, 1959). After leaving medical school, Kraepelin's early research involved applying Wundt's behavioral methods to experimental studies of persons with mental disorders. Thus, Kraepelin adopted a descriptive, behavioral approach to understanding mental disorders. Because he believed that mental disorders reflected some underlying neuropathology, he extended his behavioral analysis to a longitudinal analysis of patients' symptoms. Kraepelin assumed that syndromes (i.e., clusters of co-occurring behaviors) with a common course were most likely associated with a common underlying etiology.

In addition to performing research and clinical work, Kraepelin authored a textbook on psychiatry (Blashfield, 1984). Perhaps in part because of his carefully behavioral descriptions of patients, the various editions of his textbook gained popularity in Germany. Like most textbook authors, Kraepelin organized his book into chapters, each discussing a particular mental disorder. What are now known as Kraepelin's classifications are simply the tables of contents to the various editions of his textbooks (Menninger, 1963). As Kraepelin gathered clinical data, particularly on the courses of various syndromes, he changed the concepts that he used as chapter headings.

In the sixth edition of his textbook (Kraepelin, 1899), two chapters became the foci of an international controversy. One chapter was on *dementia praecox* (now called schizophrenia), and the other concerned *manic–depressive insanity*. Dementia praecox was controversial because Kraepelin combined two other popular concepts of the time, hebephrenia and catatonia, as subtypes of dementia praecox (Mickle, 1909). Kraepelin's discussion of dementia praecox also had a number of parallels to another well-known disorder of the time, *dementia paralytica* (now called paresis or tertiary syphilis of the central nervous system). Manic–depressive insanity was controversial because Kraepelin was combining two concepts, mania and melancholia, that had been separately recognized for over 2,000 years since the medical writings of the Greeks (Drapes, 1909).

Due to Kraepelin's stature in Germany and the ensuing international controversy over the concepts of dementia praecox and manic–depressive insanity, Kraepelin's chapter headings became the basis of the first official classification adopted by the American Psychiatric Association in 1917 (Menninger, 1963). This classification was revised in 1932 (APA, 1933). However, psychiatry in the United States, unlike in Europe, was dominated by the psychoanalytic revolution. Many psychoanalysts eschewed classification as a superficial analysis of symptoms rather than as providing an understanding of the psychodynamic bases of the symptoms. Thus, psychiatric classification was largely an ignored topic during the first part of the twentieth century in the United States.

As a result, at the end of World War II, various competing classification systems were in use in the United States. American psychiatrists were embarrassed by this "Tower of Babel" situation and decided to form one consensual system that all American psychiatrists would use. A committee was formed to create a classification system that the members of the committee felt would be acceptable to most psychiatrists. A draft of the classification was sent to 150 American psychiatrists for feedback. The resulting system, published by APA in 1952, was called the *Diagnostic and Statistical Manual of Mental Disorders*. This system is now known by the abbreviation DSM-I, since this system became the first edition of a series of psychiatric classifications.

DSM-I contained 108 different categories organized under eight major headings. The various disorders in this classification were defined by short, prose definitions, similar to dictionary definitions of concepts.

The World Health Organization (WHO) was impressed by DSM-I. During the late 1950s and early 1960s, this organization used a comparable strategy to generate an international psychiatric classification that was acceptable to psychiatrists around the world. This classification was part of the *International Classification of Diseases,* eighth edition (ICD-8) (WHO, 1969). Because American psychiatry had agreed to revise its DSM to match the new international classification, DSM-II (APA, 1968) was published. DSM-II contained 185 categories that were virtually the same as categories in ICD-8; however, DSM-II retained the same style of prose definitions used in DSM-I. In contrast to DSM-II, ICD-8 was only a "nomenclature"; that is, ICD-8 simply listed the diagnostic categories, without definitions.

The Neo-Kraepelinians

By the 1950s, American psychiatry was controlled by the psychoanalytic perspective. In the decade following World War II, New York City was the ideological "Mecca" of American psychiatry, with its numerous psychoanalytic institutes and growing population of psychoanalytic and insight-oriented psychiatrists. The first major assault on the psychoanalytic perspective was associated with the mental health movement in the early 1960s and the federally funded growth of community mental health centers. The mental health movement was critical of the de facto emphasis by psychoanalysts on treating only the rich who could afford labor-intensive therapy and by the exclusivity of the psychoanalytic institutes that admitted only psychiatrists for training. The community mental health movement developed from a politically liberal, humanistic ethic that disparaged the boundaries between the different mental health professionals.

The second assault on the psychoanalytic perspective was associated with the neo-Kraepelinians (Klerman, 1978). The originators of this perspective were psychiatric researchers at Washington University in St. Louis, who believed that psychiatry, with its psychoanalytic emphasis, had drifted too far from its roots in medicine. The neo-Kraepelinians emphasized that psychiatry should be concerned with medical diseases, that extensive research was needed on the biological bases of psychopathology, and that much more emphasis needed to be placed upon classification if knowledge about psychopathology was to grow. Klerman (1978, p. 104) summarized the tenets of the neo-Kraepelinian approach to psychiatry:

1. Psychiatry is a branch of medicine.
2. Psychiatry should utilize modern scientific methodologies and base its practice on scientific knowledge.
3. Psychiatry treats people who are sick and who require treatment.
4. There is a boundary between the normal and the sick.
5. There are discrete mental illnesses. Mental illnesses are not myths. There is not one, but many mental illnesses. It is the task of scientific psychiatry, as of other medical specialties, to investigate the causes, diagnosis, and treatment of these mental illnesses.
6. The focus of psychiatric physicians should be particularly on the biological aspects of mental illness.
7. There should be an explicit and intentional concern with diagnosis and classification.
8. Diagnostic criteria should be codified, and a legitimate and valued area of research should be to validate such criteria by various techniques. Further, departments of psychiatry in medical schools should teach these criteria and not depreciate them, as has been the case for many years.
9. In research efforts directed at improving the reliability and validity of diagnosis and classification, statistical techniques should be utilized.

In 1972, a group of the psychiatric researchers at Washington University published a paper entitled, "Diagnostic Criteria for Use in Psychiatric Research" (Feighner et al., 1972). This paper listed 15 mental disorders that the researchers believed had sufficient empirical evidence to establish validity and listed a set of diagnostic criteria for defining these disorders. The authors argued that a major problem in research about these disorders had been the lack of uniform definitions by different researchers, and they suggested that future research on any of these disorders utilize the diagnostic criteria proposed in their paper.

Feighner et al.'s paper had a dramatic impact on American psychiatry (Blashfield, 1982). It was probably the most frequently referenced journal article in psychiatry during the 1970s. The diagnostic criteria were immediately adopted and became a standard for much of the psychiatric research of the decade. Moreover, the criteria were expanded into a broader set of categories, focusing primarily on the schizophrenic and affective disorders (Spitzer, Endicott, & Robins, 1975). This new classification was called the Research Diagnostic Criteria (RDC) and had an associated structured interview known as the Schedule For Affective Disorders And Schizophrenia (SADS). Because the lead author of the RDC, Robert Spitzer, had been appointed as the chairperson responsible for organizing DSM-III, the RDC became the foundation from which DSM-III was developed.

DSM-III was a revolutionary classification. First, unlike DSM-I and DSM-II, in which clinical consensus was the major organizing principle, DSM-III attempted to be a classification based on scientific evidence. For instance, the classification of depression in DSM-III was much different from that in DSM-I and DSM-II, largely because of family history data gathered in research studies performed by the neo-Kraepelinians. Second, DSM-III discontinued the use of prose definitions of the mental disorders. The neo-Kraepelinians were impressed by the research data suggesting that the reliability of psychiatric classification, as represented in DSM-I and DSM-II, was less than optimal (Spitzer & Fleiss, 1974). To try to improve diagnostic reliability, the writers of DSM-III defined virtually all mental disorders by using diagnostic criteria, the innovation stimulated by Feighner et al.'s (1972) paper. Third, DSM-III was a multiaxial classification. Because DSM-I and DSM-II were "committee products," the subsections had different implicit organizing principles. For instance, in DSM-I and DSM-II, the organic brain syndromes were organized by etiology, the psychotic disorders were organized by syndromes, and the neurotic disorders were organized according to ideas from psychoanalytic theory. To avoid the confusion inherent in the use of multiple organizing principles, the writers of DSM-III adopted a multiaxial system that permitted the separate description of the patient's psychopathology by syndrome (Axis I), personality style (Axis II), medical etiology (Axis III), environmental factors (Axis IV), and role disturbances (Axis V).

DSM-III, which was published in 1980, contained 265 mental disorders. The DSM-III contained 482 pages, a huge increase over the 92 pages of DSM-II. In 1987, APA published a revision of DSM-III (DSM-III-R), primarily to update the diagnostic criteria used for defining mental disorders.

The number of mental disorders in DSM-III-R increased from 265 to 292. Even though new disorders were added in DSM-III-R (primarily the sleep disorders), the major changes from DSM-III to DSM-III-R were the diagnostic criteria, which were altered per category as a function of descriptive research on the initial criteria.

As this chapter was being written, DSM-IV was also being developed. Because of the dramatic changes in classification during the 1980s with DSM-III and DSM-III-R, the developers of DSM-IV are trying to keep this new classification as much like DSM-III-R as possible, except where the data suggesting change are overwhelmingly clear (Frances, Widiger, & Pincus, 1989). Moreover, the chairperson of the DSM-IV committee, Allen Frances, is actively working with the international group of psychiatrists who are creating ICD-10 to make these two classifications as compatible as possible.

SECTION II: ALTERNATIVE MODELS OF CLASSIFICATION

Neo-Kraepelinian Approach to Classification

Klerman (1978) outlined the approach to classification that the neo-Kraepelinians have favored:

1. Diagnostic categories = medical diseases.
2. Each diagnosis is a discrete entity.
3. Operational criteria are used to define a category.
4. Structured interviews are used to gather the symptom information.
5. Diagnostic algorithms specify objective rules for combining symptoms to reach a diagnosis.
6. Good reliability is necessary before any type of validity can be established.
7. Good internal validity will show that the category refers clearly described patterns of symptoms.
8. Good external validity will mean that the diagnosis can be used to predict prognosis, course, and treatment response.

The fundamental tenet of the neo-Kraepelinian approach to classification is that diagnostic categories refer to specific medical diseases. Most researchers concerned with psychopathology recognize that the claim that diagnostic categories refer to medical diseases is an assumption rather than an established fact (Wing, 1978). Like Kraepelin, the neo-Kraepelinians have been interested in elucidating what the underlying disease processes are for the various mental disorders.

Second, the neo-Kraepelinians believe that the diagnostic categories in a psychiatric classification refer to discrete entities. Each disorder should have a describable etiology, course, and pattern of occurrence. The assertion that diagnostic categories are discrete entities does not mean, however, that a patient can be diagnosed as having one and only one disorder. Since diseases can co-occur in the same host organism, data showing diagnostic overlap are interpreted as reflecting comorbidity.

Third, the neo-Kraepelinians have strongly favored improving the objectivity in psychiatric diagnosis. Toward this ends, they advocate the use of explicit diagnostic criteria (i.e., operational definitions), specified diagnostic algorithms, and systematic, structured interviews to gather symptom information. By improving the objectivity in making diagnoses, the reliability among clinicians in the diagnostic process should increase. Reliability has been asserted to provide an upper limit on the validity that a classification can obtain; thus, improving the reliability of a classification will help improve both the internal (descriptive) and external (predictive) validity of the classification.

DSM-III and DSM-III-R, in many ways, attempted to satisfy the neo-Kraepelinian tenets of classification. The emphasis on diagnostic criteria in DSM-III and DSM-III-R provides an approximation to the operational definitions that the neo-Kraepelinians advocate. Moreover, the "Chinese menu" decision rules associated with the diagnostic criteria (i.e., two symptoms are needed from Group A, three from Group B, etc.) are the diagnostic algorithms. Also associated with DSM-III and DSM-III-R are a number of structured interviews (McReynolds, 1989) that have been created for assessing whether given diagnostic criteria are present in a patient. Generally, the results with DSM-III and DSM-III-R have suggested that the reliability of psychiatric diagnosis, especially when structured interviews are used, is much better than existed with DSM-I and DSM-II systems (Matarazzo, 1983).

The only significant way in which DSM-III and DSM-III-R do not satisfy the neo-Kraepelinian tenets concerns the postulate that all diagnostic categories refer to medical diseases. The authors of DSM-III and DSM-III-R were explicit that they were not adopting a specific theoretical perspective regarding the etiological bases of the mental disorders (see Bayer & Spitzer, 1985). They believed that (a) there is insufficient evidence to support any one theoretical perspective about all mental disorders, and (b) advocacy of an inadequately supported theoretical perspective could alienate clinicians who believe in other approaches to understanding psychopathology.

Prototype Model of Psychiatric Classification

An alternative approach to psychiatric classification that has become popular in the 1980s has been associated with the title "prototype model." A number of commentators (Cantor, Smith, French, & Mezzich, 1980; Clarkin, Widiger, Frances, Hurst, & Gilmore, 1983; Horowitz, Post, French, Wallis, & Siegelman, 1981; Livesley, 1985a, 1985b) have suggested that this model is superior to the standard model of psychiatric classification.

For those readers who are unfamiliar with the prototype model, the easiest way of thinking about this model is in terms of an example. According to the prototype model, if a mother wanted to teach her 2-year-old son what a bird is, she would *not* say something like, "Now, Brice, a bird is a little animal that lives outdoors; it has feathers, it eats bugs, and it lives in nests where it lays its eggs." The child would not understand such a complex, abstract definition of bird. Instead, the mother would teach Brice what a bird is by pointing at a robin in a tree and saying the word, "bird." Later, the mother might point out a sparrow to Brice and say, "bird." In effect, a child learns a concept by being presented with instances of the concept. Once the child is able to associate the instances with a verbal label (i.e., the noun "bird"), then the child has grasped the concept. Later, the child learns to abstract the essential features of the classificatory concept by making observations of the similarities among the instances of the concept (such as that birds have feathers, lay eggs, have wings, can fly, etc.).

Another important idea underlying the prototype model is that not all instances of a concept are equally good representatives of the concept. A robin, for instance, is a good exemplar of a bird. A penguin is not. Robins are about the same size as most birds, they have feathers, they can fly, and so forth. Penguins, on the other hand, are larger than most birds and cannot fly. Although they have feathers, to a child, their covering probably seems more like fur than feathers. Stated in other terms, a robin is a good prototype of the concept of bird, whereas a penguin is a poor prototype.

Advocates of the prototype model argue that this model is radically different from the neo-Kraepelinian model of psychiatric classification. In the neo-Kraepelinian model, classificatory concepts are defined by listing the features that are sufficient for making a diagnosis. If a given instance has a sufficient number of these features, then that instance is a member of the classificatory concept. Moreover, all members of a concept are equal: A square is a square; one square is not "squarer" than another square.

The prototype model was developed by Rosch and her colleagues in cognitive psychology (Rosch, 1973, 1978; Rosch & Mervis, 1975). The first direct application of the model to psychiatric classification was in a paper published by Cantor et al. (1980), who contrasted the prototype model to what they described as the "classical" (i.e., neo-Kraepelinian) model of psychiatric classification. The neo-Kraepelinian classical model, according to Cantor et al., emphasized two attributes of a classificatory system: *homogeneity* and *reliability*. Concerning homogeneity, the classical model attempts to minimize the variability among patients with the same diagnosis. Moreover, the neo-Kraepelinian model assumes that clear boundaries can be established between instances of different classificatory concept (i.e., diagnostic categories are "discrete entities"). A closed geometric figure is either a square or a triangle. There are no borderline "tri-squares." According to Cantor's view of the neo-Kraepelinian model, the goal of complete homogeneity will be accomplished when the necessary and sufficient features of a diagnostic concept are identified.

Concerning reliability, the neo-Kraepelinian model suggests that any interclinician disagreement is undesirable. Because a given instance either is or is not a member of concept, less than perfect reliability suggests that there is error in the judgment of the diagnosticians. Because good reliability is a necessary precondition for developing a valid classificatory system (Spitzer & Fleiss, 1974), reducing interclinician disagreement and establishing complete homogeneity have been the major goals of the neo-Kraepelinian model.

Cantor et al. (1980) argued that the prototype model, in contrast to the neo-Kraepelinian model, does not assume that certain features are necessary and sufficient for membership to a diagnostic category. Instead, the prototype model assumes only that there are features that are correlated with category membership. The more of these features a patient has, the more typical the patient is of the category. Stated differently, a good exemplar of a category is an instance that contains most or all of the features of a category. For example, a robin is a good exemplar of a bird because a robin has all of the features commonly associated with the concept of bird—that is, it has wings and feathers, can fly, eats bugs, and so on—whereas a penguin does not. Nevertheless, penguins, as well as albatrosses, ostriches, hummingbirds, and chickens, are all legitimate members of the category of birds. Variability among features is standard among natural categories. Moreover, imperfect reliability is normative according to the prototype model. Chickens, for instance, are birds, but they do not fly and are often associated with farm animals. Even young children will quickly agree that a robin is a bird; however, children are less likely to agree among themselves that chickens are birds. Thus, reliability varies directly with prototypicality of the instances of the concept.

The basic tenets of the prototype model are as follows:

1. Nominalism; that is, diagnostic categories = concepts that mental health professionals use.
2. Categories are not discrete.
3. There is a graded membership among different instances of a concept.
4. Categories are defined by exemplars.
5. Features (symptoms) are neither necessary nor sufficient to determine membership.
6. Membership in a category is correlated with the number of features (symptoms) that a patient has.

First, unlike the neo-Kraepelinian perspective, the prototype model offers no metaphysical speculations regarding the nature of psychopathology or the referents of diagnostic categories. Restated, the prototype model can be applied to concepts that are associated with things in the real world (e.g., birds), but it also can be applied to concepts that have no existential status (e.g., angels, unicorns).

Second, the prototype model, unlike the neo-Kraepelinian model, does not assume that categories are discrete. Categories can blur together. Birds and Arctic animals are viable categories according to the prototype model. The fact that penguins are legitimate members of both categories is perfectly reasonable from the perspective of the prototype model.

Third, the prototype model emphasizes that not all members of a category are equally good representatives of the concept. Some members of a concept are more prototypical of the concept than are others. This view differs from the neo-Kraepelinian perspective, which implicitly assumes, for instance, that, since two schizophrenic patients have the same disease, they should receive the same treatment (Livesley, 1985a; cf. Spitzer & Williams, 1987).

Fourth, the prototype model suggests that definition by example is the standard way in which concepts are learned, rather than definition by lists of features. The emphasis on definition by example suggests that a fruitful use of the prototype model would be to identify case histories that are clear prototypes for different mental disorders and to use these cases when teaching students about the disorders.

In addition to suggesting that categories are learned through definition by example, the prototype model questions that the best definition lists a set of necessary and sufficient features. Instead, the prototype model suggests that the degree of membership to a category is correlated with the number of features that a member has. Thus, a set of defining features is neither necessary nor sufficient.

A digression is relevant here. Some authors have equated the prototype model with polythetic definitions of categories (Clarkin et al., 1983; Widiger & Frances, 1985). Since the Chinese menu form of definition in DSM-III-R is a polythetic definition, these authors have argued that the DSM-III-R system utilizes the prototype model of classification. To understand this argument, the concepts of *monothetic* and *polythetic* definitions must be explained. A monothetic definition has the form:

$$a * b * c,$$

where a, b, and c are the defining features of a concept and * refers to the conjunction "and." In a monothetic definition, all defining features associated with a concept must be present if the entity is to be a member of that concept. More simply stated, if symptoms a, b, and c are the defining symptoms for a mental disorder, all three must be present for the diagnosis to be made.

In contrast, a polythetic definition has the form:

$$(a * b) \lor (a * c) \lor (b * c) \lor (a * b * c),$$

where a, b, c, and * are as defined above and v refers to the disjunction "or." Notice that the polythetic definition shown above is equivalent to listing three defining symptoms for a disorder and requiring at least two of these symptoms for the diagnosis to be made. Since most DSM-III-R definitions of diagnostic categories list sets of defining symptoms, of which some subset must be present to make the diagnosis, DSM-III-R uses polythetic definitions. In a polythetic definition, no one feature is necessary; however, subsets of the features are sufficient for making a diagnosis.

The reason that the prototype model has been equated to polythetic definitions is that both allow variability among features within a category. Notice, however, that the view of category definition by the prototype model is quite different from that inherent in polythetic definitions. First, the prototype model focuses on definition by example (e.g., comparing a manipulative, suicidal patient to a prototypical "borderline personality disorder" patient, such as the Glenn Close character in *Fatal Attraction* [Jaffee, Lansing, & Lyne, 1988]. In contrast, a polythetic definition is a definition by features (such as a list of defining symptoms for a borderline personality disorder is given, rather like Brice's being told that birds have wings, can fly, etc.). Moreover, the prototype model asserts that the level of membership in a category is correlated with the number of features. Thus, features are neither necessary *nor* sufficient since membership is not an absolute. The polythetic definition, in contrast, does require that subsets of the defining features for a concept are sufficient.

From the neo-Kraepelinian perspective, research based on the prototype model has limited value. In particular, researchers from the neo-Kraepelinian perspective believe that changes in psychiatric classification should be dictated by evidence from biological research on patients. In contrast, research using the prototype model involves the use of clinicians as subjects. To the neo-Kraepelinians, studying clinicians is simply studying the biases, stereotypes, and illusory correlations of ordinary clinicians (Chapman & Chapman, 1969; Hamilton, 1981). Only the empirical analyses of patients have the potential to lead to improvements in classification from the neo-Kraepelinian perspective.

In contrast, advocates of the prototype model suggest that research on clinicians does have a number of potential uses. First, although a range of purposes might be met by a classification of psychopathology, most taxonomists have agreed that providing a basis for communication among mental health professionals is the fundamental purpose of a psychiatric classification (Blashfield & Draguns, 1976; Deutsch, 1966). Research using the prototype model allows an assessment of how well a psychiatric classification serves as a basis of communication. For example, Livesley (1986) and Blashfield and Haymaker (1988) performed prototype studies on the meanings that American clinicians associate with the DSM-III and DSM-III-R diagnostic criteria for the personality disorders. Their results suggested that a number of diagnostic criteria have meanings that can be confused across categories of personality disorders. In descriptive studies of patients with personality disorders, researchers using structured interviews have noted a high level of diagnostic overlap among the various personality disorders (Morey, 1988; Pfohl, Coryell, Zimmerman, & Stangl, 1986). To some, this high overlap suggests comorbidity among these personality disorders. However, the results from Livesley's and Blashfield and Haymaker's prototype studies suggest that the high level of diagnostic overlap instead is likely to be caused by the blurred meanings among these disorders.

A second reason for studying clinicians is that, because clinicians are the intended audience of the DSM classifications, diagnostic categories must be acceptable to the clinicians who use them. Gathering information about what clinicians mean by the different diagnostic categories is important. Moreover, the concern about biases, illusory correlations, and stereotypes implies that researchers have "objective" data about patients, whereas clinicians use "subjective" data. This distinction between objective research data and subjective clinical data is not very persuasive in the mental health field, in which assessment is still a complex topic and most assessments, clinical or research, are based on the self-report statements by patients (Faust & Miner, 1987).

In short, the major difference between the neo-Kraepelinian perspective of classification and the prototype model is that the neo-Kraepelinian perspective is exclusively concerned with what Hempel called *validity analysis,* whereas the prototype model emphasizes *meaning analysis* (Hempel, 1965;

Schwartz & Wiggins, 1986). In meaning analysis, the researcher's goal is to understand the concepts that are used in a science so that these concepts can be made more precise and so that the relationships among concepts can be more clearly enunciated by the scientists in the field. In validity analysis, the concepts are embedded in scientific theories (or, at least, hypotheses) that can be subjected to empirical tests to determine whether the theories are correct or incorrect. Hempel (1965) argued that both types of analysis were important when developing useful classifications within a science.

Structural Models of Psychiatric Classification

Two other models of psychiatric classification should be mentioned because they are repeatedly discussed in the literature. These two models are the *categorical* and the *dimensional* models (Kendell, 1975). Typically, these two models are discussed as if they are competing and inconsistent. The categorical and dimensional models are called "structural" models because both are atheoretical and are primarily measurement models rather than models that comment on the existential status or the reliability–validity of concepts.

Categorical Model

The categorical model is usually assumed to be the structural model of psychiatric classification. The tenets of this model are as follows:

1. The basic objects of a psychiatric classification are patients.
2. Categories should be discrete, in the sense that the conditions for membership should be able to be clearly ascertained.
3. Patients either belong or do not belong to specified classes (categories).
4. The members of a category should be relatively homogeneous.
5. Categories may or may not overlap.
6. In the borderline areas where categories may overlap, the number of patients should be relatively small.
7. Cluster analytic methods can be used to initially identify categories. Discriminant analysis is used to validate categories.

In the categorical model, the unit of analysis is the patient (cf. Spitzer & Williams, 1987). Categories refer to classes of patients, and patients either are or are not members of the categories. The categorical model assumes that some type of definitional rule exists by which the membership in a category can be determined. Moreover, membership in a category is considered to be a discrete, all-or-nothing event. An animal is either a cat or not a cat. A patient is either a schizophrenic or not a schizophrenic.

An important assumption to the categorical model is that members of a category are relatively homogeneous. All animals that belong to the class of house cats should be reasonably similar morphologically. This is not to say that all house cats must be alike. Certainly, a Siamese cat and an Argyle cat have a number of obvious differences, yet they are more like each other than either is like a lynx, for instance. In the same way, two schizophrenic patients should be relatively similar. Both may have different symptom "pictures," but those pictures should be more similar to each other than either is to an antisocial patient, for instance (Sneath & Sokol, 1973).

Classes in a categorical model may or may not overlap. Most uses of the categorical model typically assume that nonoverlapping categories are an ideal, but rarely realized condition. Thus, overlap among categories is often treated like measurement error might be treated in the dimensional model— a condition to be tolerated, but minimized. It should be noted, however, that specific categorical models have been developed in which the categories are assumed to overlap (Hartigan, 1975; Jardine & Sibson, 1971). In these models, overlap is not similar to error.

Because of the assumption of relative homogeneity, the number of patients who clearly belong to one and only one category should be relatively frequent, whereas patients who fall in the overlapping, "borderline" areas between categories should be relatively infrequent. If no "points of rarity" occur, then the categories will lack the relative homogeneity postulated in Tenet 4 (Friedman & Rubin, 1967; Grinker & Werble, 1967).

Finally, the methods that have been developed to find categories are called "cluster analytic methods" (Everitt, 1980). Generally, these methods analyze a large matrix of descriptive data on patients, and attempt to form "clusters" (categories) of relatively homogeneous patients in terms of the descriptive variables that were gathered on the patients. A large number of cluster analytic methods exist, and these methods can often generate different solutions for the same data. The development and refinement of useful cluster analytic methods remains an area of active research.

Dimensional Model

The second structural model is the dimensional model. The tenets for this model are as follows:

1. The basic unit of the dimensional model is a descriptive variable (e.g., a symptom, a scale from a self-report test, a laboratory value).
2. Dimensions refer to higher-order, abstract variables.
3. A dimension refers to a set of correlated descriptive variables.
4. There are a relatively small number of dimensions compared with the number of descriptive variables, yet the dimensions account for almost as much reliable variance as do the larger number of descriptive variables.
5. Dimensions themselves may be correlated or independent.
6. The methods used to identify dimensions are exploratory factor analysis and multidimensional scaling. Confirmatory factor analysis can be used to test a specific dimensional model.

For the dimensional model, the basic units of analysis are the descriptive variables. Thus, the dimensional model focuses on symptoms, behaviors, diagnostic criteria, scales from self-report tests, and the like. The dimensional model summarizes these descriptive variables by forming higher-order, abstract variables that can serve to represent the original measurement variables. Each of these higher-order, abstract variables is a dimension since these variables are usually conceptualized as continua. Patients can have scores anywhere along these dimensions.

An important tenet of the dimensional model is that the dimensions refer to sets of correlated variables (Eysenck, 1953). Suppose, for instance, that guardedness, a preoccupation with envy, a concern with the motivations of others, and pathological jealousy all tend to occur in the same patients. They are described as being correlated: When one is present, most, if not all, of the others are present. A dimension called "suspiciousness" (Clark, 1989) might be formed that serves to represent this correlation of highly intercorrelated symptoms.

A major test of a dimensional model is parsimony. The specific dimensions in such a system should account for most of the systematic, reliable variance that exists among the original set of descriptive variables. If they do not, then using the dimensions will sacrifice a great deal of information and the original variables should be used rather than the smaller set of dimensions.

Rather like categories can be overlapping or nonoverlapping, dimensions can be correlated or uncorrelated. Many researchers suggest that uncorrelated, independent dimensions are optimal. Others have argued, however, that uncorrelated dimensions are probably unrealistic.

Finally, the two methods most commonly used to form dimensions from descriptive data are exploratory factor analysis and multidimensional scaling (Rummel, 1970; Shepard, 1980). Both procedures, especially exploratory factor analysis, have extensive histories in the literature on psychopathology. For testing a dimensional model, a relatively new procedure has been discussed in the last two decades. This procedure is confirmatory factor analysis (Haydak, 1987).

Although the categorical model and the dimensional model are often presented as if they are conflicting, the two models can be interpreted as being complementary (Skinner, 1986). The dimensional model is a measurement model that is the more fundamental of the two. The dimensional model basically assumes only that there are descriptive variables that can be summarized by a smaller set of abstract variables (i.e., dimensions). The categorical model is a somewhat stronger model in its postulations. It assumes not only that there are "clusters" of patients with relatively homogeneous symptoms, but also that these clusters are reasonably separate and discriminable. If so, patients whose symptoms put them in a certain part of the measurement space (i.e., those who have a collection of certain symptoms) can be said to belong to a specific category. If relatively homogeneous clusters of patients cannot be found, then the dimensional model is the simpler and more parsimonious measurement model to use.

In the last decade, Golden and Meehl (1979) proposed a procedure to determine whether a specific categorical model obtains. They applied their procedure to the concept of "schizotypy" to suggest that it is a category (i.e., representative of a relatively homogeneous cluster of patients), whereas Trull, Widiger, and Guthrie (1990) applied the same procedure to "borderline personality disorder" and found this concept not to be categorical.

Discussions of the DSM systems usually assume that the official psychiatric classifications are categorical (Panzetta, 1974). This assumption may not be accurate, however. Consider, for instance, DSM-III-R. The authors of this classification system (Spitzer & Williams, 1987) specifically stated that DSM-III was *not a classification of patients, but of disorders*. In effect, the authors of DSM-III were saying that the primary focus of their system was on symptoms, rather than patients. Also, most of the disorders in DSM-III were said to be "syndromes," collections of co-occurring (correlated) symptoms (i.e., binary dimensions that are either present or absent). Moreover, the recent emphasis on refining diagnostic criteria in DSM-III-R and DSM-IV has many parallels to the issues of test item development in psychological testing, an area in which factor analysis is a frequently used tool. In short, a strong case could be made that the DSM systems, especially DSM-III and DSM-III-R as created by the neo-Kraepelinians, utilize a dimensional model (except that the dimensions are binary, rather than continuous).

Neglected Topics

Although the literature on psychiatric classification has shown more growth in the last two decades than it did for most of the twentieth century, most of the discussions are rather narrowly focused. In the 1950s and 1960s, most empirical interest was in exploring the reliability of the DSM-I and DSM-II systems (Kreitman, 1961) and the use of factor analysis and cluster analysis to create new classifications (Blashfield, 1984). More recently, authors of a number of journal articles have attempted to analyze the diagnostic criteria that were proposed for certain mental disorders. Also, some authors have attempted to analyze the internal–external validity of particular disorders. Despite these areas of development, a number of significant topics have been neglected. Three will be briefly discussed below: enunciating alternative taxonomic models of classification, explicating the hierarchical arrangement of the mental disorders in the DSMs, and exploring the political and economic issues associated with psychiatric classification.

Alternative Taxonomic Models

In biology, the general field of classification is subdivided into three areas: classification in the specific sense, which refers to the formation of groups of similar organisms; identification (or diagnosis), which is the assignment of a new organism to already existing groups; and taxonomy, which is the theoretical study of classification. Discussions of taxonomy are infrequent in the literature on psychopathology. Kendell's (1975) book probably remains the best presentation of a theoretical view of classification. Recently, Millon and Klerman (1986) edited an interesting volume that contains a wide selection of theoretical views about psychiatric classification.

Hierarchies

The DSM systems, like biological classifications, are hierarchical. Paranoid schizophrenia is a subset of schizophrenia in DSM-III. Paranoid personality disorder is a subset of the Cluster A disorders, which is a subset of the more general personality disorders. Moreover, a number of psychiatrists have discussed a hierarchical ordering of categories in terms of diagnosis. If a patient presents with hallucinations and delusions, the first general disorders to rule out are the organic mental disorders. If an organic basis can be found, an organic mental disorder is used as the diagnosis and the process stops; however, if no organic mental disorder is found, then diagnoses such as schizophrenia and bipolar mood disorder are considered. Elsewhere, I have argued that the clinical hierarchy used when assigning diagnoses has a very different logical structure compared with the organization of categories in the DSM systems (Blashfield, 1989). I also suggested (Blashfield, 1986) that the concepts of mental disorder and disease have different logical status in a hierarchical organization of categories.

Politics and Economics of Classification

Mental health professionals are being made increasingly aware of the political and economic issues associated with psychiatric classification. For instance, when DSM-III-R was being proposed, three new disorders (paraphiliac rapism, masochistic personality disorder, and premenstrual disorder) led to strong protest from feminists who viewed all three as dangerous categories for women. These categories became the objects of intense and heated discussions. Earlier, disorders such as homosexuality and depressive neurosis were the foci of equally intense political movements (Bayer, 1981; Bayer & Spitzer, 1985).

Another reason for the increased interest in classification by mental health professionals is economic. Thirty years ago, health insurance did not commonly cover psychological or psychiatric services. Private patients paid for psychotherapy from their incomes. When this economic condition was normative, assigning diagnoses was not a major issue. With the growth of health insurance, however, the effects of health maintenance organizations and preferred provider organizations, and the requirements of Joint Commission on Accreditation of Health Care Organization standards, assigning diagnoses is required in almost all cases of patient care. Moreover, clinicians must learn how to use these diagnoses correctly since the diagnoses that are assigned can and do affect the level of payment that third-party payers will permit.

Although both economic and political forces have had and will continue to have strong influences on psychiatric classification, there are few detailed discussions of these influences. Also, no empirical literature has attempted to analyze these influences and their effects. Studying the political and economic factors in psychiatric classification is an important topic for future researchers to consider.

> The last trip to the state hospital was in '66. I thought something was controlling me. I hadn't figured out it was my own mind.

> In the hospital the higher-ups with thick German accents pinned me down and questioned me. I told them they were full of shit. I was there for the treatment of my mental health, not to be harassed by the staff.

When I got out I looked into all kinds of esoteric philosophies and came upon the works of Sigmund Freud. I learned about the body of Freudian knowledge, and I psychoanalyzed myself. It opened my eyes to what this "mental illness" thing is.

Psychoanalytic thought is a compound complexification of knowing the dynamicism of how the unconscious mind works. I was able to find my own mind, which never happened in the state hospital with the behavioralist nerds.

My concern is for the people I see on the street. I know how they came down because I came down the same way. Mental health funding should be diverted from locked wards to community services, to help people get back to a lifestyle that's not such a nightmare. Being crazy is being the victim of mind-fuck situations all the time. If you beat a dog, you're going to turn it mean. The whole system is a madness machine.

(Shavelson, 1986, p. 70)

REFERENCES

American Psychiatric Association. (1933). Notes and Comment: Revised classified nomenclature of mental disorders. *American Journal of Psychiatry, 90,* 1369–1376.

American Psychiatric Association. (1952). *Diagnostic and statistical manual of mental disorders* (1st ed.). Washington, DC: Author.

American Psychiatric Association. (1968). *Diagnostic and statistical manual of mental disorders* (2nd ed.). Washington, DC: Author.

American Psychiatric Association. (1980). *Diagnostic and statistical manual of mental disorders* (3rd ed.). Washington, DC: Author.

American Psychiatric Association. (1987). *Diagnostic and statistical manual of mental disorders* (3rd ed. rev.). Washington, DC: Author.

Bayer, R. (1981). *Homosexuality and American psychiatry: The politics of diagnosis.* New York: Basic Books.

Bayer, R., & Spitzer, R. L. (1985). Neurosis, psychodynamics and DSM-III. *Archives of General Psychiatry, 42,* 187–196.

Berrios, G. E., & Hauser, R. (1988). The early development of Kraepelin's ideas on classification: A conceptual history. *Psychological Medicine, 18,* 813–821.

Blashfield, R. K. (1982). Feighner et al., Invisible colleges, and the Matthew effect. *Schizophrenia Bulletin, 8,* 1–6.

Blashfield, R. K. (1984). *Classification of psychopathology.* New York: Plenum Press.

Blashfield, R. K. (1986). Structural approaches to classification. In T. Millon & G. L. Klerman (Eds.), *Contemporary issues in psychopathology* (pp. 363–380). New York: Guilford Press.

Blashfield, R. K. (1989). Co-morbidity and classification. In J. Maser & C. R. Cloninger (Eds.), *Comorbidity in anxiety and mood disorders* (pp. 61–82). American Psychiatric Press.

Blashfield, R. K., & Draguns, J. G. (1976). Towards a taxonomy of psychopathology: The purposes of psychiatric classification. *British Journal of Psychiatry, 129,* 574–583.

Blashfield, R. K., & Haymaker, D. (1988). A prototype analysis of the diagnostic criteria for DSM-III-R personality disorders. *Journal of Personality Disorders, 2,* 272–280.

Cantor, N., Smith, E. E., French, R., & Mezzich, J. (1980). Psychiatric diagnosis as prototype categorization. *Journal of Abnormal Psychology, 89,* 181–193.

Chapman, L. J., & Chapman, J. P. (1969). Illusory correlation as an obstacle to the use of valid psychodiagnostic signs. *Journal of Abnormal Psychology, 74,* 271–280.

Clark, L. A. (1990). Toward a consensual set of symptom clusters for assessment of personality disorder. In J. N. Butcher & C. D. Spielberger (Eds.), *Advances in personality assessment* Volume 8 (pp. 243–266). Hillsdale, NJ: Erlbaum.

Clarkin, J. F., Widiger, T. A., Frances, A., Hurst, S. W., & Gilmore, M. (1983). Prototypic typology and the borderline personality disorder. *Journal of Abnormal Psychology, 92,* 263–275.

Deutsch, K. W. (1966). On theories, taxonomies and models vs communication codes for organizing information. *Behavioral Science, 11,* 1–7.

Drapes, T. (1909). On the maniacal–depressive insanity of Kraepelin. *Journal of Mental Science, 55,* 58–64.

Everitt, B. S. (1980). *Cluster analysis* (2nd ed.). London: Halstead Press.

Eysenck, H. J. (1953). *The structure of human personality.* London: Mithsun.

Faust, D. A., & Miner, R. A. (1987). Empiricist and his new clothes: DSM-III in perspective. *American Journal of Psychiatry, 143,* 962–967.

Feighner, J. P., Robins, E., Guze, S., Woodruff, R. A., Winokur, G., & Munoz, R. (1972). Diagnostic criteria for use in psychiatric research. *Archives of General Psychiatry, 26,* 57–63.

Frances, A. J., Widiger, T. A., & Pincus, H. A. (1989). The development of DSM-IV. *Archives of General Psychiatry, 46,* 373–375.

Friedman, H. P., & Rubin, J. (1967). On some invariant criteria for grouping data. *Journal of American Statistical Association, 62,* 1159–1178.

Golden, R. R., & Meehl, P. E. (1979). Detection of the schizoid taxon with MMPI indicators. *Journal of Abnormal Psychology, 88,* 217–223.

Grinker, R., & Werble, B. (1967). *The borderline patient.* New York: Aronson.

Hamilton, D. L. (1981). Illusory correlation as a basis for stereotyping. In D. L. Hamilton (Ed.) *Cognitive processes in stereotyping and intergroup behavior* (pp. 115–144). Hillsdale, NJ: Erlbaum.

Hartigan, J. A. (1975). *Clustering algorithms.* New York: Wiley.

Haydak, L. A. (1987). *Structural equation modeling with LISREL.* Baltimore, MD: Johns Hopkins University Press.

Hempel, C. G. (1965). *Aspects of scientific explanation and other essays in the philosophy of science.* New York: Free Press.

Horowitz, L., Post, D., French, R., Wallis, K., & Siegelman, E. (1981). The prototype as a construct in abnormal psychology: 2. Clarifying disagreement in psychiatric judgments. *Journal of Abnormal Psychology, 90,* 575–585.

Jaffee, S. R. & Lansing, S. (Producers), & Lyne, A. (Director). (1988). *Fatal attraction* [Film]. Hollywood, CA: Paramount Pictures.

Jardine, N., & Sibson, R. (1971). *Mathematical taxonomy.* New York: Wiley.

Kahn, E. (1959). The Emil Kraepelin memorial lecture. In D. Pasamanick (Ed.), *Epidemiology of mental disorders.* Washington, DC: American Association for the Advancement of Science.

Kendell, R. E. (1975). *The role of diagnosis in psychiatry.* Oxford: Blackwell Scientific Publications.

Klerman, G. L. (1978). The evolution of a scientific nosology. In J. C. Shershow (Ed.), *Schizophrenia: Science and practice* (pp. 99–121). Cambridge, MA: Harvard University Press.

Kraepelin, E. (1899). *Psychiatrie, Ein Lehrbuch fur studirende und aerzte* (6th ed., Vol. 1–2). Leipzig, Germany: Verlag von Johann Ambrosius Barth.

Kreitman, N. (1961). The reliability of psychiatric diagnosis. *Journal of Mental Science, 107,* 878–886.

Livesley, W. J. (1985a). Classification of personality disorders: I. The choice of category concept. *Canadian Journal of Psychiatry, 30,* 353–358.

Livesley, W. J. (1985b). Classification of personality disorders: II. The problem of diagnostic criteria. *Canadian Journal of Psychiatry, 30,* 359–362.

Livesley, W. J. (1986). Trait and behavioral prototypes of personality disorder. *American Journal of Psychiatry, 143,* 728–732.

Matarazzo, J. D. (1983). The reliability of psychiatric and psychological diagnosis. *Clinical Psychology Review, 3,* 103–145.

McReynolds, P. (1989). Diagnosis and clinical assessment: Current status and major issues. *Annual Review of Psychology, 40,* 83–108.

Menninger, K. (1963). *The vital balance.* New York: Viking Press.

Mickle, W. J. (1909). Catatonia: In relation to dementia praecox. *Journal of Mental Science, 55,* 22–36.

Millon, T., & Klerman, G. L. (Eds.). (1986). *Contemporary directions in psychopathology.* New York: Guilford Press.

Morey, L. (1988). Personality disorders in DSM-III and DSM-III-R: Convergence, coverage and internal consistency. *American Journal of Psychiatry, 145,* 573–577.

Panzetta, A. F. (1974). Towards a scientific psychiatric nosology: Conceptual and pragmatic issues. *Archives of General Psychiatry, 30,* 154–161.

Pfohl, B., Coryell, W., Zimmerman, M., & Stangl, D. (1986). DSM-III personality disorders: Diagnostic overlap and internal consistency of individual DSM-III criteria. *Comprehensive Psychiatry, 27,* 21–34.

Rosch, E. (1973). Natural categories. *Cognitive Psychology, 4,* 328–350.

Rosch, E. (1978). Principles of categorization. In E. Rosch & B. B. Lloyd (Eds.), *Cognition and categorization* (pp. 27–48). Hillsdale, NJ: Erlbaum.

Rosch, E., & Mervis, C. B. (1975). Family resemblances: Studies in the internal structure of categories. *Cognitive Psychology, 7,* 573–605.

Rummel, R. J. (1970). *Applied factor analysis.* Evanston, IL: Northwestern University Press.

Schwartz, M. A., & Wiggins, O. P. (1986). Logical empiricism and psychiatric classification. *Comprehensive Psychiatry, 27,* 101–114.

Shavelson, L. (1986). *I'm not crazy, I just lost my glasses.* Berkeley, CA: DeNovo Press.

Shepard, R. N. (1980). Multidimensional scaling, tree-fitting and clustering. *Science, 210,* 390–398.

Skinner, H. A. (1986). Construct validation approach to psychiatric classification. In T. Millon & G. L. Klerman (Eds.), *Contemporary directions in psychopathology* (pp. 307–330). New York: Guilford Press.

Sneath, P. H. E., & Sokol, R. R. (1973). *Numerical taxonomy.* San Francisco: Freeman.

Spitzer, R. L., Endicott, J., & Robins, E. (1975). *Research diagnostic criteria (RDC) for a selected group of functional disorders.* New York: New York State Psychiatric Institute.

Spitzer, R. L., & Fleiss, J. L. (1974). A re-analysis of the reliability of psychiatric diagnosis. *British Journal of Psychiatry, 125,* 341–347.

Spitzer, R. L., & Williams, J. B. W. (1987). Introduction. In *Diagnostic and statistical manual of mental disorders* (3rd ed. rev.) (pp. xvii–xxvii). Washington, DC: American Psychiatric Association.

Trull, T., Widiger, T., & Guthrie, P. (1990). The categorical versus dimensional status of borderline personality disorder. *Journal of Abnormal Psychology, 99,* 40–48.

Widiger, T. A., & Frances, A. (1985). The DSM-III personality disorders: Perspectives from psychology. *Archives of General Psychiatry, 42,* 615–623.

Wing, J. K. (1978). *Reasoning about madness.* London: Oxford University Press.

World Health Organization. (1969). *International classification of diseases* (8th ed.). Geneva: Author.

CHAPTER 2

Practical Use of DSM-III-R

SHAWN SHEA

INTRODUCTION

Nearly 100 years ago, D. H. Tuke, one of a long line of Tuke family members who fought for the compassionate care of the mentally ill, caustically commented that, "The wit of man has rarely been more exercised than in the attempt to classify the morbid mental phenomena covered by the term insanity. The result has been disappointing . . ." (Tuke, 1892). In 1980, the American Psychiatric Association (APA) published a diagnostic system, the *Diagnostic and Statistical Manual of Mental Disorders,* third edition (DSM-III). It was a classification that proved to be a good deal less witty than the systems ridiculed by D. H. Tuke and a good bit more practical.

This chapter is an introduction to the clinical use of DSM-III and its 1987 revision, DSM-III-R (APA, 1987). Hopefully, the chapter will appeal to contemporary mental health professionals from a variety of disciplines, including psychiatry, psychology, counseling, social work, nursing, and psychoanalysis. Although DSM-III and DSM-III-R have met with reasonable acceptance among the range of contemporary mental health professionals, I have found that this acceptance is frequently a begrudging one.

The hesitancy to enthusiastically utilize DSM-III and DSM-III-R often is related to one of the following concerns: (a) the DSM-III-R represents "the medical model" of classification and can lead to dehumanization of the person seeking help, (b) the DSM-III-R provides little of use in providing clues to the practical treatment of mental disorders, and (c) the DSM-III-R is too complicated to be useful in everyday practice. If any of these assertions were true, then I would probably be best advised to write a chapter describing why DSM-III-R should not be used. But all three statements are false. Moreover, I can think of no better way to introduce the novice clinician to the convincing utility of DSM-III-R than to carefully explore the reasons that these three statements are misconceptions.

This chapter is meant to be a guide for the clinician in the field, a clinician who, generally speaking—if my observations in community mental health centers and university centers are accurate—is enormously overloaded with work. Consequently, the chapter is designed to be simplifying by emphasizing practical tips on how to mine the DSM-III-R system for all that it is worth. The chapter is neither a review of the field of psychopathology nor a manual for differential diagnosis. It is designed to generate a sound foundation for the clinical application of DSM-III-R. To accomplish this task, it is divided into the following five sections:

1. The advantages and limitations of diagnostic systems in general
2. A brief historical survey of the development of diagnostic systems and the consequent evolution of DSM-III-R
3. An overall description of the DSM-III-R system and its advantages
4. A practical review of the use of each axis of DSM-III-R
5. A case illustration demonstrating the utility of DSM-III-R.

ADVANTAGES AND LIMITATIONS OF DIAGNOSTIC SYSTEMS

For clinicians, diagnosis serves one major purpose: to discover information that may lead to more effective methods of helping the patient. A diagnostic schema provides this avenue by allowing clinicians and researchers the opportunity to share their experiences in a common language. For example, when a clinician discovers a treatment plan that is useful in relieving a resistant major depression, these findings may be applicable to a patient being treated by a fellow clinician, who might benefit from the shared knowledge. Diagnosis should not be an intellectual game or a pastime used to placate insurance companies. It is a practical passport to the knowledge housed in journals and books, and to that deriving from the experiences of fellow clinicians.

Diagnoses can provide clinicians with prognostic information that can be of immediate value to both patients and their family members. By studying diagnostic categories that seem to present characteristic symptoms as well as characteristic outcomes, the clinician can help both the patient and the family members to understand what the future may hold. For instance, a patient suffering from a bipolar disorder may be reassured to learn that bipolar disorders frequently are episodic. This knowledge—that the condition may have periods of relief—can be powerfully reassuring. In addition, it is known that people with bipolar disorders respond well to the use of lithium. This fact can also be used to bring hope to the patient, as well as to increase the patient's motivation for treatment.

This association between diagnosis and possible treatment modalities represents one of the major advantages of using a diagnostic system. It is becoming increasingly apparent that certain diagnoses suggest specific treatment modalities. For instance, major depressions frequently respond to antidepressants. Bipolar disorder (manic phase) is usually approached with lithium, antipsychotic medications, or sometimes antiseizure medications such as carbamazepine. Phobias are frequently alleviated by using behavioral techniques. Milder forms of major depression can be approached using dynamic and cognitive psychotherapy, behavioral approaches, or numerous counseling techniques. The above list merely represents a terse survey, but it nevertheless highlights the potential power of a diagnostic system to help generate flexible treatment approaches.

A personal clinical vignette may help to make this abstract discussion more concrete. I was working with a couple whose marriage was riddled with a nasty streak of passive–aggression and strained communication. After several sessions, the marital therapy seemed to be bogging down.

The husband, a rather narcissistic man, kept insisting that nothing was being done for him. In reviewing my notes, I discovered that the referring clinician had diagnosed the husband as suffering from a dysthymic disorder. I had recently read an article in which certain types of dysthymic disorders responded well to antidepressant medication. My patient fit one of these descriptions, and consequently was begun on an appropriate antidepressant. He quickly found significant relief; however, to the chagrin of both spouses, their marital friction remained painfully present. Up to this point, the husband had balked at couples therapy, for he felt that it was his depression that was causing all the problems. Now he realized the relationship itself needed attention. He no longer had an excuse for avoiding the work of therapy; thanks to the antidepressant, suddenly the marital therapy was able to move ahead more effectively.

Before proceeding, it seems expedient to review some of the important limitations of diagnostic systems in general, such as DSM-III-R. Only through a knowledge of a system's weaknesses can its strengths be utilized safely.

One of the most obvious limitations of diagnostic systems is the fact that diagnoses are labels. As labels, they can be abused. One such abuse occurs when clinicians fall into the trap of using diagnoses as stereotypical explanations for human behavior. It should be remembered that a diagnosis provides no particular knowledge about any given patient. It merely suggests possible characteristics that may or may not be generalizable to the patient in question. Diagnostic formulations are evolving processes and, as such, should be periodically reexamined. There is a realistic danger that patients can become stuck with inappropriate diagnoses. This problem can be avoided only through persistent reappraisal.

The clinician also should remain healthily aware of the potential ramifications of certain diagnostic labels with regard to the patient's culture and family. For example, the label "schizophrenia" can result in the loss of a job or in the development of a scapegoating process within a given family. Considerations of these problematic aspects of diagnoses should be integral parts of sound clinical care.

The significance of a specific diagnostic label to the patient can also be of marked importance. For this reason, the clinician may find it useful to frequently ask patients whether anyone has given them a diagnosis in the past. If the answer is yes, one can follow with questions such as, "What is your understanding of the word schizophrenia?" or "Do you think that diagnosis is right?" The answers to these questions can provide invaluable insights into a patient's self-image, intellectual level, and previous care.

It is also very important to remind oneself that a correct diagnosis does not necessarily provide much information about the patient as a unique individual. Other conceptualizations must be used to provide this critical understanding. In this sense, the diagnosis should not be used as a method of putting the person "behind the label" at a distance. Instead, it represents one effective method of trying to enter into the patient's world by understanding, descriptively, what the patient's symptoms and perceived problems have been. A diagnosis by DSM-III-R is not meant to replace invaluable methods of understanding a patient's pain and perspectives, such as a psychodynamic formulation, an understanding of the behavioral cues to pathologic behavior, an understanding of the patient's religious beliefs, and an exploration of his or her family interactions. Instead, diagnosis is meant to provide a complementary method of helping to explore a patient's world, eventually providing symptom relief through sound treatment.

HISTORICAL ROLE AND DEVELOPMENT OF DSM-III-R

As mentioned in the introduction, one common misconception is that DSM-III-R represents the medical model. Seeking the roots of this misconception leads one into a fascinating sojourn into the history of psychiatry, including its interface with mainstream medicine, psychology, and the world of politics. A few principles concerning the development of diagnostic systems in general can function as a useful map during this historical journey.

Diagnostic systems tend to fall into one of two broad domains: (a) systems that attempt to arrive at diagnoses primarily by delineating the symptom picture and the course of the disorder, and (b) systems that attempt to arrive at a diagnosis by organizing disorders according to their causative agents. The latter technique can result in rather dramatically differing schema, depending upon theorists' beliefs of etiology. For instance, two strongly opposing systems, the biological and the psychodynamic, are both examples of diagnostic systems that depend upon an etiologic classification. A biological diagnostic system (often attacked as the medical model) would be based on the premise that abnormal behaviors are the result of true diseases, which have organic agents as the causative element, such as the bacterial spirochete in syphilis of the brain. A psychological diagnostic system, such as the one proposed by Sigmund Freud, would postulate that a specific abnormality, such as a phobia, is caused by a specific psychological agent, perhaps an unconscious conflict. In any case, both the biological and psychologic classifications are similar in the sense that both are based on supposed etiology.

The question now becomes one of uncovering which diagnostic approach historically led to psychiatric systems of diagnoses. Even more germane to this chapter is the question as to which type of diagnostic system is the DSM-III-R. To find the answer, one must go back to the middle years of the last century.

In the mid-1800s, psychiatric diagnosis was in a directionless quagmire. It was unclear whether diagnoses should proceed along clinical descriptive lines or etiologic lines. The main role of the diagnostician was frequently reduced to the mere determination of whether someone was sane or not sane. Without a sound underlying diagnostic schema, even this decision was fraught with controversy, as Welhelm Griesinger, the father of university psychiatry, so aptly noted:

> I have had submitted to me opinions of special medical psychologists, who, after six months observations of a patient in their asylum, could not come to a decision whether they should declare him insane or not; and older and recent cases have been published in which the opinions based upon long observation, instituted ad hoc, of eminent psychologists have been quite contradictory: the reading of these is very instructive.
>
> *(Griesinger, 1882/1989, p. 80.)*

Griesinger was a pivotal figure with regard to alleviating much of the confusion, which he had found so "instructive." In 1845, he published the first edition of an influential work, *Mental Pathology and Therapeutics,* in which he proposed an innovative classification of mental disorders. His system was based almost entirely upon clinical description, for, as he said in a later translation, "A classification of mental diseases according to their nature—that is, according to the anatomical changes of brain which lie at their foundation is, at the present time, impossible" (Griesinger, 1882/ 1989, p. 144). This statement clearly suggests that he believed in a biological cause of mental disorders. In the opening paragraph of his book, he was quite explicit:

> The first step towards a knowledge of the symptoms is their locality—to which organ do the indications of the disease belong. . . . physiological and patholog-ical facts show us that this organ can only be the brain; we therefore primarily, and in every case of mental disease, recognize a morbid action of that organ.
>
> *(Griesinger, 1882/1989, p. 1.)*

With such words, the medical model was born. From our current level of sophistication, it is easy to attack Griesinger as sounding reductionistic, but such a reflection is grossly unjust, for Griesinger's thoughts must be considered in a political and sociological context. Four points are worth considering:

1. Griesinger was talking primarily about severe mental illnesses, such as major psychotic disorders, severe mood disturbances, and dementia.
2. He clearly felt that brain malfunction was present in these disorders, but he felt that the brain malfunction could be caused by numerous biological, environmental, and psychological factors. The brain happened to be the end-organ of the insult.
3. Griesinger believed in a variety of psychological mechanisms and helped to develop the concept of "the ego."
4. The movement toward viewing insanity as a focus of medical attention (an affliction of the brain) was based primarily on a response to the cruel and inhuman conditions to which the mentally disabled had been subjected when left to the care of nonmedical institutions.

In this latter regard, Griesinger was one of the leaders in the battle to end physical restraints. His voice for compassionate care of the severely mentally disabled was clear and loud:

> One great principle, however, pervades the whole system of modern psychiatry—the great principle of humanity in the treatment of the insane, in contradistinction to that former barbarism which sometimes persecuted the mentally afflicted with trials for sorcery and death at the stake; sometimes, and this in the most favorable cases, cast them into dungeons, to be associated with criminals, where, beyond the influence of the medical art, and, deprived of all human aid, they were consigned to the realms of despotic cruelty and brutality. Certainly, it was that forced acknowledgment of insanity to be a disease—that first achieved their recognition as human beings by society, towards whom protection and help was due.
>
> *(Griesinger, 1882/1989, p. 326.)*

Toward the end of the century, a second German, Emil Kraepelin, added further clarification to psychiatric diagnoses (see Chapter 1). His two major diagnostic accomplishments remain hallmarks in the ongoing understanding of severe mental illness: He was the first to clearly recognize schizophrenia (which he called dementia praecox) and manic–depression. Kraepelin is also of major significance because he was a contemporary of Sigmund Freud but was not overly impressed with the theories of his Viennese colleague. Their debate is at the heart of the controversy over the medical model.

Freud was the first influential psychiatrist to move the focus of psychiatry away from serious psychopathology toward neurotic symptoms, where biological mechanisms were frequently less important. His psychiatric theories emphasized etiology as exemplified by unconscious conflicts, defense mechanisms, and the rumblings of the id. Kraepelin found Freud's nonbiological theories of psychotic process and manic–depression to be wishful thinking and threatening, in the sense that an overemphasis on such theories could lead research away from hunting for the biological agents at the roots of severe psychopathology.

When Nazi Germany became hostile to psychoanalysis, the analytic community chose the United States as its new home. It was in the United States that the first DSM diagnostic system evolved. From the 1940s to the 1960s, an interest in descriptive psychopathology, as pioneered by Griesinger and Kraepelin, hit an all-time low under the influence of pscyhoanalysis. There was also little interest in diagnosis because there was primarily only one treatment available—psychoanalysis—no matter what the disorder. Consequently, diagnosis did not seem like a pressing clinical issue. DSM-I was created within this culture, and it bore the stamps required for passing through this culture: relatively vague diagnostic distinctions and an emphasis upon psychodynamic etiologies with regard to neuroses and personality disorders.

As the 1960s dawned, new treatment modalities were blossoming, and a renewed interest in neuroscience and research was under way. Consequently, a need for a more reliable diagnostic system arose. In 1968, DSM-II appeared.

Classifications were defined more carefully and much of the psychodynamic influence was gone. This system began the move away from classification based upon etiology, either biological or psychological, for history had shown that basing a diagnostic system upon etiology essentially guaranteed nonacceptance of the given classification system by anyone who disagreed with its etiologic assumptions.

Norman Sartorius, a leading expert on international diagnostic systems, noted another reason why the medical model is not being used in contemporary systems. Even with the prominent impact of neuroscience research since the 1960s, there has been precious little development of specific disease entities in which a specific biological agent has been found (Sartorius, 1988). Moreover, mental health professionals from all disciplines have further increased their interest in helping people with problems not directly tied to biological disruption, such as marital problems, family disturbances, stress reactions, and crisis intervention. Consequently, a diagnostic system that is not based on biological etiology is needed.

During this period, an influential classification system was being developed to help researchers increase their interrater reliability (Feighner et al., 1972). This system emphasized the need for specific criteria that would decrease the sloppiness and subjectivity that plagued earlier systems. Feighner et al. developed their criteria at the department of psychiatry at Washington University in St. Louis. This system delineated fifteen diagnostic categories by using both exclusion and inclusion criteria. Building upon this base, the *Research Diagnostic Criteria* (RDC) were developed by Spitzer, Endicott, and Robins (1978). With the RDC system, the psychopathological range was increased to include twenty-three disorders. Spitzer became the spearhead in the development of DSM-III, which appeared in 1980, and was followed by its revision, DSM-III-R, in 1987. The authors of DSM-III and DSM-III-R, having learned from the past, developed these systems to be atheoretical. Consequently, they opened the door for cross-discipline interaction and the seeding of a new collaborative spirit among mental health disciplines.

ADVANTAGES OF DSM-III-R

DSM-III-R attempts to classify abnormal behaviors into a variety of mutually exclusive behavioral patterns. It covers psychopathology ranging from childhood through old age. DSM-III and DSM-III-R represent a variety of major advances. First, compared with the Feighner criteria, the system was designed primarily for clinical practice and only secondarily for application to a research setting. This clinical orientation mandated that all areas of psychopathology be delineated. The actual diagnoses were intended to be relatively distinct from one another.

A second major advance, in comparison with the DSM-I and DSM-II systems, was an emphasis upon well-defined criteria. Clinicians could no longer report that someone was schizophrenic, simply because they had an intuitive feeling that schizophrenia was present. Instead, clinicians needed to document the criteria upon which the diagnosis of schizophrenia was being made.

A third major advance, as mentioned earlier, was that DSM-III and DSM-III-R were essentially atheoretical. (It should be noted that if a clear-cut etiologic agent has been proven, such as the spirochete in the psychosis associated with syphilis, then an organic etiology is accepted.) Thus, the authors of DSM-III and DSM-III-R did not espouse a specific school of thought with regard to etiology, such as the medical model or the behavioral model. Because DSM-III-R focuses upon a concrete description of psychopathology and abnormal behavior, it can be utilized by mental health professionals from all disciplines. The ability of the DSM-III-R system to allow clinicians from various disciplines to discuss and share sophisticated clinical and research information cannot be underestimated.

A fourth major advance of DSM-III and DSM-III-R is the fact that an attempt was made to actually test for reliability in the field. Never before had statistical evidence been produced concerning issues such as interrater reliability, validity, and ease of use.

A fifth major advance, and perhaps the most important, is the utilization of a multiaxial system, in which the patient's presentation is not limited to a single diagnosis. The clinician was encouraged to look at the patient's primary psychiatric diagnosis within the context of a variety of interacting systems, such as the patient's personality structure, physical health, level of stress, and level of functioning. As Mezzich (1985) pointed out, DSM-III evolved from pioneering work with multiaxial systems around the world, including England (Rutter, Schaffer, & Shepherd, 1975; Wing, 1970), Germany (Helmchen, 1975; von Cranach, 1977), Japan (Kato, 1977), and Sweden (Ottosson & Perris, 1973).

In DSM-III-R, the clinical formulation is summarized in the following five axis:

   I. All clinical syndromes and V codes except for personality disorders and developmental disorders
  II. Personality disorders and developmental disorders
 III. Physical disorders and conditions
  IV. Severity of psychosocial stress
   V. Global assessment of functioning.

PRACTICAL USE OF EACH DSM-III-R AXIS

Axis I

At first glance, Axis I may appear confusing because of the large number of diagnostic entities it contains. There is little need for concern, however. The diagnostic task is to first uncover the general diagnostic possibilities, and then delineate the specific diagnoses, a process described by Shea (1988) in *Psychiatric Interviewing: The Art of Understanding,* from which this section has been adapted.

As the interviewer listens during the initial interview, the symptoms of the patient will suggest large diagnostic regions worthy of further exploration. This primary delineation will lead the clinician to one or more of the following easily remembered regions:

1. Mood disorders
2. Schizophrenia and related disorders
3. Anxiety disorders
4. Organic disorders (including dementia and delirium)
5. Alcohol and drug abuse disorders
6. Somatiform disorders (e.g., hypochondriasis)
7. Adjustment disorders
8. Other miscellaneous disorders (e.g., sexual disorders, factitious disorders, and impulse control disorders)
9. No disorder
10. V code.

The childhood disorders are similarly listed into large clusters, as follows:

1. Disruptive behavior disorders
2. Anxiety disorders of childhood or adolescence
3. Eating disorders
4. Gender identity disorders
5. Tic disorders
6. Elimination disorders
7. Speech disorders not elsewhere classified
8. Other disorders of infancy, childhood, or adolescence.

If a childhood disorder presents in much the same manner as its adult counterpart, it is not specifically listed or described in the section devoted to childhood disorders. This absence does not mean that these disorders do not occur in childhood; it simply means that the same criteria are used for children as for adults. Examples of disorders occurring with both children and adults include schizophrenia, bipolar disorder, major depression, dysthymia, and obsessive–compulsive disorder.

Looked at in this simplified fashion, the first step in utilizing DSM-III-R appears considerably more manageable than at first glance. To succeed, the clinician must be well grounded in psychopathology. This knowledge base will allow the interviewer to quickly determine which of the major areas may be pertinent. As the interview proceeds, the clinician can reflect upon whether each of these broad areas has at least been considered, thus avoiding errors of omission.

Once the primary delineation has been made (e.g., "Does this patient appear anxious? Does this patient appear depressed?"), the interviewer can proceed with the secondary delineation, in which the specific diagnoses assumed under the broad diagnostic areas are explored in a more exacting diagnostic fashion. Thus, if a clinician suspects a mood disorder, the clinician eventually hunts for criteria substantiating the specific mood diagnoses, such as major depression, bipolar disorder, dysthymia, cyclothymia, bipolar disorder not otherwise specified, and depressive disorder not otherwise specified. This secondary delineation is performed in each broad diagnostic area deemed pertinent.

The interviewer should explore the diagnostic areas in a fluid fashion. Most important, the interviewer should be highly flexible, always patterning the questioning in the fashion most compatible with the defenses and needs of the patient in the clinical situation. The clinician explores these diagnostic regions in a unique fashion with each patient, mixing them with various other areas of nondiagnostic information, such as psychodynamic issues and immediate stressors. When done well, the interview feels unstructured to the patient, yet delineates an accurate diagnosis.

With each Axis I diagnosis, the clinician can also rate the severity of the symptom presentation at the time of the interview. Severity is designated by one of five classifications: mild, moderate, severe, in partial remission or residual state, or in full remission. These severity ratings are defined as follows by the DSM-III-R (APA, 1987):

> *Mild*—Few, if any, symptoms in excess of those required to make the diagnosis, and symptoms result in only minor impairment in occupational functioning or usual social activities or relationships with others.
>
> *Moderate*—Symptoms or functional impairment between "mild" and "severe."
>
> *Severe*—Several symptoms in excess of those required to make the diagnosis, and symptoms markedly interfere with occupational functioning or with usual social activities or relationships with others.
>
> *Partial Remission*—Full criteria for the disorder were previously met, but currently only some of the symptoms or signs of the illness are present.
>
> *Full Remission*—There are no longer any symptoms or signs of the disorder.

Additionally, the No Disorder category serves as a reminder to the clinician to look for the strengths and normal coping mechanisms of the patient. Too many clinicians fall into the bias and perspective of seeing only with "the eyes of psychopathology" as apposed to the equally important "eyes of health."

V codes represent conditions not attributable to a mental disorder that have nevertheless become a focus of therapeutic intervention. Examples include academic problems, occupational problems, uncomplicated bereavement, noncompliance with medical treatment, marital problems, parent–child problems, and others. Sometimes these codes are used because no mental disorder is present, although the patient is coping with a stress. They can also be used if the clinician feels that not enough information is available to rule out a psychiatric syndrome, but, in the meantime, an area for specific intervention is being highlighted. Finally, these V codes can be used for the patient with a specific psychiatric syndrome that is not the immediate problem or focus of intervention. For example, an individual with chronic schizophrenia in remission may present with marital distress.

Axis II

Axis II emphasizes the realization that all of the Axis I diagnoses exist in the unique psychological milieu we call personality. Many mental health problems are primarily related to the vicissitudes of personality development. The underlying personality of the patient can greatly affect the manner in which clinicians choose to relate to the patient, both in the initial interview and in subsequent therapy. Consequently, it is expedient to conceptualize which personality characteristics have evolved in any given interviewee.

The basic approach to diagnosis follows the same two-step delineation discussed for Axis I. In the first delineation, one asks whether the interviewee's story suggests evidence of long-term interpersonal dysfunction that has remained relatively consistent since adolescence. If so, the patient may very well fulfill the criteria for a personality disorder or disorders.

After determining that a personality disorder may be present, the clinician proceeds with the secondary delineation, in which specific regions of personality diagnoses are expanded. This secondary delineation results in the generation of a differential from the following list:

1. Paranoid personality disorder
2. Schizoid personality disorder
3. Schizotypal personality disorder
4. Histrionic personality disorder
5. Narcissistic personality disorder
6. Antisocial personality disorder
7. Borderline personality disorder
8. Avoidant personality disorder
9. Compulsive personality disorder
10. Passive–aggressive personality disorder
11. Personality disorder, not otherwise specified.

In many cases, the interviewee does not demonstrate psychopathology warranting the diagnosis of a personality disorder. Instead, he or she possesses traits (sometimes adaptive in nature) found in these disorders in smaller degrees. DSM-III-R is very flexible in such cases, allowing the clinician to simply list the traits that are present. One might simply write on Axis II that "the patient displayed some histrionic and paranoid traits."

Besides personality traits, on Axis II, the clinician may also list specific defense mechanisms, which may be pertinent with regard to future treatment.

These defense mechanisms range from those commonly seen in neurotic disorders, such as rationalization and intellectualization, to those seen in more severe disorders, such as denial, projection, and splitting. These defense mechanisms are defined in Appendix C of DSM-III-R.

It should be noted that Axis II was further revised in DSM-III-R to include all forms of developmental delay. Mental retardation is included on this axis, as well as specific developmental disorders, such as developmental reading disorder or an articulation disorder. Also included on this axis are the more debilitating pervasive developmental disorders, such as infantile autism.

Axis II of DSM-III-R represents a flexible method of understanding symptoms within the context of personality structure and development. As such, its inclusion in the multiaxial system is a significant step. However, it is worth noting some of the problems that are inherent in the system and that hopefully, with time, will be resolved.

One difficulty is that many of the personality disorders seem to share characteristics with each other. A significant number of people with borderline personality disorder also fit the criteria for histrionic personality disorder, because these two disorders share many of the same characteristics. (More specifically, both the borderline and the histrionic personalities are apt to have frequent suicidal gestures or to threaten suicide when feeling interpersonally stressed.) The greater the overlap found among diagnoses, the more difficult it becomes to distinguish among them. At some level, this problem results in patients' carrying multiple diagnoses on this axis. Hopefully, in the future much of this overlap will be decreased, but some overlap is a natural outcome of the complexity of personality structure. One would expect to see some overlap in this area, because these diagnostic categories are actually labels onto which reality is sometimes uncomfortably forced. This problem is less disturbing when one keeps in mind that personality disorders are descriptions of behavioral patterns not of "types" of people.

The second, and perhaps more disturbing, problem is the issue of cultural bias in DSM-III-R. For example, some of the criteria listed for the antisocial personality may appear abnormal to the white middle class but not to a different culture. Occupational history is a good example of this problem. Some individuals enjoy switching jobs relatively frequently, and their culture may accept this behavior as reasonably normal. Even more interesting is the fact that certain criteria listed in DSM-III-R, such as criminal behavior, frequent fighting, drunken driving, and the use of aliases, seem to describe a personality pattern that is commonly known as a criminal. These are also characteristics of an antisocial personality as seen in the lower socioeconomic classes. DSM-III-R seems to imply that there are no sociopaths among the educated elite because the manual does not list as criteria for the antisocial personality the frequently exhibited behaviors of the white-collar sociopath: tax evasion, sexual harassment of employees, stealth in business dealings, broken commitments, backbiting, slander, and longstanding extramarital affairs. The psychodynamics of this person may differ very little from the pimp on Eighth Avenue, but DSM-III-R might not even acknowledge such a person as having a specific personality disorder.

This criticism leads to a related problem. Some criteria used in the diagnostic descriptions tend to be vague or depend on subjective interpretation by the interviewer. In the diagnosis of a histrionic personality, we find the following items listed:

1. Expresses emotion with inappropriate exaggeration
2. Has a style of speech that is excessively impressionistic and lacking in detail
3. Is overly concerned with physical attraction
4. Is inappropriately sexually seductive in appearance or behavior.

Although these characteristics seem straightforward, one wonders how flirtatious one has to be to fulfill the last criterion. What exactly is an exaggerated expression of emotions that will cause it to be viewed as pathologic? Obviously, each clinician is left to decide these issues somewhat idiosyncratically. One real danger arises when clinicians are unaware of their own personality traits (both pathologic and nonpathologic). In these instances, the clinician may accept clearly pathologic behavior in a patient as being not bad enough to fulfill a specific criteria. For example, a clinician may possess a hefty dose of dramatic and reactive behavior. This clinician may subsequently view the patient's dramatic behavior as "quite all right, might do the same thing myself if feeling pressured." Such blind spots can significantly affect the interrater reliability of the Axis II diagnoses.

Axis III

On Axis III, the clinician considers the role of the patient's physical disorders and conditions. Stated differently, this axis reminds the clinician to adopt a holistic approach to the patient, considering both the mind and the body as parts of the same organism.

I do not think this axis can be emphasized too much. In my opinion, all patients who exhibit psychological complaints for an extended time period should be evaluated by a physician to rule out any underlying physiologic condition or causative agent. To avoid this examination is to risk a disservice to the patient, because entities such as endocrine disorders and malignancies can easily present with psychological symptoms.

In this same light, a medical review of systems and a past medical history should become standard parts of an initial assessment. Other physical conditions that are not diseases may also provide important information concerning the holistic state of the interviewee. For instance, it is relevant to know if the interviewee is pregnant or a trained athlete, for these conditions may point toward germane psychological issues.

Axis IV

On Axis IV, the clinician examines the current stresses affecting the interviewee. The axis is concerned with the crucial interaction between the patient and the environment in which he or she lives. All too often, interviewers put emphasis on diagnostic intrigues and fail to uncover the reality-based problems confronting the patient; however, these reality-based concerns frequently suggest avenues for therapeutic intervention.

For instance, the interviewer may discover that, secondary to a job layoff, the patient's home is about to be foreclosed. With such information, the clinician may be able to help by referring the patient to a specific social agency or to a social worker.

This axis also is of paramount importance in crisis intervention. It is generally useful for the clinician to determine what perceived stressors caused the patient to seek professional help. Questions such as the following are often useful: "What stresses have you been coping with recently?" or "What thoughts made you decide to actually come here tonight as opposed to coming tomorrow or some other time?" The answers may provide another pathway for both understanding and treatment planning.

Axis V

A variety of changes were made in Axis V when DSM-III was revised. In DSM-III, this axis solely differentiated the highest functioning of the patient over a 2-month period in the preceding year. This relatively narrow perspective did not provide much practical information. Consequently, in DSM-III-R, this axis was broadened. It now includes not only a rating of the highest functioning in the past year, but also a rating of the current functioning, which provides immediate data pertinent to treatment planning and the decision as to whether hospitalization is warranted. These ratings are to be made by combining both symptoms and occupational and interpersonal functioning on the 90-point Global Assessment Functioning Scale.

The first rating, the highest level of functioning in the past year that is sustained for at least a 2-month period, may help to predict ultimate outcome, for some clinicians feel that higher levels of recent functioning may suggest better hopes prognostically. Probably of more practical importance to the clinician is the insight gained into the patient's adaptive skills and coping mechanisms. Access to this axis can be made with questions such as, "In the past year what 2 months were best for you?" or "If you were forced to relive 2 months from the last year, which 2 months would you choose to go through again?"

The following inquires, including both open and closed-ended questions, can help the clinician uncover coping skills possessed by the patient:

- When you are functioning well, what do you do to help yourself relax?
- What kinds of things do you like to do in your spare time?
- How do you go about making important decisions in your life?
- What are some of your hobbies?
- How many people have you shared your problems with? [This question may indirectly give the clinician some views on the patient's communication skills and his or her support systems.]
- Do you enjoy sports or dancing?
- Do you enjoy reading or the arts?

- Have you ever kept a journal?
- If someone asked you to list two of your best skills or talents, what would you say?

These types of questions may uncover important coping skills of a patient in crisis. For instance, one might discover that a patient has frequently kept a journal or diary as a method of sorting out problems. The clinician might use this information to remind the patient of past successes in dealing with problems, thus helping the patient to regain confidence. The clinician may also choose to have the patient solve problems, using his or her journal before the next session, a therapeutic technique that utilizes the patient's natural skills while rekindling feelings of mastery during a time of crisis.

For the second rating, a global assessment of current functioning, the clinician carefully reviews evidence of immediate coping skills as affected by symptomatology. It is important that the clinician utilize quite specific questions in this exploration, because patients, if asked for vague opinions, may give very misleading answers. For example, an acutely psychotic patient who does not want to enter the hospital may reply with a simple "not often" when asked, "Are the voices bothering you frequently?" By using a more behaviorally concrete approach, the clinician may find that the dialogue develops more along the following lines.

CLIN: During the last 2 days, how many times have you heard the voices per day? A hundred times? Ten times?

PT: [Pausing and glancing away for a moment] Probably, well . . . maybe a good fifty times a day.

CLIN: What types of things do they say?

PT: [Pause] They tell me I'm ugly.

CLIN: What do you feel when the voices say mean things like that to you?

PT: It hurts, but I try to push them out of mind.

CLIN: Do they ever tell you to hurt yourself?

PT: You could say that.

CLIN: What exactly do they tell you?

By using such specific questioning, the clinician has learned not only that the voices are bothersome, but also that they are quite frequent.

The clinician should also keep in mind that sources outside the patient, such as family and friends, frequently provide more valid information about current functioning than can the patient. Once again, when questioning corroborative sources, behaviorally specific questioning should be used to ensure validity.

CASE APPLICATION OF DSM-III-R

One of the best ways for the clinician to become familiar with the usefulness of DSM-III-R is to see the diagnostic schema in actual practice. As noted earlier, the utility of any diagnostic system is most evident when it is tied to therapeutic decision making. In the middle decades of this century, few therapeutic modalities were available; consequently, diagnosis played a minimal role in psychiatric intervention. The contemporary clinician, however, is faced with a bountiful array of treatment interventions, which, in themselves, can sometimes present a confusing arena.

The DSM-III-R system can help to provide a framework from which to base practical treatment planning, both medical and psychosocial. An entire axis of DSM-III-R is devoted to items such as social distress, allowing the clinician to suggest significant avenues for immediate psychosocial intervention. Also, the final axis, essentially nonbiological in nature, emphasizes adaptive level of functioning and severity of the symptom picture, once again providing the clinician the opportunity to consider necessary psychosocial interventions.

In the following case description, an attempt has been made to provide the information available to the clinician following the initial patient interview, as well as a corroborative interview with the patient's mother. Based on this information, the utility of the DSM-III-R system for providing a holistic understanding of various important clinical issues is discussed, including the following:

- An understanding of the symptom presentation of the patient
- An understanding of the prognosis associated with the patient's diagnoses
- A more thorough understanding of the immediate stresses on the patient and their impact
- Specific issues concerning treatment interventions.

Presentation of Mr. Graham

Mr. Graham entered the room with a lumbering gait that seemed appropriate for his large-framed body. Although his jet black hair seemed to be consistent with his stated age of 28 years, his unusual openness to questioning and the bluntness of some of his answers suggested a naivete more consistent with a younger age. When asked about recent stress, he commented with a wry smile on his face that "I need a woman bad, but nobody wants me." Although he came from a wealthy family, he was dressed in a plaid shirt and somewhat baggy jeans that, despite their large size, were barely able to contain a gradually enlarging beer belly. His facial features seemed somewhat coarse. There was a thickness to his skin, almost as if his cheeks had been stuffed, as indeed they frequently were when he was chewing tobacco. There was also a sallow color to his complexion, and he reported that, at times, he had been vomiting recently.

During the interview, Mr. Graham appeared calm except for a mild shuffling of his feet. His affect was pleasant and only mildly restricted. He reported his mood as being intermittently depressed. He frequently had vegetative symptoms of depression, but they had been intermittent for years. He related a complex history starting during his teenage years. Apparently he had had an early breakdown in which he heard auditory hallucinations and had become violent. It was unclear whether street drugs were being used at the time of this first break. Since that time, he had had several hospitalizations during which he would hear voices saying things such as "You gotta walk softly."

Recently, Mr. Graham had become progressively more violent, and on two occasions had shot items in his house with a gun, including a silver serving tray and a radio. When questioned about the serving tray, he became animated and said that when he had been looking into it, he felt that he saw a demon invading his body. He also related that at times he became paranoid and felt worried that a neighbor might be trying to harm him. He frequently experienced periods of time in which he felt agitated and restless inside. This restlessness seemed to increase several days after he received his shots of haldol.

During his high school years, Mr. Graham had used a variety of street drugs, including marijuana, mescaline, cocaine, LSD, speed, and alcohol. During the past several months, he had used marijuana and had been binge drinking. While on a binge, he could consume close to a fifth of whiskey. He related that his psychotic symptoms seemed to get worse at such times. He had been having frequent suicidal ideation, with thoughts of shooting himself and running his car off the road, although he had not acted on these ideas and felt in control of such impulses. He also described periods of time when he felt unusually excitable and did not require sleep. He had frequent sexual ideation and fantasies of rape, although he denied any actions on these fantasies.

Mr. Graham's mother, who spoke with a gentle animation and presented an attitude of resignation, painted a somewhat different picture about her son. She related that he was probably drinking more than he was admitting to the clinicians. She also felt that he had been having significant problems with sleep, frequently staying awake into the early morning hours and occasionally shrieking out an unintelligible yell. She commented, "Frankly he scares me, and I don't always know what to do with him." She added that the police had been called to the house on several occasions. Over the previous few weeks, however, he had been much calmer and had been drinking less. She commented that she felt that there were periods of time when he clearly heard the voices although he had not been using alcohol. She denied seeing persistent manic symptoms.

Mr. Graham lived at home with his mother and had not been employed for years. She related, "Oh, sometimes he tinkers around with an antique Ford in the garage, but I don't think he has any intention of really becoming a mechanic." He was supposed to pay $200 in rent per month, but in actuality squandered his money. His mother frequently gave him over $200 a month for cigarettes and magazines.

Discussion of Mr. Graham

On Axis I, Mr. Graham presents a complex diagnostic picture. His history of active psychotic process, spanning many years, strongly suggests schizophrenia or a schizoaffective disorder. The chronicity of the disorder, and its lack of episodicity, is more suggestive of schizophrenia than a mood disorder, such as a bipolar disorder. At times, psychosis seems to be present without substance abuse. On the other hand, it appears that both his impulsivity and his psychotic process are frequently exacerbated by the use of street drugs and alcohol. His intermittent depressed symptoms, of a long-standing nature, may merely represent manifestations of schizophrenia and/or substance abuse, or they may represent an actual dysthymia.

In summary, on Axis I, Mr. Graham is probably best described in the following manner. He seems to be suffering from schizophrenia, alcohol dependence, and possible marijuana abuse. One would want to rule out a schizoaffective disorder, dysthymia, and an alcohol-induced hallucinosis (by history). Although at the time of the interview he appeared to have symptoms of only moderate severity, his symptoms have been very severe within the past several months.

Because of Mr. Graham's severe Axis I disorder, schizophrenia, practical therapeutic interventions are suggested. The schizophrenia immediately raises the possibility of intervention with antipsychotic medications, such as the haldol he is taking. The diagnosis of schizophrenia also automatically suggests that extensive counseling and education, concerning his schizophrenia, should occur with both patient and his family members.

This diagnosis of schizophrenia also implies that Mr. Graham may have difficulty dealing with intense confrontation and/or interpersonal intimacy. These potential difficulties are of therapeutic importance, for they suggest that he may have difficulty dealing with group therapy or, at this point in time, with an intervention such as Alcoholics Anonymous in which self-disclosure, intimacy, and confrontation are common. The appearance of substance abuse, on the other hand, strongly implies that counseling of a long-term nature is indicated. Medications such as Antabuse®, which are useful in preventing drinking behavior, could also be considered. His complexity on Axis I, combined with the chronicity, provide strong indicators that his care should be given to an experienced clinician who intends to be in the system for an extended time.

Concerning Axis II, the database is currently incomplete. The information that is available, including Mr. Graham's chronic unemployment and irresponsibility with rent, hints at the possibility of an antisocial personality disorder. Further interviewing revealed that he also had had numerous fights in the past, which also suggest this diagnosis. On the other hand, some of these traits may actually be related to the schizophrenia or alcohol abuse. On Axis II, it is probably best to defer the diagnosis and rule out an antisocial personality disorder.

Axis II is where the clinician also describes defense mechanisms and personality traits. In this instance, it is probably appropriate to relate that Mr. Graham has antisocial traits. Also, he appears to be at risk for developing psychotic transferences with female therapists. The listing of this primitive defense mechanism has immediate treatment ramifications with regard to the style of interventions to be used by a female therapist, if indeed a female therapist is working with the patient. Its presence implies the need for immediately addressing transference as it develops in an effort to prevent psychotic transference. it also suggests the need to carefully ensure that the patient does not misinterpret clinician behaviors in a sexual fashion.

On Axis III, the clinician would record that Mr. Graham probably is suffering from akathisia, as noted by his restlessness. The presence of akathisia, a side effect of the haldol, suggests the possibility of either decreasing the haldol or adding another medication, such as propranolol, to reduce the side effect.

Also on Axis III, one would want to rule out hepatitis, a chronic liver dysfunction. The sallow coloring of Mr. Graham's skin, his vomiting, and his history of alcohol abuse suggest that it may be present. Laboratory evaluations such as liver function tests should be performed.

On Axis IV, four specific stresses seem to be of importance:

1. Intense social isolation
2. Lack of employment
3. Poor financial support
4. Interpersonal stress with mother (with a major focus upon his keeping guns).

The Axis IV diagnoses suggest a variety of therapeutic interventions. Because of his social isolation, one must wonder whether Mr. Graham has adequate social skills for his stage of life. The clinician could consider the use of interventions, such as social skills training or possibly support group therapy or day activities as might be seen in a partial hospital. Mr. Graham's lack of employment raises complicated issues. To determine his vocational aptitude, Mr. Graham should be given neuropsychiatric tests, which may indicate a need for vocational rehabilitation. Regardless of the test results, counseling related to vocational issues and also to the scheduling of his time would seem important. The presence of both schizophrenia and alcohol dependence raises the issue of the role of boredom and lack of activity in precipitating Mr. Graham's drinking bouts, which could function to trigger the schizophrenia.

Mr. Graham's financial stress, which ties in with his vocational problems, also suggests the need for vocational intervention, as well as work with the family to encourage setting limits to his spending. Counseling with both the family and the patient may help to decrease tensions concerning both Mr. Graham's lack of motivation and his fiscal irresponsibility. The financial issues also suggest the need to provide family members with supportive counseling concerning the severe stressed created by Mr. Graham's constant presence in the household and his apparent irresponsibility. Helping the family to delineate what aspects of his irresponsibility may be related to his schizophrenia and what aspects may represent issues on which limits should be set could become one of the focuses of therapy.

The final concern showing up on Axis IV, the family's stress caused by Mr. Graham's guns, certainly suggests a need for intervention. Family counseling and the patient's removing the guns from the house, or at least removing all bullets, may play a key role not only in decreasing family tensions, but also in preventing possible suicide or homicide.

On Axis V, two ratings can be made concerning Mr. Graham's global assessment of functioning. His immediate presentation suggests a rating of somewhere around 50, which indicates that serious symptoms are still present. This rating indicates that, although Mr. Graham is calm, his occupational functioning remains seriously impaired. On the other hand, over the past year, he has not persistently shown, for a 2-month period, a functioning level much above 20. This low value on a chronic scale is of immediate importance for treatment planning. It suggests the need for intensive case management and counseling. The patient might be referred to an intensive treatment team (e.g., a continuous treatment team), in which clinicians carry small case loads and provide intensive counseling, home visits, family therapy, and medications.

As the clinician utilizes the DSM-III-R categorization for Mr. Graham, he or she begins to see a clearer picture of the patient's functioning on a daily basis and its impact on his family. By looking at all five axes, a clinician can quickly recognize that Mr. Graham is seriously impaired. The DSM-III-R schema allows the clinician to truly utilize the biopsychosocial model in which interventions may range from medication to family therapy or vocational counseling.

SUMMARY

This chapter was intended to provide an introduction to the DSM-III-R system. In particular, an effort has been made to address the three concerns that commonly prevent clinicians from wholeheartedly accepting the system. An effort also has been made to demonstrate that the DSM-III-R system is not based on the medical model, but rather represents an atheoretical approach that provides useful information and critical communication across all mental health disciplines. The case illustration was intended to demonstrate both the flexibility of the DSM-III-R system and the fact that it can provide an excellent foundation for treatment planning. Treatment planning that evolves from the DSM-III-R system is not medication specific, but rather addresses a multitude of interventions from psychotherapy to biological intervention. Finally, the common concern that the DSM-III-R system is too complicated for practical use has been addressed by demonstrating, with a few simple principles, that DSM-III-R is a system that can be readily learned and applied in a practical fashion.

In summary, the DSM-III-R system has been designed to provide a broad spectrum of assessment procedures and interventions for patients. The system attempts to push the clinician toward a compassionate understanding of the patient, forcing the clinician to always look at the symptom picture in conjunction with underlying personality structure, the possible presence of physical illness, and the interplay of complex psychosocial issues, such as family relationships and vocational aptitude. This attempt, inherent in the DSM-III-R system, to compassionately understand the patient can be no better stated than by Francis Peabody in 1927, who commented, "One of the essential qualities of the clinician is interest in humanity, for the secret of the care of the patient is caring for the patient."

REFERENCES

American Psychiatric Association. (1980). *Diagnostic and statistical manual of mental disorders* (3rd ed.). Washington, DC: Author.

American Psychiatric Association. (1987). *Diagnostic and statistical manual of mental disorders* (3rd ed.-rev.). Washington DC: Author.

Feighner, J. P., Robins, E., Guze, S. B., Woodruff, R. A., Winokur, G., & Munoz, R. (1972). Diagnostic criteria for use in psychiatric research. *Archives of General psychiatry, 26,* 57–63.

Griesinger, W. (1989). *Mental pathology and therapeutics* (2nd ed.). Birmingham, AL: Classics of Psychiatry and Behavioral Science Library. (Originally published in 1882).

Helmchen, H. (1975). Schizophrenia. Diagnostic concepts in the ICD-8. In M. H. Lader (Ed.), Studies in schizophrenia, [Special issue]. *British Journal of Psychiatry, 10,* 10–18.

Kato, M. (1977). *Multiaxial diagnosis in adult psychiatry.* Paper presented at the VIth World Congress of Psychiatry, Honolulu.

Mezzich, J. (1985). Multiaxial diagnostic systems in psychiatry. In H. Kaplan & B. Sadock (Eds.), *Comprehensive textbook of psychiatry* (4th ed.). Baltimore: Williams and Wilkins.

Ottosson, J. O., & Perris, C. (1973). Multidimensional classification of mental disorders. *Psychological medicine, 3,* 238–243.

Peabody, F. W. (1927). The case of the patient. *Journal of the American Medical Association, 88,* 877.

Rutter, M., Shaffer, D., & Shepherd, M. (1975). *A multiaxial classification of child psychiatric disorders.* Geneva: World Health Organization.

Sartorius, N. (1988). International perspectives of psychiatric classification. *British Journal of Psychiatry, 152,* 9–14.

Shea, S. C. (1988). *Psychiatric interviewing: The art of understanding.* Philadelphia: W. B. Saunders.

Spitzer, R. L., Endicott, J., & Robins, E. (1978). Research diagnostic criteria. *Archives of General Psychiatry, 35,* 773–782.

Tuke, D. H. (1892). *A dictionary of psychological medicine* (Vol. 2). Philadelphia: Blakiston.

von Cranach, M. (1977). *Categorical vs. multiaxial classification.* Paper presented at the VIth World Congress of Psychiatry, Honolulu.

Wing, L. (1970). Observations on the psychiatric section of the International Classification of Diseases and the British Glossary of Mental Disorders. Psychological Medicine, 1, 79-85.

PART TWO

Specific Disorders

CHAPTER 3

Organic Mental Disorders

GERALD GOLDSTEIN

INTRODUCTION

In 1987, The American Psychiatric Association (APA) published the revised third edition of the *Diagnostic and Statistical Manual of Mental Disorders* (DSM-III;1980). Ordinarily, the revision of descriptions of the organic mental disorders written only 7 years earlier would not be viewed as a great challenge in that most neurological disorders of mankind are ancient diseases, and developments in treatment and cure have been painfully slow. On this occasion, however, two substantive developments—one unfortunate and one fortunate—had taken place during those 7 years. The unfortunate event was the appearance of a new disease, acquired immune deficiency syndrome (AIDS) dementia. AIDS dementia is a consequence of human immunovirus infection and apparently represents an illness that has not appeared on the planet previously. It has been characterized as a progressive "subcortical dementia" of the type seen in patients with Huntington's disease and other neurological disorders in which the major neuropathology is in the subcortex. The syndrome itself has not been completely described, but there is substantial evidence of neuropsychological abnormalities. The first papers in this area appeared circa 1987, with the most well-known study being that of Grant et al. (1987). A recent review was written by Van Gorp, Miller, Satz, and Visscher (1989).

The fortunate news is that the marker for the Huntington's disease gene has been discovered on Chromosome 4 (Gusella et al., 1983). Although the gene itself has not been identified, geneticists are apparently coming close to doing so. Discovery of the gene will open treatment possibilities for this currently incurable illness, likely through methods involving recombinant DNA (deoxyribonucleic acid). There have been other less dramatic developments in the organic mental disorders, as well as some minor reformulations and changes in nomenclature associated with the appearance of the revised version of DSM-III, commonly termed DSM-III-R (APA, 1987). These matters are discussed below under specific topical areas.

A traditional distinction is made in psychopathology between the so-called functional and organic disorders. The functional disorder is generally viewed as a reaction to some environmental or psychosocial stress (e.g., anxiety disorder) or as a condition in which the presence of a specific organic etiologic factor is strongly suspected, but not proven (e.g., schizophrenia). The organic mental disorders can be more or less definitively associated with temporary or permanent dysfunction of the brain. Individuals with these illnesses are frequently described as "brain damaged" patients or patients with "organic brain syndromes."

Recent developments in psychopathological research and theory have gone a long way toward breaking down this distinction, and it is becoming increasingly clear that many of the schizophrenic, affective, and attentional disorders have their bases in some alteration of brain function. Nevertheless, the clinical phenomenology, assessment methods, and treatment management procedures associated with patients generally described as brain damaged are sufficiently unique that the traditional functional versus organic distinction is probably worth retaining. To delineate the subject matter of this chapter as precisely as possible, however, I prefer to think of the content as being concerned with individuals having structural brain damage rather than with "organic patients."

The theoretical approach taken here is neuropsychological in orientation, in that it will be based on the assumption that clinical problems associated with brain damage can be understood best in the context of what is known about the relationships between brain function and behavior. Thus, the presentation is expanded beyond the descriptive psychopathology of DSM-III-R in the direction of attempting to provide some material related to basic brain–behavior mechanisms. There are many sources of brain dysfunction, and the nature of the source has a great deal to do with determining behavioral consequences: morbidity and mortality. Thus, a basic grasp of key neuropathological processes is crucial to understanding the differential consequences of brain damage. Furthermore, it is important to have some conceptualization of how the brain functions. We do not know a great deal about this matter yet, so it remains necessary to think in terms of brain models or conceptual schema concerning brain function. For example, we still do not know how memories are preserved in brain tissue; however, there are several neuropsychological models and hypotheses concerning memory, portions of which have been supported by neurochemical and neurophysiological research.

In recognition of the complexities involved in relating structural brain damage to behavioral consequences, a field called clinical neuropsychology has emerged as a specialty area within psychology. Clinical neuropsychological research has provided a number of specialized instruments for assessment of brain damaged patients and, more recently, a variety of rehabilitation methods aimed at remediation of neuropsychological deficits. This research has also pointed out that "brain damage," far from being a single clinical entity, actually represents a wide variety of disorders. Initially, neuropsychologists were strongly interested in the relationship between localization of the brain damage and behavioral outcome. In recent years, however, localization has come to be seen as only one determinant of outcome, albeit often a very important one. Other considerations include such matters as the current age of the individual, the individual's age when the brain damage was acquired, the premorbid personality and level of achievement, and the type of pathological process producing the brain dysfunction. Furthermore, neuropsychologists are now cognizant of the possible influence of various "nonorganic" factors on their assessment methods, such as educational level, socioeconomic status, and mood states. Thus, this chapter is concerned with concepts of brain dysfunction in historical and contemporary perspectives, the various causes of brain dysfunction, and the clinical phenomenology of a number of syndromes associated with brain damage in relation to such factors as localization, age of the individual, age of the lesion, and pathological process.

CHANGING VIEWS OF BRAIN FUNCTION AND DYSFUNCITON

Concepts of how mental events are mediated have evolved from vague philosophical speculations concerning the "mind–body problem" to rigorous scientific theories supported by objective experimental evidence. According to studies of the history of science, it was not always understood that the "mind" was in the brain, and mental events were thought to be mediated by other organs of the body. Boring (1950) indicated that Aristotle thought that the mind was in the heart. Once the discovery was made that it was in the brain, scientists turned their interests to how the brain mediates behavior, thus beginning a line of investigation that to this day is far from complete.

Two major methodologies were used in this research: direct investigations of brain function through lesion generation or brain stimulation in animal subjects, and studies of patients who had sustained brain damage, particularly localized brain damage. The latter method, with which I am mainly concerned here, can be reasonably dated back to 1861 when Paul Broca produced his report on the case of a patient who had suddenly developed speech loss. An autopsy done on this patient revealed that he had sustained an extensive infarct in the area of the third frontal convolution of the left cerebral hemisphere. Thus, an important center in the brain for speech had been discovered, but, perhaps more significantly, this case produced what many would view as the first reported example of a neuropsychological or brain–behavior relationship in a human. Indeed, to this day, the third frontal convolution of the left hemisphere is known as Broca's area, and the type of speech impairment demonstrated by the patient is known as Broca's aphasia. Following Broca's discovery, much effort was devoted to relating specific behaviors to discrete areas of the brain. Wernicke made the very important discovery that the area that mediates comprehension, as opposed to expression, of speech is not Broca's area, but is a more posterior region in the left temporal lobe, the superior temporal gyrus.

Other investigators sought to localize other language, cognitive, sensory, and motor abilities in the tradition of Broca and Wernicke, some using animal lesion and stimulation methods, and others using clinical autopsy investigations of human brain damaged patients. Various syndromes were described, and centers or pathways whose damage or disconnection produced these syndromes were suggested. These early neuropsychological investigations not only provided data concerning specific brain–behavior relationships, but also explicitly or implicitly evolved a theory of brain function, now commonly known as classical localization theory. In essence, the brain was viewed as consisting of centers for various functions connected by neural pathways. In human subjects, the presence of these centers and pathways was documented through studies of individuals who had sustained damage to either a center or the connecting links between two centers such that they became disconnected. To this day, the behavioral consequences of this latter kind of tissue destruction is referred to as a "disconnection syndrome" (Geschwind, 1965). For example, some patients can speak and understand, but cannot repeat what was just said to them. In such cases, it is postulated that there is a disconnection between the speech and auditory comprehension centers.

From the beginnings of the scientific investigation of brain function, not all investigators advocated localization theory. The alternative view is that, rather than functioning through centers and pathways, the brain functions as a whole in an integrated manner. Views of this type are currently known as mass action, holistic, or organismic theories of brain function. Although we generally think of holistic theory as a reaction to localization theory, it actually preceded localization theory, in that the early concepts of brain function proposed by Galen and Descartes can be understood as holistic in nature. What is viewed as the first scientific presentation of holistic theory, however, was made in 1824 by Flourens, who proposed that the brain may have centers for special functions (*action propre*), but that there is a unity to the system as a whole (*action commune*) that dominates the entire system. Boring (1950) quoted Flourens's statement, "Unity is the great principle that reigns; it is everywhere, it dominates everything."

The legacy of holistic theory has come down to us from Flourens through the neurologist Hughlings Jackson. Jackson proposed a distinction between primary and secondary symptoms of brain damage. The primary symptoms are the direct consequences of the insult to the brain itself, whereas the secondary symptoms are the changes that take place in the unimpaired stratum. Thus, a lesion produces changes not only at its site, but throughout the brain.

In contemporary neuropsychology, the strongest advocates of holistic theory were Kurt Goldstein, Martin Scheerer, and Heinz Werner. K. Goldstein and Scheerer (1941) are best known for their distinction between abstract and concrete behavior, their description of the "abstract attitude," and the tests they devised to study abstract and concrete functioning in brain damaged patients. Their major proposition was that many symptoms of brain damage can be viewed not as specific manifestations of damage to centers or connecting pathways, but as some form of impairment of the abstract attitude. The abstract attitude is not localized in any region of the brain, but depends upon the functional integrity of the brain as a whole. K. Goldstein (1959) described the abstract attitude as the capacity to transcend immediate sensory impressions and consider situations from a conceptual standpoint. Generally, it is viewed as underlying such functions as planning, forming intentions, developing concepts, and separating ourselves from immediate sensory experience. The abstract attitude is evaluated objectively primarily through the use of concept formation tests that involve sorting or related categorical abilities. In language, it is evaluated by testing the patient's ability to use speech symbolically. Often, such testing is accomplished by asking the patient to produce a narrative about some object that is not present in the immediate situation.

Werner and various collaborators applied many of Goldstein's concepts to studies of brain injured and mentally retarded children (e.g., Werner & Strauss, 1942). Their analyses and conceptualizations reflected an orientation toward Gestalt psychology and holistic concepts, dealing with such matters as figure–ground relationships and rigidity. Halstead (1947) made use of the concept of the abstract attitude in his conceptualizations of brain function, but in a modified form. Like most contemporary neuropsychologists, Halstead viewed abstraction as one component or factor in cognitive function among many, and did not give it the central role attributed to it by Goldstein and his followers. Correspondingly, rather than adhering to an extreme position concerning the absence of localization, Halstead provided evidence to suggest that the frontal lobes were of greater importance in regard to mediation of abstract behavior than were other regions of the brain. K. Goldstein (1936) also came to accept the view that the frontal lobes were particularly important in regard to mediation of the abstract attitude.

The notion of a nonlocalized generalized deficit underlying many of the specific behavioral phenomena associated with brain damage has survived to some extent in contemporary neuropsychology, but in a greatly modified form. Similarly, some aspects of classical localization theory are still with us, but also with major changes (Mesulam, 1985). None of the current theories accepts the view that there is no localization of function in the brain and, correspondingly, none would deny that there are some behaviors that cannot be localized to some structure or group of structures. This synthesis is reflected in a number of modern concepts of brain function, the most explicit probably being that of Luria (1973). Luria developed the concept of functional systems as an alternative to both strict localization and mass action theories. Basically, a functional system consists of a number of elements involved in the mediation of some complex behavior. For example, there may be a functional system for auditory comprehension of language. The concept of pluripotentiality is substituted for Lashley's (1960) older concept of equipotentiality. Equipotentiality theory suggests that any tissue in a functional area can carry out the functions previously mediated by destroyed tissue. Pluripotentiality is a more limited concept, suggesting that one particular structure or element may be involved in many functional systems. Thus, no structure in the brain is involved in only a single function. Depending upon varying conditions, the same structure may play a role in several functional systems.

Current neuropsychological thought reflects some elements of all of the general theories of brain function briefly outlined above. In essence, the brain is thought to be capable of highly localized activity directed toward control of certain behaviors, but also of mediating other behaviors through means other than geographically localized centers. Indeed, since the discovery of the neurotransmitters (chemical substances that appear to play an important role in brain function), there appears to have been a marked change in how localization of function is viewed. To some authorities at least, localization is important only because the receptor sites for specific neurotransmitters appear to be selectively distributed in the brain. As we will see later, neuroscientists now tend to think not only in terms of geographical localization, but also in terms of neurochemical localization.

With regard to clinical neuropsychology, however, the main point seems to be that there are both specific and nonspecific effects of brain damage. Evidence for this point of view has been presented most clearly by Teuber and his associates (Teuber, 1959) and by Satz (1966). Teuber and his collaborators were able to show that patients with penetrating brain wounds that produced very focal damage had symptoms that could be directly attributed to the lesion site, but they also had other symptoms that were shared by all patients studied, regardless of their specific lesion sites. For example, a patient with a posterior lesion might have an area of cortical blindness associated with the specific lesion site in the visual projection areas, but he or she might also have difficulties in performing complex nonvisual tasks, such as placing blocks into a formboard while blindfolded. Most of Teuber's patients had difficulty with the formboard and other complex tasks, regardless of specific lesion site. In clinical settings, we may see brain damaged patients with this combination of specific and nonspecific symptoms, as well as patients with only nonspecific symptoms. One of the difficulties with early localization theory is that, because investigators tended to be unaware of the problem of nonspecific symptoms, they reported only the often more dramatic specific symptoms.

An old principle of brain function in higher organisms that has held up well and that is commonly employed in clinical neuropsychology involves contralateral control: the right half of the brain controls the left side of the body, and vice versa. Motor, auditory, and somatosensory fibers cross over at the base of the brain and thus control the contralateral side of the body. In the case of vision, the crossover is atypical. The optic nerve enters a structure called the optic chiasm, at which point fibers coming from the outer or temporal halves of the retinas go to the ipsilateral side of the brain, while fibers from the inner or nasal halves cross over and go to the contralateral cerebral hemispheres. However, the pattern is thought to be complete and all fibers coming from a particular hemiretina take the same course. For somesthesis, hearing, and motor function, the crossover is not complete, but the majority of fibers do cross over. Thus, for example, most of the fibers from the right auditory nerve find their way to the left cerebral hemisphere. The contralateral control principle is important for clinical neuropsychology because it explains why a patient with damage to one side of the brain may become paralyzed or develop sensory disturbances only on the opposite side of the body. We see this condition most commonly in individuals who have had strokes, but it is also seen in some patients with head injuries or brain tumors.

Although aphasia, or impaired communicative abilities as a result of brain damage, was recognized before Broca (Benton & Joynt, 1960), it was not recognized that it was associated with destruction of a particular area of one side of the brain. Thus, the basic significance of Broca's discovery was not the discovery of aphasia, but of cerebral dominance. *Cerebral dominance* is the term commonly employed to denote the fact that the human brain has a hemisphere that is dominant for language and a nondominant hemisphere. In most people, the left hemisphere is dominant, and left hemisphere brain damage may lead to aphasia; however, some individuals have dominant right hemispheres and others do not appear to have a dominant hemisphere. What was once viewed as a strong relationship between handedness and dominant hemisphere has not held up in recent studies, but the answers to questions regarding why the left hemisphere is dominant in most people and why some people are right dominant or have no apparent dominance remain unknown. In any event, it seems clear that aphasia is common in individuals who sustain left hemisphere brain damage, but rare with damage to the right hemisphere.

Following Broca's discovery, other neuroscientists discovered that, just as the left hemisphere has specialized functions in the area of language, the right hemisphere also has specialized functions. These functions all seem to relate to nonverbal abilities, such as visual–spatial skills, perception of complex visual configurations, and, to some extent, appreciation of nonverbal auditory stimuli such as music. Some investigators have conceptualized the problem in terms of sequential as opposed to simultaneous abilities. The left hemisphere is said to deal with material in a sequential, analytic manner, while the right hemisphere functions more as a detector of patterns or configurations (Dean, 1986). Thus, whereas patients with left hemisphere brain damage tend to have difficulty with language and other activities that involve sequencing, patients with right hemisphere brain damage have difficulties with such tasks as copying figures and producing constructions. In view of these findings regarding specialized functions of the right hemisphere, many neuropsychologists now prefer to use the expression "functional asymmetries of the cerebral hemispheres" rather than "cerebral dominance." The former terminology suggests that one hemisphere does not actually dominate or lead the other, but rather that each hemisphere has its own specialized functions.

As indicated above, localization alone is not the sole determinant of the behavioral outcomes of brain damage. Although age, sociocultural, and personality factors also are contributors, perhaps the most important consideration is the type of brain damage. Some would argue that neuropsychological assessment is rarely the best method of determining type of brain damage because other techniques, such as the computed tomography (CT) scan, cerebral blood flow studies, and, more recently, magnetic resonance imaging (MRI), are more adequate for that purpose. Their point may be well taken, but the problem remains that different types of lesions produce different behavioral outcomes even when they involve precisely the same areas of the brain. Thus, the clinician should be aware that the assessment methodology he or she uses may not be the best one to meet some specific diagnostic goal, and it is often necessary to use a variety of methods deriving from different disciplines to arrive at an adequate description of the patient's condition. In the present context, an adequate description generally involves identification of the kind of brain damage the patient has as well as its location. To point out the implications of this principle, it is necessary to provide a brief outline of the types of pathology that involve the brain and their physical and behavioral consequences.

NEUROPATHOLOGICAL CONSIDERATIONS

The brain may incur many of the illnesses that afflict other organs and organ systems. It may be damaged by trauma or may become infected. The brain can become cancerous or lose adequate oxygen through occlusion of the blood vessels that supply it. The brain can be affected through acute or chronic exposure to toxins, such as carbon monoxide or other poisonous substances. Nutritional deficiencies can alter brain function, just as they alter the function of other organs and organ systems.

In addition to these general systemic and exogenous factors, other diseases more or less specifically have the central nervous system as their target. These conditions, generally known as degenerative and demyelinating diseases, include Huntington's disease, multiple sclerosis, Parkinson's disease, and a number of disorders associated with aging. From the point of view of neuropsychological considerations, it is useful to categorize the various disorders according to temporal and topographical parameters. Certain neuropathological conditions are static and do not change substantially, others are slowly progressive, and some are rapidly progressive. Also, certain conditions tend to involve focal, localized disease, others multifocal lesions, and still others diffuse brain damage without specific localization. Another very important consideration has to do with morbidity and mortality. Some brain disorders are more or less reversible, some are static and do not produce marked change in the patient over lengthy periods of time, and some are rapidly or slowly progressive, producing increasing morbidity and eventually leading to death. Thus, some types of brain damage produce a stable condition with minimal changes, some types permit substantial recovery, and other types are in actuality terminal illnesses. It is therefore apparent that the kind of brain disorder from which the patient suffers is a crucial clinical consideration in that it has major implications for treatment, management, and planning.

Head Trauma

Although the skull affords the brain a great deal of protection, severe blows to the head can produce temporary brain dysfunction or permanent brain injury. The temporary conditions, popularly known as concussions, are generally self-limiting and follow a period of confusion, dizziness, and perhaps double vision; however, there seems to be complete recovery. In these cases, the brain is not thought to be permanently damaged. More serious trauma is generally classified as closed-head or open-head injury.

In closed-head injury, which is more common, the vault of the skull is not penetrated, but the impact of the blow crashes the brain against the skull and thus may create permanent structural damage. A commonly occurring type of closed-head injury is the subdural hematoma, in which a clot of blood forms under the dura, one of the protective layers on the external surface of the brain. These clots produce pressure on the brain that may be associated with clear-cut neurological symptoms. They may be removed surgically, but sometimes residual symptoms of a localized nature persist, such as weakness of one side of the body.

In open-head injury, the skull is penetrated by a missile of some kind. Open-head injuries occur most commonly during wartime as a result of bullet wounds; however, they sometimes occur as a result of vehicular or industrial accidents, if some rapidly moving object penetrates the skull. Open-head injuries are characterized by the destruction of brain tissue in a localized area. Remote effects often occur as well, but usually the most severe symptoms are associated with the track of the missile through the brain. Thus, an open-head injury involving the left temporal lobe could produce an aphasia, whereas a similar injury to the back of the head could produce a visual disturbance.

A major neuropsychological difference between open- and closed-head injuries is that the open-head injury typically produces specific, localized symptoms, whereas the closed-head injury, with the possible exception of subdural hematoma, produces diffuse dysfunction without specific focal symptoms. In both cases, some symptoms may disappear with time, but others may persist. Generally, a sequence of phases applies to the course of both closed- and open-head injuries. Often, the patient is initially unconscious and may remain that way for a widely varying amount of time, ranging from minutes to weeks or months. After consciousness is regained, the patient generally goes through a so-called acute phase, during which there may be confusion and disorientation.

Very often, a condition called posttraumatic amnesia is present, in which the patient cannot recall events that immediately preceded the trauma up to the present time. Research has shown that the length of time spent unconscious as well as the length of posttraumatic amnesia are reasonably accurate prognostic signs; the longer either persists, the worse the prognosis. During this stage, seizures are common, and treatment with anticonvulsant drugs is often necessary. When the patient emerges from this acute phase, the confusion diminishes, amnesia may persist but may not be as severe as previously, the seizures may abate, and one gets a better picture of what the long-term outcome will be. The range of variability is extremely wide, extending from patients remaining in persistent vegetative states to patients who regain complete recovery of function. In general, the residual difficulties of the head trauma patient, when they are significant, represent a combination of cognitive and physical symptoms. With regard to the latter, these patients are often more or less permanently confined to wheelchairs because of partial paralysis. Frequently, there are sensory handicaps, such as partial loss of vision or hearing.

It should be remembered that trauma to the head can do damage not only to the brain but to other parts of the head as well, such as the eyes and ears. Additionally, substantial disfigurement sometimes occurs in the form of scars, some of which can be treated with cosmetic surgery. The cognitive residual symptoms of head trauma are extremely varied since they are associated with whether the head injury was open or closed and whether there was clear tissue destruction. Most often, patients with closed-head injuries have generalized intellectual deficits involving abstract reasoning ability, memory, and judgment. Sometimes, marked personality changes occur, often having the characteristic of increased impulsiveness and exaggerated affective responsivity. Patients suffering from the residual of open-head injury may have classic neuropsychological syndromes, such as aphasia, visual–spatial disorders, and specific types of memory or perceptual disorders. In these cases, the symptoms tend to be strongly associated with the lesion site. For example, a patient with left hemisphere brain damage may have an impaired memory for verbal material, such as names of objects, whereas the right hemisphere patient may have an impaired memory for nonverbal material, such as pictures or musical compositions. In these cases, there is said to be both modality (e.g., memory) and material (e.g., verbal stimuli) specificity.

Head trauma is generally thought to be the most frequently seen type of brain damage in adolescents and young adults. It therefore generally occurs in a reasonably healthy brain. When the injury occurs in a young person with a previously healthy brain, the prognosis for recovery is generally good if the wound itself is not devastating in terms of its extent or the area of the brain involved. For practical purposes, residual brain damage is a static condition that does not generate progressive changes for the worse. Some research (Walker, Caveness, & Critchley, 1969) indicates that, following a long quiescent phase, head injured individuals may begin to deteriorate more rapidly when they become elderly; nevertheless, head injured individuals may have many years of productive functioning.

Since the first edition of this chapter appeared, interest in outcome following mild head injury has increased (Levin, Eisenberg, & Benten, 1989), as well as interest in the specific problems associated with head injury in children (Goethe & Levin, 1986). In recent years, trauma has frequently been reported as the major cause of death in children, and head trauma among children is not uncommon.

Brain Tumors

Brain cancer is a complex topic, particularly since cancer in general is not as yet completely understood. However, the conventional distinction between malignant and nonmalignant tumors is useful for the brain, as it is for other organs and organ systems. Some brain tumors are destructive, rapidly progressive, and essentially untreatable. Generally, these tissue structures are known as intrinsic tumors since they directly infiltrate the parenchyma of the brain. The most common type is a class of tumor known as glioma. Other types of tumors grow on the external surface of the brain and produce symptoms through the exertion of pressure on brain tissue. This type of tumor is described as being extrinsic, and the most common type is called a meningioma. In addition to these two types, there are metastases in which tumors have spread to the brain from some other organ of the body, often the lung. The extrinsic tumors are often treatable surgically, but metastases are essentially untreatable.

The clinical symptoms of tumor include headaches that frequently occur at night or on awakening, seizures, and vomiting. There are often progressive cognitive changes, perhaps beginning with some degree of confusion and poor comprehension and progressing to severe dementia during the terminal stages. Because tumors often begin in quite localized areas of the brain, the symptoms tend to depend on the particular location affected. For example, there is a large literature on frontal lobe tumors in which impairment of judgment, apathy, and general loss of the ability to regulate and modulate behavior are the major symptoms. As in the case of head injury, patients with left hemisphere tumors may develop aphasia, whereas patients with right hemisphere tumors may have visual–spatial disorders as their most prominent symptoms. The difference from head injury is that, short of surgical intervention, the severity of symptoms increases with time, sometimes at a very slow and sometimes at a very rapid rate, depending upon the type of tumor.

On rare occasions, the clinical psychologist or psychiatrist may see patients with tumors that affect particular structures in the brain, thereby generating characteristic syndromes. Among the most common of these are the cranial pharyngiomas, the pituitary adenomas, and the acoustic neuromas. The cranial pharyngiomas are cystic growths that lie near the pituitary gland and often depress the optic chiasm so that the primary symptoms may involve delayed development in children and waning libido and amenorrhea in adults, in combination with weakening of vision. The pituitary adenomas are similar in location, but the visual loss is often more prominent, frequently taking the form of what is called a bitemporal hemianopia (i.e., a loss of vision in both peripheral fields). The acoustic neuromas, tumors of the auditory nerve, produce hearing loss as the earliest symptom; however, because the auditory nerve also has a vestibular component, there may be progressive unsteadiness of gait and dizziness.

Clinicians may also see patients who have had surgically treated tumors and who demonstrate residual neuropsychological symptoms. They seem like patients with histories of open-head injury, perhaps because the brain lesion has, in a manner of speaking, been converted from a mass of abnormal tissue to a stable, nonmalignant wound. When neurosurgery has been successful, the changes are often rapid and very substantial. Because recurrence is possible, these patients should remain under continued medical care. Successful surgical treatment, however, may leave the patient with many years of productive life.

Brain Malformations and Early Life Brain Damage

A great deal of difference exists between destruction of a brain function already acquired and destruction of the brain mechanisms needed to acquire that function before it has been developed. The consequences of being born with an abnormal brain or acquiring brain damage during the early years of life may be quite different from the consequences of acquiring brain damage as an adult. On the positive side, the young brain generally has greater plasticity than the older brain, and it is somewhat easier for preserved structures to take over functions of impaired structures. On the negative side, when the brain mechanisms usually involved in the acquisition of some function are absent or impaired, that function is often not learned or not learned at a normal level. The relationship between age and consequences of brain damage remains an intensively researched area (Finger & Stein, 1982); however, for practical purposes it can be said that there is a population of individuals who were born with abnormal brain function, or who sustained structural brain damage at or shortly after birth, who go on to have developmental histories of either generalized or specific cognitive subnormality.

Generalized deficits, when sufficiently severe, are frequently described by a variety of terms, such as minimal brain damage, learning disability, and attention deficit disorder. One common generalized deficit becomes apparent in children who fail to learn to read normally despite adequate educational opportunity and average intelligence. These children are described as having dyslexia or developmental dyslexia.

With regard to neuropathological considerations, several types of brain disorder may occur during the prenatal period. Some are developmental in that either the brain itself or the skull does not grow normally during gestation. When the skull is involved, the brain is damaged through the effects of pressure on it. Sometimes a genetic factor is present, as is clearly the case with Down's syndrome. Sometimes poor prenatal care is responsible, the fetal alcohol syndrome perhaps being an extreme case of this condition. Sometimes an infection acquired during pregnancy, notably rubella (German measles), can produce severe mental retardation. Probably most often, however, the causes of the developmental abnormalities are unknown.

Damage to the brain can also occur as the result of a traumatic birth. Following birth, brain damage may occur due to such conditions as cerebral anoxia, infection, and brain dysfunction associated with such ongoing conditions as malnutrition or exposure to toxic substances. Children also have strokes and brain tumors, but they are quite rare. In essence, brain damage can occur in the very young before, during, and after birth. Although the neuropathological distinctions among the various disorders are quite important, the life span development of individuals from all three categories share some common characteristics. Retrospectively, it is often difficult to identify the responsible agent in the school-age child or adult. Thus, it is sometimes useful to think in terms of some general concept, such as perinatal or early life brain damage, rather than to attempt to specifically relate a particular developmental course or pattern of functioning to a single entity.

Although early life brain damage is usually a static condition in the sense that the lesion itself does not change, it may have varying consequences throughout a person's life. During the preschool years, the child may not achieve the generally accepted landmarks, such as walking and talking, at the average times. In school, these children often do not do well academically and may be either poor learners in general or have specific disabilities in such areas as reading, arithmetic, or visual–spatial skills. These academic difficulties may be accompanied by some form of behavioral disorder, often manifested in the form of hyperactivity or diminished attentional capacity. During adulthood, these individuals often do not make satisfactory vocational adjustments, and many researchers now feel that they are particularly vulnerable to certain psychiatric disorders, notably alcoholism (Tarter, 1976) or schizophrenia (Mednick, 1970).

Although this volume does not specifically address child psychopathology, several disorders classed as organic mental, or neurobehavioral, disorders begin during childhood and persist into adulthood. Growing evidence (McCue & Goldstein, in press; Spreen, 1987) indicates that learning disability frequently persists into adulthood. Autism, which is now generally viewed as a neurobehavioral disorder (Minshew & Payton, 1988a, 1988b), also generally persists into adulthood. A recent study (Rumsey & Hamburger, 1988) that followed up some of Kanner's (1943) original cases demonstrated the persistence of neuropsychological deficit in these autistic adults.

Diseases of the Circulatory System

Current thinking about the significance of vascular disease has changed in recent years. It once was felt that cerebral arteriosclerosis, or hardening of the arteries, was the major cause of generalized brain dysfunction in middle-aged and elderly adults. Although this condition is much less common than was once thought, the status of the heart and the blood vessels is significantly related to the intactness of brain function. Basically, the brain requires oxygen to function, and oxygen is distributed to the brain through the cerebral blood vessels. When these vessels become occluded, circulation is compromised and brain function is correspondingly impaired. Such impairment occurs in a number of ways, perhaps the most serious and abrupt of which is stroke. A stroke is a sudden total blockage of a cerebral artery caused by a blood clot or a hemorrhage. The clot may be a thrombosis, formed out of atherosclerotic plaque at branches and curves in the cerebral arteries, or an embolism, which is a fragment that has broken away from a thrombus in the heart and has migrated to the brain. Cerebral hemorrhages are generally fatal, but survival from thrombosis or embolism is not at all uncommon. Following a period of stupor or unconsciousness, the most common and apparent postacute symptom is hemiplegia, paralysis of one side of the body. There is also a milder form of stroke, known as a transient ischemic attack (TIA), which is basically a temporary, self-reversing stroke that does not produce severe syndromes, or may be essentially asymptomatic.

A somewhat different picture emerges in another cerebral vascular disorder known as multi-infarct dementia. As opposed to the abruptly rapid onset seen in stroke, multi-infarct dementia is a progressive condition based on a history of small strokes associated with hypertension. Patients with multi-infarct dementia experience a stepwise deterioration of function, with each small stroke making the dementia worse in some way. There are parallels between multi-infarct dementia and the older concept of cerebral arteriosclerosis in that they both relate to the role of generalized cerebral vascular disease in producing progressive brain dysfunction; however, multi-infarct dementia is actually a much more precisely defined syndrome that, although not rare, is also not extremely common.

As discussed later, many patients once diagnosed as having cerebral arteriosclerosis would now be diagnosed as having one of the degenerative diseases associated with the presenile or senile period of life. Other relatively common cerebrovascular disorders are associated with aneurysms and other vascular malformations in the brain. An aneurysm is an area of weak structure in a blood vessel that may not produce symptoms until it balloons out to the extent that it creates pressure effects or it ruptures. A ruptured aneurysm is an extremely serious medical condition in that it may lead to sudden death; however, surgical intervention in which the aneurysm is ligated is often effective.

Arteriovenous malformations are congenitally acquired tangles of blood vessels. They may be asymptomatic for many years, but can eventually rupture and hemorrhage. They may appear anywhere in the brain, but commonly they occur in the posterior half. The symptoms produced, when they occur, may include headache and neurological signs associated with the particular site.

The individual with a focal vascular lesion, most commonly associated with stroke, and the patient with generalized vascular disease such as multi-infarct dementia exhibit major neuropsychological differences. The stroke patient is characterized not only by the hemiplegia or hemiparesis, but sometimes by an area of blindness in the right or left visual fields and commonly by a pattern of behavioral deficits associated with the hemisphere of the brain affected and the locus within that hemisphere. If the stroke involves a blood vessel in the left hemisphere, the patient will be paralyzed or weak on the right side of the body; the area of blindness, if present, will involve the right field of vision; and there will frequently be an aphasia. Right hemisphere strokes may produce left-sided weakness or paralysis and left visual fields defects but no aphasia. Instead, a variety of phenomena may occur. The patient may acquire a severe difficulty with spatial relations, a condition known as constructional apraxia. The ability to recognize faces or to appreciate music may be affected. A phenomenon known as unilateral neglect may develop in which the patient does not attend to stimuli in the left visual field, although basic vision is found to be intact. Sometimes affective changes occur in which the patient denies that he or she is ill, and may even develop euphoria.

In contrast with this specific, localized symptom picture seen in the stroke patient, the individual with multi-infarct dementia or other generalized cerebral vascular disease has a different set of symptoms. Generally, this patient has no unilateral paralysis, no visual field deficit, no gross aphasia, and none of the symptoms characteristic of patients with right hemisphere strokes. Rather, generalized intellectual, and to some extent physical, deterioration occurs. If weakness is present, it is likely to affect both sides of the body, and typically there is general diminution of intellectual functions, including memory, abstraction ability, problem solving ability, and speed of thought and action. In the case of the patient with multi-infarct dementia, there tend to be several localizing signs that do not point to a single lesion in one specific site.

The more common forms of cerebral vascular disease are generally not seen until at least middle age, and for the most part are diseases of the elderly. Clinically significant cerebral vascular disease is often associated with a history of generalized cardiovascular or other systemic diseases, notably hypertension and diabetes. Some genetic or metabolic conditions promote greater production of atheromatous material than is normal, and some people are born with arteriovenous malformations or aneurysms, placing them at higher than usual risk for serious cerebral vascular disease. When a stroke is seen in a young adult, it is usually because of an aneurysm or other vascular malformation. Most authorities agree that stroke is basically caused by atherosclerosis, and acknowledge that genetic and acquired conditions that promote atherosclerotic changes in blood vessels generate risk of stroke. With modern medical treatment, there is a good deal of recovery from stroke with substantial restoration of function. In the case of the diffuse disorders, however, there is no concept of recovery since they tend to be slowly progressive. The major hope is to minimize the risk of future strokes, through such means as controlling blood pressure and weight.

Interest has developed recently in the long-term effects of hypertension on cerebral function, as well as the long-term effects of antihypertensive medication. Recent reviews (Elias & Streeten, 1980; King & Miller, 1990) have demonstrated that both hypertension and antihypertensive medication can impair cognitive function, but there are no definite conclusions in this area as yet, with studies reporting mixed as well as benign outcomes associated with prudent use of antihypertensive medication (G. Goldstein, 1986).

Degenerative and Demyelinating Diseases

The degenerative and demyelinating diseases comprise a variety of disorders that have a number of characteristics in common, but that also differ from each other in many ways. They specifically attack the central nervous system, they are slowly progressive and incurable, and, although they are not all hereditary diseases, they appear to stem from some often unknown but endogenous defect in physiology. Certain diseases, once thought to be degenerative, have been found not to be so, or are thought not to be so at present. For example, certain dementias have been shown to be caused by a so-called "slow virus," whereas multiple sclerosis, the major demyelinating disease, is strongly suspected of having a viral etiology. Thus, for these two examples, the classification would change from degenerative to infectious diseases.

The term degenerative disease means that, for some unknown reason, the brain or the entire central nervous system gradually wastes away. In some cases, this wasting, or atrophy, resembles what happens to the nervous system in very old people; however, it occurs substantially earlier than the senile period, perhaps as early as the late 40s. These diseases are known as presenile dementia, the most common type being Alzheimer's disease. Alzheimer's disease also occurs in a senile form, but there is some controversy as to whether the senile and the presenile forms are in actuality the same disease. Senile dementia is generally diagnosed in elderly individuals when the degree of cognitive deficit is substantially greater than one would expect with normal aging. In other words, not all old people become significantly demented before death. Most of those who do, but do not have another identifiable disease of the central nervous system, are generally thought to have Alzheimer's disease. Indeed, Alzheimer's disease is now thought to account for more senile dementia than does cerebral arteriosclerosis.

A disorder related to Alzheimer's disease, called Pick's disease, is difficult to distinguish from Alzheimer's disease in living individuals. The distinction becomes apparent only on autopsy, since the neuropathological changes in the brain are different. Within psychiatry, there is no longer an attempt to differentiate clinically among Alzheimer's, Pick's, and some rarer degenerative diseases. DSM-III describes them all with the single term "primary degenerative dementia." DSM-III-R uses the term "primary degenerative dementia of the Alzheimer type."

Another frequently occurring degenerative disease found in younger adults is called Huntington's chorea or Huntington's disease. The disease is characterized by progressive intellectual deterioration and a motor disorder involving gait disturbance and involuntary jerky, spasmodic movements. It has definitely been established as hereditary, and there is a 50 percent chance of acquiring the disease if born to a carrier of the gene. Symptoms may begin to appear during the second or third decade, and survival from the time symptoms appear is generally about 8 years. The intellectual deterioration is characterized by progressively profound impairment of memory, with most cognitive functions eventually becoming involved. Often, speech articulation is difficult because of the loss of control of the musculature involved in speech.

Although much is still not known about the degenerative disorders, much has been discovered in recent years. The major discovery was that Alzheimer's and Huntington's diseases are apparently based on neurochemical deficiencies. In the case of Alzheimer's disease, the deficiency is thought to be primarily the group of substances related to choline, one of the neurotransmitters. The disease process is characterized by progressive death of the choline neurons, the cells that serve as receptor sites for cholinergic agents. Huntington's disease is more neurochemically complex because three neurotransmitters are involved: choline, gamma-aminobutyric acid (GABA), and substance P. The reasons for these neurochemical deficiency states remain unknown, but the states have been described and treatment efforts have been initiated based on this information. For example, some Alzheimer's patients have been given choline or lecithin, a substance related to choline, in hopes of achieving symptomatic improvement.

Multiple sclerosis is the most common of the demyelinating diseases. Its pathology involves progressive erosion of the myelin sheaths that surround fibers in the central nervous system. Both the brain and the spinal cord are involved in this illness. Nerve conduction takes place along the myelin sheaths, and therefore cannot occur normally when these sheaths erode. This abnormality leads to motor symptoms, such as paralysis, tremor, and loss of coordination, but characteristic changes occur in vision if the optic nerve is involved, as well as in cognitive function. Obviously, cognitive skills that involve motor function tend to be more impaired than those that do not. Until its final stages, multiple sclerosis does not have nearly as devastating an effect on cognitive function as do the degenerative diseases.

The crippling motor disorder may be the only apparent and significantly disabling symptom for many years. Less often, but not infrequently, progressive loss of vision also occurs. Multiple sclerosis acts much like an infectious disease, and some authorities feel that it is, in fact, caused by some unknown viral agent. Symptoms generally appear during young adulthood and may progress rapidly or slowly, leading some authorities to differentiate between acute and chronic multiple sclerosis. Individuals with this disorder may live long lives, and there may be lengthy periods during which no deterioration takes place. Sometimes, temporary remission of particular symptoms is seen. In recent years, extensive neuropsychological studies of multiple sclerosis have been done (reviewed in Peyser & Poser, 1986), with a particular interest in differences between relapsing–remitting and chronic–progressive forms of the disease (Heaton, Nelson, Thompson, Burks, & Franklin, 1985).

Alcoholism

The term alcoholism, in the context of central nervous system function, involves not only the excessive consumption of alcoholic beverages, but a complex set of considerations involving nutritional status, related disorders such as head trauma, physiological alterations associated with the combination of excessive alcohol consumption and malnutrition, and possible genetic factors. These elements, and perhaps others, may influence the status of the central nervous system in alcoholic patients. Long-term chronic alcoholics often experience deterioration of intellectual function, similar to that of patients with primary degenerative dementia. It is not clear, however, that the deteriorative process is specifically associated with alcohol consumption per se. Thus, although some clinicians use the term "alcoholic dementia," this characterization lacks sufficient specificity, since it is rarely clear that the observed dementia is solely a product of excessive use of alcohol.

Looking at the matter in temporal perspective, first, there may be a genetic propensity for the acquisition of alcoholism that might ultimately have implications for central nervous system function (Goodwin, 1979). Second, Tarter (1976) suggested that there may be an association between having minimal brain damage or a hyperactivity syndrome as a child and acquiring alcoholism as an adult. These two considerations suggest that at least some individuals who eventually become alcoholics may not have completely normal brain function preceding the development of alcoholism. Third, during the course of becoming chronically alcoholic, dietary habits tend to become poor and multiple head injuries may be sustained as a result of fights or accidents. As the combination of excessive alcohol abuse and poor nutrition progresses, major physiological changes may occur, particularly in the liver and to some extent in the pancreas and gastrointestinal system. Thus, the dementia in long-term alcoholic patients may well involve a combination of all of these factors in addition to the always present possibility of other neurological complications.

Although the majority of alcoholics who develop central nervous system complications demonstrate general deterioration of intellectual abilities, some develop specific syndromes. The most common is the Wernicke–Korsakoff syndrome, a disorder that begins with the patient's going into a confusional state accompanied by difficulty in walking and controlling eye movements, and by polyneuritis, a condition marked by pain or loss of sensation in the arms and legs. The latter symptoms may gradually disappear, but the confusional state may evolve into a permanent, severe amnesia. When this transition has taken place, the patient is generally described as having Korsakoff's syndrome or alcohol amnestic disorder, and is treated with large dosages of thiamine, since the etiology of the disorder appears to be a thiamine deficiency rather than a direct consequence of alcohol ingestion. Evidence (Blass & Gibson, 1977) indicates that the thiamine deficiency must be accompanied by an inborn metabolic defect related to an enzyme that metabolizes thiamine.

The amnesic and intellectual disorders found in chronic alcoholics are permanent and present even when patients are not intoxicated. The acute effects of intoxication or withdrawal (e.g., delirium tremens [DTs]) are superimposed on these permanent conditions. These disorders are also progressive as long as alcohol abuse and malnutrition persist. Other than abstinence and improved nutrition, there is no specific treatment. Even thiamine treatment for the Korsakoff patient does not restore memory; it is used primarily to prevent additional brain damage.

A major interest in recent years has been the genetics of alcoholism. Findings have been impressive thus far, and there is a growing, probably well-justified belief that a positive family history of alcoholism increases an individual's risk for becoming alcoholic, if exposed to the beverage alcohol. A broad range of research has been done, including extensive family adoption studies (Goodwin, Schulsinger, Hermansen, Guze, & Winokur, 1973); neuropsychological studies of relatives (Schaeffer, Parsons, & Yohman, 1984) and children of alcoholics (Tarter, Hegedus, Goldstein, Shelly, & Alterman, 1984); psychophysiological studies, emphasizing brain event-related potentials in siblings (Steinhauer, Hill, & Zubin, 1987) and children (Begleiter, Porjesz, Bihari, & Kissin, 1984) of alcoholics; and laboratory genetic studies. In summary, extensive efforts are being made to find the biological markers of alcoholism (Hill, Steinhauer, & Zubin, 1987) and to determine the transmission of alcoholism in families. One reasonable assumption is that alcoholism is a heterogeneous disorder, and there may be both hereditary and nonhereditary forms (Cloninger, Bohman, & Sigvardsson, 1981).

Toxic, Infectious, and Metabolic Illnesses

The brain may be poisoned by exogenous or endogenous agents, or it may become infected. Sometimes these events occur with such severity that the person dies, but usually the individual survives with a greater or lesser degree of neurological dysfunction. The major exogenous toxin, alcohol, has already been discussed. However, excessive use of drugs, such as bromides and barbiturates, may produce at least temporary brain dysfunction. This temporary condition, called delirium in DSM-III-R, is basically a loss of capacity to maintain attention and a reduced awareness of the environment.

Tremors and lethargy may be accompanying symptoms. Delirium is reversible in most cases, but may evolve into a permanent dementia or other neurological disorder.

In psychiatric settings, a frequently seen toxic disorder is carbon monoxide poisoning. This disorder and its treatment are quite complex, because it usually occurs in an individual with a major mood or psychotic disorder who has attempted to commit suicide by inhaling car fumes in a closed garage. The brain damage sustained often is permanent, resulting in significant intellectual and physical dysfunction in addition to the previously existing psychiatric disorder. Other toxic substances that may affect central nervous system function include certain sedative and hypnotic drugs, plant poisons, heavy metals, and toxins produced by certain bacteria leading to such conditions as tetanus and botulism. The specific effects depend on the substance, as well as on whether exposure is acute (as in the case of tetanus or arsenic poisoning) or chronic (as in the case of addiction to opiates and related drugs).

A large number of brain disorders are associated with inborn errors of metabolism. In some way, a fault in metabolism produces a detrimental effect on the nervous system, generally beginning in early life. Although many of these disorders exist, only two of the more well-known ones are used here as illustrations. The first is phenylketonuria (PKU). PKU is an amino acid uria, a disorder that involves excessive excretion of some amino acid into the urine. It is genetic and, if untreated, can produce mental retardation accompanied by poor psychomotor development and hyperactivity. The treatment involves a diet low in phenylalanine. The second disorder is Tay–Sach's disease, an enzyme abnormality due to a deficiency in hexasaminidase A, which is important for the metabolism of protein and polysaccharides. It is hereditary, occurs mainly in Jewish children, and is present from birth. The symptoms are initially poor motor development and progressive loss of vision, followed by dementia, with death usually occurring before age 5. These two examples illustrate similarity in process, which is basically an inherited enzyme deficiency, but variability in outcome. PKU is treatable, with a relatively favorable prognosis, whereas Tay–Sachs is a rapidly progressive, incurable terminal illness.

Bacterial infections of the brain are generally associated with epidemics, but sometimes occur when no epidemics are at large. These infections are generally referred to as encephalitis, when the brain itself is infected, or meningitis, when the infection is in the meninges, the membranous tissue that lines the brain. Infections, of course, are produced by microorganisms that invade tissue and produce inflammation. During the acute phase of the bacterial infections, the patient may be quite ill and survival is an important issue. Headaches, fever, and a stiff neck are major symptoms. There may be delirium, confusion, and alterations in state of consciousness ranging from drowsiness, through excessive sleeping, to coma. Some forms of encephalitis were once popularly known as "sleeping sickness." Following the acute phase of bacterial infection, the patient may be left with residual neurological and neuropsychological disabilities and personality changes. Sometimes infections are local, and the patient is left with neurological deficits that correspond with the lesion site. The irritability, restlessness, and aggressiveness of postencephalitic children are mentioned in the literature. Jervis (1959) described these children as overactive, restless, impulsive, assaultive, and wantonly destructive.

Neurosyphylis is another type of infection that has a relatively unique course. In addition to progressive dementia, the disorder is characterized by major personality changes involving the acquisition of delusions and a tendency toward uncritical self-aggrandizement. Although neurosyphilis or general paresis played a major role in the development of psychiatry, it is now a relatively rare disease and is seldom seen in clinical practice. Similarly, the related neurosyphilitic symptoms, such as tabes dorsalis and syphilitic deafness, are also rarely seen.

During recent years, the incidence and perhaps the interest in bacterial infections and neurosyphilis have diminished, whereas interest in viral infections has increased substantially. Perhaps four reasons account for this phenomenon: Jonas Salk's discovery that poliomyelitis was caused by virus and could be prevented by vaccination; the recent increase in the incidence of herpes simplex, a viral disorder; the appearance of AIDS; and the discovery of the "slow viruses." The latter two reasons are probably of greatest interest in the present context. Recent discoveries indicate that certain viruses have a long incubation period and may cause chronic degenerative disease, resembling Alzheimer's disease in many ways. Thus, some forms of dementia may be produced by a transmittable agent. A disease known as kuru and another known as Creutzfeldt–Jakab disease appear to be such dementias. The importance of the finding is that the discovery of infection as the cause of a disease opens the possibility of developing preventive treatment in the form of a vaccine. As indicated above, AIDS dementia is another form of viral encephalopathy.

Epilepsy

Despite the usual manner in which this condition is described, epilepsy is actually a symptom of many diseases and not a disease in itself. Patients are generally diagnosed as "epileptics" when seizures are the major or only presenting symptoms and the cause cannot be determined. However, seizures are commonly associated with diagnosable disorders, such as brain tumors, alcoholism, or head trauma. Furthermore, the view that epilepsy means that the patient has "fits" or episodes of falling and engaging in uncontrolled, spasmodic movements is also not completely accurate. Although these fits or convulsions represent one form of epilepsy, there are other forms as well. Several attempts have been made to classify epilepsy into subtypes, but only the most recent one generally accepted by neurologists is mentioned here (Gastaut, 1970).

The major distinction made is between generalized and partial seizures. In the case of generalized seizures, there is a bilaterally symmetrical abnormality of brain function, with one of two things generally happening: (a) a massive convulsion with a sequence of spasmodic movements and jerking, or (b) a brief abrupt loss of consciousness with little in the way of abnormal motor activity. There may be some lip smacking or involuntary movements of the eyelids. The former type used to be called a grand mal seizure, whereas the latter type was called a petit mal seizure or absence.

The partial seizures may have a simple or a complex symptomatology. In the simple case, the seizure may be confined to a single limb and may involve either motor or sensory function. Motor seizures are often characterized by a turning movement of the head, accompanied by contractions of the trunk and limbs. A relatively rare form of this disorder is called a Jacksonian motor seizure in which the spasmodic movements spread from the original site to the entire side of the body, a phenomenon referred to as a march. In the case of sensory seizures, the epileptic activity may consist of a variety of sensory disorders, such as experiencing a sudden numbness, feeling "pins and needles," seeing spits of light, or hearing a buzzing or roaring in the ears.

The complex partial seizures involve confused but purposeful appearing behavior, followed by amnesia for the episode. In this condition, sometimes known as temporal lobe or psychomotor epilepsy, the patient may walk around in a daze, engage in inappropriate behavior, or have visual or auditory hallucinations. From this description, it is clear that not all seizures involve massive motor convulsions. What all of these phenomena have in common is that they are based on a sudden, abrupt alteration of brain function produced by an excessive, disorganized discharge of neurons. Thus, if one were looking at an epileptic individual's brain waves on an electroencephalograph (EEG) and a seizure occurred, a sudden and dramatic alteration would occur in the characteristics of the EEG. The presence and particular pattern of these alterations are often used to identify and diagnose various forms of epilepsy.

The question of whether an association exists between epilepsy and intellectual impairment is complex. According to Klove and Matthews (1974), individuals having complex partial (temporal lobe) seizures demonstrate little intellectual impairment; however, individuals with generalized seizures of unknown etiology that appear early in life are likely to have significant intellectual deficit. The matter is also complicated by the cause of the seizure. If an individual has seizures related to a brain tumor, neuropsychological deficits generally associated with the lesion sites involved are likely to appear as well as the seizures. The question of intellectual deficit seems to arise primarily in the case of individuals who are epileptic and have no other apparent neurological signs of symptoms. This condition is known as recurrent seizures of unknown cause or as idiopathic epilepsy. The tentative answer to the question appears to be that there is a higher probability of significant intellectual deficit when the disorder involves generalized seizures and appears early in life.

The mental health practitioner should be aware that, although epilepsy can be treated through the use of a variety of "anticonvulsant" medications, the epileptic patient may have many difficulties of various types. The disorder has retained some degree of social stigma, in the form of either superstitious beliefs or the inaccurate stereotype that epileptics tend to be violent or impulsive people. More realistically, epileptics do have difficulties with such matters as obtaining drivers' licenses or insurance coverage that allows them to work around potentially hazardous equipment. It is possible that, during a complex partial seizure, an individual can perform an antisocial act over which he or she honestly has no control and cannot remember. Epileptic seizures may be symptoms of some life-threatening illness. Children with petit mal epilepsy may have school difficulties because of their momentary lapses of consciousness. Individuals with motor seizures may injure their heads during the seizure and produce additional brain dysfunction through trauma. Thus, the epileptic may have many problems in living that are not experienced by the nonepileptic, and frequently may be assisted through an understanding of the nature of the condition, and through counseling and support in coping with it.

Recently, Myslobodsky and Mirsky (1988) edited an extensive work on petit mal epilepsy that covers its genetic, neurophysiological, neuropsychological, metabolic, and electrophysiological aspects. Interest in the psychosocial aspects of epilepsy is growing. Having seizures clearly produces an impact on one's environment, and people in the environment may maintain the older superstitions and false beliefs about epilepsy. Furthermore, modifications of behavior in epileptics may be largely biologically determined because of the cerebral dysfunction associated with the disorder. Dodrill (1986) recently reviewed the extensive literature on psychosocial consequences of epilepsy, providing a useful outline of the types of psychosocial difficulties epileptics commonly experience, the relationship between psychosocial and neuropsychological function, and treatment-related issues.

SOME COMMON SYNDROMES

In this section, I provide descriptions of the more commonly occurring disorders associated with structural brain damage. Clearly, what is common in one setting may be rare in another. Thus, the focus is on what is common in an adult neuropsychiatric setting. The neuropsychological syndromes found in childhood are often quite different from what is seen in adults and deserve separate treatment. Furthermore, the emphasis is on chronic rather than acute syndromes since, with relatively rare exceptions, the psychologist and psychiatrist encounter the former far more frequently than the latter. However, initially acute conditions, such as stroke, that evolve into chronic conditions also are dealt with in some detail.

Thus far, matters have been discussed from the standpoints of general concepts of brain function and of neuropathological processes. The following material is on the behavioral manifestations of the interaction between various brain mechanisms and different types of pathology. It is useful to view these manifestations in the form of identified patterns of behavioral characteristics that might be described as neuropsychological syndromes. Although neuropsychological deficits can be described and classified in other ways, the syndrome approach has the advantage of providing rather graphic phenomenological descriptions of different kinds of brain damaged patients. However, it runs the risk of suggesting that every brain damaged patient can be classified as having some specific, identifiable syndrome—something that is not at all true. It is therefore important to keep in mind that this discussion involves classic types of various disorders that are in fact seen in some actual patients; however, many brain damaged patients do not have classic-type syndromes, their symptomatology reflecting an often complex combination of portions of several syndromes.

Heilman and Valenstein (1985), in the way in which they outlined their recently revised clinical neuropsychology text, suggested a useful and workable classification of syndromes. First, there are communicative disorders, which may be subdivided into aphasia and the specialized language or language-related disorders, including reading impairment (alexia), or writing disorders (agraphia), and calculation disorders (acalculia). Second, there are syndromes associated with some aspect of perception or motility. These include the perception of one's body (the body schema disturbances), the various visual–spatial disorders (which may involve perception, constructional abilities, or both), the gnostic disorders (impairment of visual, auditory, and tactile recognition), the neglect syndromes, and the disorders of skilled and purposeful movement, called apraxias. Third, there are syndromes that primarily involve general intelligence and memory–dementia and the amnesic disorders. Associated with this latter type are the relatively unique syndromes associated with damage to the frontal lobes. These general categories account for most of the syndromes seen in adults, and the discussion here is limited to them.

Communicative Disorders

In general, aphasia and related language disorders are associated with unilateral brain damage to the dominant hemisphere, which in most individuals is the left hemisphere. Most aphasias result from stroke, but they can also be acquired on the basis of left hemisphere head trauma or brain tumor. Although the definition has changed over the years, the most current one requires impairment of communicative ability associated with focal, structural brain damage. Thus, the term is not coextensive with all disorders of communicative ability and does not include, for example, the language disorders commonly seen in demented individuals with diffuse brain damage. The study of aphasia has in essence become a separate area of scientific inquiry, having its own literature and several theoretical frameworks.

The term aphasia itself does not convey a great deal of clinically significant information since the various subtypes are quite different from each other. Although numerous attempts have been made to classify the aphasias, no system is universally accepted. Contemporary theory indicates that perhaps the most useful major distinction is between fluent and nonfluent aphasias. To many authorities, this distinction is more accurate than the previously more commonly made distinction between expressive and receptive aphasias. The problem is that aphasics with primarily expressive problems do not generally have normal language comprehension, and it is usually true that aphasics with major speech comprehension disturbances do not express themselves normally. However, there are aphasics who talk fluently and others whose speech is labored, very limited, and halting, if present at all in a meaningful sense. Although speech is fluent in the former group, it is generally more or less incomprehensible because of a tendency to substitute incorrect words for correct ones, a condition known as verbal paraphasia. The primary disturbance in these patients involves profoundly impaired auditory comprehension. This combination of impaired comprehension and paraphasia is generally known as Wernicke's aphasia. The responsible lesion is generally in the superior gyrus of the left temporal lobe. In nonfluent aphasia, comprehension is generally somewhat better, but speech is accomplished with great difficulty and is quite limited. This condition is generally known as Broca's aphasia, because the responsible lesion is in the lower, posterior portion of the left frontal lobe (i.e., Broca's area). Several other types of aphasia are relatively rare and are not described here. It is important to point out, however, that most aphasias are mixed, having components of the various pure types. Furthermore, the type of aphasia may change in the same patient, particularly during the course of recovery.

The disorders of reading, writing, and calculation may also be divided into subtypes. In the case of reading, the interest here is in the so-called acquired alexias in which an individual formerly able to read has lost that ability because of focal, structural brain damage. The ability to read letters, words, or sentences may be lost. Handwriting disturbances, or agraphia, might involve a disability in writing words from dictation or a basic disability in forming letters. Some agraphic patients can write, but with omissions and distortions relative to what was dictated, whereas others can no longer engage in the purposive movements needed to form letters. Calculation disturbances, or acalculias, are also of several types. The patient may lose the ability to read numbers, to calculate even if the numbers can be read, or to arrange numbers in a proper spatial sequence for calculation.

The various syndromes associated with communicative disorders sometimes exist in pure forms, but more often merge together. For example, alexia is frequently associated with Broca's aphasia, and difficulty with handwriting is commonly seen in patients with Wernicke's aphasia. Generally, however, the pattern is such that a clear primary disorder, such as impaired auditory comprehension, occurs with associated defects, such as difficulty with reading or writing. Sometimes, rather unusual combinations occur, as in the case of the syndrome of alexia without agraphia. In this case, the patient can write but cannot read, often to the extent that the patient cannot read what he or she has just written. Research done since the first version of this chapter was written indicates that academic deficits are frequently seen in adults that are not the product of brain damage acquired during adulthood or of inadequate educational opportunity. Rather, people with these deficits have developmentally based learning disabilities that they never outgrew. The view that learning disability is commonly outgrown has been rejected by most students of this area (McCue & Goldstein, in press).

Disorders of Perception and Motility

The disorders of perception can involve perception of one's body as well as perception of the external world. In the case of the external world, the disorder can involve some class of objects or some geographical location. The disorders of motility discussed here are not primary losses of motor function, as in paralysis or paresis, but losses in the capacity to perform skilled, purposive acts. This set of impairments is called apraxia. There is also a borderline area in which the neuropsychological defect has to do with the coordination of a sense modality, usually vision, and purposive movement. These disorders are sometimes described as impairment of constructional or visual-spatial relations ability. In some patients the primary difficulty is perceptual, whereas in others it is mainly motoric.

The body schema disturbances most commonly seen are of three types. In one type, the patient is unable to point to his or her own body parts on command. This syndrome is called autotopognosia, meaning lack of awareness of the surface of one's body. A more localized disorder of this type is finger agnosia in which, while identification of body parts is otherwise intact, the patient cannot identify the fingers of his or her own hands, or of another person's hands. Finger agnosia has been conceptualized as a partial dissolution of the body schema. The third type of body schema disturbance is right–left disorientation, in which the patient cannot identify body parts in regard to whether they are on the right or left side. For example, a patient who is asked to show you his or her right hand may become confused or show you his or her left hand. More commonly, however, a more complex command is required to elicit this deficit, such as asking the patient to place his or her left hand on his or her right shoulder. Traditionally, both finger agnosia and right–left disorientation are considered part of a syndrome, with the responsible brain damage being in the region of the left angular gyrus. Benton (1985), however, pointed out that the matter is in fact more complicated, and the issue of localization involves the specific nature of these defects in terms of the underlying cognitive and perceptual processes affected.

Perceptual disorders in which the patient has difficulty recognizing some class of external objects are called gnostic disorders or agnosias. These disorders may be classified with regard to modality and verbal or nonverbal content. Thus, one form of the disorder might involve visual perception of nonverbal stimuli, and would be called visual agnosia. By definition, an agnosia is present when primary function of the affected modality is intact, but the patient cannot recognize or identify the stimulus. For example, in visual agnosia, the patient can see but cannot recognize what he or she has seen. To determine whether visual agnosia is present, one should establish whether the patient can recognize and name an object when it is placed in his or her hand, so that it can be recognized by touch, or when it produces some characteristic sound, so that it can be recognized by audition.

The brain lesions involved in the agnosias are generally in the association areas for the various perceptual modalities. Thus, visual agnosia is generally produced by damage to association areas in the occipital lobes. When language is involved, there is obviously a great deal of overlap between the agnosias and the aphasias. For example, visual–verbal agnosia can actually be viewed as a form of alexia. In these cases, it is often important to determine through detailed testing whether the deficit is primarily a disturbance of perceptual recognition or a higher level conceptual disturbance involving language comprehension. A wide variety of gnostic disorders are reported in the literature involving such phenomena as the inability to recognize faces, colors, or spoken works; however, they are relatively rare conditions and, when present, may persist only during the acute phase of the illness. In general, agnosia has been described as "perception without meaning," and it is important to remember that it is quite a different phenomenon from what we usually think of as blindness or deafness.

Sometimes a perceptual disorder involves a portion of geographical space rather than a class of objects. Although this phenomenon is described by many terms, the most frequently used terms are neglect and inattention. This disorder is seen most dramatically in vision, where the patient may neglect the entire right or left side of the visual world. It also occurs in the somatosensory modality, in which case the patient may neglect one side of his or her body. Although neglect can occur on either side, it is more common on the left side, since it is generally associated with right hemisphere brain damage.

In testing for neglect, it is often useful to employ the method of double stimulation, for example, in the form of simultaneous finger wiggles in the areas of the right and left visual fields. Typically, the patient may report seeing the wiggle in the right field but not in the left. Similarly, when the patient with neglect is touched lightly on the right and left hand at the same time, he or she may report feeling the touch in only one hand or the other. As in the case of the gnostic disorders, neglect is defined in terms of the assumption of intactness of the primary sensory modalities. Thus, the patient with visual neglect should have otherwise normal vision in the neglected half field, whereas the patient with tactile neglect should have normal somatosensory function.

Clinically, neglect may be a symptom of some acute process and should diminish in severity or disappear as the neuropathological condition stabilizes. For example, visual neglect of the left field is often seen in individuals who have recently sustained right hemisphere strokes, but can be expected to disappear as the patient recovers.

The apraxias constitute a group of syndromes in which the basic deficit involves impairment of purposive movement occurring in the absence of paralysis, weakness, or unsteadiness. For some time, the distinction has been made among three major types of apraxia: ideomotor, limb-kinetic, and ideational. In ideomotor apraxia, the patient has difficulty performing a movement to verbal command. In limb-kinetic apraxia, movement is clumsy when the patient performs on command or is asked to imitate a movement. In ideational apraxia, the difficulty is with organizing the correct motor sequences in response to language. In other words, it may be viewed as a disability in regard to carrying out a series of acts. In addition, there are facial apraxias in which the patient cannot carry out facial movements to command. These four types are thought to involve different brain regions and different pathways; however, each is generally conceptualized as a destruction or disconnection of motor engrams or traces that control skilled, purposive movement. Certain of the visual–spatial disorders are referred to as apraxias, such as constructional or dressing apraxia, but they are different in nature from the purer motor apraxias described above.

The basic difficulty met by the patient with a visual–spatial disorder relates to comprehension of spatial relationships and, in most cases, coordination between visual perception and movement. In extreme cases, the patient may readily become disoriented and lose his or her way when going from one location to another. In most cases, however, the difficulty appears to be at the cognitive level and may be examined by asking the patient to copy figures or solve jigsaw or block design type puzzles. Patients with primarily perceptual difficulties have problems in localizing points in space, judging direction, and maintaining geographical orientation, as tested by asking the patient to describe a route or use a map. Patients with constructional difficulties have problems with copying and block building. So-called dressing apraxia may be seen as a form of constructional disability in which the patient cannot deal effectively with the visual–spatial demands involved in such tasks as buttoning clothing. Although visual–spatial disorders can result from lesions found in most parts of the brain, they are most frequently seen, and seen with the greatest severity, in patients with right hemisphere brain damage. Generally, the area that most consistently produces the severest deficit is the posterior portion of the right hemisphere. Whereas some patients show a dissociation between visual–spatial and visual–motor or constructional aspects of the syndrome of constructional apraxia, most patients have difficulties on both purely perceptual and constructional tasks.

Dementia

Dementia is probably the most common form of organic mental disorder. There are several types of dementia, and they all usually involve slowly progressive deterioration of intellectual function. Deterioration is frequently patterned, with loss of memory generally being the first function to decline, followed by deterioration of other abilities at later stages of the illness. As the term is used now, dementia may occur at any age. One major class of dementia consists of those disorders that arise during late life, either during late middle age—presenile dementia—or during old age—senile dementia. In children, dementia is differentiated from mental retardation on the basis of deterioration from a formerly higher level. Dementia may result from head trauma or essentially any of the neuropathological conditions discussed above. One common cause of dementia appears to be alcoholism and the nutritional disorders that typically accompany it. A specific type of dementia that generally appears before the presenile period is Huntington's disease.

The term dementia, when defined in the broad way suggested here, is not particularly useful and does not provide more information than do such terms as "organic brain syndrome" or "chronic brain syndrome." When the term is used in a more specific way, however, it becomes possible to point out specific characteristics that may be described as syndromes. Such specificity may be achieved by defining the dementias as those disorders in

which, for no exogenous reason, the brain begins to deteriorate and continues to do so until death. DSM-III-R describes these conditions as "progressive degenerative dementia."

The most common type of progressive degenerative dementia is Alzheimer's disease, but sufficient diagnostic methods are not yet available to
diagnose Alzheimer's disease in the living patient. Its presence becomes
apparent only on examination of the brain at autopsy. Clinically, the course
of the illness generally begins with signs of impairment of memory for
recent events, followed by deficits in judgment, visual–spatial skills, and
language. In recent years, the language deficit has become a matter of particular interest, perhaps because the communicative difficulties of dementia
patients are becoming increasingly recognized. Generally, the language difficulty does not resemble aphasia, but can perhaps be best characterized
as an impoverishment of speech, with word finding difficulties and progressive inability to produce extended and comprehensible narrative speech.
Recently, basically the same finding was noted in the descriptive writing
of Alzheimer's disease patients (Neils, Boller, Gerdeman, & Cole, 1989).
The patients wrote shorter descriptive paragraphs than age-matched controls and also made more handwriting errors of various types.

The end state of dementia is generalized, severe intellectual impairment
involving all areas, with the patient sometimes surviving for various lengths
of time in a persistent vegetative state. The progressive dementia seen in
Huntington's disease also involves significant impairment of memory, with
other abilities becoming gradually affected through the course of the illness.
It differs from Alzheimer's disease, however, in that it is accompanied by the
choreic movements described earlier and by the fact that the age of onset is
substantially earlier than is the case for Alzheimer's disease. Because of the
chorea, a difficulty in speech articulation is also frequently seen, which is
not the case for Alzheimer's patients. A form of dementia that has a known
etiology but that is slowly progressive is multi-infarct dementia. This disorder is known to be associated with hypertension and a series of strokes, with
the end result being substantial deterioration. However, the course of the
deterioration is not thought to be as uniform as in Alzheimer's disease, but
rather is generally stepwise and patchy. The patient may remain relatively
stable between strokes, and the symptomatology produced may be associated with the site of the strokes.

During the bulk of the illness' course, the dementia patient typically
appears confused, possibly disoriented, and lacking in the ability to recall
recent events. Speech may be very limited and, if fluent, is likely to be
incomprehensible. Thus, these patients do not have the specific syndromes
of the type described above surrounded by otherwise intact function. Instead, the deficit pattern tends to be global in nature, with all functions
more or less involved.

Although distinctions between multi-infarct and primary degenerative
dementia are clearly described, a definitive differential diagnosis cannot
always be made in individual patients. Even such sophisticated radiological
methods as CT scan and MRI do not always contribute to the diagnosis.
Some investigators have attempted to identify syndromal subtypes, with

some having more deficit in the area of abstraction and judgment, some in the area of memory, and some in regard to affect and personality changes. This proposed typology has not been well established, however, as most patients have difficulties with all three areas.

Some dementias are treatable, particularly dementias associated with endocrine disorders or normal pressure hydrocephalus, but there is no curative treatment for progressive degenerative dementia. Current research offers the hope that pharmacological treatment may eventually be able to ameliorate the course of Alzheimer's disease, but thus far no such effective treatment is available.

One type of dementia appears to be specifically associated with frontal lobe brain damage. The damage may occur as a result of a number of processes, such as head trauma, tumor, or stroke, but the syndrome produced is more or less the same. Indeed, clinicians speak of a "frontal lobe syndrome." The outstanding features all may be viewed as relating to impaired ability to control, regulate, and program behavior. Such impairment is manifested in numerous ways, including poor abstraction ability, impaired judgment, apathy, and loss of impulse control. Language is sometimes impaired, but in a rather unique way. Rather than having a formal language disorder, the patient loses the ability to control behavior through language. Often, the patient has a difficulty with narrative speech that has been interpreted as a problem in forming the intention to speak or in formulating a plan for a narrative. Such terms as lack of insight or of the ability to produce goal-oriented behavior are used to describe the frontal lobe patient. In many cases, these activating, regulatory, and programming functions are so impaired that the outcome looks like a generalized dementia with implications for many forms of cognitive, perceptual, and motor activities.

Amnesia

Although some degree of memory impairment is a part of many brain disorders, in a number of conditions, memory loss is clearly the outstanding deficit. When memory loss is particularly severe and persistent, and other cognitive and perceptual functions are relatively intact, the patient can be described as having an amnesic syndrome. Dementia patients are often amnesic, but their memory disturbance is embedded in significant generalized impairment of intellectual and communicative abilities. The amnesic patient generally has normal language and may be of average intelligence. As in the case of aphasia and several other disorders, there is more than one amnesic syndrome. The differences among these syndromes revolve around what the patient can and cannot remember. The structures in the brain that are particularly important for memory are the limbic system, especially the hippocampus, and certain brain stem structures, including the mammillary bodies and the dorsomedial nucleus of the thalamus.

Many systems are described in the literature for distinguishing among types of amnesia and types of memory. With regard to the amnesias, perhaps the most basic distinction is between anterograde and retrograde amnesia. Anterograde amnesia involves the inability to form new memories from the time of the onset of the illness producing the amnesia, whereas retrograde amnesia refers to the inability to recall events that took place before the onset of the illness. This distinction dovetails with the distinction between recent and remote memory. It also corresponds to some extent with the distinction made between short-term and long-term memory in the experimental literature. However, because various theories define these latter terms somewhat differently, perhaps it is best to use the more purely descriptive terms recent and remote memory in describing the amnesic disorders. It then can be stated that the most commonly appearing amnesic disorders involve dramatic impairment of recent memory with relative sparing of remote memory. This sparing becomes greater as the events to be remembered become more remote. Thus, most amnesic patients can recall their early lives, but may totally forget what occurred during that last several hours. The distinction between recent and remote memory possibly aids in explaining why most amnesic patients maintain normal language function and average intelligence. In this respect, an amnesic disorder is not so much an obliteration of the past as it is an inability to learn new material.

Probably the most common type of relatively pure amnesic disorder is alcoholic Korsakoff's syndrome. These patients, while often maintaining average levels in a number of areas of cognitive function, demonstrate a dense amnesia for recent events with relatively well-preserved remote memory. Alcoholic Korsakoff's syndrome has been conceptualized by Butters and Cermak (1980) as an information processing defect in which new material is encoded in a highly degraded manner, leading to high susceptibility to interference. Butters and Cermak (1980), as well as numerous other investigators, have carried out detailed experimental studies of alcoholic Korsakoff's patients in which the nature of their perceptual, memory, and learning difficulties have been described in detail. The results of this research aid in explaining numerous clinical phenomena noted in Korsakoff's patients, such as their capacity to perform learned behaviors without recall of when or if those behaviors were previously executed, or their tendency to confabulate or "fill in" for the events of the past day that they do not recall. It may be noted that, although confabulation was once thought to be a cardinal symptom of Korsakoff's syndrome, it is seen in only some patients.

Another type of amnesic disorder results from direct, focal damage to the temporal lobes and, most importantly, to the hippocampus. These temporal lobe or limbic system amnesias are less common than Korsakoff's syndrome, but have been well studied because of the light they shed on the neuropathology of memory. Such patients share many of the characteristics of Korsakoff's patients, but have a much more profound deficit in regard to basic consolidation and storage of new material. When Korsakoff's patients are sufficiently cued and given enough time, they can learn. Indeed, sometimes they can demonstrate normal recognition memory. Patients with temporal lobe amnesias, however, may find it almost impossible to learn new material under any circumstances.

In some cases, amnesic disorders are modality specific. If one distinguishes between verbal and nonverbal memory, the translation can be made from the distinction between language and nonverbal abilities associated with the specialized functions of each cerebral hemisphere. It has, in fact, been reported that patients with unilateral lesions involving the left temporal lobe may have memory deficits for verbal material only, whereas right temporal patients have corresponding deficits for nonverbal material. Thus, the left temporal patient may have difficulty with learning word lists, whereas the right temporal patient may have difficulty with geometric forms.

In summary, although there are several amnesic syndromes, they all have in common the symptom of lack of ability to learn new material following the onset of the illness. Sometimes the symptom is modality specific, involving only verbal or nonverbal material, but usually it involves both modalities. Although there are several relatively pure types of amnesia, notably Korsakoff's syndrome, memory difficulties also are cardinal symptoms of many other brain disorders, notably the progressive dementias and certain disorders associated with infection. For example, people with Herpes encephalitis frequently have severely impaired memories, but they have other cognitive deficits as well.

ALTERNATIVE DESCRIPTIVE SYSTEMS

As has been indicated, not all clinicians or researchers associated with brain damaged patients have adopted the neuropsychologically oriented syndrome approach briefly described above. Many methodological and substantive reasons underlie these differing views. The methodological issues largely revolve around the operations used by investigators to establish the existence of a syndrome. Critics suggest that syndromes may be established on the basis of overly subjective inferences, as well as on incomplete examinations. The alternative method proposed is generally described as a dimensional approach in which, rather than attempting to assign patients to categories, they are measured on a variety of neuropsychologically relevant dimensions, such as intellectual function, language ability, and memory. Advocates of this approach are less concerned with determining whether the patient has a recognizable syndrome, and more interested in profiling the patient along a number of continuous dimensions, and relating that profile to underlying brain mechanisms. Rourke and Brown (1986) recently clarified this issue in a full discussion of similarities and differences between behavioral neurology and clinical neuropsychology.

Utilizing a dimensional philosophy, there is no need to develop a classification system, except perhaps in terms of certain characteristic profiles. For purposes of providing an overview of the descriptive phenomenology of structural brain damage, however, the substantive matters probably are of more relevance. In essence, the disciplines of neurology, neuropsychology, and psychiatry have all developed descriptive classificatory systems that differ in many respects. We have already discussed the ways in which brain damage is described and classified by neurologists and neuropsychologists; however, the psychiatric descriptions are also quite important, because they point to problems not uncommonly seen in brain damaged patients that are not always clearly identifiable in the neurological and neuropsychological systems. There is an area of overlap in regard to dementia and the amnesias, but DSM-III and DSM-III-R contain a number of categories that are not clearly defined neurologically or neuropsychologically.

The first of these categories is the organic delusional syndrome. Patients with this disorder have, as the primary symptom, delusional beliefs while in a normal state of consciousness. It must be established that the delusions have an organic basis and that the patient is not actually delusional because of a paranoid or schizophrenic disorder. The neurological basis for this syndrome is varied, and may involve drug abuse, right hemisphere brain damage, or Huntington's disease or another dementia. Related to this diagnosis, but different from it, is organic hallucinosis. In this syndrome, hallucinations rather than delusions are the primary symptoms, but again the disorder must have an organic basis. DSM-III and DSM-III-R also describe organic affective and organic personality syndromes, in which the primary symptoms are, respectively, a mood disturbance (either mania or depression) and a personality change. The personality changes noted generally involve increased impulsiveness, emotional lability, or apathy. Perhaps these are actually mainly frontal lobes syndromes, but the syndrome may also be seen in conjunction with temporal lobe epilepsy.

There are some minor differences between the terms in DSM-III and those in DSM-III-R. In general, the term "syndrome" has been changed to "disorder" (e.g., organic delusional syndrome has become organic delusional disorder). Consistent with the remainder of DSM-III-R, the term "affect" has been changed to "mood." Thus, organic affective syndrome has been changed to organic mood disorder, and one specifies whether the mood disorder is manic, depressed, or mixed. A disorder called organic anxiety disorder has been added in DSM-III-R. Under organic personality disorder, one specifies in DSM-III-R whether it is of the explosive type.

DSM-III and DSM-III-R also classify under the organic mental disorders substance-induced intoxication, withdrawal states, and other symptom complexes associated with various sympathomimetic and hallucinogenic drugs. Typically, these conditions are acute phenomena and do not persist beyond a matter of days. Certain of them, however, notably those associated with alcohol abuse, may eventually evolve into permanent disorders, notably dementia. Their behavioral correlates generally involve personality changes, such as euphoria, agitation, anxiety, hallucinations, and depersonalization. Cognitive changes might include impairment of memory and inability to concentrate. Within the context of psychopathology, the commonality between these conditions and those related to more permanent, structural brain damage is that they all have an identified or presumed organic basis and are therefore distinct from the functional psychiatric disorders. The phraseology used to describe the organic mental disorders in DSM-III and DSM-III-R is as follows: "Evidence, from the history, physical examination, or laboratory test, of a specific organic factor that is judged to be etiologically related to the disturbance."

The psychiatrically based categorization can perhaps be most productively viewed as supplemental to the type of neuropsychological system used by Heilman and Valenstein (1985), rather than as an alternative to it. It plays a major role in describing the noncognitive kinds of symptomatology that are often associated with structural brain damage, particularly for those cases in which these personality and affective changes are the predominant symptoms. These considerations are of the utmost clinical importance, because the failure to recognize the organic basis for some apparently functional symptom, such as a personality change, may lead to the initiation of totally inappropriate treatment or the failure to recognize a life-threatening physical illness.

Although alterations in brain function can give rise to symptoms that look like functional personality changes, the reverse can also occur. That is, a nonorganic personality change, notably acquisition of a depression, can produce symptoms that look like they have been produced by alterations in brain function. The term generally applied to this situation is "pseudodementia," and is most frequently seen in elderly people who become depressed. The concept of pseudodementia or depressive pseudodementia is not universally accepted, but it is not uncommon to find elderly patients diagnosed as demented when in fact the symptoms of dementia are actually produced by depression. The point is proven when the symptoms disappear or diminish substantially after the depression has run its course or the patient is treated with antidepressant medication. Wells (1979, 1980) pointed out that this differential diagnosis is difficult to make, and cannot be accomplished satisfactorily with the usual examinational, laboratory, and psychometric methods. He suggested that perhaps the most useful diagnostic criteria are clinical features. For example, patients with pseudodementia tend to complain about their cognitive losses, whereas patients with dementia tend not to complain. In a more recent formulation, Caine (1986) pointed to the many complexities of differential diagnosis in the elderly, referring in particular to the abundant evidence for neuropsychological deficits in younger depressed patients, and to the not uncommon coexistence of neurological and psychiatric impairments in the elderly.

SUMMARY

The organic mental disorders are a large number of conditions in which behavioral changes may be directly associated with some basis in altered brain function. Although the general diagnostic term "organic brain syndrome" has commonly been used to describe these conditions, the wide variability in the manifestations of brain dysfunction make this term insufficiently precise in reference to clinical relevance. Variability is attributable to a number of factors, including the following considerations: (a) the location of the damage in the brain, (b) the neuropathological process producing the damage, (c) the length of time the brain damage has been present, (d) the age and health status of the individual at the time the damage is sustained, and (e) the individual's premorbid personality and level of function.

The neuropsychological approach to the conceptualization of the organic mental disorders has identified a number of behavioral parameters along which the manifestations of brain dysfunction can be described and classified. The most frequently considered dimensions are intellectual function, language, memory, visual–spatial skills, perceptual skills, and motor function. Some important concepts related to brain function and brain disorders include the principle of contralateral control of perceptual and motor functions and functional hemisphere asymmetries. In addition, studies of brain damaged patients have shown that particular structures in the brain mediate relatively discrete behaviors. Neurologists and neuropsychologists have identified a number of syndromes in such areas as language dysfunction, memory disorder, and general intellectual impairment. Also, there are major variations in the courses of the organic mental disorders. Some are transient, leaving little or no residual; some are permanent but not progressive; and others are either slowly or rapidly progressive. Although these disorders most profoundly and commonly involve impairment of cognitive, perceptual, and motor skills, sometimes personality changes of various types are the most prominent symptoms. More often than not, personality and affective changes appear in brain damaged patients along with their cognitive, perceptual, and motor disorders. Thus, an affective disorder or such symptoms as delusions and hallucinations may be sequelae of brain damage for various reasons.

Since the writing of the first version of this chapter, two major events have occurred: the appearance of AIDS dementia and the discovery of the marker for the Huntington's disease gene. Also, new, productive work has been done in the area of alcoholism genetics. There have also been important advances in neurodiagnostic technologies, notably major increases in the sophistication of magnetic resonance imaging and capacities to measure cerebral activity through various cerebral blood flow techniques and positron emission tomography (see Bigler, Yeo, & Turkheimer, 1989, for a comprehensive review). The capacity to visualize the brain with increasingly fine resolution, as well as to measure brain function at rest and under activation conditions, is growing rapidly.

REFERENCES

American Psychiatric Association. (1980). *Diagnostic and statistical manual of mental disorders* (3rd ed.). Washington DC: Author.

American Psychiatric Association. (1987). *Diagnostic and statistical manual of mental disorders* (3rd ed. rev.). Washington DC: Author.

Begleiter, H., Porjesz, B., Bihari, B., & Kissin, B. (1984). Event-related potentials in boys at high risk for alcoholism. *Science, 225,* 1493–1496.

Benton, A. (1985). Body schema disturbances: Finger agnosia and right left disorientation. In K. M. Heilman & E. Valenstein (Eds.), *Clinical neuropsychology* (2nd ed., pp. 115–129). New York: Oxford University Press.

Benton, A. L., & Joynt, R. J. (1960). Early descriptions of aphasia. *Archives of Neurology, 3,* 205–222.

Bigler, E. D., Yeo, R. A., & Turkheimer, E. (1989). *Neuropsychological function and brain imaging.* New York: Plenum.

Blass, J. P., & Gibson, G. E. (1977). Abnormality of a thiamine-requiring enzyme in patients with Wernicke–Korsakoff syndrome. *The New England Journal of Medicine, 297,* 1367–1370.

Boring, E. G. (1950). *A history of experimental psychology* (2nd ed.). New York: Appleton-Century-Crofts.

Broca, P. (1861). Perte de la parole. Ramollissement chronique et destruction partielle du lobe anterieur gauche du cerveau. *Bulletin de la Societe d'Anthropologie, 2,* 235–238.

Butters, N., & Cermak, L. S. (1980). *Alcoholic Korsakoff's syndrome.* New York: Academic Press.

Caine, E. D. (1986). The neuropsychology of depression: the pseudodementia syndrome. In I. Grant & K. M. Adams (Eds.), *Neuropsychological assessment of neuropsychiatric disorders* (pp. 221–243). New York: Oxford University Press.

Cloninger, C. R., Bohman, M., & Sigvardsson, S. (1981). Inheritance of alcohol abuse: Cross-fostering analysis of adopted men. *Archives of General Psychiatry, 38,* 861–868.

Dean, R. S. (1986). Lateralization of cerebral functions. In D. Wedding, A. M. Horton Jr., & J. Webster (Eds.), *The neuropsychology handbook: Behavioral and clinical perspectives* (pp. 80–102). New York: Springer.

Dodrill, C. B. (1986). Psychosocial consequences of epilepsy. In S. B. Filskov & T. J. Boll (Eds.), *Handbook of clinical neuropsychology* (Vol. 2, pp. 338–363). New York: Wiley.

Elias, M. F., & Streeten, D. H. P. (1980). *Hypertension and cognitive processes.* Mount Desert, ME: Beech Hill.

Finger, S. & Stein, D. G. (1982). *Brain damage and recovery: Research and clinical perspectives.* New York: Academic Press.

Flourens, M. J. P. (1824). *Recherches experimentales sur les proprietes et les fonctons du systeme nerveux dans les animaux vertebres.* Paris: Crevot.

Gastaut, H. (1970). Clinical and electroencephalographical classification of epileptic seizures. *Epilepsia, 11,* 102–103.

Geschwind, N. (1965). Disconnection syndromes in animals and man. *Brain, 88,* 237–294.

Goethe, K. E., & Levin, H. S. (1986). Neuropsychological consequences of head injury in children. In G. Goldstein & R. E. Tarter (Eds.), *Advances in clinical neuropsychology* (Vol. 3, pp. 213–242). New York: Plenum Press.

Goldstein, G. (1986, February). *Neuropsychological effects of five antihypertensive agents.* Poster presented at annual meeting of International Neuropsychological Society, Denver.

Goldstein, K. (1936). The significance of the frontal lobes for mental performance. *Journal of Neurology and Psychopathology, 17,* 27–40.

Goldstein, K. (1959). Functional disturbances in brain damage. In S. Arieti (Ed.), *American handbook of psychiatry.* (pp. 770–794). New York: Basic Books.

Goldstein, K., & Scheerer, M. (1941). Abstract and concrete behavior: An experimental study with special tests. *Psychological Monographs, 53*(2, Whole No. 239).

Goodwin, D. W. (1979). Alcoholism and heredity: A review and hypothesis. *Archives of General Psychiatry, 36,* 57–61.

Goodwin, D. W., Schulsinger, F., Hermansen, L., Guze, S. B., & Winokur, G. (1973). Alcohol problems in adoptees raised apart from alcoholic biological parents. *Archives of General Psychiatry, 28,* 238–243.

Grant, I., Atkinson, J. H., Hesselink, J. R., Kennedy, C. J., Richman, D. D., Spector, S. A., & McCutchan, J. A. (1987). Evidence for early central nervous system involvement in the acquired immunodeficiency syndrome (AIDS) and other human immunodeficiency virus (HIV) infections. *Annals of Internal Medicine, 107,* 828–836.

Gussella, J. F., Wexler, N. S., Conneally, P. M., Naylor, S. L., Anderson, M. A., Tanzi, R. E., Watkins, P. C., Ottina, K., Wallace, M. R., Sakaguchi, A. Y., Young, A. B., Shoulson, I., Bonilla, E., & Martin, J. B. (1983). A polymorphic DNA marker genetically linked to Huntington's disease. *Nature, 306,* 234–238.

Halstead, W. C. (1947). *Brain and intelligence.* Chicago: University of Chicago Press.

Heaton, R. K., Nelson, L. M., Thompson, D. S., Burks, J. S., & Franklin, G. M. (1985). Neuropsychological findings in relapsing-remitting and chronic-progressive multiple sclerosis. *Journal of Consulting and Clinical Psychology, 53,* 103–110.

Heilman, K. M., & Valenstein, E. (Eds.). (1985). *Clinical neuropsychology* (2nd ed.). New York: Oxford University Press.

Hill, S. Y., Steinhauer, S. R., & Zubin, J. (1987). Biological markers for alcoholism: A vulnerability model conceptualization. In C. Rivers (Ed.), *Nebraska symposium on motivation. Vol. 34: Alcohol and addictive behavior* (pp. 207–256). Lincoln, NE: University of Nebraska Press.

Jervis, G. A. (1959). The mental deficiencies. In S. Arieti (Ed.), *American handbook of psychiatry* (Vol. 2, pp. 1289–1314). New York: Basic Books.

Kanner, L. (1943). Autistic disturbances of affective contact. *Nervous Child, 2,* 217–250.

King, H. E., & Miller, R. E. (in press). Hypertension: Cognitive and behavioral considerations. *Neuropsychology Review, 1,* 31–73

Klove, H., & Matthews, C. G. (1974). Neuropsychological studies of patients with epilepsy. In R. M. Reitan & L. A. Davison (Eds.), *Clinical neuropsychology: Current status and applications* (pp. 237–265). New York: Winston-Wiley.

Lashley, K. S. (1960). In search of the engram. In F. A. Beach, D. O. Hebb, C. T. Morgan, & H. W. Nissen (Eds.), *The neuropsychology of Lashley* (pp. 478–505).New York: McGraw-Hill. [Originally published in 1950]

Levin, H. S., Eisenberg, H. M., & Benton, A. L. (1989). *Mild head injury.* New York: Oxford University Press.

Luria, A. R. (1973). *The working brain.* New York: Basic Books.

McCue, M., & Goldstein, G. (in press). Neuropsychological aspects of learning disability in adults. In B. P. Rourke (Ed.), *Neuropsychological validation of learning disability subtypes.* New York: Guilford.

Mednick, S. A. (1970). Breakdown in individuals at high risk for schizophrenia: Possible predispositional perinatal factors. *Mental Hygiene, 54,* 50–63.

Mesulam, M. M. (1985). *Principles of behavioral neurology.* Philadelphia: F. A. Davis.

Minshew, N. J., & Payton, J. B. (1988a). New perspectives in autism: Part 1. The clinical spectrum of infantile autism. *Current Problems in Pediatrics, 18,* 561–610.

Minshew, N. J., & Payton, J. B. (1988b). New perspectives in autism: Part 2. The differential diagnosis and neurobiology of autism. *Current Problems in Pediatrics, 19,* 615–694.

Myslobodsky, M. S., & Mirsky, A. F. (1988). *Elements of petit mal epilepsy.* New York: Peter Lang.

Neils, J., Boller, F., Gerdeman, B., & Cole, M. (1989). Descriptive writing abilities in Alzheimer's disease. *Journal of Clinical and Experimental Neuropsychology, 11,* 692–698.

Peyser, J. M., & Poser, C. M. (1986). Neuropsychological correlates of multiple sclerosis. In S. B. Filskov & T. J. Boll (Eds.), *Handbook of clinical neuropsychology* (Vol. 2, pp. 364–397). New York: Wiley.

Rourke, B. P., & Brown, G. G. (1986). Clinical neuropsychology and behavioral neurology: Similarities and differences. In S. B. Filskov & T. J. Boll (Eds.), *Handbook of clinical neuropsychology* (Vol. 2, pp. 3–18). New York: Wiley.

Rumsey, J. M., & Hamburger, S. D. (1988). Neuropsychological findings in high-functioning men with infantile autism, residual state. *Journal of Clinical and Experimental Neuropsychology, 10,* 201–221.

Satz, P. (1966). Specific and nonspecific effects of brain lesions in man. *Journal of Abnormal Psychology, 71,* 65–70.

Schaeffer, K. W., Parsons, O. A., & Yohman, J. R. (1984). Neuropsychological differences between male familial and nonfamilial alcoholics and nonalcoholics. *Alcoholism: Clinical and Experimental Research, 8,* 347–351.

Spreen, O. (1987). *Learning disabled children growing up: A follow-up into adulthood.* Lisse, The Netherlands: Swets & Zeitlinger.

Steinhauer, S. R., Hill, S. Y., & Zubin, J. (1987). Event related potentials in alcoholics and their first-degree relatives. *Alcoholism, 4,* 307–314.

Tarter, R. E. (1976). Neuropsychological investigations of alcoholism. In G. Goldstein & C. Neuringer (Eds.), *Empirical studies of alcoholism* (pp. 231–256). Cambridge, MA: Ballinger.

Tarter, R. E., Hegedus, A., Goldstein, G., Shelly, C., & Alterman, A. I. (1984). Adolescent sons of alcoholics: Neuropsychological and personality characteristics. *Alcoholism: Clinical and Experimental Research, 8,* 216–222.

Teuber, H.-L. (1959). Some alterations in behavior after cerebral lesions in man. In A. D. Bass (Ed.), *Evolution of nervous control from primitive organisms to man* (pp. 157–194). Washington, DC: American Association for the Advancement of Science.

Van Gorp, W. G., Miller, E. N., Satz, P., & Visscher, B. (1989). Neuropsychological performance in HIV-1 immunocompromised patients: A preliminary report. *Journal of Clinical and Experimental Neuropsychology, 11,* 763–773.

Walker, A. E., Caveness, W. F., & Critchley, M. (Eds.). (1969). *Late effects of head injury.* Springfield, IL: Charles C. Thomas.

Wells, C. E. (1979). Pseudodementia. *American Journal of Psychiatry, 136,* 895–900.

Wells, C. E. (1980). The differential diagnosis of psychiatric disorders in the elderly. In J. O. Cole & J. E. Barrett (Eds.), *Psychopathology in the aged* (pp. 19–31). New York: Raven Press.

Werner, H., & Strauss, A. (1942). Experimental analysis of the clinical symptom "perseveration" in mentally retarded children. *American Journal of Mental Deficiency, 47,* 185–188.

CHAPTER 4

Psychoactive Substance Use Disorder (Alcohol)

TONY TONEATTO, LINDA C. SOBELL, MARK B. SOBELL, and GLORIA I. LEO

Alcohol abuse is a serious social, economic, and medical problem. In addition to being a major psychiatric disorder, alcohol abuse is a common factor in numerous medical problems, highway fatalities, homicides, industrial accidents, work-related deaths, drownings, fatal fires, and falls. The economic costs of alcohol abuse and its consequences are in the billions of dollars per year in North America (e.g., Addiction Research Foundation, 1985; MacDonald, 1985), and the human costs are incalculable. Although alcohol abuse is clearly a long-standing social problem of immense proportions, its etiology and effective treatment remain elusive.

EARLY VIEWS ON ALCOHOL ABUSE

The writings of Alcoholics Anonymous (AA; 1939) and Jellinek (1960) have been viewed as statements of traditional conceptualizations of alcohol problems (Pattison, Sobell, & Sobell, 1977). According to AA, alcohol abusers were victims of psychological and physical aberrations and the fact that only some drinkers suffered alcohol problems was attributed to a biological predisposition. Alcoholics were considered to be "allergic" to alcohol (i.e., after some amount of drinking experience, such individuals were thought to rapidly become dependent on alcohol whenever it was consumed). Even small amounts of alcohol were thought to trigger dependence, which would then necessitate further drinking to forestall the onset of withdrawal symptoms. Alcoholism was also viewed as a progressive disorder (i.e., deterioration would proceed as long as drinking continued).

In contrast to the lay nature of AA's formulations, the model developed by Jellinek (1960) was considerably more professional and sought to endow medicine with the responsibility for helping alcohol abusers. Jellinek did not speculate as to why only some drinkers developed problems, although he alluded to possible genetic components. He considered alcohol abusers as

The views expressed in this paper are those of the authors and do not necessarily reflect those of the Addiction Research Foundation.

persons who had learned to drink as a means of coping with life problems. With increasing drinking experience, tolerance made it necessary for alcoholics to increase the amount consumed to achieve the desired effect. Jellinek hypothesized that prolonged drinking produced physiologic changes such that even small amounts of drinking would initiate physical dependence on alcohol, a state that he referred to as "loss of control." When physical dependence was evident, Jellinek considered alcoholism to be a disease, because it involved a clear departure from normal health. He also recognized that there were many types of alcohol problems that did not involve physical dependence. Furthermore, he considered alcohol problems to be a progressive disease, with a natural history of fairly well-defined stages that could be "arrested" only through abstinence.

Historically, the population of major concern in the alcohol field, as represented by the views of Jellinek and AA, has been individuals who are severely dependent on alcohol. Recognition of the needs of individuals who are not severely dependent on alcohol (i.e., those with identifiable alcohol-related problems but who have not experienced major alcohol withdrawal symptoms) has been very recent (M. B. Sobell & Sobell, 1987). These so-called problem drinkers (Kissin, 1983) greatly outnumber severely dependent drinkers, ranging from 3:1 to 7:1, depending on the criteria used to define alcohol problems (Cahalan, 1970; Cahalan & Room, 1974; Fillmore & Midanik, 1984; Polich, 1981). Thus, traditional conceptualizations of alcoholism have centered on individuals who have developed severe dependence problems, to the exclusion of what has been termed the "underserved majority" (M. B. Sobell & Sobell, 1987).

THE NATURAL HISTORY OF ALCOHOL PROBLEMS

Progressivity?

Until recently, problem severity has been a neglected issue in the alcohol field. One reason may relate to conventional views of alcoholism as an inexorably progressive disease. In its simplest version, this model dictates that alcohol problems will increasingly worsen unless the individual stops drinking. The progressivity concept, which has been a hallmark of the alcohol field for decades, evolved from an error in logic, however. Proponents assumed that, since people who had severe problems reported having suffered from less severe problems in the past, all those who experience less severe problems will go on to deteriorate unless they cease drinking. The error is that, when inferences are based only on the experiences of persons whose problems became severe, one has no knowledge of whether other people have had less serious problems that did not worsen, or perhaps even abated. To determine whether a disorder is progressive (i.e., that, barring effective treatment, the condition will worsen), studies are needed whereby individuals are followed beginning early in their problem careers.

Over the past two decades, several well-designed scientific studies of progressivity have been conducted, and their findings have serious implications for the way the alcohol field has offered treatment services (Fillmore, 1988a;

M. B. Sobell & Sobell, 1987). According to this research base, which includes both longitudinal studies of alcohol problems in the general population and attempts to replicate Jellinek's progression, symptom severity increases over time for only a minority of cases (25 to 30 percent by most estimates). For the majority of cases, the natural history of the disorder can be described as an oscillation between periods of alcohol problems of varying severity and periods either of abstinence or of drinking limited quantities without problems. Thus, if at one point in time an individual is experiencing problems with alcohol, it is not possible to predict, in the absence of treatment, what the individual's circumstances will be at a later time.

The above conclusion has serious implications. For years, treatment agencies generally have considered individuals with less serious drinking problems to be in an early stage of the progressive development of alcoholism and, therefore, as needing to be treated similarly to severe cases. Consequently, the full range of persons entering alcohol treatment programs have been faced with the same prospect and given the same message: their illness or disease is progressive. Such an approach is regressive and generally inconsistent with medical practice (e.g., patients who are diagnosed with angina typically do not undergo triple bypass surgery). In the alcohol field, however, all alcohol abusers, from problem drinkers to chronic alcoholics, are typically prescribed a single course of treatment: inpatient hospitalization with a traditional disease orientation (Cook, 1988; Wright, 1988). The research literature, however, does not support this approach and suggests that intensive treatments be reserved for very chronic alcoholics, and that services be individualized (i.e., by using a treatment tiering approach similar to that used with most other health problems). A tiering approach incorporates a range of services, and provides the level or type of treatment that best matches each person's presenting problem. If the initial treatment of choice is unsuccessful, clients are referred to an alternative (e.g., more intensive) treatment, and so on, until recovery occurs or all options have been tried.

The Fates of Untreated Alcohol Abusers

Several studies have shown that a sizable proportion of alcohol abusers are reluctant to enter traditional treatment (Hingson, Mangione, Meyers, & Scotch, 1982; Thom, 1986; Weisner, 1987). In fact, the ratio of untreated to treated alcohol abusers has been estimated to range from 3:1 to 13:1 (Roizen, 1977). However, not all untreated alcohol abusers continue to suffer problems. Although exact prevalence rates are lacking, a growing body of literature suggests that recoveries without treatment are not uncommon (Edwards, 1989; Fillmore, 1988b; Vaillant, 1983). Unfortunately, at present, little is known about what motivates and maintains those recoveries.

In summary, what we know from the available literature is that alcohol problems are not progressive for a large majority of individuals with alcohol problems, that the roads to recovery are many and varied, that most people with alcohol problems do not seek treatment, and that some of these people recover on their own.

EPIDEMIOLOGY

Although alcohol is the most widely consumed psychoactive drug in the Western world, determining the incidence of alcohol problems in the general population is difficult because few agree on how to define and measure alcohol problems. A popular approach is Ledermann's (1956) model, which postulates a direct relationship between the total amount of alcohol consumption in a society and the number of alcohol abusers. This model has received some support from positive correlations between per capita consumption and measures of alcohol-related problems (e.g., alcohol-related death rates, driving offenses, and liver cirrhosis). Another method of measuring alcohol abuse is based on the incidence of alcohol-related diseases, such as liver cirrhosis (Schmidt, 1977). For example, decreases in alcohol availability, as occurred during the two world wars, were associated with decreases in cirrhosis-related deaths. Reliance on death rates from cirrhosis may underestimate the extent of alcohol problems, however, since not all alcohol abusers will develop cirrhosis. Also, cirrhosis does not always result from alcohol abuse. Similarly, a variety of other alcohol-related health and social problems frequently occur in the absence of cirrhosis.

Surveys indicate that approximately two-thirds of males in Western countries drink regularly, with between 5 and 10 percent of adult men in the United States developing some type of drinking problem during their lives (Schuckit, 1989). Williams, Aitken, and Malin (1985) place the number of alcohol abusers at 10.4 million in the United States (7.1 million men, 3.3 million women). Such estimates, however, are dependent on the method of measuring alcohol problems. For example, using the Short Michigan Alcohol Screening Test (SMAST) (Selzer, Vinokur, & van Rooijen, 1975) and counting as problem drinkers those endorsing a "yes" response to 3 or more of the 13 items, Hilton (1987) estimated that 5.7 million men and 2.5 million women in the United States had drinking problems. Hilton (1989), however, demonstrated the arbitrariness of definitions of alcohol problems by showing that requiring "yes" responses to at least 4 SMAST items produced estimates of 3.7 million men and 1.5 million women alcohol abusers, whereas requiring "yes" responses to at least 2 SMAST items produced problem drinking estimates of 8.8 million men and 4.2 million women.

Less stringent criteria for alcohol abuse, as employed in a recent large-scale epidemiological survey, found alcohol abuse was the most common of 15 psychiatric disorders (Robins, Helzer, Przybeck, & Regier, 1988). Data from three of the five mental health centers in this study showed current prevalence (6-month) rates to be 9 percent for men and 1.5 percent for women (6:1 ratio), with lifetime prevalence rates of 24.3 and 4.4 percent, respectively. Although agreement on specific criteria for alcohol problems remains elusive, it is clear that a significant proportion of the male population reports alcohol-related problems at some time during their lives.

MORTALITY AND MORBIDITY

The causes of alcohol-related deaths are multiple (e.g., alcohol-related diseases, secondary nutritional deficiencies, immunosuppression, accidents, suicides). Death rates are considerably higher (two to four times for men and three to seven times for women) for alcohol abusers than for nonabusers (Edwards, 1989). The suicide rate among alcohol abusers is also higher than that for the general population (Berglund, 1984).

Depending on the amount consumed and the pattern of drinking, excessive drinking can cause a variety of medical complications. For example, alcohol abusers show higher cancer rates than the general population (e.g., cancers of the digestive tract, lungs, esophagus, liver, pancreas, stomach) (Gallant, 1987). Although consumption of moderate to high quantities of alcohol (more than 80 grams per day) has been related to adverse effects upon the liver (Frank & Raicht, 1985; Nouchi, Worner, Sato, & Lieber, 1987), as little as 40 grams (e.g., 3 ounces of 80-proof spirits) per day of alcohol in men and 20 grams in women may acutely affect the liver (Frank & Raicht, 1985). Heavy alcohol consumption can cause hepatitis, and repeated episodes of hepatitis can ultimately lead to liver cirrhosis, which afflicts 10 to 15 percent of severe alcohol abusers (Senior, 1985/1986). Fatty liver, the most common alcohol-related hepatic disorder, is less serious than hepatitis or cirrhosis, and often develops following prolonged heavy drinking (Morgan, 1980; Morgan, Colman, & Sherlock, 1981), but can be reversed upon cessation of drinking.

The most common effects of alcohol on the brain include acute brain syndromes (e.g., intoxication and confusional states), which clear several hours following cessation of drinking. Chronic brain syndromes, which can result from prolonged very heavy alcohol consumption (greater than 150 grams per day; Turner, Mezey, & Kimball, 1977), can occur through direct damage from alcohol or through nutritional deficiencies (e.g., Wernicke–Korsakoff syndrome) and can lead to severe disturbances in memory, cognitive processes, and personality (Grant, 1987; Harper, Kril, & Daly, 1987). Although chronic abusive drinking has been shown to be related to cerebrovascular accidents (Hillbom & Kaste, 1981), especially among younger alcoholics who binge heavily (Taylor et al., 1985), studies of individuals who drink moderately show no consistent relationship between drinking history and neuropsychological functioning (Grant, 1987; Parsons, 1987).

DIAGNOSIS OF ALCOHOL PROBLEMS

The classification of alcohol problems has undergone considerable evolution over the last two decades, reflecting both the state of knowledge and the predominant attitudes of the time. The continuing revisions to the *Diagnostic and Statistical Manual of Mental Disorders* (DSM) of the American Psychiatric Association (APA) reflect this evolution. For instance, the DSM-III (APA, 1980) diagnosis for alcohol disorders consisted of two types: "1) abuse, requiring a pattern of pathological use and social or occupational impairment, and 2) dependence, requiring either physiological tolerance or withdrawal in addition to pathological use and/or social or occupational impairment" (Rounsaville, Kosten, Williams, & Spitzer, 1987, p. 351). The revised third edition (DSM-III-R; APA, 1987), however, has replaced the DSM-III distinction with one category of alcohol dependence. Alcohol abuse is retained, primarily as a residual diagnosis for individuals who have only recently begun to abuse alcohol or who have used alcohol in a manner damaging to their biopsychosocial functioning (e.g., a drunk driving arrest), but who fail to meet the criteria for dependence. In DSM-III-R, the diagnostic criteria also form a diagnostic index so that alcohol dependence no longer depends on any particular symptom. The core symptoms comprising the dependence syndrome need not always be present, or present with the same magnitude on any given occasion, for dependence to be diagnosed. Furthermore, the criteria for dependence have been broadened to incorporate behavioral, physiological, and cognitive symptoms of alcohol abuse.

DSM-III-R Criteria for Psychoactive Substance Dependence

The following nine symptoms constitute DSM-III-R (APA, 1987) criteria for psychoactive substance dependence, including alcohol. At least three of these symptoms need to be present for a dependence diagnosis to be made.

1. Substance is consumed in larger amounts or over a longer period than the person intended.
2. Desire persists or one or more efforts to cut down or control substance use have been unsuccessful.
3. A disproportionate amount of time is spent in activities necessary to get the substance (e.g., theft), take the substance (e.g., chain smoking), or recover from its effects.
4. Frequent intoxication or withdrawal symptoms interfere with major role obligations at work, school, or home, or when substance use is physically hazardous.
5. Important social, occupational or recreational activities are neglected or discontinued because of substance use.
6. Substance use is continued despite knowledge of having a persistent or recurrent social, psychological, or physical problem that is caused or exacerbated by the use of the substance.
7. There is marked tolerance, that is, need for markedly increased amounts of the substance in order to achieve intoxication or desired effect, or markedly diminished effect with continued use of the same amount.
8. Withdrawal symptoms occur when the substance is not consumed.
9. Substance often is taken to relieve or avoid withdrawal symptoms.

The DSM-III-R also views alcohol dependence as a graded phenomenon, ranging from mild (one or more psychosocial consequences, but no major withdrawal symptoms; e.g., problem drinkers) to severe (major withdrawal symptoms and pervasive drug seeking; e.g., chronic alcohol abusers experiencing delirium tremens).

Utility of Diagnostic Formulations

A proper diagnosis should permit the differentiation between alcohol use and abuse, distinguish between primary and secondary substance abuse, and suggest the most effective treatment approach. Although the majority of North Americans consume alcohol and although a large minority of young males may develop temporary psychosocial problems as a result of excessive alcohol use, most will not develop alcohol dependence (Cahalan, 1970; Schuckit, 1989). Thus, alcohol-related difficulties, although they help define the clinical picture of diagnosed alcohol abusers, are not, in and of themselves, sufficient to predict alcohol dependence, because many people who do not develop more severe forms of dependence will also experience such problems.

Diagnostic formulations may also play an important role in decisions about treatment goals and intensity (M. B. Sobell & Sobell, 1987). For example, some research suggests that severity of alcohol dependence may interact with response to treatment goals (abstinence or nonproblem drinking) and different treatment intensities (Annis, 1986; Heather & Robertson, 1983; Orford & Keddie, 1986a). A fit between the level of alcohol dependence and the most appropriate treatment is consistent with the notion of client–treatment matching (Finney & Moos, 1986; Miller & Hester, 1986b).

A diagnosis of alcohol dependence must distinguish between a disorder that is secondary to other psychiatric disorders and a disorder that can produce other psychiatric disorders (i.e., a primary disorder). For example, psychotic symptoms in an individual who abuses alcohol may be diagnosed as primary alcohol dependence with secondary psychosis or as an acute psychotic disorder with secondary alcohol dependence, although in both cases the alcohol problem needs to be addressed. The former diagnosis implies that the psychotic symptoms should disappear once the drinking remits, whereas the latter diagnosis suggests that the psychotic symptoms require direct treatment. Distinguishing between primary and secondary substance abuse problems has important prognostic implications. For example, one study (Rounsaville, Dolinsky, Babor, & Meyer, 1987) found that alcohol abusers who had pronounced psychiatric symptoms prior to treatment had the worst treatment outcomes and were hospitalized more often than clients with few or no psychiatric symptoms.

The three most common psychiatric disorders associated with alcohol problems are affective, anxiety, and conduct disorders. Approximately 15 percent of male and 5 percent of female alcohol abusers have been shown to carry an additional diagnosis of antisocial personality (Schuckit, 1985). Some workers have diagnosed between 7 and 50 percent of their alcohol abusers with an antisocial personality disorder (Hesselbrock, Meyer, & Keener, 1985; Powell, Read, Penick, Miller, & Bingham, 1987). The prevalence of major affective disorder varies among studies: lifetime rates have ranged from 18 to 25 percent (Hesselbrock et al., 1985; Powell et al., 1987;

Weissman & Meyers, 1980), with current rates for treated alcohol abusers ranging from 9 to 38 percent (Dorus, Kennedy, Gibbons, & Ravi, 1987; Keeler, Taylor, & Miller, 1979). Anxiety disorders also appear to be more prevalent in alcohol abusers, with lifetime rates for panic disorder ranging from 8 to 16 percent and for phobias from 3 to 55 percent (Bowen, Cipywnyk, D'Arcy, & Keegan, 1984; Hesselbrock et at., 1985; Schuckit, 1985; Smail, Stockwell, Cante, & Hodgson, 1984). The Epidemiologic Catchment Area Program found lifetime prevalence rates for a variety of anxiety disorders among alcohol abusers to range between 10 and 25 percent across the three study sites (Robins et al., 1988).

Recent years have witnessed a growing trend for other drug abuse to accompany alcohol abuse (Craddock, Bray, & Hubbard, 1985; Kaufman, 1982; L. C. Sobell, Sobell, & Nirenberg, 1988; Wilkinson, Leigh, Cordingley, Martin, & Lei, 1987). Also, abusers of substances other than alcohol (e.g., heroin, cocaine, cannabis) frequently abuse alcohol (Belenko, 1979; Craig, 1984; Kaufman, 1982). In addition to these illicit drugs, tobacco and caffeine use have been shown to be strongly related to alcohol consumption (Istvan & Matarazzo, 1984). For example, 80 to 90 percent of all alcohol and drug abusers smoke cigarettes, compared with 30 percent of the general population (reviewed in L. C. Sobell, Sobell, Kozlowski, & Toneatto, 1990). A diagnosis of polydrug abuse has important treatment implications in that treatment for multiple substance abuse may not parallel that for abuse of only one drug (Battjes, 1988; Burling & Ziff, 1988; Kaufman, 1982).

ETIOLOGY

Theories to account for alcohol abuse are not scarce (see Lettieri, Sayers, & Pearson, 1980, for a summary of 43 theoretical accounts). The diversity of explanatory accounts bears witness to the complexity of alcohol abuse, but it also reflects the limitations of any individual theory. Most theories of alcohol abuse may be considered as limited perspectives on alcohol abuse that stem from differing models of human behavior (e.g., moral, medical, psychological, sociological) and of the level of etiologic origin (e.g., molecular, biochemical, behavioral, anthropological, sociological, economic).

A comprehensive summary of the literature on major theories of alcoholism is well beyond the scope of this chapter. Interested readers are referred to Chaudron and Wilkinson (1988) and Blane and Leonard (1987) for excellent reviews of this literature. The next section briefly highlights recent developments and major features of the more influential theories of alcohol problems.

Genetic Theory

The clinical observation of the clustering of alcohol abusers in some families suggests that there may be a genetic predisposition to develop alcohol problems. Twin studies present a unique opportunity to compare individuals who are genetically 100 percent identical (identical twins) with twins who share a

50 percent genetic loading (fraternal twins). Twin studies, once thought to be quite promising, have recently come under serious scrutiny (Lester, 1988; Searles, 1988). Searles (1988) concluded that the results of twin studies are not consistent: some show little effect, some show a considerable effect, and others are equivocal.

Adoption studies provide a more controlled test of the genetic contribution to alcohol abuse, because they permit the assessment of environmental and genetic factors independently. Strong support for the hypothesis that biological relatives contribute to the development of alcohol problems in adopted-out male offspring comes from Sweden (Cloninger, Bohman, & Sigvardsson, 1981; Cloninger, Bohman, Sigvardsson, & von Knorring, 1984) and the United States (Cadoret, Cain, & Grove, 1980). Although the adoption studies do suggest that heritable factors play a role in alcohol problems for males (although not for females), gene X environment interactions appear to be important. An example of the complexity of how genetic factors may relate to alcohol problems is shown by Cloninger's (e.g., Cloninger et al., 1981) research on two types of genetically influenced alcohol problems: Type I (milieu type), which is associated with both mild and severe alcohol abuse, minimal criminal behavior, no history of alcoholism treatment in the biological parents, and an environment conducive to the development of alcohol problems (e.g., heavy drinking parental model), and Type II, which is limited to males and is characterized by high criminality and severe alcohol abuse (relatively independent of environmental influences), as well as biological parents with a history of alcohol abuse treatment.

Another line of research relevant to genetic theory concerns offspring of alcohol abusers who are not abusing alcohol. Although studies of these high-risk individuals cannot disentangle genetic and environmental factors, they may shed light on the genetics of alcohol abuse. Compared with a control group of low-risk individuals (i.e., offspring of families with no history of alcohol abuse), high-risk individuals have not been shown to be consistently different on biological markers (e.g., blood acetaldehyde levels; Behar et al., 1983); ethanol absorption or clearance rates (Nagoshi & Wilson, 1987; Schuckit, 1981); neuropsychological markers (Hesselbrock et al., 1985; Workman-Daniels & Hesselbrock, 1987); psychological profiles (Schuckit, 1982; Tarter, Hegedus, Goldstein, Shelly, & Alterman, 1984); and cognitive functioning (Tarter, Jacob, & Bremer, 1989). Some evidence suggests however, that alcohol may produce differential effects on mood (Moss, Yao, & Maddock, 1989) and stress (i.e., unavoidable shock; Finn & Pihl, 1987, 1988) in high-risk individuals. Because much of this research fails to control for current levels of alcohol use, differences in the postnatal environment, and ethnic and sex differences, it is not possible to draw any firm conclusions at the present time regarding differences between people at higher risk for alcohol abuse (as measured by family history) and those at lower risk.

Finally, although several recent reviews have been extremely critical of the design, conduct, and interpretation of genetic studies (Finn & Pihl, 1987; Lester, 1988; Murray et al., 1983; Peele, 1986; Searles, 1988), the existence of a heritable component to alcohol problems appears to be likely in males with multigenerational alcohol abuse histories. It also should be recognized, however, that only a small proportion of all individuals with alcohol problems can, at present, be accounted for by such means.

Learning Theory

An aversive conditioning treatment for alcohol problems, based on Pavlovian conditioning principles, was reported in 1929 by Kantorovich. Although some private treatment programs also reported using aversive conditioning procedures in the early 1940s (Voetglin & Lemere, 1942), it was not until Wikler's (1948) important contributions toward a learning theory account of drug relapse that learning theory became a serious contender for explaining substance abuse. Wikler postulated that withdrawal symptoms following abstinence from a psychoactive substance could become conditioned to exteroceptive cues (e.g., visual or olfactory stimuli) and interoceptive cues (e.g., emotions) that reliably preceded the withdrawal symptoms. Exposure to such cues at a later time was hypothesized to elicit conditioned withdrawal symptoms, which, in turn, made substance use (i.e., relapse) likely. Although Wikler's model was originally developed to explain opiate addiction, Ludwig and Stark (1974) extended it to alcohol abuse and suggested that craving could be considered a useful cognitive indicator of conditioned withdrawal antecedent to alcohol consumption.

More recently, several conditioning models of addiction and relapse have been introduced, influenced by the work of Wikler and his colleagues and supported by considerable basic research (see Niaura et al., 1988, for a review). The development of these models was spurred by research showing that Pavlovian processes play an important role in the development of tolerance, previously considered a purely physiological adaptation. For example, Siegel and his colleagues (e.g., Poulos, Hinson, & Siegel, 1981; Siegel, Krank, & Hinson, 1987) developed a conditioned compensatory responding model in which the body reacts homeostatically to ingestion of a drug by responses that are opposite in direction to the drug effects. With repeated trials, these compensatory responses become conditioned to environmental correlates of the drug effect. When such stimuli are present, but the drug has not been ingested, conditioned compensatory responses can occur that may be experienced as similar to withdrawal symptoms. Because such symptoms can be eliminated through alcohol consumption, the likelihood of relapse is high.

Appetitive motivational models have been proposed by Stewart, deWit, and Eikelboom (1984) and by Baker, Morse, and Sherman (1987). These models suggest that positive affective motivational states can become conditioned to alcohol use, in addition to the more commonly observed link between alcohol use and negative affective motivational states. Urge to consume alcohol, a hypothesized important moderating variable in precipitating alcohol abuse (Baker et al., 1987), is considered to be a conditioned affect associated with approach behavior. The appetitive model further hypothesizes that alcohol has a rewarding effect on the central nervous system, and that stimuli associated with drug use come to acquire an incentive function (i.e., they motivate drug seeking).

Whereas Pavlovian conditioning theories of addiction have spawned considerable basic research in recent years, treatments based on operant learning theory (e.g., token economies, contingency management) were influential during the 1960s. These typically were based on unelaborated social learning accounts of alcohol abuse. For instance, the use of skills training procedures (e.g., Lovibond & Caddy, 1970; M. B. Sobell & Sobell, 1973) was based on the premise that alcohol use is functional, and that, for the person to forgo or reduce drinking, the functions served by drinking needed to be replaced by alternative, less problematic behaviors. The theoretical basis for these treatments was not well specified, however.

A more elaborate, cognitive social learning account of alcohol abuse and the process of relapse following treatment was developed by Marlatt and his colleagues (e.g., Marlatt & Gordon, 1985). This approach stresses the importance of cognitive mediators of the environment–behavior interface, such as beliefs, expectancies, attributions, and attitudes, in the understanding of alcohol abuse. Treatments based on this approach typically focus on the high-risk situations that make alcohol overconsumption likely (e.g., associating with heavy-drinking friends), the cognitive mediators of relapse (e.g., low self-efficacy, unawareness of negative consequences of alcohol abuse), and the necessity of enhancing self-efficacy through the development of nonpharmacological means of coping with identified high-risk situations (e.g., Sanchez-Craig, Annis, Bornet, & MacDonald, 1984).

ASSESSMENT

Because the literature on the assessment of alcohol abuse is very large, it is not summarized here. Interested readers are referred to L. C. Sobell, Sobell, and Nirenberg (1988) for a summary of current assessment issues and techniques. What follows is an overview of key assessment issues that need to be considered in treatment planning. For alcohol abusers, areas of assessment cover both alcohol and nonalcohol (e.g., family, work) related events, and information may derive from a variety of sources (e.g., clients' self-reports, clinical and other official records, physical and mental health indices of cognitive functioning, liver function, and drug toxicity; L. C. Sobell, Sobell, & Nirenberg, 1988). Because no data source is error free, it has been recommended that assessment information be gathered from multiple sources and cross-validated whenever possible (L. C. Sobell & Sobell, 1990).

Assessment of Alcohol Use

Assessing drinking behavior involves the measurement of both the quantity and the frequency of past and present use. The method of choice for assessing drinking behavior depends on time constraints and the precision of measurement sought. Reviews of drinking behavior assessment methods have identified two major retrospective methods. The first involves quantity–frequency (QF) approaches, which measure estimated average drinking patterns over a specified time period. Although QF methods provide reliable information about overall consumption and number of drinking days, they mask certain types of drinking days, particularly atypical heavy days, which are often associated with health risks but do not form part of an individual's typical drinking pattern (L. C. Sobell, Cellucci, Nirenberg, & Sobell, 1982). The Lifetime Drinking History (LDH; Skinner & Sheu, 1982), a variant of QF approaches, assesses lifetime drinking based on subjectively defined discrete phases involving major changes in a person's average drinking pattern. LDH provides a valuable overview of shifts in a person's drinking style over the life course. It lacks precision, however, for the most recent drinking period.

The second method, the Time-Line (TL; L. C. Sobell, Maisto, Sobell, & Cooper, 1979; L. C. Sobell, Sobell, Leo, & Cancilla, 1988) or daily estimation approach, asks subjects to estimate their daily alcohol consumption over a specified time interval ranging from 30 to 360 days back from the date of the interview. This method has been shown to have good psychometric characteristics across multiple populations of drinkers (L. C. Sobell, Sobell, Leo, & Cancilla, 1988; L. C. Sobell, Sobell, Riley, et al., 1988). Self-monitoring, another method of assessing daily drinking, unlike QF and TL approaches, is prospective. Use of this method requires clients to record various aspects of their daily drinking behavior (e.g., amount, frequency) and can provide clinically useful feedback about treatment effectiveness.

Recent alcohol use can also be objectively assessed with breath alcohol tests and through the measurement of various bodily fluids (e.g., urine, sweat, breath, and blood). The alcohol dipstick (Kapur & Israel, 1983, 1984), which determines ethanol concentrations in urine, saliva, or blood, can be used conveniently and reliably in a variety of clinical settings (e.g., emergency rooms, outpatient programs, doctors' offices).

Liver function tests are one of the most common methods of objectively assessing alcohol use over extended time periods. Several studies have demonstrated that elevations on certain biochemical tests (e.g., gamma-glutamyl transpeptidase) correlate well with recent heavy drinking. These tests have their limitations, however (e.g., considerable intersubject variability; differential effects of drinking patterns; the fact that certain medical conditions—heart failure, diabetes—also affect test values; O'Farrell & Maisto, 1987; L. C. Sobell, Sobell, & Nirenberg, 1988).

Assessment of Alcohol-Related Events

The functions of alcohol use should also be assessed through events, moods, and cognitions that precede and follow alcohol use. Especially important is the identification of high-risk events that are highly correlated with heavy drinking (Marlatt & Gordon, 1985). Annis has developed two instruments that yield profiles of high-risk situations: Inventory of Drinking Situations, which assesses situations in which clients drank heavily during the past year, and Situational Confidence Questionnaire, which requires clients to rate their present ability to resist urges to drink heavily in various situations (Annis & Davis, 1988).

Both the positive (e.g., social reinforcement from drinking, relief from tension and other undesired affects) and the negative (e.g., health, occupational, and family problems) short-term and long-term consequences of alcohol use should be assessed. Although several short self-administered checklists have been developed to assess psychosocial consequences and dependence symptoms of alcohol abuse (e.g., Michigan Alcohol Screening Test; Selzer, 1971), many of these scales have serious drawbacks (L. C. Sobell, Sobell, & Nirenberg, 1988). Two of the most common scales assessing alcohol dependence are the Substance Abuse Dependence Questionnaire (Stockwell, Murphy, & Hodgson, 1983), a 20-item scale, and the Alcohol Dependence Scale (Skinner & Horn, 1984), a 25-item scale, which can also be used to help screen clients for severity of dependence and appropriateness of a reduced drinking goal.

TREATMENT

Issues in Treatment Planning

Involving clients in their own treatment planning is important because clients can provide valuable information about the desirability, feasibility, and ease with which treatment strategies can be implemented. Client involvement early in treatment planning also sets the stage for continued participation and compliance and ensures that treatment goals have been mutually determined. Such involvement can also provide clients with a sense of self-mastery over their difficulties. A good treatment plan should clearly define goals and problems that are amenable to measurement and evaluation. For example, long-term goals should be partitioned into multiple short-term goals, which can be used to assess progress, provide the client early success experiences in treatment, and maintain motivation for making further changes. In planning treatment, the most effective but least restrictive treatments should be provided (i.e., those requiring the least total lifestyle change by the client yet still likely to be effective; L. C. Sobell, Sobell, & Nirenberg, 1988). For example, low-dependence problem drinkers may benefit as much or more from relatively brief treatments as from longer treatments (M. B. Sobell & Sobell, 1987).

Treatment Goals

Effective treatment planning needs to clearly specify treatment goals. For problem drinkers, one of the most important goals is whether the client will attempt to abstain or to drink moderately. Traditionally, most alcohol abuse treatment programs have promoted an abstinence goal for all clients (see Riley, Sobell, Leo, Sobell, & Klajner, 1987; Rounsaville, 1986; M. B. Sobell & Sobell, 1987); this goal is usually based on the rationale of progressivity, which states that anyone with a diagnosable alcohol problem will go on to develop severe dependence on alcohol unless he or she ceases drinking. For example, Kissin (1983), in his reformulation of the disease concept of alcoholism, suggested that physically dependent alcohol abusers are biologically incapable of achieving nonabstinence drinking goals. Of course, this reconceptualization excludes the large number of individuals with alcohol problems who do not exhibit significant physical dependence, and who presumably would not a priori be incapable of achieving moderation outcomes.

The rationale for an alternative to abstinence is multifaceted: alcohol is legally available, and its use in moderation is socially sanctioned; when used in moderation, it does not produce marked impairment or dysfunction; abstinence has not succeeded as an enduring outcome for most alcohol abusers (L. C. Sobell, Toneatto, & Sobell, 1990; M. B. Sobell & Sobell, 1987); for some individuals, especially young males, a rigid adherence to abstinence may be unacceptable; and several treatment and longitudinal studies (Edwards, 1989; Fillmore, 1988b; Riley et al., 1987; M. B. Sobell & Sobell, 1987) have shown that many persons evaluated as having significant alcohol problems at one point in time will be drinking in moderation and without problems at a later time (even with abstinence-oriented treatments). Permitting some clients, especially low-dependence problem drinkers, to choose their own drinking goals (unless contraindicated) has become an increasingly common feature of many behavioral treatment programs. Such a goal choice procedure is thought to increase motivation for change and contribute to treatment success (Booth, Dale, & Ansari, 1984; Elal-Lawrence, Slade, & Dewey, 1986; Eriksen, Björnstad, & Götestam, 1986; Fink et al., 1985; Foy, Nunn, & Rychtarik, 1984; Orford & Keddie, 1986a; Rychtarik, Foy, Scott, Lokey, & Prue, 1987).

Polydrug Abuse

If the alcohol abuser is also abusing other drugs, a decision to treat the problems simultaneously or sequentially needs to be addressed. The most significant example of multiple substance use is the common co-occurrence of smoking and alcohol abuse (Bobo, Gilchrist, Schilling, Noach, & Schinke, 1987; Burling & Ziff, 1988; Kozlowski, Jelinek, & Pope, 1986; L. C. Sobell, Sobell, et al., 1990). Although simultaneous cessation of the use of multiple substances has been hypothesized to increase risk of relapse, conditioning theory might suggest the opposite: that continued use of one substance while treating use of another may precipitate relapse. As noted recently (L. C. Sobell, Sobell, & Nirenberg, 1988), since there is virtually no research to indicate whether multiple drug problems should be treated concurrently or sequentially, the best approach, at present, is to make decisions on a case-by-case basis.

Relapse Prevention

Another important issue in treatment planning is relapse prevention (Marlatt & Gordon, 1985). Because alcohol abusers have very high relapse rates, especially within the first 6 months following treatment (L. C. Sobell, Sobell, & Nirenberg, 1988), relapse prevention skills training would appear to be a wise treatment choice. Relapse prevention is concerned with inculcating a long-term perspective on recovery from alcohol abuse, acquiring coping skills to prevent, as well as to deal constructively with, relapses that do occur (e.g., terminating the relapse as quickly as possible), and viewing a relapse as a learning, rather than as a failure, experience (Eriksen et al., 1986; Ito, Donovan, & Hall, 1988).

Treatment Matching

One approach to increasing the effectiveness of treatment of alcohol abuse has been to match treatments to the specific needs of the client. Although the concept of treatment matching in the alcohol field is not new (Glaser, 1980; Miller & Hester, 1986b), in the United States, clinical practice in the alcohol field has long been dominated by a relatively standardized treatment approach viewed as suitable for all cases, the so-called Minnesota Model (Cook, 1988; Zimmerman, 1988). With respect to patient–treatment matching, Miller and Hester (1986b) offered the following conclusions based on a review of the alcohol literature: broad-spectrum treatments are beneficial to the extent that these components specifically address the client's problems; clients benefit most from a treatment approach compatible with their cognitive style; more intensive treatments are likely to benefit clients with more severe alcohol-related problems, and vice versa; and clients actively involved in choosing their treatment from among alternatives are more compliant with treatment and more likely to be successful than clients not offered a choice.

Studies relevant to the matching hypothesis show that less dependent clients benefit as much from brief, self-management oriented treatments as from more intensive ones (Orford & Keddie, 1986a, 1986b). Unfortunately, much of the existing matching research is limited to post hoc correlational analyses exploring client characteristics predictive of outcome. Few studies have used an a priori design to test a matching hypothesis. Despite this, the value of a matching approach seems clear, at least at a rudimentary level. For example, it is unrealistic to expect alcoholics with serious brain damage to respond well to cognitively complex treatments (Wilkinson & Sanchez-Craig, 1981), or to refer an adolescent who occasionally consumes alcohol to extended inpatient treatment. At some level, therefore, the need for an individualized approach is incontestable. Beyond such obvious considerations, however, the issue of matching becomes more complex (Finney & Moos, 1986).

A major issue is whether matching research is warranted when clearly effective treatments for alcohol abuse have not yet been demonstrated. On the one hand, it can be argued that it is imprudent to attempt to maximize effectiveness in the absence of an effective treatment. On the other hand, it is possible that failure to take account of patient–treatment interactions might obscure evidence of treatment effectiveness. By combining the results of clients who respond well to a treatment with those who respond poorly, the grouped outcome would be unimpressive and misleading.

Treatment Outcome

Behavioral treatments have produced comparable and sometimes superior outcomes to nonbehavioral treatments (Miller & Hester, 1986a; Riley et al., 1987), but no approach has had more than modest success. The limited efficacy (both short and long term) of traditional, first-generation, behavioral treatments (e.g., relaxation training, aversion conditioning, covert conditioning, social skills training, assertiveness training, contingency contracting; reviewed in L. C. Sobell, Toneatto, & Sobell, 1990; Wilson, 1987), coupled with the more complex behavioral conceptualizations of alcohol abuse (Marlatt & Gordon, 1985; M. B. Sobell & Sobell, 1987) and the growing influence of cognitive factors in behavior therapy (Bandura, 1986; Beck, 1976; Marlatt & Gordon, 1985), has led to the development of more sophisticated, and hopefully more efficacious, behavioral interventions.

The central features of second-generation behavioral treatments blend old approaches with new. A recent review (L. C. Sobell, Toneatto, & Sobell, 1990) of these second-generation treatments shows that they include the following components: self-management approaches (e.g., self-monitoring of drinking, self-selection of goals, bibliotherapy), functional analysis of drinking (i.e., identifying antecedents and consequences of high- and low-risk drinking situations), cognitive restructuring, development of coping strategies to deal with high-risk drinking situations, and, when indicated, provision of marital or family therapy.

A recent review of behavioral self-management (BSM) techniques with alcohol abusers (L. C. Sobell, Toneatto, & Sobell, 1990) found self-management approaches to significantly reduce problem drinking but not to be clearly superior to other behavioral or nonbehavioral treatments. This finding is consistent with the conclusion reached a few years earlier by Carey and Maisto (1985), who, in their review of behavioral self-control treatments, concluded that "no technique or combination of techniques is superior to any other in ameliorating alcohol problems. Self-control training appears to result in improvement that is at least comparable to the interventions against which it has been evaluated" (p. 242). Furthermore, since there is no Empirical basis for determining the relative importance of any of the several treatment components that comprise BSM (e.g., functional analysis, self-monitoring, cognitive restructuring, stress management, group therapy), one goal of future research is to identify the elements of BSM necessary to produce the most efficient and enduring outcomes. The efficacy of nonbehavioral treatments also suggests that the effectiveness of BSM strategies may not lie in the specific treatment components (e.g., problem solving, cognitive restructuring, functional analysis), but rather in the activation of therapeutic change processes common to any intervention.

Treatment Intensity

It is not always true that more treatment is better. In general, the most effective, but least restrictive treatment should be provided. Early reviews of the treatment literature (Armor, Polich, & Stambul, 1978; Edwards et al., 1977; Emrick, 1974, 1975) suggested that successful outcomes of alcohol abuse treatment are not a direct function of the intensity of treatment. Recent research has continued to provide strong support for this view (Antti-Poika, Karaharju, Roine, & Salaspuro, 1988; Chapman & Huygens, 1988; Chick, Ritson, Connaughton, Stewart, & Chick, 1988; Fink et al., 1985; Heather,

1989; Orford & Keddie, 1986b; Powell, Penick, Read, & Ludwig, 1985; Skutle & Berg, 1987; L. C. Sobell, Toneatto, & Sobell, 1990).

Deterrent Drugs

Deterrent (e.g., antialcohol) drugs result in aversive side effects when alcohol is ingested (e.g., rapid heart rate, palpitations, flushing, nausea). Disulfiram (Antabuse®) is the most commonly prescribed pharmacotherapeutic treatment for alcohol abuse; however, there have been relatively few controlled studies of the efficacy of antialcohol drugs. For example, a study by the Veterans Administration found that disulfiram and counseling did not produce greater treatment effects (as measured by latency to first drink, periods of abstinence, and social stability) than did a control placebo condition with counseling (Fuller et al., 1986). Also, disulfiram should not be prescribed for individuals with serious medical problems (e.g., cirrhosis, heart disease, hypertension), because these conditions may be exacerbated in an alcohol-disulfiram reaction (Kitson, 1977).

Several other pharmacological agents are currently being examined for their utility in decreasing alcohol consumption. One class of drugs is the serotonin-uptake inhibitors (e.g., zimelidine, citalopram, fluoxetine, viqualine), which have been shown in animals to reduce ethanol consumption (Lawrin, Naranjo, & Sellers, 1986; Naranjo, Sellers, & Lawrin, 1986; Spinosa, Perlanski, Leenen, Stewart, & Grupp, 1988). These drugs are hypothesized to pharmacologically block receptors that mediate reinforcing and toxic effects of the abused substance and/or suppress cravings for alcohol. Naranjo and Sellers (1988) suggest that the efficacy of such drugs may best be maximized in combination with psychosocial interventions.

Alcoholics Anonymous (AA)

The intention of the AA program is to help alcohol abusers achieve abstinence through an alteration of the individuals' major belief systems and attitudes, often accomplished by changes in spiritual awareness. The AA program consists of "Twelve Steps," which, it is believed, an individual must complete for recovery from alcohol abuse. These steps include the surrendering of the belief that the alcohol abuser can ever adopt normal drinking, acceptance that outside guidance is needed to remain sober, conducting an honest self-analysis, and, whenever possible, making restitution to those the alcohol abuser has harmed. The fellowship of AA attracts universal acclaim, and is often believed to be the most effective treatment for alcohol abuse. It is also a central component of most traditional alcohol treatment programs. However, the effectiveness of AA, admittedly very difficult to evaluate (i.e., because of the anonymous and independent nature of the organization), remains undemonstrated. The few evaluations that have been done have found AA to be no more or less effective than other existing alcohol treatments (Miller & Hester, 1986a). Emrick (1987), in a review of the treatment efficacy of AA, concluded that on the basis of the current evidence, "AA has not been proven to be more effective than no or comparison treatments when evaluated in randomized clinical trials for court-mandated patients" (p. 419). Finally, because the development of AA was based on the experience of severely dependent alcohol abusers, AA may not be well suited to the needs of problem drinkers. This difficulty increases in significance when one considers that the majority of individuals with alcohol problems are not severely dependent on alcohol.

SUMMARY

Alcohol abuse continues to be a problem involving major social, psychological, and economic consequences that affects a significant minority of the general population. Unfortunately, useful theoretical conceptualizations of alcohol abuse have been slow to develop, although the genetic, conditioning, and social learning theories discussed in this chapter are receiving a great deal of attention and may help contribute to a biopsychosocial understanding of alcohol abuse. Historically, the scientific study of alcohol abuse has focused primarily on individuals who have been severely dependent on alcohol, even though such persons constitute a minority of the alcohol abusing population. Over the past several years, there has been an increased recognition of the needs of the underserved majority of alcohol abusers who experience negative consequences of alcohol abuse, but who are not severely dependent on alcohol. Despite the abundance of treatments for alcohol abuse, effective treatments with enduring outcomes are still elusive; hopefully, new theoretical developments may yield significant insights into the most effective manner to treat this refractory disorder. Although effective psychopharmacological treatments have yet to be discovered, this area of inquiry holds promise for combined psychological and pharmacological interventions.

REFERENCES

Addiction Research Foundation. (1985). *Statistics on alcohol and drug use in Canada and other countries. Vol. 1: Statistics on alcohol use.* Toronto: Author.

Alcoholics Anonymous. (1939). New York: Works Publishing.

American Psychiatric Association. (1980). *Diagnostic and statistical manual of mental disorders* (3rd ed.). Washington, DC: Author.

American Psychiatric Association. (1987). *Diagnostic and statistical manual of mental disorders* (3rd ed. rev.). Washington, DC: Author.

Annis, H. M. (1986). Is inpatient rehabilitation of the alcoholic cost effective? Con position. *Advances in Alcohol and Substance Abuse, 5,* 175–190.

Annis, H. M., & Davis, C. S. (1988). Assessment of expectancies. In D. M. Donovan & G. A. Marlatt (Eds.), *Assessment of addictive behaviors* (pp. 84–111). New York: Guilford Press.

Antti-Poika, I., Karaharju, E., Roine, R., & Salaspuro, M. (1988). Intervention of heavy drinking—A prospective and controlled study of 438 consecutive injured male patients. *Alcohol and Alcoholism, 23,* 115–121.

Armor, D. J., Polich, J. M., & Stambul, H. B. (1978). *Alcoholism and treatment*. New York: Wiley.

Baker, T. B., Morse, E., & Sherman, J. E. (1987). The motivation to use drug: A psychobiological analysis of urges. In C. Rivers (Ed.), *The Nebraska symposium on motivation: Alcohol use and abuse* (pp. 257–323). Lincoln: University of Nebraska Press.

Bandura, A. (1986). *Social foundations of thought and action: A social cognitive theory*. Englewood Cliffs, NJ: Prentice-Hall.

Battjes, R. J. (1988). Smoking as an issue in alcohol and drug abuse treatment. *Addictive Behaviors, 13,* 225–230.

Beck, A. T. (1976). *Cognitive therapy and the emotional disorders*. New York: International Universities Press.

Behar, D., Berg, C. J., Rapoport, J. L., Nelson, W., Linnoila, M., Cohen, M., Bozevich, C., & Marshall, T. (1983). Behavioral and physiological effects of ethanol in high-risk and control children: A pilot study. *Alcoholism: Clinical and Experimental Research, 7,* 404–410.

Belenko, S. (1979). Alcohol abuse by heroin addicts: Review of research findings and issues. *International Journal of the Addictions, 14,* 965–975.

Berglund, M. (1984). Suicide in alcoholism. A prospective study of 88 suicides: I. The multidimensional diagnosis at first admission. *Archives of General Psychiatry, 41,* 888–891.

Blane, H. T., & Leonard, K. E. (Eds.). (1987). *Psychological theories of drinking and alcoholism*. New York: Guilford Press.

Bobo, J. K., Gilchrist, L. D., Schilling, R. F. I., Noach, B., & Schinke, S. P. (1987). Cigarette smoking cessation attempts by recovering alcoholics. *Addictive Behaviors, 7,* 209–215.

Booth, P. G., Dale, B., & Ansari, J. (1984). Problem drinkers' goal choice and treatment outcome: A preliminary study. *Addictive Behaviors, 9,* 357–364.

Bowen, R. C., Cipywnyk, D., D'Arcy, C., & Keegan, D. (1984). Alcoholism, anxiety disorders, and agoraphobia. *Alcoholism: Clinical and Experimental Research, 8,* 48–50.

Burling, T. A., & Ziff, D. C. (1988). Tobacco smoking: A comparison between alcohol and drug inpatients. *Addictive Behaviors, 13,* 185–190.

Cadoret, R., Cain, C., & Grove, W. (1980). Development of alcoholism in adoptees raised apart from alcoholic biologic relatives. *Archives of General Psychiatry, 37,* 561–563.

Cahalan, D. (1970). *Problem drinkers: A national survey*. San Francisco: Jossey-Bass.

Cahalan, D., & Room, R. (1974). *Problem drinking among American men*. New Brunswick, NJ: Rutgers Center of Alcohol Studies.

Carey, K. B., & Maisto, S. A. (1985). A review of the use of self-control techniques in the treatment of alcohol abuse. *Cognitive Therapy and Research, 9,* 235–251.

Chapman, P. L. H., & Huygens, I. (1988). An evaluation of three treatment programmes for alcoholism: An experimental study with 6- and 18-month follow-ups. *British Journal of Addiction, 83,* 67–81.

Chaudron, C. D., & Wilkinson, D. A. (Eds.). (1988). *Theories on alcoholism*. Toronto: Addiction Research Foundation.

Chick, J., Ritson, B., Connaughton, J., Stewart, A., & Chick, J. (1988). Advice versus extended treatment for alcoholism: A controlled study. *British Journal of Addiction, 83,* 159–170.

Cloninger, C. R., Bohman, M., & Sigvardsson, S. (1981). Inheritance of alcohol abuse: Cross-fostering analysis of adopted men. *Archives of General Psychiatry, 38,* 861–868.

Cloninger, C. R., Bohman, M., Sigvardsson, S., & von Knorring, A. L. (1984). Psychopathology in adopted-out children of alcoholics. In M. Galanter (Ed.), *Recent developments in alcoholism* (pp. 37–51). New York: Plenum.

Cook, C. C. H. (1988). The Minnesota Model in the management of drug and alcohol dependency: Miracle, method or myth? Part I. The philosophy and the programme. *British Journal of Addiction, 83,* 625–634.

Craddock, S. G., Bray, R. M., & Hubbard, R. L. (1985). *Drug use before and during drug abuse treatment: 1979–1981 TOPS admission cohorts* (DHHS Publication No. ADM 85-1387). Rockville, MD: National Institute on Drug Abuse.

Craig, R. J. (1984). MMPI substance abuse scales on drug addicts with and without concurrent alcoholism. *Journal of Personality Assessment, 48,* 495–499.

Dorus, W., Kennedy, J., Gibbons, R. D., & Ravi, S. D. (1987). Symptoms and diagnosis of depression in alcoholics. *Alcoholism: Clinical & Experimental Research, 11,* 150–154.

Edwards, G. (1989). As the years go rolling by: Drinking problems in the time dimension. *British Journal of Psychiatry, 154,* 18–26.

Edwards, G., Orford, J., Egert, S., Guthrie, S., Hawker, A., Hensman, C., Mitcheson, M., Oppenheimer, E., & Taylor, C. (1977). Alcoholism: A controlled trial of "treatment" and "advise." *Journal of Studies on Alcohol, 38,* 1004–1031.

Elal-Lawrence, G., Slade, P. D., & Dewey, M. E. (1986). Predictors of outcome type in treated problem drinkers. *Journal of Studies on Alcohol, 47,* 41–47.

Emrick, C. D. (1974). A review of psychologically oriented treatment of alcoholism: I. The use and interrelationships of outcome criteria and drinking behavior following treatment. *Quarterly Journal of Studies on Alcohol, 35,* 523–549.

Emrick, C. D. (1975). A review of psychologically oriented treatment of alcoholism: II. The relative effectiveness of different treatment approaches and the effectiveness of treatment versus no treatment. *Quarterly Journal of Studies on Alcohol, 36,* 88–108.

Emrick, C. D. (1987). Alcoholics Anonymous: Affiliation processes and effectiveness as treatment. *Alcoholism: Clinical and Experimental Research, 11,* 416–423.

Eriksen, L., Björnstad, S., & Götestam, K. G. (1986). Social skills training in groups for alcoholics: One-year treatment outcome for groups and individuals. *Addictive Behaviors, 11,* 309–329.

Fillmore, K. M. (1988a). *Alcohol use across the life course: A critical review of 70 years of international longitudinal research.* Toronto: Addiction Research Foundation.

Fillmore, K. M. (1988b, February). *Spontaneous remission of alcohol problems.* Paper presented at the National Conference on Evaluating Recovery Outcomes, San Diego.

Fillmore, K. M., & Midanik, L. (1984). Chronicity of drinking problems among men: A longitudinal study. *Journal of Studies on Alcohol, 45,* 228–236.

Fink, E. B., Longabaugh, R., McCrady, B. M., Stout, R. L., Beattie, M., Ruggieri-Authelet, A., & McNeil, D. (1985). Effectiveness of alcoholism treatment in partial versus inpatient settings: Twenty-four month outcomes. *Addictive Behaviors, 10,* 235–248.

Finn, P. R., & Pihl, R. O. (1987). Men at risk for alcoholism: The effect of alcohol on cardiovascular response to unavoidable shock. *Journal of Abnormal Psychology, 96,* 230–236.

Finn, P. R., & Pihl, R. O. (1988). Risk for alcoholism: A comparison between two different groups of sons of alcoholics on cardiovascular reactivity and sensitivity to alcohol. *Alcoholism: Clinical and Experimental Research, 12,* 742–747.

Finney, J. W., & Moos, R. H. (1986). Matching patient with treatments: Conceptual and methodological issues. *Journal of Studies on Alcohol, 47,* 122–134.

Foy, D. W., Nunn, L. B., & Rychtarik, R. G. (1984). Broad-spectrum behavioral treatment for chronic alcoholics: Effects of training controlled drinking skills. *Journal of Consulting and Clinical Psychology, 52,* 218–230.

Frank, D., & Raicht, R. F. (1985). Alcohol-induced liver disease. *Alcoholism: Clinical and Experimental Research, 9,* 66–82.

Fuller, R. K., Branchey, L., Brightwell, D. R., Derman, R. M., Emrick, C. D., Iber, F. L., James, K. E., LaCoursiere, R. B., Lee, K. K., Lowenstain, I., Maany, I., Neiderhiser, D., Nocks, J. J., & Shaw, S. (1986). Disulfiram treatment of alcoholism: A Veteran's Administration cooperative study. *Journal of the American Medical Association, 250,* 1449–1455.

Gallant, D. M. (1987). *Alcoholism: A guide to diagnosis, intervention, and treatment.* New York: Norton.

Glaser, F. (1980). Anybody got a match? Treatment research and the matching hypothesis. In G. Edwards & M. Grant (Eds.), *Alcoholism treatment in transition* (pp. 178–196). London: Croom Helm.

Grant, I. (1987). Alcohol and the brain: Neuropsychological correlates. *Journal of Consulting and Clinical Psychology, 55,* 310–324.

Harper, C., Kril, J., & Daly, J. (1987). Are we drinking our neurones away? *British Medical Journal, 294,* 534–536.

Heather, N. (1989). Psychology and brief interventions. *British Journal of Addiction, 84,* 357–370.

Heather, N., & Robertson, I. (1983). *Controlled drinking* (2nd ed.). New York: Methuen.

Hesselbrock, M. N., Meyer, R. E., & Keener, J. J. (1985). Psychopathology in hospitalized alcoholics. *Archives of General Psychiatry, 42,* 1050–1055.

Hillbom, M., & Kaste, M. (1981). Ethanol intoxication: A risk factor for ischemic brain infarction in adolescents and young adults. *Stroke, 12,* 422–425.

Hilton, M. (1987). Drinking patterns and drinking problems in 1984: Results from a general population survey. *Alcoholism: Clinical and Experimental Research, 11,* 167–175.

Hilton, M. E. (1989). How many alcoholics are there in the United States? *British Journal of Addiction, 84,* 459–460.

Hingson, R., Mangione, T., Meyers, A., & Scotch, N. (1982). Seeking help for drinking problems: A study in the Boston metropolitan area. *Journal of Studies on Alcohol, 43,* 273–288.

Istvan, J., & Matarazzo, J. D. (1984). Tobacco, alcohol, and caffeine use: A review of their interrelationships. *Psychological Bulletin, 95,* 301–326.

Ito, J. R., Donovan, D. M., & Hall, J. J. (1988). Relapse prevention in alcohol aftercare: Effects on drinking outcome, change process, and aftercare attendance. *British Journal of Addiction, 83,* 171–181.

Jellinek, E. M. (1960). *The disease concept of alcoholism.* New Brunswick, NJ: Hillhouse Press.

Kantorovich, N. V. (1929). An attempt at association reflex therapy in alcoholism. *Nov. Refleksol. Fizl. Nervous Syst., 3,* 435–447.

Kapur, B. M., & Israel, Y. (1983). A dipstick methodology for rapid determination of alcohol in body fluids. *Clinical Chemistry, 29,* 1178.

Kapur, B. M., & Israel, Y. (1984). Alcohol dipstick for ethanol and methanol. *Clinical Biochemistry, 17,* 201.

Kaufman, E. (1982). The relationship of alcoholism and alcohol abuse to the abuse of other drugs. *American Journal of Drug and Alcohol Abuse, 9,* 1–17.

Keeler, M. H., Taylor, I., & Miller, W. C. (1979). Are all recently detoxified alcoholics depressed? *American Journal of Psychiatry, 136,* 586–588.

Kissin, B. (1983). The disease concept of alcoholism. In R. G. Smart, F. B. Glaser, Y. Israel, H. Kalant, R. E. Popham, & W. Schmidt (Eds.), *Research advances in alcohol and drug problems* (Vol. 7, pp. 93–126). New York: Plenum Press.

Kitson, T. M. (1977). The disulfiram–ethanol reaction. *Journal of Studies on Alcohol, 38,* 96–113.

Kozlowski, L. T., Jelinek, L. C., & Pope, M. A. (1986). Cigarette smoking among alcohol abusers: Continuing and neglected problem. *Canadian Journal of Public Health, 77,* 205–207.

Lawrin, M., Naranjo, C., & Sellers, E. (1986). Identification and testing of new drugs. *Psychopharmacology, 22,* 1020–1025.

Ledermann, S. (1956). *Alcool, alcoolisme, alcoolisation: Données Scientifiques de Caractere Physiologique Economique et Social [Alcohol, alcoholism, alcoholization: Scientific data of economic and social psychological character].* (Institut National d'Etudes Demographiques, Travaux et Documents; Cahier No. 29). Paris: Presses Universitaires de France.

Lester, D. (1988). Genetic theory: An assessment of the heritability of alcoholism. In C. D. Chaudron & D. A. Wilkinson (Eds.), *Theories on alcoholism* (pp. 1–28). Toronto: Addiction Research Foundation.

Lettieri, D. J., Sayers, M., & Pearson, H. W. (Eds.). (1980). *Theories on drug abuse: Selected contemporary perspectives.* Rockville, MD: National Institute on Drug Abuse.

Lovibond, S. H., & Caddy, G. (1970). Discriminated aversive control in the moderation of alcoholics' drinking behavior. *Behavior Therapy, 1,* 437–444.

Ludwig, A. M., & Stark, L. H. (1974). Alcohol craving: Subjective and situational aspects. *Quarterly Journal of Studies on Alcohol, 35,* 899–905.

MacDonald, D. I. (1985). *Statement before a Hearing of the Select Committee on Children, Youth, and Families: Alcohol Abuse and Its Implications for Families* (Alcohol, Drug Abuse, and Mental Health Administration, Department of Health and Human Services). Rockville, MD: U.S. Government Printing Office.

Marlatt, G. A., & Gordon, J. R. (Eds.). (1985). *Relapse prevention.* New York: Guilford Press.

Miller, W. R., & Hester, R. K. (1986a). The effectiveness of alcoholism treatment: What research reveals. In W. R. Miller & N. Heather (Eds.), *Treating addictive behaviors: Processes of change* (pp. 121–174). New York: Plenum Press.

Miller, W. R., & Hester, R. K. (1986b). Matching problem drinkers with optimal treatments. In W. R. Miller & N. Heather (Eds.), *Treating addictive behaviors: Processes of change* (pp. 175–203). New York: Plenum Press.

Morgan, M. Y. (1980). Markers for detecting alcoholism, and monitoring for continued abuse. *Pharmacology, Biochemistry and Behavior, 13,* 1–8.

Morgan, M. Y., Colman, J. C., & Sherlock, S. (1981). The use of a combination of peripheral markers for diagnosing alcoholism and monitoring for continued abuse. *British Journal of Alcohol and Alcoholism, 16,* 167–177.

Moss, H. B., Yao, J. K., & Maddock, J. M. (1989). Responses by sons of alcoholic fathers to alcoholic and placebo drinks: Perceived mood, intoxication, and plasma prolactin. *Alcoholism: Clinical and Experimental Research, 13,* 252–257.

Murray, R. M., Clifford, C., Gurling, H. M. D., Topham, A., Clow, A., & Bernadt, M. (1983). Current genetic and biological approaches to alcoholism. *Psychiatric Developments, 2,* 179–192.

Nagoshi, C. T., & Wilson, J. R. (1987). Influence of family alcoholism history on alcohol metabolism sensitivity, and tolerance. *Alcoholism: Clinical and Experimental Research, 11,* 392–398.

Naranjo, C. A., & Sellers, E. M. (1988). Serotonin uptake inhibitors attenuate ethanol intake in humans. *Australian Drug and Alcohol Review, 7,* 109–112.

Naranjo, C. A., Sellers, E. M., & Lawrin, M. O. (1986). Modulation of ethanol intake by serotonin uptake inhibitors. *Journal of Clinical Psychiatry, 47,* 16–22.

Niaura, R. S., Rohsenow, D. J., Binkoff, J. A., Monti, P. M., Abrams, D. B., & Pedraza, M. (1988). Relevance of cue reactivity to understanding alcohol and smoking relapse. *Journal of Abnormal Psychology, 97,* 133–152.

Nouchi, T., Worner, T. M., Sato, S., & Liber, C. S. (1987). Serum procallagen type III N-terminal peptides and laminin P1 peptide in alcoholic liver disease. *Alcoholism: Clinical and Experimental Research, 11,* 287–291.

O'Farrell, T. J., & Maisto, S. A. (1987). The utility of self-report and biological measures of alcohol consumption in alcoholism treatment outcome studies. *Advances in Behavior Research and Therapy, 9,* 91–125.

Orford, J., & Keddie, A. (1986a). Abstinence or controlled drinking in clinical practice: A test of the dependence and persuasion hypotheses. *British Journal of Addiction, 81,* 495–504.

Orford, J., & Keddie, A. (1986b). Abstinence or controlled drinking in clinical practice: Indications at initial assessment. *Addictive Behaviors, 11,* 71–86.

Parsons, O. (1987). Intellectual impairment in alcoholics. *Acta Medica Scandanavica, 17,* 33–46.

Pattison, E. M., Sobell, M. B., & Sobell, L. C. (Eds.). (1977). *Emerging concepts of alcohol dependence.* New York: Springer.

Peele, S. (1986). The implications and limitations of genetic models of alcoholism and other addictions. *Journal of Studies on Alcohol, 47,* 63–73.

Polich, J. M. (1981). Epidemiology of alcohol abuse in military and civilian populations. *American Journal of Public Health, 71,* 1125–1132.

Poulos, C. X., Hinson, R., & Seigel, S. (1981). The role of Pavlovian processes in drug tolerance and dependence: Implications for treatment. *Addictive Behaviors, 6,* 205–211.

Powell, B. J., Penick, E. C., Read, M. S. W., & Ludwig, M.D. (1985). Comparison of three outpatient treatment interventions: A twelve-month follow-up of men alcoholics. *Journal of Studies on Alcohol, 46,* 309–312.

Powell, B. J., Read, M. R., Penick, E. C., Miller, N. S., & Bingham, S. F. (1987). Primary and secondary depression in alcoholic men: An important distinction? *Journal of Clinical Psychiatry, 48,* 98–101.

Riley, D. M., Sobell, L. C., Leo, G. I., Sobell, M. B., & Klajner, F. (1987). Behavioral treatment of alcohol problems: A review and a comparison of behavioral and non-behavioral studies. In W. M. Cox (Ed.), *Treatment and prevention of alcohol problems: A resource manual* (pp. 73–115). New York: Academic Press.

Robins, L. N., Helzer, J. E., Przybeck, T. R., & Regier, D. A. (1988). Alcohol disorders in the community: A report from the Epidemiologic Catchment area. In R. M. Rose & J. Barrett (Eds.), *Alcoholism: Origins and outcome* (pp. 15–28). New York: Raven Press.

Roizen, R. (1977). *Barriers to alcoholism treatment.* Berkeley, CA: Alcohol Research Group.

Rounsaville, B. J. (1986). Clinical implications of relapse research. In F. M. Tims & C. G. Leukefeld (Eds.), *Relapse and recovery in drug abuse* (Research Monograph No. 72, pp. 172–184). Rockville, MD: National Institute on Drug Abuse.

Rounsaville, B. J., Dolinsky, Z. S., Babor, T. F., & Meyer, R. E. (1987). Psychopathology as a predictor of treatment outcome in alcoholics. *Archives of General Psychiatry, 44,* 505–513.

Rounsaville, B. J., Kosten, T. R., Williams, J. B. W., & Spitzer, R. L. (1987). A field trial of DSM-III-R psychoactive substance dependence disorders. *American Journal of Psychiatry, 144,* 351–355.

Rychtarik, R. G., Foy, D. W., Scott, T., Lokey, L., & Prue, D. M. (1987). Five–six-year follow-up of broad spectrum behavioral treatment for alcoholism: Effects of training controlled drinking skills. *Journal of Consulting and Clinical Psychology, 55,* 106–108.

Sanchez-Craig, M., Annis, H., Bornet, A., & MacDonald, K. (1984). Random assignment to abstinence and controlled drinking: Evaluation of cognitive–behavioral program for problem drinkers. *Journal of Consulting and Clinical Psychology, 52,* 390–403.

Schmidt, W. (1977). Cirrhosis and alcohol consumption: An epidemiologic perspective. In G. Edwards & M. Grant (Eds.), *Alcoholism: New knowledge and new responses* (pp. 15–47). London: Croom Helm.

Schuckit, M. A. (1981). Peak blood alcohol levels in men at high risk for the future development of alcoholism. *Alcoholism: Clinical and Experimental Research, 5,* 64–66.

Schuckit, M. A. (1982). Anxiety and assertiveness in sons of alcoholics and controls. *Journal of Clinical Psychiatry, 43,* 238–239.

Schuckit, M. A. (1985). Chapter 1: Overview: Epidemiology of alcoholism. In M. A. Schuckit (Ed.), *Alcohol patterns and problems* (pp. 1–42). New Brunswick, NJ: Rutgers University Press.

Schuckit, M. A. (1989). *Drug and alcohol abuse* (3rd ed.). New York: Plenum Medical Book.

Searles, J. S. (1988). The role of genetics in the pathogenesis of alcoholism. *Journal of Abnormal Psychology, 97,* 153–167.

Selzer, M. L. (1971). The Michigan Alcoholism Screening Test: The quest for a new diagnostics instrument. *American Journal of Psychiatry, 127,* 89–94.

Selzer, M. L., Vinokur, A., & van Rooijen, L. (1975). A self-administered Short Michigan Alcoholism Screening Test (SMAST). *Journal of Studies on Alcohol, 36,* 117–126.

Senior, J. R. (1985/1986, Winter). Alcohol hepatitis. *Alcohol Health and Research World,* pp. 40–47.

Siegel, S., Krank, M. D., & Hinson, R. E. (1987). Anticipation of pharmacological and nonpharmacological events: Classical conditioning and addictive behavior. *Journal of Drug Issues, 17,* 83–110.

Skinner, H. A., & Horn, J. L. (1984). *Alcohol Dependence Scale (ADS) user's guide.* Toronto, Ontario: Addiction Research Foundation.

Skinner, H. A., & Sheu, W. J. (1982). Reliability of alcohol use indices: The lifetime drinking history and the MAST. *Journal of Studies on Alcohol, 43,* 1157–1170.

Skutle, A., & Berg, G. (1987). Training in controlled drinking for early-stage problem drinkers. *British Journal of Addiction, 82,* 493–501.

Smail, P., Stockwell, T., Cante, S., & Hodgson, R. (1984). Alcohol dependence and phobic anxiety states: I. A prevalence study. *British Journal of Psychiatry, 144,* 53–57.

Sobell, L. C., Celluccci, T., Nirenberg, T., & Sobell, M. B. (1982). Do quantity-frequency data underestimate drinking-related health risks? *American Journal of Public Health, 72,* 823–828.

Sobell, L. C., Maisto, S. A., Sobell, M. B., & Cooper, A. M. (1979). Reliability of alcohol abuser's self-reports of drinking behavior. *Behaviour Research and Therapy, 17,* 157–160.

Sobell, L. C., & Sobell, M. B. (1990). Self-report issues in alcohol abuse: State of the art and future directions. *Behavioral Assessment, 12,* 91–106.

Sobell, L. C., Sobell, M. B., Kozlowski, L. T., & Toneatto, T. (1990). Alcohol or tobacco research versus alcohol and tobacco research. *British Journal of Addiction, 85,* 263–269.

Sobell, L. C., Sobell, M. B., Leo, G. I., & Cancilla, A. (1988). Reliability of a timeline method: Assessing normal drinkers' reports of recent drinking and a comparative evaluation across several populations. *British Journal of Addiction, 83,* 393–402.

Sobell, L. C., Sobell, M. B., & Nirenberg, T. D. (1988). Behavioral assessment and treatment planning with alcohol and drug abusers: A review with an emphasis on clinical application. *Clinical Psychology Review, 8,* 19–54.

Sobell, L. C., Sobell, M. B., Riley, D. M., Schuller, R., Pavan, D. S., Cancilla, A., Klajner, F., & Leo, G. I. (1988). The reliability of alcohol abusers' self-reports of drinking and life events that occurred in the distant past. *Journal of Studies on Alcohol, 49,* 225–232.

Sobell, L. C., Toneatto, A., & Sobell, M. B. (1990). Behavior therapy (alcohol and other substance abuse). In A. S. Bellack & M. Hersen (Eds.), *Handbook of comparative treatments for adult disorders (pp. 479–505).* New York: Wiley.

Sobell, M. B., & Sobell, L. C. (1973). Individualized behavior therapy for alcoholics. *Behavior Therapy, 4,* 49–72.

Sobell, M. B., & Sobell, L. C. (1987). Conceptual issues regarding goals in the treatment of alcohol problems. In M. B. Sobell & L. C. Sobell (Eds.), *Moderation as a goal or outcome of treatment for alcohol problems: A dialogue (pp. 1–37).* New York: Haworth Press.

Spinosa, G., Perlanski, E., Leenen, F. H. H., Stewart, R. B., & Grupp, L. A. (1988). Angiotensin converting enzyme inhibitors: Animal experiments suggest a new pharmacological treatment for alcohol abuse in humans. *Alcoholism: Clinical and Experimental Research, 12,* 65–68.

Stewart, J., deWit, H., & Eikelboom, R. (1984). Role of unconditioned and conditioned drug effects in the self-administration of opiates and stimulants. *Psychological Review, 91,* 251–268.

Stockwell, T., Murphy, D., & Hodgson, R. (1983). The Severity of Alcohol Dependence Questionnaire: Its use, reliability and validity. *British Journal of Addiction, 78,* 145–155.

Tarter, R. E., Hegedus, A. M., Goldstein, G., Shelly, C., & Alterman, A. I. (1984). Adolescent sons of alcoholics: Neuropsychological and personality characteristics. *Alcoholism: Clinical and Experimental Research, 8*, 216–222.

Tarter, R. E., Jacob, T., & Bremer, D. A. (1989). Cognitive status of sons of alcoholic men. *Alcoholism: Clinical and Experimental Research, 13*, 232–235.

Taylor, C., Brown, D., Duckitt, A., Edwards, G., Oppenheimer, E., & Sheehan, M. (1985). Patterns of outcome: Drinking histories over ten years among a group of alcoholics. *British Journal of Addiction, 80*, 45–50.

Thom, B. (1986). Sex differences in help-seeking for alcohol problems: 1. The barriers to help-seeking. *British Journal of Addiction, 81*, 777–788.

Turner, T. B., Mezey, E., & Kimball, A. W. (1977). Measurement of alcohol-related effects in man: Chronic effects in relation to levels of alcohol consumption. Part A. *Johns Hopkins Medical Journal, 141*, 235–248.

Vaillant, G. E. (1983). Natural history of male alcoholism V: Is alcoholism the cart or the horse to sociopathy? *British Journal of Addiction, 78*, 317–326.

Voetglin, W. L., & Lemere, F. (1942). The treatment of alcohol addiction: A review of the literature. *Quarterly Journal of Studies on Alcohol, 2*, 717–803.

Weisner, C. (1987). The social ecology of alcohol treatment in the U.S. In M. Galanter (Ed.), *Recent developments in alcoholism* (Vol. 5, pp. 203–243). New York: Plenum Press.

Weissman, M. M., & Meyers, J. K. (1980). Clinical depression in alcoholism. *American Journal of Psychiatry, 137*, 372–373.

Wikler, A. (1948). Recent progress in research on the neurophysiologic basis of morphine addiction. *American Journal of Psychiatry, 105*, 329–338.

Wilkinson, D. A., Leigh, G. M., Cordingley, J., Martin, G. W., & Lei, H. (1987). Dimensions of multiple drug use and a typology of drug users. *British Journal of Addiction, 82*, 259–287.

Wilkinson, D. A., & Sanchez-Craig, M. (1981). Relevance of brain dysfunction to treatment objectives: Should alcohol-related deficits influence the way we think about treatment? *Addictive Behaviors, 6*, 253–260.

Williams, G. D., Aitken, S. S., & Malin, H. (1985). Reliability of self-reported alcohol consumption in a general population survey. *Journal of Studies on Alcohol, 46*, 223–227.

Wilson, G. T. (1987). Chemical aversion conditioning as a treatment for alcoholism: A re-analysis. *Behavior Research and Therapy, 25*, 503–516.

Workman-Daniels, K. L., & Hesselbrock, V. M. (1987). Childhood problem behavior and neuropsychological functioning in persons at risk for alcoholism. *Journal of Studies on Alcohol, 48*, 187–193.

Wright, M. D. (1988). *Physical medicine and rehabilitation: Rehabilitation of the alcoholic* (Vol. 2). Philadelphia: Hanley & Belfus.

Zimmerman, R. (1988, January). Britons balk at U.S. treatment methods. *U.S. Journal of Drug and Alcohol Dependence*, pp. 7,18.

CHAPTER 5

Psychoactive Substance Use Disorder (Drugs)

JESSE B. MILBY and ROBERT D. STAINBACK

The variety of drugs used for spiritual and recreational purposes and abuse has changed throughout the years, in accordance with shifting societal standards, discovery of new compounds, and drug availability. Drug use may have begun as early as 4000 to 7000 B.C., with use and cultivation of opium poppies (Bejerot, 1970; Brown, 1961; Maurer & Vogel, 1973). Coca use can be traced back to 600 A.D. Indeed, archeological digs have revealed South American Indian mummies buried with supplies of coca leaves. Recovered pottery from this period portrays the characteristic cheek bulge of the coca leaf chewer (Milby, 1981a). However, cocaine, derived from coca, is only a little more than 100 years old.

This chapter examines drug abuse and dependence in contemporary society. Topics include prevalence, natural history, course, and etiology, especially roots of adolescent drug abuse and theoretical concepts of etiology. We sample current classification schemes and briefly review evolution of classification, using the American Psychiatric Association's (APA's) *Diagnostic and Statistical Manual of Mental Disorders* (DSM) as an illustration. We focus on DSM-III-R (APA, 1987) criteria and current issues in differential diagnosis. Typical clinical pictures for various types of substance use disorders and their implications for diagnosis and assessment are reviewed in detail. Finally, we cover the assessment of related disorders and dysfunction and briefly discuss clinical management of illustrative disorders.

EPIDEMIOLOGY OF SUBSTANCE USE DISORDERS

Prevalence

Drug abuse prevalence and type vary over time and across social systems. In their review of drug abuse epidemiology, Kozel and Adams (1986) found that incidence of heroin abuse increased and peaked during the 1960s and has generally declined since that time. The addict population appears to have remained relatively stable during the past 10 years, with estimates ranging from 400 thousand to 600 thousand. O'Malley, Bachman, and Johnston

(1988), summarizing data from annual surveys of drug use among high school seniors and young adults, suggested that patterns of drug abuse are complex. Drugs of abuse are subject to period effects (changes over time regardless of age groups), age effects (maturational changes that occur consistently for all groups of individuals at the same age), and cohort effects (sustained differences among different groups). Their data indicate that nicotine, alcohol, and cocaine are used frequently and consistently among young people. Prevalence of other drug use appears to fluctuate, demonstrating relatively strong period effects. Other studies have suggested that polydrug use is not uncommon among youthful users (Clayton & Ritter, 1985; Lester, Math, Guy, & Johnson, 1987). In particular, nicotine, marijuana, and cocaine use have been found to be related in college students (Lester et al., 1987).

Sharp increases in cocaine use occurred in the middle to late 1970s. Lifetime prevalence of cocaine use among young adults and high school students increased from 5.4 million to 22.2 million between 1974 and 1985. Estimates of current prevalence, defined as use in the past 30 days, increased from 1.6 million in 1977 to 5.8 million in 1985. The increase in cocaine abuse among adults aged 26 to 34, an age range in which a decrease in drug use typically would be expected, is particularly disturbing. This finding suggests that the age range for risk of cocaine abuse differs from that of other drugs (Adams, Gfroerer, Rouse, & Kozel, 1986; Kozel & Adams, 1986).

Natural History and Course of Drug Dependence

Initiation of drug use is most likely to occur in adolescence or young adulthood. Major risk periods for initiating cigarette, alcohol, and marijuana use typically end by age 20, and for illicit drugs, except cocaine, by age 21. Initiation of prescribed, psychoactive drug use occurs at a later age (Kandel & Logan, 1984). Young adult drug users differ from their peers along various dimensions. They typically have more difficulty making a successful transition to adult role responsibilities, engage in more deviant behavior, and become immersed in a social network supportive of their drug use (Kandel, 1984; Newcomb & Bentler, 1986). As drug use increases, these tendencies become more pronounced and often lead to family, school, social, health, and occupational problems (Kandel, Davies, Karus, & Yamaguchi, 1986; Schwartz, Hoffman, & Jones, 1987). Kandel and Logan (1984) indicated that marijuana and alcohol use decline after peaking at age 20 to 21, in sharp contrast with cigarette smoking, which continues to climb during the early 20s.

The nature of drug use patterns and the resulting consequences are difficult to track following young adulthood. It is reasonable to assume that many of those adults who continue use will become dependent on their drug(s) of choice. If these drugs are illicit, legal consequences are likely (Benson & Holmberg, 1984; Hammersley & Morrison, 1987). Long-term drug abuse is also associated with increased use of psychiatric, medical, and social services and with lower income (Holmberg, 1985).

Outcomes of addiction are variable and difficult to predict. A small portion of addicts discontinue the habit without formal treatment

(Tuchfeld, 1981; Winick, 1962), a process that is poorly understood. Some enter treatment and make sufficient changes to terminate drug use. Others respond to treatment only after repeated attempts and relapses. Finally, an unfortunate percentage continues unrelenting abuse until premature death due to the drug's direct effects on health or to other consequences of their drug use. For a detailed discussion of factors influencing the change process in addiction, the reader is referred to a book edited by Miller and Heather (1986), entitled *Treating Addictive Behaviors: Processes of Change.*

Predicting course and outcome of treatment for substance abuse is difficult. Positive outcomes occur in a variety of treatment settings (inpatient, outpatient, therapeutic communities) and intensities (Miller & Hester, 1986a); however, high relapse rates following treatment are common across addictions (W. A. Hunt, Barnett, & Branch, 1971). The consequences of unsuccessful treatment represent tremendous liabilities to the individual abuser and to society (Benson, 1985). Therefore, understanding treatment factors associated with negative and positive outcome is imperative.

Presence of other psychiatric illness in substance abusers has been well documented (Jainchill, DeLeon, & Pinkham, 1986; Ross, Glaser, & Germanson, 1988). Diagnoses frequently associated with substance abuse include personality disorders (Craig, 1988; Weller & Halikas, 1985), mood disorders (Weiss, Mirin, Griffin & Michael, 1988), posttraumatic stress disorders (Jelinek & Williams, 1984), eating disorders (Jonas, Gold, Sweeney, & Pottash, 1987), and schizophrenia (Schneier & Siris, 1987). Unfavorable substance abuse treatment outcomes have been associated with primary psychiatric symptoms prior to substance abuse treatment (Allgulander, Ljungberg, & Fisher, 1987) and with increasing severity of the symptoms (McLellan, Luborsky, Woody, O'Brien, & Druley, 1983). Early recognition of these comorbidities is important for treatment decisions and affects eventual treatment outcome.

Perhaps the most favorable prognostic indicator for substance abuse treatment is participation in aftercare following treatment. Ito and Donovan (1986) indicated that aftercare following alcoholism treatment improves treatment outcome, and its effects are independent of intake prognostic indicators. Aftercare provides a supportive structure that can assist in recovery. It enables early detection of relapse episodes, encourages development of coping skills, and provides an opportunity for family members to become involved constructively in the addict's recovery.

Continued substance abuse results in deleterious effects. No organ system is spared. Depending on the type, frequency, and duration of abuse, neurological (Leeds, Malhotra, & Zimmerman, 1983), cardiovascular (Jaffe, 1983; Yeager, Hobson, Padberg, Lynch, & Chakravarty, 1987), respiratory (Glassroth, Adams, & Schnoll, 1987), and musculoskeletal (Firooznia, Golimbu, Rafii, & Lichtman, 1983) problems are common. In addition, infectious complications can occur (Blanck, Ream, & Deleese, 1984), most notably the increased probability of contracting human immunovirus (HIV) infections for intravenous drug users (D'Aquila & Williams, 1987).

ETIOLOGY OF SUBSTANCE USE DISORDERS

Drug abuse is a multifaceted biological, pharmacological, and sociopsychological phenomenon. Animals with no previous exposure to drugs readily self-administer psychoactive drugs, and their consummatory patterns are similar to those of human users. This phenomenon suggests that psychoactive drugs can exert abuse and dependence properties on a human biological system, with no preexisting psychopathology or addictive liability required to establish initial use and self-administration. A comprehensive understanding of the etiology of substance use disorders requires a recognition of the basic biological and molecular mechanisms underlying the reinforcing effects of psychoactive substances. These mechanisms provide the foundations for other etiologic factors operating at the intrapersonal, interpersonal, and social levels, and in no way diminishes the importance of well-established precursors for drug abuse and variables that contribute to individual vulnerability.

Most drug abuse includes a variety of substances in any user (Wilkinson, Leigh, Cordingley, Martin, & Lei, 1987), with their use being independent, sequential, or concurrent with varying degrees of frequency and intensity. Research has shown that experimentation with many drugs is the statistical norm among U.S. adolescents. For example, graduating high school seniors reported the following lifetime prevalence rates for three compounds: marijuana 58.7 percent, alcohol 92.8 percent, and tobacco 70.1 percent (Johnston, Bachman, & O'Malley, 1982). Most drug users, however, *do not* become chronic abusers. Thus, most users experiment with drugs a few times and discontinue or continue to use occasionally. For example, Kandel and Yamaguchi (1985) found that only 25 percent of youngsters who experimented with drugs were still using drugs at age 23. Unlike the more common adolescent drug user, the chronic abuser becomes seriously involved with and dependent on drugs over many years.

Numerous cross-sectional and longitudinal studies have been done to determine the correlates and antecedents of adolescent drug use. Murray and Perry (1985) listed 12 studies since 1977 and grouped the variables examined into four general categories: demographic, social–environmental, intrapersonal, and behavioral. Demographic factors other than age and gender account for little additional variance in predicting future adolescent drug use. Probability and extent of drug use, except for tobacco and stimulant use, increase with age during adolescence and young adulthood. Males are more likely than females to use legal and illegal substances.

Murray and Perry (1985) reported a compendium of social–environmental factors associated with increased drug use: family and/or peer approval or tolerance for drug use, family and/or peers as models for use, family and/or peer pressure to use drugs, greater influence by peers than parents, incompatibility between parents and peers, greater involvement in peer-related activities such as dating or parties, greater reliance on peers than parents, low educational aspiration for children by parents, lack of parental involvement in children's activities, weak parental controls and discipline, and ready access to drugs. These correlations seem fairly constant across gender and ethnic group. Also, many of them predict future drug usage, with predictive strength varying as a function of the different compounds used. Thus, results from these studies of antecedents of later use and abuse suggest that future users typically live in an environment peopled by multiple models for drug use and significant others who tolerate or even encourage drug use, and an environment in which drugs are readily available. Adolescents who spend most of their time with peers are more likely to experience an environment that supports drug use than are those who spend their free time with their family or who tend to stay alone.

Murray and Perry (1985) also found a number of intrapersonal factors that correlated with drug use, many of which predicted future drug usage relative to nonusers. These factors include unconventional and nonconforming interpersonal styles, more openness to new experiences, more spontaneity, and placing a lower value on and expecting less from traditional avenues for achievement, when compared with age peers. Behavioral factors associated with adolescent use of particular drugs include use of other drugs, delinquency, sexual activity, political activism, and declining academic performance. Longitudinal studies suggest that many of these factors *precede* heavy drug use rather than result from it (Kandel, 1980).

Although the social environment may provide necessary background conditions for drug use, not all young people in high-risk environments choose to experiment or use drugs regularly. Murray and Perry (1985) suggested that intrapersonal and behavioral factors may be critical for determining the response of each adolescent. The relative value placed on conventional goals and activities and nondrug alternatives that meet the adolescent's needs appears to be critical. Although drug experimentation seems to be a peer phenomenon, dysfunctional use and severe abuse are associated with family conflict, failure in school, and antisocial behavior (Hawkins, Lishner, & Catalano, 1985). Thus, many theories of addiction and the body of research on the correlates and precursors of drug use in adolescence strongly suggest that drug use in the young serves a purpose for them and is therefore functional. This notion has important implications for clinicians who assess and diagnose substance use disorders.

MAJOR THEORIES OF ETIOLOGY

Milby (1981a, Chapter 8) critically reviewed theories of addiction and found that they can be conveniently divided into two broad types:

1. *Circumscribed theories,* which aim to explain a limited domain, such as the development of heroin addiction or tolerance.
2. *Comprehensive theories,* which attempt to explain the broad spectrum of phenomena from initiation of use to maintenance of abuse or dependence.

Types of circumscribed theories include psychoanalytic theories, metabolic disease theories, moral models, and learning theories. For the most part, the more rigorous scientific theories from which testable hypotheses can be drawn are found among circumscribed theories. The problem for the clinician is that the account of circumscribed phenomenon in drug abusing clients is of minor interest and usefulness. What are most useful are more comprehensive theories, which try to account for the multiple phenomena of initial use, experimentation, abuse, and addiction. Fortunately, a few general theories do meet reasonable standards of scientific rigor and usefulness and are having an important impact on the field (Koob & Bloom, 1988; Solomon & Corbit, 1974; Wikler, 1973).

Most rigorous scientific theories have focused on postulated mechanisms underlying physical dependence and tolerance and have based their explanatory concepts on varieties of evidence that physical dependence and tolerance generally develop and decay on a similar time course. Tolerance and dependence have been explained by postulating opponent adaptive biological processes that seek to return the system to its predrug state. This homeostatic process opposes the drug action and becomes a disruptive state itself when drug administration ceases and it remains unopposed. Until the last decade, these explanatory mechanisms remained hypothetical constructs; however, recent research indicates that tolerance and dependence not only are separable processes (Ternes, Erhman, & O'Brien, 1985), but have reliably identifiable brain sites and measurable molecular mechanisms of action. A recent comprehensive theory postulates a neurobiological basis for drug dependence, which utilizes known and postulated linkages between cellular and behavioral effects of three classes of drugs: opiates, psychostimulants, and alcohol (Koob & Bloom, 1988).

Several theories on the etiology of abuse have been developed in association with research on precursors of abuse in adolescence. These theories focus on how drug use is initiated and maintained in adolescence, and many look to social phenomena in adolescence to explain development of abuse. Milby (1981b) counted 63 such theories, Lettieri (1985) reviewed 43, and new theories are being developed constantly (e.g., Koob & Bloom, 1988; Wise & Bozarth, 1987). Space does not permit a detailed review of these theories of etiology; however, the interested reader will find excellent reviews in Milby (1981) and Lettieri (1985) and summaries of nine models of etiology in adolescence by Murray and Perry (1985).

DSM-III-R DIAGNOSTIC CRITERIA AND DIFFERENTIAL DIAGNOSIS

Rationale for Classification

We see the process of differential diagnosis as a fundamental exercise in the logical process of scientific classification. DSM-III-R is one of many classification schemes for substance use disorders that may be divided into two types: partial and complete (Milby, 1981a). Most partial schemes organize and classify one subtype of dependence according to severity. Complete schemes attempt to organize drug dependence into a unified whole, with categories typically based on the pharmacological class of drug. The most widely used complete classification scheme is DSM-III-R (APA, 1987). Of 12 schemes compared on type of dependence, level of use in research and clinical practice, logical structure, number of organizing principles, and potential usefulness, Milby (1981a) found one-third to be of limited utility and another third to be of moderate usefulness. Since that review, several new and useful classification schemes have been added, including DSM-III-R (APA, 1987; Cancrini, Cingolani, Compagnoni, Constantini, & Mazzoni, 1988; Wilkinson et al., 1987). Recent research supports the utility of the notion of a common dependence syndrome with psychosocial sequelae for all psychoactive drugs (Kosten, Rounsaville, Babor, Spitzer, & Williams, 1987).

Classification in clinical science is an active rather than static process. Useful classification schemes should be in a continuous state of refinement and evolution as our understanding of substance use disorders expands. The type and number of psychoactive drugs available are growing. Also, modes of use and the type and degree of physical and emotional dysfunction are changing. A good example of the evolution of a functional classification scheme is found in the elaboration of the APA's diagnostic and statistical manuals. The classification scheme for substance use disorders in DSM-II (APA, 1968) was based on the pharmacological properties of the drugs used and was not concerned with degree of dysfunction. Beyond establishing a need for a certain type of drug to be employed in detoxification, it was worthless as a tool to differentially assess degree of personal and social disruption caused by the drug abuse pattern, and therefore worthless for establishing treatment goals and evaluating response to rehabilitation. DSM-III (APA, 1980), using a multiaxial classification scheme, included additional classification variables, which aided in developing treatment plans and recommending modes of treatment.

DSM-III-R Descriptions of the Disorders: Diagnostic Criteria and Differential Diagnosis

DSM-III-R (APA, 1987) represents the state of the art in the diagnosis of mental disorders and reflects much current research and theory. Drug use and related psychopathology can be examined under two different major diagnostic categories within DSM-III-R: psychoactive substance use disorders and organic mental disorders. The major organizing principle across these two diagnostic categories is pharmacological type. Parameters for psychoactive substance use disorder are organized by dependence and abuse. Subsumed within the diagnostic category of psychoactive substance-induced organic mental disorders are toxic drug states, such as intoxication, withdrawal, delirium, delusional disorders, mood disorders, and other syndromes (e.g., amnestic disorder, perception disorder). Both a diagnosis of psychoactive substance-induced organic mental disorder (e.g., intoxication) and one of substance use disorder are often given to people with drug problems.

Substance Use Disorders

Two types of substance use disorder are described: dependence and abuse. For dependence to be diagnosed, at least three of nine characteristic symptoms of dependence must be met:

1. Substance is often taken in larger quantities or over longer time periods than intended.

2. Desire persists or efforts to reduce or control substance use are unsuccessful.
3. A great deal of time is spent acquiring, using, or recovering from the effects of the substance.
4. Frequent intoxication or withdrawal prevents fulfillment of major role obligations (e.g., at work, home, school), or substance is used in physically hazardous situations.
5. Important social, occupational, and recreational activities are sacrificed or diminished due to substance use.
6. Substance use is continued despite knowledge of persistent, related problems.
7. There is marked tolerance, requiring increased amounts of substance (at least a 50 percent increase) to achieve desired effect, or there are markedly reduced effects with use of the same amount.
8. Identifiable withdrawal symptoms occur.
9. Substance is often taken to reduce and prevent withdrawal symptoms.

In addition, some of the symptoms of dependence must have been present for a minimum of 1 month.

Severity of dependence is categorized as mild, moderate, severe, in partial remission, or in full remission. Symptoms of the dependence syndrome are the same across substances; however, with some drug classes, symptoms may be less pronounced or absent.

Psychoactive substance abuse is a residual category used to describe maladaptive patterns of substance use not meeting the criteria for dependence. Diagnostic criteria include a maladaptive pattern of use indicated by the following:

1. continued use despite knowledge of having a persistent or recurrent social, occupational, psychological, or physical problem that is caused or exacerbated by use of the psychoactive substance, and/or
2. recurrent use in situations in which use is physically hazardous (e.g. driving while intoxicated). (APA, 1987 p. 169)

Duration criteria are the same as for substance dependence. In order to be diagnosed as an abuser, a person must not have previously met criteria for dependence with that particular substance.

Substance-Induced Organic Mental Disorder

For substance-induced organic mental disorders, DSM-III-R provides diagnostic criteria for toxic states associated with each drug class. Unique criteria are used, which include intoxication, withdrawal, delirium, delusional disorders, mood disorders, and other syndromes (e.g., amnestic disorder, perception disorder).

For intoxication and withdrawal, DSM-III-R criteria differ based on the substance. Diagnostic signs of delirium may include, but are not limited to, reduced ability to maintain or shift attention, disorganized thinking, reduced level of consciousness, perceptual disturbance, disorientation, and memory impairment. Symptoms develop over a brief period of time (hours to days) and fluctuate. DSM-III-R criteria for an organic delusional disorder include prominent delusions that do not occur exclusively during the course of delirium. Criteria for the organic mood disorder are the presence of "prominent and persistent depressed, elevated, or expansive mood" (APA, 1987) and the fact that symptoms are not associated exclusively with delirium. The organic amnestic disorder includes diagnostic criteria of demonstrated short- and long-term memory impairment, not occurring exclusively in delirium, and not meeting criteria for dementia. Included in the criteria for delirium, delusional disorder, mood disorder, and amnestic disorder is evidence from history, physical exam, or laboratory tests that a specific organic factor can be etiologically linked to the disturbance. The perception disorder occurs only with hallucinogens and is characterized by the person's reexperiencing of perceptual symptoms that occurred during intoxication and marked distress regarding the recurrent symptoms. Other causes of the symptoms, such as lesions, infections, and delirium, must be ruled out before this diagnosis is assigned.

Changes from DSM-III to DSM-III-R

DSM-III-R incorporates several changes in criteria by which substance use disorders were diagnosed using DSM-III. Nine symptoms of dependence, which are more consistent with contemporary views of addiction, replaced DSM-III dependence criteria. A minimum of three symptoms are required for a diagnosis of dependence. The symptoms focus more on early warning signs (behavioral and cognitive) that occur in dependence rather than on the late-stage problems (high-volume drinking, tolerance, withdrawal, social or occupational impairment) emphasized in DSM-III (Landry, 1987). Also, the severity index ranging from mild to in full remission was added, permitting a more refined description of the substance use disorder. New categories of dependence were added for cocaine, phencyclidine, hallucinogens, and inhalants. The substance abuse diagnosis was originally to be deleted from DSM-III-R, but was reinstated as a residual category for cases in which dysfunctional or hazardous use is present without other dependence symptoms (Rounsaville, Kosten, Williams, & Spitzer, 1987). It was intended primarily for adolescents and young adults whose substance use might be problematic but not sufficient to warrant a diagnosis of dependence.

DSM-III-R represents a significant advancement in diagnosis of substance use disorders. The diagnostic criteria for dependence are more consistent across substances and have been supported by reliability studies (see Kosten et al., 1987). A field trial comparing the DSM-III and DSM-III-R systems demonstrated a high level of agreement, suggesting that the disorders are sufficiently robust so as to be readily diagnosed with different criteria (Rounsaville et al., 1987). Although the DSM-III-R criteria increase the number of individuals receiving a diagnosis of dependence, this change may result in the identification of substance use disorders before late-stage problems occur. Treatment is likely to be more effective earlier in the course of the disorder.

Despite the significant improvements of DSM-III-R over DSM-III, it is not without potential problems. By redefining most, if not all, substance abusers as dependent, incidence of substance dependence will increase. Although this change in labeling may result in earlier identification of substance-dependent individuals needing treatment, it may also invite unnecessary treatment of individuals who do not need intervention. The term dependence still carries pejorative overtones, which will be applied to more people with the DSM-III-R criteria. Blackwell (1987) suggested that, by replacing "dependence" with "use disorder," the potential negative effects of labeling might be reduced. Despite this concern, the DSM-III-R criteria for substance use disorders appear to be a significant contribution to diagnostic accuracy, reliability, and clinical research.

CLINICAL PICTURES

Aside from the common phenomena described below, there is no one clinical picture for substance use disorders. Instead, there are many clinical pictures, which vary according to the pharmacological action of the substance, the substance's legal status, and important individual differences. Limited space renders it impossible to describe clinical pictures for each type. Therefore, characteristics commonly seen in the development of most drug dependence are described, and then representative clinical pictures are described for prototypes of each pharmacological class.

Abuse usually begins with curiosity, excitement, peer pressure, or a prescription. Dose size, frequency, tolerance, and psychological dependence increase due to the reinforcing effects of pleasure and social and peer approval; consequently, an obsessive preoccupation with the drug occurs. The person then begins elaborate drug seeking behavior and masters drug abuse skills (e.g., drug acquisition, drug language, drug administration).

Development of dependence begins when the initial drug effects are reduced due to tolerance. Drug craving develops and is perceived as a "need" for the drug. For most drugs, the dosage is gradually increased until the level remains fairly constant. At that point, a relatively stable dose level is maintained with dependence until something interrupts it. Periods of abstinence occur when the individual attempts to stop usage or, more frequently, when the drug source becomes unavailable. Use is typically resumed, with subsequent periods of abstinence and relapse. If physical dependence develops, tolerance and/or the abstinence syndrome occur. When the drug of choice is unavailable, cross-tolerance is manifested if drugs are substituted within the same class (e.g., Valium™ for Barbiturates). The abstinence syndrome (withdrawal) occurs when drug use is discontinued, resulting in unpleasant physical symptoms. The user usually becomes obsessed with drugs and spends increasing time and energy finding and consuming drugs. Because of this obsessive preoccupation, most nondrug interests decline.

Additional characteristics are associated with the use of illegal drugs. Criminal activities often provide money for drug acquisition, sometimes leading to incarceration and the introduction of a criminal lifestyle. When illegal activities are undertaken to support the "habit," self-esteem frequently deteriorates along with grooming, general hygiene, and health.

Clinical pictures are reviewed for the following prototypes: morphine (class: opiates); barbiturates (class: barbiturates/hypnotic sedatives); amphetamine, caffeine, cocaine, and nicotine (class: psychostimulants); LSD (class: hallucinogens); cannabis sativa (class: cannabinols); and steroids. Two prototypes for concurrent dependence also are discussed: opiates/barbiturates and barbiturates/stimulants. Initial dosing effects, chronic use effects, abstinence syndromes, and overdose effects are covered for each prototype.

Opiates

Because morphine has been studied in great detail, we selected it as our prototype for the opiate class. Initial injections produce a "rush" sensation focused in the abdomen, in addition to pleasurable flushing and itching of the skin. This "rush" is followed by intense feelings of euphoria. "Nodding" (dozing in light sleep), "driving" (purposeless motoric activity), or alternating nodding and driving usually occur. Dry mouth, light-headedness, pain relief, constipation, reduced appetite and sexual desire, are often reported. Other symptoms include decreased physiological responses: body temperature, heart rate, respiration, blood pressure, and urination (Andrews, 1943; Kay, Eisenstein, & Jasinski, 1969; Wikler, 1973a). Effects diminish in 4 to 6 hours and, as tolerance develops, the duration of euphoric effects becomes shorter.

Chronic users (multiple daily use) manifest constipation, increased urination, decreased sex drive, impaired ejaculation, irregular menstruation, and weight loss (Bejerot, 1970; Eisenman, Sloan, Martin, Jasinski, & Brooks, 1969). Other effects may include lowered motivation for activity (contrasted to the driving state with initial use), low social involvement, irritation with social situations, and frequent somatic complaints (Haertzen & Hooks, 1969).

The primary phase of the abstinence syndrome occurs 5 to 6 hours after cessation of morphine use, peaks in 36 to 48 hours, and lasts about 10 days. Symptoms include nervousness, irritability, weakness, leg and back aches, cramps, nausea, decreased appetite, yawns, watery eyes, runny nose, constricted pupils, perspiration, gooseflesh, and chills. After 10 days, physiological functioning slowly begins to stabilize near normal values, but complete return to preaddiction baselines may take 30 weeks. Although the physical distress is serious, death is seldom associated with this abstinence syndrome.

Either during the withdrawal stage or after a period of abstinence, reuse usually occurs and compulsive use resumes. Periods of abstinence before reuse are common and may occasionally occur without treatment. Such periods usually are seen during and following treatment or are induced by incarceration or a period of unavailability of the drug or means to get it. Long-term follow-up studies show that, before sustained abstinence is established, several cycles of abstinence followed by relapse usually occur (Vaillant, 1973). Periods of abstinence are often marked by higher levels of stable functioning, then relapse occurs, associated and perhaps precipitated by increases in stress, psychosocial problems, reduced levels of functioning, and recent cocaine abuse (Kosten, Rounsaville, & Kleber, 1986a, 1986b, 1987). Assessments of stable abstinence in long-term follow-up studies range from about

24 percent after 11 years (Haastrup & Jepsen, 1988) to 42 percent after 20 years (Vaillant, 1973).

Most opioid addicts seek treatment at some point, and it is important to consider the impact of such treatment on the overall clinical picture. Of course, treatment varies greatly, and what treatment an addict enters depends on his or her personal characteristics and preferences, but is also a function of treatment availability and admission criteria. Space does not permit a review of treatment for opioid addiction, but the most widely available treatment, methadone maintenance, is often effective (Milby, 1981a, 1989). Controlled studies show that counseling and psychotherapy enhance methadone's treatment effects (Woody, Luborsky, McLellan, et al., 1983) and that psychotherapy perhaps provides the greatest benefit for patients with most severe psychopathology (Woody, McLellan, Luborsky, O'Brien, Beck, Blaine, Herman, & Hole, et al., 1984). When abstinence is achieved from opioids, concurrent improvement tends to occur in many other areas of functioning: reduced criminal activity, improved medical status, social functioning, and less abuse of other drugs (Rounsaville, Kosten, & Kleber, 1987). Achieving abstinence also is related to being in a drug treatment program, especially methadone maintenance; the long-range benefits of abstinence are observed even for those addicts who have relapsed at the time of follow-up.

Opiate overdose is typified by a slowing of physical functions with pulmonary edema and respiratory distress (Millman, 1978). Death may occur due to respiratory failure and collapse of the circulatory system (Bejerot, 1970). Most of these adverse effects are from true overdoses, but a portion are probably the result of allergic reactions to the drug or dilutants, nonsterile syringes, opiate-induced arrhythmias, and failure of tolerance effects (Millman, 1978; Seigel, 1981).

Some important implications can be derived from the clinical picture. First, it should be clear that successful treatment is usually a long-term process and may involve several cycles of stability–improvement–relapse, before a final level of stable adjustment, abstinence, and a functional lifestyle are achieved. Second, it is becoming increasingly clear that opioid addicts respond to active counseling and often need focused psychotherapy for concurrent disorders. Third, a program that maintains contact and rapport with the addict through multiple cycles is probably going to be in the best position to provide the sustained outpatient counseling and psychotherapy that is needed to attain stable functioning most efficiently.

Barbiturates/Hypnotic Sedatives

Because barbiturates have been studied experimentally in much detail, they are discussed as the prototype for the barbiturate/hypnotic sedative class. Drugs within this class are central nervous system depressants and include alcohol and the benzodiazepines.

Detectable effects of a single dose—for example, 200 milligrams of secobarbital—disappear within 4 to 6 hours. If this dose is administered at 5-hour intervals, however, effects overlap and signs of intoxication can be seen. Addicts may stagger, slur speech, be uncoordinated, and appear drunk. They show oscillatory movement of the eyes (nystagmus) and decreased muscle tone. They may become loud, boisterous, irritable, or aggressive. Sexual inhibitions may be reduced with low doses (Millman, 1978). There is a marked variation in response to barbiturates between individuals and within an individual given the same dose repeatedly.

Chronic consumption of more than 400 milligrams for several weeks puts the individual at risk for addiction and produces a clinical picture marked by articulation difficulties and lack of coordination in motor acts (e.g., walking). In contrast to low doses, which may reduce sexual inhibition, a chronic pattern of high doses leads to impaired sexual functioning and may be the etiologic factor in concurrent psychosexual dysfunction. Residual effects of barbiturates, including drowsiness and irritability, may last for hours, and disturbance with normal sleep patterns is common (Morin & Kwentus, 1988).

The abstinence syndrome for barbiturates, unlike opiates, can be life-threatening due to the possibility of convulsions. After withdrawal of the drug for 24 hours, anxiety, restlessness, fatigue, irritability, insomnia, and nightmares frequently occur (Kales & Kales, 1974). These symptoms may be accompanied by faintness, sweating, shivering, and convulsions. There may be a delirious psychotic reaction with paranoid delusions; however, complete recovery from the psychotic reaction usually occurs within 3 weeks. Many experts think hospitalization is mandatory for safe, effective treatment of barbiturate withdrawal.

Barbiturate overdose is frequent and one of the most prevalent causes of drug-related deaths. Barbiturates are often used in suicide attempts. Accidental overdose with barbiturates occurs among alcoholics, as they substitute or mix barbiturates with alcohol at bedtime to treat insomnia (thereby potentiating effects of both drugs). Memory impairment often contributes to drug automatism—that is, the user forgets the amount consumed and ingests more, resulting in the increased possibility of overdose (Mirin, 1977). With overdose, all symptoms described earlier are exaggerated, leading to stupor and coma. Death is due to circulatory failure and respiratory collapse.

The benzodiazepines (Valium™ and similar drugs) are frequently used for treatment of anxiety-mediated disorders. Common medical practice has been to prescribe them widely because the risk of dependence was thought to be small; however, research has shown frequent normal therapeutic dose dependence, with objective and measurable signs of withdrawal associated with mixed signs of tolerance (Kales & Kales, 1974; Lader, 1983; McKinnon & Parker, 1982). Appearance of a withdrawal syndrome in patients taking prescribed doses of sedatives or hypnotics may or may not meet DSM-III-R criteria for dysfunctional abuse dependence. Those patients dependent on these compounds often do not recognize their dependence and are identified only when they seek treatment for some other disorder, often anxiety-mediated disorders or insomnia. For patients who are more clearly dependent, a steady source of the drug is obtained from many unwary physicians, each of whom assumes he or she is the patient's primary physician and the only one prescribing benzodiazepines. Effective treatment for chronic insomnia or the underlying primary anxiety disorder can lead to successful treatment of the secondary drug dependence as well.

The treatment and long-term outcome for primary dependence on seda-tive and hypnotic drugs are hard to evaluate because of the dearth of studies available. Current data show an outcome and follow-up picture similar to, or worse than, that for opiate dependence. Allgulander, Borg, and Vikarder (1984) completed a 4- 6-year follow-up study on 50 patients originally hos-pitalized for primary sedative–hypnotic dependence and found that 84 percent resumed sedative–hypnotic use, 52 percent were abusing drugs at follow-up, and 42 percent had been readmitted for abuse. Three had experi-enced delirious states and 6 had seizures during withdrawal. Social deterio-ration was observed in 48 percent. A recent long-term study in Sweden by Allgulander et al. (1987) showed similar unfavorable outcomes for 221 pa-tients admitted for dependence on sedative–hypnotics. Poor outcomes were significantly related to primary psychiatric symptoms before first admis-sion, concomitant alcohol abuse, familial drug and alcohol abuse, and health care occupation. Of those with primary sedative–hypnotic dependence, 46 percent continued abuse until death or follow-up. There also was higher than expected unnatural death: 11 percent of the men and 23 percent of the women.

Concurrent Dependence

Opioid addiction is often thought of as a single-class substance phenomenon, but the use of opioids to the exclusion of all other classes of drugs is rare (Siegal, 1981). Opioid addicts often abuse alcohol, barbiturates and synthetic hypnotics, cocaine, and other compounds (Anglin, Almog, Fisher, & Peters, 1989). Findings suggest that alcohol use during methadone treatment reflects a lifetime pattern of increased alcohol use following any decline in heroin intake.

Weiss et al. (1988) studied 329 hospitalized drug abusers for current or past diagnosis of alcoholism and found that 51 percent carried current or pre-vious diagnoses of alcoholism. The alcoholics were significantly more likely to receive a DSM-III diagnosis of major depression and to have a concurrent antisocial personality disorder.

The clinical picture for concurrent dependence (i.e., dependence on two classes of drugs) is extremely complex. A typical concurrent dependence in-volves combined use of opiates and barbiturates. The user may substitute one drug for another and show a mixed clinical picture. For instance, instead of showing the "nod" state common to opiates, opiate–barbiturate addicts will, despite a recent dose of an opiate, show signs of barbiturate withdrawal, in-cluding anxiety, irritability, and sleep difficulty. They may show some slur-ring of speech, difficulty walking, trouble keeping their balance, and general incoordination in the absence of any odor of alcohol. Frequently, the user does not realize the symptoms are from barbiturate withdrawal, but at-tributes the effects to opiate withdrawal, the "primary" addiction.

Another typical concurrent dependence involves barbiturates and stimu-lants. The clinical picture is for concurrent and alternating use. To prevent aversive symptoms from chronic amphetamine dosage, barbiturates are of-ten consumed to reduce sleeplessness and hyperexcitability. Amphetamines are used to reduce barbiturate sedation after a large dose or to reduce morning drowsiness.

Another common pattern of concurrent dependence is that of opiates and cocaine. With the widespread use of "crack" cocaine, this pattern is widely seen in methadone maintenance and drug-free treated patients (Hanbury, Sturiano, Cohen, Stimmel, & Aguillaume, 1986; D. Hunt, Spunt, Lipton, Goldsmith, & Strug, 1986; Strug, Hunt, Goldsmith, Lipton, & Spunt, 1985). There is some evidence that depression may lead to increased vulnerability for such cocaine abuse (Kosten, Rounsaville, & Kleber, 1987).

Psychostimulants: Amphetamine, Caffeine, Cocaine, and Nicotine

Amphetamine

One type of psychostimulant is amphetamine. Initial low to moderate doses (1 to 50 milligrams) of amphetamine elevate mood, increase alertness, and induce euphoria. Increased motor activity and respiration, agitation, insomnia, and decreased appetite are common effects of moderate doses. With chronic use of high doses (100 milligrams or more), an intense, pleasurable feeling or "rush" is produced, especially when intravenous (IV) administration is used. These levels reduce fatigue, promote wakefulness, and suppress appetite. Administered hourly, such levels increase the likelihood of a psychotic reaction (Angrist & Gershon, 1970). A behavior pattern similar to schizophrenia may occur, marked by disorganized behavior, confused thought and speech patterns, and repetition of meaningless acts. Individuals may become overly suspicious, paranoid, and verbally and physically aggressive.

There is disagreement as to whether an abstinence syndrome occurs with amphetamines. After termination of high doses, certain symptoms do reliably appear (e.g., sleep, depression, hunger, and high fluid intake), and suicidal behavior may occur due to severe depression. Administration of amphetamines during this stage, however, does not restore normal physiological and psychological functions. Thus, a clearly defined abstinence syndrome, as in opiate and barbiturate addictions, is not demonstrated (Himmelsbach, 1939; Sapira & MacDonald, 1970).

Overdose may occur with amphetamines. Overdose symptoms, labeled amphetamine psychosis (Connell, 1958), resemble paranoid psychotic reactions. Cardiovascular symptoms (circulatory collapse, irregular heartbeat), gastrointestinal symptoms (nausea, cramps, diarrhea) and psychological symptoms (confusion, hallucinations, persecutory delusions, panic attacks) occur. Death from overdose is rare, although in some instances a large increase in arterial blood pressure leads to ruptured vessels and death (Julien, 1975).

Caffeine

Caffeine is found in coffee, tea, cola, and cocoa. Caffeine amounts vary in accordance with type of beverage or food and with the method in which it is prepared. For example, a cup of coffee contains 70 to 140 milligrams of caffeine, with brewed coffee containing more. A cup of coffee contains twice as much caffeine as a cup of tea and three times as much as one cola (Schuckit, 1979). With doses of less than 100 milligrams, effects are negligible, but mild psychological and physiological effects occur with doses in excess of 200 milligrams. Motor activity and speed of thought increase, whereas sleepiness and fatigue decrease. These symptoms are accompanied by an increase in heart rate, blood pressure, and gastrointestinal problems. With high doses of more than 500 milligrams, intoxification may occur. Symptoms of intoxification include decreased need for sleep and rest, restlessness, muscle twitches, rambling thoughts and speech, diuresis, and flushing. Caffeine dependence, also called caffeinism, has been investigated by several groups of researchers (Goldstein & Kaizer, 1969; Rieman, 1967). Consumption of 5 or more cups of coffee daily results in weight loss, reduced appetite, and insomnia. Although not frequently recognized, an abstinence syndrome with caffeine has been documented (Griffiths, Bigelow, & Liebson, 1986; Griffiths & Woodson, 1988). The abstinence syndrome begins 12 to 24 hours following cessation of use, peaks 20 to 48 hours following cessation, and lasts approximately 1 week. Reported and observed symptoms include increased headaches and fatigue, and decreased alertness and activity. Less frequent symptoms include anxiety, nausea and vomiting, and craving. Overdose is rare, since 10 grams of caffeine (70 to 100 cups of coffee) would be needed (Schuckit, 1979).

Cocaine

Cocaine is available in various forms and is administered in various ways. Effects of cocaine depend partly on how it is consumed: snorted, smoked (freebased), or injected. Effects of snorting a typical intranasal dose (25 to 150 milligrams) of pure, pharmaceutical cocaine hydrochloride include euphoria; increased energy, alertness, and sensory awareness; and decreased appetite. Freebase and intravenous cocaine users report an intense rush of euphoria, often referred to as "power" or "energy." The rush fades in seconds, but the euphoria remains for several minutes. The euphoria is followed by dysphoria, agitation, and restlessness, prompting the user to use again (Gold, Dackis, Pottash, Extein, & Washton, 1986).

With continued use of cocaine, maladaptive cognitive–behavioral changes may occur, including feelings of grandiosity, hypervigilance, agitation, and impaired judgment. General signs of sympathetic arousal may include tachycardia, pupillary dilation, elevated blood pressure, and perspiration. Severe intoxication may be characterized by rambling speech, psychomotor agitation, anxiety, apprehension, impaired judgment, and fighting. Other symptoms might include transient ideas of reference, paranoid ideation, increased sexual interest, and visual or tactile hallucinations. Immediate abstinence effects with cocaine (the "crash") include dysphoria, craving, anxiety, tremulousness, irritability, fatigue, and depression. Beyond 24 hours of abstinence, the withdrawal syndrome may include insomnia or hypersomnia and psychomotor agitation (APA, 1987).

Both animal studies (Bozarth & Wise, 1985) and clinical observations (Valladares & Lemberg, 1987) attest to the toxic effects of cocaine. In reviewing emergency room visits and hospital admissions at a major metropolitan hospital, Lowenstein et al. (1987) noted acute neurologic and psychiatric symptoms as primary complaints. Neurologic complications included seizures, focal neurologic signs, headache, and transient loss of consciousness. Agitation, anxiety, depression, psychosis, paranoia, and suicidal ideation were the most frequent psychiatric symptoms. Pulmonary problems have been noted in freebasers (Kissner, Lawrence, Selis, & Flint, 1987; Salzman, Khan, & Emory, 1987).

The minimum lethal dose of cocaine is difficult to determine, because much of the street supply of the drug is adulterated. Also, death has occurred with various blood levels of cocaine in otherwise healthy individuals, prompting Smart and Anglin (1987) to suggest that "virtually no dose, however small, can be guaranteed safe for 100% of cases." Death associated with cocaine use is frequently due to a cardiovascular complication, such as myocardial infarction, arrhythmia, or aortic rupture (Bates, 1988).

Nicotine

Since the report of the surgeon general in 1988 concerning the addictive qualities of nicotine, public awareness of this drug has increased (Byrne, 1988; Gunby, 1988). Although nicotine is consumed in a variety of forms (cigarettes, pipe, cigars, chewing tobacco, snuff), with related negative consequences, cigarette smoking is the most common. At low doses, similar to those from cigarette smoking, nicotine increases heart rate and blood pressure. Many smokers report that smoking increases arousal and relaxation, and produces positive effects on mood, concentration, anger, and depression (Benowitz, 1988). With continued use of nicotine via cigarette smoking, tolerance to many of its effects occurs rapidly.

In novice smokers, for example, tolerance to the initial unpleasant response of the body (dizziness, nausea) may occur within several episodes of use. In regular smokers, tolerance to the subjective effects and heart rate acceleration occur within a day (West & Russell, 1987). An abstinence syndrome, appearing within 24 hours of cigarette abstinence or reduced consumption, has been documented (Henningfield, 1984). The syndrome is characterized by craving for nicotine, irritability, anxiety, impaired concentration, and restlessness. Symptoms typically reach maximal intensity 24 to 48 hours after cessation and gradually diminish in intensity over a period of 2 weeks. Exsmokers, however, have reported that the desire to smoke persists for months or even years after quitting (Benowitz, 1988). Nicotine overdose has been documented in cases of accidental exposure to nicotine containing pesticides or occupational exposure to tobacco leaves (Saxena & Scheman, 1985). In the case of cigarette smoking, overdose does not appear to be a risk.

Hallucinogens

The drug class hallucinogens contains diverse drugs with wide differences in chemical structure and mechanism of action. Little in the literature suggests that severe dependence develops to hallucinogens, but researchers may have ignored its dependence-inducing capacity because most of the drugs in this class do not produce the classical withdrawal illness and physical dependence.

Tennant (1983), in a review of the literature, could not find one study that documented abstinence in the majority of any group of hallucinogen users for as long as 90 days following treatment. Thus, it may be that abuse and psychological dependence on hallucinogens are more difficult to treat than has been generally assumed.

D-lysergic acid diethylamide (LSD), our prototype, has two phases of dose effects: autonomic nervous system effects and psychological symptoms. Autonomic nervous system effects are decreased appetite, dizziness, increased body temperature and blood sugar, chills, restlessness, gooseflesh, nausea, vomiting, and variations in pulse and blood pressure. Psychological symptoms include depersonalization and body image distortion of internal stimuli (i.e., visual, auditory, tactile, olfactory, gustatory, and thermal illusions).

Chronic dosage does not cause physical dependence, but tolerance to physical and psychological effects occurs. Individuals having a history of psychological disturbances, living in insecure environments, or undergoing crisis situations frequently have adverse reactions. Lasting adverse reactions have not been adequately documented, although anecdotal reports indicate that flashbacks and panic reactions ("bad trips") occur (McWilliams & Tuttle, 1973; Millman, 1978). Psychological dependence occurs relatively infrequently. No overdose deaths have been reported in the literature.

Cannabinols

Cannabis sativa and cannabis sativa resin are the prototypes for the class cannabinols. Although this drug is considered an hallucinogen, hallucinations rarely occur with usual doses. Thus, the drug is considered in a separate class.

Use of cannabis sativa (marijuana) and its resin (hashish) produces physiological, perceptual, and psychological effects (Hollister, 1971). Tetrahydrocannabinol (THC) is the prevalent psychoactive ingredient in marijuana and hashish, so dosage levels refer to THC content. With low doses of 5 to 25 milligrams (one "joint" equals approximately 7.5 milligrams of THC), typical physiological effects include bloodshot eyes, dry mouth, unusual sensations such as tingling (parasthesias), increased appetite, and craving for sweets. Heightened senses of taste, touch, smell, sound, and vision are typical perceptual effects (Hollister, 1971). Psychological effects are elated mood; slowed time sense; difficulties in thinking, comprehending, and expressing; poor memory; and uncontrollable laughter. Impaired performance on visuomotor and cognitive tasks, such as driving an automobile and piloting an aircraft, have been reported (Hollister, 1988; Yesavage, Leirer, Denari, & Hollister, 1985). These effects often are not recognized by the user.

With chronic high doses of 200 milligrams, more intense symptoms occur. Emotional responses are magnified, sensations are distorted, and hallucinations may occur. Acute panic reactions, toxic delirium, psychosis, and transient paranoid states have been reported to occur (Hollister, 1988; Schwartz, 1987). Chronic marijuana use may exacerbate existing mental illness, such as schizophrenia (Maycut, 1985). Decreased performance on perceptual motor tasks (Varma, Malhotra, Dang, Das, & Nehra, 1988) and on reaction time, speed, and accuracy tests (Mendhiratta et al., 1988) have been associated with chronic, heavy marijuana use. No clinical or experimental evidence indicates that an abstinence syndrome is produced, although tolerance and reverse tolerance have been noted (Ferraro & Grisham, 1972; Weil, Zinberg, & Nelson, 1969). An amotivational syndrome, consisting of lowered activity, goallessness associated with apathy, sluggish mental and physical responses, loss of interest in personal appearance, flattening of affect, symptoms of mental confusion, and a slowed time sense, has been described (Maugh, 1974), but its validity is still controversial (Hochman & Brill, 1973).

Anabolic Steroids

Anabolic steroids are testosterone derivatives developed to maximize the anabolic effects of testosterone and minimize its androgenic effects. The primary anabolic effect of steroids is an increase in body weight and lean muscle mass. The androgenic effects include changes in sex characteristics, both primary (increases in penis size and sperm production) and secondary (increase of facial hair, deepening of voice). The drugs have an accepted medical use for induction of sexual development in hypogonadal males (Haupt & Rovere, 1984); however, their illicit use is the reason they have been included in this chapter on drug abuse. Some athletes use anabolic steroids, mostly without prescription or medical supervision, to increase weight and muscle mass. Some experts feel that use of anabolic steroids is pervasive in the sports world at the elite level of competition (see review by Donahoe & Johnson, 1986). Furthermore, increasing evidence indicates that their use has become more common among adolescent athletes and nonathletes (Buckley et al., 1988).

The first reported use of anabolic steroids in athletics was by Russian weight lifters in the 1950s. American weight lifters followed their lead later in that decade. Since that time, steroid use has become increasingly popular and has spread to other sports, such as football, swimming, and track and field.

Although the use of steroids is now widespread, their effect on athletic performance remains controversial. Athletes using the drugs typically have strong beliefs that their performance is improved while taking steroids; however, results of controlled studies on the effects of steroids on athletic performance are mixed. In a recent literature review, Haupt and Rovere (1984) suggested that anabolic steroids yield significant strength increases in athletes intensively trained in weight lifting before and during steroid use, in those athletes who maintain high-protein diets, and in those events in which strength is measured by the single repetition–maximal weight technique. The belief that steroids will enhance strength may also play a strong role in their ultimate effect.

A second major controversy about steroids is the frequency with which physical and emotional side effects occur. Athletes taking the drugs often believe that side effects are not serious or permanent. The medical and scientific communities suggest otherwise, citing reports of abnormal liver function tests, reproductive system change, liver tumors, and cholesterol imbalance in chronic heavy steroid users (American College of Sports Medicine; Wright & Stone, 1985). Psychological effects of steroid use, including affective and psychotic symptoms, also have been reported (Pope & Katz, 1988).

The controversies surrounding the effects of steroids on athletic perform-ance and the incidence and seriousness of side effects have created an unfor-tunate rift between the athletic and scientific communities. The athlete, under pressure to win and without definitive knowledge of benefits and risks associated with steroid use, is left to a combination of "faith and fear" that stimulates his or her use of steroids (Donahoe & Johnson, 1986): faith that steroids will build muscle and increase strength, and fear that, without the use of steroids, he or she will be at a disadvantage to steroid-using competitors. Fuller and LaFountain (1987) suggested that athletes, when put under these conditions, resort to defensive mechanisms to justify their use of steroids. These psychological strategies might include denial of potential health risks, condemnation of nonathletes who criticize their steroid use, and appeal to the "higher loyalties" of sport. These justification strategies are not unlike those that might be used by other illicit drug users.

Although anabolic steroids are not included in the traditionally recog-nized drugs of abuse, their use among athletes is cause for concern. In 1975, their use was banned in amateur athletic competition; however, evidence indicates that, rather than reducing steroid use, such banning has led athletes to find new and improved methods of disguised use (Donahoe & Johnson, 1986). Each new method of drug testing has spawned a variety of methods to avoid detection. A reexamination of the goals of sport participation will likely be necessary before steroid use can be significantly altered.

ASSESSMENT

Because drug abuse and dependence are often secondary to some underlying mental or emotional disorder, we think that early and thorough assessment is the cornerstone of good treatment. Ample evidence shows that substance use disorders often present with other forms of psychopathology, especially anxiety-mediated disorders, depression, and history of suicide behavior (Ward & Schuckit, 1980). When psychopathology is diagnosed and treated, a more favorable outcome of treatment can be expected (Woody et al., 1984). Thus, we feel that assessment of drug abuse and dependence is similar to the assessment of any form of psychopathology, but with one added feature. Be-cause the pharmacological component of the maladaptation adds complica-tions, additional evaluation is required. Although the psychologist does not usually use pharmacological assessment procedures, they are an important component of evaluation for this population, and for that reason are included in our discussion.

Assessment of drug abuse and dependence is usually done in a hospital, a general clinic such as a mental health center, or a drug dependence clinic or program. Assessment approaches vary according to the site and purpose of assessment. For example, an assessment carried out in an emergency room because of behavior that suggests an overdose or drug-induced psychosis differs from an assessment of a self-referred heroin addict seeking admis-sion to a therapeutic community. The former focuses on pharmacological variables: what drug was used, how much was used, and when and how it was administered. The latter focuses on psychosocial variables, marital and family history, friendship and recreation patterns, vocational history, target behaviors, and so on. Pharmacological variables are assessed, but they receive less emphasis. Thus, the only assessment strategy that makes sense is one that is idiographic and sensitive to the site, role, and goals of the program in which the assessment is done.

Drug abuse and dependence can be primary or secondary to other forms of psychopathology. When primary, it exists as the dominant form of psychopathology and is the dysfunction from which other problems develop. When secondary, other forms of psychopathology are the major disorder, and drug abuse or dependence becomes an adaptation to deal with the psychopathology. For example, drug abuse may develop in a depressed individual, who discovers chemical means of treating his or her dysphoria, or in an individual with an anxiety-mediated disorder, such as agoraphobia, who develops dependence on hypnotic sedatives to escape generalized anxiety and intense panic attacks. Drug abuse and dependence can also be concurrent with other forms of psychopathology, not clearly playing a primary or a secondary role. Obviously, these inferences are of strategic importance, suggesting treatment modalities and priorities. Unfortunately, no instruments or procedures are available by which such inferences can be systematically derived. They depend on the clinician's judgment, as he or she sorts through facts, scores, and observations; however, these inferences are more likely to be valid and useful when assessment is broad, detailed, and, most importantly, idiographic.

Assessment Strategies and Techniques

Assessment of drug abuse or dependence is a relatively underdeveloped area. However, the following assessment techniques may be employed: structured interviews, self-reports, direct observations, urine and blood sampling, pharmacological procedures, and psychometrics.

Structured Interview

A structured interview may be conducted with the patient or with a significant other (Cautela & Upper, 1976). The interview not only should focus on drug use, but should address numerous areas of the client's life. One of the most important aspects of the interview should be the discovery of the functionality of drug use for the particular person. Although such information may not contribute to establishment of a DSM-III-R differential diagnosis, it can be immensely important, even critical, for the development of a successful intervention plan. We would submit that *any* intervention plan is likely to fail if it does not take into account what function drug use serves for a particular person. A plan that utilizes such information is more likely to help the drug user discover less destructive and socially acceptable ways to meet legitimate needs.

Topics to be covered in an interview include type of drug used and pattern of use; physical health; emotional–cognitive, marital, social, vocational, and recreational functioning; and possible legal difficulties. After determining the type of drug or drugs used, the clinician should evaluate the quantity, frequency, and duration of use (including abstinence periods). Drug administration techniques are also important (e.g., intravenous, intramuscular, or subcutaneous injection; inhalation; ingestion). The possibility of cross-tolerance and mixed addictions should be assessed. Structured questioning of precipitating and maintaining factors should include the following: social environment, emotions and cognitions, and physiological processes. Furthermore, consequences of use (e.g., incarceration, financial costs, interpersonal costs) should be noted.

In evaluating the physical condition of the patient, the interviewer should be concerned with drug-related disease (e.g., skin infections, hepatitis, and HIV virus), iatrogenic abuse, serious withdrawal symptoms, and drug-induced psychotic states. In medical settings, evaluation by a physician and careful review of medical records augment interview data. In nonmedical settings, assessment of the patient's physical status may require referral for medical assessment.

The patient's emotional and cognitive state may be addressed in part by a structured interview. Of particular importance is the assessment of the extent to which the client self-medicates in an effort to ameliorate primary psychological symptomatology. Fears about detoxification should be ascertained. Presence of detoxification phobia has recently been documented in the literature and may have ramifications for treatment, especially detoxification (Milby, Garrett, & Meredith, 1980; Milby, Rice, & Garrett, 1979).

Assessing family and marital history renders information on stability, the presence of marital stress, and the presence of social support. Marriages often dissolve when one spouse is a heavy user. In addition, the spouse's drug use should be determined, since it usually affects use patterns.

The social environment may be assessed by inquiring about social affiliations (e.g., friends, clubs) and recreational pursuits. Often, drug users' only friends are part of the drug culture, and their recreational pursuits revolve solely around acquiring and using drugs.

Questioning about vocational status yields information about income available for drugs. The clinician should ascertain any employment terminations, difficulties, or absences due to drug "hangover" or being "high."

Legal status is important for assessing the degree of maladaptive behavior that is due to drug use. Arrests for shoplifting, prostitution, and stealing drugs and property are common, as are arrests for selling drugs.

The structured interview lends itself to checks on reliability and validity of data by facilitating comparisons from independent interviews of the same patient. In addition, data can be collected in a systematic manner, facilitating program and treatment evaluation.

One brief structured interview is the Addiction Severity Index (ASI), introduced by McLellan et al. (1980) and refined through further research (McLellan et al., 1985). ASI assesses severity in seven areas: medical problems, employment and types of financial support, alcohol use, drug use, legal problems, family and social functioning, and psychiatric disorders. It yields a severity index and profile that is sensitive to gains in treatment. Derived composite scores, along with the severitd index, have been used in clinical outcome research for alcohol and substance use disorder studies.

Another structured interview that is useful for diagnosing other disorders in substance abusers is the National Institute of Mental Health (NIMH) Diagnostic Interview Schedule (DIS). The validity and utility of

DIS early in treatment may be compromised in drug-dependent patients by neurological deficits and impaired recollection of their previous symptoms (Bergman, Borg, & Holm, 1980; Griffin, Weiss, Mirin, Wilson, & Bouchard-Voelk, 1987). A modified version of DIS, with an expanded section on substance use, is available based on DSM-III.

Self-Report

When screening a patient for the presence of any psychopathology, the clinician must assume within reason that information given by the client is reliable and valid. In the case of substance abusers, alcoholics in particular, this assumption has been questioned. Watson, Tilleskjor, Hoodecheck-Schow, Pucel, and Jacobs (1984) suggested that alcoholics tend to give a more favorable report of their drinking history than do collaterals. Recent reviews of the literature on reliability and validity of self-reported alcohol use (Midanik, 1982; Polich, 1982) suggest that self-reports are reasonably accurate, given that the conditions of the interview support truthful reporting. If negative consequences are to follow self-reported alcohol use (e.g., a return to jail), then the likelihood of inaccurate reporting increases. In a treatment setting in which the client is not punished for reporting alcohol use, self-reports are likely to be valid. Setting of the appropriate demand characteristics to increase the probability of valid self-reports is partly the responsibility of the clinician. A similar relationship between self-report accuracy and demand characteristics appears to exist for drug abusers (Ben-Yehuda, 1980). Furthermore, Skinner (1984) found that report accuracy increases with length of stay in treatment. Computer-administered interviews have also been shown to yield reliable alcohol and drug use histories (Skinner & Allen, 1983).

In the treatment setting, self-monitoring data may be kept by the patient, including drug use frequency, time, place, antecedents, consequences, and amount. Other self-report assessments require the individual to record all urges (cravings) to use the drug (Boudin, 1972). With another self-report technique (Boudin, Valentine, & Ingraham, 1977), the individual telephones the drug treatment facility between one and six times per day and reports on such things as drug use, anxiety, urges, or arguments. Most self-report monitoring is aimed at obtaining a functional analysis of behavior (Callahan, Price, & Dahlkoetter, 1980; Nurnberger & Zimmerman, 1970).

Other self-report methods employed with drug users are questionnaires. A general screening may be conducted by using a Life History Questionnaire, such as that developed by Lazarus (1980). Problem checklists can be employed, such as the Mooney Problem Checklist (Mooney and Gordon, 1950). The many self-report surveys are too numerous to review here. Focused surveys and questionnaires, such as for sexual dysfunction, generally are administered only when specific problems are indicated during a more general assessment.

Direct Observation

Direct observation is extremely important in assessing the client's initial presentation to treatment personnel. Careful observation can reveal signs of withdrawal symptoms, drug-related diseases or disorders, general health and cognitive status, and quality of interpersonal skills and social support. Direct observation can be systematized, and ratings can be derived. For example, the Objective Opiate Withdrawal Scale provides an index of opiate withdrawal based on thirteen physically observable signs, which are rated present or absent during a timed observation period (Handelsman et al., 1987).

Observational assessment strategies have been studied experimentally in controlled settings to record, for example, the euphoric effects of heroin (Babor, Meyer, & Mirin, 1976; McNamee, Mirin, Kuhnle, & Meyer, 1976; Mirin, Meyer, & McNamee, 1976). Observational assessment has also been carried out by allowing patients free access to a variety of substances in a lab setting (Blanchard, Libet, & Young, 1973). Elkin, Williams, Barlow, and Stewart (1974) videotaped users "shooting up," and later replayed the tape and assessed the users' physiological arousal. O'Brien, Testa, and O'Brien (1977) observed and measured heroin addicts' conditioned withdrawal symptoms to stimuli associated with heroin use.

Urine and Blood Samples

Urine and blood samples are frequently obtained in treatment of drug abuse. Toxicologic procedures are used for various therapeutic reasons: to verify the abused substance in cases of acute intoxication; to provide a basis for distinguishing intoxication or withdrawal from other psychopathology; to prevent recent drug use from interfering with accuracy of other diagnostic tests, such as psychological testing; and to monitor possible drug use during rehabilitation. Laboratory tests fall into two broad categories: competitive binding assays and chromatographic assays (Lehrer & Gold, 1986). The former include radioimmunoassays and enzyme immunoassays. The latter include thin layer chromatography (TLC), gas liquid chromatography (GLC), and combined gas chromatography and mass spectrometry (GC-MS). Commercial urine assays vary in their sensitivity and specificity (Cone, Menchen, Paul, Mell, & Mitchell, 1989; Cone & Mitchell, 1989). GC-MS is generally regarded as the most powerful analytical technique for identifying drugs, and therefore is recommended for forensic work. For clinical use, a screening test high in sensitivity (e.g., TLC) is typically used initially; positive results are confirmed with a test higher in specificity (e.g., GLC).

Because drugs vary in their rates of metabolism and excretion, assessment timing and frequency affect accuracy of detection. Callahan et al. (1980) recommended random urine or blood sampling to validate self-report. Compared with random-interval sampling, fixed-interval sampling has been shown to miss detection of drug use by as much as 50 percent (Harford & Kleber, 1978). Blood sampling is more invasive and costly, and therefore is used less frequently as a routine assessment procedure.

Pharmacological Procedures

Pharmacological assessment is used to assess tolerance and dependence on opiates, barbiturates, and hypnotic sedatives (Kolb, 1973; Schuckit, 1979). Opiate dependence may be determined by administration of a narcotic antagonist, such as naloxone, which will precipitate an acute abstinence state if the person is opioid dependent. To establish opiate tolerance levels, test doses of methadone are administered on a timed schedule until signs of intoxication appear. A similar procedure is used with some short-acting barbiturates, such as pentobarbital, to establish barbiturate and hypnotic sedative tolerance.

Psychometrics

Although traditional psychometric instruments have been widely employed with drug abusers, in our view they have not been shown to be specifically applicable to this population or to be very helpful in diagnosis. The Minnesota Multiphasic Personality Inventory (MMPI), however, may offer pertinent assessment information for screening out substance use problems from a general psychiatric population. Several scales have been developed from MMPI item pools (Cavior, Kurtzberg, & Lipton, 1967; Dahlstrom, Welsh, & Dahlstrom, 1975; Panton & Brisson, 1971).

The most commonly used MMPI scale in substance abuse assessment is the MacAndrew Alcoholism Scale (MacAndrew, 1965). For example, Lachar, Berman, Grisell, and Schoof (1976) found that alcoholics, heroin addicts, and polydrug users obtained similar elevated scores on this scale. All three groups had significantly higher scores than matched controls. An abbreviated version of this scale was a significant predictor of marijuana, cocaine, and amphetamine use (Rathus, Fox, & Ortins, 1980).

Although the MMPI can be useful in screening for psychopathology, the Millon Clinical Multiaxial Inventory (MCMI) may be a better measure of the presence and type of personality disorder often found in the addicted population (Marsh, Stile, Stoughton, & Trout-Landen, 1988). A brief general screening test of psychopathology is the widely used Symptoms Checklist (SCL-90), developed by Derogatis, Rickels, and Rock (1976). A shorter version, referred to as the Brief Symptom Inventory (BSI), has also shown ability to distinguish among groups with various levels of drug abuse and indicate number of life areas affected by the substance use disorder (Royse & Drude, 1984).

Some specialized measures are available for a drug population. Because narcotic addicts often have phobias (Ling, Holmes, Post, & Litaker, 1973), the Fear Survey Schedule could be helpful. Instruments designed to measure social skills and aggressive behaviors may be employed. The astute clinician may use instruments to detect a thought disorder or to measure intelligence. In other words, the full range of intellectual and personality assessment techniques may be employed in making diagnostic and treatment formulations for substance abuse populations.

CLINICAL MANAGEMENT

The Change Process

Clinicians treating drug dependence need to understand that clients change their addictive behaviors for a variety of reasons and under numerous conditions. Outcomes of addictive behavior are variable and difficult to predict (Orford, 1986). Positive changes occur without treatment (Saunders &

Kershaw, 1979; Tuchfeld, 1981) and in a variety of treatment circumstances. In the alcoholism literature, for instance, favorable treatment outcomes have been reported with one-session "advice" giving (Edwards et al., 1977), self-help manuals (Heather, 1986), and traditional inpatient and outpatient therapy (Miller & Hester, 1986b). Psychological models developed to account for changes in addiction suggest three basic stages of the change process. In the first stage, the addict is contemplating the seriousness of the problem, surveying and selecting solutions, and making a commitment to change. The second stage involves taking necessary actions to change (e.g., self-help measures or treatment). The final stage involves maintaining changes made in earlier stages through monitoring and evaluating progress, and adhering to previously established goals.

The stage model of change has implications for substance abuse treatment. First, the clinician must have a basic understanding of the dynamics of each stage. A patient struggling with issues characterizing the first stage, such as deciding whether the consequences of the addictive behavior are serious enough to change the behavior, requires different intervention strategies from those required by the patient in the third stage, when treatment generally focuses on ways to sustain progress and prevent relapse. A second implication of the stage theory is that therapeutic gains may be short-lived if extended follow-up is not provided for the patient. The challenges of the maintenance stage are significant, and positive long-term outcome depends on patients' successfully adjusting to life stressors without substance abuse. A final implication, as obvious as it may sound, is that patients are responsible for changing their addictions. Therefore, patients should be active in making decisions about their treatment. Patients allowed this input are less likely to drop out of treatment and more likely to adhere to an established remedial plan (Parker, Winstead, & Willi, 1979; Parker, Winstead, Willi, & Fisher, 1979).

Motivation to Change

Changing addictive behavior requires a sustained high level of motivation. Miller (1985) operationally defined motivation for treatment as the probability of entering into, continuing in, and complying with treatment. He suggested that patient motivation depends primarily on characteristics of the patient–therapist relationship and the appropriateness of treatment alternatives offered. In their work with problem drinkers, Miller and his colleagues suggested three therapeutic goals for motivational interviewing (Miller, 1983; Miller, Sovereign, & Krege, 1988):

1. Increase the patient's perceived discrepancy between the present state (e.g., current daily alcohol use) and the perceived objective (e.g., long-term abstinence)
2. Facilitate increased self-efficacy (feelings of control) by providing realistic alternatives to reach the perceived objective
3. Enhance the patient's self-esteem through empathy, positive regard, and an "active helping attitude."

Motivational interviewing and similar interventions intended to increase patients' motivation to change have been effective with problem drinkers (Edwards et al., 1977; Kristenson, 1982). It is reasonable to assume that these methods would also be helpful with other addictions. For an extensive review of the motivation-for-treatment literature, see Miller (1985).

Treatment Modality Decisions

Treatment for substance abuse has been fairly standard and typically includes inpatient detoxification, individual and/or group therapy, self-help groups, deterrent medications (e.g., disulfiram, methadone), and aftercare. Although this approach is the standard, Miller and Hester (1986a) suggested that it is, at best, modestly effective. Recent attention has been given to the idea that substance abusers could be more effectively treated if they were matched to the treatment modality most appropriate for their situation. Although this "matching hypothesis" sounds reasonable and has existed in the literature for years (Ewing, 1977; Glaser & Skinner, 1981), it has had limited influence to date. This is primarily due to the fact that few studies have been carried out that establish the concept's validity and that yield clear guidelines by which patients can be matched with treatment. In their review of matching problem drinkers with appropriate treatment, Miller and Hester (1986a) suggested that progress is being made. In a prospective study of patient–treatment matching in a substance abuse population, McLellan, Woody, Luborsky, O'Brien, and Druley (1983) found superior treatment outcome for matched versus mismatched patients.

Other studies have shown that less severe alcoholism is best treated in less intensive settings (Orford, Oppenheimer, & Edwards, 1976) and that patients given treatment choices show a better response to treatment and better recovery rates (Kissin, Platz, & Su, 1971). Progress in establishing guidelines for patient–treatment matching has been made; however, much ground has yet to be covered. Allison and Hubbard (1985) perhaps accurately summarized the situation when they concluded that many treatment-related variables have been identified, but no clear picture of the relative strength of each variable and the way they interact to influence treatment outcome has emerged.

Trend Toward Outpatient Care

A clear trend in substance abuse treatment has been toward reducing length of hospitalization, and in some cases omitting it in favor of outpatient treatment. There are obvious cost benefits to this approach, as well as evidence to suggest that outpatient treatment is as beneficial as, and in some cases more beneficial than, inpatient care (Miller & Hester, 1986b). Some patients, due to the nature of their problems, do require hospitalization (e.g., those showing medical or psychiatric complications, concurrent dependencies, severe psychosocial impairment, or inability to discontinue use); however, long-term hospitalization is often used when less expensive, more appropriate alternatives would suffice. Various studies have suggested that brief hospitalization followed by outpatient aftercare can be equally or more effective than longer hospitalization (Page & Schaub, 1979; Pittman & Tate, 1979; Walker, Donovan, Kivlahan, & O'Leary, 1983). Some investigators have suggested that inpatient or residential treatment should be regarded as an "orientation program" (Page & Schaub, 1979) or "launching platform" (Zweben, 1986) for recovery, not as the stage of treatment during which major changes will occur.

Aftercare and Relapse

Relapse to substance use is the most frequent outcome of substance abuse treatment. W. A. Hunt et al. (1971) found relapse rates to be between 70 and 80 percent at 12 months posttreatment for heroin addicts, tobacco smokers, and alcoholics. The relapse phenomenon in addictions has received much attention in the literature, particularly by Marlatt and Gordon (1980, 1985), resulting in a well-researched relapse prevention model. Although their work has a clear implication for clinical decision making, a discussion of their model is beyond the scope of this chapter. Aftercare is an essential component of the treatment armamentarium to prevent relapse to drug use. The term aftercare is used to describe interventions with various intensity, scope, and length. It can be viewed as an appropriate extension of any form of primary care preceding it, with a specific intention to maintain earlier treatment gains (Harmon, Lantinga, & Costello, 1982). Aftercare options for substance abusers include outpatient treatment, methadone maintenance, therapeutic communities, and halfway houses. For a complete discussion of aftercare with substance abusers, see Stainback and Walker (1990). Ito and Donovan (1986) emphasized the importance of aftercare in alcoholism treatment because they found that aftercare attendance improves treatment outcome, independent from intake prognostic indicators. Aftercare is a treatment component that can be included to increase the probability of favorable long-term outcome.

SUMMARY

This chapter has reviewed the following major topics of psychoactive substance use disorders: prevalence, natural history and course, etiology, etiological theories, diagnostic classification schemes, clinical pictures of selected substance use disorders, and common assessment and clinical management strategies. The ubiquity of drug use in contemporary America is presented, along with selected prevalence data on opiate and cocaine use. Drugs of choice and prevalence are shown to vary over time and across social groups. Treatment course and outcome is described as variable and difficult to predict. The etiology of drug abuse is regarded as multifaceted, including biological, pharmacological, and sociopsychological factors. Specific attention is paid to correlates and antecedents of adolescent drug use and abuse. A brief review of common etiological theories is included.

The section on diagnosis includes a discussion of the rationale for classification, description of DSM-III-R diagnostic criteria for substance use disorders and substance-induced organic mental disorders, and a review of the changes occurring from the DSM-III to the DSM-III-R.

Clinical pictures, which included initial, chronic, and overdose effects, and abstinence syndromes where they occur, were presented on the following drugs as prototypes for their respective pharmacological classes: morphine for opioids; barbiturates for barbiturate/hypnotic sedatives; amphetamine, caffeine, cocaine, and nicotine for psychostimulants; LSD for hallucinogens, and cannabis sativa for cannabinols. While not traditionally regarded as an abused drug, anabolic steroids are included due to their illicit use primarily by athletes.

Various assessment strategies, techniques, and instruments were reviewed, including structured interviews and other self-report measures, direct observation, urine and blood samples, pharmacological procedures, and psychometrics. The general assessment strategy we recommend is an idiographic approach, sensitive to individual differences in the client, but which also meets the needs, goals, and purposes of the program in which it is conducted.

The final section is an overview of clinical management. We discussed processes involved in changing drug abuse behavior, motivation-to-change issues, treatment modality decisions, recent trends toward outpatient care, and aftercare.

REFERENCES

Adams, E. H., Gfroerer, J. C., Rouse, B. A., & Kozel, N. J. (1986). Trends in prevalence and consequences of cocaine use. *Advances in Alcohol and Substance Abuse, 6*(2), 49–71.

Allgulander, C., Borg, S., & Vikander, B. (1984). A 4–6 year follow-up of 50 patients with primary dependence on sedative and hypnotic drugs. *American Journal of Psychiatry, 141,* 1580–1582.

Allgulander, C., Ljungberg, L., & Fisher, L. D. (1987). Long-term prognosis in addiction on sedative hypnotic drugs analyzed with the Cox regression model. *Acta Psychiatrica Scandinavica, 75,* 521–531.

Allison, M., & Hubbard, R. L. (1985). Drug abuse treatment process: A review of the literature. *International Journal of the Addictions, 20,* 1321–1345.

American College of Sports Medicine. (1984). *Position stand on the use of anabolic-androgenic steroids in sports.* Indianapolis: Author.

American Psychiatric Association. (1968). *Diagnostic and statistical manual of mental disorders* (2nd ed.). Washington, DC: Author.

American Psychiatric Association. (1980). *Diagnostic and statistical manual of mental disorders* (3rd ed.). Washington, DC: Author.

American Psychiatric Association (1987). *Diagnostic and statistical manual of mental disorders* (3rd ed. rev.). Washington, DC: Author.

Andrews, H. L. (1943). Changes in the electroencephalogram during a cycle of morphine addiction. *Psychosomatic Medicine, 5,* 143–146.

Anglin, M. D., Almog, I. J., Fisher, D. G., & Peters, K. R. (1989). Alcohol use by heroin addicts: Evidence for an inverse relationship. A study of methadone maintenance and drug-free treatment samples. *American Journal of Drug and Alcohol Abuse, 15,* 191–207.

Angrist, B. M., & Gershon, S. (1970). The phenomenology of experimentally induced amphetamine psychosis—Preliminary observations. *Biological Psychiatry, 2,* 95–107.

Babor, T. F., Meyer, R. E., & Mirin, S. M. (1976). Behavioral and social effects of heroin self-administration and withdrawal. *Archives of General Psychiatry, 33,* 363–367.

Bates, C. K. (1988). Medical risks of cocaine use. *Western Journal of Medicine, 148,* 440–444.

Bejerot, N. (1970). *Addiction and society.* Springfield, IL: Charles C. Thomas.

Benowitz, N. L. (1988). Pharmacologic aspects of cigarette smoking and nicotine addiction. *New England Journal of Medicine, 319,* 1318–1330.

Benson, G. (1985). Course and outcome of drug abuse and medical and social conditions in selected young drug abusers. *Acta Psychiatrica Scandinavica, 71,* 48–66.

Benson, G., & Holmberg, M. B. (1984). Drug-related criminality among young people. *Acta Psychiatrica Scandinavica, 70,* 487–502.

Ben-Yehuda, N. (1980). Are addicts' self-reports to be trusted? *International Journal of the Addictions, 15,* 1265–1270.

Bergman, H., Borg, S., & Holm, L. (1980). Neuropsychological impairment and exclusive abuse of sedatives or hypnotics. *American Journal of Psychiatry, 137,* 215–217.

Blackwell, J. (1987). Proposed changes in DSM-III substance dependence criteria [Letter to the editor]. *American Journal of Psychiatry, 144,* 258.

Blanchard, E. B., Libet, J. M., & Young, L. D. (1973). Apneic aversion and covert sensitization in the treatment of hydrocarbon inhalation addiction: A case study. *Journal of Behavior Therapy and Experimental Psychiatry, 4,* 383–387.

Blanck, R. R., Ream, N. W., & Deleese, J. S. (1984). Infectious complications of illicit drug use. *International Journal of the Addictions, 19,* 221–232..

Boudin, H. M. (1972). Contingency contracting as a therapeutic tool in the declaration of amphetamine use. *Behavior Therapy, 3,* 604–605.

Boudin, H. M., Valentine, V. E., & Ingraham, R. D. (1977). Contingency contracting with drug abusers in the natural environment. *International Journal of the Addictions, 12,* 1–16.

Bozarth, M. A., & Wise, R. A. (1985). Toxicity associated with long-term intravenous heroin and cocaine self-administration in the rat. *Journal of the American Medical Association, 254,* 81–83.

Brown, T. T. (1961). *The enigma of drug addiction.* Springfield, IL: Charles C. Thomas.

Buckley, W. E., Yesalis, C. E., Friedl, K. E., Anderson, W. A., Streit, A. L., & Wright, J. E. (1988). Estimated prevalence of anabolic steroid use among male high school seniors. *Journal of the American Medical Association, 260,* 3441–3445.

Byrne, G. (1988). Nicotine likened to cocaine, heroin. *Science, 240,* 1143.

Callahan, E. J., Price, K., & Dahlkoetter, J. A. (1980). Drug abuse. In R. Daitzman (Ed.), *Clinical behavior therapy and behavior modification* (Vol. 1).

Cancrini, L., Cingolani, S., Compagnoni, F., Constantini, D., & Mazzoni, S. (1988). Juvenile drug addiction: A typology of heroin addicts and their families. *Family Process, 27,* 261–271.

Cautela, J. R., & Upper, D. (1976). The behavioral inventory battery: The use of self-report measures in behavioral analysis and therapy. In M. Hersen & A. S. Bellack (Eds.), *Behavioral assessment: A practical handbook* (pp. 77–109). New York: Pergamon Press.

Cavior, N., Kurtzberg, R. L., & Lipton, D. S. (1976). The development of validation of a heroin addiction scale with the MMPI. *International Journal of the Addictions, 2,* 129–137.

Clayton, R. R., & Ritter, C. (1985). The epidemiology of alcohol and drug abuse among adolescents. *Advances in Alcohol and Substance Abuse, 4*(3–4), 69–97.

Cone, E. J., Menchen, S. L., Paul, B. D., Mell, L. D., & Mitchell, J. (1989). Validity testing of commercial urine cocaine metabolite assays: I. Assay detection times, individual excretion patterns, and kinetics after cocaine administration to humans. *Journal of Forensic Sciences, 34,* 15–31.

Cone, E. J., & Mitchell, J. (1989). Validity testing of commercial urine cocaine metabolite assays: II. Sensitivity, specificity, accuracy, and confirmation by gas chromatography/mass spectrometry. *Journal of Forensic Sciences, 34,* 32–45.

Connell, P. H. (1958). *Amphetamine psychosis.* New York: Oxford University Press.

Craig, R. (1988). A psychometric study of the prevalence of DSM-III personality disorders among treated opiate addicts. *International Journal of the Addictions, 23,* 115–124.

Dahlstrom, W. G., Welsh, G. S., & Dahlstrom, L. E. (1975). *An MMPI handbook: Vol. 2. Research applications.* Minneapolis: University of Minnesota Press.

D'Aquila, R. T., & Williams, A. B. (1987). Epidemic human immunodeficiency virus (HIV) infection among intravenous drug users (IVDU). *Yale Journal of Biology and Medicine, 60,* 545–567.

Derogatis, L. R., Rickels, K., & Rock, A. F. (1976). The SCL-90 and the MMPI: A step in the validation of a new self-report scale. *British Journal of Psychiatry, 128,* 280–289.

Donahoe, T., & Johnson, N. (1986). *Foul play: Drug abuse in sports.* New York: Basil Blackwell.

Edwards, G., Orford, J., Egert, S., Guthrie, S., Hawker, A., Hensman, C., Mitcheson, M., Oppenheimer, E., & Taylor, C. (1977). Alcoholism: A controlled trial of "treatment" and "advice." *Journal of Studies on Alcohol, 38,* 1004–1031.

Eisenman, A. J., Sloan, J. W., Martin, W. R., Jasinski, D. R., & Brooks, J. W. (1969). Catecholamine and 17-hydroxycorticosteroid excretion during a cycle of morphine dependence in man. *Journal of Psychiatric Research, 7,* 19–28.

Elkin, T. E., Williams, J. G., Barlow, P. H., & Stewart, W. R. (1974). *Measurement and modification of intravenous drug abuse. A preliminary study using succinyl choline.* Unpublished manuscript, University of Mississippi Medical School, University, MS.

Ewing, J. (1977). Matching therapy and patients: The cafeteria plan. *British Journal of Addiction, 72,* 13–18.

Ferraro, D. P., & Grisham, M. G. (1972). Tolerance to the behavioral effects of marijuana in chimpanzees. *Physiology and Behavior, 9,* 49–54.

Firooznia, H., Golimbu, C., Rafii, M., & Lichtman, E. A. (1983). Radiology of musculoskeletal complications of drug addiction. *Seminars in Roentgenology, 18,* 198–206.

Fuller, J. R., & LaFountain, M. J. (1987). Performance-enhancing drugs in sport: A different form of drug abuse. *Adolescence, 22,* 969–976.

Glaser, F. B., & Skinner, H. A. (1981). Matching in the real world: A practical approach. In E. Gottheil, A. McClellan, & K. Druley (Eds.), *Matching patient needs and treatment methods in alcoholism and drug abuse* (pp. 295–324). Springfield, IL: Charles C. Thomas.

Glassroth, J., Adams, G. D., & Schnoll, S. (1987). The impact of substance abuse on the respiratory system. *Chest, 91,* 596–602.

Gold, M. S., Dackis, C. S., Pottash, A. L., Extein, I., & Washton, A. (1986). Cocaine update: From bench to bedside. *Advances in Alcohol and Substance Abuse, 5*(1–2), 35–60.

Goldstein, A., & Kaizer, S. (1969). Psychotropic effects of caffeine in man: III. A questionnaire survey of coffee drinking and its effects on a group of housewives. *Clinical Pharmacology and Therapeutics, 10,* 477–478.

Griffin, M. L., Weiss, R. D., Mirin, S. M., Wilson, H., & Bouchard-Voelk, B. (1987). The use of the Diagnostic Interview Schedule in drug-dependent patient. *American Journal of Drug and Alcohol Abuse, 6,* 97–106.

Griffiths, R. R., Bigelow, G. E., & Liebson, I. A. (1986). Human coffee drinking: Reinforcing and physical dependence producing effects of caffeine. *Journal of Pharmacology and Experimental Therapeutics, 239,* 416–425.

Griffiths, R. R., & Woodson, P. P. (1988). Caffeine physical dependence: A review of human and laboratory animal studies. *Psychopharmacology, 94,* 437–451.

Gunby, P. (1988). Surgeon general emphasizes nicotine addiction in annual report on tobacco use, consequences. *Journal of the American Medical Association, 259,* 2811.

Haastrup, S., & Jepsen, P. W. (1988). Eleven year follow-up of 300 young opioid addicts. *Acta Psychiatrica Scandinavica, 77,* 22–26.

Haertzen, C. A. & Hooks, N. T. (1969). Changes in personality and subjective experience associated with the administration and withdrawal of opiates. *Journal of Nervous and Mental Disease, 148,* 606–614.

Hammersley, R., & Morrison, V. (1987). Effects of polydrug use on the criminal activities of heroin-users. *British Journal of Addiction, 82,* 899–906.

Hanbury, R., Sturiano, V., Cohen, M., Stimmel, B., & Aquillaume, C. (1986). Cocaine use in persons on methadone maintenance. *Advances in Alcohol and Substance Abuse, 6*(2), 97–106.

Handelsman, L., Cochrane, K. J., Aronson, M. J., Ness, R., Rubenstein, K. J., & Kanof, P. D. (1987). Two new rating scales for opiate withdrawal. *American Journal of Drug and Alcohol Abuse, 13,* 293–308.

Harford, R. J., & Kleber, H. D. (1978). Comparative validity of random-interval and fixed-interval urinalysis schedules. *Archives of General Psychiatry, 35,* 356–359.

Harmon, S. K., Lantinga, L. J., & Costello, R. M. (1982). Aftercare in chemical dependence treatment. *Bulletin of the Society of Psychologists in Substance Abuse, 1,* 107–109.

Haupt, H. A., & Rovere, G. (1984). Anabolic steroids: A review of the literature. *American Journal of Sports Medicine, 12,* 469–483.

Hawkins, J. D., Lishner, D., & Catalano, R. F. (1985). Childhood predictors and the prevention of adolescent substance abuse. National Institute on Drug Abuse Research Monograph Series. *Etiology of Drug Abuse: Implications for Treatment, 56,* 75–126.

Heather, N. (1986). Change without therapists: The use of self-help manuals by problem drinkers. In W. Miller & N. Heather (Eds.), *Treating addictive behaviors: Processes of change* (pp. 331–359). New York: Plenum Press.

Henningfield, J. E. (1984). Pharmacologic basis and treatment of cigarette smoking. *Journal of Clinical Psychiatry, 45*(12), 24–34.

Himmelsbach, C. K. (1939). Studies of certain addiction characteristics of (a) dehydromorphine ("Paramorphan") (b) dihydrodesoxymorphine-D ("Desomorphine") (c) dihydrodesoxycodein-D ("Desocodeine") and (d) methyldihydromorphinone ("Metopon"). *Journal of Pharmacology and Experimental Therapeutics, 67,* 239–254.

Hochman, J. S., & Brill, N. D. (1973). Chronic marijuana use and psychosocial adaptation. *American Journal of Psychiatry, 130,* 132.

Hollister, L. E. (1971, May). *Human pharmacology of marijuana (cannabis).* Paper presented at the American Federation for Clinical Research Symposium on Drug Abuse, Atlantic City, NJ.

Hollister, L. E. (1988). Cannabis–1988. *Acta Psychiatrica Scandinavica, 78,* 108–118.

Holmberg, M. B. (1985). Longitudinal studies of drug abuse in a fifteen-year-old population: I. Chronic drug abusers. *Acta Psychiatrica Scandinavica, 71,* 201–203.

Hunt, D., Spunt, B., Lipton, D., Goldsmith, D., & Strug, D. (1986). The costly bonus: Cocaine related crime among methadone treatment clients. *Advances in Alcohol and Substance Abuse, 6*(2), 107–122.

Hunt, W. A., Barnett, W., & Branch, L. G. (1971). Relapse rates in addiction programs. *Journal of Clinical Psychology, 27,* 455–456.

Ito, J. R., & Donovan, D. M. (1986). Aftercare in alcoholism treatment: A review. In W. R. Miller & N. Heather (Eds.), *Treating addictive behaviors: Processes of change* (pp. 435–456). New York: Plenum Press.

Jaffe, R. B. (1983). Cardiac and vascular involvement in drug abuse. *Seminars in Roentgenology, 18,* 207–212.

Jainchill, N., DeLeon, G., & Pinkham, L. (1986). Psychiatric diagnoses among substance abusers in therapeutic community treatment. *Journal of Psychoactive Drugs, 18,* 209–213.

Jelinek, J. M., & Williams, T. (1984). Post-traumatic stress disorder and substance abuse in Vietnam combat veterans: Treatment problems, strategies and recommendations. *Journal of Substance Abuse Treatment, 1,* 87–97.

Johnston, L. D., Bachman, J. G., & O'Malley, P. M. (1982). *Student drug use in America 1971–1981* (DHHS Publication No. ADM 82-1221). Washington, DC: U.S. Government Printing Office.

Jonas, J. M., Gold, M. S., Sweeney, D., & Pottash, A. L. (1987). Eating disorders and cocaine abuse: A survey of 259 cocaine abusers. *Journal of Clinical Psychiatry, 48,* 47–50.

Julien, R. M. (1975). *A primer of drug action.* San Francisco: W. H. Freeman.

Kales, A., & Kales, J. D. (1974). Sleep disorders: Recent findings in the diagnosis and treatment of disturbed sleep. *New England Journal of Medicine, 290,* 487–499.

Kandel, D. (1980). Drug and drinking behavior among youth. *Annual Review of Sociology, 6,* 235–285.

Kandel, D. B. (1984). Marijuana users in young adulthood. *Archives of General Psychiatry, 41,* 200–209.

Kandel, D. B., Davies, M., Karus, D., & Yamaguchi, K. (1986). The consequences in young adulthood of adolescent drug involvement. *Archives of General Psychiatry, 43,* 746–754.

Kandel, D. B., & Logan, J. A. (1984). Patterns of drug use from adolescence to young adulthood: 1. Periods of risk for initiation, continued use, and discontinuation. *American Journal of Public Health, 74,* 660–666.

Kandel, D. B., & Yamaguchi, K. (1985). Development patterns of the use of legal, illegal, and medically prescribed psychotropic drugs from adolescence to young adulthood. National Institute on Drug Abuse Research Monograph Series. *Etiology of Drug Abuse: Implications for Treatment, 56,* 193–235.

Kay, A., Eisenstein, R. B., & Jasinski, D. R. (1969). Morphine effects on human REM state, waking state and NREM sleep. *Psychopharmacologia, 14,* 404.

Kissin, B., Platz, A., & Su, W. (1971). Selective factors in treatment choice and outcome in alcoholics. In N. Mello & J. Mendelson (Eds.), *Recent advances in studies of alcoholism: An interdisciplinary symposium* (pp. 781–802). Washington, DC: U.S. Government Printing Office.

Kissner, D. G., Lawrence, W. D., Selis, J. E., & Flint, A. (1987). Crack lung: Pulmonary disease caused by cocaine abuse. *American Review of Respiratory Disease, 136,* 1250–1252.

Kolb, L. C. (1973). *Modern clinical psychiatry* (8th ed.). Philadelphia: W. B. Saunders.

Koob, G. F., & Bloom, F. E. (1988). Cellular and molecular mechanisms of drug dependence. *Science, 242,* 715–723.

Kosten, T. R., Rounsaville, B. J., Babor, T. F., Spitzer, R. L., & Williams, J. B. (1987). Substance-use disorders in DSM-III-R: Evidence for the dependence syndrome across different psychoactive substances. *British Journal of Psychiatry, 151,* 834–843.

Kosten, T. R., Rounsaville, B. J., & Kleber, H. D. (1986a). Antecedents and consequences of cocaine abuse among opioid addicts: A 2.5 year follow-up. *Journal of Nervous and Mental Disease, 176*(3), 176–181.

Kosten, T. R., Rounsaville, B. J., & Kleber, H. D. (1986b). A 25 year follow-up treatment retention and reentry among opioid addicts. *Journal of Substance Abuse Treatment, 3,* 181–189.

Kosten, T. R., Rounsaville, B. J., & Kleber, H. D. (1987). A 25 year follow-up of cocaine use among treated opioid addicts: Have our treatments helped? *Archives of General Psychiatry, 44*(3), 201–204.

Kozel, N. J., & Adams, E. H. (1986). Epidemiology of drug abuse: An overview. *Science, 234,* 970–974.

Kristenson, H. (1982). *Studies on alcohol-related disabilities in a medical intervention programme in middle aged males* (2nd ed.). Malmo, Sweden: University of Lund.

Lachar, D., Berman, W., Grisell, J. L., & Schoof, K. (1976). The MacAndrew Alcoholism Scale as a general measure of substance misuse. *Journal of Studies on Alcohol, 37,* 1609–1615.

Lader, M. (1983). Dependence on benzodiazepines. *Journal of Clinical Psychiatry, 44,* 121–127.

Landry, M. (1987). Addiction diagnostic update: DSM-R psychoactive substance use disorders. *Journal of Psychoactive Drugs, 19,* 379–381.

Lazarus, A. A. (1980). Multimodal Life History Questionaire Kingston, N.J.: Multimodal Publications Inc.

Leeds, N. E., Malhotra, V., & Zimmerman, R. D. (1983). The radiology of drug addiction affecting the brain. *Seminars in Roentgenology, 18,* 227–233.

Lehrer, M., & Gold, M. S. (1986). Laboratory diagnosis of cocaine: Intoxication and withdrawal. *Advances in Alcohol and Substance Abuse, 6,* 123–141.

Lester, D., Math, Y. S., Guy, K. S., & Johnson, K. O. (1987). Drugs used by students: Caffeine, tobacco, marijuana, cocaine, and alcohol. *Psychological Reports, 61,* 158.

Lettieri, D. J. (1985). Drug abuse: A review of explanations and models of explanation. *Advances in Alcohol and Substance Abuse, 43*(3–4), 9–40.

Ling, W., Holmes, E. D., Post, G. R., & Litaker, M. B. (1973). A systematic psychiatric study of the heroin addict. In *Proceedings of the Fifth National Conference on Methadone Treatment* (pp. 429–432).

Lowenstein, D. H., Massa, S. M., Rowbotham, M. C., Collins, S. D., McKinney, H. E., & Simon, R. P. (1987). Acute neurologic and psychiatric complications associated with cocaine abuse. *The American Journal of Medicine, 83,* 841–846.

MacAndrew, C. (1965). The differentiation of male alcoholic outpatients from nonalcoholic psychiatric patients by means of the MMPI. *Quarterly Journal of Studies on Alcohol, 26,* 238–246.

Marlatt, G. A., & Gordon, J. R. (1980). Determinants of relapse: Implications for the maintenance of behavioral change. In P. Davidson & S. Davidson (Eds.), *Behavioral medicine: Changing health lifestyles* (pp. 410–452). New York: Bruner/Mazel.

Marlatt, G. A., & Gordon, J. R. (Eds.). (1985). *Relapse prevention: Maintenance strategies in the treatment of addictive behaviors.* New York: Guilford Press.

Marsh, D. T., Stile, S. A., Stoughton, N. L., & Trout-Landen, B. L. (1988). Psychopathology of opiate addiction: Comparative data from the MMPI and MCMI. *American Journal of Drug and Alcohol Abuse, 14*(1), 17–27.

Maugh, T. H. (1974). Marijuana (II): Does it damage the brain? *Science, 185,* 775–776.

Maurer, D. W., & Vogel, V. H. (1973). *Narcotics and narcotic addiction* (4th ed.). Springfield, IL.: Charles C. Thomas.

Maycut, M. O. (1985). Health consequences of acute and chronic marijuana use. *Progress in Neuro-psychopharmacology and Biological Psychiatry, 9,* 209–238.

McKinnon, G. L., & Parker, W. A. (1982). Benzodiazepine withdrawal syndrome: A literature review and evaluation. *American Journal of Drug and Alcohol Abuse, 9*(1), 19–33.

McLellan, A. T., Luborsky, L., Cacciola, J., Griffith, J., Evans, F., Barr, H. L., & O'Brien, C. P. (1985). New data from the Addiction Severity Index: Reliability and validity in three centers. *The Journal of Nervous and Mental Disease, 173*(7), 412–423.

McLellan, A. T., Luborsky, L., O'Brien, C. P., & Woody, G. E. (1980). An improved evaluation instrument for substance abuse patients: The Addiction Severity Index. *The Journal of Nervous and Mental Disease, 168,* 26–33.

McLellan, A. T., Luborsky, L., Woody, G. E., O'Brien, C. P., & Druley, K. A. (1983). Predicting response to alcohol and drug abuse treatments: Role of psychiatric severity. *Archives of General Psychiatry, 40,* 620–625.

McLellan, A. T., Woody, G. E., Luborsky, L., O'Brien, C. P., & Druley, K. A. (1983). Increased effectiveness of substance abuse treatment: A prospective study of patient-treatment "matching." *Journal of Nervous and Mental Disease, 171,* 597–605.

McNamee, H. B., Mirin, S. M., Kuhnle, J. C., & Meyer, R. E. (1976). Affective changes in chronic opiate users. *British Journal of Addiction, 71,* 275–280.

McWilliams, S. A., & Tuttle, R. J. (1973). Long-term psychological effects of LSD. *Psychological Bulletin, 79,* 341–351.

Mendhiratta, S., Varma, V. K., Dang, R., Malholtra, A. K., Das, K., & Nehra, R. (1988). Cannabis and cognitive functions: A re-evaluation study. *British Journal of Addiction, 83,* 749–753.

Midanik, L. (1982). The validity of self-reported alcohol consumption and alcohol problems: A literature review. *British Journal of Addictions, 77,* 357–382.

Milby, J. B. (1981a). *Addictive behavior and its treatment.* New York: Springer.

Milby, J. B. (1981b, August). *The status of theories of addiction.* Paper presented at the annual meeting of the American Psychological Association, Los Angeles.

Milby, J. B. (1989). Methadone maintenance to abstinence: How many make it? *Journal of Nervous and Mental Disease, 176*(7), 409–422.

Milby, J. B., Garrett, C., & Meredith, C. (1980). Iatrogenic phobic disorders in methadone maintenance treated patients. *The International Journal of Addictions, 15,* 747–757.

Milby, J. B., Rice, J., & Garrett, C. (1979, September). *Iatrogenic phobia of detoxification in methadone maintenance: Reliability, prevalence.* Paper presented at the American Psychological Association Meeting, New York.

Miller, W. R. (1983). Motivational interviewing with problem drinkers. *Behavioral Psychotherapy, 11,* 147–172.

Miller, W. R. (1985). Motivation for treatment: A review with special emphasis on alcoholism. *Psychological Bulletin, 98,* 84–107.

Miller, W. R., & Heather, N. (Eds.). (1986). *Treating addictive behaviors: Processes of change.* New York: Plenum Press.

Miller, W. R., & Hester, R. K. (1986a). The effectiveness of alcoholism treatment: What research reveals. In W. Miller & N. Heather (Eds.), *Treating addictive behaviors: Processes of change* (pp. 121–174). New York: Plenum Press.

Miller, W. R., & Hester, R. K. (1986b). Inpatient alcoholism treatment: Who benefits? *American Psychologist, 41,* 794–805.

Miller, W. R., Sovereign, R., & Krege, B. (1988). Motivational interviewing with problem drinkers: II. The drinker's checkup as a preventive measure. *Behavioral Psychotherapy, 16,* 251–268.

Millman, R. B. (1978). Drug and alcohol abuse. In B. J. Wolman, J. Egan, & A. O. Ross (Eds.), *Handbook of treatment of mental disorders in childhood and adolescence* (pp. 238–267). New Jersey: Prentice-Hall.

Mirin, S. M. (1977). Drug abuse. In E. L. Bassuk & S. C. Schoonover (Eds.), *The practitioners' guide to psychoactive drugs* (pp. 235–300). New York: Plenum Medical.

Mirin, S. M., Meyer, R. E., & McNamee, B. (1976). Psychopathology and mood during heroin use: Acute vs. chronic effects. *Archives of General Psychiatry, 33,* 1503–1580.

Mooney, R. L. & Gordon, L. V. (1950). Manual to accompany the Mooney Problem Check Lists, Forms C, H, and J. New York: The Psychological Corporation.

Morin, C. M., & Kwentus, J. A. (1988). Behavioral and pharmacological treatments for insomnia. *Annals of Behavioral Medicine, 10*(3), 91–100.

Murray, D. M., & Perry, C. L. (1985). The prevention of adolescent drug abuse: Implications of etiological, developmental, behavioral, and environmental models. In C. L. Jones & R. J. Battjes (Eds.), *Etiology of drug abuse: Implications for treatment* (DHHS Publication No. ADM 85-1335). Washington, DC: U.S. Government Printing Office. 236–255.

Newcomb, M. D., & Bentler, P. M. (1986). Cocaine use among young adults. *Advances in Alcohol and Substance Abuse, 6*(2), 73–96.

Nurnberger, J. I., & Zimmerman, J. (1970). Applied analysis of human behavior: An alternative to conventional motivational inferences and unconscious determination in therapeutic programming. *Behavior Therapy, 1,* 59–69.

O'Brien, C. P., Testa, T., & O'Brien, T. J. (1977). Conditioned narcotic withdrawal in humans. *Science, 195,* 1000–1002.

O'Malley, P. M., Bachman, J. G., & Johnston, L. D. (1988). Period, age, and cohort effects on substance use among young Americans. *American Journal of Public Health, 78,* 1315–1321.

Orford, J. (1986). Critical conditions for change in addictive behaviors. In W. Miller & N. Heather (Eds.), *Treating addictive behaviors: Processes of change* (pp. 91–108). New York: Plenum Press.

Orford, J., Oppenheimer, E., & Edwards, G. (1976). Abstinence or control: The outcome for excessive drinkers two years after consultation. *Behavior Research and Therapy, 14,* 409–418.

Page, R. D., & Schaub, L. H. (1979). Efficacy of a three- versus a five-week alcohol treatment program. *International Journal of the Addictions, 14,* 697–714.

Panton, J. H., & Brisson, R. C. (1971). Characteristics associated with drug abuse within a state prison population. *Corrective Psychiatry and Journal of Social Therapy, 17,* 3–33.

Parker, M. W., Winstead, D. K., & Willi, F. J. (1979). Patient autonomy in alcohol treatment: I. Literature review. *International Journal of the Addictions, 14,* 1015–1022.

Parker, M. W., Winstead, D. K., Willi, F. J., & Fisher, P. (1979). Patient autonomy in alcohol treatment: II. Program evaluation. *International Journal of the Addictions, 14,* 1177–1184.

Pittman, D. J., & Tate, R. L. (1979). A comparison of two treatment programs for alcoholics. *Quarterly Journal of Studies on Alcohol, 30,* 888–899.

Polich, J. M. (1982). The validity of self-reports in alcoholism research. *Addictive Behaviors, 7,* 123–132.

Pope, H. G., & Katz, D. L. (1988). Affective and psychotic symptoms associated with anabolic steroid use. *American Journal of Psychiatry, 145,* 487–490.

Rathus, S. A., Fox, J. A., & Ortins, J. B. (1980). The MacAndrew Scale as a measure of substance abuse and delinquency among adolescents. *Journal of Clinical Psychology, 36,* 579–583.

Rieman, H. A. (1967). Caffeinism: A case of long continued low grade fever. *Journal of the American Medical Association, 202,* 1105–1107.

Ross, H. E., Glaser, F. B., & Germanson, T. (1988). The prevalence of psychiatric disorders in patients with alcohol and other drug problems. *Archives of General Psychiatry, 45,* 1023–1031.

Rounsaville, B. J., Kosten, T. R., & Kleber, H. D. (1987). The antecedents and benefits of achieving abstinence in opioid addicts: A 2.5 year follow-up study. *American Journal of Drug and Alcohol Abuse, 13*(3), 213–229.

Rounsaville, B. J., Kosten, T. R., Williams, J. B., & Spitzer, R. L. (1987). A field trial of DSM-III-R psychoactive substance dependence disorders. *American Journal of Psychiatry, 144,* 351–354.

Royse, D., & Drude, K. (1984). Screening drug abuse clients with the Brief Symptom Inventory. *The International Journal of the Addictions, 19,* 849–857.

Salzman, G. A., Khan, F., & Emory, C. (1987). Pneumomediastinum after cigarette smoking. *Southern Medical Journal, 80,* 1427–1429.

Sapira, J. D., & McDonald, R. H., Jr. (1970, November). Drug abuse—1970. *Disease-a-Month,* pp. 1–47.

Saunders, W., & Kershaw, P. (1979). Spontaneous remission from alcoholism: A community study. *British Journal of Addictions, 74,* 251–265.

Saxena, K., & Scheman, A. (1985). Suicide plan by nicotine poisoning: A review of nicotine toxicity. *Veterinary and Human Toxicology, 27,* 495–497.

Schneier, F. R., & Siris, S. G. (1987). A review of psychoactive substance use and abuse in schizophrenia: Patterns of drug choice. *The Journal of Nervous and Mental Disease, 175,* 641–652.

Schuckit, M. A. (1979). *Drug and Alcohol Treatment.* New York: Plenum Press.

Schwartz, R. H. (1987). Marijuana: An overview. *Pediatric Clinics of North America, 34,* 305–317.

Schwartz, R. H., Hoffmann, N. G., & Jones, R. (1987). Behavioral, psychological and academic correlates of marijuana usage in adolescence. *Clinical Pediatrics, 26,* 264–270.

Siegal, H. A. (1981). Current patterns of psychoactive use: Some epidemiological observations. In S. E. Gardner (Ed.), *Drug and alcohol abuse: Implications for treatment.* Washington, DC: NIDA Treatment Research Monograph.

Siegel, S. (1981, August). *The conditioning theory of tolerance.* Paper presented at the meeting of the American Psychological Association, Los Angeles.

Skinner, H. A. (1984). Assessing alcohol use by patients in treatment. In R. G. Smart, H. D. Cappell, F. B. Glaser, Y. Israel, H. Kalant, R. E. Popman, W. Schmidt, & E. M. Sellers (Eds.), *Research advances in alcohol and drug problems* (pp. 183–287). New York: Plenum Press.

Skinner, H. A., & Allen, B. A. (1983). Does the computer make a difference? Computerized versus face-to-face versus self-report assessment of alcohol, drug, and tobacco use. *Journal of Consulting and Clinical Psychology, 51,* 267–275.

Smart, R. G., & Anglin, L. (1987). Do we know the lethal dose of cocaine? [Letter to the editor]. *Journal of Forensic Sciences, 32,* 303–312.

Solomon, R. L., & Corbit, J. D. (1974). An opponent-process theory of motivation: I. Temporal dynamics of affect. *Psychological Review, 81*(2), 119–145.

Stainback, R. D., & Walker, C. P. (1990). Discharge planning and selection of aftercare for substance abusers. In W. D. Lerner & M. A. Barr (Eds.), *Handbook of hospital-based substance abuse treatment* (pp. 184–201). New York: Pergamon Press.

Strug, D. L., Hunt, D. E., Goldsmith, D. S., Lipton, D. S., & Spunt, B. (1985). Patterns of cocaine use among methadone clients. *The International Journal of the Addictions, 20*(8), 1163–1175.

Tennant, F. S. (1983). Treatment of dependence upon stimulants and hallucinogens. *Drug and Alcohol Dependence, 11,* 111–114.

Ternes, J. W., Ehrman, R. N., & O'Brien, C. P. (1985). Nondependent monkeys self-administer hydromorphine. *Behavioral Neuroscience, 99,* 583–588.

Tuchfeld, B. S. (1981). Spontaneous remission in alcoholics: Empirical observations and theoretical implications. *Journal of Studies on Alcohol, 42,* 626–641.

Vaillant, G. E. (1973). A 20-year follow-up of New York narcotic addicts. *Archives of General Psychiatry, 29,* 237–241.

Valladares, B. K., & Lemberg, L. (1987). The Miami Vices in the CCU: Part I. Cardiac manifestations of cocaine use. *Heart and Lung, 16,* 456–458.

Varma, V. K., Malhotra, A. K., Dang, R., Das, K., & Nehra, R. (1988). Cannabis and cognitive functions: A prospective study. *Drug and Alcohol Dependence, 21,* 147–152.

Walker, R. D., Donovan, D. M., Kivlahan, D. R., & O'Leary, M. R. (1983). Length of stay, neuropsychological performance, and aftercare: Influences on alcohol treatment outcome. *Journal of Consulting and Clinical Psychology, 51,* 900–911.

Ward, N. G., & Schuckit, M. A. (1980). Factors associated with suicidal behavior in polydrug abusers. *Journal of Clinical Psychiatry, 41,* 379–385.

Watson, C. G., Tilleskjor, C., Hoodecheck-Schow, E. A., Pucel, J., & Jacobs, L. (1984). Do alcoholics give valid self-reports? *Journal of Studies on Alcohol, 45,* 344–348.

Weil, A. T., Zinberg, N. E., & Nelson, J. M. (1969). Clinical and psychological effects of marijuana in man. *The International Journal of the Addictions, 4,* 427–451.

Weiss, R. D., Mirin, S. M., Griffin, M. L., & Michael, J. L. (1988). Psychopathology in cocaine abusers: Changing trends. *The Journal of Nervous and Mental Disease, 176,* 719–725.

Weller, R. A., & Halikas, J. A. (1985). Marijuana use and psychiatric illness: A follow-up study. *American Journal of Psychiatry, 142,* 848–850.

West, R. J., & Russell, M. A. (1987). Cardiovascular and subjective effects of smoking before and after 24 hours of abstinence from cigarettes. *Psychopharmacology, 92,* 118–121.

Wikler, A. (1973a). Drug dependence. In A. B. Baker & L. H. Baker (Eds.), *Clinical neurology* (Vol. II). Philadelphia: Harper and Row.

Wikler, A. (1973b). Dynamics of drug dependence: Implications of a conditioning theory for research and treatment. *Archives of General Psychiatry, 28,* 611–616.

Wilkinson, D. A., Leigh, G. M., Cordingley, J., Martin, G. W., & Lei, H. (1987). Dimensions of multiple drug use and a typology of drug users. *British Journal of Addiction, 82,* 259–273.

Wise, R. H., & Bozarth, M. A. (1987). A psychomotor theory of addiction. *Psychological Review, 94,* 469–492.

Winick, C. (1962). Maturing out of narcotic addiction. *Bulletin on Narcotics, 14,* 1–7.

Woody, G. E., Luborsky, L., McLellan, A. T., O'Brien, C. P., Beck, A. T., Blaine, I., Herman, I. & Hole, A. (1983). Psychotherapy for opiate addicts: Does it help? *Archives of General Psychiatry, 40,* 639–645.

Woody, G. E., McLellan, A. T., Luborsky, L., O'Brien, C. P., Blaine, I., Fox, S., Herman, I., & Beck, A. T. (1984). Psychiatric severity as a predictor of benefits from psychotherapy; The Penn–VA Study. *American Journal of Psychiatry, 141*(10), 1172–1177.

Wright, J. E., & Stone, M. H. (1985). NSCA statement on anabolic drug use: Literature review. *National Strength and Conditioning Association Journal, 7*(5), 45–59.

Yeager, R. A., Hobson, R. W., Padberg, F. T., Lynch, T. G., & Chakravarty, M. (1987). Vascular complications related to drug abuse. *The Journal of Trauma, 27,* 305–308.

Yesavage, J. A., Leirer, V. O., Denari, M., & Hollister, L. E. (1985). Carry-over effects of marijuana intoxication on aircraft pilot performance: A preliminary report. *American Journal of Psychiatry, 142,* 1325–1329.

Zweben, J. E. (1986). Treating cocaine dependence: New challenges for the therapeutic community. *Journal of Psychoactive Drugs, 18,* 239–245.

CHAPTER 6

Schizophrenia

RANDALL L. MORRISON

Schizophrenia is one of the most grave and disruptive of the psychiatric illnesses. Each episode of the disorder is disabling and, by definition, runs a prolonged course involving marked losses in occupational and role functioning. For most patients, the first episode, which typically occurs during adolescence or early adulthood, signals a progression of subsequent episodes of acute symptoms, often accompanied by continued poor interepisodic functioning. In short, the first episode may signal a lifetime of incapacitation and trauma, with a markedly reduced opportunity to participate in, or contribute to, life in a meaningful way. The disorder also introduces tremendous emotional and financial strains on the families of schizophrenics, as they embark on what for many becomes a virtually endless travail of obtaining ongoing care for their afflicted relatives. No cure for the illness exists, and the cause is unknown. Somatic and psychosocial intervention for chronic patients is most accurately described as symptom management.

Although the future for many schizophrenics and their families has been unquestionably bleak, we are currently witnessing a tremendous explosion of new research for the disorder. Influenced by improved, more objective diagnostic criteria for schizophrenia, as well as ongoing attempts to subclassify the disorder into more homogeneous subgroups, and spurred by the development of more sophisticated physiologic assessment techniques, researchers have made considerable progress in evaluating the myriad dysfunctions associated with the disorder. Tremendous advances have been made in understanding particular brain pathology that may relate to those dysfunctions and, more recently, the genetics of the disorder. Recent findings have already resulted in improved treatment interventions that show considerable promise in forestalling relapse, and further treatment progress is anticipated.

In keeping with the applied pragmatic clinical orientation that characterizes this text, this chapter emphasizes recent empirical findings as they relate to the clinical phenomena and treatment outcome of schizophrenia. It must be recognized, however, that current concepts regarding the disorder may change markedly in short order, as neurophysiologic investigation continues at a rapid pace.

DESCRIPTION OF THE DISORDER

Schizophrenia is a heterogeneous disorder, for which no singular symptomatology is pathognomonic. Despite the tremendous recent neuroscientific progress in this area, schizophrenia remains a clinical entity, which is diagnosed based on the presence of a minimum subset of reported or observed symptoms from a broad constellation of possible symptomatology. The primary features of schizophrenia are marked distortions of reality (i.e., psychotic symptoms), including delusions, hallucinations, and/or disordered thought processes. Other symptoms include attentional impairments, and disturbances in motor behavior, affect, and life role functioning.

Owing to the range of clinical phenomena that can be present, considerable attention has been devoted to identifying subtypes of the disorder. Some investigators (e.g., Crow, 1985) have suggested that schizophrenia may actually represent a heterogeneous collection of syndromes, as opposed to a single group of disorders. Several conflicting diagnostic criteria exist for the disorder: the third revised edition of the *Diagnostic and Statistical Manual of Mental Disorders* (DSM-III-R; American Psychiatric Association [APA], 1987), Research Diagnostic Criteria (Spitzer, Endicott, & Robins, 1978), and the Washington University or St. Louis criteria (Feighner et al., 1972). DSM-III-R lists five types of the disorder (i.e., catatonic, disorganized, paranoid, undifferentiated, residual) and provides criteria for subtyping the course of the disorder (i.e., subchronic, chronic, subchronic with acute exacerbation, chronic with acute exacerbation). Other subclassification issues that have been emphasized include distinguishing between the positive and negative symptoms of schizophrenia (e.g., Andreasen, 1982; Andreasen & Olsen, 1982; Crow, 1980, 1985) and differentiating cognitive deficits as indicative of different variants of the disorder (Neale, Oltmanns, & Harvey, 1985). Data suggest the presence of differential physiologic–organic impairment associated with subtypes of the disorder. For example, the paranoid–nonparanoid distinction has been associated with differential electroencephalograms (Etevenon, Peron-Magnan, Campistron, Verdeaux, & Deniker, 1983) and brain anatomical abnormalities (Nasrallah et al., 1983). Patients with predominantly negative symptoms have been shown to be more likely than patients with predominantly positive symptoms to have structural brain abnormalities (Andreasen & Olsen, 1982). Findings of this sort lend further support to the notion that schizophrenia may actually comprise several differentiable syndromes.

An additional aspect of the heterogeneity of schizophrenia is that symptoms typically vary during the course of the illness. Differences in prominent psychotic symptomatology may be present during successive acute episodes, and fluctuations in levels of residual symptoms, such as social and/or cognitive dysfunction, may occur interepisodically. Crow's (1980) data suggested that, at least in some patients, the disorder exhibits a progression toward increasingly negative symptoms and/or an increasingly prominent organic pathology as the disorder progresses; however, these issues are controversial and require further longitudinal study. Another issue is that the clinical presentation of schizophrenia is confounded by somatic therapies for the disorder, which are typically instituted for significant periods of time and/or as maintenance treatment. In addition to their desired effects of reducing prominent psychotic symptoms of the disorder, neuroleptics can produce a number of deleterious side effects, which are discussed later.

CLINICAL PRESENTATION

As noted, the clinical presentation of schizophrenia can be quite variable, with no specific pathognomonic symptoms or symptom sets. All of the existing diagnostic classification systems for the disorder typically specify that, for the diagnosis to be met, a minimum number or set of symptoms must be present from a broader collection of possible symptoms. Specification of clinical presentation cannot be divorced from diagnostic systems, because what constitutes an acceptable minimum constellation of symptoms varies across systems. Indeed, a number of investigations have considered differences in definitions of the disorder across diagnostic systems, and found resulting differences in classification of patients from the same sample according to the different diagnostic requirements (e.g., Endicott, Nee, Cohen, Fleiss, & Simon, 1986; Endicott et al., 1982; Gruenberg, Kendler, & Tsuang, 1985; Kendler, Gruenberg, & Tsuang, 1985). Thus, the "typical" clinical presentation is affected by the particular diagnostic system that is utilized to define patient groups.

According to DSM-III-R, to meet criteria for schizophrenia, a patient must exhibit (or have exhibited during some active phase of the disorder) psychotic symptoms, as well as a deterioration in work, social, and/or self-care functioning. Psychotic symptom criteria are presented in Table 6.1. A further criterion pertains to duration: Continuous signs of the illness must be present for at least 6 months (a duration of less than 6 months suggests a schizophreniform disorder). During this minimum 6-month course, the patient must have symptoms indicative of an active phase of the illness (i.e., meeting the psychotic symptom criteria listed in Table 6.1). The course may also comprise a prodromal and/or residual phase (see Table 6.2). Finally, the diagnosis of schizophrenia is to be made only when a specific organic factor cannot be established as having initiated and maintained the disturbance.

Typically, age of onset is late adolescence or early adulthood, although later onset is possible. As noted, variability is symptomatology is marked. Specific schizophrenic subtypes are described below, prior to further discussion of the major symptoms.

Thought Disorder

The disturbances of thought that typify schizophrenia involve disruptions in thought form (i.e., the organization of ideas) and deviant thought content. Thought form disturbances are evidenced by unusual speech, which can be illogical, disorganized, and potentially incomprehensible. Characteristic disturbances of thought form include loose associations, blocking,

TABLE 6.1. DSM-III-R Psychotic Symptom Criteria for Schizophrenia

Presence of characteristic psychotic symptoms (1, 2, or 3 below) during the active phase for at least 1 week (unless the symptoms are successfully treated):

1. Two of the following:
   a. Delusions
   b. Prominent hallucinations (throughout the day for several days or several times a week for several weeks, with each hallucinatory experience longer than a few brief moments)
   c. Incoherence or marked loosening of associations
   d. Catatonic behavior
   e. Flat or grossly inappropriate affect.
2. Bizarre delusions (involving a phenomenon that the person's culture would regard as totally implausible, e.g., thought broadcasting).
3. Prominent hallucinations (as defined in 1b above) of a voice with content having no apparent relation to depression or elation, or a voice keeping up a running commentary on the person's behavior or thoughts, or two or more voices conversing with each other.

Source: Adapted with permission from the *Diagnostic and Statistical Manual of Mental Disorders* (3rd ed., revised). Copyright 1987 American Psychiatric Association.

neologisms, poverty of speech and of speech content, perseveration, echolalia, and clanging.

Delusions represent the most typical manifestation of deviant thought content in schizophrenia. Common examples include delusions of being controlled, bizarre delusions (i.e., thought insertion, thought broadcasting, and thought withdrawal), grandiose delusions, persecutory delusions, and delusions of reference. Although thought disorder is one principal criterion for diagnosing schizophrenia, its presence does not discriminate between schizophrenia and other psychotic disorders (e.g., mood disorder with psychotic features) (Andreasen, 1979).

Perceptual Disturbances

Hallucinations are a common schizophrenic symptom, occurring in approximately 75 percent of newly hospitalized schizophrenic patients (Ludwig,

TABLE 6.2. DSM-III-R Prodromal or Residual Schizophrenic Symptoms

1. Marked social isolation or withdrawal
2. Marked impairment in role functioning as wage earner, student, or homemaker
3. Markedly peculiar behavior (e.g., collecting garbage, talking to self in public, hoarding food)
4. Marked impairment in personal hygiene and grooming
5. Blunted or inappropriate affect
6. Digressive, vague, overelaborate, or circumstantial speech; or poverty of speech; or poverty of content of speech
7. Odd beliefs or magical thinking, influencing behavior and inconsistent with cultural norms (e.g., superstitiousness, belief in clairvoyance, telepathy, "sixth sense," "others can feel my feelings," overvalued ideas, ideas of reference)
8. Unusual perceptual experiences (e.g., recurrent illusions, sensing the presence of a force or person not actually present)
9. Marked lack of initiative, interests, or energy

Source: Adapted with permission from the *Diagnostic and Statistical Manual of Mental Disorders* (3rd ed., revised). Copyright 1987 American Psychiatric Association.

1986). Auditory hallucinations are most prevalent and are present in almost 90 percent of hallucinating patients (Ludwig, 1986). Less common hallucinations include visual, olfactory, tactile, somatic, and gustatory. These are uncommon, however, in the absence of hallucinatory voices.

Attentional Disturbances

Primary disruptions of elementary cognitive processes may underlie the various psychotic symptoms of schizophrenia. The attentional disturbances of schizophrenia were first described by Bleuler (1924–1976), who noted that schizophrenic patients were "incapable of holding the train of thought in the proper channels" (p. 377). Numerous studies of the cognitive functioning of acutely psychotic schizophrenics, as well as patients in relative remission, have been conducted. In a review of findings regarding the attentional abilities of schizophrenics, Nuechterlein and Dawson (1984) concluded that actively symptomatic schizophrenics, relatively remitted patients, and populations at risk for the disorder exhibit deficits on tasks that require relatively high processing loads and/or active rehearsal. Only tasks involving low demands on processing capacity have differentiated between symptomatic patients (who show deficits on such tasks) and remitted patients or at-risk groups. Thus, impaired higher level processing abilities, and/or the ability to respond to effortful processing demands, may reflect vulnerability factors for schizophrenia.

It is well known, however, that motivational and arousal disturbances, as well as affective symptoms, can contribute to the information processing difficulties of schizophrenics, in contrast to "pure" cognitive processing impairments. Gjerde (1983) has noted that organismic factors will most likely impact on tasks with high processing loads:

> Controlled, effortful processes are more labile than processes that have been automaticized, and individual differences, both within and among individuals, are most likely to manifest themselves on tasks requiring effortful processing. Organismic variables (e.g., arousal, mood, and age) are therefore more likely to influence performance when the task at hand . . . has high attentional requirements than when the demand is for automatic processing.
>
> *(p. 59)*

Little research has been done on the relationship between specific symptomatic/behavioral referents of schizophrenia and particular cognitive deficits. Recently, Neale et al. (1985) critiqued the empirical literature pertaining to cognitive deficits and schizophrenia on these grounds, and emphasized that few investigations have gone beyond demonstrating a simple correlation between a psychological variable and schizophrenia. For example, although it is hypothesized that cognitive dysfunction mediates impaired language production–communication in schizophrenia, the most prevalent research design has been the comparison of a heterogeneous sample of schizophrenic patients (without regard for subclassification in terms of communication impairment) with control samples. However, as Neale et al. indicated, within a group of schizophrenic patients with heterogeneous symptoms, "it seems reasonable that, for example, patients who experience auditory hallucinations may exhibit one form of cognitive impairment while those whose verbal conversation is difficult to follow may exhibit another" (p. 290).

Negative Symptoms

Negative symptoms may provide another important consideration with regard to both the diminished motivation and the cognitive performance of schizophrenic patients. Contemporary interest in subtyping schizophrenic symptomatology along positive and negative symptom dimensions was fueled by Strauss, Carpenter, and Bartko (1974). Positive symptoms include the manifest psychotic features of the disorder (See Table 6.1). Negative symptoms involve a diminution or loss of functioning, and typically include avolition, anhedonia–asociality, affective flattening or blunting (and/or inappropriate affect), alogia, and attentional impairment (Andreasen, 1982; Andreasen & Olsen, 1982). The results of several investigations have indicated that schizophrenic patients with prominent negative symptoms tend to be cognitively impaired and are more likely than patients with predominantly positive symptoms to have structural brain abnormalities (Andreasen & Olsen, 1982; Rieder, Donnelly, Herdt, & Waldman, 1979).

Social Functioning Impairment

As discussed, deterioration in social functioning is included among DSM-III-R criteria as characteristic of the prodromal phase, and difficulty in interpersonal relations is almost invariably present throughout an episode (APA, 1987).

Summary

Despite the heterogeneity of schizophrenic symptoms, the degree of relationship across symptoms is unclear. Some symptoms may underlie others; for example, disruptions in basic attentional and/or information processing mechanisms may ultimately prove responsible for aspects of the psychotic phenomena of the disorder. Alternatively, the motivational deficits that are common to the disorder may relate to the poor information processing abilities, and, in turn, motivational disturbances can comprise an aspect of the negative symptoms of the disorder. Also, although investigators have discussed the social deficits of schizophrenic patients for some time as though they were independent phenomena, the similarity of the so-called negative symptoms of the disorder to the sorts of social skills deficits that have been noted among schizophrenic patients based on behavioral observation techniques is striking and conceptually difficult to sort out. Finally, it is possible, in light of the far-reaching heterogeneity of the disorder and the relative paucity of knowledge regarding it, that similar symptoms could result from markedly different mechanisms, either within or across different subtypes. For example, considerable recent attention has been devoted to the affect recognition abilities of schizophrenic patients, and deficits have been recorded as common. The reason(s) for such deficits remains unclear, however, although proposed explanations have included lack of social experience and/or social isolation associated with the disorder, general cognitive impairment, and altered patterns of hemispheric lateralization and/or specific right hemisphere lesions (e.g., Morrison, Bellack, & Mueser, 1988).

DSM-III-R CRITERIA AND DIFFERENTIAL DIAGNOSIS

The primary DSM-III-R criteria for the diagnosis of schizophrenia were discussed above and were identified in Tables 6.1 and 6.2. DSM-III-R also specifies criteria for five types of the disorder:

1. *Catatonic Schizophrenia* is characterized by severe psychomotor disturbance, involving stupor, negativism, rigidity, excitement, or posturing. Catatonic schizophrenia has apparently decreased in frequency, and is now rare in North America and Europe.
2. *Disorganized Schizophrenia* involves incoherence, prominent loose associations, or markedly disorganized behavior, in conjunction with flat or grossly inappropriate affect. Systematized delusions are absent.
3. *Paranoid Schizophrenia* is characterized either by preoccupation with a systematized delusion(s) or by frequent auditory hallucinations that are related to a single theme. The paranoid subclassification has received the most attention, with several investigators reporting a later age of onset and a better prognosis (e.g., Klein, 1982; Lewine, Watt, & Fryer, 1978).
4. *Undifferentiated Schizophrenia* involves a clinical presentation comprising prominent delusions, hallucinations, incoherence, or grossly disorganized behavior, but does not meet criteria for catatonic, disorganized, or paranoid types.
5. *Residual Schizophrenia* involves an absence of prominent psychotic symptoms, but continuing evidence of the disturbance is indicated by the presence of at least two residual symptoms, outlined in Table 6.2.

A significant number of disorders can present with symptoms that are similar, or even identical, to those comprising schizophrenia. Accurate diagnosis is of utmost importance, because it dictates treatment. DSM-III-R and other sources (e.g., Roth, 1986) place considerable emphasis on the differentiation between organic mental disorders and schizophrenia. DSM-III-R criteria specify that, for a diagnosis of schizophrenia to be made, an organic factor cannot be identified as relating to the initiation or maintenance of the illness. Organic delusional syndromes, such as those induced by amphetamines or phencyclidine, can be cross-sectionally identical in symptomatology to schizophrenia (APA, 1987); however, an organic syndrome diagnosis is suggested by the presence of persistent disorientation, memory impairment, clouding of consciousness, progressive dementia, or delirious state (Roth, 1986). Included among the organic syndromes that must be considered in the differential diagnosis of schizophrenia is anticholinergic delirium. Cognitive toxicity can be a result of the anticholinergic effects of neuroleptic medications, and/or the combined effects of neuroleptics and ancillary anticholinergic drugs, as prescribed for the management of the extrapyramidal side effects associated with neuroleptic treatment (See "Course and Complications" below).

One of the most difficult differentials to establish is that between schizophrenia and psychotic forms of mood disorder and schizoaffective disorder (Doran, Breier, & Roy, 1986). This differentiation is especially hard if the differential is to be made during an isolated admission based only upon a cross-sectional evaluation (Deutsch & Davis, 1983). Data compiled during the last several decades have documented changing proportions in the diagnosis of schizophrenia versus affective disorders in clinical settings. For example, Baldessarini (1970) recorded an inverse relation between diagnostic rates for schizophrenia and those for manic–depressive and schizoaffective disorder over a 24-year period. An increase in one diagnosis was associated with a corresponding decrease in the other. An increased rate of schizophrenic diagnoses and a corresponding reduction in affective illness was noted to coincide with the introduction of antipsychotic medications. An opposite trend occurred with the introduction of lithium treatment for bipolar illness. Pope and Lipinski (1978) reviewed the findings from 18 investigations and concluded that 20 to 50 percent of patients with manic–depressive illness have symptoms that are considered to be important in the diagnosis of schizophrenia; however, evidence to support a distinction between schizophrenia and psychotic affective disorders also has been reported. Winokur, Morrison, Clancy, and Crowe (1972) and Tsuang (1978) reported greater morbid risk of affective disorder in the families of affectively disordered probands than in those of schizophrenic probands, and vice versa. Certain biological variables also have been reported to differ between schizophrenia and mania (See, e.g., Abrams & Taylor, 1979; Buchsbaum, 1978), as have behavioral ratings of thought disorder in studies utilizing DSM-III diagnostic criteria (Solovay, Shenton, & Holzman, 1987). DSM-III-R, while acknowledging that mood disturbance is common during all three phases of schizophrenia, emphasizes temporal factors in the appearance of schizophrenic syndrome and symptoms of mood disturbance in this differential. For example;

> If the total duration of all episodes of a mood syndrome are brief relative to the duration of Schizophrenia (active and residual phases), then the mood disturbance is considered an associated feature of Schizophrenia, and no additional diagnosis need be made. If the total duration of the mood disturbance is not brief, then a diagnosis of Schizophrenia is not made, and Schizoaffective Disorder and Mood Disorder with Psychotic Features must be considered.
>
> *(APA, 1987, p. 192)*

The differentiation between schizophrenia and schizoaffective disorder historically has been particularly controversial. Although some investigators have been skeptical regarding the validity of the schizoaffective diagnosis (e.g., Pope, Lipinski, Cohen, & Axelrod, 1980), diagnostic criteria for schizoaffective disorder were refined for DSM-III-R based on empirical findings (DSM-III listed no specific symptom criteria for schizoaffective disorder). The application of these improved criteria in longitudinal studies will help to better specify the differential diagnosis of these disorders. A remaining problem with DSM-III-R criteria for schizoaffective disorder is that they emphasize the sequence of appearance and duration of psychotic versus affective symptoms in the differential diagnosis of the disorder. This sequence can be difficult to determine accurately, as it must often be based on the patient's report and recall.

Schizophreniform disorder is also differentiated from schizophrenia on the basis of symptom duration. The duration of schizophreniform disorder is specified in DSM-III-R as less than 6 months.

Other mental disorders listed in DSM-III-R to be considered in the differential diagnosis of schizophrenia include delusional disorder, autistic disorder, obsessive–compulsive disorder, factitious disorder with psychological symptoms, and certain personality disorders, including schizotypal, borderline, schizoid, and paranoid types.

ETIOLOGY

In all likelihood, schizophrenia has multiple causes. Current etiologic models emphasize genetic, neurobiological, and psychosocial factors, as well as their interplay. Given the heterogeneity of schizophrenic symptoms, different etiologic factors may ultimately be implicated in different subtypes of the disorder. For example, findings implicating structural pathology in the brains of patients with a predominance of negative symptoms are suggestive of specific neurobiological factors that may play an etiologic role in these patients. Alternatively, the suggestion that schizophrenia may involve a progression from predominantly positive symptomatology to more pronounced negative symptoms in later stages may argue against different etiologic factors in these various subtypes.

The remarkable recent scientific progress in the development of investigational technology pertinent to neurobiological and genetic bases of schizophrenia has propelled significant advances in etiologic theory in these areas. With regard to neurobiology, the most widely advanced of the numerous biochemical hypotheses of schizophrenia has been the dopamine hypothesis. According to this model, schizophrenia results from hyperdopaminergic activity in the mesolimbic or mesocortical dopamine (DA) nerve terminal regions. Evidence in support of this hypothesis derives from data regarding the effects of antipsychotic medications. Carlsson (1978) showed that the therapeutic action of these drugs derives primarily from their antagonism of dopamine receptor interactions in the central nervous system. The increased dopaminergic activity associated with schizophrenia may be due to an increased number of DA receptors and/or to DA receptor abnormalities (Sedvall, Farde, & Wiesel, 1987; D. Seeman, 1980).

Other neurological abnormalities in brain structure and activity that have been associated with schizophrenia are enlarged ventricles (Keilp et al., 1988; Pfefferbaum et al., 1988) and hypofrontality (i.e., lowered metabolic activity in the frontal cortex) (Ariel et at., 1983; Buchsbaum et al., 1984; Farkas et al., 1984; Kling, Metter, Riege, & Kuhl, 1986; Weinberger, Berman, & Zec, 1986; Wolkin et al., 1988; Wolkin et al., 1985). Although findings suggest altered neuronal substrates and metabolic pathways in schizophrenia, ultimate understanding of the neurobiological basis of schizophrenia will require the discovery of specific genes and/or particular pathophysiologic mechanisms that produce these sorts of brain pathology.

Clearly, schizophrenia has an hereditary component, as cases tend to cluster in families. Morbid risk has been estimated in cohorts with varying genetic relationships, and a positive correlation between morbid risk and degree of genetic relationship has consistently been observed. Estimated lifetime risk is approximately 2 percent in uncles and aunts of schizophrenics, 4 percent in parents, 8 percent in siblings, and 12 percent in children (Helzer, 1988). However, these data do not provide conclusive support for genetic transmission of the illness, because family members typically share the same environment. Thus, genetic versus environmental transmission is confounded.

Twins have been studied in an attempt to resolve such confounding, by comparing monozygotic (MZ) and dizygotic (DZ) concordance. Data from twin studies almost invariably indicate a concordance rate for MZ twins that is several times greater than that for DZ twins. In their review of epidemiological findings, Gottesman and Shields (1982) derived estimates of concordance rates of approximately 50 percent for MZ pairs and 17 percent for DZ pairs. Increased concordance among MZ twins provides further support for genetic transmission; the 50 percent discordance among twins sharing the identical genome points to strong nongenetic factors. Findings of a link between cases of schizophrenia and a genetic defect on an as yet unknown gene on chromosome 5 were recently reported (Sherrington et al., 1988); however, it was found that those carrying the gene do not invariably develop the disease, but are merely susceptible to it. Furthermore, it is not known whether the specific deficit is a sufficient cause of schizophrenia, or whether other conditions must be met before the disease develops ("Where Next with Psychiatric Illness?" November 1988).

Psychosocial stress may precipitate onset in predisposed individuals. Stressful life events have been found to precede onset of schizophrenia (e.g., Birley & Brown, 1970; Jacobs & Myers, 1976), and such events tend to cluster in the 2 to 3 weeks immediately preceding an episode onset (e.g., Day et al., 1987). As such, psychosocial phenomena may play a critical role in the course of the illness, especially in regard to relapse. Considerable attention has been devoted to expressed emotion (EE) and relapse. EE represents a range of overt family attitudes toward the patient, including criticism, hostility, dissatisfaction, and overinvolvement (Brown & Rutter, 1966). A series of investigations has demonstrated that patients discharged to high EE families relapse more rapidly (50 percent or higher 9-month relapse rates) than those residing with low EE families (approximately 15 percent 9-month relapse rate) (Brown, Birley, & Wing, 1972; Vaughn & Leff, 1976; Vaughn, Snyder, Jones, Freeman, & Falloon, 1984).

NATURAL HISTORY

No illness has an outcome *in vacuo,* or even a natural history per se (Kendell, 1988). Treatment and other environmental influences invariably affect outcome. The "typical" course of schizophrenia may be particularly difficult to specify. Its heterogeneity results in considerable variability at the "starting point," and different subtypes may actually represent different syndromes with different outcomes. In many cases, schizophrenia has a chronic course and is affected by prolonged use of pharmacological and psychosocial treatment regimens, as no curative treatments exist. Also, evidence suggests differential outcome for male and female patients. A further consideration is that schizophrenics may be especially susceptible to the effects of various environmental stressors, as discussed above.

Medication and Psychosocial Treatment Effects

In a review of findings regarding "natural" (i.e., unmedicated) course, Davis (1985) concluded that schizophrenia has a constant relapse rate of 10 percent per month in unmedicated patients. Antipsychotic medication reduced this rate, with reported decreases ranging from 2.5-fold to 10-fold. Relapse rates for schizophrenic patients on neuroleptics have been shown to average approximately 40 percent per year, for both injected and orally administered medication (Falloon, Watt, & Shepperd, 1978; Hogarty, 1984; Hogarty et al., 1979; Schooler et al., 1980).

Combined treatment with maintenance neuroleptics and psychosocial intervention can significantly forestall relapse during the first year following hospital discharge. Hogarty et al. (1986) reported that combined family therapy and social skills training resulted in a significant reduction in relapse rates (19 and 20 percent, respectively) compared with a medication-only condition (41 percent). Most notably, the relapse rate for a combined treatment consisting of social skills training, family therapy, and maintenance medication was 0 percent during the first year postdischarge.

Differential Outcome Across Subtypes

Numerous retrospective data have shown that premorbid and/or preepisodic adjustment relates to outcome in schizophrenia: the better the premorbid functioning, the better the outcome (e.g., Strauss, Kokes, Klorman, & Sacksteder, 1977). In a prospective investigation, Gaebel and Pietzcker (1987) reported that outcome 1 year postdischarge was related to continuous neuroleptic treatment, initial (preepisodic) level of work adjustment, and heterosexual adjustment.

Recent findings have emphasized symptomatology as an outcome predictor, and have suggested that variation in symptomatology may represent a predictor of outcome as good as or better than premorbid functioning. Results indicate a relation between symptom severity and course (e.g., Harrow, Marengo, & McDonald, 1986; Marengo & Harrow, 1987), and, in particular, negative symptoms have been implicated in poor prognosis (e.g., Kay & Lindenmayer, 1987). Symptomatology is not entirely independent of other factors, however. For example, although negative symptoms were earlier regarded as intractible to treatment, data have been reported that indicate responsivity of negative syndrome patients to neuroleptics (e.g., Goldberg, 1985). Breier et al. (1987) demonstrated that negative and positive symptoms were significantly reduced by neuroleptic treatment, and that a similar pattern of reduction and exacerbation of negative and positive symptoms occurred during neuroleptic treatment and withdrawal, respectively.

Differential Outcome for Male and Female Patients

In terms of hospitalization data, long-term course appears to be better for female patients. Females evidence a superior response to neuroleptics and improved residential status (M. V. Seeman, 1986). These observations may relate to social phenomena (e.g., women may be more likely to have basic housekeeping skills needed for survival, and also represent less of a threat of violence to others). Also, the fact that women have a later age of onset suggests that there may be an intrinsic difference between the sexes in development of schizophrenia (Kendell, 1988).

COURSE AND COMPLICATIONS

Unquestionably, schizophrenia is a disorder of young adulthood. Its peak incidence is in the early 20s, and the range of onset is typically regarded as the mid-teens through approximately age 45. It is also apparent that schizophrenia is a malignant psychiatric disease with a poor prognosis. Estimates suggest that 15 to 30 percent of patients have no further recurrence of the disorder after the resolution of one or several acute episodes (Ludwig, 1986), but some of these persons may represent misdiagnoses. More typically, there is a chronic course with frequent relapses and poor interepisodic functioning. Some patients experience chronic, unremitting psychosis, with or without acute exacerbations. Almost all patients have sharply reduced psychosocial accomplishments, and the work and dating/marriage histories of patients are frequently quite dysfunctional. Schizophrenic patients also have a reduced life expectancy, as evidenced by increased rates of suicide, accidents, and abuse of psychoactive drugs, as well as diminished self-care abilities.

Unfortunately, in addition to the debilitating impact of the disorder itself, significant complications are associated with pharmacological treatments for schizophrenia. The potential complications of neuroleptic medications, which are currently considered to be critical to the amelioration of acute psychotic symptoms and as maintenance treatment, range from mild drowsiness to occasional serious and irreversible effects (Simpson, Pi, & Sramek, 1981, 1984). In general, excessive sedation, cardiovascular changes, and anticholinergic effects, including dry mouth, blurred vision, and constipation, result from low-potency neuroleptics (e.g., chlorpromazine, thioridozine). High-potency neuroleptics (e.g., haloperidol, fluphenazine) produce more extrapyramidal side effects, such as muscle spasm, restlessness, and parkinsonian symptoms (see Simpson & Pi, 1987, for a more detailed discussion of neuroleptic side effects). The adverse effects of neuroleptics can be compounded when they are prescribed in combination with other medications. Tune, Strauss, Lew, Breitlinger, and Coyle (1982) reported an inverse correlation between memory performance and serum anticholinergic levels in a sample of 24 outpatient schizophrenics. All patients were symptomatically stable and were taking the equivalent of 200 milligrams per day of chlorpromazine. Fifteen of the patients were also taking anticholinergic drugs as prescribed for the management of extrapyramidal side effects. A 0.77 percent incidence of toxic delirium associated with low-potency neuroleptics was reported by Schmidt et al. (1987), who also reported a 1.54 percent risk of toxic delirium associated with combined low-potency neuroleptics and anticholinergic antidepressants.

Tardive dyskinesia (TD) is a serious, late-onset, neurologic side effect of treatment with neuroleptics. TD involves spontaneous irregular (nonrhythmical) movements, primarily affecting the mouth and tongue, fingers, arms, and legs. Constant chewing movements, facial grimacing, pouting, puffing of the lips and cheeks, tongue protrusion, abnormal trunk movements, and rocking of the pelvis can also occur (Simpson, Pi, & Sramek, 1982). Symptoms of TD typically first appear or worsen when a neuroleptic dose is reduced or the medication is discontinued. Prevalence rates ranging from 0.5 to 56 percent have been reported (Kane & Smith, 1982). Results from a recent prospective investigation indicate a 24 percent incidence after 7 years of cumulative neuroleptic treatment (Kane et al., 1984). Wegner, Catalano, Gibralter, and Kane (1985) observed that schizophrenics with TD had more neurologic soft signs, were more frequently rated as evidencing poor premorbid social functioning, performed more poorly on psychometric testing, and had a higher familial loading for affective disorders in first-degree relatives than did non-TD schizophrenics. Non-TD patients had received neuroleptics for a longer period of time than patients with TD. Wegner et al. speculated that these factors may represent evidence of an increased vulnerability to the development of TD and, in particular, that individuals evidencing early schizoid withdrawal may be at a higher risk for TD development.

Individual susceptibility to side effects is unpredictable. However, elderly patients (Morrison & Katz, 1989) and patients with organic cerebral disease are at particular risk for the development of adverse effects (Norman, Judd, Marriott, & Burrows, 1986).

Schizophrenics may be more likely than other psychiatric patient groups and nonpatients to abuse psychoactive drugs. In a recent review, Schneier and Siris (1987) concluded that schizophrenics' use of amphetamines and cocaine, cannabis, hallucinogens, inhalants, caffeine, and tobacco was significantly greater than or equal to use by psychiatric controls or nonpatients. Numerous reports have established that short-term use of moderately large doses of stimulants can induce the development of acute psychoses (e.g., Angrist & Gershon, 1970; Bell, 1973; Griffith, Oates, & Cavanaugh, 1968), and, as noted, psychostimulant-induced psychotic reactions can present a difficult differential vis-à-vis other psychotic diagnoses. After examining recent psychostimulant use in hospitalized schizophrenics, Richard, Liskow, and Perry (1985) reported that relapsing schizophrenics utilized stimulants prior to hospitalization more often than did nonschizophrenic patients, and that outpatient antipsychotic prophylaxis did not prevent these relapses. These investigators concluded that stimulants may partially contribute to relapse.

CLINICAL MANAGEMENT

The principal issues in the clinical management of schizophrenia are the reduction of psychotic symptoms during an acute episode, the enhancement of interepisodic functioning, and the prevention of relapse. Unquestionably, the most important development in the treatment of schizophrenia was the advent in the late 1950s of neuroleptic medications. The term *neuroleptic* denotes the integrating neurological effects of these drugs in the brain. The term *antipsychotic* refers to the primary therapeutic action of the drugs. The two terms are frequently used interchangeably in the literature. The first neuroleptic (chlorpromazine) was discovered in the early 1950s. Since then, these agents have superseded all other biological treatments for schizophrenia. Currently, many different chemical classes of neuroleptics are available for psychiatric practice. The primary chemical class is the phenothiazines, which includes chlorpromazine (see Table 6.3).

The mainstay of treatment for all phases of the disorder remains treatment with an antipsychotic medication. During an acute phase, the majority of patients will require inpatient care. Inpatient treatment provides the opportunity to isolate the patient from further environmental stress, to provide the patient with assistance in the area of basic self-care skills with which he or she

TABLE 6.3.   Chemical Classification of
Commonly Used Antipsychotics

Phenothiazines
Aliphatic group
   Chlorpromazine (Thorazine®)
   Promazine (Sparine®)
Piperidine group
   Thioridazine (Mellaril®)
   Mesoridazine (Serentil®)
Piperazine group
   Fluphenazine (Prolixin®)
   Long-acting (depot) forms: decanoate/enanthate
   Trifluoperazine (Stelazine®)
   Perphenazine (Trilafon®)
   Prochlorperazine (Compazine®)
Thioxanthenes
   Chlorprothixene (Taractan®)
   Thiothixene (Navane®)
Butyrophenones
   Haloperidol (Haldol®)
Dibenzoxazepines
   Loxapine (Loxitane®)
Dihydroindolones
   Molindone (Moban®)
Rauwolfia
   Reserpine

may have particular difficulty during acute episodes, and to conduct a careful evaluation and formulate a treatment plan, including the initiation or increase of neuroleptics and subsequent titration upon symptom reduction.

Neuroleptics are used to induce and maintain remission of psychotic symptoms. Most patients require maintenance drug therapy following acute episodes to maintain remission. The "natural" course of the disorder in the absence of neuroleptic treatment and the effects of maintenance neuroleptics in forestalling relapse were discussed above. All antipsychotic drugs have equal efficacy and similar impacts on different symptoms (Norman et al., 1986); however, potency varies across different antipsychotics, as does potential to produce side effects, as discussed previously.

Clearly, a factor relating to relapse among many outpatient schizophrenics is their failure to comply with ongoing maintenance pharmacotherapy, and patients on long-acting depot medication have been shown to have a significantly lower rehospitalization rate than patients on oral maintenance therapy (Babiker, 1987). As we have seen, however, neuroleptic treatment is only one of several factors affecting outcome. Investigations reviewed above demonstrated that stressful life events and/or certain family behaviors precede relapse, and suggest that schizophrenic patients may exhibit a particular sensitivity to certain types of stressors. Therefore, the role of psychosocial interventions aimed at reducing interpersonal and familial stress and/or at providing the patient with increased coping abilities has become increasingly apparent. A combination of maintenance neuroleptic treatment and psychosocial interventions has been recommended as the treatment of choice to enhance interepisodic functioning and to forestall relapse (e.g., Schooler, 1986). Indeed, the data reported by Hogarty et al. (1986) suggest that the particular combination of behavioral family therapy and social skills training can provide a particularly efficacious complement to ongoing neuroleptic treatment.

In addition to evaluating the effects of combined pharmacological and psychosocial interventions, researchers have put considerable effort into devising improved pharmacological interventions. One such approach has been to supplement neuroleptics with other compounds. For example, Wolkowitz, Dickar, Doran, Breier, and Paul (1986) reported that the addition of alprazolam under double-blind conditions to a stable neuroleptic regimen in 2 schizophrenic patients resulted in clinically apparent improvement in positive and negative schizophrenic symptoms. Both patients exhibited significant worsening of symptoms following reduction or discontinuation of alprazolam. Later, Wolkowitz et al. (1988) demonstrated that alprazolam augmented the antipsychotic effects of fluphenazine in schizophrenic patients.

Also, during the past decade, researchers have put considerable effort into developing and testing "atypical" antipsychotic compounds. Ideally, a new antipsychotic would have limited extrapyramidal effects and produce enhanced symptom reduction in treatment-resistant patients. One such compound that exhibits considerable promise is clozapine, which has been demonstrated not to induce dystonia when administered on a short-term basis. Although akinesia and akathisia develop in some patients, the incidence appears to be low (Juul Povlsen, Noring, Fog, & Gerlach, 1985). In a recent double-blind comparison with chlorpromazine for treatment-resistant schizophrenic patients, clozapine produced significantly greater clinical improvement; 30 percent of the clozapine-treated patients were categorized as responders compared with 4 percent of chlorpromazine-treated patients (Kane, Honigfeld, Singer, Meltzer, & the Clozaril Collaborative Study Group, 1988). However, an increased risk of agranulocytosis has been identified as being related to clozapine administration (Lieberman et al., 1988), and careful hematologic monitoring is recommended.

Much further work is needed to develop treatment strategies that may prove differentially effective with particular subgroups of schizophrenic patients and at different stages of the disorder. Given the recent emphasis on subtyping of schizophrenic patients and continuing refinement of neuroscientific procedures to further investigate the organic pathology of schizophrenia, it is hoped that the future will see more successful efforts in these areas.

SUMMARY

Schizophrenia is a complex, heterogeneous disorder. Despite tremendous recent progress in diagnostic practice and neurobiological assessment, the etiology of the disorder remains unknown. There are no curative treatments, and the primary maintenance pharmacological treatments can result in considerable adverse effects. However, recent applications of combined pharmacological and psychosocial interventions appear promising, as does ongoing development of new pharmacological agents for the treatment of the disorder. Different subtypes of the disorder may exhibit different symptomatology, including cognitive deficits and/or organic pathology, as well as different longitudinal course and treatment response. The priority for assessment and treatment research in the immediate future is the continued scrutiny of subdiagnostic differences using longitudinal (cross-episodic), as opposed to cross-sectional, designs.

REFERENCES

Abrams, R., & Taylor, M. A. (1979). Differential EEG patterns in affective disorder and schizophrenia. *Archives of General Psychiatry, 36,* 1355–1358.

American Psychiatric Association. (1987). *Diagnostic and statistical manual of mental disorders* (3rd ed., rev.). Washington, DC: Author.

Andreasen, N. C. (1979). Affective flattening and the criteria for schizophrenia. *American Journal of Psychiatry, 136,* 944–946.

Andreasen, N. C. (1982). Negative symptoms in schizophrenia. *Archives of General Psychiatry, 39,* 784–788.

Andreasen, N. C., & Olsen, S. (1982). Negative vs. positive schizophrenia: Definition and validation. *Archives of General Psychiatry, 39,* 789–794.

Angrist, B. M., & Gershon, S. (1970). The phenomenology of experimentally induced amphetamine psychosis—Preliminary observations. *Biological Psychiatry, 2,* 95–107.

Ariel, R. N., Golden, C. J., Berg, R. A., Quaife, A., Dirksen, J. W., Forsell, T., Wilson, J., & Graber, B. (1983). Regional cerebral blood flow in schizophrenics. *Archives of General Psychiatry, 40*, 258–263.

Babiker, I. E. (1987). Comparative efficacy of long-acting depot and oral neuroleptic medications in preventing schizophrenic recidivism. *Journal of Clinical Psychiatry, 48*, 94–97.

Baldessarini, R. J. (1970). Frequency of diagnosis of schizophrenia vs affective psychoses from 1944–1968. *American Journal of Psychiatry, 127*, 759–763.

Bell, D. S. (1973). The experimental reproduction of amphetamine psychosis. *Archives of General Psychiatry, 29*, 35–40.

Birley, J., & Brown, G. (1970). Crises and life changes preceding the onset of acute schizophrenia: Clinical aspects. *British Journal of Psychiatry, 116*, 327–333.

Bleuler, E. (1976). *Textbook of psychiatry* (A. A. Brill, Trans.). New York: Arno Press. (Original work published 1924)

Breier, A., Wolkowitz, O. M., Doran, A. R., Roy, A., Boronow, J., Hommer, D. W., & Pickar, D. (1987). Neuroleptic responsivity of negative and positive symptoms in schizophrenia. *American Journal of Psychiatry, 144*, 1549–1555.

Brown, G. W., Birley, J. L. T., & Wing, J. K. (1972). Influence of family life on the course of schizophrenic disorders: A replication. *British Journal of Psychiatry, 121*, 241–258.

Brown, G. W., & Rutter, M. (1966). The measurement of family activities and relationships: A methodological study. *Human Relations, 19*, 241–263.

Buchsbaum, M. S. (1978). The average evoked response technique in differentiation of bipolar, unipolar, and schizophrenic disorders. In H. S. Akiskal & W. L. Webb (Eds.), *Psychiatric diagnosis: Explorations of biological predictors* (chap. 22). New York: Spectrum.

Buchsbaum, M. S., DeLisi, L. E., Holcomb, H. H., Cappelletti, J., King, A. C., Johnson, J., Hazlett, E., Dowling-Zimmerman, S., Post, R. M., Morihisa, J., Carpenter, W., Cohen, R., Pickar, D., Weinberger, D. R., Margolin, R., & Kessler, R. M. (1984). Anteroposterior gradients in cerebral glucose use in schizophrenia and affective disorders. *Archives of General Psychiatry, 41*, 1159–1166.

Carlsson, A. (1978). Antipsychotic drugs, neurotransmitters, and schizophrenia. *American Journal of Psychiatry, 135*, 164–173.

Crow, T. J. (1980). Molecular pathology of schizophrenia: More than one disease process? *British Medical Journal, 280*, 66–68.

Crow, T. J. (1985). The two-syndrome concept: Origins and current status. *Schizophrenia Bulletin, 11*, 471–486.

Davis, J. M. (1985). Maintenance therapy and the natural course of schizophrenia. *Journal of Clinical Psychiatry, 46*, 18–21.

Day, R., Nielsen, J. A., Korten, A., Ernberg, G., Dube, K. C., Gerhart, J., Jablensky, A., Leon, C., Marsella, A., Olatawura, M., Sartorius, N., Stromgren, E., Takahashi, R., Wig, N., & Wynne, L. C. (1987). Stressful life events preceding the acute onset of schizophrenia: A cross-national study from the World Health Organization. *Culture, Medicine, and Psychiatry, 11*, 123–205.

Deutsch, S. I., & Davis, K. L. (1983). Schizophrenia: A review of diagnostic and biological issues. *Hospital and Community Psychiatry, 34*, 313–322.

Doran, A. R., Breier, A., & Roy, A. (1986). Differential diagnosis and diagnostic systems in schizophrenia. *Psychiatric Clinics of North America, 9*, 17–34.

Endicott, J., Nee, J., Cohen, J., Fleiss, J., & Simon, R. (1986). Diagnosis of schizophrenia. *Archives of General Psychiatry, 43,* 13–19.

Endicott, J., Nee, J., Cohen, J., Fleiss, J., Williams, J. B. W., & Simon, R. (1982). Diagnostic criteria for schizophrenia: Reliabilities and agreement between systems. *Archives of General Psychiatry, 39,* 884–889.

Etevenon, P., Peron-Magnan, P., Campistron, D., Verdeaux, G., & Deniker, P. (1983). Differences in EEG symmetry between patients with schizophrenia and normals assessed by Fourier analysis. In P. Flor-Henry & J. H. Gruzelier (Eds.), *Laterality and psychopathology* (pp. 269–290). New York: Elsevier.

Falloon, I., Watt, D. C., & Shepperd, M. (1978). A comparative controlled trial of pimozide and fluphenazine decanoate in the continuation therapy of schizophrenia. *Psychological Medicine, 8,* 59–70.

Farkas, T., Wolf, A. P., Jaeger, J., Brodie, J. D., Christman, D. R., & Fowler, J. S. (1984). Regional brain glucose metabolism in chronic schizophrenia. *Archives of General Psychiatry, 41,* 293–300.

Feighner, J. P., Robins, E., Guze, S. B., Woodruff, R. A., Winokur, G., & Munoz, R. (1972). Diagnostic criteria for use in psychiatric research. *Archives of General Psychiatry, 26,* 57–63.

Gaebel, W., & Pietzcker, A. (1987). Prospective study of course of illness in schizophrenia. *Schizophrenia Bulletin, 13,* 307–316.

Gjerde, P. F. (1983). Attentional capacity dysfunction and arousal in schizophrenia. *Psychological Bulletin, 93,* 57–72.

Goldberg, S. C. (1985). Negative and deficit symptoms in schizophrenia do respond to neuroleptics. *Schizophrenia Bulletin, 11,* 453–456.

Gottesman, I. I., & Shields, J. (1982). *Schizophrenia: The epigenetic puzzle.* New York: Cambridge University Press.

Griffith, J. D., Oates, J., & Cavanaugh, J. (1968). Paranoid episodes induced by drugs. *Journal of American Medical Association, 205,* 39–46.

Gruenberg, A. M., Kendler, K. S., & Tsuang, M. T. (1985). Reliability and concordance in the subtyping of schizophrenia. *American Journal of Psychiatry, 142,* 1355–1358.

Harrow, M., Marengo, J., & McDonald, C. (1986). The early course of schizophrenic thought disorder. *Schizophrenia Bulletin, 12,* 208–224.

Helzer, J. E. (1988). Schizophrenia: Epidemiology. In J. O. Cavenar, Jr., (General Editor) *Psychiatry* (Vol. 1, 1–17). Philadelphia: J. B. Lippincott.

Hogarty, G. E. (1984). Depot neuroleptics: The relevance of psycho-social factors. *Journal of Clinical Psychiatry, 45,* 36–42.

Hogarty, G.E., Anderson, C. M., Reiss, D. J., Kornblith, S. J., Greenwald, D. P., Javna, C. D., Madonia, M. J., & Environmental/Personal Indicators in the Course of Schizophrenia Research Group. (1986). Family psychoeducation, social skills training, and maintenance chemotherapy in the aftercare treatment of schizophrenia. *Archives of General Psychiatry, 43,* 633–642.

Hogarty, G. E., Schooler, N. R., Ulrich, R. F., Mussare, F., Herron, E., & Ferro, P. (1979). Fluphenazine and social therapy in the aftercare of schizophrenic patients: Relapse analyses of a two-year controlled study of fluphenazine decanoate and fluphenazine hydrochloride. *Archives of General Psychiatry, 36,* 1283–1294.

Jacobs, S., & Myers, J. K. (1976). Recent life events and acute schizophrenic psychosis: A controlled study. *Journal of Nervous and Mental Disease, 162,* 75–87.

Juul Povlsen, U., Noring, U., Fog, R., & Gerlach, J. (1985). Tolerability and therapeutic effect of clozapine: A retrospective investigation of 216 patients treated with clozapine for up to 12 years. *Acta Psychiatrica Scandinavia, 71,* 176–185.

Kane, J., Honigfeld, G., Singer, J., Meltzer, H., and the Clozaril Collaborative Study Group. (1988). Clozapine for the treatment-resistant schizophrenic: A double-blind comparison with chlorpromazine. *Archives of General Psychiatry, 45,* 789–796.

Kane, J. M., Woerner, M., Weinhold, P., Wegner, J., Kinon, B., & Borenstein, M. (1984). Incidence of tardive dyskinesia: Five-year data from a prospective study. *Psychopharmacology Bulletin, 20,* 39–40.

Kane, J. M., & Smith, J. M. (1982). Tardive dyskinesia: Prevalence and risk factors. *Archvies of General Psychiatry, 39,* 473–481.

Kay, S. R., & Lindenmayer, J. P. (1987). Outcome predictors in acute schizophrenia. Prospective significance of background and clinical dimensions. *The Journal of Nervous and Mental Disease, 175,* 152–160.

Keilp, J. G., Sweeney, J. A., Jacobsen, P., Soloman, C., St. Louis, L., Deck, M., Frances, A., & Mann, J. J. (1988). Cognitive impairment in schizophrenia: Specific relations to ventricular size and negative symptomatology. *Biological Psychiatry, 24,* 47–55.

Kendell, R. E. (1988). Schizophrenia: Clinical features. In J. O. Cavenar, Jr., (General Editor) *Psychiatry* (Vol. 1, pp. 1–20). Philadelphia: J. B. Lippincott, Kendler, K. S., Gruenberg, A. M., & Tsuang, M. T. (1985). Subtype stability in schizophrenia. *American Journal of Psychiatry, 142,* 827–832.

Klein, D. N. (1982). Relation between current diagnostic criteria for schizophrenia and the dimensions of premorbid adjustment, paranoid symptomatology, and chronicity. *Journal of Abnormal Psychology, 91,* 319–325.

Kling, A. S., Metter, E. J., Riege, W. H., & Kuhl, D. E. (1986). Comparison of PET measurement of local brain glucose metabolism and CAT measurement of brain atrophy in chronic schizophrenia and depression. *American Journal of Psychiatry, 143,* 175–180.

Lewine, R. R. J., Watt, N. F., & Fryer, J. H. (1978). A study of childhood social competence, adult premorbid competence, and psychiatric outcome in three schizophrenic subtypes. *Journal of Abnormal Psychology, 87,* 271–294.

Lieberman, J. A., Johns, C. A., Kane, J. M., Rai, K., Pisciotta, A. V., Saltz, D. L., & Howard, A. (1988). Clozapine induced agranulocytosis: Non-cross reactivity with other psychotropic drugs. *Journal of Clinical Psychiatry, 49,* 271–277.

Ludwig, A. M. (1986). *Principles of clinical psychiatry.* New York: Free Press.

Marengo, J. T., & Harrow, M. (1987). Schizophrenic thought disorder at follow-up: A persistent or episodic course? *Archives of General Psychiatry, 44,* 651–659.

Morrison, R. L., Bellack, A. S., & Mueser, K. T. (1988). Facial affect recognition deficits and schizophrenia. *Schizophrenia Bulletin, 14,* 67–83.

Morrison, R. L., & Katz, I. R. (1989). Drug-related cognitive impairment: Current progress and recurrent problems. In C. Eisdorfer, R. W. Besdine, J. E. Birren, V. Cristofalo, M. P. Lawton, G. L. Maddox, & B. D. Starr (Eds.), *Annual review of gerontology and geriatrics* (Vol. 9, pp. 232–284). New York: Springer Publishing.

Nasrallah, H. A., McCalley-Whiters, M., Bigelow, L. B., & Rauscher, F. P. A histological study of the corpus callosum in chronic schizophrenia. *Psychiatry Research, 8,* 251–260.

Neale, J. M., Oltmanns, T. F., & Harvey, P. D. (1985). The need to relate cognitive deficits to specific behavioral referents of schizophrenia. *Schizophrenia Bulletin, 11,* 286–291.

Norman, T. R., Judd, F. K., Marriott, P. F., & Burrows, G. D. (1986). Pharma-cotherapy of schizophrenia: Clinical aspects. In G. D. Burrows, T. R. Norman, & G. Rubinstein (Eds.), *Handbook of studies on schizophrenia: Part 2. Management and research* (pp. 1–12). New York: Elsevier.

Neuchterlein, K. H., & Dawson, M. E. (1984). Information processing and attentional functioning in the developmental course of schizophrenic disorders. *Schizophrenia Bulletin, 10,* 160–202.

Pfefferbaum, A., Zipursky, R. B., Lim, K. O., Zatz, L. M., Stahl, S. M., & Jernigan, T. L. (1988). Computerized tomographic evidence for generalized sulcal and ventricular enlargement in schizophrenia. *Archives of General Psychiatry, 45,* 633.

Pope, H. G., & Lipinski, J. F. (1978). Diagnosis in schizophrenia and manic–depressive illness: A reassessment of the specificity of "schizophrenic" symptoms in the light of current research. *Archives of General Psychiatry, 35,* 811–828.

Pope, H. G., Lipinski, J. F., Cohen, B. M., & Axelrod, D. T. (1980). "Schizoaffective disorder": An invalid diagnosis? A comparison of schizoaffective disorder, schizophrenia, and affective disorder. *American Journal of Psychiatry, 137,* 921–927.

Richard, M. L., Liskow, B. I., & Perry, P. J. (1985). Recent psychostimulant use in hospitalized schizophrenics. *Journal of Clinical Psychiatry, 46,* 79–83.

Rieder, R. O., Donnelly, E. F., Herdt, J. R., & Waldman, I. N. (1979). Sulcal prominence in young chronic schizophrenic patients: CT scan findings associated with impairment on neuropsychological tests. *Psychiatry Research, 1,* 1–8.

Roth, M. (1986). Diagnosis and prognosis of schizophrenia. In G. D. Burrows, T. R. Norman, & G. Rubinstein (Eds.), *Handbook of studies on schizophrenia: Part 1. Epidemiology, aetiology and clinical features,* (pp. 169–182). New York: Elsevier.

Schmidt, L. G., Grohmann, R., Strauss, A., Spiess-Kiefer, C., Lindmeier, D., & Muller-Oerlinghausen, B. (1987). Epidemiology of toxic delirium due to psychotrophic drugs in psychiatric hospitals. *Comprehensive Psychiatry, 28,* 242–249.

Schneier, F. R., & Siris, S. G. (1987). A review of psychoactive substance use and abuse in schizophrenia. Patterns of drug choice. *The Journal of Nervous and Mental Disease, 175,* 641–652.

Schooler, N. R. (1986). The efficacy of antipsychotic drugs and family therapy in the maintenance treatment of schizophrenia. *Journal of Clinical Psychopharmacology, 6,* 11s–19s.

Schooler, N. R., Levine, J., Severe, J. B., Brauzer, B., DiMascio, A., Klerman, G. L., & Tuason, V. B. (1980). Prevention of relapse in schizophrenia: An evaluation of fluphenazine decanoate. *Archives of General Psychiatry, 37,* 16–24.

Sedvall, G., Farde, L., & Wiesel, F. A. (1987). Quantitative determination of D2 dopamine receptor characteristics in healthy human subjects and psychiatric patients. Symposium on analysis of neurotransmitters. *Life Sciences, 41,* 813–816.

Seeman, M. V. (1986). Current outcome in schizophrenia: Women vs men. *Acta Psychiatrica Scandinavica, 73,* 609–617.

Seeman, P. (1980). Brain dopamine receptors. *Pharmacological Reviews, 32,* 229–313.

Sherrington, R., Brynjolfsson, J., Petursson, H., Potter, M., Dudleston, K., Barraclough, B., Wasmuth, J., Dobbs, M., & Gurling, H. (1988). Localization of a susceptibility locus for schizophrenia on chromosome 5. *Nature, 336,* 164–167.

Simpson, G. M., & Pi, E. H. (1987). Issues in pharmacological treatment. In R. L. Morrison & A. S. Bellack (Eds.), *Medical factors and psychological disorders: A handbook for psychologists* (pp. 19–40). New York: Plenum Press.

Simpson, G. M., Pi, E. H., & Sramek, J. J. (1981). Adverse effects of antipsychotic agents. *Drugs, 21,* 138–151.

Simpson, G. M., Pi, E. H., & Sramek, J. J. (1982). Management of tardive dyskinesia: Current update. *Drugs, 23,* 381–383.

Simpson, G. M., Pi, E. H., & Sramek, J. J. (1984). Neuroleptics and antipsychotics. In M. N. G. Dukes (Ed.), *Meyler's side effects of drugs* (10th ed. pp. 105–131). Amsterdam: Elsevier.

Solovay, M. R., Shenton, M. E., & Holzman, P. S. (1987). Comparative studies of thought disorders. *Archives of General Psychiatry, 44,* 13–20.

Spitzer, R. L., Endicott, J., & Robins, E. (1978). *Research Diagnostic Criteria (RDC) for a selected group of functional disorders* (3rd ed.). New York: Biometrics Research, New York State Psychiatric Institute.

Strauss, J. S., & Carpenter, W. T., & Bartko, J. J. (1974). The diagnosis and understanding of schizophrenia. Part III. Speculation on the processes that underlie schizophrenic symptoms and signs. *Schizophrenia Bulletin, 1* (11), 61–69.

Strauss, J. S., Kokes, R. F., Klorman, R., & Sacksteder, J. L. (1977). Premorbid adjustment in schizophrenia: Concepts, measures, and implications: I. The concept of premorbid adjustment. *Schizophrenia Bulletin, 3,* 182–185.

Tsuang, M. T. (1978). Familial subtyping of schizophrenia and affective disorder. In R. Spitzer & D. Klein (Eds.), *Critical Issues in Psychiatric Diagnosis* (pp. 203–211). New York: Raven Press.

Tune, L. E., Strauss, M. E., Lew, M. F., Breitlinger, E., & Coyle, J. T. (1982). Serum levels of anticholinergic drugs and impaired recent memory in chronic schizophrenic patients. *American Journal of Psychiatry, 139,* 1460–1462.

Vaughn, C. E., & Leff, J. P. (1976). The influence of family and social factors on the course of psychiatric illness: A comparison of schizophrenic and depressed neurotic patients. *British Journal of Psychiatry, 129,* 125–137.

Vaughn, C. E., Snyder, K. S., Jones, S., Freeman, W. B., & Falloon, I. R. H. (1984). Family factors in schizophrenic relapse: Replication in California of British research on expressed emotion. *Archives of General Psychiatry, 41,* 1169–1177.

Wegner, J. T., Catalano, F., Gibralter, J., & Kane, J. M. (1985). Schizophrenics with tardive dyskinesia. *Archives of General Psychiatry, 42,* 860–865.

Weinberger, D. R., Berman, K. F., & Zec, R. F. (1986). Physiologic dysfunction of dorsolateral prefrontal cortex in schizophrenia: I. Regional cerebral blood flow evidence. *Archives of General Psychiatry, 43,* 114–124.

Where next with psychiatric illness? *Nature, 336,* 95–96 (editorial).

Winokur, G., Morrison, J., Clancy, J., & Crowe, R. (1972). The Iowa 500. *Archives of General Psychiatry, 27,* 462–464.

Wolkin, A., Angrist, B., Wolf, A., Brodie, J. D., Wolkin, B., Jaeger, J., Cancro, R., & Rotrosen, J. (1988). Low frontal glucose utilization in chronic schizophrenia: A replication study. *American Journal of Psychiatry, 145,* 251–253.

Wolkin, A., Jaeger, J., Brodie, J. D., Wolf, A. P., Fowler, J., Rotrosen, J., Gomez-Mont. F., & Cancro, R. (1985). Persistence of cerebral metabolic abnormalities in chronic schizophrenia as determined by positron emission tomography. *American Journal of Psychiatry, 142,* 564–571.

Wolkowitz, O. M., Breier, A., Doran, A. R., Kelsoe, J., Lucas, P., Paul, S. M., & Pickar, D. (1988). Alprazolam augmentation of the antipsychotic effects of fluphenazine in schizophrenic patients: Preliminary results. *Archives of General Psychiatry, 45,* 664–671.

Wolkowitz, O. M., Pickar, D., Doran, A. R., Breier, A., & Paul, S. M. (1986). Combination alprazolam-neuroleptic treatment of the positive and negative symptoms of schizophrenia. *American Journal of Psychiatry, 143,* 85–87.

CHAPTER 7

Mood Disorders (Unipolar Depression)

CONSTANCE L. HAMMEN

As a mood state or symptom accompanying life circumstances and medical and psychological events, depression is part of the human condition. It is a familiar and, indeed, normal experience in the lives of most individuals. For a substantial part of the population, however, depression is a debilitating or even life-threatening syndrome. It is a constellation of somatic, mood, behavioral, and cognitive symptoms that endure over varying periods of time and impair a person's ability to function normally in typical roles.

The various syndromes that constitute unipolar depression represent one of the most common forms of diagnosable psychiatric disorder. Lifetime rates of major depression assessed in randomly selected residents of four cities, using the most sophisticated methods available, ranged from 4.0 to 8.4 percent (Karno et al., 1987). Past studies that used somewhat different criteria and included more mild forms of depression estimated the lifetime rates to be even higher, up to 18 percent, in samples of U.S. and Western industrialized cities (Boyd & Weissman, 1981). Boyd and Weissman (1981) asked community residents to report depressive symptoms on questionnaires rather than in interviews, and found that between 9 and 20 percent of respondents indicated the presence of significant symptoms. Although the majority of individuals who experience even major depressions do not seek treatment, significant segments of the population at any given moment, or across lifetimes, experience debilitating depressive conditions. The demoralization of depression, the resultant disrupted functioning at work or in family and social roles, and the health implications constitute an enormous toll on the public health of the community.

No major segment of the population escapes significant rates of clinical depression. Evidence is growing that the incidence of lifetime diagnosable major depression is as high in adolescents as in adults (Kashani et al., 1987; Lewinsohn, Hops, Roberts, & Seeley, 1988). This suprisingly high rate in youngsters in the community is compatible with reports that depressive disorders are growing in frequency in younger populations (Gershon, Hamovit, Guroff, & Nurnberger, 1987; Klerman et al., 1985). Even school-age children in community samples appear to meet adult criteria for depressive disorders, with a prevalence of 2 percent in a sample of 11-year-olds (Anderson, Williams, McGee, & Silva, 1987). Diagnosable depression and depressive symptoms are more commonly reported by women than men, typically at a ratio of 2:1 or more (Boyd & Weissman, 1981; Nolen-Hoeksema, 1987; L. N. Robins et al., 1984), although some evidence suggests that this gap may be narrowing (Klerman et al., 1985).

CLINICAL PRESENTATION

As a mood state, depression is usually transitory, lasts a few hours or a few days, and generally has minimal impact on the functioning of the individual. When the depressed mood is accompanied, however, by a variety of other features of the syndrome called major depression, or when it persists over a lengthy period, it is likely to cause a degree of suffering and impairment that we consider to be clinically significant.

Clinical depression is much more than a disturbance of mood in which the individual feels sad, low, blue, or despondent. It is also a disorder that affects the way people think about themselves and their worlds, and that alters intellectual functioning; it is a disturbance accompanied by characteristic physical and behavioral changes. A depressed person is likely to feel apathetic, listless, low in energy, unable to enjoy activities or people that were previously pleasurable, and lacking in motivation to engage in typical activities or to initiate or plan new activities. Depressed persons are likely to feel critical of themselves, to feel guilty, and to experience themselves as deficient in important positive qualities that make them desirable, worthwhile, competent, and capable of managing their lives. In severe depression, a person may feel that the future is bleak, and feelings of hopelessness may be associated with thoughts of death or suicide. The more severe the depression, the more likely the person may be to experience cognitive impairment: Making decisions becomes a heavy burden, memory may be impaired, and concentration is difficult. Also, with more severe depression, changes in sleeping are likely (difficulty staying asleep or sleeping more than usual), and changes in appetite may lead to weight gain or loss. Depressed people commonly experience aches and pains, or the accentuation of previously present medical problems. Frequently, the inner experiences of listlessness and low energy are visible in the form of slowness of movement and sad facial expression, although in many cases the person is restless and agitated instead of slowed down.

Depressed individuals and their family members often are unaware that the varying manifestations form a syndrome in which the various symptoms affect each other. Instead, a depressed man may feel even more depressed and guilty because he feels apathetic toward his wife, and a depressed woman may feel worse when she does not have the energy to go to work or feels impatient toward her children.

DIAGNOSTIC CRITERIA AND DIFFERENTIAL DIAGNOSIS

DSM-III-R Criteria

Unipolar depression is not itself a diagnostic category, but refers to a conceptual distinction separating a class of depressive disorders whose course does not include evidence of mania or hypomania. Unipolar depressions not only are fairly common, as noted earlier, but also are considered to be a very heterogeneous group of disorders. The American Psychiatric Association (APA), in the revised third edition of its official diagnostic manual, the *Diagnostic and Statistical Manual of Mental Disorders,* (DSM-III-R; 1987), lists two forms of unipolar depression: major depression and dysthymia.

Major Depression

Table 7.1 presents the criteria for major depression. Additionally, major depression may be rated for level of severity, presence or absence of psychotic features, and whether it is single episode, recurrent, or chronic. Also, DSM-III-R provides criteria for the melancholic subtype of major depression, for which diagnosis requires presence of at least five of the following: loss of interest or pleasure in activities, lack of reactivity to usually pleasurable stimuli such that the person does not feel better even temporarily when pleasant

TABLE 7.1.   DSM-III-R Criteria for Major Depressive Episode

A. At least five of the following symptoms have been present during the same 2-week period and represent a change from previous functioning; and at least one of the symptoms is either (a) depressed mood or (b) loss of interest or pleasure. (Do not include symptoms that are clearly due to a physical condition, mood-incongruent delusions or hallucinations, incoherence, or marked loosening of associations.)
  1. Depressed mood (or irritable mood in children and adolescents) most of the day, nearly every day, as indicated either by subjective account or observation by others
  2. Markedly diminished interest or pleasure in all, or almost all, activities most of the day, nearly every day (as indicated either by subjective account or observation by others of apathy most of the time)
  3. Significant weight loss or weight gain when not dieting (e.g., more than 5% of body weight in a month), or decrease or increase in appetite nearly every day (in children, consider failure to make expected weight gains)
  4. Insomnia or hypersomnia nearly every day
  5. Psychomotor agitation or retardation nearly every day (observable by others, not merely subjective feelings of restlessness or being slowed down)
  6. Fatigue or loss of energy nearly every day
  7. Feelings of worthlessness or excessive or inappropriate guilt (which may be delusional) nearly every day (not merely self-reproach or guilt about being sick)
  8. Diminished ability to think or concentrate, or indecisiveness, nearly every day (either by subjective account or as observed by others)
  9. Recurrent thoughts of death (not simply fear of dying), recurrent suicidal ideation without a specific plan, or a suicide attempt or a specific plan for committing suicide
B. 1. It cannot be established that an organic factor initiated and maintained the disturbance.
  2. The disturbance is not a normal reaction to the death of a loved one (uncomplicated bereavement).
    Note: Morbid preoccupation with worthlessness, suicidal ideation, marked functional impairment or psychomotor retardation, or prolonged duration suggest bereavement complicated by major depression.
C. At no time during the disturbance have there been delusions or hallucinations for as long as 2 weeks in the absence of prominent mood symptoms (i.e., before the mood symptoms developed or after they have remitted).

Source: Adapted with permission from the *Diagnostic and Statistical Manual of Mental Disorders* (3rd ed., revised). Copyright 1987 American Psychiatric Association.

things happen, diurnal variation of mood (e.g., worse in A.M.), early morning awakening, observable psychomotor changes (slowed or agitated), and significant weight loss. Also included as criteria are lack of significant personality disturbance prior to major depression, one or more previous major depressions followed by complete or near-complete recovery, and previous good response to antidepressant medication. The rationale for these criteria and the evolution of the present definition of melancholia from that of the earlier DSM-III (APA, 1980), are reported in Zimmerman and Spitzer (1989).

Dysthymia

Dysthymia, previously termed depressive neurosis, refers to a chronic depression lasting most of the time for at least 2 years, during which at least two of six symptoms of the depression syndrome occur. This condition is further characterized as primary or secondary (to some preexisting Axis I disorder or medical condition) and as early or late onset (age 21 or after). Like major depression, dysthymia is considered to be heterogeneous. Akiskal (1983) and Depue and Monroe (1986) proposed several subtypes of chronic depression, as discussed below.

The use of DSM-III and DSM-III-R has greatly improved the reliability of the diagnosis of depressive disorders. Nevertheless, as with any classification system, validity and completeness of the diagnoses are limited by the available knowledge about characteristics of the condition. Two recent studies suggest that additional naturally occurring forms of depression exist that do not meet current official criteria. Barrett, Barrett, Oxman, and Gerber (1988) interviewed a subset of patients in a general medical practice who had been screened as scoring high on depressive symptoms on self-report checklists. In addition to those who met DSM-III criteria for depressive disorders, another reasonably large subset (10.5 percent) had significant depressive symptoms that did not fall in one of the official categories; one group had a mix of depression and anxiety, and another group had observed depressive features but denied other symptoms (termed "masked/suspected" depression). Blazer et al. (1988) used multivariate statistical techniques to characterize the symptoms reported by community residents participating in the Epidemiological Catchment Area survey. They found that several depression symptom profiles emerged, but only one corresponded to DSM-III major depression. The most notable additional pattern suggested a mixed anxiety–depression type characterizing a substantial proportion of the more severely depressed respondents. Blazer et al. (1988) noted that such conditions may not be properly recognized by diagnosticians because they do not meet full DSM-III-R criteria for either major depression or anxiety disorders. Thus, it is important to keep in mind that significant clinical depression may take forms other than those contained in DSM-III or DSM-III-R.

Differential Diagnosis

The most important differential diagnostic issue is the distinction between unipolar and bipolar depression because the two appear to have very different etiologic and treatment implications (e.g., Depue & Monroe, 1978). The differences between unipolar depression and bipolar I disorder (depression with history of mania) are especially important in terms of course, etiology, and treatment, whereas the implications of a distinction between bipolar II disorders (depression with history of hypomania) and unipolar major depression are somewhat more ambiguous (e.g., Keller, 1988). Although major depression may look similar in unipolar and bipolar patients, careful analysis of the past history of manic or hypomanic periods is essential and facilitates the diagnosis of unipolar or bipolar disorder.

Depression may coexist with a variety of psychiatric and medical conditions. It is a common accompaniment to eating disorders, alcohol and drug abuse, and anxiety disorders, and may arise prior to or as a consequence of such conditions (Lehmann, 1985). A major depression that is concurrent with symptoms of schizophrenia may meet criteria for schizoaffective disorder, a condition that remains controversial with respect to whether it is truly a form of affective disorder or of schizophrenia, or whether it is an independent disorder. Similarly, mood symptoms and even diagnosable depressions may be common features of personality disorders; those disorders with marked affective lability, such as borderline, narcissistic, or histrionic types, may complicate differential diagnosis. For instance, in their recent review of borderline personality disorder, Widiger and Frances (1989) noted the overlap of symptoms for affective disorders and borderline disorder. They suggested that the relationship between the two is complex, and that a subgroup of borderline patients may have depressive disorders.

Numerous extant medical conditions are known to cause depressive symptoms, including a variety of endocrinological, neurological, and viral diseases (reviewed in Cassem, 1988). Schulberg, McClelland, and Burns (1987) reviewed physical symptoms of depression, depressive symptoms of medical illness, and depressive reactions to medical illness, noting their differential clinical and etiologic implications.

Subtypes of Depression

The concept of unipolar depression is very broad, containing heterogeneous conditions that complicate the search for etiologic models and effective treatments. Various strategies are used for classifying the possible subtypes, including grouping individuals, symptom patterns, or presumed etiologic features. On balance, however, as Keller (1988) concluded, scant evidence supports the utility of contemporary unipolar subtype distinctions in terms of their contributions to treatment, or to understanding the course or etiology.

A theme that has run through most past and current efforts to describe depression subtypes is whether a biological "disease" type can be distinguished from psychosocial "disorder" types. A widely held corollary is that the former types are best treated with somatic interventions, whereas the latter should be treated with psychotherapy. The empirical data, however, do not support either notion. Some years ago, a reactive–endogenous distinction was drawn, with the implication that reactive depressions were caused by stressors and differed qualitatively from endogenous depressions that arose from biological dysfunction of some kind; however, little evidence has supported the validity of this categorical distinction. Depressions preceded by stressors do not necessarily differ in symptoms from those without apparent stressors, whereas depressions characterized by "endogenous" symptoms frequently follow stressful life events. Efforts to define a "situational" subtype retaining the idea of stress-precipitated depression met with mixed results (Hirschfeld, 1981). Although certain symptoms did appear to distinguish stress-induced situational depressions from nonsituational depressions, the groups did not differ on endogenous symptoms, overall recovery rates, or overall stress levels. Therefore, Keller (1988) and Leber, Beckham, and Danker-Brown (1985) concluded that the validity of the situational subtype is questionable.

Endogenous–Nonendogenous Distinction

Although little evidence has supported the idea of "autonomous" or endogenous depressions arising from biological rather than psychological processes, an endogenous–nonendogenous distinction based on qualitative aspects of symptom profiles seems to have some validity (Leber et al., 1985). In DSM-III and DSM-III-R, this concept is retained as "melancholia" so as to avoid an etiologic presumption. However, despite evidence that certain symptom clusters do appear with enough consistency and frequency to warrant such a diagnostic distinction, the meaning and implications are less clear. For instance, studies using Research Diagnostic Criteria (RDC; Spitzer, Endicott, & Robins, 1975) or DSM-III criteria of melancholia have found no evidence of greater presumed genetic loading or family aggregation (Andreasen et al., 1986; Zimmerman, Black, & Coryell, 1989; Zimmerman & Spitzer, 1989), and mixed evidence of differential time to recovery or relapse (Keller, 1988; Zimmerman et al., 1989). The presumption that melancholia marks a type of severe depression particularly responsive to medication or electroconvulsive therapy has not been supported (Zimmerman & Spitzer, 1989). Also, symptom severity is a known correlate of melancholia, but some evidence suggests that it may be merely a severe variant of depression rather than a qualitatively different subtype (reviewed in Zimmerman & Spitzer, 1989).

Partially because of the empirical failure to support the presumed correlates of DSM-III melancholia, the criteria were revised in DSM-III-R to include certain nonsymptom features (e.g., previous good response to somatic therapy, previous major depressive episode with complete recovery, lack of personality disturbance before first episode; Zimmerman & Spitzer, 1989). Using the new criteria, Zimmerman et al. (1989) found that melancholic patients had more severe symptoms only for melancholic signs of depression, but not for nonmelancholic symptoms, thus providing some support for the idea that melancholia, as defined in DSM-III-R, is not merely a more severe depression. Also, the authors found support for their hypothesis that the melancholic subtype is characterized by less stress, less personality disorder, less likelihood of blaming others, and less family history of drug abuse and antisocial personality. Additional work is needed to validate the DSM-III-R version of melancholia.

Seasonal Affective Disorder

In addition to the presumed biological endogenous or melancholic subtype of depression, another possible biological subtype has recently been proposed: seasonal affective disorder (SAD). At a recent workshop sponsored by the National Institute of Mental Health, the syndromal validity of this type of depression was said to be strong, perhaps more so than for melancholia (Blehar & Rosenthal, 1989), although definitive conclusions are not yet warranted. Typified by a pattern of winter depression, the syndrome tends to include atypical depressive symptoms, such as overeating, carbohydrate craving, weight gain, fatigue, and hypersomnia. It appears to occur in both unipolar and bipolar depression. Because SAD has been reported to be effectively treated with phototherapy (exposure to full-spectrum light) and may have a unique pathophysiology related to circadian rhythm disruption (see review by Blehar & Rosenthal, 1989), it could prove to be an important diagnostic subtype.

Neurotic Depression

Another distinction that has been drawn historically is neurotic versus psychotic depression. Unfortunately, the distinction has been described variously as presumed biological (psychotic) versus nonbiological (neurotic) depression or as severe (psychotic) versus mild (neurotic) depression. In DSM-III-R, psychotic depression is marked by the presence of hallucinations, delusions, or thought disorder, along with affective symptoms. The course of psychotic depression appears to be different from that of nonpsychotic depression (Keller, 1988).

Neurotic depression no longer exists in the official DSM usages, having been replaced by the concept of dysthymia, referring to chronic mild depressions. Relatively recent research on possible subtypes of depression, however, appear to have revived an interest in the construct, as a variant of major depression with an implied psychosocial origin. Zimmerman, Coryell, Stangl, and Pfohl (1987) developed operational criteria for a neurotic subtype to classify a series of hospitalized depressed patients. The system included six criteria: personality disorder, psychosocial stressors, age of onset before 40, blaming others for depression, nonserious suicide attempts, and marital separation or divorce. The authors found that neurotic depression, so defined, had low rates of abnormal dexamethasone suppression test results, family history of alcoholism, less improvement in the hospital, and more frequent relapses in a 6-month follow-up. Although neurotic subtyping was negatively associated with DSM-III melancholic features, Zimmerman et al. (1987) viewed the two as orthogonal dimensions and suggested a four-fold dual classification system.

Winokur (1985) also presented criteria for a neurotic subtype that overlap with his concept of depression spectrum disease. The defining features included personality disturbances, evidence of a stormy life-style, and, importantly, familial alcoholism. He essentially excluded persons with significant melancholic symptoms, and he stated that melancholic (endogenous) depression criteria may have less resolving power, defining a more heterogeneous group than a neurotic reactive subtype.

Winokur's Iowa Classification System

Winokur and colleagues proposed subtypes of unipolar depression based on familial constellations rather than on symptom presentation. They proposed three types: familial pure depressive disease, depressive spectrum disease, and sporadic depressive disease (Winokur, 1979). The first type is thought to afflict late-onset males who have male and female first-degree relatives with depression, and the disorder is thought to be severe, frequently becoming chronic. The second type, depressive spectrum disease (largely synonymous with the neurotic–reactive subtype noted above), by contrast, is viewed as typically a female affliction with onset before age 40, and characterized by a history of depression in female relatives but alcoholism and sociopathy in male relatives. This disorder is seen as less severe, and more likely to arise from chaotic life-styles. The sporadic depressive disease type has no history of family psychiatric disorder. Support for these proposed subtypes has been inconsistent (Keller, 1988; Leber et al., 1985). Zimmerman, Coryell, and Pfohl (1986) found evidence that the depressive spectrum disease type over-laps with neurotic depression and that the familial pure depressive disease overlaps with endogenous depression; differences between these groups of patients on psychosocial factors were especially pronounced when stringent criteria for family history of depression and alcoholism were used. There was little support for a separate sporadic depression as distinct from familial pure depressive disease.

Other subtypes

Additional classification systems have been the focus of research and specula-tion over the years. The primary–secondary distinction (E. Robins & Guze, 1972) attempted to determine whether depression appeared chronologically before or after any other nonaffective psychiatric condition. Secondary de-pressions refer to those arising subsequent to anxiety disorder, alcoholism, organic brain syndrome, and the like. Such distinctions are often difficult to make, however, and the clinical utility is questionable; research usages of the distinction aimed at yielding more homogeneous groups may be useful, but the concept has not led to clear findings with respect to differential etiology or course (Leber et al., 1985).

Age of onset has shown some utility in distinguishing among possible subgroups of unipolar depressed individuals, generally suggesting greater family aggregation of depressive disorders in those individuals with earlier onset of depression (Bland, Newman, & Orn, 1986). Bland et al. found that both relatively early age of onset and history of recurrent major depression independently predicted higher rates of depression in first-degree relatives. They proposed that these two dimensions be used to classify unipolar de-pressives in research, and that they may account for the variability that often emerges from morbidity studies when the dimensions are ignored.

Additional subtypes have been proposed for the mild, chronic dys-thymic disorders. Akiskal, Bitar, Puzantian, Rosenthal, and Walker's (1978) work was instrumental among contemporary research in suggesting heterogeneity in mild depressions, and Akiskal (1983) proposed a variety of subtypes differentiated by presumed etiologic and clinical features. Depue and Monroe (1986) subsequently enlarged on the list to suggest five subgroups of dysthymic depressives as a subset of an even larger list of chronic depressions. The validity of these distinctions remains to be estab-lished. Recently, however, Klein, Taylor, Dickstein, and Harding (1988) attempted to investigate the validity of the new DSM-III-R category of primary early-onset dysthymia. Klein et al. (1988) found that such patients, as a group, show high levels of melancholic symptoms and high family rates of affective disorder, and concluded that these patients represent an affective illness that is a relatively severe form of the disorder compared with nonchronic major depressives. Further work on subtypes of chronic depression seems important to pursue.

Overall, it appears that current diagnostic categories of major depression and dysthymia represent highly heterogeneous mixtures of symptom and etiologic pictures. Thus far, attempts to define essential subgroups have proven elusive, but efforts have focused particularly on melancholic–nonmelancholic subtypes, and a potentially orthogonal neurotic–nonneurotic distinction. These distinctions may cut across the severity and chronicity dimensions, and seem to differ with respect to the presence either of early onset, with psychogenic patterns related to chaotic lifestyle or of later onset, with a better premorbid functioning pattern that is less related to life circumstances. Thus, major clinical, treatment, and etiologic breakthroughs in depression must await valid characterization of subtypes.

ETIOLOGIC MODELS OF UNIPOLAR DEPRESSION

Psychological Approaches to Causation

Cognitive Theories

Based on the observation of depressed patients' characteristic negativism, Aaron Beck (1967, 1976) introduced a model that has served as a dominant approach to depression among psychologists for 15 years. Interpretations of the self, events, and the future that are negative, self-deprecating, and pessimistic are seen as causes of dysphoric mood and the related symptoms of depression. The tendency to construe the self and situations in such ways imparts a vulnerability to develop depression, and is thought to arise from traumatic or depriving childhood experiences in which negativistic schemas are formed. Such schemas, viewed in information processing terms, give rise to cognitive distortions in the interpretation of current information (or information retrieved from memory). A somewhat similar cognitive model of depression, evolved from earlier versions of the learned helplessness model (Seligman, 1975), construes depression as arising from the expectation of uncontrollability, a cognition that results from encountering an important personally meaningful event and interpreting it to have been caused by unchanging, global, personal characteristics (Abramson, Alloy, & Metalsky, 1988; Peterson & Seligman, 1984). Such internal, stable, and global causal explanations for events mark the depressive attributional style (Abramson, Seligman, & Teasdale, 1978; Seligman, Abramson, Semmel, & von Baeyer, 1979), which is assumed to be a stable trait, developed over time, including childhood experiences (e.g., Seligman et al., 1984).

Both the cognitive vulnerability approach of Beck and the attributional model of depression have undergone revisions over time (see Abramson et al.,

1988; Hammen, 1988) in response to empirical and conceptual challenges (e.g., Coyne & Gotlib, 1983; Hammen, 1985). Early research generally supported the picture of currently depressed individuals as likely to selectively attend to negative information; construe themselves and their future in disparaging, futile ways; and view the causes of negative events as due to internal, stable, and global characteristics (e.g., Hammen & Krantz, 1985; Sweeney, Anderson, & Bailey, 1986). More recent research, however, has moved away from the largely descriptive, nonclinical, cross-sectional methods of past research to address the critical issue of cognitions as causes of depression. The emergent picture is much less supportive of simple cognitive primacy models. Vulnerability cognitions, including dysfunctional attitudes, self-schemas, automatic negative thoughts, and depressive attributional style, appear to be mood dependent (see review by Barnett & Gotlib, 1988); that is, in contrast to the prediction that underlying vulnerable cognitions predict depression onset in currently nondepressed individuals or remain stable in remitted depressives, a volume of research suggests that negativistic cognitions are instead concomitants of the depressed state. When no longer depressed, individuals appear similar to nondepressed persons in their tendencies to subscribe to negative attitudes, attributions, and other cognitions. On the other hand, dysfunctional cognitions may prolong or intensify dysphoria, even if they do not precipitate a diagnosable onset (e.g., Barnett & Gotlib, 1988; Lewinsohn, Hoberman, & Rosenbaum, 1988).

More promising trends move away from global cognitive bias models of initial onset of depression, toward stress-diathesis approaches, which integrate the appraisals of specific life events and specific kinds of vulnerability cognitions (Abramson et al., 1988; Barnett & Gotlib, 1988; Hammen, 1988). Individuals may have specific domains of the self, such as achievement goals or interpersonal relationships, that are central to self-worth, such that losses and disruptions in these particular contents may be construed as significant depletions that cannot be replaced or coped with effectively, leading to depressive reactions (e.g., Hammen, Ellicott, Gitlin, & Jamison, 1989; Hammen, Marks, deMayo, & Mayol, 1985). Additionally, investigators emphasize the need for more specific models that apply to subtypes of depression and account for differences between onset, maintenance, relapse, and recovery, in contrast to the broad models of the past. There is considerable agreement that appraisals of stressful life events mediate depressive reactions to negative events, so that the cognitive approach continues to exert influence. The mechanisms of operation of this process, whether as schematic information processing or some other mechanism, warrant further research (e.g., Segal, 1988). Pyszczynski and Greenberg (1987) presented an integrative "self-regulatory perseveration" model of depression that is compatible with this approach. It emphasizes self-focused attention as a response to disruptive events that threaten self-esteem. Self-focus, in turn, perpetuates and intensifies depressive cognitions, such as self-blame, that worsen symptoms. This promising integrative approach requires empirical support before taking a place as a major theory of depression.

An additional notable trend in contemporary cognitive models of etiology emphasizes self-processes, the ways in which individuals derive a sense of self-worth from particular goals or objects whose losses or disruptions lead to reduced self-esteem and to the activation of a variety of cognitive processes that intensify self-criticism and selective interpretation of negative information about the self and the world (e.g., Barnett & Gotlib, 1988; Hammen, 1988; Rehm, 1990). In a recent review and metatheoretical analysis of theories of depression, Hyland (1987) noted that most major cognitive theories about depression, whether they focus on self-esteem processes or self-efficacy and control processes, share features and interact in ways that emphasize commonalities, thus prohibiting a view of them as incompatible approaches to depression etiology.

Stressful Life Event Approaches

Research has consistently indicated an association between stressful life events and depression, both in community samples and in patients (e.g., reviews by Billings & Moos, 1982; Lloyd, 1980; Paykel, 1979; Thoits, 1983). The statistical relationship is generally a small one, however, and most individuals who experience even major disruptions in their lives do not show clinically significant depression. The observed overall associations may be influenced especially by individuals with histories of past depression or chronic symptoms (e.g., Depue & Monroe, 1986; Hammen, Mayol, deMayo, & Marks, 1986; Lewinsohn et al., 1988). Improved methods of assessing both episodic and chronic stressors have contributed to developments in this area (Brown & Harris, 1978; Thoits, 1983). Most of the recent research, however, has focused on conceptual development: clarification of aspects of stressors and the processes by which they affect lives. Exploration of mediators, such as individual appraisals, personality characteristics, social supports, and coping, has also improved the prediction of responses to stressors (see Billings, Cronkite, & Moos, 1983; Brown & Harris, 1978; Lazarus & Folkman, 1984; Paykel, 1979; Thoits, 1983).

Increasingly, the concept of "meaning" has been incorporated into stress–depression models (reviewed in Hammen, 1988), moving away from the simple notion that change causes illness, including depression, because of the burden placed on the individual's adaptive mechanisms. Instead, investigators emphasize the role of meaning of events, the individual appraisals of the impact and implications of events. Emphasis on the meaning of events with respect to self-worth as a unique predictor of depression has grown (Brown & Harris, 1978; Oatley & Bolton, 1985; Pyszczynski & Greenberg, 1987; Thoits, 1983). The work of George Brown and colleagues has been especially influential, due both to painstaking methods of assessing and dating stressors in the context of respondents' lives, and to the rich and integrative analysis of multiple psychosocial factors. This work demonstrates the significance to depression onset of highly personally stressful events, especially those occurring in the context of chronic ongoing difficulties and those that may make the individual feel hopeless (Brown, Bifulco, & Harris, 1987; Brown & Harris, 1978).

The inherently cognitive emphasis on meaning opens the door for a profitable integration with other psychological models of depression. Recent focus on processes relevant to the self emphasizes interpretations of stressors with respect to personal meaning (e.g., Abramson et al., 1988; Arieti & Bemporad, 1980; Linville, 1985; Thoits, 1983) and invites integration of life stress, role functioning, social characteristics, personality, and developmental processes. Hammen (1989) describes a cognitive–environmental perspective in which depression is the specific response to interpretations that stressful life events deplete beliefs in self-worth and self-efficacy. Such appraisals can be predicted from characteristic attitudes, beliefs, and memories, and are hypothesized to arise in the context of family relationships in which dysfunctional mother–child communications contribute to vulnerable self-regard (Hammen et al., 1989; Hammen & Goodman-Brown, 1990; Hammen et al., 1985). A related example of an integrative approach is Barnett and Gotlib's (1988) emphasis on psychosocial deficits as a vulnerability factor in depression. Noting that dependency and introversion, low social integration, and marital distress have been found to be common in depressed persons, the authors argued that the depression may result from disruption of the interpersonal domain in which self-esteem may be overinvested without sufficient alternative roles as a source of compensatory self-regard.

Two additional areas concerning stressors warrant mention because of continuing research activities. Loss of a parent in childhood has been hypothesized to be a stressful event uniquely predictive of depressive reactions in adulthood. The research has yielded inconsistent results that vary according to whether loss is due to death or separation, quality of assessments, and use of appropriate controls. One well-controlled study examined 300 patients and indicated a significantly higher rate of permanent separation from both mothers and fathers for depressed patients than for medical controls (Roy, 1985). Recent research has suggested that it is likely not loss itself, but rather the quality of parental relationships and family support that follow loss of a parent that may be associated with vulnerability to adult psychopathology, especially depression (Breier et al., 1988).

An additional stressful situation that appears to be highly predictive of depression, at least in children, is having a mother with an affective disorder (Hammen, Gordon, et al., 1987; Weissman, 1988). Although this situation is commonly construed as reflecting a genetic basis of depression, offspring research, as well as retrospective reports by adult depressives about their childhoods, implicates dysfunctional, negative, and critical mother–child relationships and communication as contributors to children's depression (Gordon et al., 1989). Additionally, women with affective disorders are frequently highly stressed both as a cause and as a consequence of their disorders, and even stressed women without major affective disorders have increased risk of children with depression and other forms of psychopathology (e.g., Hammen, Adrian, et al., 1987; Hammen, Burge, & Stansbury, 1990; Holahan & Moos, 1987). Thus, both general stressful conditions and, specifically, disturbed parent–child relationships, appear to contribute to risk for depression.

In sum, ample evidence supports the role of psychosocial stressors in depression, their impact mediated by cognitions concerning their meaning and consequences; however, the search for vulnerability factors continues. The trend appears to be away from simple, unidirectional, grand theories, toward more integrative, complex models concerning specific aspects of depression's course or subtypes. As discussed next, similar trends are occurring in the search for biological origins of depression.

Biological Models of Depression

Genetic Transmission of Depression

The traditional twin, adoption, and family study methodologies have supported to some extent the hypothesis of heritability of depressive disorders. The findings are not as strong or consistent as those for bipolar disorders, however, and frequently must be qualified by characteristics of the depression being investigated. Twin studies generally show higher concordance for monozygotic (MZ) than dizygotic (DZ) twin pairs; however, as Torgersen (1986) found in his twin study, heritability could not be demonstrated for certain forms of major depression and for milder forms, such as dysthymic disorder. Adoption studies have been relatively rare, but have not clearly supported the case for heritability, except for severe forms of depression occurring in the biological relatives (Wender et al., 1986). Wender et al. (1986) did not find significant differences between biological and adoptive families of depressed probands in milder forms of depression.

Family studies of depression in relatives of patients with depression provide the most consistent data supporting genetic hypotheses. In a recent review, Goldin and Gershon (1988) noted that, across four studies based on direct interviews of first-degree relatives of unipolar patients, probands' families had significantly higher rates of unipolar depression than did control families. The authors pointed out, however, that such familial aggregations do not rule out environmental explanations (see the previous discussion of children of depressed mothers).

The extensive work of Weissman and colleagues on genetic epidemiology points to the likelihood of depressive subgroup differences in familial patterns (Weissman et al., 1986). They found that early-onset (before age 30) concomitant anxiety disorder and secondary alcoholism were independently related to increased family risk for major depression. Other traditional subtypes, such as endogenous, delusional, melancholic, and recurrent depression, were not associated with greater rates of depression in families of probands. Others (e.g., Andreasen et al., 1986) have also found that endogenous depression is not associated with increased risk for family aggregation of depression, compared with nonendogenous depressed probands.

Recent developments in molecular genetics using recombinant deoxyribonucleic acid (DNA) techniques for mapping genes have produced hundreds of markers that can be studied to determine if they are linked to hypothesized genetically transmitted disorders. The most common method is to investigate the statistical likelihood of linkage of disease genes and marker loci in large families, where linkage would lead to an association in predictable ways that would not occur in the general population. Goldin and Gershon (1988) reviewed the relatively few such studies of families of unipolar depressed patients, and concluded that there was no evidence of linkage. They noted, however, that the heterogeneity of unipolar depression and the possibility of diagnostic variation in the studies precluded firm conclusions. Linkage studies would be very difficult for heterogeneous disorders, and it is likely that polygenic modes of transmission are involved rather than single loci (e.g., Goldin & Gershon, 1988). Overall, therefore, a meeting of investigators of family and genetic aspects of affective disorders noted that, although certain subtypes of unipolar disorders may aggregate in families, considerably more research is needed to identify clear genetic transmission. Moreover, nongenetic factors that may modify the expression of the disorders must be vigorously pursued (Blehar, Weissman, Gershon, & Hirschfeld, 1988).

Neurochemical Abnormalities

Investigation of neurotransmitter systems in the brain has had a long and active history in the search for biological bases of affective disorders. Successful treatment of major depression by antidepressants encouraged the development of the monoamine hypothesis in the 1960s, based on the observation that functional levels of norepinephrine and serotonin in the synaptic cleft were increased with antidepressant medications. Other observations were also consistent with the hypothesis of depression as a functional deficiency of such monoamine neurotransmitters (and mania as an excess of catecholamines). The deficiency was believed to arise in various ways: decreased synthesis or increased degradation, impaired reuptake, and changes in the sensitivity or number of receptors. Subsequently, numerous studies of the metabolites of norepinephrine, especially 3-methoxy-4-hydroxylphenylglycol (MHPG), revealed inconsistent and contradictory findings (Thase, Frank, & Kupfer, 1985). Dopamine, another catecholamine, has also been studied widely in major depression, although with ambiguous interpretation of results. Thase and Howland (1989) reviewed the results of additional studies of neurotransmitters, such as serotonin, and acetylcholine, which is known to interact with monoamines, noting evidence of cholinergic hyperactivity in depression. They concluded that there is insufficient support for the original monoamine hypothesis of depression, noting that complex interrelationships between neurotransmitters and other biological systems likely preclude a simple deficit model.

Subsequent research on the effects of antidepressants has also undermined the simple monoamine uptake theories of depression. Studies of the effects of antidepressant medications, for example, have noted that the clinical effects develop more slowly than the immediate neurochemical effects, and that some of the newer generation of antidepressants do not have effects on the uptake of norepinephrine or other hypothesized mechanisms consistent with the monoamine deficit theory (McNeal & Cimbolic, 1986). Indeed, as McNeal and Cimbolic noted, the long-term effects of antidepressants seem to be lower postsynaptic beta-adrenergic receptor density and sensitivity, and other receptors also seem to be altered. Such time-related changes, along with evidence of highly complex interactions between neurotransmitters and neuroendocrine functioning, have led Siever and Davis (1985) to postulate a dysregulation hypothesis of depression, rather than simple increases or decreases in noradrenergic activity. Dysregulation refers to impairment in neurotransmitter homeostatic regulatory mechanisms, and Siever and Davis (1985) outlined specific criteria for testing such a model, indicating at least preliminary support from clinical and animal model data. The dysregulation concept, if not its specific content, appears to be widely echoed in contemporary biological research, with acknowledgment of complex interactions between systems that are believed to be implicated in the etiology of depression (e.g., Ballenger, 1988; Gold, Goodwin, & Chrousos, 1988a; Thase & Howland, 1989).

Neuroendocrine Hypotheses

The contiguity and interconnection between the hypothalamus and pituitary glands on the one hand, and between centers of the brain that regulate vegetative functions (e.g., appetite and sleep) that commonly mark major symptoms of depression on the other hand, contributed to an interest in the potential link between the hypothalamic–pituitary–adrenal cortex axis (HPA) and depression. It is also known that certain disorders of the endocrinological system are associated with depression. Studies of HPA functioning, therefore, have been common, and have clearly indicated dysregulation. The most consistent finding has been cortisol hypersecretion; however, disinhibition of nocturnal secretion of cortisol and loss of normal circadian variation of cortisol have also been observed (Ballenger, 1988; Thase & Howland, 1989). Gold, Goodwin, and Chrousos (1988b) cited evidence to support the hypothesis of a defect at the level of the hypothalamus, resulting in the hypersecretion of corticotropin-releasing hormone (CRH). Because neurohormones modulate the influence of neurotransmitters, Gold and colleagues emphasized the mutual influence of CRH and the locus ceruleus–norepinephrine systems, suggesting that the CRH neuron may provide a final common pathway in melancholic depression for various disturbances in central nervous system functioning. Because of the association between stress and disruption of HPA functioning, Gold et al. (1988b) argued that melancholic depression arises from an acute generalized stress response that has escaped the usual homeostatic restraint mechanisms.

The common finding of cortisol dysregulation in major depression contributed to the widely heralded dexamethasone suppression test (DST) as the first psychiatric "test" of a presumed biological disorder. Initial enthusiasm has given way, however, to criticism and caution (Ballenger, 1988; Thase & Howland, 1989). The DST has turned out to be neither sufficiently sensitive nor specific to depression to be of major clinical relevance. Abnormal cortisol functioning appears to be related to increasing age, certain stressful conditions, drug and alcohol abuse, and other circumstances (Ballenger, 1988; Thase & Howland, 1989), and DST nonsuppression is not a reliable predictor of clinical response to antidepressant medication, as was once hoped. Despite the disappointing results of the DST experience, considerable work continues on a variety of neuroendocrinological fronts (see Thase & Howland, 1989).

Circadian Rhythm Dysfunction

Certain characteristics of depression have lent support to speculations of chronobiological abnormalities as causal factors. For example, depressed patients are frequently observed to enter rapid eye movement (REM) sleep unusually early, termed "shortened REM latency" (reviewed in Ballenger, 1988; Gold et al., 1988a), a sleep change possibly attributable to disruptions in the circadian rhythm. Other phenomena that suggest chronobiological rhythm disruptions in depression include changes in cortisol secretion, seasonal patterns of symptomatology in subgroups of patients, sleep disruption, diurnal variation in mood, and antidepressant-induced rapid cycling. Recently, several investigators studied circadian rhythms, 24-hour variations in sleeping, waking, body temperature, endocrine function, and neural activity. Two subsystems apparently oscillate independently. One, regulating sleep–wake cycles, is controlled by a "weak" generator located in the suprachiasmatic nuclei of the hypothalamus and neurally connected to the retina, pineal gland, and limbic system. The other, regulating body temperature, REM sleep, and cortisol secretion, appears to be controlled by a different generator. One theory (Wehr & Goodwin, 1981) is that an advance in the timing of the circadian rhythms can be attributed to a phase advance of the strong oscillator (body temperature, REM propensity, and cortisol secretion) in relation to the weak oscillator (sleep–wake cycle). This dissociation may account for early morning awakening and diurnal mood variation (reviewed in Thase & Howland, 1989). Preliminary evidence supporting the phase advance theory in the etiology of depression beyond the sleep pattern data includes nocturnal hypercortisolemia and early onset of cortisol secretion during sleep in some patients (Thase & Howland, 1989). Additionally, antidepressant effects following sleep deprivation to reset the abnormally advanced circadian rhythm have been reported (e.g., Wehr & Wirz-Justice, 1982). Additional studies, however, including those on body temperature regulation, are consistent with a blunting or dysregulation of the circadian rhythm, rather than with phase advance (see review by Healy & Williams, 1988; Thase & Howland, 1989).

Circadian rhythms may also be implicated in neurochemical functioning, possibly related to receptor density or sensitivity in certain cities. These rhythms are affected by certain hormones, such as estrogen, and may be altered by antidepressant medications (reviewed in Thase & Howland, 1989).

The finding of seasonal patterns of mood disorders with regular annual cycles in certain individuals, apparently associated with changes in daylight, has been interpreted by some to reflect faulty entrainment of circadian rhythms. The hormone melatonin has been implicated in the process, although recently its role has been challenged (Sack, Rosenthal, Parry, & Wehr, 1987). Moreover, as Thase and Howland (1989) reported, patients with seasonal affective disorders often have a bipolar form of affective disorder, and generally do not show biological abnormalities consistent with disrupted circadian rhythms.

Thase and Howland (1989) reminded us that the complex regulatory and inhibitory relationships between neurotransmitters argue against isolated deficits as etiologic factors. They also noted that the heterogeneity of depression, with many findings relatively more robust for endogenous or melancholic subtypes, is consistent with a need for multiple etiologic models. Nevertheless, they concluded that, at a general level, there is "compelling evidence of the existence of some underlying neurochemically mediated regulatory disturbance(s) involving the limbic system in many depressed patients" (p. 34). Whether such disturbances are causes or consequences of depression is unclear, however. As Thase et al. (1985) noted, the kinds of biological irregularities that may be found in depression, especially severe depression, do not necessarily indicate etiologic processes; that is, there is relatively little evidence that many of the biological disturbances are enduring trait markers, or consequences rather than state markers of the depressed condition. As such, some of the abnormalities may represent epiphenomena; alternatively, they may reflect the results of some additional unknown processes. As in most areas of research on psychopathology, therefore, improvements in theory-driven investigations, including longitudinal studies, will increase our confidence in the implications of research for etiologic processes.

Integrations of Biological and Psychological Approaches

Although many investigators from both biological and psychosocial perspectives acknowledge the contributions of the alternative perspectives, only relatively recently have truly integrative models begun to appear. None is conceptually elaborated or empirically grounded to date, but they are worth noting briefly as important directions for new research. A selected sample of provocative approaches is noted briefly.

Linking early childhood family disruption following parental loss to incidence of adult psychopathology (observed to be affective disorders in 86 percent of subjects), Breier et al. (1988) found that cortisol and adrenocorticotropic hormone (ACTH) levels were significantly correlated with reported disruption. They found that subjects with childhood parental loss who evidenced lifetime psychopathology had significantly increased plasma cortisol and beta-endorphin immunoreactivity compared with those having no significant psychopathology. Because the majority of individuals diagnosed with lifetime incidence of disorder were asymptomatic at testing, Breier et al. argued that the changes were permanent responses to childhood loss. The stress of early loss and disruption may result in enduring neurobiological alterations in the form of increased HPA activity that may represent a predisposition or vulnerability marker for depression. The authors noted the large body of nonhuman species studies of neurobiological changes associated with early parental separation.

Post, Rubinow, and Ballenger (1984) discussed features of the course of affective disorders, such as recurrence, and possible increasing independence of stressors and recurrence, in terms of phenomena of sensitization, kindling, and conditioning, based largely on animal research. These authors contended that stressors may alter neurochemical activity such that early and/or repeated exposures to stress sensitize or condition the person to respond with biochemical, physiologic, and behavioral features of an affective response. Eventually, affective reactions may be triggered merely by anticipatory cognitions, interpretations of current events, and images associated with previous depressive onsets. This approach, although not directly tested, is intriguingly compatible with research on the course of depression, especially implicating aversive childhood experiences as altering the brain and thereby the likelihood of recurring adult depressions. The model includes the role of cognitive interpretations in precipitating affective reactions.

Recently, Healy and Williams (1988) proposed that psychological factors, such as perceptions of helplessness, may disrupt circadian rhythms, and that such disruption may account for symptoms of endogenous depression. Although compatible with certain research from animal models, this hypothesis requires direct investigation. Similarly, Ehlers, Frank, and Kupfer (1988) hypothesized that one way to integrate biological and psychosocial models is to consider the impact that severe life events may have in disrupting circadian rhythms. To the extent that biological clocks are partially entrained to social patterns (social zeitgebers), loss of social relationships or major roles may affect biologically vulnerable circadian systems.

Gold et al. (1988b) suggested that melancholic depression is a response to a generalized physiological stress reaction that has escaped the counterregulatory restraints aimed at preventing excessive activation. According to this model, the corticotropin-releasing hormone and locus ceruleus–norepinephrine systems are the biological effectors of the generalized stress response, and Gold et al. cited evidence that these systems are dysregulated in melancholic depression. The causes of such dysregulation are unclear, but could be due to inherited defects in the neurohormonal regulation of stress. The authors further argued that early life stress experiences may lead to sensitization and/or damage to systems that regulate neurohormonal functioning. In this way, stressful conditions and biology interact to produce vulnerability to recurrent bouts of melancholic depression. Although considerable research on humans is needed to test elements of this model, it is particularly noteworthy for its potential integration of biological, stress, and cognitive–developmental approaches to major depression.

NATURAL HISTORY OF UNIPOLAR DEPRESSION

Information about the natural history of depression must be recognized as based on samples of unknown generality to the entire population of depressive experiences. The reason is that the studies of the course of unipolar depression are based on treated samples of individuals attending clinics or university facilities. Because the majority of depressed individuals do not seek treatment, it is unclear whether treated samples have the same characteristics as individuals who are not included in study samples. Also, the untreated course of disorder cannot be known in such groups. Moreover, very few longitudinal studies exist.

Age of Onset

Although it was once believed that unipolar depression was primarily a disorder of middle age, it is now seen that the age of onset varies widely in the adult years. For instance, Lewinsohn, Duncan, Stanton, and Hautzinger (1986) dated community residents' episodes of various RDC unipolar diagnoses and found that the onsets were very low in childhood, increased dramatically in adolescence, peaked in middle age, and decreased sharply in the elderly years. Although the sample was not representative (it was self-selected), the patterns nonetheless generally agree with recent epidemiological surveys based on random samples that find the highest rates of diagnosable depression in young- and middle-adult years (e.g., L.N. Robins et al., 1984). Some even argue that the ages of onset for depression are decreasing, with growing numbers of depressed young adults (e.g., Klerman et al., 1985).

Some evidence indicates that earlier onset of depression predicts a more negative course (Bland et al., 1986; Klein et al., 1988). Lewinsohn, Fenn, Stanton, and Franklin (1986), however, did not find that earlier onset was associated with longer duration of episodes. Evidence also indicates that childhood depression, although relatively rare, may nevertheless predict high rates of recurrence, chronicity, and psychosocial impairment (Kovacs, Feinberg, Crouse-Novak, Paulauskas, & Finkelstein, 1984).

Duration

Major depressive episodes have generally been considered time limited, and most people recover without the need for professional help. Clayton (1984) summarized research on duration and concluded that most depressions last 10 to 11 months. Keller, Shapiro, Lavori, and Wolfe (1982a) found that 64 percent of help-seeking patients had recovered within 6 months of entry into their study. Lewinsohn, Fenn, et al. (1986), in a community rather than treatment sample, found that about 40 percent of major or minor depressions lasted less than 3 months. In a later section on treatment, issues concerning the length of episodes can be seen to take on both theoretical and practical significance.

Number of Episodes and Typical Course

It has become apparent in recent research that depression is a recurrent disorder (Zis & Goodwin, 1979). Keller (1985) reported that between 50 and 85 percent of patients with one major episode who seek treatment will have at least one additional episode. Clayton (1984) estimated that 85 percent of hospitalized depressed patients will have more than one episode. Angst et al. (1973) estimated that the mean number of lifetime episodes of depression is five or six. Angst (1984) reported that, in his 20-year longitudinal study of 190 unipolar patients, they spent about 20 percent of their lives in episodes after onset of the disorder. Although, as Clayton (1984) noted, most unipolar depressed individuals experience depressions separated by symptom-free intervals of years, there is growing recognition that a sizeable subset experience intermittent or chronic symptoms and impairment (this topic will be reviewed under "Complications in the Course of Disorder").

Angst (1984) suggested that, over the course of affective disorders, episodes recur with shorter intervals. Although not a great deal of information is available about the predictors of the timing of recurrences, Ezquiaga, Gutierrez, and Lopez (1987) suggested that earlier episodes are more reactive to stressful life events whereas later episodes are less so (or react to milder stressors). In general, it is widely acknowledged that the best predictor of future episodes is past depression (e.g., Clayton, 1984; Hammen et al., 1986; Lewinsohn et al., 1988). Further discussion of predictors of relapse is presented in the next section.

COMPLICATIONS IN THE COURSE OF DISORDER

Chronicity

One significant complication of unipolar depression is chronic symptomatology, which has been estimated to occur in at least 25 percent of cases (e.g., Depue & Monroe, 1986). For instance, in their longitudinal study of patients with unipolar major depression, Keller, Lavori, Rice, Coryell, and Hirschfeld (1986) found that approximately 20 percent of patients failed to recover after a recurrent episode following initial recovery from the index episode. Over time, this led to a 30 percent cumulative rate of chronicity in their sample. Recent reports of chronicity are higher than the rate of 15 percent initially reported by E. Robins and Guze (1972), and indicate the likelihood of substantial ongoing impairment for a significant minority of individuals with major depressive episodes.

Research on the predictors of chronicity is made difficult by the heterogeneity of this construct, as indicated earlier. For example, Akiskal et al. (1978) found that secondary depression was far more associated with chronicity than was primary depression. According to Akiskal, King, Rosenthal, Robinson, and Scott-Strauss (1981), however, chronic depressions may vary by early or late onset, by presence or absence of major depressive episodes, and by association with preexisting illness (secondary) or not (primary).

Within the category of primary chronic depression, both features of the course of illness and psychosocial factors apparently predict chronicity. For instance, Keller, Lavori, Rice, et al. (1986) found that previous *duration* of major episodes, but not *number* of episodes, was associated with increased likelihood of chronicity. Severity of episode was not associated with likelihood of chronicity (Akiskal, 1982; Keller, Lavori, Rice, et al., 1986). Keller, Lavori, Rice, et al. (1986) also found that older age at relapse and low family income predicted protracted course of symptoms. Akiskal (1982) found that chronicity was correlated with family history of affective disorder, as well as with a variety of current psychosocial stressful conditions. Hirschfeld, Klerman, Andreasen, Clayton, and Keller (1986), however, did not find differences between matched chronic and recovered depressives on stressful life events or role functioning, but they did find that chronic depressed persons were more dissatisfied with their major life role. Also, they found that chronic depressives showed certain personality differences, reflective of poorer ego resiliency and higher neuroticism, but noted that such differences are not indicators of premorbid functioning and may reflect differences in current symptoms. Interestingly, there is some indication that chronicity may also reflect lack of adequate treatment. Both Berti Ceroni, Neri, and Pezzoli (1984) and Keller, Lavori, Rice, et al. (1986) found that a substantial subset of chronic major depressed patients were not treated, suggesting that the course might have been different had they been vigorously treated early in the depression.

Relapse and Recurrence

Another complication of major depression is the relatively high likelihood of developing new episodes (or experiencing exacerbation of symptoms). In a recent review, Belsher and Costello (1988) noted that the trends in various studies converge: Around 20 percent of individuals relapse at 2 months postrecovery, increasing to 30 percent at 6 months, and stabilizing at about 50 percent relapse within 2 years. Keller (1988) reported that, by 5 years, 76 percent of patients in their NIMH sample had experienced a recurrence.

In general, the patterns suggest that the period of greatest risk is the few months after recovery from the previous episode (e.g., Keller, 1988). Most of the studies indicate that the longer a person stays well, the less likely he or she is to relapse (Belsher & Costello, 1988; Keller, 1988). Also, individuals with more previous episodes have significantly higher probabilities of recurrence (Belsher & Costello, 1988; Keller, 1988).

Psychosocial predictors of recurrence include stressful life events that follow initial recovery, but there are conflicting results regarding demographic characteristics, such as age and gender (reviewed in Belsher & Costello, 1988). For instance, Lewinsohn, Hoberman, and Rosenbaum (1988) recently reported higher relapse rates among young women in their community sample, whereas earlier studies found no gender effects. Additionally, evidence is growing that lack of supportive relationships with family members is associated with increased likelihood of recurrence of depression (Hooley, Orley, & Teasdale, 1986; Vaughn & Leff, 1976).

The condition termed "double depression," the superimposition of a major depression on a preexisting dysthymic disorder, should be mentioned. Keller, Lavori, Endicott, Coryell, and Klerman (1983) found that 25 percent of more than 300 patients they followed evidenced this pattern, and that the course of disorder is particularly pernicious for this group. For instance, although these patients are more likely to recover from their major depression within 2 years than are those with major depression alone, they have higher rates of relapse into major depression, and they relapse faster. Also, nearly 60 percent remained chronically symptomatic even after recovering from the major depression (Hirschfeld, 1984; Keller, 1988).

Bipolar Outcomes

A significant minority of individuals diagnosed with unipolar depression may, on follow-up, turn out to evidence hypomania or even mania, although mania is not truly a "complication" of unipolar disorders in the sense of causality. For instance, the NIMH Consensus Development Conference on Pharmacologic Prevention of Recurrences estimated the rate to be about 15 percent (NIMH/NIH, 1985). Not only would a past clinical history of hypomanic symptoms identify such bipolar patients, but also possible predictors might include age (not yet through the age of risk for development of bipolar disorders), family history of bipolar disorder, and pharmacologically induced hypomania.

Health and Mortality

Apart from the extreme debilitation of the symptomatology of depression and the disruptive effects on social and work adjustment of recurrent and chronic symptoms, depression may also prove to be life threatening. Suicidal thoughts are, of course, a serious symptom of the depression syndrome, and depression is, indeed, a risk factor for suicide. For instance, Hirschfeld and Davidson (1988) reviewed a number of studies of suicide among psychiatric patients, and noted that depression was the most common diagnosis. Brent, Kupfer, Bromet, and Dew (1988) indicated that psychological autopsy studies report that between 40 and 70 percent of suicide victims have an affective disorder (including bipolar disorder), and that follow-up studies of patients with affective disorder indicate that 10 to 15 percent go on to commit suicide. Although there are a variety of empirical predictors of suicide (see Brent et al., 1988; Hirschfeld & Davidson, 1988), it is noteworthy that hopelessness, another symptom of the depression syndrome, seems particularly associated with suicidal thinking and completed suicide (e.g., Beck, Steer, Kovacs, & Garrison, 1985).

Other research suggests that depressive disorders in patients are associated with increased mortality, due not only to suicide, but also to accidents and medical illness (e.g., Tsuang & Simpson, 1985). A recent community study of individuals followed for 16 years indicated 1.5 times the number of deaths in depressed compared with nondepressed individuals, with depressed men showing significantly higher risk than depressed women. These differences occurred even after the effects of age and baseline physical disorders were controlled, and appeared to apply to medical causes as well as to "unnatural" deaths (Murphy, Monson, Olivier, Sobol, & Leighton, 1987). Recent research on immune functioning, although in its infancy and yielding inconsistent results, suggests a possible link between depression and altered immunological responding in at least some subtypes of depression (e.g., Schleifer, Keller, Bond, Cohen, & Stein, 1989).

CLINICAL MANAGEMENT

Somatic Treatments

Antidepressant Medication

Since their introduction to the United States in the late 1950s, tricyclic antidepressants (TCAs) have been widely and effectively used to treat depression. Currently, approximately seven such drugs, along with four of the new generation heterocyclic preparations and three monoamine oxidase inhibitors (MAOIs), are in use. In general, the tricyclics are reported to have about 65 to 75 percent effectiveness compared with placebos in controlled blind trials (Klein et al., 1988; Prien, 1988). No one drug appears to be superior in efficacy to the others, and selection between cyclic medications seems to be largely a matter of clinical judgment based on previous history of response and side effect and symptom profiles (Gitlin, 1990; Prien, 1988). These are highly important clinical matters, concerning such judgments as how suicidal the individual may be, tolerance for delay in treatment efficacy (since it commonly takes up to 2 weeks or more for the medications to have observable effects), and medical contraindications (reviewed in Gitlin, 1990). Nonresponse on one drug is likely to lead to trials on a different one that may differ in serotonergic or noradrenergic properties. Typical dosages are reported in Gitlin (1990). A clear relationship between blood level and response has been established only for nortriptyline, imipramine, and probably desipramine (Joyce & Paykel, 1989).

Indications for use of tricyclic medications include moderate depression (Joyce & Paykel, 1989), but mildly depressed patients may also respond as long as initial symptom levels are not *too* low (e.g., Hamilton scores below 12; Paykel, Freeling, & Hollyman, 1988). There is some controversy about whether those with more severe and endogenous symptoms are better responders (Prien, 1988) or not (Joyce & Paykel, 1989, note that moderate levels of endogenous symptoms may mark better responding). There appears to be agreement that psychomotor retardation is a good predictor of response, whereas agitation is a poor prognostic indicator (Joyce & Paykel, 1989). In addition, depression with psychotic features does not seem to respond well to TCAs (Joyce & Paykel, 1989; Prien, 1988), but may be more effectively treated with electroconvulsive therapy or a combination of antidepressants and antipsychotic medications.

So-called atypical depressions and depressions not responsive to TCAs are commonly treated with MAOIs, with report of efficacy compared with placebos in controlled trials. There is considerable variation in what is considered to be atypical depression, but recent reviews suggest that MAOIs may be especially effective, compared with TCAs, in depressed patients with significant anxiety symptoms, especially panic attacks (Joyce & Paykel, 1989; Prien, 1988). Joyce and Paykel (1989) noted that additional studies of MAOIs in patients with endogenous or more severe symptoms are needed, especially with higher dosages than in past research. Decision rules for switching between medications or combining drugs in unresponsive patients are reported in Gitlin (1990) and Prien (1988).

Additional factors that have been associated with responsiveness to antidepressants include features of the course of disorder and psychosocial variables. For instance, Joyce and Paykel's (1989) review suggests that longer duration, more previous episodes, and more abrupt onset predict a poorer response to medication. There is also consensus that depressed individuals with significant personality disorders, and with neurotic, histrionic, and hypochondriacal traits respond less well to TCAs (Joyce & Paykel, 1989). There is no evidence, however, that "situational" depressions apparently precipitated by adverse circumstances respond less well to medications than do alleged biological depressions (Joyce & Paykel, 1989; Prien, 1988).

The search for biological markers that predict responsiveness to medications has been fueled by the original monoamine hypothesis of depression (reviewed above). It has become clear, however, that no simple theory can account either for depression or for the mechanisms by which the various antidepressant medications have their effects. The widely heralded DST as a marker of cortisol nonsuppression has generally failed to identify groups of patients who respond better to medications than other patients (Joyce & Paykel, 1989), although these authors suggest that DST nonsuppressors may do better with biological treatment than with psychotherapy. Additionally, there is little consistent evidence of a predictive relationship between other biological markers and effectiveness of specific antidepressants (Joyce & Paykel, 1989).

Continuation treatment after the initial control of acute symptoms appears to be important, since controlled studies comparing continuing antidepressants with switching to placebos have shown high rates of relapse in placebo subjects (Prien, 1988). Typically, such symptoms recurred within a short time after drug withdrawal. As Prien (1988) noted, it is not known whether antidepressants primarily suppress symptoms until the episode runs its natural course, or whether they actually shorten the episode. Thus, the duration of the continuation treatment is a matter of clinical judgment, usually indicating several months of symptom-free functioning before discontinuation. Important research activities are ongoing to identify markers of relapse that might identify those at particular risk of recurrence (e.g., Prien & Kupfer, 1986).

In addition to continuation treatment after initial acute symptoms abate, other issues concern maintenance treatment for the long-term prevention of recurrence, and treatment of chronic depression. Preventive treatment is often warranted because of the high likelihood of numerous recurrences in some individuals with major depression. The Consensus Development Conference on Mood Disorders: Pharmacologic Prevention of Recurrences (NIMH/NIH, 1985) noted that both TCAs and lithium have demonstrated effectiveness in the prevention of recurrent depression. Prien (1988) noted that clinical judgment determines who is a candidate for preventive treatment, acknowledging the empirically established relationship between episode frequency and risk of recurrence. Thus, someone who may have had two or more episodes relatively close together and who responded well to prior TCA medication, might be considered for preventive maintenance dosages. He further noted that there appear to be no advantages to the use of lithium for this purpose, except in cases with suspected bipolar disorder, and that prior responsiveness to antidepressant medications would indicate continuation on the same drug (Prien, 1988).

Treatment of chronic depression has been far less studied, and is additionally complicated by the heterogeneity of such individuals, with a high likelihood of comorbid disorders. Akiskal (1983) speculated that two subtypes that are likely to be responsive to medications (as well as to require psychotherapy) are the late-onset chronic depressions that are unrecovered major depressions, and the early-onset subaffective primary depression. To date, however, there is no empirical validation of these hypotheses. Kocsis et al. (1988) reported the only known placebo-controlled double-blind study of response to antidepressants in a chronic sample. Their chronic patients responded significantly better to imipramine than to placebo; however, nearly all of their chronic depressives met criteria for major depression (moderate severity). Thus, medication treatment for milder chronic depressives remains relatively unexplored.

Two final issues of major clinical relevance concerning medication are "aggressiveness" of treatment and compliance with medication regimen. It has always been known that the majority of depressive episodes go untreated, but surprisingly it has also been shown that those who are treated may not receive adequate trials of medication when they are referred for somatotherapy. For example, Keller, Lavori, Klerman, et al. (1986) recently examined treatment of carefully diagnosed patients referred to the NIMH–Clinical Research Branch Collaborative Program on the Psychobiology of Depression: Clinical Study at Five U.S. Sites. They found that only 49 percent of inpatients and 19 percent of outpatients received at least 200 milligrams of imipramine or its equivalent for 4 consecutive weeks. Thirty-one percent of inpatients and 53 percent of outpatients received either no antidepressants or very low or unsustained levels. The authors concluded that depressed patients were substantially undertreated, and that treatment was not related to patient characteristics. They could not account for the findings, other than to speculate that research results from published articles are not finding their way into clinical practice.

The other difficulty with medication use is the suspected rate of noncompliance. This phenomenon has been much more extensively studied in bipolar samples taking maintenance lithium, and has been reported to be as high as 57 percent in terms of patients not taking the medication at the prescribed dosage or frequency, or refusing the medication altogether (Cochran, 1986). Apparently stemming from beliefs about undesirability of medication control of moods and reactions to side effects, as well as resistance to the idea of a psychological disorder, especially one with chronic or recurrent features, potential noncompliance requires physician monitoring and direct discussion in many cases.

Electroconvulsive Therapy (ECT)

Because of past abuses and medical complications, because it is an invasive procedure, and because of the general effectiveness of antidepressant medication, the use of ECT as a primary treatment for major depression has declined substantially over the past decades. However, it remains the treatment of choice under certain conditions: where there are prominent psychotic or melancholic features of depression and especially where severe depression has not responded to medication; where severe, life-threatening situations require rapid response; and where prior clinical response to ECT has been positive (Weiner & Coffey, 1988). These authors reviewed the treatment efficacy studies, and concluded that controlled studies, including the use of sham ECT, strongly support the antidepressant properties of ECT. As for antidepressant medications, however, the neurobiological mechanisms accounting for the effectiveness of ECT are not known (Sackheim, 1988).

Other Somatotherapies for Depression

Seasonal affective disorders have been treated with apparent effectiveness by exposure to high-intensity full-spectrum light (Blehar & Rosenthal, 1989). Although there is controversy over the effective parameters of phototherapy, such as exposure time and whether A.M. exposure is better than P.M. treatment, phototherapy is clearly superior to placebo conditions. Such treatment is relatively new, however, and active efforts are under way to account for the mechanisms by which phototherapy has its effects (see Blehar & Rosenthal, 1989).

Sleep deprivation has been shown to produce transitory but significant mood improvement in depressed patients (Roy-Byrne, Uhde, & Post, 1984). Moreover, the effects are specific to depression, compared with anxiety disorders (Roy-Byrne, Uhde, & Post, 1986). The parameters of sleep deprivation therapy are an intriguing area of ongoing exploration.

Psychotherapy for Depressive Disorders

For many years, clinical lore held that psychotherapy for depression was limited in value, and that depressed patients were highly resistant and difficult to treat. In recent years, however, there have been a number of developments in effective, brief psychotherapy treatments for depression. In a recent meta-analysis, Nietzel, Russell, Hemmings, and Gretter (1987) identified forty-five such studies, and included thirty-one that used the Beck Depression Inventory as a measure of outcome. They concluded that psychotherapies for unipolar depression were indeed successful, resulting in moderate clinical improvement that is maintained over follow-up periods. For the most part, however, the research has not progressed sufficiently to identify specific predictors of response, including features of the clinical course, depression characteristics, or patient qualities (e.g., Nietzel et al., 1987; Shea, Elkin, & Hirschfeld, 1988).

Cognitive–Behavioral therapies

One of the major developments of the last 15 years in psychotherapy has been Beck's cognitive therapy of depression (Beck, Rush, Shaw, & Emery, 1979). Its impact has been broad throughout psychotherapy beyond treatment of depression, and throughout psychology for its cognitive theory of depression. It is a behavioral, active, generally time-limited intervention that attempts to systematically alter maladaptive thinking and dysfunctional attitudes that contribute to depression, while also changing problematic behaviors and dealing with life circumstances. Cognitive therapy of depression has been the subject of numerous controlled outcome studies. Dobson (1989) presented a meta-analysis of cognitive therapies, and found them to be more effective than comparison treatments. In a recent review, Hollon and Najavits (1988) distinguished between outcomes of acute treatment and prevention of relapse. Their overall conclusion was that, for treatment of acute symptoms, cognitive therapy was at least comparable to TCAs in effectiveness. There is little evidence that TCAs in combination with cognitive therapy enhance outcomes compared with cognitive therapy alone; on the other hand, the majority of relevant studies suggest that cognitive therapy combined with TCAs is superior to the use of TCAs alone.

With respect to relapse, cognitive therapy seems to show a clear superiority to medication in reducing rates of relapse after treatment is discontinued. Hollon and Najavits (1988) found relapse rates of about 30 percent for cognitive therapy compared with rates of about 60 percent for medication (e.g., Blackburn, Eunson, & Bishop, 1986; Simons, Murphy, Levine, & Wetzel, 1986). Based on differences between cognitive therapy and medication on maintenance of treatment gains, Hollon, Evans, and DeRubeis (1988) hypothesized that medications may serve to suppress the symptoms of depression but do not alter underlying causal mechanisms. On the other hand, cognitive therapy may actually alter causal mechanisms or induce compensatory activities that result in reduced risk of relapse and recurrence.

Cognitive therapy for depression has also been successfully administered in group format (e.g., Covi & Primakoff, 1988), and with a variety of special populations, such as the depressed elderly (Steuer et al., 1984) and others (see Hollon & Najavits, 1988).

Indications for cognitive therapy compared with medication have not yet been identified. The endogenous–nonendogenous distinction does not appear to be predictive of differential outcomes for medication or cognitive therapy (Hollon & Najavits, 1988).

A number of additional behavioral or cognitive–behavioral forms of brief therapy for depression have appeared over the past decade. They include Self-Control Therapy based on Rehm's self-regulation theory of depression (O'Hara & Rehm, 1983), Nezu's (1986) Problem-Solving Training, and Lewinsohn's psychoeducational approach, termed Coping with Depression (Teri & Lewinsohn, 1985). To date, each of these has received empirical support, but has not been widely tested or compared with antidepressant medications.

Other Psychotherapies

Interpersonal therapy was developed by Klerman, Weissman, Rounsaville, and Chevron (1984) as a time-limited form of psychodynamic psychotherapy focused on interpersonal events, especially current relationships, conflicts, communication difficulties, social integration, and the like. Although few outcome studies have been reported (see Shea et al., 1988), because of its inclusion in the NIMH Treatment of Depression Collaborative Research Program, discussed below, it has had a thorough test and was shown to be as effective as cognitive therapy and imipramine (Elkin et al., 1986). Moreover, in a unique study of predictors of recurrence during maintenance conditions following acute treatment, a once-per-month maintenance form of interpersonal therapy was significantly related to survival time compared with maintenance antidepressants: 50 percent of those assigned to medication experienced a recurrence by 21 weeks, whereas the 50 percent recurrence rate did not occur until 61 weeks in the interpersonal therapy maintenance condition (Frank, Kupfer, & Perel, 1989).

Another therapy with an interpersonal focus was recently introduced, based on a systems approach (Gotlib & Colby, 1987), although it has not yet been investigated in controlled trials. Additionally, it is worth mentioning that a number of self-help books on treatment of depression have appeared over the years, aimed at the vast segment of the depressed population that does not seek formal treatment. Among them are Lewinsohn's behavioral and psychoeducational manual (Lewinsohn, Munoz, Youngren, & Zeiss,

1978) and two books based largely on Beck's cognitive model (Burns, 1980; Emery, 1981).

Comparisons between Psychotherapies for Depression

A number of relatively limited studies have compared different forms of psychotherapy, such as cognitive versus behavioral, or cognitive versus interpersonal therapies. The most ambitious comparative study was mounted by the NIMH as a multisite collaborative investigation of cognitive, interpersonal, antidepressant (combined with clinical management contact), and pill–placebo (plus clinical management) treatments (Elkin, Parloff, Hadley, & Autry, 1985). To date, the results have not been published, but a preliminary report indicates no significant differences between the two psychotherapies or between psychotherapy and medication (Elkin et al., 1986). Shea et al. (1988) located fourteen comparative outcome studies and concluded that the majority found no significant differences between modalities. Exceptions occurred mainly when the comparison was a nonspecific form of psychotherapy, such as "insight-oriented" or "psychodynamic." Rehm (in press) drew a similar conclusion, observing that structured, clearly defined psychotherapies for depression probably derive effectiveness from shared features, such as presence of rationale, structure, and feedback. Others have also observed that processes derived from theory, such as cognitive changes, interpersonal functioning, or behavioral changes, do not seem to be specifically linked to the psychotherapy from which they are drawn (Hollon & Najavits, 1988; Rehm, 1988; Shea et al., 1988).

Thus, as with antidepressant medication, there is little basis for claiming superiority of one psychotherapy over another, and little clear consensus about the processes that account for successful outcomes. Nevertheless, because they have been shown to be as effective as antidepressant medications, well-developed psychotherapies for depression offer important alternatives for individuals who fail to respond to medications, who require prophylactic treatment, who cannot tolerate medication because of medical contraindications or side effects, or who simply do not want to take medication (Shea et al., 1988). Moreover, to the degree that they may actually alter depressogenic processes, or life circumstances, psychotherapies may be the treatment of choice of certain depressed individuals.

SUMMARY

Unipolar depression is one of the most common of psychiatric disorders, and affects a substantial minority of the population in a lifetime, even though most people do not seek treatment. We are increasingly coming to realize that it is also one of the most debilitating disorders in terms of impairment of role functioning as a worker, parent, and spouse. Such impairment is intensified by the likelihood of recurrence and, for some, of chronicity. It is further noteworthy that the incidence of significant depression appears to be increasing in younger samples, including children and adolescents, and peaking in young adulthood. Depression takes various forms, involving different modes of symptom expression, as well as likely differences in etiologic factors. Research is hampered by insufficient agreement on what the subtypes of depression are, which would enable study of more homogeneous populations.

Theories of the causes of depression have prompted extremely active research efforts to study both biological and psychosocial hypotheses. In the biological realm, genetic studies clearly indicate that depression runs in families, but the methods do not permit clarification of what part might be due to heritability and what part to family environment. Genetic marker studies that are proving to be useful in bipolar affective disorder may not yield solid results because of the apparent heterogeneity of unipolar depression. Neurochemical and neuroendocrinological studies are similarly affected by the heterogeneity of depression, and by the difficulty in separating what might be causative factors from those that might be consequences of the depressed state. Growing awareness of the complexity and interconnectedness of neurotransmitter and neurohormonal systems make definitive conclusions difficult. Interesting hypotheses are being pursued, however, that concern circadian rhythm abnormalities, neurotransmitter dysregulation, and dysfunctional stress responses.

The psychological front has experienced a similar movement away from overly simple, unidirectional models. Versions of the cognitive approaches and life stress approaches have evolved over time, toward greater integration. A variety of cognitive, developmental, and environmental perspectives generally view depression as a result of vulnerability of the sense of self, leading to the propensity to interpret personally stressful life events as depleting or overwhelming. Some of the models that integrate biological vulnerability and psychosocial factors offer an exciting direction for future research.

Both biological and psychological treatments have proven to be successful with clinical depressions. Numerous questions remain unanswered, however, concerning what the limits of applicability of the various treatments are, what parameters are actually altered by the medications or psychotherapies, and, most important, how to match the person to the ideal treatment.

REFERENCES

Abramson, L. Y., Alloy, L. B., & Metalsky, G. I. (1988). The cognitive diathesis-stress theories of depression: Toward an adequate evaluation of the theories' validities. In L. B. Alloy (Ed.), *Cognitive processes in depression* (pp. 3–30). New York: Guilford Press.

Abramson, L. Y., Seligman, M. E. P., & Teasdale, J. D. (1978). Learned helplessness in humans: Critique and reformulation. *Journal of Abnormal Psychology, 87,* 49–74.

Akiskal, H. S. (1982). Factors associated with incomplete recovery in primary depressive illness. *Journal of Clinical Psychiatry, 43,* 266–271.

Akiskal, H. S. (1983). Dysthymic disorder: Psychopathology of proposed chronic depressive subtypes. *American Journal of Psychiatry, 140,* 11–20.

Akiskal, H. S., Bitar, A. H., Puzantian, V. R., Rosenthal, T. L., & Walker, P. W. (1978). The nosological status of neurotic depression: A prospective three- to four-year follow-up examination in light of the primary–secondary and unipolar-bipolar dichotomies. *Archives of General Psychiatry, 35,* 756–766.

Akiskal, H. S., King, D., Rosenthal, T. L., Robinson, D., & Scott-Strauss, A. (1981). Chronic depressions: Clinical and familial characteristics in 137 probands. *Journal of Affective Disorders, 3,* 297–315.

American Psychiatric Association. (1980). *Diagnostic and statistical manual of mental disorders* (3rd ed.). Washington, DC: Author.

American Psychiatic Association. (1987). *Diagnostic and statistical manual of mental disorders* (3rd ed. rev.). Washington, DC: Author.

Anderson, J. C., Williams, S., McGee, R., & Silva, P. A. (1987). DSM-III disorders in preadolescent children: Prevalence in a large sample from the general population. *Archives of General Psychiatry, 44,* 69–76.

Andreasen, N. C., Scheftner, W., Reich, T., Hirschfeld, R. M. A., Endicott, J., & Keller, M. B. (1986). The validation of the concept of endogenous depression. *Archives of General Psychiatry, 43,* 246–251.

Angst, J. (1984, April). *A prospective study on the course of affective disorders.* Paper presented at the National Institute of Mental Health Consensus Development Conference, Washington, DC.

Angst, J., Baastrup, P. C., Grof, P., Hippius, H., Poeldinger, W., & Weiss, P. (1973). The course of monopolar depression and bipolar psychoses. *Psychiatrie, Neurologie et Neurochirurgie, 76,* 246–254.

Arieti, S., & Bemporad, J. (1980). The psychological organization of depression. *American Journal of Psychiatry, 136,* 1369.

Ballenger, J. C. (1988). Biological aspects of depression: Implications for clinical practice. In A. J. Frances & R. E. Hales (Eds.), *Review of psychiatry* (pp. 169–187). Washington, DC: American Psychiatric Press.

Barnett, P. A., & Gotlib, I. H. (1988). Psychosocial functioning and depression: Distinguishing among antecendents, concomitants, and consequences. *Psychological Bulletin, 104,* 97–126.

Barrett, J. E., Barrett, J. A., Oxman, T. E., & Gerber, P. D. (1988). The prevalence of psychiatric disorders in primary care practice. *Archives of General Psychiatry, 45,* 1100–1106.

Beck, A. T. (1967). *Depression: Clinical, experimental and theoretical aspects.* New York: Harper & Row.

Beck, A. T. (1976). *Cognitive therapy and the emotional disorders.* New York: International Universities Press.

Beck, A., Rush, A. J., Shaw, B., & Emery, G. (1979). *Cognitive therapy of depression.* New York: Guilford Press.

Beck, A. T., Steer, R. A., Kovacs, M., & Garrison, B. (1985). Hopelessness and suicidal behavior: An overview. *American Journal of Psychiatry, 142,* 559–563.

Belsher, G., & Costello, C. G. (1988). Relapse after recovery from unipolar depression: A critical review. *Psychological Bulletin, 104,* 84–96.

Berti Ceroni, G., Neri, C., & Pezzoli, A. (1984). Chronicity in major depression: A naturalistic prospective study. *Journal of Affective Disorders, 7,* 123–132.

Billings, A. G., Cronkite, R. C., & Moos, R. H. (1983). Social–environmental factors in unipolar depression: Comarisons of depressed patients and nondepressed controls. *Journal of Abnormal Psychology, 92,* 119–133.

Billings, A. G., & Moos, R. H. (1982). Psychosocial theory and research on depression: An integrative framework and review. *Clinical Psychology Review, 2,* 213–237.

Blackburn, I. M., Eunson, K. M., & Bishop, S. (1986). A two-year naturalistic follow-up of depressed patients treated with cognitive therapy, pharmacotherapy and a combination of both. *Journal of Affective Disorders, 10,* 67–75.

Bland, R. C., Newman, S. C., & Orn, H. (1986). Recurrent and nonrecurrent depression: A family study. *Archives of General Psychiatry, 43,* 1085–1089.

Blazer, D., Swartz, M. Woodbury, M., Manton, K. G., Hughes, D., & George, L. K. (1988). Depressive symptoms and depressive diagnoses in a community population. *Archives of General Psychiatry, 45,* 1078–1084.

Blehar, M. C., & Rosenthal, N. E. (1989). Seasonal affective disorders and phototherapy. *Archives of General Psychiatry, 46,* 469–474.

Blehar, M. C., Weissman, M. M., Gersohn, E. S., & Hirschfeld, R. M. A. (1988). Family and genetic studies of affective disorders. *Archives of General Psychiatry, 45,* 289–292.

Boyd, J. H., & Weissman, M. M. (1981). Epidemiology of affective disorders. *Archives of General Psychiatry, 38,* 1039–1046.

Breier, A., Kelsoe, Jr., J. R., Kirwin, P. D., Beller, S. A., Wolkowitz, O. M., & Pickar, D. (1988). Early parental loss and development of adult psychopathology. *Archives of General Psychiatry, 45,* 987–993.

Brent, D. A., Kupfer, D. J., Bromet, E. J., & Dew, M. A. (1988). The assessment and treatment of patients at risk for suicide. In A. J. Frances & R. E. Hales (Eds.), *Review of psychiatry* (pp. 353–385). Washington, DC: American Psychiatric Press.

Brown, G. W., Bifulco, A., & Harris, T. O. (1987). Life events, vulnerability and onset of depression: Some refinements. *British Journal of Psychiatry, 150,* 30–42.

Brown, G. W., & Harris, T. (1978). *Social origins of depression.* London: Free Press.

Burns, D. (1980). *Feeling good.* New York: Morrow.

Cassem, E. H. (1988). Depression secondary to medical illness. In A. J. Frances & R. E. Hales (Eds.), *Review of psychiatry* (pp. 356–373). Washington, DC: American Psychiatric Press.

Clayton, P. J. (1984, April). *Overview of recurrent mood disorders: Definitions and natural course.* Paper presented at the National Institute of Mental Health Consensus Development Conference, Washington, DC.

Cochran, S. D. (1986). Compliance with lithium regimens in the outpatient treatment of biploar affective disorders. *Journal of Compliance in Health Care, 1,* 153–170.

Covi, L., & Primakoff, L. (1988). Cognitive group therapy. In A. J. Frances & R. E. Hales (Eds.), *Review of psychiatry* (pp. 608–626). Washington, DC: American Psychiatric Press.

Coyne, J. C., & Gotlib, I. H. (1983). The role of cognition in depression: A critical appraisal. *Psychological Bulletin, 94,* 472–505.

Depue, R. A., & Monroe, S. M. (1978). The uniploar–bipolar distinction in the depressive disorders. *Psychological Bulletin, 88,* 1001–1030.

Depue, R. A., & Monroe, S. M. (1986). Conceptualization and measurement of human disorder and life stress research: The problem of chronic disturbance. *Psychological Bulletin, 99,* 36–51.

Dobson, K. (1989). A meta-analysis of the efficacy of cognitive therapy for depression. *Journal of Consulting and Clinical Psychology, 57,* 414–419.

Ehlers, C. L., Frank, E., & Kupfer, D. J. (1988). Social zeitgebers and biological rhythms. *Archives of General Psychiatry, 45,* 949–952.

Elkin, I., Parloff, M. B., Hadley, S. W., & Autry, J. H. (1985). NIMH treatment of depression collaborative research program. *Archives of General Psychiatry, 42,* 305–316.

Elkin, I., Shea, T., Imber, S., Pilkonis, P., Sotsky, S., Glass, D., Watkins, J., Leber, W., & Collins, J. (1986). *NIMH treatment of depression collaborative research program: Intial outcome findings.* Unpublished manuscript.

Emery, G., (1981). *A new beginning: How can you change your life through cognitive therapy.* New York: Simon and Schuster.

Ezquiaga, E., Gutierrez, J. L. A., & Lopez, A. G. (1987). Psychosocial factors and episode number in depression. *Journal of Affective Disorders, 12,* 135–138.

Frank, E., Kupfer, D. J., & Perel, J. M. (1989). Early recurrence in unipolar depression. *Archives of General Psychiatry, 46,* 397–400.

Gershon, E. S., Hamovit, J. H., Guroff, J. J., & Nurnberger, J. I. (1987). Birth-cohort changes in manic and depressive disorders in relatives of bipolar and schizoaffective patients. *Archives of General Psychiatry, 44,* 314–319.

Gitlin, M. (1990). *Therapists' guide to psychopharmacology.* New York: Free Press.

Gold, P. W., Goodwin, F. K., & Chrousos, G. P. (1988a). Clinical and biochemical manifestations of depression: Relation to the neurobiology of stress. Part I. *The New England Journal of Medicine, 319,* 348–413.

Gold, P. W., Goodwin, F. K., & Chrousos, G. P. (1988b). Clinical and biochemical manifestations of depression: Relation to the neurobiology of stress. Part II. *The New England Journal of Medicine, 319,* 413–420.

Goldin, L. R., & Gershon, E.S. (1988). The genetic epidemiology of major depressive illness. In A. J. Frances & R. E. Hale (Eds.), *Review of psychiatry* (pp. 149–168). Washington, DC: American Psychiatric Press.

Gordon, D., Burge, D., Hammen, C., Adrian, C., Jaenicke, C., & Hiroto, D. (1989). Observations of interactions of depressed women with their children. *American Journal of Psychiatry, 146,* 50–55.

Gotlib, I., & Colby, C. (1987). *Treatment of depression: An interpersonal systems approach.* New York: Pergamon Press.

Hammen, C. (1985). Predicting depression: A cognitive–behavioral perspective. In P. C. Kendall (Ed.), *Advances in cognitive–behavioral research and therapy* (pp. 29–71). Orlando, FL: Academic Press.

Hammen, C. (1988). Self-cognitions, stressful events, and the prediction of depression in children of depressed mothers. *Journal of Abnormal Child Psychology, 16,* 347–360.

Hammen, C. (1989). Understanding depression in women: The cognitive approach as an ally. *Canadian Psychology, 30,* 52–54.

Hammen, C., Adrian, C., Gordon, D., Burge, D., Jaenicke, C., & Hiroto, D. (1987). Children of depressed mothers: Maternal strain and symptom predictors of dysfunction. *Journal of Abnormal Psychology, 96,* 190–198.

Hammen, C., Burge, D., & Stansbury, K. (1990). Relationship of mother and child variables to child outcomes in a high risk sample: A causal modeling analysis. *Developmental Psychology, 26,* 24–30.

Hammen, C., Ellicott, A., Gitlin, M., & Jamison, K. R. (1989). Sociotropy/autonomy and vulnerability to specific life events in unipolar and bipolar patients. *Journal of Abnormal Psychology, 98,* 154–160.

Hammen, C., & Goodman-Brown, T. (1990). Self-schemas and vulnerability to specific life stress in children at risk for depression. *Cognitive Therapy and Research, 14,* 215–227.

Hammen, C., Gordon, D., Burge, D., Adrian, C., Jaenicke, C., & Hiroto, D. (1987). Maternal affective disorders, illness, and stress: Risk for children's psychopathology. *American Journal of Psychiatry, 144,* 736–741.

Hammen, C., & Krantz, S. (1985). Measures of psychological processes in depression. In E. E. Beckham & W. R. Leber (Eds.), *Handbook of depression: Treatment, assessment, and research* (pp. 408–444). Homewood, IL: Dorsey Press.

Hammen, C., Marks, T., deMayo, R., & Mayol, A. (1985). Self-schemas and risks for depression: A prospective study. *Journal of Personality and Social Psychology, 49,* 1147–1159.

Hammen, C., Mayol., A., deMayo, R., & Marks, T. (1986). Initial symptom levels and the life event–depression relationship. *Journal of Abnormal Psychology, 95,* 114–122.

Healy, D., & Williams, J. M. G. (1988). Dysrhythmia, dysphoria, and depression: The interaction of learned helplessness and circadian dysrhythmia in pathogenesis of depression. *Psychological Bulletin, 103,* 163–178.

Hirschfeld, R. M. A. (1981). Situational depression: Validity of the concept. *British Journal of Psychiatry, 139,* 297–305.

Hirschfeld, R. M. A. (1984, April). *NIMH collaborative study on psychobiology of illness.* Paper presented at the National Institute of Mental Health Consensus Development Conference, Washington, DC.

Hirschfeld, R. M. A., & Davidson, L. (1988). Risk factors for suicide. In A. J. Frances & R. E. Hales (Eds.), *Review of psychiatry* (pp. 307–333). Washington, DC: American Psychiatric Press.

Hirschfeld, R. M. A., Klerman, G. L., Andreason, N. C., Clayton, P. J., & Keller, M. B. (1986). Psycho-social predictors of chronicity in depressed patients. *British Journal of Psychiatry, 148,* 648–654.

Holahan, C. J., & Moos, R. H. (1987). Risk, resistance, and psychological distress: A longitudinal analysis with adults and children. *Journal of Abnormal Psychology, 96,* 3–13.

Hollon, S. D., Evans, M. D., & DeRubeis, R. (1988). Preventing relapse following treatment for depression: The cognitive pharmacotherapy project. In T. M. Field, P. M. McCabe, & N. Schneiderman (Eds.), *Stress and coping across development* (pp. 227–243). Hillsdale, NJ: Erlbaum.

Hollon, S. D., & Najavits, L. (1988). Review of empirical studies on cognitive therapy. In A. J. Frances & R. E. Hales (Eds.), *Review of psychiatry* (pp. 643–666). Washington, DC: American Psychiatric Press.

Hooley, J. M., Orley, J., & Teasdale, J. D. (1986). Levels of expressed emotion and relapse in depressed patients. *British Journal of Psychiatry, 148,* 642–647.

Hyland, M. E. (1987). Control theory interpretation of psychological mechanisms of depression: Comparison and integration of several theories. *Psychological Bulletin, 102,* 109–121.

Joyce, P. R., & Paykel, E. S. (1989). Predictors of drug response in depression. *Archives of General Psychiatry, 46,* 89–99.

Karno, M., Hough, R. L., Burnam, A., Escobar, J. I., Timbers, D. M., Santana, F., & Boyd, J. H. (1987). Lifetime prevalence of specific psychiatric disorders among Mexican Americans and non-Hispanic whites in Los Angeles. *Archives of General Psychiatry, 44,* 695–701.

Kashani, J. H., Carlson, G. A., Beck, N. C., Hoeper, E. W., Corcoran, C. M., McAllister, J. A., Fallahi, C., Rosenberg, T. K., & Reid, J. C. (1987). Depression, depressive symptoms, and depressed mood among a community sample of adolescents. *American Journal of Psychiatry, 144,* 931–934.

Keller, M. B. (1985). Chronic and recurrent affective disorders: Incidence, course, and influencing factors. In D. Kemali & G. Recagni (Eds.), *Chronic treatments in neuropsychiatry.* New York: Raven Press.

Keller, M. B. (1988). Diagnostic issues and clinical course of unipolar illness. In A. J. Frances & R. E. Hales (Eds.), *Review of Psychiatry* (pp. 188–212). Washington, DC: American Psychiatric Press.

Keller, M. B., Lavori, P. W., Endicott, J., Coryell, W., & Klerman, G. L. (1983). "Double depression": Two-year follow-up. *American Journal of Psychiatry, 140,* 689–694.

Keller, M. B., Lavori, P. W., Klerman, G. L., Andreasen, N. C., Endicott, J., Coryell, W., Fawcett, J., Rice, J. P., & Hirschfeld, R. M. A. (1986). Low levels and lack of predictors of somatotherapy and psychotherapy received by depressed patients. *Archives of General Psychiatry, 43,* 458–466.

Keller, M. B., Lavori, P. W., Rice, J., Coryell, W., & Hirschfeld, R. M. A. (1986). The persistent risk of chronicity in recurrent episodes of nonbipolar major depressive disorder: A prospective follow-up. *American Journal of Psychiatry, 143,* 24–28.

Keller, M. B., Shapiro, R. W., Lavori, P. W., & Wolfe, N. (1982a). Recovery in major depressive disorder: Analysis with the life table and regression models. *Archives of General Psychiatry, 39,* 905–910.

Klein, D. N., Taylor, E. B., Dickstein, S., & Harding, K. (1988). Primary early-onset dysthymia: Comparison with primary nonbipolar nonchronic major depression on demographic, clinical, familial, personality, and socioenvironmental characteristics and short-term outcome. *Journal of Abnormal Psychology, 97,* 387–398.

Klerman, G. L., Lavori, P. W., Rice, J., Reich, T., Endicott, J., Andreasen, N. C., Keller, M. C., & Hirschfeld, R. M. A. (1985). Birth-cohort trends in rates of major depressive disorder among relatives of patients with affective disorder. *Archives of General Psychiatry, 42,* 689–695.

Klerman, G., Weissman, M., Rounsaville, B., & Chevron, E. (1985). *Interpersonal psychotherapy of depression.* New York: Basic Books.

Kocsis, J. H., Frances, A. J., Voss, C., Mann, J. J., Mason, B. J., Sweeney, J. (1988). Imipramine treatment for chronic depression. *Archives of General Psychiatry, 45,* 253–257.

Kovacs, M., Feinberg, T. L., Crouse-Novak, M. A., Paulauskas, S. L., & Finkelstein, R. (1984). Depressive disorders in childhood. *Archives of General Psychiatry, 41,* 229–237.

Lazarus, R. S., & Folkman S. (1984). *Stress, appraisal and coping.* New York: Springer.

Leber, W. R., Beckham, E. E., & Danker-Brown, P. (1985). Diagnostic criteria for depression. In E. E. Beckham & W. R. Leber (Eds.), *Handbook of depression: Treatment, assessment, and research* (pp. 343–371). Homewood, IL: Dorsey Press.

Lehmann, H. E. (1985). Affective disorders: Clinical features. In H. I. Kaplan & B. J. Sadock (Eds.), *Comprehensive textbook of psychiatry.* Baltimore: Williams & Wilkins.

Lewinsohn, P. M., Duncan, E. M., Stanton, A. K., & Hautzinger, M. (1986). Age at first onset for nonbipolar depression. *Journal of Abnormal Psychology, 95,* 378–383.

Lewinsohn, P. M., Fenn, D. S., Stanton, A. K., & Franklin, J. (1986). Relation of age at onset to duration of episode in unipolar depression. *Journal of Psychology and Aging, 1,* 63–68.

Lewinsohn, P. M., Hoberman, H. M., & Rosenbaum, M. (1988). A prospective study of risk factors for unipolar depression. *Journal of Abnormal Psychology, 97,* 251–264.

Lewinsohn, P. M., Hops, H., Roberts, R., & Seeley, J. R. (1988, November). *Adolescent depression: Prevalence and psychosocial aspects.* Paper presented at the American Public Health Association's Annual Meeting, Boston, MA.

Lewinsohn, P., Munoz, R., Youngren, M., & Zeiss, A. (1978). *Control your depression.* Englewood Cliffs, NJ: Prentice Hall.

Linville, P. (1985). Self-complexity and affective extremity: Don't put all your eggs in one cognitive basket. *Social Cognition, 3,* 94–110.

Lloyd, C. (1980). Life events and depressive disorder reviewed: Events as predisposing factors. *Archives of General Psychiatry, 37,* 529–535.

McNeal, E. T., & Cimbolic, P. (1986). Antidepressants and biochemical theories of depression. *Psychological Bulletin, 99,* 361–374.

Murphy, J. M., Monson, R. R., Oliver, D. C., Sobol, A. M., & Leighton, A. H. (1987). Affective disorders and mortality. *Archives of General Psychiatry, 44,* 473–480.

NIMH/NIH Consensus Development Conference Statement. (1985). *American Journal of Psychiatry, 142,* 469–476.

Nezu, A. M. (1986). Efficacy of a social problem-solving therapy approach for unipolar depression. *Journal of Consulting and Clinical Psychology, 54,* 196–202.

Nietzel, M. Y., Russell, R. L., Hemmings, K. A., & Gretter, M. L. (1987). Clinical significance of psychotherapy for unipolar depression: A meta-analytic approach to social comparison. *Journal of Consulting and Clinical Psychology, 55,* 156–161.

Nolen-Hoeksema, S. (1987). Sex differences in unipolar depression: Evidence and theory. *Psychological Bulletin, 101,* 259–282.

Oatley, K., & Bolton, W. (1985). A social-cognitive theory of depression in reaction to life events. *Psychological Review, 92,* 372–388.

O'Hara, M. W., & Rehm, L. P. (1983). Self-control group therapy of depression. In A. Freeman (Ed.), *Cognitive therapy with couples and groups.* New York: Plenum Press.

Paykel, E. S. (1979). Causal relationships between clinical depression and life events. In J. E. Barrett (Ed.), *Stress and mental disorder* (pp. 71–86). New York: Raven.

Paykel, E. S., Freeling, P., & Hollyman, J. A. (1988). Are tricyclic antidepressants useful for mild depression? A placebo controlled study. *Pharmacopsychiatry, 21,* 15–18.

Peterson, C., & Seligman, M. E. P. (1984). Causal explanations as a risk factor for depression: Theory and evidence. *Psychological Review, 91,* 347–374.

Post, R. M., Rubinow, D. R., & Ballenger, J. C. (1984). Conditioning, sensitization, and kindling: Implications for the course of affective illness. In R. Post & J. Ballenger (Eds.), *Neurobiology of mood disorders* (pp. 432–466). Baltimore: Williams & Wilkins.

Prien, R. F. (1988). Somatic treatment of unipolar depressive disorder. In A. J. Frances & R. E. Hales (Eds.), *Review of psychiatry* (pp. 213–234). Washington, DC: American Psychiatric Press.

Prien, R. F., & Kupfer, D. J. (1986). Continuation drug therapy for major depressive episodes: How long should it be maintained? *American Journal of Psychiatry, 143,* 18–23.

Pyszczynski, T., & Greenberg, J. (1987). Self-regulatory perseveration and the depressive self-focusing style: A self-awareness theory of reactive depression. *Psychological Bulletin, 102,* 122–138.

Rehm, L. (1990). A memory model of emotion. In R. Ingram (Ed.), *Contemporary psychological approaches to depression: Treatment, research, and theory*. New York: Plenum Press.

Rehm, L. P. (in press). Psychotherapies for depression. B. Bloom & K. Schlesinger (Eds.), *Boulder Sympsium on Clinical Psychology: Depression*. Hillsdale, NJ: Lawrence Erlbaum.

Robins, E., & Guze, S. B. (1972). Classification of affective disorders: The primary-secondary, the endogenous, and the neurotic–psychotic concepts. In T. A. Williams, M. M. Katz, & J. A. Shield (Eds.), *Recent advances in the psychobiology of depressive illness*. Washington, DC: Department of Health, Education & Welfare.

Robins, L. N., Helzer, J. E., Weissman, M. M., Orvaschel, H., Gruenberg, E., Burke, J. D., & Regier, D. A. (1984). Lifetime prevalence of specific psychiatric disorders in three sites. *Archives of General Psychiatry, 41,* 949–958.

Roy, A. (1985). Early parental separation and adult depression. *Archives of General Psychiatry, 42,* 987–995.

Roy-Byrne, P. P., Uhde, T. W., & Post, R. M. (1984). Antidepressant effects of one night's sleep deprivation: Clinical and theoretical implications. In R. M. Post & J. C. Ballenger (Eds.), *Neurobiology of mood disorders* (pp. 817–835). Baltimore: Williams & Wilkins.

Roy-Byrne, P. P., Uhde, T. W., & Post, R. M. (1986). Effects of one night's sleep deprivation on mood and behavior in panic disorder: Patients with panic disorder compared with depressed patients and normal controls. *Archives of General Psychiatry, 43,* 895–899.

Sack, D. A., Rosenthal, N. E., Parry, B. L., & Wehr, T. A. (1987). Biological rhythms in psychiatry. In H. Y. Meltzer (Ed.), *Psychopharmacology: The third generation of progress* (pp. 669–685). New York: Raven Press.

Sackheim, H. A. (1988). Mechanisms of action of electroconvulsive therapy. In A. J. Frances & R. E. Hales (Eds.), *Review of psychiatry* (pp. 436–457). Washington, DC: American Psychiatric Press.

Schleifer, S. J., Keller, S. E., Bond, R. N., Cohen, J., & Stein, M. (1989). Major depressive disorder and immunity. *Archives of General Psychiatry, 46,* 81–87.

Schulberg, H. C., McClelland, M., & Burns, B. J. (1987). Depression and physical illness: The prevalence, causation and diagnosis of comorbidity. *Clinical Psychology Review, 7,* 145–167.

Segal, Z. V. (1988). Appraisal of the self-schema construct in cognitive models of depression. *Psychological Bulletin, 103,* 147–162.

Seligman, M. E. P. (1975). *Helplessness*. San Francisco: Freeman.

Seligman, M. E. P., Abramson, L. Y., Semmel, A., & von Baeyer, C. (1979). Depressive attributional style. *Journal of Abnormal Psychology, 88,* 242–247.

Seligman, M. E. P., Peterson, C., Kaslow, N. J., Tanenbaum, R. L., Alloy, L. B., & Abramson, L. Y. (1984). Attributional style and depressive symptoms among children. *Journal of Abnormal Psychology, 93,* 235–241.

Shea, M. T., Elkin, I., & Hirschfeld, R. M. A. (1988). Psychotherapeutic treatment of depression. In A. J. Frances & R. E. Hales (Eds.), *Review of psychiatry* (pp. 235–255). Washington, DC: American Psychiatric Press.

Siever, L. J., & Davis, K. L. (1985). Overview: Toward a dysregulation hypothesis of depression. *American Journal of Psychiatry, 142,* 1017–1031.

Simons, A. D., Murphy, G. E., Levine, J. E., & Wetzel, R. (1986). Cognitive therapy and pharmacotherapy for depression: Sustained improvement over one year. *Archives of General Psychiatry, 43,* 43–49.

Spitzer, R. L., Endicott, J., & Robins, E. (1975). *Research diagnostic criteria (RDC) for a selected group of functional disorders.* New York: New York State Psychiatric Institute.

Steuer, J., Mintz, J., Hammen, C., Hill, M., Jarvik, L., McCarley, T., Motoike, P., & Rosen, R. (1984). Cognitive–behavioral and psychodynamic group psychotherapy in treatment of geriatric depression. *Journal of Consulting and Clinical Psychology, 52,* 180–189.

Sweeney, P. D., Anderson, K., & Bailey, S. (1986). Attributional style in depression: A meta-analytic review. *Journal of Personality and Social Psychology, 50,* 974–991.

Teri, L., & Lewinsohn, P. M. (1985). Group intervention for unipolar depression. *Behavior Therapist, 8,* 109–123.

Thase, M. E., Frank, E., & Kupfer, D. J. (1985). Biological processes in major depression. In E. E. Beckham & W. R. Leber (Eds.), *Depression: Basic mechanisms, diagnosis, and treatment* (pp. 816–913). New York: Dow Jones/Irwin.

Thase, M. E., & Howland, R. (1989, April). *The biology of depression.* Paper presented at the Boulder Symposium on Clinical Psychology: Depression. Boulder, CO.

Thoits, P. A. (1983). Multiple identities and psychological well-being: A reformulation and test of the social isolation hypothesis. *American Sociological Reviews, 48,* 174–187.

Torgersen, S. (1986). Genetic factors in moderately severe and mild affective disorders. *Archives of General Psychiatry, 43,* 222–226.

Tsuang, M. T., & Simpson, J. C. (1985). Mortality studies in psychiatry: Should they stop or proceed? *Archives of General Psychiatry, 42,* 98–103.

Vaughn, C. E., & Leff, J. P. (1976). The influence of family and social factors on the course of psychiatric illness: A comparison of schizophrenic and depressed neurotic patients. *British Journal of Psychiatry, 129,* 125–137.

Wehr, T. A., & Goodwin, F. K. (1981). Biological rhythms and psychiatry. In S. Arieti & H. K. H. Brodie (Eds.), *American handbook of psychiatry* (Vol. 7, pp. 46–74). New York: Basic Books.

Wehr, T. A., & Wirz-Justice, A. (1982). Circadian rhythm mechanisms in affective illness and in antidepressant drug action. *Pharmacopsychiatry, 15,* 31–39.

Weiner, R. D., & Coffey, C. E. (1988). Indications for use of electroconvulsive therapy. In A. J. Frances & R. E. Hales (Eds.), *Review of psychiatry* (pp. 458–481). Washington, DC: American Psychiatric Press.

Weissman, M. (1988). Psychopathology in the children of depressed parents: Direct interview studies. In D. L. Dunner, E. S. Gershon, & J. E. Barrett (Eds.), *Relatives at risk for mental disorder,* (pp. 143–159). New York: Raven Press.

Weissman, M. M., Merikangas, K. R., Wickramaratne, P., Kidd, K. K., Prusoff, B. A., Leckman, J. F., & Pauls, D. L. (1986). Understanding the clinical heterogeneity of major depression using family data. *Archives of General Psychiatry, 43,* 430–434.

Wender, P. H., Kety, S. S., Rosenthal, D., Schulsinger, F., Ortmann, J., & Lunde, I. (1986). Psychiatric disorders in the biological and adoptive families of adopted individuals with affective disorders. *Archives of General Psychiatry, 43,* 923–929.

Widiger, T. A., & Frances, A. J. (1989). Epidemiology, diagnosis, and comorbidity of borderline personality disorder. In A. Tasman, R. E. Hales, & A. J. Frances (Eds.), *Review of psychiatry* (pp. 8–24). Washington, DC: American Psychiatric Press.

Winokur, G. (1979). Familial (genetic) subtypes of pure depressive disease. *American Journal of Psychiatry, 136,* 911–913.

Winokur, G. (1985). The validity of neurotic-reactive depression. *Archives of General Psychiatry, 42,* 1116–1122.

Zimmerman, M., Black, D. W., & Coryell, W. (1989). Diagnostic criteria for melancholia: The comparative validity of DSM-III and DSM-III-R. *Archives of General Psychiatry, 46,* 361–368.

Zimmerman, M., Coryell, W., & Pfohl, B. (1986). Validity of familial subtypes of primary unipolar depression. *Archives of General Psychiatry, 43,* 1090–1096.

Zimmerman, M., Coryell, W., Stangl, D., & Pfohl, B. (1987). Validity of an operational definition for neurotic unipolar major depression. *Journal of Affective Disorders, 12,* 29–40.

Zimmerman, M., & Spitzer, R. L. (1989). Melancholia: From DSM-III to DSM-III-R. *The American Journal of Psychiatry, 146,* 20–28.

Zis, A. P., & Goodwin, F. K. (1979). Major affective disorder as a recurrent illness: A clinical review. *Archives of General Psychiatry, 36,* 835–839.

CHAPTER 8

Mood Disorders (Bipolar)

ROBERT E. SMITH and GEORGE WINOKUR

Bipolar disorder is characterized by episodes of mania and depression. The episodes are usually discrete and show clusterings of depressive or manic symptoms (Feighner et al., 1972). Common symptoms in depression are complaints of being sad, blue, despondent, or hopeless; poor appetite; weight loss; sleep difficulties, such as insomnia or waking up early in the morning; loss of energy or a feeling of fatigability; agitation or retardation; loss of interest in usual activities such as work or play; decrease in sexual drive; feelings of self-reproach or guilt; inability to concentrate; recurrent thoughts of death or suicide; and diurnal variation (e.g., feeling worse in the morning). Although not all of these symptoms have to be present, several should be present before one would consider depression a possibility. An episode of mania is manifested by euphoric mood, hyperactivity, push of speech, racing thoughts, feelings of grandiosity, decreased need for sleep, distractibility, extravagance, and intrusiveness.

Most patients considered to have bipolar disorder show one or more depressions and manias, but occasional patients show only manias and no depressions. Also, some patients who have bipolar disorder probably show only depressions and no manias. Bipolar disorder is familial. In a family in which one manic patient exists, between 36 and 75 percent of the affectively ill relatives will exhibit only depression. The remainder will show either manias or manias and depressions (Winokur, 1979).

To best understand the concept of bipolar disorder, it is necessary to separate it from unipolar affective disorder, in which an individual shows only depressions and no manic episodes. The occurrence of bipolar disorder was noted as far back as 1686 when Bonet used the term "maniaco-melancholicus" in describing a group of patients. In the 1850s, Falret adopted the term "circular insanity" for the same kinds of patients, and Baillarger used the term "double-form insanity." In 1883, Kraepelin published his textbook on psychiatry, in which he separated manic–depressive illness from dementia praecox or schizophrenia on the basis of clinical descriptions and the natural history of the illnesses. The natural history of manic–depressive illness was characterized by episodes and that of schizophrenia by a chronic deteriorating course (Kraepelin, 1921). Although the original descriptions clearly noted the presence of both manias and depressions in the same patient, it was generally accepted practice to assume that those patients who had only depressions, in fact, belonged in the group of manic–depressive illnesses.

In 1959, Leonhard suggested that the bipolar and unipolar forms of affective illness might be separate illnesses. He studied 238 bipolar and 288 unipolar patients and looked at the incidence of endogenous psychosis in parents and siblings of the probands. Of the first-degree relatives of the bipolar sample, 39.9 percent were ill, whereas 25.7 percent of the relatives of the unipolar sample were ill. Thus, the bipolar patients had a larger yield of psychiatric illness in their families than did unipolar patients. By 1962, however, Leonhard, Korff, and Schulz showed differences in personality traits between the two groups of probands.

In 1966, a concatenation of findings from Sweden, Switzerland, and the United States put the bipolar–unipolar distinction on a firm basis. In that year, Angst in Switzerland and Perris in Sweden published their results, and Winokur and Clayton presented their data at the annual meeting of the Society of Biological Psychiatry in Washington, D.C. Angst (1966) reported that the morbidity risk (MR) for affective disorders in the first-degree relatives of bipolar probands was higher than for those of unipolar probands. Furthermore, bipolar probands had more bipolar illness. Perris (1966) in Sweden also showed that bipolar probands were more likely than unipolar probands to have bipolar illness in their families. Winokur and Clayton (1967) showed that one-third of the first-degree relatives of bipolar patients had bipolar illness. These data are presented in Table 8.1.

Over time, other differences have been noted between patients with unipolar depression (depressive disease) and patients with bipolar affective disorder (manic–depressive disease). The bipolar patients are more likely to have multiple episodes (Winokur, 1973), to become ill earlier in life, and to have affective illness in parents or extended family. Table 8.2 presents some of these data. Besides the presence of mania in a proband, a number of other factors separate bipolar from unipolar patients. Despite marked differences in clinical picture, course, family history, and treatment, not all investigators accept the concept of two distinct illnesses. Gershon and colleagues (Gershon, Bunney, Leckman, vanEerdewegh, & DeBauche, 1976; Gershon et al., 1982), in reviewing available family study data, concluded that an alternative hypothesis—that is, a common genetic diathesis—might account for both bipolar and unipolar illnesses. This viewpoint depends

TABLE 8.1.   Initial Family Studies Supporting the Distinction between Unipolar and Bipolar Affective Disorders

Study	Probands	First-Degree Relative Morbidity Risk (%)	
		Unipolar	Bipolar
Angst (1966)	Unipolar	5.1	0.3
	Bipolar	13.0	4.3
Perris (1966)	Unipolar	6.4	0.3
	Bipolar	0.5	10.1
Winokur & Clayton (1967)	Bipolar	20.4	10.2

TABLE 8.2.   Differences between Manic–Depressive Disease
(Bipolar) and Depressive Disease (Unipolar)

	Bipolar	Unipolar
Presence of mania in proband	yes	no
Age of onset in proband (median)	28 years	36 years
Bi- or triphasic immediate course (D,M,D) or (M,D) or (D,M)	yes	no
Six or more episodes of illness	57%	18%
Affective illness in parent	51%	26%
Families having two generations of affective illness (proband parent, proband child)	54%	32%
Affective illness in parents or extended family	63%	36%
Bipolar psychosis in first-degree relatives	3.7–10.8%	.29–.35%

Note: D = depressive, M = manic.

on the finding that the more severe illnesses (e.g., psychotic affective illnesses) would have a higher incidence in family history than the less severe
illnesses and that the bipolars would have a higher incidence in family history than the unipolars. This viewpoint would also support a kind of continuum, with nonpsychotic unipolars having the mildest type of affective
disorder and bipolars with psychotic symptoms having the most severe
forms of the illness. Winokur (1984), however, presented data that showed
that psychotic and nonpsychotic bipolars and unipolars (four groups) all
suffered the same amount of familial affective illness. This argument may
not be possible to resolve until a specific gene is identified in one or both
forms.

CLINICAL PICTURE OF BIPOLAR ILLNESS

An individual experiencing an episode of bipolar affective illness may
present in a manic phase, a depressed phase, or occasionally a mixed
clinical state in which symptoms of both phases of the illness occur together. Thus, a description of the symptomatic behavior of bipolar illness
encompasses the uniqueness of manic and hypomanic behavior, the ubiquity of depressive symptomatology, and the clinically confusing mixed
state. Investigators delineating the clinical picture of mania and hypomania are describing the signs and symptoms of a relatively homogeneous
patient population. All manic episodes are attributed to bipolar affective
illness when neurological or medical etiologies are ruled out. The situation
with depressive episodes is more complex. Depressed patients are diagnosed or suspected of having bipolar illness only if they have a past history
of a manic episode and/or a familial history of mania or hypomania. These
individuals are the source of our clinical picture of bipolar depression.
Unfortunately, this clinical picture of bipolar depression is not easily differentiated from that seen in the unipolar depressive disorders. Subtle
differences exist, but none is pathognomonic.

Mania

The manic phase of bipolar illness is divided by severity into hypomania and mania. Both of these are defined in the third revised edition of the *Diagnostic and Statistical Manual of Mental Disorders* (DSM-III-R) as a distinct period of abnormally and persistently expansive, elevated, or irritable mood (American Psychiatric Association [APA], 1987). Hypomania is characterized by the loss of ability for goal-directed work and an incapacity to complete a definite series of thoughts. The rate of thought production is accelerated, but derailment does not occur. These individuals lack insight and do not identify themselves as ill. Their moods are cheerful, but irritability may appear at the slightest provocation. Self-confidence is high and actions may be impulsive. Psychomotor activity is increased with a lively quality. Speech rate may be minimally increased, and these individuals are often verbose and bombastic.

A manic episode is characterized by a clustering of three or more of the following behavioral changes (APA, 1987):

1. Increased self-esteem or grandiosity
2. Decreased need for sleep
3. Increased speech, talkativeness, or pressure of speech
4. Flight of ideas or racing thoughts
5. Distractibility
6. Increased goal-directed activities, such as professional, social, or sexual activities
7. Psychotic acceleration or agitation.

Acute mania may be heralded by a period of hypomanic signs and symptoms or begin acutely in its full form. All the characteristics of hypomania are increased in severity. Thoughts and speech become disconnected, fleeting grandiose delusions may be present, and the individual's mood becomes expansive and exalted. Extreme irritability may appear and be associated with destructive actions. If changes in consciousness or psychotic features are present, they often dominate the clinical picture. Delusions are frequently religious in nature, and visual and auditory hallucinations are not infrequent.

Irrespective of the severity of the behavioral symptoms, a patient with psychotic symptoms (delusions or hallucinations) is always classified as experiencing a manic episode. The clinical picture of a manic episode can vary considerably, but most often contains the three cardinal symptoms of mania: elevated mood, flight of ideas, and psychomotor overactivity.

Depression

The clinical pictures of unipolar and bipolar depressive episodes generally share a broad range of affective symptomatology. The wise clinician will attempt to differentiate one from the other by utilizing information on the course of the patient's illness and the family history of affective illness and not by eliciting subtle behavioral differences in depressive symptomatology. Many researchers cited below have found these subtle differences; however, other investigators reported no differences between bipolar and unipolar depressive episodes when cross-sectional symptoms are compared (Abrams & Taylor, 1980). With such discrepancies in the literature, it may be best to initiate a description of the depressive states with the classical material of Kraepelin.

In presenting the clinical picture of depression, Kraepelin (1921) separated groups according to severity. The resulting six groups were melancholia simplex, stupor, melancholia gravis, paranoid melancholia, fantastic melancholia, and delirious melancholia. In melancholia simplex, a sense of profound inward dejection dominates the mood. The patient's view of life is markedly pessimistic and flavored with hopelessness and despair. Feelings of worthlessness are prominent, and torment from guilt is frequent. Endogenous features of decreased libido, anorexia, weight loss, and sleep disturbance with early morning awakening often are present. Energy is markedly decreased, and psychomotor retardation is demonstrated. Phobias may also be part of the clinical picture. Various combinations of these signs and symptoms characterize simple melancholia.

In depressive stupor, the prominent feature is the patient's difficulty in perceiving surroundings and assimilating these external stimuli. Apathy is readily observed, and the patient makes detached statements with confused ideas. However, the patient is most commonly observed to be mute and shows minimal physical activity. The other features of depression are present, but the stuporous quality is most striking clinically.

Melancholia gravis is characterized by the presence of ideas of sin and persecution. The patient is preoccupied with his or her present and past sins, both real and imaginary. His or her life has been without any saving grace, and damnation is viewed as the final reward. Somatic delusions concerning the rotting away of various organs may be experienced, as well as hallucinations of figures or spirits of relatives. Persecutory ideation, when present, is closely related to sinful delusions. Paranoid melancholia is characterized by persecutory ideation centering on beliefs that the patient is being watched or spied upon. He or she often imagines being the target of others, and auditory hallucinations reflect the paranoid theme. The patient's mood is gloomy and despondent; the risk for suicide is significant.

Fantastic melancholia is characterized by multiple delusions and hallucinations. A single patient will have delusions of guilt and persecution, bizarre somatic dysfunction, and hypochondriasis. Abundant hallucinations of spirits, the devil, monsters, and angels are present. Cognitive function appears impaired, and psychomotor activity may range from one extreme to the other. If cognitive function and consciousness are significantly impaired within this total clinical picture, a diagnosis of delirious melancholia is made.

The currently utilized description of an episode of bipolar depression is given in DSM-III-R. This reference does not differentiate the clinical picture of bipolar depression from that of unipolar (major) depression. The central feature of either depression is a pervasive (at least 2 weeks in duration) dysphoric mood. The elderly not uncommonly experience a greater loss of interest or presence of apathy and complain less of sadness or discouragement. Children or adolescents often present with irritable mood. In addition, a clinical picture mimicking a conduct disorder may confound diagnosis in this age group. At least four or more of the following signs and symptoms must accompany the dysphoria or loss of interest to satisfy the criteria for an episode of depression:

1. Appetite disturbance, usually manifested by loss of appetite, but sometimes by increased appetite
2. Sleep disturbance, classically presenting as early morning awakening
3. Loss of interest or pleasure in usual activities, such as hobbies, work, or sexual function
4. Changes in psychomotor activity level, manifested as either agitation or retardation of speech and movement
5. Subjective complaints or objective evidence of impaired ability to concentrate, remember, process information, or make decisions
6. Decreased self-esteem, manifested by feelings of worthlessness, self-reproach, or excessive or inappropriate guilt
7. Decreased energy and a sense of sustained fatigue even in the absence of physical exertion
8. Thoughts of death or suicide.

The literature suggests that symptomatic differences exist between bipolar and unipolar depression. Further research is needed in this area, however, since considerable overlap exists on most variables. Detre et al. (1972) found that the type of sleep disturbance a patient is experiencing may be associated with the classification of the depressive episode. Bipolar depressive patients more frequently have hypersomnia, whereas unipolar patients more commonly have hyposomnia. The presence or absence of anxiety does not differentiate the two groups, but anger may. Beigel and Murphy (1971) reported that bipolar depressives rarely experience anger directed inward or displaced outward toward others. They also reported that unipolar patients had significantly higher ratings for somatic complaints than did matched bipolar patients. Prolonged periods of psychomotor retardation characterize the bipolar depressed patient (Bunney & Murphy, 1973). Psychomotor agitation, in contrast, is more frequent and severe in the unipolar patient (Beigel & Murphy, 1971).

Psychotic symptoms (delusions, hallucinations, or catatonia) may be seen during episodes of bipolar or unipolar depression. It is estimated that between 20 and 30 percent of all psychotically depressed patients are bipolar. This percentile is about twice that predicted by epidemiological data. Bipolar psychotically depressed patients are also characterized by childhood or adolescent age of onset, profound psychomotor retardation, antidepressant-induced periods of mania or hypomania, and a strong family history of affective illnesses, often in three consecutive generations. Psychotic symptoms do not differentiate unipolar from bipolar illness, but the likelihood of bipolar disease is greatly increased.

From the above data, we can delineate some characteristics that differentiate the unipolar depressive from the bipolar depressive. The characteristics
hold for groups, but, because of overlap, application to the individual patient
will be less certain. Unipolar depressed patients appear to have more anger
directed at self or others, to present more frequently with multiple somatic
complaints as part of their depression, to experience hyposomnia, and to have
higher levels of psychomotor agitation. Bipolar depressed patients have minimal anger, few somatic complaints, more hypersomnia, and more psychomotor retardation. In a recent study, Winokur and Wesner (1987) found a high
incidence of reproach and guilt in bipolar depression, but those features were
not seen in unipolar depression.

Mixed Episodes

A mixed form of bipolar illness may be seen, with both manic and depressive
features. Once given little attention and thought to be rare, the patient experiencing a mixed episode is now being recognized frequently in the clinical
setting. The identification of this phase of the bipolar illness is critical, since
it may be the first time lithium or anticonvulsants are considered in the
therapeutic management of the patient's recurring "depression."

COURSE OF ILLNESS

Bipolar illness starts generally before the age of 30. Table 8.3 presents the
cumulative risk for age of onset for both males and females (Winokur,
1970). Over half the patients become ill prior to the age of 30, and in fact, a
quarter of the patients become ill prior to 20. Although it has become clear
that bipolar illness frequently begins in adolescence, in the past, the simple
fact of an early onset frequently suggested that the clinician was dealing
with schizophrenia.

Bipolar disorder may first manifest itself by a depression. In a recent study,
225 unipolar depressive patients were identified and then followed for as long
as 40 years. Within the first few years after follow-up, about 4 percent of the
patients went from unipolarity to bipolarity (Winokur & Morrison, 1973);

TABLE 8.3.   Age of Onset and Age at Index Admission (N = 89 Manics)

Age of Onset	Admission Age (Both Sexes)	Age at Onset of Illness			Cumulative Risk (Both Sexes)
		Males	Females	Both Sexes	
10–19	6	8	14	22	25%
20–29	16	12	13	25	53%
30–39	18	3	12	15	70%
40–49	18	5	8	13	84%
50–59	18	5	6	11	97%
60–69	11	2	1	3	100%
70–79	2	0	0	0	—
Total	89	35	54	89	

however, in the long-term follow-up, 9.7 percent became bipolar (Winokur, Tsuang, & Crowe, 1982). When compared with the stable unipolars, potential bipolars at the time of admission for their depression had a history of more episodes and more hospital admissions. Likewise, they were more likely to show marked reproach or guilt (Winokur & Wesner, 1987).

The episodes are often biplasic or triplasic. Often, there is a short depression (few weeks), followed by a mania (2 to 3 months), followed in turn by a longer depression (6 to 9 months). Short-term follow-ups in bipolar patients are in reasonable agreement. Bratfos and Haug (1968) followed 42 patients for 6 years. They found that 7 percent recovered without relapse, 48 percent had one or more episodes, and 45 percent had chronic courses. Winokur, Clayton, and Reich (1969) followed 28 bipolar patients for 18 to 36 months after index admission. Table 8.4 presents the results. Notably, about 39 percent were consistently chronically ill or only partially remitted, and 14 percent were well in every way. Commonly, the patient has subsequent episodes, either superimposed on partial remission or wellness.

A large study on the course of bipolar illness was published by Angst and coworkers (1973). They evaluated 393 bipolar patients from five countries. The analysis was based on case histories and verbal information. Only 2 of the 393 bipolars suffered single episodes of illness. Sixty-four percent of the bipolar psychoses have been followed for at least 10 years and 49 percent for 15 years. The median number of episodes for the observation period was seven to nine, and the mean number of episodes in patients who had been observed for 40 years was not higher than in patients who had been observed for only 15 years. The authors concluded that there was a certain self-limitation in the mean number of episodes. It is important to note that these data refer to bipolars who have been treated. Between 70 and 80 percent of the patients had been treated in the hospital, and very few patients had received no treatment at all. The length of the episodes remains rather constant, varying only between 2.7 months in the first episode to 2.4 months in the tenth. The cycle length, or the time from the beginning of one episode to the beginning of the next, shortens from episode to episode, but approaches a certain threshold value.

The data presented by Angst from modern times do not jibe with data presented by Pollock in the early part of the century (1909 to 1920). About 55 percent of manic patients had only one recorded episode (Pollock, 1931). Like the Angst study, Pollock's also depended on hospital admissions. Also, Fukuda, Etoh, and Iwandate (1983) followed 100 bipolars in Japan for 12

TABLE 8.4.   Course of Illness in Bipolar Patients (18 to 36 Months Following Admission)

	N	Chronically Ill	Partial Remission with Episodes	Partial Remission without Episodes	Well with Episodes	Well in Every Way
Male	10	0	1	3	3	3
Female	18	3	4	0	10	1
Total	28	3	5	3	13	4

years, and reported a much higher percentage (39 percent) of patients who had only one or two episodes. The reasons for the differences between the modern Japanese study and Angst's study, as well as the reasons for the differences in the material from today and Pollock's material, are not apparent.

In any follow-up of bipolar disorder, it is necessary to evaluate the consequences of the illness. Although suicide is the major concern, increased mortality in bipolar patients from natural causes has been reported. Tsuang, Woolson, and Fleming (1980), reporting data from the "Iowa 500," found excessive death from unnatural causes in both primary unipolar depressives and manics. The unnatural deaths, mainly suicides, were higher in the unipolar depressives, but manic patients experienced excessive natural death. These data result from a follow-up of patients admitted to the hospital in the 1930s.

In a large modern study of hospitalized patients with affective disorders, excessive death from natural causes was found in female bipolar depression and in male and female manics who had concurrent organic mental disorders or serious medical illness (Black, Winokur, & Nasrallah, 1987). In the absence of these conditions, however, natural death was not excessive. Alternately, unnatural deaths, mainly suicides, were significantly increased in follow-up bipolar men and women if admitted for depression. If the index admission was for mania, unnatural deaths were not significantly increased. Taken together (bipolars of both sexes admitted for either depression or mania), no increased natural death rate was found after the patients with organic medical disorders were omitted; however, unnatural deaths (mainly suicides) were significantly increased, mainly in males. The increase in the unnatural death rate of bipolars was not as large as that in unipolars. A reasonable conclusion is that bipolar illness causes an increased suicide rate, but the increased natural death rate is the result of patients with two diseases, bipolar illness and serious medical disease.

EPIDEMIOLOGY

Results from epidemiological studies may be used to estimate the prevalence of bipolar illness in the general population. We must clearly understand the definitions for the relevant terms used in these studies, however, and also appreciate that many of the epidemiological studies conducted prior to use of criteria-based psychiatric diagnoses ascertained the prevalence of psychiatric symptomatology and not of psychiatric disorder. Prevalence rates for bipolar illness may be either point prevalence (i.e., the number of individuals ill at some time in a given year) or lifetime prevalence, a potentially more meaningful piece of information.

It is becoming increasingly apparent that all forms of affective illness (unipolar plus bipolar) are more prevalent than once thought. Prior to the 1970s, meaningful data were available only from studies done outside the United States. European investigators at that time were reporting on specific psychiatric disorders, not simply symptomatology; however, their definitions for given illnesses must be carefully noted because they differ from present-day nosology. These conservative estimates of prevalence represented the state of the art of epidemiology at that time.

One European study that is often cited was conducted by Helgason (1964) in Iceland. Using the biographic method (long-term follow-up of a randomly obtained sample), Helgason reported the lifetime prevalence for manic–depressive psychosis. Again, we encounter the problem of a nosology that combines bipolar illness with some forms of unipolar illness. Helgason defined manic–depressive psychosis as an illness characterized by attacks of affective disturbance, either elated or depressed, without apparent external cause and associated with psychomotor dysfunction and periods of disability. He also included involutional depression, a form of unipolar illness. Results were reported for both certain and uncertain diagnosis as a single diagnostic group.

Helgason drew his sample by identifying all Icelanders born in Iceland from 1895 to 1897 and living there on December 1, 1910. His period of observation began on that date and extended to July 1, 1957. Information was obtained on 99.4 percent of his probands, including those who had emigrated. Probands were followed from 13 to 15 years of age through 59 to 62 years of age. Thus, all had essentially passed through the age of risk for bipolar illness. A lifetime prevalence (certain plus uncertain diagnoses) was found to be 1.50 and 2.07 for men and women, respectively. The combined prevalence figure was 1.80 percent. It is impossible to determine what portion of these probands had bipolar illness and what portion had a form of unipolar illness; therefore, we can only conclude that these figures are high estimates for the true bipolar lifetime prevalence. No data exist that prevent generalization of this information to other populations of European descent.

Helgason (1979) reanalyzed his data, using criteria that differentiated bipolar disorder from other affective illnesses, and reported the expectancy (morbidity risk) for bipolar illness in his probands. The resultant finding, 0.79 percent, is not the lifetime prevalence, but approximates this figure closely because of the protracted period of follow-up. Tsuang, Winokur, and Crowe (1980) also reported morbidity risk for bipolar illness in the relatives of their surgical controls. Their value of 0.30 percent is generally considered to be a conservative figure that underestimates the true lifetime risk.

A contemporary study, reported by Weissman and Myers (1978), determined illness in an urban population in the United States. These investigators interviewed 515 randomly selected adults 25 years of age or older using a structured interview. Diagnoses were made using Research Diagnostic Criteria (Spitzer, Endicott, & Robins, 1977). Weissman and Myers found a lifetime prevalence for bipolar illness (depressions associated with mania or hypomania) to be 1.2 percent.

The National Institute of Mental Health's Epidemiological Catchment Area study is the largest study currently available that gives prevalence rates for criteria-based affective disorders (Weissman, Leaf, & Tischler, 1988). Five urban sites in the United States were used to assess over 18,000 people. Bipolar illness was defined as depression occurring with at least one manic or hypomanic episode. The 2-week prevalence rate of bipolar disorder was

0.7 percent. The lifetime prevalence rate was 1.2 percent. Bipolar illness was found to be significantly less prevalent than unipolar depression. The study reported the prevalence rate for major depression for the 2 weeks prior to the interview to be 4.4 percent. In contrast to unipolar illness, bipolar disorder was also found to have an earlier age of onset and no significant sex differences for prevalence rates.

An earlier study by Robins, Helzer, Weissman, et al. (1984) reported lifetime prevalence of psychiatric disorders in three U.S. sites. The authors differentiated the rate for Bipolar Type I (mania plus depression) from Bipolar Type II (hypomania plus depression). Bipolar Type I had a lifetime prevalence rate of 0.8 percent. When combined with other data, these findings appear to indicate that approximately two-thirds of patients with bipolar disorder will have depressive disorders with at least one full manic episode at some point in their lives.

ETIOLOGY

There are two sets of etiologic findings in bipolar illness: a distal etiology, that is, evidence in favor of a genetic background, and a proximal etiology, which covers findings of pathophysiology or neurochemistry.

Genetics

In a study of 57 bipolar probands, the morbidity risk for parents was 34 percent plus or minus 4.6, and for siblings 35 percent or minus 5.0 (Winokur et al., 1969). In that study, no male proband had an ill father, which suggested the possibility of X chromosome linkage. Females, on the other hand, had ill fathers and ill mothers. In the relatives of the probands, females were much more likely to be affected than males. Of 99 male first-degree relatives at risk, 19 had an affective disorder, and of 100 female relatives at risk, 50 had an affective disorder.

A modern twin study was reported from Denmark. Bertlesen, Harvald, and Hauge (1977) showed a concordance rate in bipolar monozygotic and dizygotic twins of 74 and 17 percent, respectively, clearly suggesting a genetic factor in bipolar illness. Mendlewicz and Rainer (1977), in a study of adoptees with bipolar illness, reported that 31 percent of biological parents and 12 percent of adopted parents of hospitalized bipolar adoptees had an affective disorder. The percentage in biological parents was comparable to the risk reported in parents of nonadopted bipolar patients. Again, this is strong evidence of the presence of a genetic factor in bipolar illness.

Clearly, family studies, twin studies, and adoption studies all suggest the possibility of a genetic factor in bipolar illness, but the matter of transmission has been argued. Reich, Clayton, and Winokur (1969) reported positive findings on X-linkage. Two families showed clear evidence of the possibility of a dominant gene on the X chromosome being related to bipolar illness. Mendlewicz, Linkowski, and Wilmotte (1980) studied a large family of bipolars from Israel, and reported that the illness was specifically linked to the G6PD region of the X chromosome; however, the results are somewhat contradictory. Gershon, Targum, Mattysse, and Bunney (1979) published results for linkage with red–green color blindness and ruled out close linkage. Gershon and his collaborators concluded that bipolar illness is not transmitted by a single gene close to the region on the X chromosome that transmits color blindness. Del Zompo, Bocchetta, Goldin, and Corsini (1984) presented data that supported linkage between bipolar illness and the color blindness–G6PD region of the X chromosome in two Sardinian pedigrees.

Within the past couple of years, however, new data have been reported. Baron et al. (1987) reported a positive finding of linkage between bipolar disorders and X chromosome markers. Mendlewicz et al. (1987) reported a study of linkage with a known X-linked marker using molecular genetics techniques. Finally, however, it seems clear that X-linkage cannot account for all of the transmission in bipolar illness. Many cases of male-to-male transmission have been reported. A finding of an autosomal linkage was reported by Egeland and her coworkers (1987) in a large Amish pedigree, in whom the linkage was to the Harvey-Ras locus and the insulin gene locus, both on chromosome 11.

The genetic findings are probably the strongest etiologic findings reported in psychiatry. More proximal etiologic findings are less reliable. One of the larger problems in the more proximal etiologies is that it is impossible to determine whether the illness causes the abnormality or the abnormality causes the illness. Suffice it to say that there may be findings that seem to be related to bipolar illness.

In evaluating the etiologic factors in bipolar illness, one falls back on the series of theories and a series of findings, but no unequivocal set of data exist that show clear evidence of a neurochemical or neurophysiological basis for depression. Probably the most popular concept is the amine hypothesis, which states that, in depression, a functional deficit of either norepinephrine or serotonin occurs at critical synapses in the central nervous system. Alternatively, an excess of these amines are present in mania. Other biogenic amines, such as dopamine, have been implicated, and an affective state may be relevant to a balance between central cholinergic and adrenergic neurotransmitters. Mania may be a disorder of adrenergic predominance in this balance (Janowski et al., 1983). However, no unchallenged body of evidence supports any of these theories.

Lewis and McChesney (1985) reported significantly fewer tritiated imipramine binding sites on platelet membranes in patients with bipolar illness when compared with controls. Such a study requires replication.

Abnormalities in endocrine parameters have been reported. Schlesser, Winokur, and Sherman (1980) presented evidence of inability to suppress serum cortisol after administration of dexamethasone the night before. Eighty-five percent of bipolar depressives were abnormal suppressors. On the other hand, manics suppressed normally the morning after dexamethasone administration. This has not been replicated by everyone. The implication of the finding is that a hypothalamic–pituitary–adrenal abnormality exists in bipolar patients, as well as in some unipolar patients. In the sleep laboratory, bipolar depressed patients have shortened rapid eye movement (REM) latency, higher REM density, and problems with sleep continuity (Kupfer, 1983).

On a more clinical basis, cases of secondary mania have been reported in conjunction with brain tumors and with the administration of various drugs, such as corticosteroids. Other reports of various associations have appeared in the literature through the years. These cases appear to be more similar to a concept of "induced" mania. The concept of "secondary" suggests only a temporal association and no etiology, but, in these reports, a biological etiology is, in fact, suggested. In any event, unlike most bipolar patients, patients with secondary or induced mania have a negative family history (Krauthammer & Klerman, 1978). Such reports may have value for their heuristic reasons. They may suggest studies of more specific pathophysiology and etiology.

THERAPY IN BIPOLAR DISORDER

Current approaches to the treatment of bipolar illness emphasize the somatic therapies. Lithium carbonate remains the drug of first choice for therapy, but lithium-resistive illness has spurred intensive research directed toward finding alternate interventions. Strategies for the treatment of acute episodes of either mania or depression are distinct from each other and also from the prophylactic or preventive therapies designed to eliminate or significantly dampen subsequent episodes of illness.

In the acute treatment of manic episodes, the primary pharmacological therapy is lithium. If a fulminant manic psychosis is present, adjunctive therapy with antipsychotic medications of the phenothiazine or butyrophenone classes is often required. These drugs have potent sedating effects, but appear not to have a specific antimanic effect. Lithium carbonate, however, does posses this specific antimanic effect and, thus, should be solely used in patients who are manageable without antipsychotics. Recently, the benzodiazepines, lorazepam and clonazepam, have been suggested as possessing specific antimanic effects while being less likely to induce the intolerable side effects so often seen with the neuroleptics (phenothiazine, butyrophenone, etc.). Thus, they are often utilized along with lithium in the acute treatment. As control of the episode is obtained, the antipsychotic or other adjunctive medication is tapered and ultimately discontinued while the lithium is continued for maintenance and ultimately prophylactic therapy. It has been estimated that approximately 40 percent of manic patients present with a dysphoric or mixed-mania state. These patients often do not benefit from lithium, and alternate therapies are indicated.

In addition to lorazepam and clonazepam, the past decade has seen the introduction of other medications with antimanic properties. The major contribution has come from drugs of the anticonvulsant class. Other promising drugs include calcium channel blocking agents, the alpha-2 agonist clonidine, and the beta-blocker propanolol. These latter medications are primarily experimental at this time; however, the anticonvulsants are currently in widespread clinical use.

Carbamazepine, an anticonvulsant, has emerged as the primary alternative therapy when lithium proves ineffectual. In responsive individuals, carbamazepine has a rapid onset of action, which is comparable to that seen with neuroleptics. If combined with lithium, benefits may be better than those of either agent alone. Carbamazepine has a low risk for bone marrow suppression (its most notorious adverse effect), and other side effects are usually well tolerated. Valproic acid and the benzodiazepines, clonazepam and lorazepam, are gaining ground as both alternate and adjunctive therapies for acute mania. Their beneficial activity appears to arise from their anticonvulsant properties.

Electroconvulsive therapy (ECT) is a very effective treatment for acute mania and may be the treatment of choice if the illness is life threatening. It is rarely used for mania today, primarily because of the efficacy of the pharmacotherapies. ECT is discussed further below as a treatment for depression, where its utilization is currently increasing.

In the acute treatment of depressive episodes, the primary pharmacological therapy is antidepressant medications. The 1950s saw the development of the first drugs with truly effective antidepressant properties. Two classes of antidepressants, monoamine oxidase inhibitors (MAOIs) and tricyclic antidepressants, were serendipitously discovered during this period. The MAOIs came from research in drug therapy for tuberculosis, whereas the tricyclics were derived from work with the neuroleptic antipsychotics. Since that time, other heterocyclic antidepressants have been developed. The most recent additions have been bupropion and fluoxetine. These two drugs may indeed possess unique therapeutic benefits, but their roles in the treatment of bipolar disorder remain unclear. The tricyclics and MAOIs treat acute depression, but do not stabilize the mood as does lithium and the anticonvulsants. Some evidence suggests that antidepressants may precipitate mania or induce more frequent episodes of illness (rapid cycling). In contrast, some investigators regard bupropion as a potential lithium alternative because of purported prophylaxes for recurring mania. The generic names for various drugs identified by major class are shown in Table 8.5.

ECT as an organic treatment in psychiatry dates back to 1938 when Cerletti first reported its use. Its introduction was a refinement in artificially

TABLE 8.5. Major Classes of Antidepressant Medications

Tricyclics	MAO Inhibitors	New Antidepressants
Amitriptyline	Phenelzine	Amoxapine
Nortriptyline	Tranylcypromine	Maprotiline
Imipramine	Isocarboxazid	Trazodone
Desipramine		Fluoxetine
Protriptyline		Bupropion
Doxepin		
Trimipramine		

induced convulsive therapy in use at that time. Although schizophrenia was the illness that was thought to benefit by convulsive therapy, it soon became apparent that ECT's most dramatic effects were in depression. Early reports were anecdotal in nature, but, as scientific methodology improved in psychiatry, well-designed, controlled studies demonstrated the efficacy of this treatment modality for depression. The therapeutic response of depressive signs and symptoms to ECT appears not to be a function of diagnosis (unipolar vs. bipolar illness). An American Psychiatric Association task force reviewed the literature and practice of ECT, and the following conclusions were drawn (APA Task Force Report, 1978): ECT is clinically indicated for the treatment of major depressive episodes if the patient has proven unresponsive to antidepressant medication or has serious suicidal risk, or if the depression is especially severe as demonstrated by a profound degree of weight loss or psychotic thought content.

The safety of ECT was increased dramatically by the introduction of two methodological advances in the 1950s. A short-acting hypnotic and a muscle relaxant are administered prior to the production of the seizure; thus, a modified convulsion is produced. The most recent advance is the use of unilateral ECT: The electrode placement is on the nondominant hemisphere, which minimizes transient memory impairment and confusion. Pharmacotherapy remains the mainstay for the treatment of severe depression, but ECT retains indications under certain clinical situations.

Because bipolar disorder is an episodic illness characterized by recurrence, prevention of future manic and depressive episodes is central to therapy. The Consensus Development Panel (1985) concluded that studies addressing the prevention of recurrence of bipolar episodes support the determination that lithium carbonate possesses prophylactic properties. It is estimated, however, that 50 percent or more of bipolar patients receive incomplete or no preventive benefit from lithium. Clinical practice suggests that the anticonvulsants that are beneficial for acute mania may also possess preventive properties, either alone or in combination with lithium. Current clinical research is attempting to validate these observations.

REFERENCES

Abrams, R., & Taylor, M. A. (1980). A comparison of unipolar and bipolar depressive illness. *American Journal of Psychiatry, 137,* 1084–1087.

American Psychiatric Association. (1978). *The APA task force report on electroconvulsive therapy.* Washington, DC: Author.

American Psychiatric Association. (1987). *Diagnostic and statistical manual of mental disorders* (3rd ed., rev.). Washington, DC: Author.

Angst, J. (1966). *Etiologie und nosologie endogener depressiver psychogen.* Berlin: Springer.

Angst, J., Baastrup, P., Grof, P., Hippius, H., Poldinger, W., & Weis, P. (1973). The course of monopolar depression and bipolar psychoses. *Psychiatrica Neurologia, Neurochirurgia, 76,* 489–500.

Baron, M., Risch, N., Hamburger, R., Mandel, B., Kushner, S., Newman, M., Drumer, D., & Belmaker, R. (1987). Genetic linkage between X-chromosome markers and affective illness. *Nature, 326,* 289–292.

Bartelsen, A., Harvald, B., & Hauge, N. (1977). A Danish twin study of manic depressive disorders. *British Journal of Psychiatry, 133,* 330–351.

Beigel, A., & Murphy, D. (1971). Unipolar and bipolar affective illness: differences in clinical characteristics accompanying depression. *Archives of General Psychiatry, 24,* 215–220.

Black, D., Winokur, G., & Nasrallah, A. (1987). Is death from natural causes still excessive in psychiatric patients. *Journal of Nervous and Mental Disease, 175,* 674–680.

Bratfos, O., & Haug, J. (1968). The course of manic–depressive psychosis. *Acta Psychiatrica Scandinavica, 44,* 89–112.

Bunny, W. & Murphy, D. (1973). The behavioral switch process and psychopathology. In J. Mendels (Ed.), *Biological Psychiatry.* New York: Wiley—Interscience.

Consensus Development Panel. (1985). Mood disorders: Pharmacologic prevention of recurrence. *American Journal of Psychiatry, 142,* 469–476.

Del Zompo, M., Bocchetta, A., Goldin, L., & Corsini, G. (1984). Linkage between X-chromosome markers and manic depressive illness. *Acta Psychiatrica Scandinavica, 70,* 282–287.

Detre, T., Himmelhoch, J. Swartzburg, M., Anderson, C., Byck, R. & Kuper, D. (1972). Hypersomnia and manic-depressive disease. *American Journal of Psychiatry, 128,* 1303–1305.

Egeland, J., Gerhard, D., Pauls, D., Sussex, J., Kidd, K., Allen, C., Hostetter, A., & Houseman, D. (1987). Bipolar affective disorders linked to DNA markers on chromosome 11. *Nature, 325,* 783–787.

Feighner, J., Robins, E., Guze, S., Woodruff, R., Winokur, G., & Munoz, R. (1972). Diagnostic criteria for use in psychiatric research. *Archives of General Psychiatry, 26,* 57–63.

Fukuda, K., Etoh, T., & Iwandate T. (1983). The course and prognosis of manic–depressive psychosis: A quantitative analysis of episodes and intervals. *Journal of Experimental Medicine, 139,* 299–307.

Gershon, E., Bunney, W., Leckman, J., vanEerdewegh, N., & DeBauche, B. (1976). The inheritance of affective disorders: A review of data and hypothesis. *Behavior Genetics, 6,* 227–261.

Gershon, E., Hamovit, J., Guroff, J., Dibble, E., Leckman, J., Sceery, W., Targum, S., Nurnberger, J., Goldin, L., & Bunney, W. (1982). The family study of schizoaffective bipolar I, bipolar II, unipolar, and normal control probands. *Archives of General Psychiatry, 39,* 1157–1167.

Gershon, E., Targum, S., Mattysse, S., & Bunney, W. (1979). Color blindness not closely linked to bipolar illness. *Archives of General Psychiatry, 36,* 1423–1430.

Helgason T. (1964). Epidemiology of mental disorders in Iceland. *Acta Psychiatrica Scandinavica, 40,* Supplement No. 173.

Helgason, T. (1979). Epidemiological investigations concerning affective disorders. In M. Schou & E. Stromgren (Eds.), *Origin, prevention and treatment of affective disorders.* New York: Academic Press.

Janowski, D., Risch, S., Judd, L., Parker, D., Kalin, N., & Huey, L. (1983). Behavioral and neuroendocrine effects of physostigmine in affective disorder patients.

In P. Clayton & J. Barrett (Eds.), *Treatment of depression, old controversies and new approaches.* New York: Raven Press.

Kraepelin, E. (1921). *Manic depressive insanity and paranoia.* Edinburgh: Livingstone.

Krauthammer, C., & Klerman, G. (1978). Secondary mania. *Archives of General Psychiatry, 35,* 1333–1339.

Kupfer, D. (1983). Application of sleep EEG in affective disorders. In J. Davis & J. Maas (Eds.), *The affective disorders.* Washington, DC: American Psychiatric Press.

Leonhard, K. (1959). *Aufterlung der Endogenen Psychosen* (2nd ed.). Berlin: Academie Verlag.

Leonhard, K., Korff, I., & Schulz, H. (1962). Die temperamente in den familien der monopolaren und bipolaren phasichen psychosen. *Psychiatria et Neurologia, 143,* 416–434.

Lewis, D., & McChesney, C. (1985). Tritiated imipramine binding distinguishes among subtypes of depression. *Archives of General Psychiatry, 42,* 485–488.

Mendlewicz, J., Linkowski, P., & Wilmotte, J. (1980). Linkage between glucose-6-phosphate dehydrogenase deficiency and manic depressive psychosis. *British Journal of Psychiatry, 137,* 337–342.

Mendlewicz, J., & Rainer, J. (1977). Adoption studies supporting genetic transmission in manic–depressive illness. *Nature, 268,* 327–329.

Mendlewicz, J., Simon, P., Sevy, S., Charon, F., Legros, S., & Vasanrt, G. (1987, May 30). Polymorphine DNA marker on X-chromosome and manic depression. *Lancet,* pp. 1230–1232.

Perris, C. (1966). A study of bipolar (manic-depressive) and unipolar recurrent depressive psychoses. *Acta Psychiatrica Scandinavica, 42,* (Suppl. 194).

Pollock, H. (1931). Recurrence of attacks in manic–depressive psychoses. *American Journal of Psychiatry, 22,* 567–574.

Reich, T., Clayton, P., & Winokur, G. (1969). Family history studies: V. The genetics of mania. *American Journal of Psychiatry, 125,* 358–360.

Robins, L., Helzer, J., Weissman, M., Orvaschel, H., Gruenberg, E., Burke, J., Regier, D. (1984). Lifetime prevalence of psychiatric disorders in three sites. *Archives of General Psychiatry, 41,* 949–958.

Schlesser, M., Winokur, G., & Sherman, B. (1980). Hypothalamic–pituitary-adrenal axis activity in depressive illness. *Archives of General Psychiatry, 37,* 737–743.

Spitzer, R., Endicott, J., & Robins, E. (1977). *Research diagnostic criteria: Rationale and reliability.* Paper presented at the Annual Meeting of the American Psychiatric Association, Toronto.

Tsuang, M., Winokur, G., & Crowe, R. (1980). Morbidity risk of schizophrenia and affective disorders among first-degree relatives of patients with schizophrenia, mania, depression, and surgical conditions. *British Journal of Psychiatry, 137,* 497–504.

Tsuang, M., Woolson, R., & Fleming, J. (1980). Causes of death in schizophrenia and manic depression. *British Journal of Psychiatry, 136,* 239–242.

Weissman, M., Leaf, P., Tischler, G., Blazer, D., Karno, M., Bruce, M., Florio, L. (1988). Affective disorder in five United States communities. *Psychological Medicine, 18,* 141–153.

Weissman, M., & Myers, J. (1978). Affective disorders in a U.S. urban community. *Archives of General Psychiatry, 35,* 1304–1311.

Winokur, G. (1970). Genetic findings and methodological considerations in manic–depressive disease. *British Journal of Psychiatry, 117,* 267–274.

Winokur, G. (1973). The types of affective disorders. *Journal of Nervous and Mental Disease, 156,* 82–97.

Winokur, G. (1979). Unipolar depression, is it divisible into autonomous subtypes? *Archives of General Psychiatry, 36,* 47–52.

Winokur, G. (1984). Psychosis in bipolar and unipolar affective illness with special reference to schizoaffective disorder. *British Journal of Psychiatry, 145,* 236–242.

Winokur, G., & Clayton, P. (1967). Family history studies—Two types of affective disorder separated according to genetic and clinical factors. In J. Wortis (Ed.), *Recent advances in biological psychiatry.* New York: Plenum Press.

Winokur, G., Clayton, P., & Reich, T. (1969). *Manic depressive illness.* St. Louis: Mosby.

Winokur, G., & Morrison, J. (1973). The Iowa 500: Follow up of 225 depressives. *British Journal of Psychiatry, 123,* 543–548.

Winokur, G., Tsuang, M., & Crowe, R. (1982). The Iowa 500: Affective disorder in relatives of manic and depressed patients. *American Journal of Psychiatry, 139,* 209–212.

Winokur, G., & Wesner, R. (1987). From unipolar depression to bipolar illness: 29 who changed. *Acta Psychiatrica Scandinavica, 73,* 59–63.

CHAPTER 9

Anxiety Disorders

DEBORAH C. BEIDEL and SAMUEL M. TURNER

The decade of the 1980s marked a watershed in the study of anxiety disorders. Prior to that time, these conditions were subsumed under three rather broad categories: phobic neurosis, obsessive–compulsive neurosis, and anxiety neurosis (American Psychiatric Association, 1968). With the introduction of the third edition of the *Diagnostic and Statistical Manual of Mental Disorders* (DSM-III; APA, 1980), classification of the anxiety disorders was radically altered. A major change was the "splitting" of anxiety neurosis into panic disorder and generalized anxiety disorder (GAD). Other significant changes included the introduction of agoraphobia, social phobia, and post-traumatic stress disorder (PTSD) as distinct diagnostic categories. The revision of DSM-III (DSM-III-R; APA, 1987) provided further classificatory changes, with agoraphobia being subsumed under the panic disorder diagnosis. The anxiety disorders appear to be the second most common psychiatric disorder in the general population of the United States, after substance abuse disorders (Blazer et al., 1985; Burnam et al., 1987; Robins et al., 1984), and they are equally common among children and adults (Anderson, Williams, McGee, & Silva, 1987).

Data from the large-scale National Institute of Mental Health's (NIMH) Epidemiological Catchment Area (ECA) study provided some estimates of the prevalence of anxiety disorders in the adult population, although not for the specific DSM-III-R categories. Six-month prevalence rates (adjusted to control for slight variations in the age and sex distributions across the five ECA sites) for the combined anxiety/somatoform categories ranged from 6.6, 7.2, and 7.4 percent (St. Louis, Los Angeles, and New Haven sites, respectively) to 14.8 percent (Baltimore and Piedmont sites) of the general adult population (Burnam et al., 1987). Somatoform disorders contributed only minimally to these prevalence rates (less than 0.4 percent for somatization disorder). In contrast, the phobia category, which included agoraphobia, social phobia, and simple phobia, accounted for the majority of the anxiety diagnoses. No data were obtained on the prevalence of PTSD for the general population. The 6-month prevalence rates for the specific anxiety disorder categories covered in the study and reported for each site are presented in Table 9.1.

Several issues with respect to the ECA studies should be noted. First, the semistructured interview that was used did not include assessment for every anxiety disorder diagnosis. Data were collected using the Diagnostic Interview

TABLE 9.1. Six-Month Prevalence Rates for Phobic Disorders Across Five Sites[a]

Disorder	New Haven	Baltimore	St. Louis	Piedmont	Los Angeles
Phobia	5.9	13.4	5.4	—	6.3
Agoraphobia	2.8	5.8	2.7	8.4	—
Social phobia	—	2.2	1.2	—	—
Simple phobia	4.7	11.8	4.5	—	—
Panic Disorder	0.6	1.0	0.9	—	0.9
Obsessive–Compulsive					
disorder	1.4	2.0	1.3	2.1	0.7

[a]Unadjusted for age or sex distributions across sites.

Schedule (DIS), an instrument designed for lay interviewers. Some disorders were omitted from the DIS because they were perceived as too difficult for lay interviewers to diagnose, and others were omitted from one or more sites in the interest of shortening the interview (Robins et al., 1984). Second, prevalence rates varied considerably across sites. This may be accounted for by changes in wording of the DIS, instituted after the study began in New Haven (Eaton et al., 1984). The largest change was the addition of many more examples of social situations, especially those usually associated with social phobia. This change also accounts for the lack of prevalence data for social phobia at the New Haven site.

Other potential limitations of the ECA data pertain to the use of lay interviewers rather than trained clinicians. When the lifetime diagnoses assigned by lay DIS interviewers were compared with those given by psychiatrists using the DIS or a DSM-III checklist 6 weeks later (Helzer et al., 1985), the results indicated low sensitivity for the DIS. Although the lay interviewer and the clinician agreed on the presence of one or more diagnoses, often they were not the same diagnoses. In addition, although the overall reliability coefficient was .64 (Yule's Y statistic), and 8 of the 11 DIS categories had reliability coefficients of .60 or better, some of the anxiety disorders coefficients were lower (.58 for agoraphobia, .45 for social phobia, .31 for simple phobia). Furthermore, obsessive–compulsive disorder was significantly underdiagnosed by lay interviewers. A second validity study reported low kappa coefficients for the diagnosis of current anxiety disorders, ranging from $-.02$ for panic disorder to .24 for phobic disorders and .05 for obsessive–compulsive disorder (Anthony et al., 1985). Also, for all diagnostic categories, individuals selected as "cases" by various methods were often different subjects.

Finally, a comparison of the initial lay DIS diagnoses and psychiatrists' diagnoses of ECA subjects were compared with psychiatric outcome measures a year later, including mental health visits, feeling overwhelmed by problems, a DIS diagnosis at follow-up, and psychiatric history in first-degree relatives (Helzer et al., 1985). For phobias and panic disorder, the psychiatrist checklist was a better predictor than the DIS for most of the outcome variables, and for all of the outcome variables in the case of obsessive–compulsive disorder. The DIS fared better for other diagnostic categories, such as depression, alcoholism, mania, substance abuse, or antisocial personality disorder. It appears, then, that the DIS may be particularly problematic for the diagnosis of anxiety disorders, making the ECA data on anxiety disorders suspect.

Many variations among these studies make it difficult to draw definitive conclusions, including whether the assessment pertained to lifetime prevalence (Helzer et al., 1985) or active disorders (Anthony et al., 1985). In addition, accuracy of the diagnoses differed depending on the severity of the disorder (Robins, 1985). Thus, although high concordance can be attained when no symptoms or all symptoms are endorsed, the threshold cases are the source of the unreliability because the positive endorsement of one additional symptom may be crucial to the assignment or nonassignment of a diagnosis. Since the current diagnostic system is based on meeting a certain minimum number of symptoms, however, this limitation is applicable to all methods of diagnosis, not only to the DIS.

Another major difficulty with the ECA data concerns the prevalence of anxiety disorders in minorities. Results showed that African–Americans had a higher lifetime prevalence than whites for simple phobia and agoraphobia (Blazer et al., 1985; Robins et al., 1984); however, these data are difficult to interpret due to the sampling strategy that was used. For example, there was overinclusion of severely disadvantaged African–Americans in general at the Baltimore and St. Louis sites, oversampling of elderly African–Americans, undersampling of low-income African–American males, and virtual exclusion of middle-class African–Americans (Williams, 1986). Also, the content validity of the DIS for low-income African–Americans has been questioned (Hendricks et al., 1983). For a more extended discussion of anxiety disorders research with African–Americans, see Neal and Turner (in press). In summary, although the ECA survey provided the first data on the prevalence of anxiety disorders in a large community sample, limitations with respect to data collection methods indicate that the resultant data must be interpreted cautiously.

CLINICAL PRESENTATION

The differentiation of "normal" anxiety from the clinical syndromes included in the diagnostic nomenclature is based not only on severity of symptomatology, but also on the degree of interference it presents in the individual's everyday life. For example, although up to 40 percent of the population may report "fears" of public speaking, only 2 percent of the population have fears that are severe enough to warrant a diagnosis of social phobia (Robins et al., 1984).

Anxiety is a multidimensional construct, and the most common way for it to be conceptualized is to use the tripartite model (Lang, 1977). Basically, this model divides anxiety responses into three dimensions: subjective distress (self-report), physiological response, and avoidance or escape behavior (overt behavioral response). Consistent with the transient "fight or flight" response, the somatic complaints of anxiety patients are characterized primarily by activation of the sympathetic nervous system. Thus, complaints of tachycardia, tremulousness, dizziness, lightheadedness, parasthesias, and dyspnea are common. Although a large literature attests to individual patterns of autonomic responses when assessed by laboratory tests such as cold pressor tasks (Lader, 1975), recent evidence suggests that certain types of anxiety disorder patients differentially experience somatic symptomatology. For example, in a study by Amies, Gelder, and Shaw (1983), dizziness, difficulty breathing, weakness in limbs, fainting episodes, and buzzing or ringing in the ears were endorsed significantly more often by agoraphobics than by social phobics. In contrast, patients with social phobia were significantly more likely than agoraphobics to endorse blushing and muscle twitching. Individuals with GAD report a preponderance of gastrointestinal distress, including indigestion, nausea, constipation, diarrhea, and urinary urgency and frequency. Finally, the reaction of needle–blood–injury phobics is defined by parasympathetic activation manifested by bradycardia and hypotension (Connolly, Hallam, & Marks, 1976), which is clearly different from the somatic responses found in other fear states.

Cognitive symptoms usually entail worry about the occurrence of specific events involving the possibility of danger or harm to oneself or sometimes to others. Although the cognitive symptoms are most often experienced as specific thoughts, they also may occur as ideas, images, or impulses. The occurrence of the fearful event, although a possibility, is usually of very low probability; thus, fear is out of proportion to situational demand. Anxiety patients are usually aware that their fears are excessive or unreasonable, yet this knowledge does little to assuage their emotional states. In simple or social phobias, the thought usually has a specific theme, and is most often triggered by contact with the feared stimulus or anticipation of such contact. On the other hand, those with more pervasive anxiety states, such as GAD, present with a broader constellation of anxious cognitions, termed worry, which encompasses several thematic areas, has the characteristics of mental problem solving, and carries the possibility of at least one negative outcome (Borkovec, Robinson, Pruzinsky, & DePress, 1983, p. 10).

A final category of anxious cognitions are obsessions that consist of intrusive unwanted thoughts and images, or impulses that are often horrific, and perceived by the patient as uncontrollable, yet always as a product of one's own mind and not the work of outside forces. The differentiation between these types of anxious cognitions can be quite subtle, and may be tied to the severity of the specific disorder; that is, the more chronic and disabling the condition, the more likely it is that the thoughts are consistent. Recently, an attempt to differentiate worry from obsessionality (Turner & Beidel, 1989a) highlighted several distinguishing characteristics, including thematic content (GAD patients do not often report excessive concern with dirt, contamination, aggressive impulses, or horrific images), form of cognition (GAD patients do not report images or impulses, but primarily conceptual, verbal linguistic activity, as described by Borkovec & Shadick, 1989, p. 22), and intrusive quality (worry is perceived as less intrusive and less egodystonic than obsessions). Thus, although there are some similarities in the cognitive distress experienced by various types of anxiety patients, there are a number of important differences as well.

The characteristic behavior of anxiety patients is escape from or avoidance of the feared stimulus. Many patients devise elaborate strategies, often engaging the cooperation of others to avoid the feared object or situation. In severe cases, such as those who suffer from panic disorder with agoraphobia, avoidance may become so restrictive that the affected individuals become "housebound." In the case of obsessive–compulsive disorder, avoidance is usually accompanied by the occurrence of ritualistic behaviors, such as washing or checking, which serve to "undo" or prevent the occurrence of the feared event. Although escape or avoidance is almost always present, it is not necessary for an anxiety disorder diagnosis to be made. In addition, behavioral avoidance is sometimes manifested in subtle ways that may not be readily apparent to the patient but can be detected by a trained clinician.

Other aspects of the clinical presentation include appetite or sleep disturbances, and concentration and memory difficulties. Anxiety patients often describe a dysphoric mood, usually attributed to restrictions placed on them as a result of their disorder. Many of these additional symptoms are similar to those experienced by depressed patients, making it sometimes difficult to differentiate these two mood states. In addition, certain patients may present with a mixed symptom picture. The research addressing this distinction is presented later in the "Differential Diagnosis" section. Below, the diagnostic criteria for each of the anxiety disorders are presented, along with comorbidity and differential diagnostic criteria.

DIAGNOSTIC CRITERIA AND DIFFERENTIAL DIAGNOSIS

Panic Disorder

As noted earlier, one of the most significant changes in DSM-III and DSM-III-R was the addition of panic disorder. Klein and his associates usually are credited with the impetus for differentiating panic from other forms of anxiety. Klein and Fink (1962) reported that antidepressants were effective in decreasing phobic inpatients' episodic anxiety or panic attacks, but ineffective for ameliorating anticipatory anxiety or avoidance. On the other hand, benzodiazepines were reported as being effective for anticipatory anxiety. Through a semantic drift, anticipatory anxiety became synonymous in the literature with generalized anxiety (Turner, Beidel, & Jacob, 1988). This "pharmacological dissection" strategy was thought to have delineated two distinct types of anxiety. More recent studies, however, have shown that imipramine is effective for GAD patients (e.g., R. J. Kahn et al., 1981) and that the newer high-potency benzodiazepines appear to be effective for treating panic disorder (see the "Clinical Management" section), thus calling into question this early model (Lydiard, Roy-Byrne, & Ballenger, 1988).

Panic disorder is defined by the occurrence of one or more panic attacks. An attack consists of discrete periods of intense fear or discomfort that are unexpected and are not triggered by specific fearful objects or situations in which the person is the focus of others' attention (APA, 1987, pp. 235–236). To meet diagnostic criteria, one must have had four attacks in a 4-week period, or at least one attack that was followed by a period of at least a month of persistent fear of having another attack. At least four of the following symptoms must have developed during at least one of the attacks: shortness of breath or smothering sensations, dizziness, unsteady feelings or faintness, palpitations or tachycardia, trembling or shaking, sweating, choking, nausea or abdominal distress, depersonalization or derealization, numbness or tingling sensations, hot flashes or chills, chest pain or discomfort, fear of dying, or fear of going crazy or doing something uncontrolled. Limited symptom attacks are also unexpected, but consist of three or fewer of the above symptoms.

There are two subtypes of panic disorder: with or without agoraphobia. In DSM-III-R, agoraphobia is considered to be a complication of panic disorder in which the person fears being in public places or situations where escape might be difficult or where help may be unavailable in case a panic attack occurs. As a result of this fear, the person tends to avoid leaving the house alone or traveling distances from home. Agoraphobics commonly fear being in crowded places, such as supermarkets, shopping malls, restaurants, churches, and theaters; riding in buses, cars, or planes; and·traveling over bridges or through tunnels. Earlier prevalence rates indicated that, although equal proportions of men and women had DSM-III panic disorder, those with DSM-III agoraphobia were predominantly female (Myers et al., 1984). Inasmuch as these two disorders have been combined in DSM-III-R, the current ratio of male to female patients is unclear; however, those with panic disorder and agoraphobia constitute over 50 percent of the patients seeking treatment at anxiety disorders clinics (Barlow, DiNardo, Vermilyea, Vermilyea, & Blanchard, 1986; Chambless, 1982).

Agoraphobia without History of Panic

Some agoraphobics report fear and avoidance of public places but apparently have never had panic attacks. Thus, although they behave similarly to those suffering from panic disorder with agoraphobia, they have never experienced the sudden, unexpected onset of panic. According to DSM-III-R, such patients are usually afraid of the sudden onset of one or several symptoms (limited symptom attacks), such as dizziness or falling, loss of bowel or bladder control, vomiting, or cardiac distress (APA, 1987). Persons given this diagnosis must never have met criteria for panic disorder. Interestingly, for some, the symptoms they fear have never occurred, at least not in the public places that they fear. This also differentiates the disorder from panic disorder with agoraphobia, in which the sudden onset of these symptoms is the first stage of the disorder. Agoraphobia without history of panic is seen only rarely, if at all, in clinical settings. Furthermore, recent evidence indicates that those who fear losing control of their bodily functions possess some clinical characteristics reminiscent of obsessive–compulsive disorder and may actually fall within the obsessional realm (Beidel & Bulik, 1990; Jenike, Vitagliano, Rabinowitz, Goff, & Baer, 1987). Although this condition was thought to be relatively rare, Weissman (1988) reported a prevalence of 2.9 percent in the general population. Closer examination of these data, however, led to the calculation of a more modest 1 percent prevalence rate (Jacob & Turner, 1988). Clearly, this is a controversial diagnostic category, and further research is needed to address the ambiguities.

Social Phobia

Although fears when in the presence of others date back to the days of the Hippocratic Corpus (Marks, 1985), and have been addressed in the literature since at least 1970 (Marks, 1970), social phobia was not introduced into the U.S. psychenclature until 1980. Social phobia refers to a persistent fear of one or more social situations in which the person may be exposed to possible scrutiny by others. An individual with this disorder may feel uncomfortable performing certain activities in the presence of others, such as speaking, eating, drinking, or writing, fearing that he or she may do something that will cause humiliation or embarrassment, such as forgetting a speech, mispronouncing a word, or shaking uncontrollably. Some social phobics also fear that others will detect their nervousness by observing signs of somatic distress, such as blushing or trembling. For some, the fear is not limited to circumscribed social situations, but is present in most social interactions, including one-to-one conversations. Those social phobics who fear only certain specific situations, such as speaking or writing in public, are considered to have the "specific" subtype, whereas those who fear a broad range of social situations are considered to have the "generalized" subtype. Although these subtype distinctions are listed in DSM-III-R, currently few empirical data support the subtype distinction (Turner & Beidel, 1989b).

Many social phobics (86 percent) avoid at least some social situations (Turner, Beidel, Dancu, & Keys, 1986), although strict avoidance is not necessary for the diagnosis. Unlike other anxiety disorders, social phobia appears to affect men and women in equal proportions (Amies et al., 1983; Marks, 1970; Turner et al., 1986). Recent research has revealed that, although originally considered rarely incapacitating, social phobia is a serious disorder that has significant ramifications for emotional, occupational, academic, and social functioning (Turner et al., 1986).

Simple Phobia

Simple phobia refers to a persistent fear of any object or situation that is unrelated to fears of having a panic attack (panic disorder with agoraphobia) or of embarrassment in public situations (social phobia). When confronted with the feared situation, simple phobics experience somatic and cognitive distress that may be quite intensive and disabling. In the general population, common simple phobias include fears of animals, such as dogs, snakes, insects, and mice, as well as fears of blood–injury, heights, and enclosed spaces (Agras, Sylvester, & Oliveau, 1969; APA, 1987). In clinical settings, claustrophobia (fear of closed spaces) and acrophobia (fear of heights) are most commonly encountered (Emmelkamp, 1988).

A common misconception is that simple phobias are relatively minor reactions. Certainly, the data collected from the large-scale ECA study revealed that a significant percentage of the general population suffers from some type of simple phobia, whereas this disorder accounts for a very small percentage of those treated in anxiety disorders clinics (Barlow et al., 1986). Those who do seek treatment at anxiety clinics are rarely "simple" often presenting with additional Axis I and Axis II disorders (Barlow, 1988). In addition, a patient's presenting complaint of a simple fear of knives or thunderstorms, for example, upon further questioning may be only a small part of a much larger fear complex, such as obsessive–compulsive disorder (Barlow, 1988; Turner & Beidel, 1988). The nature of the relationship of simple phobia to other anxiety disorders is unclear at this time.

Obsessive–Compulsive Disorder

Obsessive–compulsive disorder is characterized by the presence of intrusive thoughts, often coupled with repetitive behaviors that are elaborate, are time-consuming, and create significant distress for the individual and/or significant others. Obsessions are intrusive thoughts, ideas, images, or impulses that are abhorrent, horrific, or senseless, and that are experienced as intrusive and outside of voluntary control. Unlike delusions, they are recognized as products of one's own mind, and not as being imposed externally. Initially, the person attempts to ignore or suppress the intrusive thoughts. The most common forms of obsessions are doubting, thinking, impulses, fears, images, and urges. The most common content areas include dirt and contamination, aggression, inanimate–interpersonal features (e.g., locks, bolts, other safety devices, orderliness), sex, and religion (Akhtar, Wig, Verna, Pershod, & Verna, 1975; Khanna & Channabasavanna, 1988).

Compulsions are repetitive, purposeful, and intentional behaviors that are usually carried out in response to obsessions (APA, 1987), although, in a percentage of chronic cases, the obsessions or compulsions appear to exist independently (Turner & Beidel, 1988). Compulsions are performed according to rigid rules and are designed to prevent the occurrence of a future event, or to neutralize the aftereffects of an event that may have occurred, such as coming into contact with germs. Similar to obsessions, the purposelessness of these actions is recognized, but the person nonetheless feels compelled to carry out the ritual to completion. Completing the ritual may be negatively reinforcing, in that it does provide a temporary decrease in anxiety for most patients, although a few report increased anxiety (e.g., Walker & Beech, 1969). Common forms of compulsions are handwashing and bathing, cleaning, checking, counting, and ordering. Repetitive cleaning behaviors are often seen with contamination fears, whereas checking behaviors are common in those who experience self-doubt or dread the onset of some future event (Turner & Beidel, 1988). It is also common, however, for more than one type of compulsion to be present, as well as more than one type of obsession. In addition, patients with this disorder often develop elaborate strategies to avoid contact with feared objects or situations, thereby lessening their daily distress and limiting the necessity to engage in ritualistic behaviors. Thus, as noted above, fear of specific objects or events may be indicative of obsessive–compulsive disorder rather than simple phobia. Obsessive–compulsive disorder affects men and women in equal proportions (Turner & Beidel, 1989a) and is considered to have the most chronic course among the anxiety disorders.

Posttraumatic Stress Disorder

Posttraumatic stress disorder (PTSD) also was introduced in DSM-III. In DSM-III-R, those with PTSD are described as having experienced an event that is outside the realm of usual life experience and that would be significantly distressing to anyone. Examples of such events include combat experiences, assault, rape, or observing the serious injury or violent death of another person. Patients with this diagnosis report that they "reexperience" the event in one of the following ways: recurrent and intrusive recollections or dreams, suddenly acting or feeling as if the event were reoccurring, or intense psychological distress when exposed to events that symbolize or resemble some aspect of the trauma. As a result of the trauma, the person attempts to avoid stimuli associated with the event, including thoughts, feelings, activities, or situations, and the person may have difficulty recalling important aspects of the event. Furthermore, patients usually describe numbing of general emotions, including diminished interest in activities, feeling of detachment or estrangement from others, restricted range of affect, and a sense of a foreshortened future. Occurrence of general and persistent autonomic arousal is also a component of the disorder and may include difficulty sleeping, irritability or anger, difficulty concentrating, hypervigilance, exaggerated startle responses, and physiologic reactivity upon exposure to stimuli associated with the event (APA, 1987). The symptoms must persist for at least a month, and the disorder has two subtypes: immediate or delayed onset. In the case of the latter, the symptom onset occurs at least 6 months after the triggering event. Historically, this diagnosis was applied to persons who had participated in combat but currently it is also used for those who experience natural disasters and for victims of assault or rape (Kilpatrick, Saunders, Amick-McMullen, & Best, 1989). Given the multiplicity of symptoms associated with this disorder, and the reluctance of individuals to admit victimization events such as rape and physical or sexual abuse, patients may not spontaneously report the past occurrence of such events. Thus, direct questioning is often necessary to reveal such traumatic events and the presence of this disorder.

Generalized Anxiety Disorder

In DSM-III, generalized anxiety disorder (GAD) was reserved for those who did not meet criteria for any other anxiety disorder (Barlow, 1988), yet reported persistent worry and perhaps accompanying somatic distress lasting for 1 month. Basically, it was a residual diagnostic category. The diagnosis was quite controversial, producing only limited diagnostic reliability, and, due to the 1-month duration criterion, diagnostic criteria could be met by individuals responding to various acute life events. For a review of the difficulties associated with the DSM-III diagnosis and its subsequent evolution, the interested reader is referred to Barlow (1988).

In DSM-III-R, the more specific diagnostic criteria stipulate that a GAD patient must report excessive worry or overconcern about two or more life circumstances, such as finances or the health of significant others. In addition, the worries must be relatively constant and persist for a period of at least 6 months. Furthermore, the worries must be unrelated to those that might be a natural occurrence of any other anxiety disorder, such as worry about the occurrence of a panic attack or scrutiny by others.

In addition, complaints of somatic distress and cognitive apprehension, such as motor tension, autonomic hyperactivity, and vigilance or scanning, are common. Specific symptoms included under these three categories include trembling, twitching or feeling shaky, muscle tension, aches or soreness, restlessness, easy fatigability, shortness of breath or smothering sensations, palpitations or tachycardia, sweating or cold, clammy hands, dry mouth, dizziness or lightheadedness, nausea, diarrhea, other abdominal distress, flushes or chills, frequent urination, trouble swallowing or "lump in the throat," feeling keyed up or on edge, exaggerated startle response, difficulty concentrating, trouble falling or staying asleep, and irritability. According to DSM-III-R, these symptoms must persist for 6 months, rather than the 1-month criterion that was used in DSM-III. One result of requiring a 6-month symptom duration has been a sharp decrease in the prevalence figures for GAD. For example, whereas 11.5 percent of females in the general population would meet diagnostic criteria for GAD by applying the 1-month cutoff, this percentage drops to 2.4 percent if a 6-month duration criterion is used (Breslau & Davis, 1985).

Differential Diagnosis

Differential diagnosis is often difficult inasmuch as a substantial degree of comorbidity exists among the anxiety disorders. For example, Sanderson, Rapee, and Barlow (1987) reported that over 50 percent of anxiety patients actually received more than one anxiety disorder diagnosis when hierarchical rules were suspended. Social phobia was present in 25 percent of the patients with a primary diagnosis of panic disorder, and simple phobias were diagnosed in 44 percent. Similarly, 17 percent of social phobics also met criteria for a secondary diagnosis of panic disorder, and 59 percent of patients with primary GAD met criteria for a secondary diagnosis of social phobia. Because of the revised diagnostic criteria, the prevalence of GAD in large samples is unknown. Moreover, those presenting for treatment typically do not have a singular diagnosis of GAD. Even when GAD is assigned primary hierarchical status based on severity and degree of functional interference, only 9 percent of anxiety disorders patients diagnosed using DSM-III-R received GAD as the sole diagnosis (Sanderson et al., 1987). Ninety-two percent of patients receive one, two, or three additional anxiety disorders diagnoses, most commonly panic disorder with agoraphobia, social phobia, or simple phobia. The prevalence of GAD across all of the other diagnostic categories has led some investigators to suggest that it may not be a distinct disorder, but perhaps the basis from which other disorders arise and the residual state following treatment for other specific disorders (Turner, Beidel, Borden, Stanley, & Jacob, 1989). Although the anxiety disorders appear to have significant overlap, distinctions are necessary inasmuch as treatment interventions can vary depending upon the specific anxiety state present.

In addition to comorbidity among the anxiety disorders, anxiety and depressive states share many symptoms. This significant degree of overlap has led some investigators to suggest that many of the anxiety disorders, most specifically obsessive–compulsive disorder and panic disorder, are merely variants of depressive disorder. However, the bulk of the evidence—based on actual symptoms, childhood characteristics, and childhood events; differential predictors of outcome; personality characteristics; and analysis of genetic models based on large samples of twin data—supports the hypothesis that anxiety and depression are indeed different disorders (e.g., Gurney, Roth, Garside, Kerr, & Shapira, 1972; Kendler, Heath, Martin, & Eaves, 1987; Roth et al., 1972). In a recent study, Kendler et al. (1987) examined anxiety and depressive symptoms in an unselected sample of twins (3,798 pairs). The results, based on factor analysis, indicated that symptoms of anxiety and depression tend to form separate symptom clusters (depression–distress and general anxiety) and that the environment rather than any specific genetic influence was depressogenic or anxiogenic.

Although depression and anxiety may be separate disorders, the clinician is still confronted with distinguishing between these mood states, which often have a high rate of concordance. One method for drawing distinctions has been to examine the disorder's etiology and designate as "primary" the one that had the earliest onset. Thus, secondary depression would be defined as depression that occurs after the onset of the anxiety disorder. Secondary depression is common among anxiety patients, with estimates ranging from 17.5 to 60 percent, and averaging approximately 30 to 35 percent for panic disorder and agoraphobic patients (Barlow et al., 1986; Breier, Charney, & Heninger, 1984; Dealy, Ishiki, Avery, Wilson, & Dunner, 1981; Lesser et al., 1988; Uhde et al., 1985; Van Valkenberg, Akiskal, Puzantian, & Rosenthal, 1984). Another method of determining primacy is to determine the longitudinal course of the disorders. Breier et al. (1984) examined the course of depression in 60 patients with agoraphobia or panic disorder. Seventy percent of the patients had an episode of depression, with 43 percent reporting that the depression occurred before the first panic attack. The average time between the remission of the depression and the subsequent onset of the panic attacks was 4 years. In contrast, 57 percent of those patients who had both anxiety and depressive disorders reported that the depression occurred following the onset of the panic. For those patients, symptoms of panic, anticipatory anxiety, and generalized anxiety were chronic and unremitting, whereas symptoms of depression were episodic in nature, with 63 percent of those patients having remissions of depression that lasted for 1 year or more (Breier, et al., 1984). In such cases, the depressive disorder would clearly be seen as secondary to the anxiety disorder.

Depression is also common in obsessive–compulsive disorder, in which the majority of patients may experience at least some dysphoric mood (Barlow et al., 1986; Insel, Zahn, & Murphy, 1985). Again, the most common distinction has been based on the etiologic onset of the disorders. Depression that occurs after the onset of obsessive–compulsive disorder is considered to be secondary. As discussed in the "Clinical Management" section below, even though considered secondary, the presence of significant depression in a patient with obsessive–compulsive disorder could have important treatment implications.

Often, it is necessary to differentiate between cases in which anxiety is but one symptom of a primary Axis II personality disorder, and those that truly manifest comorbid Axis I and Axis II disorders. For example, although individuals with paranoid personality disorder are often anxious when in the company of others, their anxiety is due to concern about the motives of others, as opposed to social phobics who fear doing something to humiliate or embarrass themselves. Thus, a diagnosis of social phobia is not warranted in cases of paranoid personality disorder. In addition, the DSM-III-R diagnostic criteria for avoidant personality disorder are now so similar to those for social phobia that the majority of socially phobic patients meet at least some of the personality disorder criteria (Turner & Beidel, 1989b). Even with careful diagnosis and the use of hierarchical diagnostic rules, however, a subset of individuals will have anxiety disorders and personality disorders. Reich and Noyes (1987) reported that approximately 35 percent of acutely ill panic patients met criteria for a personality disorder, with the majority of these disorders falling into the Cluster C category (avoidant, dependent, passive–aggressive, and compulsive subtypes). Similarly, Mavissakalian and Hammen (1986, 1988) reported that between 30 and 40 percent of their agoraphobic samples met criteria for a personality disorder, with avoidant, dependent, and histrionic personality disorders occurring most frequently. Turner et al. (1989) found that 41 percent of a socially phobic sample met criteria for personality disorders, most commonly avoidant personality disorder or obsessive–compulsive personality disorder, and recent evidence indicates that those with obsessive–compulsive disorder and comorbid schizotypal symptoms, which may account for up to 20 percent of obsessive–compulsive patients, have a significantly poorer prognosis than those without such features (Jenike, Baer, Minichiello, Schwartz, & Carey, 1986; Stanley, Turner, & Borden, in press).

In summary, differential diagnosis among the anxiety disorders is necessary if we are to fully understand these conditions. Moreover, certain treatments that may be effective for one disorder may be relatively ineffective for another. Although differentiation is possible, it can be complicated because a substantial percentage of anxiety patients are comorbid for an additional anxiety disorder, a depressive disorder, or a personality disorder. In the majority of cases, the patients with additional diagnoses appear to be more symptomatic (Jenike et al., 1986; Mavissakalian & Hammen, 1988; Turner et al., 1989) and may have a poorer treatment prognosis (Mavissakalian & Hammen, 1988).

ETIOLOGICAL MODELS OF ANXIETY DISORDERS

Behavioral Theories

Recent surveys investigating the mode of onset for certain anxiety disorders indicate that conditioning experiences play an important role in etiology. Conditioning experiences were reported to be instrumental in the onset of agoraphobia (76.7 to 84 percent), claustrophobia (66.7 percent), and dental phobias (68.4 percent) (Öst, 1987; Öst & Hugdahl, 1983). Although still evident, conditioning experiences appear less significant in the acquisition of social phobia (58 percent), animal phobias (48 percent), and blood phobias (45 percent) (Öst, 1987). In the case of the latter two simple phobias, vicarious conditioning accounts for fear onset in approximately 25 percent of cases. Behavioral theories enjoy a prominent role in explaining the acquisition of anxiety and phobic states; however, it is clear that no single theory can adequately explain the onset or nature of these disorders. In the ensuing paragraphs, behavioral theories used to account for the acquisition and/or maintenance of the anxiety disorders are discussed. In light of the voluminous literature on the subject, this review touches briefly on important perspectives and highlights some of the more recent formulations.

The earliest accounts of fear acquisition, exemplified by the case of Little Albert (Watson & Rayner, 1920), were based on a strict Pavlovian conditioning model. Delprato and McGlynn (1984) summarized 25 studies that supported Pavlovian conditioning as a mechanism for the acquisition of fear. Also, a combination of classical and operant conditioning is inherent in the two-factor theory (e.g., Mowrer, 1947), a model frequently used to explain anxiety. Traditional conditioning models have been subject to a variety of criticisms, however. First, conditioning is evident in the case histories of many anxiety patients, yet, for some disorders, almost an equivalent number of cases experienced no apparent direct conditioning. Second, as noted by Rachman (1990), under even the most ideal traumatic conditioning situations, certain individuals fail to acquire fear. Third, types of learning other than classical conditioning have been demonstrated to be effective in explaining the acquisition of fear (Bandura, 1969). In a more recent conceptualization of fear-acquisition theory, Rachman (1977) proposed a "three-pathway" hypothesis in which classical conditioning is considered to be one method through which fear may be acquired; the other methods are vicarious learning and transmission via information and/or instruction.

Another problem for traditional conditioning models is that they do not adequately explain the unequal distribution of fears reported by the general population (Agras et al., 1969). For example, a significant proportion of the population endorsed fears of heights or snakes, yet few actually had traumatic conditioning experiences involving these stimuli. To account for this, Seligman (1971) put forth the notion of preparedness. Essentially, preparedness theory postulates that the unequal distribution of fears in the general population stems from a biological bias, such that certain fears are more easily acquired, inasmuch as they enhance the species' survival. A recent nonhuman primate study provided some support for preparedness theory. Cook and Mineka (1989) reported that fearful reactions were more easily acquired when laboratory-reared monkeys observed other monkeys behaving fearfully in the presence of fear-relevant stimuli (e.g., snakes or lizards) than when they behaved fearfully in the presence of rabbits or flowers. In each case, videotapes of a monkey behaving fearfully in the presence of a live snake were spliced and edited so that it appeared to the observer monkey that this fearful reaction was elicited by a toy snake, toy lizard, toy rabbit, or flower. Despite the identical reaction of the model, superior observational learning and fear responses occurred consistently and significantly more often in the monkeys who viewed the videotapes that included the lizard or snake, objects that are known to elicit fear in wild-bred rhesus monkeys.

According to Seligman (1971), the theory of biological preparedness accounts for the following characteristics of phobias: rapid acquisition, irrationality, belongingness, and high resistance to extinction. Belongingness describes the tendency for some conditioned stimuli (CSs) to more rapidly acquire fear-producing capabilities (through pairing with an unconditioned stimulus). Initial laboratory studies by Öhman and his colleagues (e.g., Öhman, 1986; Öhman, Eriksson, & Olafsson, 1975; Öhman, Fredrikson, Hugdahl, & Rimmo, 1976), conducted with human subjects, appeared to provide some initial support for the concept of preparedness. However, McNally's (1987) comprehensive and thoughtful review of the preparedness literature argues persuasively that the entire body of experimental evidence supporting the model is equivocal. Of the studies designed to investigate the characteristic properties listed above, only enhanced resistance to extinction of laboratory-conditioned electrodermal responses has been demonstrated consistently. Results of investigations examining ease of acquisition, belongingness, and irrationality have received only minimal support. Prior to discarding the theory, however, several mitigating issues need to be considered. Factors that may be potentially important in mediating the ability to acquire fear via these conditioning paradigms include human subject constraints that prevent researchers from attempting to experimentally condition strong fears, inability to control for prior information about and experience with the stimulus selected as the CS, and perception of the stimulus as dangerous (see McNally, 1987).

The study by Cook and Mineka (1989) partially addressed the issue of inability to control for prior information. The observer monkeys in this study had no prior information about any of the stimuli as dangerous or safe, yet conditioning was more evident for those objects feared "naturally" by wild-bred monkeys. Other studies by these investigators provide further evidence that prior information and experience pertaining to the "dangerousness" of the situation may be significant mediating factors. With respect to prior information, Mineka and Cook (1986) demonstrated that monkeys could be immunized against snake fear by prior observational learning. Laboratory-bred monkeys first observed other monkeys behaving nonfearfully in the presence of a toy snake, and then observed monkeys who behaved fearfully when confronted with the same snake. When the observer monkeys were exposed to the snake stimulus, they failed to acquire a fear response. Thus, it appears that prior exposure to nonfearful models served to "immunize" the observer monkeys against the later acquisition of fear. These data suggest that prior positive environmental experiences may play a significant role in explaining why only some individuals become fearful after experiencing a traumatic event. Also, recent data suggest that conditioning experiences can be cumulative (Mineka, 1985), and that there are factors before, within, and following the conditioning experience that have relevance for fear acquisition (Mineka & Zinbarg, in press).

Another issue in the conditioning literature that deserves further investigation is whether the CS is actually perceived as dangerous or frightening. As Cook and Mineka (1989) demonstrated, superior conditioning in nonhuman primates may occur for particular classes of stimuli that are considered to have potential survival relevance. Many studies with humans, however, have failed to document such a relationship. An alternative explanation for the nonrandomness of fears in the general population was examined by Merckelbach, van den Hout, Jansen, and van der Molen (1988). Undergraduate students rated 38 stimuli commonly used in preparedness research for fearfulness, objective dangerousness, and spatiotemporal unpredictability. The same items were rated for survival relevance by fifteen biologists. Spatiotemporal unpredictability refers to the stimuli's potential to behave in an expected fashion. For example, snakes and spiders, which have locomotive properties, have a higher degree of spatiotemporal unpredictability than flowers or mushrooms. This difference may be of considerable theoretical importance in that unpredictable or underpredicted aversive events produce strong emotional responses (Merckelbach et al., 1988). These data suggest that factors other than survival relevance may be important in explaining preparedness, and also may explain the negative findings of many conditioning studies. For example, spiders and snakes are used as phobia-relevant stimuli, and mushrooms and flowers as non-phobia-relevant stimuli. However, an analysis of survival-relevance scores indicated that, although scores for snakes were significantly higher than for flowers, there was no statistically significant difference between spiders and flowers, or between mushrooms and snakes. In addition, biologists rated fear of mushrooms as considerably more survival relevant than fear of spiders. Thus, one explanation for the lack of conditioning differences in some studies may be that inappropriate stimuli were used.

Intercorrelations among these four factors were also examined. Initially, all of the constructs were highly correlated; however, a somewhat different picture emerged when partial correlational analyses were used to examine the unique variance contributed by survival relevance, dangerousness, and unpredictability to the construct of fearfulness. The results indicated that controlling for survival relevance had very little effect on fear–dangerousness or fear–unpredictability correlations. On the other hand, controlling for dangerousness and unpredictability reduced the fear–survival relevance correlation from its original .51 coefficient to a nonsignificant .18. These results suggest that perceptions of dangerousness and unpredictability contribute far more to fearfulness than does survival relevance, and that future investigations should select stimuli that differ on perceived dangerousness and unpredictability rather than on survival relevance. Interestingly, Cook and Mineka's (1989) results are consistent with those of Merckelbach et al. (1988) in that the stimuli used in the former investigation (flowers and snakes) were disparate on the dimensions of dangerousness and unpredictability.

In summary, results of behavioral theories of etiology have evolved from simplistic, straightforward classical conditioning theories toward more complex conceptualizations. First, as noted by Rachman (1977), fear may be acquired as a consequence of vicarious conditioning, information transmission, or classical conditioning. Vicarious conditioning may be a particularly powerful mechanism for fear acquisition. In nonhuman primate studies, learning occurred within a very brief period of time (8 minutes) and produced strong emotional responses that were easily observable and approximately equivalent in intensity to those of the models. Although extant family studies have often attributed strong familial prevalence rates to a biological etiology, the vicarious conditioning literature clearly indicates that other pathways may be equally important, or that some combination of biological and psychological–environmental parameters might be essential. Second, the study by Merckelbach et al. (1988) shed new light on the nonrandomness of fear-producing stimuli. Although theories of survival relevance, such as preparedness, have fallen into disfavor, other characteristics of the stimulus, such as dangerousness or spatiotemporal unpredictability, may play important roles. Obviously, experimental studies designed to more carefully examine the roles of these variables are now in order. Finally, it must be noted that behavioral theories may never fully account for acquisition or maintenance of all fear. For example, even under the strictest environmental controls, not all of Mineka and Cook's (1986) subjects acquired a fear of snakes, and the reasons remain unclear. It is likely that multiple mechanisms are involved, and we turn now to an examination of some other possible contributors.

Cognitive Theories

Perhaps the best known cognitive theory related to the etiology of anxiety disorders is that of Beck and Emery (1985). This theory utilizes an information processing model in which the basic elements of cognitive organization are cognitive schemas. Schemas are organized into cognitive constellations (cognitive sets). When a set is activated, the content directly influences the person's perceptions, interpretations, associations, and memories. Meaning is then assigned to the object that instigated the cognitive schema. Furthermore, cognitive sets contain rules. For the anxiety disorders, the rules relate to the concepts of danger and vulnerability and to the person's estimation of his or her capacity for coping with the danger. If there is a perception of high vulnerability, applying the rules results in the formulation of conclusions that one is incapable of dealing with the situation. Unlike the rules for depression, which are absolute, rules for anxiety disorders have a conditional form such as the following: If A happens, it *may* (rather than *will*) have a negative result. Thus, according to Beck and Emery (1985), the crux of an anxiety disorder is "a cognitive process that may take the form of an automatic thought or image that appears rapidly, as if by reflex, after the initial stimulus that seems plausible (e.g., shortness of breath), and that is followed by a wave of anxiety" (pp. 5–6). They added that if a specific thought or image cannot be identified, it is still possible to infer that a cognitive set with a meaning relevant to danger has been activated.

Although this theory is actually a good description of the cognitions that are part of anxiety reactions, like the behavioral theories, it has several weaknesses that prevent its adoption as a full etiologic explanation. For example, if the cognitive schema are the triggering factors, from where do the schemata come? Similarly, where does the individual acquire the set of rules related to danger and vulnerability, and why do different individuals develop different rules regarding the same object? Two plausible hypotheses would be biological predisposition or prior learning experience, both of which would remove maladaptive cognitive thinking from a primary etiologic function. In recent years, several investigators have argued that, although cognitive therapy might be a useful addition to the treatment armamentarium, it does not appear to have a unique explanatory role in illuminating etiology or explaining treatment outcome (Beidel & Turner, 1986; Brewin, 1985).

Two other cognitive theories that attempt to explain the onset of anxiety disorders are the "fear of fear" model (Goldstein & Chambless, 1978) and anxiety sensitivity (Reiss & McNally, 1985). The fear of fear model posits that individuals who have experienced panic attacks may, through the process of interoceptive conditioning, learn to fear any change in their physiological state that could signal the onset of panic. In effect, low-level bodily sensations become a conditioned stimulus that triggers fear and worry regarding the onset of panic. Of course, this is not a purely cognitive model in that interoceptive conditioning has a central role. Fear of fear seems to be a particularly important characteristic of individuals with panic disorder. Behavioral treatment models, discussed below, have built upon the fear of fear hypothesis by exposing the individual not only to places where panic might occur, but also to the physical sensations of panic itself.

More recently, however, Reiss and his colleagues proposed an elaboration of the fear of fear hypothesis by introducing the construct of "anxiety sensitivity." Anxiety sensitivity is defined as an individual difference variable consisting of beliefs that the experience of anxiety causes illness, embarrassment, or additional anxiety (Reiss & McNally, 1985; Reiss, Peterson, Gursky, & McNally, 1986). According to Reiss et al. (1986), anxiety sensitivity builds upon the original fear of fear hypothesis, yet departs from it. Although Goldstein and Chambless (1978) regarded the emergence of fear of fear as a consequence of panic attacks, Reiss and McNally (1985) considered fear of fear to be the result of several factors: panic attacks, biological predisposition, and personality needs to avoid embarrassment or illness or to maintain control. Anxiety sensitivity is the quantification of belief that anxiety causes illness or embarrassment and, like fear of fear, is thought to be more prevalent in patients with agoraphobia.

Empirical investigations by Reiss and his colleagues (Holloway & McNally, 1987; Maller & Reiss, 1987; McNally & Lorenz, 1987; Peterson & Heilbronner, 1987; Reiss et al., 1986) suggest that the Anxiety Sensitivity Inventory

(ASI) assesses a dimension other than general anxiety, anxiety symptoms, or fear of fear. However, the studies have been criticized from both methodological and theoretical perspectives (Lilienfeld, Jacob, & Turner, 1989). As noted by Lilienfeld et al. (1989), Reiss et al. (1986) and Holloway and McNally (1987) stated that anxiety sensitivity refers to beliefs that anxiety has harmful consequences. This claim cannot be substantiated, however, by a perusal of the items contained in the ASI, which appear to tap fear of anxiety and anxiety symptoms (e.g., "It *scares* me when I am nervous" or "When I notice that my heart is beating rapidly, I *worry* that I might have a heart attack") rather than beliefs concerning negative consequences (an example of which might be "A rapidly beating heart is a sure signal of a heart attack"). A second, and potentially more critical, problem for the anxiety sensitivity construct is that it has not been demonstrated that the construct differs from the more parsimonious explanation of trait anxiety. A thorough discussion of this issue can be found in Lilienfeld et al. (1989); however, it may be briefly summarized by noting that, since trait anxiety measures were not included in the empirical investigations, it is difficult to state conclusively that anxiety sensitivity differs from trait anxiety. Future investigations directed at anxiety sensitivity will need to include more thorough assessments of trait anxiety. Only then can it be determined that anxiety sensitivity makes a unique contribution to the etiology or maintenance of anxiety disorders.

In summary, recently proposed cognitive theories of anxiety have allowed the clinician to examine more directly the role of beliefs and cognitions in the etiology and maintenance of these disorders. The empirical evidence to date indicates that, although these factors may be important in maintaining fear and avoidance of phobic settings, their role as catalysts in the onset of the disorders remains uncertain. High-risk studies may well be necessary to resolve the issue of whether cognitive attributes play an etiological role or if they are merely correlates or epiphenomena.

Biological Theories

As with other areas of psychopathology, there has been increased interest in biological factors in the anxiety disorders. For example, the possibility of a genetic relationship has been pursued through twin studies and family or family history studies. The prospect of a constitutional relationship has been addressed by examining psychophysiological, neurochemical, and behavioral indices. Below, we briefly examine data from both human and nonhuman primate research that bear directly on these possibilities. With the exception of the nonhuman primate studies, those reviewed are limited to studies using DSM-III or DSM-III-R diagnostic criteria.

Family and family history studies reveal an increased morbidity rate among the first-degree relatives of patients with anxiety disorders. For example, Crowe, Noyes, Pauls, and Slyman (1983) compared the morbidity risk of panic disorder among the first-degree relatives of patients with panic disorder with that of the relatives of normal controls. The results indicated a panic disorder morbidity risk of 17.3 percent among the panic disorder patients' relatives, compared with a risk of 1.85 percent among the relatives of the normal controls. An additional 7.4 percent of the panic disorder patients' relatives reported the presence of panic attacks that did not meet DSM-III criteria; this differed significantly from the 0.4 percent morbidity risk for panic attacks found in the relatives of the normal controls. No difference was found, however, in the number of relatives in each group who met criteria for GAD: 4.8 percent in the panic patients' relatives compared with 3.6 percent in the control group, which could suggest that these disorders represent distinct diagnostic syndromes. As noted by Barlow (1988), however, this study followed the DSM-III hierarchical convention that GAD was not diagnosed if panic disorder was present. The change in DSM-III-R to allow the concurrent diagnoses of panic disorder and GAD may have resulted in differing mordibity risks in the sample. A replication of this study allowing for concurrent diagnoses is necessary before these type of data can be used as evidence for validation of the diagnostic categories. Therefore, it would be premature to draw conclusions regarding differing etiologies based on these data.

In another study, Harris, Noyes, Crowe, and Chaundry (1983) evaluated the morbidity risks for panic disorder, agoraphobia, or any anxiety disorder in the relatives of agoraphobic patients and normal controls. The morbidity risk among the relatives of agoraphobic patients was 8.6 percent for agoraphobia, 7.7 percent for panic disorder, and 31.7 percent for all anxiety disorders. These rates were significantly different from the morbidity risks in the normal control group relatives, which were 4.2 percent for agoraphobia, 4.2 percent for panic disorder, and 14.8 percent for the presence of any anxiety disorder. The results of both studies indicated that relatives of patients with panic disorder and agoraphobia appeared to be at increased risk for developing an anxiety disorder, although no specific gene has yet been discovered.

The Crowe et al. (1983) and Harris et al. (1983) studies assessed all of the available first-degree relatives of anxiety patients. Other investigators have attempted to examine the issue of increased familial prevalence by focusing more specifically on the parent–child relationship. These studies are of two types: those in which a child with an anxiety disorder is the proband and the rates of anxiety disorders in the parents are the focus of the investigation, and those in which the proband is an adult with an anxiety disorder and the investigator seeks to establish the incidence and prevalence of anxiety disorders in the patient's children.

Four studies have assessed the children of patients with a DSM-III or DSM-III-R anxiety disorder. Reichler, Hyde, and Sylvester (in press) studied the presence of anxiety and depression in the children of panic patients, depressed patients, and normal controls. The children of the normal controls were significantly less anxious and depressed compared with the patients' offspring, whereas few differences were found between the children of the two patient groups. Two findings, however, suggested at least some specificity between parent diagnosis and child symptoms. First, offspring of panic patients reported higher trait anxiety than any other group. Second, children of depressed parents reported fewer pleasurable experiences and more depression than normal controls, whereas pleasurable experiences did not differ between children of panic patients and those of normal controls.

Inasmuch as these significant differences represented only a small subset of the entire data analysis, the results must be interpreted cautiously; however, they do provide some indication that certain factors related to parental disorder may be reflected in the emotional status of children.

Weissman et al. (1984) compared children of probands with major depression, with or without an additional anxiety disorder, and children of a normal control group. Those children whose parents had both depression and an anxiety disorder were found to be at greater risk for a psychiatric disorder and were more likely to have been referred for treatment. The authors concluded that the offspring of parents with comorbid anxiety and depressive disorders were at greater risk for psychopathology than those of parents with a single disorder. The conclusions are confounded, however, in that the study did not include a parent group with only an anxiety disorder. Thus, it cannot be ruled out that greater child psychopathology might have been due to the presence of anxiety alone.

A recent study by Rosenbaum et al. (1988) directly addressed this issue by comparing rates of "behavioral inhibition" in the offspring of four groups: panic disorder patients with or without comorbid major depression, patients with only major depression, and a psychiatric control group. The term behavioral inhibition (Kagan, 1982, see below) describes a child's degree of sociability as displayed by behaviors ranging along an approach–withdrawal dimension. Briefly, inhibited children consistently emit few spontaneous vocalizations when in the presence of a stranger, and cry and cling to their mothers rather than approach other children in play settings. These behaviors resemble those of individuals who consider themselves "shy or socially phobic," although empirical studies relating these constructs have yet to be conducted. Using the assessment procedures developed by Kagan, Reznick, and Snidman (1987), Rosenbaum et al. (1988) reported that 86 percent of the panic disorder offspring were judged to be behaviorally inhibited, compared with 70 percent of the anxious and depressed group, 50 percent of the major depression only group, and 15 percent of the psychiatric control group. Therefore, although these data support the hypothesis that the offspring of anxiety disorders patients exhibit inhibited behaviors, they do not support the conclusion proposed by Weissman et al. (1984) that the children of a parent with two disorders are the most deviant.

In one of the few studies to determine the actual prevalence of DSM-III disorders in children considered to be at "high risk," Turner, Beidel, and Costello (1987) compared the offspring of anxious adults to two control groups: children of dysthymic patients and normal controls. The results indicated that children of anxiety probands were almost three times as likely to have one of several DSM-III disorders as the children of dysthymic patients, twice as likely as the children of dysthymic parents to have a DSM-III anxiety disorder, and over nine times as likely to have a DSM-III disorder as the children of normal parents. The sample size in this investigation was quite small, yet the results in conjunction with the other three investigations suggest that the offspring of anxious patients appears to constitute a group at risk for the expression of anxiety symptoms, and thus the topic is worthy of further scientific investigation.

Several other studies of familial relationships have addressed the incidence and prevalence of anxiety disorders in the relatives of children with DSM-III disorders. In one investigation, rates of anxiety disorders in the parents and grandparents of children with anxiety disorders or depressive disorders did not differ (Livingston, Nugent, Rader, & Smith, 1985). The results which indicated that only one relative in each group had an anxiety disorder must be considered in light of the study's methodological limitations. First, the total sample consisted of 12 anxious children and 11 depressed children. Second, all of the relatives were not directly interviewed. Studies that utilize only one informant (e.g., the family history method) underestimate the prevalence of familial dysfunction compared with studies in which all members are personally interviewed (e.g., the family method). In another small investigation, Bernstein and Garfinkel (1988) interviewed the parents of 6 children with school phobia and 5 children with other psychiatric disorders. Seven of the 12 parents of school phobic children (58 percent) had anxiety disorder, compared with 3 of the 10 parents (30 percent) of children with another psychiatric disorder. Again, although these results are intriguing, replication with larger samples is necessary.

Last and her colleagues (Last, Hersen, Kazdin, Finkelstein, & Strauss, 1987; Last, Hersen, Kazdin, Francis, & Grubb, 1987; Last, Hersen, Kazdin, Orvaschel, & Ye, 1988) conducted an extensive family investigation of the first- and second-degree relatives of child probands diagnosed with anxiety disorders. In addition to relatives of the anxiety probands, relatives of children with attention deficit hyperactivity disorder and normal controls were included in the latest study (Last et al., 1988). To date, the results of the first year of this investigation are available for examination (see Last & Beidel, in press). Based on data obtained through structured interviews, a significantly increased risk of anxiety disorders was evident in the first- and second-degree relatives of the anxiety probands compared with the relatives of normal controls. Differences in increased risk between the relatives of the anxiety disorders and attention deficit hyperactivity disorders' probands showed a trend in the expected direction ($p < .10$). Inasmuch as this study is still ongoing, conclusions about the significance of the initial findings require confirmation.

In addition to family studies, twin studies are also important when investigating hypotheses about genetic contributions. The only twin study in which psychiatric interviews were conducted and diagnoses assigned according to DSM-III criteria was by Torgersen (1983). Results of this investigation indicated that the concordance rate for any anxiety disorders category was higher for monozygotic (MZ) than for dizygotic (DZ) twins, with the exception of GAD. The overall concordance rate for the MZ twins was 34 percent, compared with 17 percent for the DZ twins, but no co-twin had the same anxiety disorder as the proband, and concordance rates for GAD were higher for DZ than for MZ twins. Although this study often has been interpreted as supporting the genetic transmission of all of the anxiety disorders with the exception of GAD, the more appropriate observation is that the data support the hereditary transmission of a generalized predisposition for anxiety.

In summary, some general trends appear to be consistent across all of the studies that have used family or twin designs in the search for a genetic etiology. Significantly higher rates of anxiety disorders appear in the families of anxiety probands than in the families of normal controls; however, when the families of probands with other types of psychopathology are included in the investigation as a psychiatric control group, the outcome becomes less clear. Significant differences among psychiatric groups for familial prevalence or morbidity risks are not always evident. At this time, twin studies also do not support the notion of the direct transmission of a particular anxiety disorder. Therefore, two other factors warrant consideration in explaining the observed familial pattern: the increased prevalence rates among the probands' families may reflect the stress of coping with a psychiatrically ill individual within the family structure, or some underlying vulnerability is manifested in a different fashion dependent upon environmental circumstances.

Vulnerability

Recently, several groups of investigators have attempted to shed some light upon the issue of vulnerability from different perspectives. Nonhuman primate studies of individual differences in anxiety have significant implications for the study of vulnerability in humans. Suomi (1986) reported substantial individual differences in the intensity and extent of anxiety-like behaviors in infant and juvenile rhesus monkeys. For example, when in novel situations or when separated from familiar surroundings, some infant monkeys showed evidence of behavioral, autonomic, and endocrinological signs of fearfulness, whereas others responded with exploratory or play behaviors (Suomi, Kraemer, Baysinger, & Delizio, 1981). Longitudinal studies have shown that these characteristics remain stable throughout adolescence and young adulthood. Furthermore, it appears that environmental conditions cannot completely alter constitutional vulnerability. When faced with challenging situations, biological monkey siblings "adopted away" at birth and raised in adoptive families, continued to show greater similarity in both cortisol levels and behavioral fear scores than the similarity between adopted siblings (Suomi, 1986).

Kagan and his associates (Kagan, 1982; Kagan et al., 1987; Kagan et al., 1988; Reznick et al., 1986) identified a temperamental factor referred to as behavioral inhibition. From an initial pool of 300 children, these investigators identified 60 children who consistently displayed inhibited or uninhibited behaviors in the presence of novel events (Kagan, 1982). Inhibited children were those who cried, clung to their mothers when approached by a stranger, were reluctant to interact with their peers in a play situation, and emitted few spontaneous vocalizations when in the presence of an unknown investigator. When placed in these situations, inhibited children had higher heart rates and less heart rate variability than uninhibited children. Such different heart rate patterns remained stable through the toddler, preschool, and early elementary school developmental stages in two separate cohorts followed over at least a 5-year period (Kagan et al., 1987; Kagan et al., 1988). However, overt behavioral evidence was less consistent than cardiac parameters. The original index of behavioral inhibition at 14 or 20 months was not predictive of inhibition scores at age 4. Approximately 33 percent of the children changed classification, with most becoming less inhibited. Although a further reduction in the sample size, such that it then represented only 3.25 percent of the originally screened group, resulted in significant differences between the inhibited and uninhibited children at age 4, the stability of the inhibition scores from 20 months to 4 years in this reduced sample was not reported (Kagan et al., 1988). The investigators noted that both environmental and somatic factors may have contributed to the apparent instability. First, preservation of the original behavioral index was best for inhibited children who had the most stable heart rates in the group, whereas initially inhibited children who had less stable heart rates were more likely to change classification. This finding suggests that the greatest consistency between somatic and behavioral indices of inhibition was most predictive of later behavioral inhibition. A second explanation for the changing classification of some of the children was that those inhibited children whose mothers made a special effort to expose them often to interactions with their peers also moved from inhibited to uninhibited status.

Another investigation that addressed the issue of vulnerability in anxiety disorders was that of Turner, Beidel, and Epstein (in press). Skin conductance responses of children with DSM-III anxiety disorder diagnoses were compared with those of normal controls when presented with novel or fear-producing stimuli, including a 100-db tone and a picture of a snake appearing ready to "strike." Although the small number of children in this investigation (11 normal controls and 8 anxious children) precludes broad generalizations, the results suggested that differentiating the two groups on the basis of autonomic responses is possible and potentially quite important. For example, when exposed to the tone or the snake, anxious children had a higher mean response amplitude than normal controls, indicative of increased arousal. In addition, anxious children had five times the number of spontaneous fluctuations during baseline and tone conditions, and twice the number of spontaneous fluctuations during the snake condition. Furthermore, only 1 of the anxious children habituated to the sound of the tone, even after twenty consecutive presentations, whereas 10 of the 11 normal children did so. Similarly, only 38 percent of the anxious children habituated to the picture of the snake, whereas 100 percent of the normal controls did so. Interestingly, these clear physiological differences were not mirrored in the children's self-report of distress during the task. Both groups of children reported only minimal levels of distress during the assessment, as determined by scores on a 5-point rating scale. Therefore, the results indicate that, even though the anxious children did not perceive themselves as being anxious, they manifested higher somatic arousal, which appeared to be outside of their general awareness.

The studies reviewed to this point have focused on vulnerability in the general sense of the term. Although the results indicate that certain individuals may be more prone or vulnerable to anxiety reactions, no longitudinal studies, to our knowledge, have tracked vulnerable individuals over time to determine if these factors predispose one to the onset of anxiety disorders. Furthermore, these studies do not provide any indication as to the exact nature of the vulnerability. In the following sections, other research investigations that have sought to determine if specific structures or neurochemicals are related to the anxiety disorders are discussed.

The majority of studies addressing these biological parameters, and the two areas that have focused on structural abnormalities, have been directed at panic disorder. For example, although several investigations conducted during the late 1970s and early 1980s reported a high prevalence of mitral valve prolapse in patients with panic attacks (e.g., Crowe et al., 1980; Gorman, Fyer, Glicklich, King, & Klein, 1981), others have not found the prevalence rates to be higher than those in the general population (e.g., Kathol et al., 1980; Shear, Devereux, Kranier-Fox, Mann, & Frances, 1984). As noted by Shear et al. (1984), studies that used strictly defined echocardiographic criteria (a more stringent criteria by which to determine the presence of mitral valve prolapse) were less likely to find a higher prevalence in panic disorder patients. Based on the mixed results of these studies, there does not appear to be clear-cut evidence for mitral valve prolapse as a predispositional factor for panic disorder (Shear, 1988).

The vestibular system also has been the subject of investigation as a possible etiologic factor in panic disorder. For example, Jacob, Moller, Turner, and Wall (1985) reported that 67 percent of 21 panic disorder or agoraphobic patients had some type of vestibular abnormality. In 39 percent of the patients with abnormal tests, the results were consistent with a peripheral vestibular lesion. Although these results are very intriguing, this pilot study was based on panic patients specifically selected for complaints of dizziness, and no psychiatric control groups were included. Thus, it is currently unknown if these results are specific to panic disorder, may be found in anxiety disorders in general, or may be found in all psychiatric conditions. An ongoing investigation that should shed more light on this area is assessing a group of panic patients unselected for specific complaints of dizziness, and is including appropriate psychiatric and normal controls. In summary, attempts to delineate structural abnormalities that may predispose an individual to the onset of panic disorder have yet to demonstrate any conclusive role for these factors.

A much more elaborate theory based largely on animal studies has been proposed by Gray (1982). He postulated a complex central nervous system model based around a behavioral activating system and a behavioral inhibition system. The model is beyond the scope of this chapter, and the interested reader is referred to Gray (1982).

Another series of investigations have attempted to evaluate biochemical changes that may occur when panic is produced in a laboratory setting. Induction of panic in the laboratory is seen as a method by which to examine the pathophysiology of panic (Carr & Sheehan, 1984). Laboratory-induced panic has been studied most often by infusing panic patients with lactate (e.g., Pitts & McClure, 1967), and numerous studies have documented that the percentage of patients with panic disorder who appear to experience panic after lactate infusion is higher than the percentages for other anxiety disordered patients, depressed patients, or normal controls (e.g., Gorman et al., 1983; Liebowitz, Fyer, et al., 1985; Liebowitz, Gorman, Fyer, Levitt et al., 1985; Liebowitz et al., 1984). Although there appears to be some consistency across these investigations, Margraf, Ehlers, and Roth (1986) noted that these studies have serious methodological limitations. Some of the severest limitations include inadequate criteria for defining panic attacks, strict reliance on patient report that a panic attack was occurring, use of only single-blind criteria, and failure to account for group differences in baseline anxiety levels. When these baseline differences are taken into account, there appears to be no difference in the responses of panic patients compared with those of other diagnostic or control groups (see Margraf et al., 1986, for a complete listing of methodological deficiencies).

The problem of expectancy effects in the lactate-provocation studies also must be considered (Turner, Beidel, & Jacob, 1988). A study by van der Molen and van den Hout (1988) indicated the power of these expectancy effects. Two groups of healthy volunteers were infused with lactate or placebo using a double-blind cross-over design in which one group was told to expect to become anxious after infusion and the other was told to expect pleasant excitement. Although both groups showed a significant decrease in alveolar pCO_2 after lactate, increased respiration was found in the group told to expect anxiety, whereas decreased respiration was found in the group expecting anxious excitement. Therefore, panic attacks after lactate infusion may be more likely to occur when the patients are told to expect the occurrence of such an event. Furthermore, it is likely that the expectation is far more potent in patients who have previously experienced the sudden, and frightening, onset of these symptoms.

Compounding these methodological limitations, the mechanism by which lactate might produce a panic attack is unclear. Shear (1988) listed numerous possibilities, including lowered ionized calcium, metabolical alkalosis, beta-adrenergic hypersensitivity, stimulation of central noradrenergic centers, excessive peripheral catecholamine release, alteration of acid–base regulation, and chemoreceptor hypersensitivity, but noted that thus far empirical data had failed to support any of these mechanisms. Furthermore, there does not appear to be anything specific about the ability of lactate to produce panic attacks. Many other substances, including carbon dioxide, isoproterenol, caffeine, and yohimbine, also have been documented as having panic-producing properties (Turner et al., 1988). In addition, panic attacks may be induced through behavioral methods, such as putting claustrophobics in enclosed places (Rachman, 1988), thus further undermining the likelihood of any one specific biological factor in precipitating the onset of panic disorder. In summarizing the empirical literature on laboratory-induced panic, so many methodological confounds exist that it is difficult to conclude that these data indicate a biological vulnerability for the onset of panic disorder. Of late, there appears to be little interest in pursuing this line of research, and it seems likely that the findings of the lactate-provocation studies are influenced to some degree by nonbiological factors present in the individual or the environment.

Finally, other investigators have pursued the potential etiologic role of catecholamines, norepinephrine, and serotonin. Although the relationship between increased catecholamine levels and "stress" are well documented, there is little conclusive evidence that levels of catecholamines are higher in chronically anxious patients than in normal controls. For example, one study reported no differences in resting catecholamine levels between GAD patients and normal controls (Mathew, Ho, Francis, Taylor, & Weinman, 1982). Evidence for panic is mixed, with one study reporting no differences between panic patients and controls (Liebowitz, Gorman, Fyer, Levitt et al., 1985), and others reporting higher resting levels of norepinephrine and the serotonin metabolite MHPG in agoraphobics than in normal controls (Ballenger et al., 1984) or higher resting levels of norepinephrine and epinephrine in panic or agoraphobic patients than in normal controls (Nesse et al., 1984). With respect to social phobia, Levin et al. (1989) assessed plasma epinephrine and norepinephrine responses of social phobics and normal controls when giving a 10-minute speech. Plasma epinephrine and norepinephrine values rose significantly from baseline during the speaking task, but did not differ between the two groups. This was in marked contrast to behavioral and subjective distress ratings, which clearly indicated more anxiety in the social phobic patients. One difficulty for the catecholamine literature, as noted by Barlow (1988), is that elevated catecholamine levels also exist in patients with other psychiatric disorders, such as depression, mania, and schizophrenia. Thus, elevated catecholamines may be a general stress response rather than an indicator of a specific anxiety disorder.

In recent years, interest in the relationship between serotonin functioning and the anxiety disorders has increased. A thorough review of this literature can be found in Kahn, Van Praag, Wetzler, and Barr (1988). In brief, much of the interest in serotonin is derived from the successful results of pharmacological investigations that have administered drugs with potent serotonergic effects to patients with anxiety disorders. Evidence of the effectiveness of these compounds has led investigators (correctly or incorrectly) to hypothesize abnormal serotonin functioning as an etiologic determinant of the disorder (see the "Treatment" section for a review of biological treatment studies). The literature reviewed in this section is limited to studies that have attempted to address the specific mechanism of action in anxiety patients. With respect to obsessive–compulsive disorder (OCD), Thóren, Åsberg, Cronhelm, Jornestedt, and Traskman (1980a) compared OCD patients and normal controls on cerebral spinal fluid (CSF) levels of 5-hydroxyindoleacetic acid (5-HIAA), homovanillic acid (HVA), and the serotonin metabolite, MHPG. There were no differences in mean concentrations of 5-HIAA and HVA between the two groups; MHPG was more variable in the patient group than in the normal controls, but there was no overall difference. A second investigation with OCD patients (Insel et al., 1985a), however, reported higher 5-HIAA levels in OCD patients than in normals, although this study used only 8 OCD patients.

Biological challenge studies with panic patients indicated that oral doses of m-chlorophenylpiperazine (m-CPP) induced anxiety in panic patients but not in normal controls (Mueller, Murphy, & Sunderland, 1986; Mueller, Sunderland, & Murphy, 1985; Zohar & Insel, 1987). In contrast, when given intravenously, m-CPP appears to precipitate anxiety in both panic disorder patients and normal controls (Woods, 1986; cited in Kahn et al., 1988). As noted by Kahn et al. (1988), this discrepancy could be accounted for by the method of induction and receptor hypersensitivity. If serotonin receptors in panic patients are hypersensitive, then low (oral doses) could precipitate anxiety in patients but not in normal controls. Higher doses, however, could overstimulate receptors and result in similar anxiety states for both panic patients and normal controls. Although suggestive, these challenges were very similar to the lactate-induced panic studies, and, given the methodological limitations of those, the results must be interpreted cautiously. In summary, results of endocrine and neuroendocrine studies to date provide minimal support for an etiologic role of these factors in anxiety disorders. As with the laboratory-induction procedures, there are serious methodological limitations (see Turner et al., 1988). For example, measurement of bioamine activity is limited to peripheral assessment, even though its mechanism of action may be on the central nervous system. Inasmuch as the relationship between the concentration of these elements in the peripheral nervous system and that in the central nervous system is unknown, the extent to which concentration of these elements in blood, urine, and spinal fluid reflects central nervous system activity is not well known. Furthermore, even if there was a one-to-one relationship in neurotransmitter levels, this would not guarantee that neurotransmitter function was the same at both sites (Green & Costain, 1981). Therefore, until these measurement issues can be solved, if indeed they ever can be, the conclusions from these investigations must be considered tentative.

NATURAL HISTORY

It is difficult to study the natural history of any psychological disorder since most studies of psychopathology are based on patient populations. Thus, clinic samples may be skewed because only those whose disorders may significantly interfere with life functioning go to clinics for treatment. Others with equally severe symptoms may be able to adjust their lifestyles to accommodate their disorders, or may not seek treatment for a variety of reasons. Although community-based epidemiological studies do not share this problem, they have their own difficulties, as discussed earlier.

Age of Onset

As noted above, traumatic conditioning experiences can precipitate the onset of an anxiety disorder at any age. However, inasmuch as equipotentiality theories cannot fully explain the etiology of anxiety disorders, other factors must be operative. Developmental stage may be one such factor. For example, among the anxiety disorders, simple phobias have the earliest age of onset, usually appearing during early childhood. Interestingly, ages of onset for specific simple phobias mirror the developmental stages established for "normal" childhood fears. Developmentally, animal fears are common in preschool children, and two studies reported that specific animal phobias first appear between the ages of 4.4 and 6.9 years (Marks & Gelder, 1966; Öst, 1987), whereas a third found that 100 percent of a sample of animal and insect phobics reported that the age of onset was prior to age 10 (McNally & Steketee, 1985). Similarly, younger elementary school children commonly fear natural events, such as lightning and thunder, and health-related concerns, whereas fear of injury is seen in older elementary school children (Barrios, Hartman, & Shigetomi, 1981). Liddell and Lyons (1978) reported that age of onset was 11.9 years for a small sample of thunderstorm phobics, 8.8 for blood phobics, and 10.8 for dental phobics. Studies of normal fears in children often are fraught with methodological limitations, including data based almost solely on parental report rather than on child self-report or behavioral observation. Thus, it is unclear how many of these normal fears may have been the initial expression of a simple phobia. Furthermore, it is tempting to speculate that certain constitutional or environmental characteristics may be pivotal in the differentiation of normal fear from simple phobia. Certainly, the relationship between normal childhood fears and age of onset for simple phobias is deserving of further investigation.

In contrast to most other simple phobias, certain samples of specific phobics appear to have a much later average age of onset, ranging from 16.1 years to 22.7 years (Marks & Gelder, 1966; Sheehan, Sheehan, & Minichiello, 1981; Thyer, Parrish, Curtis, Nesse, & Cameron, 1985). Sheehan et al. (1981) and Thyer et al. (1985) used samples that consisted of mixed groups of simple phobics, whereas Marks and Gelder's (1966) specific phobics were claustrophobics. Age of onset for claustrophobia in Öst's (1987) investigation also was later than for other simple phobias (20.2 years). Interestingly, these ages are more similar to the age of onset for panic disorder (see below) than for other simple phobias, which lends support to the hypothesis proposed by Klein (1981), and discussed by Öst (1987), that claustrophobia may be a restricted but functional and descriptive equivalent of panic disorder with agoraphobia.

It is generally accepted that the age of onset for panic disorder usually is during early adulthood. Öst (1987) compiled data from thirteen samples of panic and agoraphobic patients, reporting an age of onset ranging from 19.7 to 32 years of age, with a mean of 26.5 years across all studies. Although some researchers have described a bimodal age distribution, with the first period occurring during late adolescence and the second around age 30 (Marks & Gelder, 1966), others found a unimodal distribution (Öst, 1987; Thorpe & Burns, 1983). As noted above, the difference between age of onset for claustrophobia and for more typical panic disorder suggests that claustrophobia may be a more restrictive form or possibly an early stage of panic disorder. Carefully controlled naturalistic studies are necessary to address this issue, however.

Age of onset for social phobia falls somewhere between those for simple phobias and panic disorder with agoraphobia, usually occurring during adolescence. The typical age of onset ranges from 15.7 to 20.0 years (Amies et al., 1983; Liebowitz, Gorman, Fryer, & Klein, 1985; Marks & Gelder, 1966; Öst, 1987; Thyer et al., 1985; Turner et al., 1986), although the critical period is likely to be early adolescence (Turner & Beidel, 1989b). Adolescence has been noted to be the crucial period for the acquisition of social fearfulness (Öhman, 1986). The importance of peer groups and of establishing one's place within a social system is critical during adolescent development and likely accounts for the onset during this period. For those who possess anxious temperament (e.g., Kagan, Reznick, Clarke, Snidman, &

Garcia-Coll, 1984), the environmental demands that emerge during adolescence may trigger the onset of social phobia (Turner & Beidel, 1989b).

For obsessive–compulsive disorder, age of onset ranges from late adolescence to early adulthood (Rachman & Hodgson, 1980; Rasmussen & Tsuang, 1986; Turner & Beidel, 1988). In addition, OCD is one of the few anxiety disorders whose symptoms are identical in children and adults, and the onset of this disorder has been witnessed in those as young as age 4 (Turner & Beidel, 1988). Furthermore, although actual onset of OCD may average around age 20, retrospective reports from OCD patients indicate that vestiges of the disorder often are present at a much earlier age.

A review of the literature revealed no figures for a "typical" age of onset for GAD or PTSD. Because PTSD is triggered by a traumatic event, onset of the disorder can occur at any age. The controversy surrounding GAD and the recent revisions in DSM-III-R may be factors that have precluded establishing an accurate age of onset for this condition.

Course and Complications

The anxiety disorders tend to have a chronic course. For example, Breier, Charney, and Heninger (1986) reported that agoraphobia appears to be a chronic disorder with an unremitting course. Similarly, a sample of 22 outpatients with severe animal phobias reported that, once established, their fear intensity remained constant or gradually increased over subsequent years (McNally & Steketee, 1985). A similar pattern has been noted for OCD, which is described as being a chronic condition with periodic exacerbations (Rasmussen & Tsuang, 1986). Although few empirical data exist on the duration of anxiety disorders, many patients note that their symptoms wax and wane over the course of several years but rarely dissipate completely. The few empirical data that do exist, along with our clinical experience, lead us to draw the following tentative conclusions. First, symptom exacerbation is often correlated with onset of significant life stressors (Klein & Fink, 1962; Turner & Beidel, 1988). Second, once the disorder is established, behavioral avoidance often functions to reduce general emotional distress, but this avoidance is associated with social impairment, and symptoms tend to reemerge or worsen when contact with the phobic environment is initiated. Third, it is likely that a subset of anxiety disorders patients do overcome their disorder without professional intervention, but the personality or environmental characteristics that might be associated with these successful outcomes are currently unknown.

TREATMENT

Pharmacological Treatments

Pharmacological treatments consist of antidepressant, antianxiety, or beta-blocking agents. It is beyond the scope of this chapter to provide a thorough review of all of the empirical evidence for each of the pharmacological agents with each of the anxiety disorders. In brief, there is no evidence for the efficacy of any drug in the treatment of simple phobia (Lydiard et al., 1988). Furthermore, although a few reports indicate that antidepressants may be useful in treating patients with PTSD (e.g., Bleich, Siegal, Garb, & Lerer, 1986;), to date there are no double-blind placebo-controlled trials (Lydiard et al., 1988). Therefore, this review highlights the major interventions that have been used with the remaining disorders, and we refer the reader to primary sources for further detail.

Antidepressants

The effectiveness of antidepressant medication for the treatment of panic attacks in hospitalized anxiety patients was reported first almost 30 years ago when several studies noted that imipramine blocked the occurrence of panic attacks, but had little effect on anticipatory anxiety or phobic avoidance (Klein, 1964, 1967; Klein & Fink, 1962). Further investigations have compared imipramine to placebo, but in each case all of the patients received some form of behavior therapy or supportive psychotherapy. Several studies reported that those treated with imipramine improved more than placebo patients (Mavissakalian & Michelson, 1986; Zitrin, Klein, & Woerner, 1978, 1980). In contrast, a study by Marks et al. (1983) did not show any superiority for imipramine over placebo when both were used in conjunction with exposure therapy. Furthermore, Zitrin et al.'s (1978) investigation included some patients diagnosed as specific phobics, and the concomitant use of imipramine was not effective for those patients. However, several recent reports have been positive regarding the use of imipramine for the treatment of GAD (Kahn et al., 1981; Kahn et al., 1986).

Imipramine is not the only tricyclic with some degree of efficacy for panic disorder. Several small-scale open trials have reported success with clomipramine (Fyer & Sandberg, 1988; Gloger, Grunhaus, Birmacher, & Troudart, 1981; Grunhaus, Gloger, & Birmacher, 1984), but definitive conclusions must await further empirical investigation.

Imipramine and other antidepressants have been used to treat obsessive–compulsive disorder. Ananth (1985) reported that treatment with amitriptyline or imipramine effectively decreased dysphoric mood, but whether these drugs have a specific antiobsessional effect remains controversial (Mavissakalian, Turner, Michelson, & Jacob, 1986). In 1977, Yaryura-Tobias and Bhagavan proposed a serotonin hypothesis for obsessive–compulsive disorder, noting that OCD patients, compared with normal controls, had decreased functional levels of serotonin at the synaptic clefts. Since that time, much of the clinical research pertaining to the pharmacological treatment of OCD has focused on drugs with selective and potent serotonergic effects, such as clomipramine and fluoxetine. A number of studies have found clomipramine to be superior to placebo (Flament et al., 1985; Marks et al., 1980; Montgomery, 1980; Thóren, Åsberg, Cronholm, Jornestedt, & Traskman 1980), with only one negative report (Mawson, Marks, & Ramm, 1982). In addition, clomipramine has been reported to be better (but not necessarily always significantly so) than nortriptyline (Ananth, Pecknold, Van Den Steen, & Angelsmann, 1981; Thóren, Åsberg, et al., 1980), desipramine (Insel, Mueller, Gillin,

Siever, & Murphy 1985; Zohar & Insel, 1987), and desipramine or zimelidine (Insel, Mueller, & Gillin 1985). Comparisons with imipramine are less clear. Patients treated with both drugs show equal improvement based on clinician ratings (Mavissakalian et al., 1985; Volavka, Neziroglu, & Yaryura-Tobias, 1985).

Fluoxetine, a new nontricyclic serotonergic compound, was reported to be effective in one open clinical trial (Fontaine & Chouinard, 1986) and one single-blind placebo-controlled study (Turner Jacob, Beidel, & Himmelhoch, 1985). Both studies, although positive, were based on very small sample sizes (7 and 10 patients, respectively). In the latter investigation, the drug decreased, but did not eliminate, the obsessive–compulsive behavior. In addition, outcome did not appear to be correlated with initial level of depression (although the lack of a significant correlation may have been due to the sample size). Replication using larger samples and double-blind placebo-controlled designs are necessary. Although there is evidence that clomipramine, imipramine, and perhaps fluoxetine can be effective in the treatment of OCD, withdrawal of these medications have produced relapse rates ranging from 23 to 86 percent (Ananth, 1986; Fontaine & Chouinard, 1989; Pato, Zohar-Kadouch, Zohar, & Murphy, 1988). Furthermore, many of these studies, and particularly the earlier ones, suffer from methodological confounds, such as the almost total reliance upon clinician and patient rating scales and the failure to assess obsessions and compulsions independent from depressive or dysphoric mood (Turner & Beidel, 1988). Increased interest in these serotonergic compounds are likely to spur further and better controlled investigations.

Monoamine oxidase inhibitors (MAOIs), particularly phenelzine, isocarboxazid, and tranylcypromine, represent another class of drugs that have been used to treat anxiety disorders. First developed as antidepressants, they were noted to be particularly effective in the treatment of "anxious depressives" (Fyer & Sandberg, 1988). Placebo-controlled studies conducted during the 1970s using mixed groups of anxious patients (Lipsedge et al., 1973; Solyom et al., 1973; Tyrer, Candy, & Delly, 1973) found little or no effectiveness for MAOIs, although there was a suggestion that MAOIs might be more effective for panic symptoms than avoidance. As noted by Fyer and Sandberg (1988), all of these studies were limited by small sample sizes, mixed diagnostic groups, and dosages that were apparently too low to produce maximal benefit. At least one better controlled study found phenelzine to be superior to placebo for agoraphobic women (Sheehan, Ballenger, & Jacobsen, 1980), outperforming imipramine on clinician ratings of disability and avoidance.

An intriguing result from some early phenelzine research was that the drug appeared superior to imipramine in reducing interpersonal sensitivity and nonpsychotic paranoia (touchiness), and in reducing complaints of social anxiety (Liebowitz et al., 1984). This led Liebowitz and colleagues to investigate phenelzine in the treatment of social phobia. After a 6-week open clinical trial, 7 of 11 patients were markedly improved, and the other 4 were moderately improved. A subsequent double-blind, placebo-controlled, and randomized trial compared phenelzine to atenolol, a beta-blocker (Liebowitz et al.,

1988). Preliminary results indicated that phenelzine was superior to placebo or atenolol on degree of improvement and change in symptom severity as assessed by independent clinician ratings. Sixty-four percent of the phenelzine group was rated as improved, compared with 36 percent of the atenolol group and 31 percent of the placebo group. None of these differences was significant, but results may change as more patients complete the study. Finally, other MAOIs are beginning to be used as a treatment for social phobia. Tranylcypromine was reported to be effective in one open clinical trial (Versiani, Mundim, Nardi, & Liebowitz, 1988). Antidepressants of various types appear to have a place in the treatment of anxiety disorders; however, except for panic disorder, the exact medication that is most effective for each condition remains to be elucidated.

Beta-Blockers

Use of beta-blockers for the treatment of anxiety disorders was suggested initially by results from several studies of mixed anxiety groups (Noyes, Kathol, Clancy, & Crowe, 1981). Similarly, at least one study indicated that propranolol was essentially equal to imipramine in treating panic disorder (Munjack et al., 1985); however, this imipramine improvement rate was lower than that reported in other imipramine studies (see above), possibly due to either the short treatment trial (6 weeks) or a lower than average mean dosage (126 milligrams per day) (Fyer & Sandberg, 1988). The bulk of the evidence at this time does not indicate that beta-blockers are effective in the treatment of anxiety disorders (Fyer & Sandberg, 1988; Gorman et al., 1983; Noyes et al., 1984), with the possible exception of social phobia.

A number of recent studies have examined the efficacy of atenolol for the treatment of social phobia. For example, Liebowitz et al. (in press) found that atenolol was inferior to phenelzine and no different from placebo, based on independent evaluator ratings of degree of improvement and change in symptom severity. When social phobics were divided into specific and generalized subtypes, however, phenelzine and atenolol were equally effective for the specific subtype. An ongoing investigation in the Anxiety Disorders Clinic at Western Psychiatric Institute and Clinic is using a three-group placebo-controlled design to compare the effectiveness of atenolol or flooding therapy (Turner, Beidel, & Jacob, 1990). Based on the preliminary results, there were no differences between atenolol and placebo in overall improvement rates, with 47 percent of each group considered at least moderately improved, compared with 76 percent for the flooding treatment. Currently, this sample is too small to examine separately the effects for specific and generalized subtypes, yet the consistent response rates between the two research sites, as well as the lack of significant differences between atenolol and placebo, have dampened the initial enthusiasm for the use of beta-blockers in the treatment of social phobia. It is possible that a specific subgroup of social phobic patients may benefit from beta-blockers, but further empirical work is needed to clearly delineate who those individuals might be. Finally, beta-blockers have been used by primary care physicians to treat GAD (Lydiard et al., 1988). In general, however, they are rarely more effective than placebo (Noyes, 1985).

Benzodiazepines

Drugs such as diazepam and chlordiazepoxide, and the newer high-potency benzodiazepines, such as alprazolam, have been used for the treatment of anxiety disorders. There are reports that diazepam (Dunner, Ishiki, Avery, Wilson, & Hyde, 1986) and clonazepam (Tesar & Rosenbaum, 1986) may be effective in the treatment of panic disorder; however, most attention has centered on alprazolam. Several small open trials (Alexander & Alexander, 1986; Liebowitz et al., 1986) found that the drug alleviated panic attacks and blocked panic that was produced by sodium lactate infusion (Liebowitz et al., 1986). A small placebo-controlled trial (Chouinard, Annable, Fontaine, & Solyom, 1982) indicated that alprazolam was more effective than placebo, although no specific rating of panic was included in the assessment battery. Two small comparative trials using alprazolam and imipramine (Rizley, Kahn, McNair, & Frankenthaler, 1986), or alprazolam, imipramine, and trazadone (Charney et al., 1986), found that alprazolam was superior to trazadone (as was imipramine), was equal in effectiveness to imipramine, and appeared to work in a shorter period of time.

The strongest results to date come from a cross-national, multicenter trial designed to evaluate alprazolam in the treatment of panic disorder. Phase 1, using a placebo-controlled, 8-week flexible-dose trial in 600 patients with agoraphobia with panic attacks or panic disorder (Ballenger et al., 1988), found that alprazolam, after only 1 week of treatment, resulted in significant improvement on ratings of spontaneous and specific panic attacks, phobic fears, avoidance behavior, general anxiety, and secondary disability. After 4 weeks of treatment, 82 percent of the alprazolam-treated patients were judged to be at least moderately improved (and 50 percent were panic free), compared with 43 percent of the placebo patients who were at least moderately improved (and 28 percent who were panic free). Phase 2 was a placebo-controlled trial of alprazolam and imipramine in 1,100 patients in four countries (Klerman, 1988). Although the complete results of Phase 2 are not yet published, preliminary results from one site using 79 patients with panic disorder indicated that all patients reported significantly greater improvement after 4 and 8 weeks of treatment, but there were no differences among the three groups (Taylor et al., 1990); however, the alprazolam group reported significantly less fear at the end of the 8-week trial than either of the other two groups. Obviously, these findings are tenuous and may change when the complete results are reported.

With respect to the other anxiety disorders, benzodiazepines have been used widely for treating GAD (Ballenger, 1984). Also, two studies suggest that alprazolam is effective in the treatment of social phobia (Lydiard et al., in press; Reich & Yates, 1988), although neither was a controlled study.

In summarizing the current status of pharmacological treatments for the anxiety disorders, it is apparent that the antidepressants, particularly imipramine and MAOIs, are to some degree effective for the treatment of panic disorder, and one particular MAOI (phenelzine) is showing promise in the treatment of social phobia. In addition, those antidepressants with a preponderance of serotonergic properties appear to be important for the treatment of

OCD. Many issues, however, remain to be addressed regarding the use of these agents, including (a) relapse rates, which range from 19 to 30 percent (Zitrin & Klein, 1983; cited in Fyer & Sandberg, 1988) for panic disorder, and up to 86 percent for OCD; (b) whether these drugs have unique antipanic or antiobsessional effects (Fyer & Sandberg, 1988; Turner & Beidel, 1988); (c) whether beneficial improvements are maintained following drug withdrawal; and (d) the effects of using these drugs over a long period of time.

In contrast to antidepressants, beta-blockers appear to have only limited usefulness in the treatment of social phobia, and are ineffective for panic disorder or GAD (Lydiard et al., 1988). Finally, benzodiazepines have been used extensively and with some degree of effectiveness in patients with GAD, and alprazolam may be effective in panic disorder. However, there are serious questions relating to addiction and the ability of patients to withdraw safely from alprazolam that need to be addressed prior to advocating its widespread use. Furthermore, most of the medication studies have relied on global clinical rating and self-report to judge effectiveness rather than on objective strategies, and only a few studies have addressed relapse rates upon withdrawal of medication.

Behavioral and Cognitive–Behavioral Treatments

There is significant agreement in most quarters that behavior therapy is the treatment of choice for many phobic disorders and obsessive–compulsive disorder. In addition, there is increasing evidence that behavioral treatments (or cognitive–behavioral treatments) are effective in treating other forms of anxiety disorders, such as panic disorder, GAD, and PTSD. In this section, both standard behavioral and the newer cognitive–behavioral therapies are discussed together since most of these treatments share the common therapeutic ingredient of exposure to the feared stimulus (Beidel & Turner, 1986). Thus, although certain therapies may expend greater or lesser effort on the patient's accompanying cognitions, utilize therapist assistance as opposed to instructions, or, in the case of GAD, include relaxation as an important additional procedure, all include some opportunity for the patient to come into direct contact with the feared stimulus (exposure).

Exposure Therapies

Of the treatment modalities that invoke the use of exposure, a review of the behavioral literature clearly demonstrates that therapies based on extinction or habituation models are the most commonly used. These procedures rely on contact with the feared stimulus in vivo or through imagination. Contact with the stimulus is maintained until a reduction in anxiety is achieved. For panic disorder with agoraphobia, in vivo exposure (with or without the concomitant use of medication) appears to be the treatment of choice (Clum, 1989; Craske et al., 1988; Lydiard et al., 1988). An early review by Jansson and Öst (1982) noted that, excluding dropouts, 60 to 70 percent of agoraphobics benefited from exposure therapies. More recent studies continue to support the effectiveness of this treatment (Clum, 1989), and have begun to address factors that may improve its efficacy even further. For example, a 5-year follow-up of agoraphobic patients revealed that, contrary to clinical lore, ungraded exposure (consisting of immediate exposure to the most feared situation) was superior to a graduated approach (Feigenbaum, 1988, cited in Craske, Rapee, & Barlow, in press). Other studies have found that treatments targeted at different aspects of the disorder, but all including an element of exposure (e.g., graduated exposure, paradoxical intention, and relaxation training), were all equally effective in generating improvement (Michelson, Mavissakalian, & Marchione, 1988). The empirical evidence for adding coping or cognitive strategies to standard exposure procedures is equivocal, and one recent review concluded that it does increase effectiveness with respect to outcome criteria, but is not superior to exposure alone in preventing relapse (Clum, 1989). Other studies have reported that the addition of cognitive components does not generate improvement rates that are higher than exposure alone (Jansson, Jerremalm, & Öst, 1986; Michelson, Mavissakalian, & Marchione, 1985); however, use of cognitive strategies does appear to reduce the number of dropouts compared with exposure alone (Clum, 1989).

Although there is minimal controversy about the conclusion that exposure is essential for the treatment of panic disorder with agoraphobia, until recently these treatments were rarely used for those with panic attacks but no avoidance. An increasing number of case reports have indicated that cognitive–behavioral treatment (e.g., cognitive restructuring, respiratory training) may be effective for those with uncomplicated panic disorder (Beck, 1988; Clark, Salkovskis, & Chalkley, 1985; Öst, 1988). Barlow, Craske, Cerny, and Klosko (1989) developed a treatment model for panic attacks that is based on exposure to somatic symptoms and reported the results of a wait-list controlled investigation comparing the merging of the exposure treatment with cognitive therapy (Beck & Emery, 1985), relaxation training, and a combination group consisting of all three elements. The results indicated few posttreatment differences among the three active treatment groups, although all three were clearly superior to the control group. Furthermore, the two groups containing exposure to somatic cues were the only groups that were significantly superior to the control group in terms of the percentage of patients who were panic free at posttreatment. These results seem to indicate that there is a promising nonpharmacological therapy for patients with panic disorder uncomplicated by agoraphobia, and that exposure to the somatic cues is the critical element of treatment.

Considered the treatment of choice for obsessive–compulsive disorder (Foa et al., 1983; Turner & Beidel, 1988), exposure (flooding), coupled with response prevention, appears to be effective in about 70 percent of patients (Foa et al., 1983; Turner & Beidel, 1988), and 70 to 80 percent of patients maintain their treatment gains at 1-year follow-up (Kirk, 1983; Steketee, Foa, & Grayson, 1982). Flooding and response prevention have been shown to be superior to relaxation training (Hodgson, Rachman, & Marks, 1972; Rachman, Marks, & Hodgson, 1973) and thought-stopping (Emmelkamp & Kwee, 1977; Stern et al., 1975). Patients with "overvalued ideation" have been known to be resistant to standard flooding procedures; however, a recent case study by Salkovskis and Warwick (1985) reported that the addition of cognitive therapy was useful in "loosening" the overvalued ideation such that then standard exposure therapy was effective in treating the entire disorder. It should be noted that the effect of cognitive therapy was minimal in terms of treating the rituals and concomitant anxiety, but addition of this treatment may be a useful first step for a group of patients long considered refractory to any form of treatment.

Similar to the literature on the pharmacological treatments for PTSD, controlled trials of behavioral treatments are virtually nonexistent. Individual case studies have indicated that flooding may be useful for the treatment of combat-related PTSD (Black & Keane, 1982; Fairbank & Keane, 1982; Keane & Kaloupek, 1982), and two controlled trials have confirmed its effectiveness in Veterans Administration patients (Cooper & Clum, 1989; Keane, Fairbank, Caddell, & Zimering, 1989). The study by Keane et al. (1989) reported that flooding reduced depression, anxiety, and the specific reexperiencing dimension of PTSD compared with a waiting list control group, but was less effective for the numbing and social avoidance aspects of PTSD. Cooper and Clum (1989) found that the addition of nine flooding sessions to 1-hour individual therapy and 2-hour group therapy sessions (all directed at treatment of the PTSD symptoms) resulted in significant improvement for state anxiety, anxiety related to the traumatic event, and sleep disturbance, but not trait anxiety or depression.

Although the literature is more limited than for agoraphobia or obsessive–compulsive disorder, flooding also appears effective for the treatment of social phobia (Biran, Augusto, & Wilson, 1981; Vermilyea, Barlow, & O'Brien, 1984). Again, exposure appears to be the key ingredient in that the addition of other therapies, such as cognitive restructuring or self-statement training, had little interactive effect. Controlled comparisons of basic exposure therapy with other interventions, such as self-instructional training, rational–emotive therapy (Emmelkamp, Mersch, Vissia, & van der Helm, 1985), or anxiety management training (Butler, Cullington, Munby, Amres, & Gelder, 1984), indicate few differences among the treatment conditions, possibly due to the inclusion of in vivo or imaginal exposure in each of the comparative conditions. Both in vivo exposure and anxiety management training were judged to be superior to an attention-placebo control group (Butler et al., 1984), and, although the authors concluded that addition of anxiety management training was superior to in vivo exposure alone, this conclusion was based on a very small number of differences in comparison with all of the outcome measures that were used in the study. Conclusions that exposure plus cognitive treatments are superior to exposure alone (Mattick & Peters, 1988; Mattick, Peters, & Clarke, 1989) are difficult to interpret. The Mattick et al. (1989) investigation compared cognitive restructuring, guided exposure, and a combination group to a waiting list control group. There were few differences among the treatment groups at posttreatment, although all of the treatments were superior to the control group. The authors concluded that within-group differences suggested superiority of the cognitive treatments, but these conclusions are suspect in that the majority of the measures, as well as composite ratings of end-state functioning and overall improvement, did not differentiate the three groups.

Similarly, social phobics treated with 12 weeks of cognitive–behavioral treatment (which included exposure assignments) produced few differences when compared with an attention-placebo control at posttreatment, although significant differences did emerge at follow-up (Heimberg et al., in press). One conclusion from these studies, as well as from our own clinical experience, is that treatment that exceeds 3 months will be necessary to deal adequately with this disorder.

Social skills training has been noted to be an effective treatment for social phobia (Falloon, Lloyd, & Harpin, 1981; Öst, Jerrmalm, & Johansson, 1981; Stravynski, Marks, & Yule, 1982). Although the mechanism of action is unclear, several authors (Heimberg, Dodge, & Becker, 1987; Stravynski, Grey, & Elie, 1987) have suggested, and we concur, that the mechanism of social skills training may be anxiety reduction via exposure that results from role playing and homework assignments rather than skills acquisition per se. This hypothesis will have to be studied empirically, however, before a definitive conclusion can be reached.

Desensitization

The most widely recognized form of exposure therapy is systematic desensitization, based on Wolpe's (1973) theory of reciprocal inhibition. Systematic desensitization, which involves the gradual pairing of a relaxation response with stimuli or events usually evocative of anxiety, has been used most often to treat simple phobias and sometimes social phobias (see Wolpe, 1982), and is a form of counterconditioning. Surprisingly, although there is a voluminous literature on college students who report simple fears of snakes, spiders, rats, dating, or testing, relatively few group studies have been done with clinic-referred patients (Borden, in press). In one of the few extant clinical studies, Öst (1978) reported that systematic desensitization was more effective than a waiting list control group in the treatment of snake or spider phobics. Other forms of desensitization that include cognitive elements (e.g., cognitive restructuring) have been used to treat simple phobias. For example, Biran and Wilson (1981) found cognitive restructuring to be inferior to exposure in vivo (see below) for treatment of height, elevator, or darkness fears, although treatment was limited to five 50-minute sessions.

Systematic desensitization has not been found to be an effective treatment for agoraphobia (Emmelkamp, 1982; Marks, 1971) or obsessive–compulsive disorder (Turner & Beidel, 1988). There appears to be no empirical literature on the use of systematic desensitization for the treatment of GAD, PTSD, or social phobia (other than those described by Wolpe, 1982).

Relaxation

Relaxation training has been used to treat panic disorder, GAD, and social phobics. Öst developed a variant of relaxation training called applied relaxation training (e.g., Öst et al., 1981). This form of relaxation combines training in progressive muscle relaxation and cue-controlled procedures, at which point the individual uses the cue-controlled procedure while engaging in items from a fear hierarchy. Treatment in applied relaxation was reported to be successful for social phobics (Öst et al., 1981) and panic patients (Öst, 1988). In the panic study, applied relaxation was compared with standard relaxation. Although 100 percent of the applied group was panic free after fourteen sessions, so was 71.7 percent of the standard group. Similarly, Barlow et al. (1989) found that 60 percent of patients who completed progressive muscle relaxation training were panic free at the end of treatment; however, this group had a 33 percent dropout rate, and when those patients were included, the number of patients who were panic free dropped to 40 percent (not different from the 30 percent in the control group). It also should be noted that applied relaxation includes an exposure component, thus making it difficult to determine what components are responsible for its effectiveness (Craske et al., in press).

In contrast to the literature on panic disorder and social phobia, relaxation training does appear to be effective in the treatment of GAD (Blowers, Cobb, & Mathews, 1987; Borkovec et al., 1987; Rapee & Barlow, 1988), although two of the studies reported that relaxation combined with cognitive restructuring produced additional improvement (Blowers et al., 1987; Borkovec et al., 1987. Thus, as in the studies reviewed above, efficacy of relaxation training *alone* for the treatment of anxiety disorders has yet to be fully determined and is likely to be most useful in conjunction with other interventions.

Cognitive Treatments

As noted at the beginning of this section, it is difficult to discuss most cognitive treatments separately from more standard behaviorally based treatments in that many cognitive therapies contain an element of exposure. For example, cognitive restructuring treatments for panic disorder (Barlow, 1988), GAD (Rapee & Barlow, 1988), and social phobia (Heimberg et al., in press) all include exposure components, although the majority of the treatment time may be spent on attempts at changing cognitions. The study by Mattick et al. (1989) was one of the few to include a cognitive restructuring group for which actual exposure to phobic situations was discouraged during the course of treatment. Results of this study were equivocal with respect to the superiority of any intervention. Although significantly larger within-group changes on "attitudinal" measures appeared for the groups that included cognitive restructuring, it must be noted that scores among these groups or the wait list control were not different at posttreatment. Craske et al. (in press) noted that data on the use of cognitive restructuring alone for the treatment of panic disorder may be forthcoming, but currently the ability to judge the effectiveness of these treatments without the beneficial effects of exposure is difficult.

In summary, there is substantial evidence that most behavioral treatments that rely on some form of exposure to the feared stimulus are powerful treatments for phobic and anxiety states. The methods differ to some degree for particular disorders, but it seems clear that exposure to the feared stimulus is the critical ingredient. At this time, few data support the conclusions that the addition of various cognitive strategies to exposure has a beneficial additive effect.

SUMMARY

Over the past decade, conceptualization of the anxiety disorders has undergone a radical evolution. Clearly, increased attention to classification and diagnostic differentiation, along with the high prevalence of these conditions in the general population, has contributed to a burgeoning interest in the area. Although many questions remain, a number of treatment interventions (behavioral and drug) now have demonstrated effectiveness. Although the treatment for some of the anxiety disorders is better understood than for others, in our opinion, treatment of these disorders has evolved to the point that few additional advances are likely possible without increased understanding of the basic psychopathology.

Questions of etiology are emerging as central to our further understanding of the nature of these disorders and will no doubt occupy the attention of researchers over the next decade. Currently, it seems clear that the anxiety disorders are familial, but the exact nature of this familial factor is unclear. Better controlled studies are needed to elucidate the basis of this familial factor. Emerging human and nonhuman primate studies suggest the high likelihood that early temperamental factors might be related to increased vulnerability to anxiety in some individuals. To fully address the issue of vulnerability, longitudinal studies with those considered to be at high risk are necessary. Based on the extant literature, however, the nature of this vulnerability is likely to be complex, encompassing biological, psychological, and environmental parameters.

REFERENCES

Agras, W. S., Sylvester, D., & Oliveau, D. (1969). The epidemiology of common fears and phobias. *Comprehensive Psychiatry, 10,* 151–156.

Akhtar, S., Wig, N. N., Verna, V. K., Pershod, D., & Verna, S. K. (1975). A phenomenological analysis of symptoms in obsessive–compulsive neurosis. *British Journal of Psychiatry, 127,* 342–348.

Alexander, P. E., & Alexander, D. D. (1986). Alprazolam treatment for panic disorder. *Journal of Clinical Psychiatry, 47,* 27–31.

American Psychiatric Association. (1968). *Diagnostic and statistical manual of mental disorders* (2nd ed.). Washington, DC: Author.

American Psychiatric Association. (1980). *Diagnostic and statistical manual of mental disorders* (3rd ed.). Washington, DC: Author.

American Psychiatric Association. (1987). *Diagnostic and statistical manual of mental disorders* (3rd ed. rev.). Washington, DC: Author.

Amies, P. L., Gelder, M. G., & Shaw, P. M. (1983). Social phobia: A comparative clinical study. *British Journal of Psychiatry, 142,* 174–179.

Ananth, J. (1985). Clomipramine in obsessive neurosis: A review. In M. Mavissakalian, S. M. Turner, & L. Michelson (Eds.), *Psychological and pharmacological treatment of obsessive–compulsive disorder* (pp. 167–211). New York: Plenum Press.

Ananth, J. (1986). Clomipramine: An antiobsessive drug. *Canadian Journal of Psychiatry, 31,* 253–258.

Ananth, J., Pecknold, J., Van Den Steen, N., & Angelsmann, F. (1981). Double-blind comparative study of clomipramine and amitriptyline in obsessive neurosis. *Progress in Neuropsychopharmacology and Biological Psychiatry, 5,* 257–262.

Anderson, J. C., Williams, S., McGee, R., & Silva, P. A. (1987). DSM-III disorders in preadolescent children. *Archives of General Psychiatry, 44,* 69–76.

Anthony, J. C., Folstein, M., Romanoski, A. J., Von Korff, M. R., Nestadt, G. R., Chahal, R., Merchant, A., Brown, C. H., Shapiro, S., Kramer, M., & Gruenberg, E. M. (1985). Comparison of the lay diagnostic interview schedule and a standardized psychiatric diagnosis. *Archives of General Psychiatry, 42,* 667–675.

Ballenger, J. C. (1984). Psychopharmacology of the anxiety disorders. *Psychiatric Clinics of North America, 7,* 757–771.

Ballenger, J. C., Burrows, G. D., DuPont, R. L., Lesser, I. M., Noyes, R., Jr., Pecknold, J. C., Rifkin, A., & Swinson, R. P. (1988). Alprazolam in panic disorder and agoraphobia: Results from a multicenter trial. *Archives of General Psychiatry, 45,* 413–422.

Ballenger, J. C., Peterson, G. A., Laraia, M., Hucek, A., Lake, C. R., Jimerson, D., Cox, D. J., Trockman, C., Shipe, J. R., & Wilkinson, C. (1984). A study of plasma catacholomines in agoraphobia and the relationship to serum. In J. C. Ballenger, (Ed.), *Biology of agoraphobia* (pp. 27–63). Washington, DC: American Psychiatric Press.

Bandura, A. (1969). *Principles of behavior modification.* New York: Holt, Rinehart and Winston.

Barlow, D. H. (1988). *Anxiety and its disorders.* New York: Guilford Press.

Barlow, D. H., Craske, M. G., Cerny, J. A., & Klosko, J. S. (1989). Behavioral treatment of panic disorder. *Behavior Therapy, 20,* 261–282.

Barlow, D. H., DiNardo, P. A., Vermilyea, B. B., Vermilyea, J. A., & Blanchard, E. B. (1986). Co-morbidity and depression among the anxiety disorders: Issues in diagnosis and classification. *Journal of Nervous and Mental Disease, 174,* 63–72.

Barrios, B. A., Hartmann, D. B., & Shigetomi, C. (1981). Fears and anxieties in children. In E. J. Mash & L. G. Terdal (Eds.), *Behavioral assessment of childhood disorders* (pp. 259–304). New York: Guilford Press.

Beck, A. T. (1988). Cognitive approaches to panic disorder: Theory and therapy. In S. Rachman & J. D. Maser (Eds.), *Panic: Psychological perspectives* (pp. 91–109). Hillsdale, NJ: Erlbaum.

Beck, A. T., & Emery, G. (1985). *Anxiety disorders and phobias: A cognitive perspective.* New York: Basic Books.

Beidel, D. C., & Bulik, C. M. (1990). Flooding and response prevention as a treatment for bowel obsessions. *Journal of Anxiety Disorders, 4,* 247–256.

Beidel, D. C., & Turner, S. M. (1986). A critique of the theoretical bases of cognitive behavior theories and therapies. *Clinical Psychology Review, 6,* 177–197.

Bernstein, G. A., & Garfinkel, B. D. (1988) Pedigrees, functioning, and psychopathology in families of school phobic children. *American Journal of Psychiatry, 145,* 70–74.

Biran, M., Augusto, F., & Wilson, G. T. (1981). In vivo exposure vs cognitive restructuring in the treatment of scriptophobia. *Behaviour Research and Therapy, 19,* 525–532.

Biran, M., & Wilson, G. T. (1981). Treatment of phobic disorders using cognitive and exposure methods: A self-efficacy analysis. *Journal of Consulting and Clinical Psychology, 49,* 886–899.

Black, J. L., & Keane, T. M. (1982). Implosive therapy in the treatment of combat related fears in a World War II veteran. *Journal of Behavior Therapy and Experimental Psychiatry, 13,* 33–40.

Blazer, D., George, L. K., Landerman, R., Pennybacker, M., Melville, M. L., Woodbury, M., Manton, K. G., Jordan, K., & Locke, B. (1985). Psychiatric disorders. *Archives of General Psychiatry, 42,* 651–656.

Bleich, A., Siegal, B., Garb, R., & Lerer, B. (1986). Post-traumatic stress disorder following combat exposure. *British Journal of Psychiatry, 149,* 365–369.

Blowers, C., Cobb, J., & Mathews, A. (1987). Generalized anxiety: A controlled treatment study. *Behaviour Research and Therapy, 25,* 493–502.

Borden, J. (in press). Simple phobia. In S. M. Turner, K. S. Calhoun, & H. E. Adams (Eds.), *Handbook of clinical behavior therapy* (2nd ed.). New York: Wiley.

Borkovec, T. D., Mathews, A. M., Chamber, A., Ebrahimi, S., Lytle, R., & Nelson, R. (1987). The effects of relaxation training with cognitive or nondirective therapy and the role of relaxation-induced anxiety in the treatment of generalized anxiety. *Journal of Consulting and Clinical Psychology, 55,* 883–888.

Borkovec, T. D., Robinson, E., Pruzinsky, T., & DePress, J. A. (1983). Preliminary exploration of worry: Some characteristics and processes. *Behaviour Research and Therapy, 21,* 9–16.

Borkovec, T. D., & Shadick, R. (1989). *The nature of normal versus pathological worry.* Paper prepared for the DSM-IV Task Force.

Breier, A., Charney, D. S., & Heninger, G. R. (1984). Major depression in patients with agoraphobia and panic disorder. *Archives of General Psychology, 41,* 1129–1135.

Breier, A., Charney, D. S., & Heninger, G. R. (1986). Agoraphobia with panic attacks. *Archives of General Psychiatry, 43,* 1029–1036.

Breslau, N., & Davis, G. C. (1985). DSM-III generalized anxiety disorder: An empirical investigation of more stringent criteria. *Psychiatry Research, 14,* 231–238.

Brewin, C. R. (1985). Depression and causal attributions: What is their relation? *Psychological Bulletin, 98,* 297–309.

Burnam, M. A., Hough, R. L., Escobar, J. I., Karno, M., Timbers, D. M., Telles, C. A., & Locke, B. Z. (1987). Six-month prevalence of specific psychiatric disorders among Mexican Americans and Non-Hispanic whites in Los Angeles. *Archives of General Psychiatry, 44,* 687–694.

Butler, G., Cullington, A., Munby, M., Amies, P., & Gelder, M. (1984). Exposure and anxiety management in the treatment of social phobia. *Journal of Consulting and Clinical Psychology, 52,* 642–650.

Carr, D. B., & Sheehan, D. V. (1984). Evidence that panic disorder has a metabolic cause. In J. D. Ballenger (Ed.), *Biology of agoraphobia* (pp. 99–111). Washington, DC: American Psychiatric Press.

Chambless, D. L. (1982). Characteristics of agoraphobia. In D. L. Chambless & A. J. Goldstein (Eds.), *Agoraphobia* (pp. 1–18). New York: Wiley.

Charney, D. S., Woods, S. W., Goodman, W. K., Rifkin, B., Kinch, M., Aiken, B., Qudrino, L. M., & Heniger, G. R. (1986). Drug treatment of panic disorder: The comparative efficacy of imipramine, alprazolam, and trazodone. *Journal of Clinical Psychiatry, 47,* 580–586.

Chouinard, G., Annable, L., Fontaine, R., & Solyom, L. (1982). Alprazolam in the treatment of generalized anxiety and panic disorders: A double-blind, placebo-controlled study. *Psychopharmacology, 77,* 229–233.

Clark, D., Salkovskis, P., & Chalkley, A. (1985). Respiratory control as a treatment for panic attacks. *Journal of Behavior Therapy and Experimental Psychiatry, 16,* 23–30.

Clum, G. (1989). Psychological interventions vs. drugs in the treatment of panic disorder. *Behavior Therapy, 20,* 429–457.

Connolly, J. C., Hallam, R. S., & Marks, I. M. (1976). Selective association of fainting with blood-injury-illness fear. *Behavior Therapy, 7,* 8–13.

Cook, M., & Mineka, S. (1989). Observational conditioning of fear to fear-relevant versus fear-irrelevant stimuli in rhesus monkeys. *Journal of Abnormal Psychology, 98,* 448–459.

Cooper, N. A., & Clum, G. (1989). Imaginal flooding as a supplementary treatment for PTSD in combat veterans: A controlled study. *Behavior Therapy, 20,* 381–391.

Craske, M. M., Rapee, R. M., & Barlow, D. H. (in press). Cognitive–behavioral treatment of panic disorder, agoraphobia and generalized anxiety disorder. In S. M. Turner, K. S. Calhoun, & H. E. Adams (Eds.), *Handbook of clinical behavior therapy* (2nd ed.). New York: Wiley.

Crowe, R. R., Noyes, R., Pauls, D. L., & Slyman, D. (1983). A family study of panic disorder. *Archives of General Psychiatry, 40,* 1065–1069.

Crowe, R. R., Pauls, D. L., Slymen, D. J., & Noyes, R. (1980). A family study of anxiety neurosis. *Archives of General Psychiatry, 37,* 77–79.

Dealy, R. R., Ishiki, D. M., Avery, D. H., Wilson, L. G., & Dunner, D. L. (1981). Secondary depression in anxiety disorders. *Comprehensive Psychiatry, 22,* 612–618.

Delprato, D. J., & McGlynn, F. D. (1984). Behavioral theories of anxiety disorders. In S. M. Turner (Ed.), *Behavioral theories and treatment of anxiety* (pp. 1–49). New York: Plenum Press.

Dunner, D. L., Ishiki, D., Avery, D. H., Wilson, L. G., & Hyde, T. S. (1986). Effect of alprazolam and diazepam on anxiety and panic attacks in panic disorder: A controlled study. *Journal of Clinical Psychiatry, 47,* 458–460.

Eaton, W. W., Holzer, C. E., III, Von Korff, M., Anthony, J. C., Helzer, J. E., George, L., Burnam, M. A., Boyd, J. H., Kessler, L. G., & Locke, B. Z. (1984). The design of the epidemiologic catchment area surveys. *Archives of General Psychiatry, 41,* 942–948.

Emmelkamp, P. M. G. (1982). *Phobic and obsessive–compulsive disorders: Theory, research, and practice.* New York: Plenum Press.

Emmelkamp, P. M. G. (1988). Phobic disorders. In C. G. Last & M. Hersen (Eds.), *Handbook of anxiety disorders* (pp. 66–86). New York: Pergamon Press.

Emmelkamp, P. M. G., & Kwee, K. G. (1977). Obsessional ruminations: A comparison between thought-stopping and prolonged exposure in imagination. *Behaviour Research and Therapy, 15,* 441–444.

Emmelkamp, P. M. G., Mersch, P. P., Vissia, E., & van der Helm, M. (1985). Social phobia: A comparative evaluation of cognitive and behavioral interventions. *Behaviour Research and Therapy, 23,* 365–369.

Fairbank, J. A., & Keane, T. M. (1982). Flooding for combat-related stress disorders: Assessment of anxiety reduction across traumatic memories. *Behavior Therapy, 13,* 499–510.

Falloon, I. R. H., Lloyd, G. G., & Harpin, R. E. (1981). The treatment of social phobia: Real life rehearsal with nonprofessional therapists. *Journal of Nervous and Mental Disease, 169,* 180–184.

Feigenbaum, W. (in press). Long-term efficacy of ungraded versus graded massed exposure in agoraphobics. In I. Hand & H. Wittchen (Eds.), *Panic and phobias.* Berlin: Springer-Verlag.

Flament, M. F., Rapoport, J. L., Berg, C. J., Sczeery, W., Kilts, C., Mellstrom, B., & Linnoila, M. (1985). Clomipramine treatment of childhood obsessive-compulsive disorder: A double-blind controlled study. *Archives of General Psychiatry, 42,* 977–983.

Foa, E. B., Grayson, J. B., Steketee, G. S., Doppelt, H. G., Turner, R. M., & Latimer, P. R. (1983). Success and failure in the behavioral treatment of obsessive–compulsives. *Journal of Consulting and Clinical Psychology, 51,* 287–297.

Fontaine, R., & Chouinard, G. (1986). An open clinical trial of fluoxetine in the treatment of obsessive–compulsive disorder. *Journal of Clinical Psychopharmacology, 6,* 98–101.

Fontaine, R., & Chouinard, G. (1989). Fluoxetine in the long-term maintenance treatment of obsessive–compulsive disorder. *Psychiatric Annals, 19,* 88–91.

Fyer, A. J., & Sandberg, D. (1988). Pharmacologic treatment of panic disorder. In A. J. Francis & R. E. Hales (Eds.), *Review of psychiatry* (Vol. 7, pp. 88–137). Washington, DC: American Psychiatric Press.

Gloger, S., Grunhaus, L., Birmacher, B., & Troudart, T. (1981). Treatment of spontaneous panic attacks with clomipramine. *American Journal of Psychiatry, 138,* 1213–1217.

Goldstein, A. J., & Chambless, D. L. (1978). A reanalysis of agoraphobia. *Behavior Therapy, 9,* 47–59.

Gorman, J., Fyer, A. F., Glicklich, J., King, D., & Klein, D. F. (1981). Effect of imipramine on prolapsed mitral valves of patients with panic disorder. *American Journal of Psychiatry, 138,* 977–978.

Gorman, J. M., Levy, G. F., Liebowitz, M. R., McGrath, P., Appleby, I. L., Dillon, D. J., Davies, S. O., & Klein, D. F. (1983). Effect of acute b-adrenergic blockade of lactate-induced panic. *Archives of General Psychiatry, 40,* 1079–1082.

Gray, J. A. (1982). The neuropsychology of anxiety. Oxford: Clarendon Press.

Green, A. R., & Costain, D. W. (1981). *Pharmacology and biochemistry of psychiatric disorders.* New York: Wiley.

Grunhaus, L., Gloger, S., & Birmacher, B. (1984). Clomipramine treatment for panic attacks in patients with mitral valve prolapse. *Journal of Clinical Psychiatry, 45,* 25–27.

Gurney, C., Roth, M., Garside, R. F., Kerr, T. A., & Shapira, K. (1972). Studies in the classification of affective disorders. The relationship between anxiety states and depressive illness—II. *British Journal of Psychiatry, 121,* 162–166.

Harris, E. L., Noyes, R., Jr., Crowe, R. R., & Chaundry, D. R. (1983). Family study of agoraphobia. *Archives of General Psychiatry, 40,* 1061–1065.

Heimberg, R. G., Dodge, C. S., & Becker, R. E. (1987). Social phobia. In L. Michelson & M. Ascher (Eds.), *Anxiety and stress disorders: Cognitive–behavioral assessment and treatment* (pp. 280–309). New York: Guilford Press.

Heimberg, R. G., Dodge, C. S., Hope, D. A., Kennedy, C. R., Zollo, L., & Becker, R. E. (in press). Cognitive behavioral treatment of social phobia: Comparison to a credible placebo control. *Cognitive Therapy and Research.*

Helzer, J. E., Robins, L. N., McEvoy, L. T., Spitznagel, E. L., Stoltzman, R. K., Farmer, A., & Brockington, I. F. (1985). A comparison of clinical and diagnostic interview schedule diagnoses. *Archives of General Psychiatry, 42,* 657–666.

Hendricks, L. E., Bayton, J. A., Collins, J. L., Mathura, C. B., McMillian, S. R., & Montgomery, T. A. (1983). The NIMH diagnostic interview schedule: A test of its validity in a population of Black adults. *Journal of the National Medical Association, 75,* 667–671.

Hodgson, R. J., Rachman, S., & Marks, I. M. (1972). The treatment of chronic obsessive–compulsive neurosis: Follow-up and further findings. *Behaviour Research and Therapy, 10,* 181–189.

Holloway, W., & McNally, R. J. (1987). Effects of anxiety sensitivity on the response to hyperventilation. *Journal of Abnormal Psychology, 96,* 330–334.

Insel, T. R., Mueller, E. A., Alterman, I., Linnoila, M., & Murphy, D. L. (1985). Obsessive–compulsive disorder and serotonin: Is there a connection? *Biological Psychiatry, 20,* 1174–1188.

Insel, T. R., Zahn, T., & Murphy, D. L. (1985). Obsessive–compulsive disorder: An anxiety disorder? In A. H. Tuma, and J. D. Maser (Eds.), *Anxiety and the anxiety disorders* (pp. 577–589). Hillsdale, N. J.: Erlbaum.

Insel, T. R., Mueller, E. A., Gillin, C., Siever, L. J., & Murphy, D. L. (1985). Tricyclic response in obsessive–compulsive disorder. *Progress in Neurological Psychopharmacology and Biological Psychiatry, 9,* 25–31.

Jacob, R. G., Moller, M. B., Turner, S. M., & Wall, C. (1985). Otoneurological examination in panic disorder and agoraphobia with panic attacks: A pilot study. *American Journal of Psychiatry, 142,* 715–720.

Jacob, R. G., & Turner, S. M. (1988). Panic disorder: Diagnosis and assessment. In A. J. Frances & R. E. Hales (Eds.), *Review of psychiatry,* vol. 7 (pp. 67–87). Washington, DC: American Psychiatric Press.

Jansson, L., Jerremalm, A., & Öst, L. G. (1986). Follow-up of agoraphobic patients treated with exposure in-vivo or applied relaxation. *British Journal of Psychiatry, 149,* 486–490.

Jansson, L., & Öst, L. G. (1982). Behavioral treatments for agoraphobia: An evaluative review. *Clinical Psychology Review, 2,* 311–336.

Jenike, M. A., Baer, L., Minichiello, W. E., Schwartz, C. E., & Carey, R. J., Jr. (1986). Concomitant obsessive–compulsive disorders and schizotypal personality disorder. *American Journal of Psychiatry, 143,* 530–532.

Jenike, M. A., Vitagliano, H. L., Rabinowitz, J., Goff, D. C., & Baer, L. (1987). Bowel obsessions responsive to tricyclic antidepressants in four patients. *American Journal of Psychiatry, 144,* 1347–1348.

Kagan, J. (1982). Heart rate and heart rate variability as signs of a temperamental dimension in infants. In C. E. Izard (Ed.), *Measuring emotions in infants and children* (pp. 38–66). Cambridge, England: Cambridge University Press.

Kagan, J., Reznick, J. S., Clarke, C., Snidman, N., & Garcia-Coll, C. (1984). Behavioral inhibition to the unfamiliar. *Child Development, 55,* 2212–2225.

Kagan, J., Reznick, J. S., & Snidman, N. (1987). The physiology and psychology of behavioral inhibition in children. *Child Development, 58,* 1459–1473.

Kagan, J., Reznick, J. S., & Snidman, N. (1988) Biological bases of childhood shyness. *Science, 240,* 167–171.

Kahn, R. J., McNair, D. M., Covi, L., Downing, R. W., Fisher, S., Lipman, R. S., Rickels, K., & Smith, V. (1981). Effects of psychotropic agents on high anxiety subjects. *Psychopharmacology Bulletin, 17,* 97–100.

Kahn, R. J., McNair, D. M., Lipman, R. S., Covi, L. Rickels, K., Downing, R., Fisher, S., & Frankenthaler, L. M. (1986) Imipramine and clordiazepoxide in depressive and anxiety disorders. *Archives of General Psychiatry, 43,* 79–85.

Kahn, R. S., Van Praag, H. M., Wetzler, G. M., & Barr, G. (1988). Serotonin and anxiety revisited. *Biological Psychiatry, 23,* 189–208.

Kathol, R. G., Noyes, R., Slyman, D. J., Crowe, R. R., Clancy, J., & Kerber, R. E. (1980). Propranolol in chronic anxiety disorders. *Archives of General Psychiatry, 37,* 1361–1365.

Keane, T. M., Fairbank, J. A., Caddell, J. M., & Zimering, R. T. (1989). Implosive (flooding) therapy reduces symptoms of PTSD in Vietnam combat veterans. *Behavior Therapy, 20,* 245–260.

Keane, T. M., & Kaloupek, D. G. (1982). Imaginal flooding in the treatment of post-traumatic stress disorder. *Journal of Consulting and Clinical Psychology, 50,* 138–140.

Kendler, K. S., Heath, A. C., Martin, N. G., & Eaves, L. J. (1987). Symptoms of anxiety and symptoms of depression: Same genes, different environments. *Archives of General Psychiatry, 44,* 451–457.

Khanna, S., & Channabasavanna, S. M. (1988). Phenomenology of obsessions in obsessive–compulsive neurosis. *Psychopathology, 21,* 12–18.

Kilpatrick, D. G., Saunders, B. E., Amick-McMullan, A., Best, C. L., Veronen, L. J., & Resnick, H. S. (1989). Victim and crime factors associated with the development of crime-related post-traumatic stress disorder. *Behavior Therapy, 20,* 199–214.

Kirk, J. W. (1983). Behavioral treatment of obsessional–compulsive patients in clinical practice. *Behaviour Research and Therapy, 21,* 57–62.

Klein, D. F. (1964). Delineation of two drug responsive anxiety syndromes. *Psychopharmacologia, 5,* 397–408.

Klein, D. F. (1967). Importance of psychiatric diagnosis in prediction of clinical drug effects. *Archives of General Psychiatry, 16,* 118–126.

Klein, D. F. (1981). Anxiety reconceptualized. In D. F. Klein & J. R. Rabkin (Eds.), *Anxiety: New research and changing concepts* (pp. 235–263). New York: Raven Press.

Klein, D. F., & Fink, M. (1962). Psychiatric reaction patterns to imipramine. *American Journal of Psychiatry, 119,* 432–438.

Klerman, G. L. (1988). Overview of the cross-national collaborative panic study. *Archives of General Psychiatry, 45,* 407–412.

Lader, M. (1975). Psychophysiological parameters and methods. In L. Levi (Ed.), *Emotions — Their parameters and measurement* (pp. 341–367). New York: Raven Press.

Lang, P. J. (1977). Physiological assessment of anxiety and fear. In J. D. Cone & R. P. Hawkins (Eds.), *Behavioral assessment: New directions in clinical psychology* (pp. 178–195). New York: Brunner/Mazel.

Last, C. G., & Beidel, D. C. (in press). Anxiety. In M. Lewis (Ed.), *Child and adolescent psychiatry: A comprehensive textbook.* Baltimore: Williams and Wilkins.

Last, C. G., Hersen, M., Kazdin, A. E., Finkelstein, R., & Strauss, C. C. (1987). Comparison of DSM-III separation anxiety and overanxious disorders: Demographic characteristics and patterns of comorbidity. *Journal of the American Academy of Child and Adolescent Psychiatry, 26,* 527–531.

Last, C. G., Hersen, M., Kazdin, A. E., Francis, G., & Grubb, H. J. (1987). Psychiatric illness in the mothers of anxious children. *American Journal of Psychiatry, 144,* 1580–1583.

Last, C. G., Hersen, M., Kazdin, A. E., Orvaschel, H., & Ye, W. (1990). *Anxiety disorders in children and their families.* Unpublished manuscript, Nova University, Ft. Lauderdale, FL.

Lesser, I. M., Rubin, R. T., Pecknold, J. C., Rifkin, A., Swinson, R. P., Lydiard, R. B., Burrows, G. D., Noyes, R., Jr., & DuPont, R. L. (1988). Secondary depression in panic disorder and agoraphobia. *Archives of General Psychiatry, 45,* 437–443.

Levin, A. P., Sandberg, D., Stein, J., Cohen, B., Strauman, T., Gorman, J. M., Fyer, A. J., Crawford, R., & Liebowitz, M. R. (1989). *Responses of generalized and limited social phobics during public speaking.* Unpublished manuscript, Columbia University, New York.

Liddell, A., & Lyons, M. (1978). Thunderstorm phobias. *Behaviour Research and Therapy, 16,* 306–308.

Liebowitz, M. R., Fyer, A. J., Gorman, J. M., Campeas, R., Levin, A., Davies, S. R., Goetz, D., & Klein, D. F. (1986). Alprazolam in the treatment of panic disorders. *Journal of Clinical Psychopharmacology, 6,* 13–20.

Liebowitz, M. R., Fyer, A. J., Gorman, J. M., Dillon, D., Davies, S., Stein, J. M., Cohen, B. S., & Klein, D. F. (1985). Specificity of lactate infusions in social phobia versus panic disorders. *American Journal of Psychiatry, 142,* 947–950.

Liebowitz, M. R., Gorman, J. M., Fyer, A. J., Campeas, R., Levin, A. P., Sandberg, D., Hollander, E., Papp, L., & Goetz, D. (1988). Pharmacotherapy of social phobia: An interim report of placebo controlled comparison of phenelzine and atenolol. *Journal of Clinical Psychiatry, 49,* 93–98.

Liebowitz, M. R., Gorman, J. M., Fyer, A. J., & Klein, D. F. (1985). Social phobia. *Archives of General Psychiatry, 42,* 729–736.

Liebowitz, M. R., Gorman, J., Fyer, A. J., Levitt, M., Dillon, D., Levy, G., Appleby, I. L., Anderson, S., Paly, M., Davies, S. O., & Klein, D. F. (1985). Lactate provocation of panic attacks. *Archives of General Psychiatry, 42,* 709–719.

Liebowitz, M. R., Quitkin, F. M., Stewart, J. W., McGrath, P. J., Harrison, W., Rabkin, J., Tricamo, E., Markowitz, J. S., & Klein, D. F. (1984). Phenelzine vs imipramine in atypical depression: A preliminary report. *Archives of General Psychiatry, 41,* 669–677.

Lilienfeld, S. O., Jacob, R. G., & Turner, S. M. (1989). Comment on Holloway and McNally's (1987) "Effects of Anxiety Sensitivity on the Response to Hyperventilation." *Journal of Abnormal Psychology, 98,* 100–102.

Lipsedge, J. S., Hajoff, J., Huggins, P., Napier, L., Pearce, J., Pike, D. J., Rich, M. (1973). The management of agoraphobia: A comparison of proniazid and systematic desensitization. *Psychopharmacology, 32,* 67–80.

Livingston, R., Nugent, H., Rader, L., & Smith, G. R. (1985). Family histories of depressed and severely anxious children. *American Journal of Psychiatry, 142,* 1497–1499.

Lydiard, R. B., Lararia, M. T., Howell, E. F., & Ballenger, J. D. (in press). Alprazolam in social phobia. *Journal of Clinical Psychopharmacology.*

Lydiard, R. B., Roy-Byrne, P. P., & Ballenger, J. C. (1988). Recent advances in psychopharmacological treatment of anxiety disorders. *Hospital and Community Psychiatry, 39,* 1157–1165.

Maller, R. G., & Reiss, S. (1987). A behavioral validation of the Anxiety Sensitivity Index. *Journal of Anxiety Disorders, 1,* 265–272.

Margraf, J., Ehlers, A., & Roth, W. T. (1986). Sodium lactate infusions and panic attacks: A review and critique. *Psychosomatic Medicine, 48,* 23–51.

Marks, I. M. (1970). The classification of phobic disorders. *British Journal of Psychiatry, 116*, 377–386.

Marks, I. M. (1971). Phobic disorders four years after treatment: A prospective follow-up. *British Journal of Psychiatry, 118*, 683–686.

Marks, I. M. (1985). Behavioral treatment of social phobia. *Psychopharmacology Bulletin, 21*, 615–618.

Marks, I., & Gelder, M. G. (1966). Different onset ages in varieties of phobias. *American Journal of Psychiatry, 123*, 218–221.

Marks, I. M., Gray, S., Cohen, D., Hill, R., Mawson, D., Ramm, E., & Stern, R. S. (1983). Imipramine and brief therapist-aided exposure in agoraphobics having self-exposure homework. *Archives of General Psychiatry, 40*, 153–159.

Marks, I. M., Stern, R. S., Mawson, D., Cobb, J., & McDonald, R. (1980). Clomipramine and exposure for obsessive–compulsive rituals. *British Journal of Psychiatry, 136*, 1–25.

Mathew, R. J., Ho, B. T., Francis, D. J., Taylor, D. L., & Weinman, M. L. (1982). Catacholamines and anxiety. *Acta Psychiatrica Scandinavica, 65*, 142–147.

Mattick, R. P., & Peters, L. (1988). Treatment of severe social phobia: Effects of guided exposure with and without cognitive restructuring. *Journal of Consulting and Clinical Psychology, 56*, 251–260.

Mattick, R. P., Peters, L., & Clarke, J. C. (1989). Exposure and cognitive restructuring for severe social phobia. *Behavior Therapy, 20*, 3–23.

Mavissakalian, M., & Hammen, M. S. (1986). DSM-III personality disorder in agoraphobia. *Comprehensive Psychiatry, 27*, 471–479.

Mavissakalian, M., & Hammen, M. S. (1988). Correlates of DSM-III personality disorder in panic disorder and agoraphobia. *Comprehensive Psychiatry, 29*, 535–544.

Mavissakalian, M., & Michelson, L. (1986). Agoraphobia: Relative and combined effectiveness of therapist-assisted in vivo exposure and imipramine. *Journal of Clinical Psychiatry, 47*, 117–122.

Mavissakalian, M., Turner, S. M., Michelson, L., & Jacob, R. G. (1986). Tricyclic antidepressants in obsessive–compulsive disorder: II. Antiobsessional or antidepressant agents? *American Journal of Psychiatry, 142*, 572–576.

Mawson, D., Marks, I. M., & Ramm, L. (1982). Clomipramine and exposure for chronic obsessive–compulsive rituals: III. Two year follow-up and further findings. *British Journal of Psychiatry, 140*, 11–18.

McNally, R. J. (1987). Preparedness and phobias: A review. *Psychological Bulletin, 101*, 283–303.

McNally, R. J., & Lorenz, M. (1987). Anxiety sensitivity in agoraphobics. *Journal of Behavior Therapy and Experimental Psychiatry, 18*, 3–11.

McNally, R. J., & Steketee, G. S. (1985). The etiology and maintenance of severe animal phobias. *Behaviour Research and Therapy, 23*, 431–435.

Merckelbach, H., van den Hout, M. A., Jansen, A., & van der Molen, G. M. (1988). Many stimuli are frightening, but some are more frightening than others: The contributions of preparedness, dangerousness, and unpredictability to making a stimulus fearful. *Journal of Psychopathology and Behavioral Assessment, 10*, 355–366.

Michelson, L., Mavissakalian, M., & Marchione, K. (1985). Cognitive and behavioral treatments of agoraphobia: Clinical, behavioral, and psychophysiological outcomes. *Journal of Consulting and Clinical Psychology, 53*, 913–925.

Michelson, L., Mavissakalian, M., & Marchione, K. (1988). Cognitive, behavioral, and psychophysiological treatment of agoraphobia: A comparative outcome investigation. *Behavior Therapy, 19,* 97–120.

Mineka, S. (1985). Animal models of anxiety-based disorders: Their usefulness and limitations. In A. H. Tuma & J. D. Maser (Eds.), *Anxiety and the anxiety disorders* (pp. 199–244). Hillsdale, NJ: Erlbaum.

Mineka, S., & Cook, M. (1986). Immunization against the observational conditioning of snake fear in rhesus monkeys. *Journal of Abnormal Psychology, 95,* 307–318.

Mineka, S., Davidson, M., Cook, M., & Heir, R. (1985). Observational conditioning of snake fear in rhesus monkeys. *Journal of Abnormal Psychology, 93,* 355–372.

Mineka, S., & Zinbarg, R. (in press). Animal models of psychopathology. In C. E. Walker (Ed.), *Clinical psychology: Historical and research foundations.*

Montgomery, S. A. (1980). Clomipramine in obsessional neurosis: A placebo controlled trial. *Pharmacology and Medicine, 1,* 189–192.

Mowrer, O. H. (1947). On the dual nature of learning: A re-interpretation of "conditioning" and "problem-solving." *Harvard Educational Review, 17,* 102–148.

Mueller, E. A., Murphy, D. L., & Sunderland, T. (1986). Further studies of the putative serotonin agonist, m-chlorophenylpiperazine: Evidence for a serotonin receptor mediated mechanism of action in humans. *Psychopharmacology, 89,* 388–391.

Mueller, E. A., Sunderland, T., & Murphy, D. L. (1985). Neuroendocrine effects of m-CPP, a serotonin agonist, in humans. *Journal of Clinical Endocrinology and Metabolism, 61,* 1179–1184.

Munjack, D. J., Rebal, R., Shaner, R., Staples, F., Braun, R., & Leonard, M. (1985). Imipramine versus propranolol for the treatment of panic attacks: A pilot study. *Comprehensive Psychiatry, 26,* 80–89.

Myers, J. K., Weissman, M. M., Tischler, G. L., Holzer, C. E., Leaf, P. J., Orvaschel, H., Anthony, J. C., Boyd, J. H., Burke, J. D., Kramer, M., & Stoetzman, R. (1984). Six-month prevalence of psychiatric disorders in three communities. *Archives of General Psychiatry, 41,* 959–967.

Neal, A. M., & Turner, S. M. (in press). Anxiety disorders research with African–Americans: Current status. *Psychological Bulletin.*

Noyes, R., Jr. (1985). Beta-adrenergic blocking drugs in anxiety and stress. *Psychiatric Clinics of North America, 8,* 119–132.

Noyes, R., Jr., Anderson, D. J., Clancy, J., Crowe, R. R., Slyman, D. J., Ghoneim, M. M., & Hinrichs, J. V. (1984). Diazepam and propranolol in panic disorder and agoraphobia. *Archives of General Psychiatry, 41,* 287–292.

Noyes, R., Jr., Kathol, R., Clancy, J., & Crowe, R. R. (1981). Antianxiety effects of propranolol: A review of clinical studies. In D. F. Klein & J. Rabkin (Eds.), *Anxiety: New research and changing concepts* (pp. 81–93). New York: Raven Press.

Öhman, A. (1986). Face the beast and fear the face: Animal and social fears as prototypes for evolutionary analyses of emotion. *Psychophysiology, 23,* 123–145.

Öhman, A., Eriksson, A., & Olafsson, C. (1975). One-trial learning and superior resistance to extinction of autonomic responses conditioned to potentially phobic stimuli. *Journal of Comparative and Physiological Psychology, 88,* 619–627.

Öhman, A., Fredrikson, M., Hugdahl, K., & Rimmo, P. A. (1976). The premise of equipotentiality in human classical conditioning: Conditioned electrodermal responses to potentially phobic stimuli. *Journal of Experimental Psychology: General, 105,* 313–337.

Öst, L. G. (1978). Fading versus systematic desensitization in the treatment of snake and spider phobia. *Behaviour Research and Therapy, 16,* 379–389.

Öst, L. G. (1987). Age of onset in different phobias. *Journal of Abnormal Psychology, 96,* 223–229.

Öst, L. G. (1988). Applied relaxation vs. progressive relaxation in the treatment of panic disorder. *Behaviour Research and Therapy, 26,* 13–22.

Öst, L. G., & Hugdahl, K. (1983). Acquisition of phobias and anxiety response patterns in clinical patients. *Behaviour Research and Therapy, 21,* 623–631.

Öst, L. G., Jerrmalm, A., & Johansson, J. (1981). Individual response patterns and the effects of different behavioral methods in the treatment of social phobia. *Behaviour Research and Therapy, 19,* 1–16.

Pato, M. T., Zohar-Kadouch, R., Zohar, J., & Murphy, D. L. (1988). Return of symptoms after discontinuation of clomipramine in patients with obsessive-compulsive disorder. *American Journal of Psychiatry, 145,* 1521–1525.

Peterson, R. A., & Heilbronner, R. L. (1987). The Anxiety Sensitivity Index: Construct validity and factor analytic structure. *Journal of Anxiety Disorders, 1,* 117–121.

Pitts, F. N., Jr., & McClure, J. N., Jr. (1967). Lactate metabolism in anxiety neuroses. *New England Journal of Medicine, 277,* 1328–1336.

Rachman, S. (1988). Panics and their consequences: A review and prospect. In S. Rachman & J. D. Maser (Eds.), *Panic: Psychological perspectives* (pp. 259–303). Hillsdale, NJ: Erlbaum.

Rachman, S. (1990). *Fear and courage* (2nd ed.). New York: Freeman.

Rachman, S., & Hodgson, R. (1980). *Obsessions and compulsions.* Englewood Cliffs, NJ: Prentice-Hall.

Rachman, S., Marks, I., & Hodgson, R. (1973). The treatment of chronic obsessive-compulsive neurosis by modeling and flooding in vivo. *Behaviour Research and Therapy, 11,* 467–471.

Rachman, S. J. (1977). The conditioning theory of fear-acquisition. A critical examination. *Behaviour Research and Therapy, 15,* 375–387.

Rapee, R. M., & Barlow, D. H. (1988). *Cognitive restructuring and relaxation in the treatment of generalized anxiety disorder: A controlled study.* Paper presented at the 22nd Annual Association of Advancement of Behavior Therapy meeting, New York, November.

Rasmussen, S. A., & Tsuang, M. T. (1986). Clinical characteristics and family history in DSM-III obsessive–compulsive disorder. *American Journal of Psychiatry, 143,* 317–322.

Reich, J. H., & Noyes, R., Jr. (1987). A comparison of DSM-III personality disorders in acutely ill panic and depressed patients. *Journal of Anxiety Disorders, 1,* 123–131.

Reich, J., & Yates, W. (1988a). A pilot study of treatment of social phobia with alprazolam. *American Journal of Psychiatry, 145,* 590–594.

Reich, J., & Yates, W. (1988b). Family history of psychiatric disorders in social phobia. *Comprehensive Psychiatry, 29,* 72–75.

Reichler, R. J., Hyde, T. S., & Sylvester, C. E. (in press). Early identification of children with anxiety disorders in an "at risk" population. In B. Garfinkel, B. Egeland, P. Kendall, & L. Stein (Eds.), *Anxiety disorders in children: Implications for school adjustment.*

Reiss, S., & McNally, R. J. (1985). The expectancy model of fear. In S. Reiss & R. R. Bootzin (Eds.), *Theoretical issues in behavior therapy* (pp. 107–121). New York: Academic Press.

Reiss, S., Peterson, R. A., Gursky, D. M., & McNally, R. J. (1986). Anxiety sensitivity, anxiety frequency and the prediction of fearfulness. *Behaviour Research and Therapy, 24,* 1–8.

Reznick, J. S., Kagan, J., Sniderman, N., Gersten, M., Boak, K., & Rosenberg, A. (1986). Inhibited and uninhibited children: A follow-up study. *Child Development, 57,* 660–680.

Rizley, R., Kahn, R. J., McNair, D. M., & Frankenthaler, L. M. (1986). A comparison of alprazolam and imipramine in the treatment of agoraphobia and panic disorder. *Psychopharmacology Bulletin, 22,* 167–172.

Robins, L. N. (1985). Epidemiology: Reflections on testing the validity of psychiatric interviews. *Archives of General Psychiatry, 42,* 918–924.

Robins, L. N., Helzer, J. E., Weissman, M. M., Orvaschel, H., Greenberg, E., Burke, J. D., Jr., & Regier, D. A. (1984). Lifetime prevalence of specific psychiatric disorders at three sites. *Archives of General Psychiatry, 41,* 949–958.

Rosenbaum, J. R., Biederman, J., Gersten, M., Hirshfeld, D. R., Meminger, S. R., Herman, J. B., Kagan, J., Reznick, J. S., & Snidman, N. (1988). Behavioral inhibition in children of parents with panic disorder and agoraphobia. *Archives of General Psychiatry, 45,* 463–470.

Salkovskis, P. M., & Warwick, H. M. (1985). Cognitive therapy of obsessive–compulsive disorder: Treating treatment failures. *Behavioral Psychotherapy, 13,* 243–255.

Sanderson, W. C., Rapee, R. M., & Barlow, D. H. (1987). *The DSM-III-R revised anxiety disorder categories: Descriptors and patterns of comorbidity.* Paper presented at the 21st Annual Association of Advancement of Behavior Therapy meeting, November, Chicago, Ill.

Seligman, M. (1971). Phobias and preparedness. *Behavior Therapy, 2,* 307–320.

Shear, M. K. (1988). Cognitive and biological models of panic: Toward an integration. In S. Rachman & J. D. Maser (Eds.), *Panic: Psychological perspectives* (pp. 51–70). Hillsdale, NJ: Erlbaum.

Shear, M. K., Devereux, R. B., Kranier-Fox, R., Mann, J. J., & Frances, A. (1984). Low prevalence of mitral valve prolapse in patients with panic disorder. *American Journal of Psychiatry, 141,* 302–303.

Sheehan, D. V., Ballenger, J. C., & Jacobsen, G. (1980). Treatment of endogenous anxiety with phobic, hysterical, and hypochondriacal symptoms. *Archives of General Psychiatry, 37,* 51–59.

Sheehan, D. V., Sheehan, K. E., & Minichiello, W. E. (1981). Age of onset of phobic disorders. *Comprehensive Psychiatry, 22,* 544–553.

Solyom, L., Heseltine, G. F. D., McClure, D. J., Solyom, C., Tedwidge, B., & Steinberg, G. (1973). Behavior therapy vs. drug therapy in the treatment of phobic neurosis. *Canadian Psychiatric Association Journal, 18,* 25–31.

Stanley, M. A., Turner, S. M., & Borden, J. W. (in press). *Schizotypal features in obsessive–compulsive disorder. Comprehensive Psychiatry.*

Steketee, G. S., Foa, E. B., & Grayson, J. B. (1982). Recent advances in the treatment of obsessive–compulsives. *Archives of General Psychiatry, 39,* 1365–1371.

Stern, R. S., Lipsedge, M. S., & Marks, I. M. (1973). Obsessive ruminations: A controlled trial of thought-stopping technique. *Behaviour Research and Therapy, 11,* 659–662.

Stravynski, A., Grey, S., & Elie, R. (1987). Outline of the therapeutic process in social skills training with socially dysfunctional patients. *Journal of Consulting and Clinical Psychology, 55,* 224–228.

Stravynski, A., Marks, I., & Yule, W. (1982). Social skills problems in neurotic outpatients: Social skills training with and without cognitive modification. *Archives of General Psychiatry, 39,* 1378–1385.

Suomi, S. J. (1986). Anxiety in young nonhuman primates. In R. Gittelman (Ed.), *Anxiety disorders of childhood* (pp. 1–23). New York: Guilford Press.

Suomi, S. J., Kraemer, G. U., Baysinger, C. M., & Delizio, R. D. (1981). Inherited and experiential factors associated with individual differences in anxious behavior displayed by rhesus monkeys. In D. Klein & J. Rabkin (Eds.), *Anxiety: New research and changing concepts* (pp. 179–200). New York: Raven Press.

Taylor, C. B., Hayward, C., King, R., Ehlers, A., Margraf, J., Maddock, R., Clark, D., Roth, W. T., & Agras, W. S. (1990). Cardiovascular and symptomatic reduction effects of alprazolam and imipramine in patients with panic disorder: Results of a double-blind, placebo-controlled study. *Journal of Clinical Psychopharmacology, 10,* 112–118.

Tesar, G. E., & Rosenbaum, J. F. (1986). Successful use of clonazepam in patients with treatment-resistant panic disorder. *Journal of Nervous and Mental Disease, 174,* 477–482.

Thóren, P., Åsberg, M., Bertilsson, L., Mellstrom, B., Sjoqvist, F., & Traskman, L. (1980). Clomipramine treatment of obsessive–compulsive disorders: II. Biochemical aspects. *Archives of General Psychiatry, 37,* 1281–1285.

Thóren, P., Åsberg, M., Cronholm, B., Jornestedt, L., & Traskman, L. (1980). Clomipramine treatment of obsessive–compulsive disorder: I. A controlled clinical trial. *Archives of General Psychiatry, 37,* 1281–1285.

Thorpe, G. L., & Burns, L. E. (1983). *The agoraphobic syndrome.* New York: Wiley.

Thyer, B. A., Parrish, R. T., Curtis, G. E., Nesse, R. M., & Cameron, O. G. (1985). Age of onset of DSM-III anxiety disorders. *Comprehensive Psychiatry, 26,* 113–121.

Torgersen, S. (1983). Genetic factors in anxiety disorders. *Archives of General Psychiatry, 40,* 1085–1089.

Turner, S. M., & Beidel, D. C. (1988). *Treating obsessive–compulsive disorder.* New York: Pergamon Press.

Turner, S. M., & Beidel, D. C. (1989a). *On the nature of obsessional thoughts and worry: Similarities and dissimilarities.* Paper prepared for the DSM-IV Task Force.

Turner, S. M., & Beidel, D. C. (1989b). Social phobia: Clinical syndrome, diagnosis and comorbidity. *Clinical Psychology Review, 9,* 3–18.

Turner, S. M., Beidel, D. C., Borden, J. W., Stanley, M. A., & Jacob, R. G. (in press). *Social phobia: Axis I and II correlates. Journal of Abnormal Psychology.*

Turner, S. M., Beidel, D. C., & Costello, A. (1987). Psychopathology in the offspring of anxiety disorders patients. *Journal of Consulting and Clinical Psychology, 55,* 229–235.

Turner, S. M., Beidel, D. C., Dancu, C. V., & Keys, D. J. (1986). Psychopathology of social phobia and comparison to avoidant personality disorder. *Journal of Abnormal Psychology, 95,* 389–394.

Turner, S. M., Beidel, D. C., & Epstein, L. H. (in press). Vulnerability and risk for anxiety disorders. *Journal of Anxiety Disorders.*

Turner, S. M., Beidel, D. C., & Jacob, R. G. (1988). Assessment of panic. In S. Rachman & J. D. Maser (Eds.), *Panic: Psychological perspectives* (pp. 37–50). Hillsdale, NJ: Erlbaum.

Turner, S. M., Beidel, D. C., & Jacob, R. G. (1990). *Behavioral and pharmacological treatment of social phobia.* Unpublished manuscript, University of Pittsburgh.

Turner, S. M., Beidel, D. C., & Nathan, R. S. (1985). Biological factors in obsessive–compulsive disorders. *Psychological Bulletin, 97,* 430–450.

Turner, S. M., Jacob, R. G., Beidel, D. C., & Himmelhoch, J. (1985). Fluoxetine treatment of obsessive–compulsive disorder. *Journal of Clinical Psychopharmacology, 5,* 207–212.

Tyrer, P., Candy, J., & Delly, D. A. (1973). A study of the clinical effects of phenelzine and placebo in the treatment of phobic anxiety. *Psychopharmacologia, 32,* 237–254.

Uhde, T. W., Boulenger, J. P., Roy-Byrne, P. P., Geraci, M. F., Vittone, B. J., & Post, R. M. (1985). Longitudinal course of panic disorder: Clinical and biological considerations. *Progress in Neuro-Psychopharmacology and Biological Psychiatry, 9,* 39–51.

van der Molen, C. G., & van den Hout, M. A. (1988). Expectancy effects on respiration during lactate infusion. *Psychosomatic Medicine, 50,* 439–443.

Van Valkenberg, C., Akiskal, H. G., Puzantian, V., & Rosenthal, T. (1984). Anxious depressions: Clinical, family history, and naturalistic outcome-comparisons with panic and major depressive disorders. *Journal of Affective Disorders, 6,* 67–82.

Vermilyea, B. B., Barlow, D. H., & O'Brien, G. T. (1984). The importance of assessing treatment integrity: An example in the anxiety disorders. *Journal of Behavioral Assessment, 6,* 1–11.

Versiani, M., Mundim, F. D., Nardi, A. E., & Liebowitz, M. R. (1988). Tranylcypromine in social phobia. *Journal of Clinical Psychopharmacology, 8,* 279–283.

Volavka, J., Neziroglu, F., & Yaryura-Tobias, J. A. (1985). Clomipramine and imipramine in obsessive–compulsive disorder. *Psychiatry Research, 14,* 83–91.

Walker, V. J., & Beech, H. R. (1969). Mood states and the ritualistic behavior of obsessional patients. *British Journal of Psychiatry, 1150,* 1261–1268.

Watson, J. B., & Rayner, R. (1920). Conditional emotional reactions. *Journal of Experimental Psychology, 3,* 1–14.

Weissman, M. M. (1988). The epidemiology of panic disorder and agoraphobia. In A. J. Frances & R. E. Hales (Eds.), *Review of psychiatry, vol. 7* (pp. 54–66). Washington, D. C.: American Psychiatric Press, Inc.

Weissman, M. M., Leckman, J. F., Merikangas, K. R., Gammon, G. D., & Prusoff, B. A. (1984). Depression and anxiety disorders in parents and children. *Archives of General Psychiatry, 41,* 845–852.

Williams, D. H. (1986). The epidemiology of mental illness in Afro-Americans. *Hospital and Community Psychiatry, 37,* 42–49.

Wolpe, J. (1973) *The practice of behavior therapy* (2nd ed.). New York: Pergamon Press.

Wolpe, J. (1982). *The practice of behavior therapy* (3rd ed.). New York: Pergamon Press.

Yaryura-Tobias, J. A., & Bhagavan, H. N. (1977). L-tryptophan in obsessive–compulsive disorders. *American Journal of Psychiatry, 134,* 1298–1299.

Zitrin, C. M., Klein, D. F., & Woerner, M. G. (1978). Behavior therapy, supportive psychotherapy, imipramine, and phobias. *Archives of General Psychiatry, 35,* 307–316.

Zitrin, C. M., Klein, D. F., & Woerner, M. G. (1980). Treatment of agoraphobia with group exposure in vivo and imipramine. *Archives of General Psychiatry, 40,* 125–138.

Zohar, J., & Insel, T. R. (1987). Obsessive–compulsive disorder: Psychobiological approaches to diagnosis, treatment, and pathophysiology. *Biological Psychiatry, 22,* 667–687.

CHAPTER 10

Dissociative Disorders

HAROLD A. SACKEIM and D. P. DEVANAND

> The whole of this doctrine leads us to a conclusion, which is of great impor-
> tance in the present affair, viz. that all the nice and subtle questions concern-
> ing personal identity can never possibly be decided, and are to be regarded
> rather as grammatical than as philosophical difficulties. Identity depends on
> the relations of ideas; and these relations produce identity, by means of that
> easy transition they occasion. But as the relations, and the easiness of the
> transition may diminish by insensible degrees, we have no just standard by
> which we can decide any dispute concerning the time when they acquire or lose
> a title to the name of identity. All the disputes concerning the identity of
> connected objects are merely verbal, except so far as the relation of parts gives
> rise to some fiction or imaginary principle of union, as we have already ob-
> served.
>
> *Hume (1738/1911, p. 248)*

Determining what is meant by personal identity is no easy matter. What and
how much would have to be different about a person for the person to be
considered different? How can everybody be forever changing and yet each
person consider himself or herself to be the same person from moment to
moment, no less from generation to generation? What gives rise to the
pervasive belief that each person is the same individuated entity through
time? Is the belief false?

In no uncertain terms, Hume (1738/1911) argued that the notion of
personal identity has no basis in reality. He disputed that we have an experience of unity that is continuous through time. He noted that, just as our
physical beings are in constant change, our perceptions of ourselves and
others are distinct and temporary. Hume argued that our firm belief in the
notion of "personal identity" is a product of illusion. The illusion stems
from our inability to notice change, when change occurs slowly and over
long duration.

Dissociative disorders, as they are currently conceptualized, present
pathology of the very type Hume claimed not to exist. In the third revised
edition of the *Diagnostic and Statistical Manual of Mental Disorders*
(DSM-III-R), the essential feature of dissociative disorders is termed
"a disturbance or alteration in the normally integrative functions of memory, consciousness, or identity" (American Psychiatric Association [APA],
1987, p. 269). For example, the diagnosis of multiple personality hinges in

part on establishing that within the same body "the individual" is characterized by two or more identities, that is, by two or more distinct personalities. If we have trouble determining what is meant by personal identity, it is difficult to accept the existence of dissociative disorders that force us to talk about individuals who have "lost their identities" or who have acquired more than one.

At the outset, it should be noted that, while raising a host of conceptual issues, careful examination of the nature of dissociative disorders may also help to clarify what we generally mean by personal identity and why we so strongly believe that each person is characterized by a unique identity. The case histories described in this chapter are typical examples of dissociative disorders. What is characteristic about people who have been diagnosed as presenting fugue states or multiple personalities is that they behave at times in ways that depart radically from their usual patterns. Furthermore, these departures are not isolated or random acts, but are integrated, complex modes of self-presentation. Hume may have been correct in pointing out that we do not possess a reliable metric by which to determine slight or subtle changes in character. He argued that our failure to perceive change is the reason that we wrongly assume that there is something constant about ourselves through time and that this constancy constitutes personal identity. The noteworthy aspect about dissociative disorders is that individuals diagnosed as presenting such disorders display marked and rapid change, often of such an extreme nature that, were personalities akin to fruit, such individuals might best be described at one time as an apple and at another time as a watermelon. It is precisely our ability to perceive the drastic behavioral alterations in cases of dissociative disorder that may indicate that Hume's dismissal of the concept of personality identity was incorrect.

Diagnosis of dissociative disorder is quite rare. Although the disorder of multiple personality, for example, is the subject of much attention in the media and films, only a few hundred case reports of this syndrome have been published. Many, if not most, clinicians go through a lifetime of practice without entertaining the notion that a patient is presenting dissociative disorder. The rarity of the disorder has precluded traditional empirical studies of the reliability and validity of diagnosis, incidence and prevalence, nature of etiology, and evaluation of treatment. Virtually all that we know about dissociative disorders stems from relatively unsystematic case reports. Furthermore, symptomatology is often not directly observable. In cases of depersonalization disorder, feelings of alienation and unreality may be the primary complaint. In cases of psychogenic amnesia, diagnosis may be based on circumstantial evidence of memory lapse, with the patient apparently indifferent to the problem. In such situations, description and interpretation of cases are often heavily influenced by the clinician's theoretical perspective. The cases that are reported also may be extreme instances and not prototypic of disorder. In reviewing the literature on dissociative disorders, we have had to rely almost exclusively on such case reports and on our clinical experience. Accordingly, we suggest caution in accepting clinical lore as fact.

DESCRIPTION AND DIAGNOSIS

As indicated above, according to DSM-III-R, the essential feature of dissociative disorders is an abrupt aberration of memory, consciousness, or identity. Dissociative disorders comprise four types of disturbance: psychogenic amnesia, psychogenic fugue, multiple personality, and depersonalization disorder. Before discussing each disorder in detail, general diagnostic issues about this grouping will be considered.

We have no commonly accepted definitions of consciousness or identity, let alone of what constitutes aberrations in these areas. The acute phases of many psychiatric disorders present behavior that might be viewed as abrupt alterations in memory, consciousness, or identity. Certainly, acute psychotic reactions involve alterations in consciousness. It is not uncommon for schizophrenic patients to claim that they are someone different from who indeed they are. Patients presenting major affective disorders commonly report that they do not feel at all like themselves and that their world views have changed. Rapid cycling bipolar patients may seem to undergo repeated changes in disposition and behavior over relatively short time spans.

One can also raise the question whether normal functioning is characterized by behaviors that are akin to dissociative disorders. Momentary forgetting, a universal experience that occurs when people lose their train of thought (Luborsky, Sackeim, & Christoph, 1979), might share features with psychogenic amnesia. Behavioral acts subsequent to hypnotic suggestion—including posthypnotic amnesia, posthypnotic writing or other motor behavior, hypnotic regression, and hypnotic personality alteration—appear to mimic dissociative states (e.g., Hilgard, 1977). Likewise, the contradictory beliefs and actions expressed by different personalities in cases of multiple personality might be modeled by nonpathological instances of self-deception, in which individuals appear to hold contradictory sets of beliefs and are aware of only one (Sackeim, 1983, 1988; Sackeim & Gur, 1978).

The pragmatics of diagnosis are such that syndromes such as schizophrenia and major affective disorder are not considered dissociative disorders. Prior to DSM-III, in psychiatric nosology, dissociative disorders were subgrouped with conversion reactions as manifestations of hysterical neurosis (APA, 1968). The basis for diagnosis was presentation of a sensorimotor disturbance or disturbance of higher cognitive function that resembled disorders produced by neuropathology but that were believed to be psychogenically based. Hysterical neurosis was given some specificity by restricting symptomatology to conditions that appeared similar to effects of neurological disease and by excluding symptoms related to other medical conditions, such as headache or digestive tract disorders (Goodwin & Guze, 1979). Neurologic-appearing disturbances in faculties of sense (e.g., blindness, deafness) were grouped as hysterical conversion reaction. Incapacity or loss of motor behavior (e.g., paralysis) was also termed conversion reaction. Disturbances of higher cognitive functions that mimicked neurological disease were grouped as dissociative reaction. The major dissociative reactions included in DSM-II were amnesia, somnambulism, fugue, and multiple personality (APA, 1968). All

four disorders are characterized by amnesia. In fact, the presence of presumed psychogenically based amnesia could serve as the cardinal sign for a
diagnosis of hysterical dissociative reaction. The requirement of amnesia
would in itself rule out most instances of schizophrenia or affective disorder
as possible cases of dissociative disorder.

The revisions in nosology embodied in DSM-III (APA, 1980) and, more
recently, DSM-III-R, make diagnosis more complex. Conversion reactions are
now viewed as a subgrouping of somatoform disorders, which, in addition,
include body dysmorphic disorder, somatoform pain disorder, hypochondriasis, and somatization disorder or Briquet's syndrome. Dissociative disorders
are a grouping unto themselves. The nosology no longer implies that conversion and dissociative disorders are both manifestations of the same underlying
psychopathological processes that result in either form of hysterical neurosis.
Depersonalization also is included as a dissociative disorder.

As acknowledged in DSM-III-R, the incorporation of depersonalization as
a dissociative disorder is perhaps the most critical and controversial issue.
Depersonalization disorder differs from the other dissociative disorders in
that amnesia is not a necessary or even likely component of symptomatology.
The primary inclusion criterion for depersonalization disorder is recurrent
or persistent experiences of depersonalization that cause marked distress,
with intact reality testing. The incorporation of depersonalization in dissociative disorders puts new emphasis on alterations in identity as a basic sign
of disturbance. Although the central problem in multiple personality and
fugue states appears to be one of identity, the requirement that amnesia also
should occur provides for better reliability. In our view, the inclusion of depersonalization as a dissociative disorder, where there is no amnesia, is likely
to result in less diagnostic reliability than were it excluded.

As a general rule of thumb, alterations in consciousness that are considered
to be essential features of dissociative disorders are problems of memory.
Psychogenic amnesia patients may appear unable to recall intense, traumatic
experiences. During fugue states, the patient has amnesia for whom he or she
is, as well as for location of home, members of family, occupation, or other
personal details. Following the fugue state, the patient may have partial or
complete amnesia for all events that occurred while he or she was unable to
recall the past. In multiple personality, the dominant personality usually
displays amnesia for events that occurred while other personalities seemed to
control behavior.

Also, as a general rule, abrupt alterations in identity are problems in the
"consistency" of personality. In fugue states and multiple personality, individuals behave in ways that appear to be out of character. People who are
timid, withdrawn, and law abiding may abruptly appear to be garrulous, ex-
troverted, and criminal. Personal preferences in clothing, food, and even sexual orientation may alter dramatically. The assumption is that the person's
normally enduring and integrated set of traits, dispositions, values, and preferences are abruptly replaced by another, often contradictory, set. In cases of
multiple personality, the dominant personality may deny amnesia. There may
not be an opportunity to interview directly subpersonalities. Nonetheless, the

diagnosis of multiple personality may be suggested by a history of behaviors that seem totally out of character for the individual. Third-party reports may indicate that, during these acts, the individual displayed a markedly different tone of voice, altered patterns of dress, and change in gait, and/or responded to a different name. In depersonalization disorder, patients rarely display overt behavior that suggests such a problem in the consistency of personality; rather, they report feeling that they are no longer themselves. Commonly, they report that they feel like their personalities have been lost and that they are unindividuated objects, without vitality or life.

It is possible, by this view, to distinguish disturbances in the consistency of personality that characterize dissociative disorders from problems of identity that arise in other psychiatric conditions. Critical here is the assumption that the personality manifested in the dissociated state is discontinuous with the previous or dominant personality of the individual and yet is integrated within itself. Patients presenting major depressive disorders may indicate that they do not feel like themselves; however, except when depersonalization is a major part of the clinical picture, they neither report nor act as if they have experienced a radical and discontinuous change in beliefs, values, or preferences. Schizophrenics may display behaviors that appear out of character with premorbid acts. In acute states, such individuals may fail to respond to their own name and may insist they are someone else (e.g., Jesus Christ). Rarely, however, is the inconsistent behavior integrated to an extent that would suggest that a different pattern of personality organization is reflected in the behavior.

Recently, attempts have been made to quantify the presence or likelihood of dissociation with the development of assessment scales. A dissociation scale has been developed and tested in normal individuals and in patients with a variety of psychopathology, and there appears to be preliminary evidence of adequate reliability and validity. A Dissociative Disorders Interview Schedule and a Dissociative Experiences Scale were recently developed by Ross and Anderson (1988). The clinical utility of these scales either in differential diagnosis or in quantifying the severity of dissociative symptomatology, remains to be established. In addition, the rarity of true dissociative states may make it difficult to validate conditions such as psychogenic fugue and psychogenic amnesia (Bernstein & Putnam, 1986).

In the sections that follow, we discuss the characteristics of each of the four types of dissociative disorder. We highlight what attempts have been made to determine objectively whether alterations in identity reflect discontinuous, but internally integrated, breaks in the consistency of personality (e.g., Osgood, Luria, Jeans, & Smith, 1976). Such attempts have rarely been made, and, in common practice, diagnostic decisions are based on subjective impressions as to whether behavior of an individual is sufficiently discontinuous with the person's past and sufficiently integrated within itself to merit the diagnosis of dissociative disorder. After a presentation of the major theories of the etiology of dissociative disorder and forms of treatment, we again raise the question of whether instances of dissociative states in normal functioning can serve as analogs of pathological dissociation.

DIAGNOSTIC CRITERIA AND COURSE

Psychogenic Amnesia

The DSM-III-R criteria for the diagnosis of psychogenic amnesia are as follows:

1. The predominant disturbance is an episode of sudden inability to recall important personal information that is too extensive to be explained by ordinary forgetfulness.
2. The disturbance is not due to multiple personality disorder or to an organic mental disorder (e.g., blackouts during alcohol intoxication).

The following description of a clinical interaction suggests a diagnosis of psychogenic amnesia:

The patient was a 40-year-old, married female. She resided at her mother's home, with her second husband and two youngest children. She was recently employed as a secretary, the sixteenth such position she had held due to frequent firing because of absenteeism. She completed high school but did not receive a diploma due to failed courses. She entered treatment shortly following a suicide attempt in which she ingested pain pills and drove aimlessly in a car. It was her second attempt. She was depressed, with feelings of hopelessness, suicidal ideation, weight loss, and disturbed sleep. She had a history of headaches that she reported as continuously present, but varying in intensity from mild to severe. She also presented with a host of interpersonal problems, including an abusive relationship with her husband.

The patient had two previous experiences with psychotherapy; both ended abruptly by her refusal to continue. As an adjunct in her current treatment, hypnosis was used as an aid in lessening the frequency and severity of her headaches. In her first exposure to hypnosis, after trance induction, it was suggested that she visualize scenes or incidents in her life that might be related to her current problems. She first reported visualizing her father, whom she had seen on only two occasions. Her father had deserted her mother for a period of 10 years prior to the patient's birth. He returned, the patient was conceived, and the father left the family shortly thereafter, never to return. She had met him once as a child and once as an adolescent, at her aunt's funeral. The images were of her father at the funeral.

The next series of images concerned an abortion she had when she was living with her aunt in a distant city. She was 14 at the time, and the abortion was performed without her family's knowledge. In reporting her images, the patient appeared to regress spontaneously. She seemed to be reexperiencing the abortion and then an ensuing rape by the abortionist. She was writhing in her chair, appeared to be fighting off the attack, and displayed profuse tears and sobbing.

After these events, it was suggested to the patient that she would awake from the hypnotic state with a clear memory of all that transpired during the session. She was instructed to nod her head yes if she understood that she was to remember these events. She so indicated.

Upon awakening, the patient inquired as to why she had been permitted to sleep for the past hour. She had no memory of her imagery concerning her father. It was unclear whether she had any recall about her images or behavior related to the abortion. She was told that she had related something about an abortion, and she reported that she had some vague feeling that that was the case. At that point, she touched her face and felt wetness. She inquired whether she had been crying. She did not remember reporting anything about the rape.

In later sessions, details of the events recalled during hypnosis were verified. She had had the experiences she reported, although she had never divulged the abortion and rape to anyone previously. She displayed marked hypnotic susceptibility, and later sessions concentrated on the use of hypnosis to control headache pain. At the end of each subsequent session, it was suggested that she would be free of pain for progressively longer periods. This technique appeared successful in that headache-free periods, by her report, were extended to a week at a time. During this period, she began to postpone or cancel appointments. Despite the fact that, in her view, her headaches were a source of continual torment, and although she acknowledged that for the first time in years she was experiencing relief, she terminated treatment.

In this vignette, the patient recalled traumatic events while hypnotized and then appeared to have forgotten the experience of remembering and reporting these events just a few moments later, after hypnosis was lifted. In psychogenic amnesia, the individual frequently is unable to recall traumatic events, and the extent of the disturbance is too great to explain by ordinary forgetfulness. This case is unusual in two respects. First, the patient did not have amnesia for the traumatic events themselves. At least by her report, she indicated that she had, from time to time, thought about her father and the events related to the abortion. Rather, she displayed almost complete amnesia for her imaging and reexperiencing of these events. Second, the case is unusual in that the behavior subject to amnesia and the report of amnesia were observed and documented by the same individual. There is no question of intervening physical trauma or drug or alcohol intoxication being related to the presence of amnesia.

Psychogenic amnesia is classified into four types (APA, 1987). *Localized amnesia* is a failure to recall events that occur during a specific period of time. This type, described in the case material above, is the most common type. Usually, localized amnesia extends for the first few hours following an intense trauma. It is commonly reported by survivors of natural disasters and by soldiers after intense combat experience. For instance, soldiers have reported complete amnesia for their behavior during a siege, although comrades have indicated that the individual was fighting alongside them. *Selective amnesia* is a less common syndrome that fulfills the same criteria as localized amnesia, but the person has partial recall of events that occurred during the circumscribed period. A rape victim may, for instance, recall items of clothing worn by an attacker, but little else. *Generalized* and *continuous amnesias* are the least common. The former refers to complete loss of memory for one's past, whereas the latter is characterized by memory loss extending from a particular point in the past up to and including the present.

Psychogenic amnesia is rarely diagnosed. Several factors may account for low incidence. First, even among patients with diagnosed hysteric disorders, amnesia is a relatively uncommon symptom. Perley and Guze (1962) examined frequency of a wide range of symptoms in a sample of hysterics (at the time, dissociative disorders were included in this grouping). Although symptoms such as dizziness, headache, fatigue, and abdominal pain occurred at extremely high rates (all in excess of 70 percent of patients), amnesia was found in only 8 percent of cases. Second, patients presenting psychogenic amnesia typically present a number of other psychiatric disorders. For instance, in the case described above, psychogenic amnesia occurred as an isolated event and no other instances were noted during treatment or by the patient. The patient met the criteria for major depressive disorder and passive–aggressive personality disorder. The possibility of multiple forms of psychopathology in patients with psychogenic amnesia likely results in an underestimation of the frequency of the latter. Third, psychogenic amnesia does not necessarily interfere with social or occupational functioning. The most common varieties involve forgetting of isolated events. Furthermore, patients with psychogenic amnesia, as in cases of conversion reaction, may display indifference to their symptomatology. Therefore, they are unlikely to present for treatment.

Psychogenic amnesia is more common in females, and is thought to occur more often in adolescence and young adulthood than in the elderly. Most cases show recovery of memory over relatively brief periods and, therefore, the disorder is usually transient. Abeles and Schilder (1935) and Herman (1938) reported on 63 cases of psychogenic amnesia, but also included fugue states in this categorization. Twenty-seven recovered within 24 hours, 21 within 5 days, 7 within a week, and 4 within 3 weeks or more. Recurrence is rare, as might be expected since onset is typically associated with highly traumatic events, as in wartime and during natural disasters.

Problems of differential diagnosis usually involve distinguishing psychogenic amnesia from two other types of conditions. In contrast to organic brain syndrome, recovery of memory is complete in psychogenic amnesia. Trauma to the brain may produce similar syndromes and amnesia may be malingered.

As we noted, historically the grouping of dissociative disorders was an attempt to categorize disturbances of higher cognitive functions that resemble effects of neurological dysfunction but that are believed to be psychogenic in origin. If amnesia can be related to organic disorder, the diagnosis of dissociative disorder is inappropriate. There have been no studies to date of the frequency with which patients diagnosed as presenting dissociative disorders concurrently or ultimately show signs of neurological disease; however, such work in the case of hysterical conversion reactions indicates that a disturbingly large number of patients so diagnosed manifest neurological disorders (at the time or shortly thereafter) that in some cases prove fatal (Slater & Glithero, 1965; Whitlock, 1967).

The difficulties of differential diagnosis in this area can be illustrated with the syndrome of transient global amnesia (Fisher & Adams, 1958, 1964).

Without warning, individuals, usually middle-aged, display retrograde amnesia for events that occurred in the previous days, weeks, or years. The amnesia is typically quite transient, lasting from minutes to several hours. Its onset may be associated with exertion or fatigue. When memory returns, the person typically experiences a progressive recall of distant events, with memory of the most recent past returning last. During the amnesia, the individual is usually well oriented, with perception, sense of identity, and other higher cognitive functions intact. Typically, the individual feels considerable concern and upset about the memory loss. The attacks may occur only once or may be recurrent (Heathfield, Croft, & Swash, 1973).

The transient nature of the amnesia and its occurrence in individuals who appear medically healthy might suggest a dissociative reaction. Heathfield et al. (1973) reported on 31 patients who were referred for transient loss of memory. Of the 31 patients, memory loss was associated with epilepsy in 6 cases, migraine in 1 case, and temporal lobe encephalitis in 2 cases. Three cases received the diagnosis of psychogenic amnesia. The remaining 19 cases were considered as presenting the syndrome of transient global amnesia. The age of these 19 patients (13 men, 6 women) ranged from 46 to 68 years; amnesic episodes lasted from 30 minutes to 5 days; 11 patients had only one attack during the period of study. Of these 19 patients, cerebrovascular dysfunction was suggested in 9 cases. The authors concluded,

> It is probable that most episodes of transient global amnesia result from bilateral temporal lobe or thalamic lesions. In some of our patients there was clear evidence of ischemia in the territory of the posterior cerebral circulation, and we consider that such ischemia is the cause of this syndrome.
>
> *(p. 735)*

Transient global amnesia exemplifies some of the difficulties in differential diagnosis because, like psychogenic amnesia, memory loss is transient and typically circumscribed. Furthermore, as in psychogenic amnesia, there is often no concurrent sign of neurologic disturbance and attacks of memory loss may not necessarily recur.

Some general guidelines may be useful in distinguishing psychogenic amnesia from the memory loss that accompanies neurological disease. Typically, the memory loss associated with head trauma (W. Russell & Nathan, 1946), Korsakoff psychosis (Talland, 1965), temporal lobe dysfunction (Milner, 1966), and electroconvulsive therapy (ECT) (Dornbusch & Williams, 1974) has both retrograde and anterograde components. The most typical type of psychogenic amnesia is sometimes reported to be anterograde (e.g., APA, 1987). Patients fail to recall details after the onset of a traumatic event. Unfortunately, this distinction is weak because determination of whether memory loss is retrograde or anterograde depends on evaluation of the precise onset of the physical or psychological trauma triggering the amnesia. For instance, if the aftermath of an outcome of a violent interaction results in psychogenic amnesia for the complete episode, the amnesia is retrograde. It is frequently impossible to determine precisely what event produced the amnesia.

Of more value in differential diagnosis is the collateral behavior of the patient and the nature of the recovery of memory. Patients who present amnesia with clouded consciousness, disorientation, and/or mood change are likely manifesting neurological disturbance. Incontinence of urine or feces should be taken as a strong sign of neurological disturbance (e.g., Geschwind, 1975). On the other hand, indifference to an amnesia that concerns events that would ordinarily be associated with guilt and shame for the patient suggests a psychogenic basis. Psychogenic amnesia usually pertains to traumatic events, and the occurrence of amnesia for the ordinary events of life would suggest a neurological disturbance. Amnesia during or following a stressful experience is not, however, a reliable sign of psychogenic origin. As noted above, stress may precipitate a transient ischemic attack (TIA) or epileptic discharge (e.g., Walton, 1977), resulting in amnesia.

Another factor that may be helpful in differential diagnosis is the age of the patient. Although without empirical verification, it is generally held that psychogenic amnesia is most likely during adolescence and young adulthood. On the other hand, amnesia accompanying neurological disorders other than head trauma and epilepsy generally increase in frequency with age.

Retrograde amnesia associated with known neurological insult typically has a standard course of recovery (e.g., E. Russell, 1981). Events in the most distant past are recalled prior to more recent events, often with orderly temporal progression. In psychogenic amnesia, memory usually returns suddenly and all at once (e.g., Nemiah, 1979).

Hypnotic and/or sodium amytal interviews may be useful to distinguish psychogenic amnesia from neurological disturbance. A number of studies reported that patients have recovered memory while under the influence of either procedure, and in some cases the recovery has been permanent (e.g., Herman, 1938). Recovery of memory with the use of hypnosis or amytal should not occur in cases of neurological disturbance.

The absence of definite or probable neurological signs is not sufficient for a diagnosis of psychogenic amnesia. Positive indications, such as indifference, a need to deny, or rapid recovery, are necessary to help establish this diagnosis. Likewise, the presence of definite neurological disturbance does not necessarily rule out psychogenic origin of the amnesia. Patients with well-documented epilepsy may also have seizures that are hysterical or psychogenic in nature.

Malingering refers to deliberate and voluntary simulation of psychological or physical disorder. The assumption in a diagnosis of psychogenic amnesia is that the loss of memory and its subsequent recovery is not under the voluntary control of the patient. Some clinicians, with considerable exposure to amnesias of psychological origin, question whether a distinction between malingering and psychogenic amnesia can or should be made. Gillespie (1936) stated, "It is difficult to believe in most of them, perhaps in any of them, that memory was ever beyond the effort of voluntary recall" (p. 1182). Parfitt and Carlyle-Gall (1944), with a sample of soldiers presenting amnesia, claimed that memory recovery could be obtained in almost all cases by "simple persuasion" (p. 520).

Differentiating between psychogenic amnesia and malingering is extremely difficult. The degree to which a malingerer is successful at simulation likely depends on the sophistication of the patient in regard to manifestations of psychological and neurological disease. In a somewhat similar context, experienced hypnotists cannot reliably distinguish hypnotized subjects from individuals simulating effects of hypnosis (e.g., Orne, 1979).

Psychogenic Fugue

The DSM-III-R criteria for psychogenic fugue are as follows:

1. The predominant disturbance is sudden unexpected travel away from home or customary place of work, with inability to recall one's past.
2. Assumption of a new identity (partial or complete).
3. The disturbance is not due to multiple personality disorder or to an organic mental disorder (e.g., partial complex seizures in temporal lobe epilepsy).

The following case description fulfills the DSM-III-R criteria for psychogenic fugue:

A man is found at the Hudson River walking up and down in a strange fashion.

A policeman is called and the man cannot identify himself, shows great bewilderment, and complains of a terrible headache. He is brought to a hospital where study establishes that he has no memory of any relevance of his personal identity, and he is aware of this fact and bewildered by it. For ten days all attempts with hypnosis and barbiturates do not avail in trying to break through this condition. On the tenth day a sodium amytal interview brings back his memories and awareness of personal identity, and reveals that he is unemployed, that he had a violent quarrel with his wife, and that he remembers nothing that happened between leaving his home after the quarrel and being approached by the policeman at the Hudson River. Two weeks later the memory of this period too is recovered in a barbiturate interview: in the eight hours, he was walking the streets in a daze, full of gnawing uneasiness and guilt, and felt he must end it all; he was scarcely aware of the path he took to the Hudson, nor of any thought, but only of his daze, guilt, and the wish to end it all. (Rapaport, 1967, p. 388)

The term *fugue* derives from the Latin word *fugere,* meaning flight. As a psychiatric diagnosis, psychogenic fugue has been applied to a wide number of conditions, some of which do not meet the current criteria for classification. For instance, Stengel (1941) described a patient who would become depressed every spring and feel compelled to leave home and wander for days or weeks at a time. During the first week of wandering, the patient would appear disoriented, neither eating nor maintaining hygiene. After a few days, however, the patient's mood would improve markedly, with a suggestion of hypomania; he would become oriented and seek employment. Upon return home, the patient did not appear to have amnesia for the period of time spent wandering. The patient did not adopt a new identity during these periods. As the compulsion to wander was annual, in later years, the patient made preparations for departure before wandering. It seemed to Stengel (1941) that the wandering brought on by the "fugue state" was voluntary. This case would not meet current criteria for psychogenic fugue because there was no evidence of at least a partial assumption of a new identity, nor could the wandering be called unexpected in an individual who prepares for departure ahead of time.

Psychogenic fugue has been diagnosed in individuals who may make unexpected trips or wander, who are amnesic for the wandering, but who maintain the same identity. In most cases, the fugue is not elaborate and consists of little more than brief, apparently purposeful travel. Rice and Fisher (1976) presented a case of wandering in an individual who had transient retrograde amnesia. During dissociated states, the patient appeared to forget that his father was dead. On one occasion, the patient left home for religious services and ended up at a hospital 5 miles away. He met an acquaintance at the hospital and, when questioned about whom he was visiting, made up an excuse and walked home. He had been on the same floor in the hospital where his father had been a patient at the time of his death. Rice and Fisher (1976) interpreted this case an an instance of fugue in which identity is preserved but there is a reversion, with retrograde amnesia, to an earlier period in life.

Other uses of the diagnosis of fugue have not required evidence of wandering or travel. Escueta, Boxley, Stubbs, Waddell, and Wilson (1974) described a case of prolonged twilight or fugue state in which the individual was first immobile and disoriented for brief periods, followed by periods of repetitive and characteristic automatic movements. None of these movements involved locomotion.

In practice, the diagnosis of fugue has been applied to a much wider variety of conditions than encompassed by the criteria in DSM-III-R. These criteria pertain mostly to the most severe and perhaps prototypic forms of psychogenic fugue. The most common fugues appear to have some loss of personal identity, but no assumption of a new one. Change of identity is not a consistent aspect of the syndrome as described in the psychiatric literature, with most episodes being brief and less elaborate than required by DSM-III-R criteria (Riether & Stoudemire, 1988).

The validity of this narrow definition cannot readily be evaluated because empirical studies that establish external criteria for diagnosis have not been conducted. It should be noted that the cases of Stengel (1941), Rice and Fisher (1976), and Escueta et al. (1974) would most likely receive quite different diagnoses in 1990. Stengel's (1941) case might be viewed as an unusual instance of obsessive–compulsive disorder, with the compulsion to travel being repetitive, subject to awareness, and disruptive of social and occupational functioning. Temporal lobe epilepsy or bipolar affective disorder are other possibilities in that case. Rice and Fisher's (1976) case might be viewed as psychogenic continuous amnesia, with the purposeful wandering being incidental. The symptoms presented by Escueta et al.'s (1974) patient, as well as concurrent electroencephalographic (EEG) testing, strongly suggested an organic brain syndrome, possibly temporal lobe epilepsy. Fugue has also been considered a somnambulistic state (Fisher, 1945). More recently, a case of familial fugue has been reported (McKinney & Lange, 1983).

Individuals with psychogenic fugue, in its most prototypic form, travel away from home or work unexpectedly. The period of travel, that is, the fugue state, may last for a few hours or days, but rarely for more prolonged periods of time. During the traveling, the individual may appear disoriented or confused. The individual may adopt a new identity and, in extreme cases, establish a new occupation and new social and familial networks. More commonly, the individual displays partial amnesia for previous identity and may retain knowledge of skills, personal information, and so forth. During the fugue, individuals commonly behave in ways that are inconsistent with previous personality, whether or not they adopt new identities. Except for the suggestion of an underlying epileptic condition, a case reported by Akhtar and Brenner (1979) fits this description precisely. The patient was a 46-year-old sheriff who, on three occasions, disappeared suddenly and traveled to locations up to 200 miles from his home. When he became aware of his departure, he called his wife, but continued the journey. He had only partial memory for the details of his trips and strongly denied improper behavior. Akhtar and Brenner (1979) reported,

> During amytal narcoanalysis [sodium amytal interview], the patient revealed that he used an alias while on these trips. He said that on these occasions, he actually felt as though he were another person, the outlaw type he had always secretly admired. He drank heavily, mingled with a "rough crowd" and went to "brothels," wild parties and drag races.
>
> *(p. 382)*

In the series of 25 cases reported by Stengel (1941), 6 patients displayed sexual promiscuity during their presumed fugue states.

In the most prototypic cases, the alteration in identity or inconsistent behavior ends abruptly, without intervention by professionals. Most patients present after the fugue has ended. The patient usually seeks help in recovering his or her identity or the memory of events during the fugue. Typically, the patient's memory returns spontaneously after someone provides a key to the past or when the patient feels psychologically safe. There is usually amnesia, partial or complete, for events that transpired during the fugue. Except under hypnosis or drug-induced hypnagogic states, later recovery of memory for these events is not generally observed.

Review of the approximately 150 cases of fugue reported as psychogenic in origin or as epileptic manifestations (e.g., Berrington, Liddell, & Foulds, 1956; Mayeux, Alexander, Benson, Brandt, & Rosen, 1979; Stengel, 1941) indicates that the majority of patients presenting fugue-like behavior show evidence of depression prior to the unexpected wandering. This is the case both in samples in which the fugue-like behavior appears psychogenic and in cases of clear neurological disturbance. Akhtar and Brenner (1979) presented a case that involved an attempt to jump from a bridge during a fugue state. In Stengel's

(1941) series of 25 cases, depressed mood preceded and/or accompanied the fugue in virtually all patients, and 12 of the patients had attempted suicide at some point in their lives. In Berrington et al.'s (1956) study, depression was observed in 29 of 37 cases, with 10 patients having a history of attempted suicide. Psychogenic fugue is a rather infrequent behavior in depressive disorders, but it would seem that depression frequently precedes and/or accompanies fugue states, whether classified as psychogenic or neurological in origin. It should also be noted that, during the fugue state, initial depression may be replaced by hypomania as the fugue progresses.

Other than the apparent association with a premorbid depressed state, we have little knowledge of the precipitants of psychogenic fugue. It is believed that the fugue state is usually preceded by an intense affect that the patient finds overwhelming, and that the dissociative state is usually accompanied by amnesia or loss of personal identity (Riether & Stoudemire, 1988). Heavy alcohol use and severe psychosocial stress are believed to be predisposing factors (APA, 1987). It is often commented that fugue, like psychogenic amnesia, is most likely to occur during wartime conditions or following natural disasters. Recovery is usually rapid and recurrences are rare. The rarity of the disorder has precluded studies of incidence or prevalence. The frequency of fugue states in seizures has been reported in up to 78 percent of cases with temporal lobe epilepsy and in 6.4 percent of cases of unspecified epilepsy (Akhtar & Brenner, 1979). Fugues have also been reported in head trauma, as part of the postconcussion syndrome, and in toxic states such as carbon monoxide poisoning (Berger, 1985). The most common fugue state is that seen in alcohol- or drug-related "blackouts" that occur during acute intoxication or withdrawal states.

The problems of differential diagnosis in cases of fugue are more complex than in cases of psychogenic amnesia. Again, the major diagnostic decisions concern differentiating psychogenic fugue from neurological disturbance and from malingering.

Neurological disturbance may produce behavioral abnormalities that are identical in features to those seen in psychogenic fugue. As Mayeux et al. (1979) pointed out, Kraepelin (1909) observed that wandering behavior may be seen in hysteria or depression. He also described *Wandertrieb,* aimless wandering in epileptic patients, followed by retrograde amnesia. The ambulatory behavior that accompanies epilepsy or other neurologic disturbance is sometimes reported to be less complex and purposeful than that observed in psychogenic fugue (e.g., APA, 1980). If this is to be taken as a general rule, it should be recognized that there are many exceptions to it. Extremely well-organized, postictal (subsequent to epileptic seizure) automatic behavior has been frequently reported (Feindel & Penfield, 1954; Pincus & Tucker, 1978). Perhaps the most well-known such case is that of a physician, Dr. Z., who correctly diagnosed and treated a case of pneumonia and was subsequently amnesic for this period (Hughlings Jackson, 1898).

The suggestion that wandering as an epileptic manifestation is typically less complex than the behavior in psychogenic fugue is appropriate for the condition of cursive epilepsy (running epilepsy). Cursive epilepsy is a rare condition seen often in children in whom apparently purposeless running occurs during the ictal state (e.g., Sethi & Rao, 1976). This condition may be more readily distinguished from psychogenic fugue because of the typically brief duration of the ambulatory behavior, other accompanying signs of seizure activity, and positive history of epilepsy. On the other hand, a number of cases of poriomania have been reported. This condition specifically refers to prolonged periods of wandering in epileptic patients, which is followed by amnesia.

Mayeux et al. (1979) described three cases of poriomania. Were it not for evidence of neurological disturbance, each case would appear to be classic psychogenic fugue. The patients displayed spontaneous, repetitive, episodic wandering from home, often traveling large distances. Following the episodes, they were disoriented for time and place and amnesic for events that took place during the wandering. It is unknown whether such individuals show identity change or behave in ways that are inconsistent with previous personality during the wandering. Including the report of Mayeux et al., at least 23 cases of poriomania have been described (e.g., Haller, 1957; Meyer-Mickeleit, 1953; Penfield & Jasper, 1954; Stengel, 1941, 1943; Wissfeld, 1957). In 13 of these cases, EEG examinations were performed; 12 showed signs of a focus involving the temporal lobe. Depression preceded the unexpected wandering in 18 of the 23 cases.

Mayeux et al. (1979) offered two alternative accounts of the syndrome of poriomania. First, poriomania was interpreted as a form of postictal automatism in patients with complex partial seizures (temporal lobe epilepsy or psychomotor seizures). The prodromal state of depression was viewed as part of the ictus or seizure period. Alterations in mood and emotional expression during epileptic seizures, particularly the psychomotor variety, are not uncommon (e.g., Daly & Mulder, 1957; Sackeim et al., 1982). It is of note that cursive or running epilepsy, perhaps a primitive form of poriomania, may be overrepresented in individuals who have uncontrollable outbursts of laughing during the ictus (e.g., Sugimoto, Matsumura, Sakamoto, & Taniuchi, 1979). In essence, Mayeux et al.'s first alternative is that the prodromal depression is a result of the seizure, whereas the prolonged wandering and subsequent amnesia reflect postseizure, nonconvulsive status epilepticus. This alternative could not be tested because no case of poriomania has undergone EEG or other testing during the episode.

The second alternative was to interpret poriomania as an interictal (between-seizures) event, not related directly to the epileptic condition, but, like many other cases of psychogenic fugue, associated with depression. Poriomania is unlikely to be a reaction to the depressive state engendered during seizures, because the 3 patients reported by Mayeux et al. responded to anticonvulsants. Poriomania, which in all 3 cases was repetitive, disappeared when seizure frequency was sharply curtailed by anticonvulsant drug therapy.

The fact that neurological conditions and psychogenic fugue may display virtually identical symptomatology makes differential diagnosis difficult. Furthermore, neurological insult may be overrepresented in cases of psychogenic fugue. In the series of 37 cases by Berrington et al. (1956), 16 had histories of head injury. A control sample had a significantly lower rate of head injury. Berrington et al. (1956) suggested that, in fact, the disorientation and amnesia experienced subsequent to head injury may "form the basis for the suggestion of a psychogenic amnesia at a later date" (p. 284).

To aid in differential diagnosis, the factors of age, sex, precipitating events, and history of psychosomatic complaints may be useful. Age of onset of first psychogenic fugue appears to be most often before the age of 50, with few observations before 20 years of age (Berrington et al., 1956; Kanzer, 1939; Stengel, 1941). Berrington et al. (1956) found that 31 of 37 cases were male. Stengel's (1941) cases were principally female, but there was a selection bias, as his case material came mostly from female wards. In addition to a depressed mood, cases of psychogenic fugue are usually preceded by stress, often reduced by the departure. Of the 37 patients in Berrington et al.'s series, "14 of the cases were escaping from justice, 3 from domestic stress, 7 from domestic and vocational stress, 2 from mental hospital, 2 from work and 2 from 'work by compensation'" (p. 283). As a rule, it is generally believed that onset of psychogenic fugue, like psychogenic amnesia, usually occurs in the context of a prior history of psychosomatic complaints of probable psychogenic origin.

The case of the misbehaving sheriff described above is one in which recall of events during the fugue appeared facilitated by interviewing the patient under the influence of sodium amytal. A number of similar cases have been reported in which postfugue amnesia remitted during amytal interviews, and the general conviction has been that the drug-related recovery of memory is specific to amnesia that is psychogenic in origin and would not occur in fugue states due to known neuropathology (e.g., Akhtar & Brenner, 1979; Berrington et al., 1956; Herman, 1938). Purposeful travel and the assumption of a new identity do not occur in psychogenic amnesia (APA, 1987). In multiple personality disorder, shifts of identity are not limited to a single episode.

Without question, a number of cases reported in the literature as psychogenic fugue were instances of deliberate simulation. Stengel (1941) described a soldier who developed fugue-like behavior while away without leave (AWOL) from his unit. The fugue involved extensive travel, including a side trip to a romantic involvement. The soldier later confessed that the "postfugue amnesia" was feigned and that his unexpected travel was deliberate. Since psychogenic fugue appears to occur frequently in contexts in which the individual is subject to stress that might be relieved by flight (e.g., impending prosecution), the possibility of malingering or simulation is quite high.

A complication in differential diagnosis of psychogenic fugue or malingering is that individuals subject to psychogenic fugue may simulate other conditions, engage in preposterous lying, or otherwise create doubt about the veracity of their self-report. Stengel (1941) reported that, in 8 of his 25 cases, there was a history of marked lying (pseudologia fantastica). Berrington et al. (1956) commented that a tendency of frequent lying was observed in 13 of 37 cases. The fact that patients presenting fugue may simulate other conditions and be found to be deceitful raises the issue as to whether the fugue behavior and subsequent amnesia are themselves instances of malingering. One should keep in mind, however, that a sophisticated malingerer who achieves secondary gains through escaping intolerable situations with fugue-like behavior is unlikely to present preposterous lies, so as to raise doubt about the veracity of the simulation.

Multiple Personality

The DSM-III-R criteria for the diagnosis of multiple personality disorder are as follows:

1. The existence within the person of two or more distinct personalities or personality states exist, each with its own relatively enduring pattern of perceiving, relating to, and thinking about the environment and self.
2. At least two of these personalities or personality states recurrently take full control of the patient's behavior.

The following case description meets the criteria for diagnosis of multiple personality. The description is based on the clinical report of Ludwig, Brandsma, Wilbur, Bendfeldt, and Jameson (1972).

The patient, a 27-year-old black male named Jonah, was admitted to a hospital with complaints of headache associated with amnesia. On the night prior to hospital admission, he had attempted to stab a man and was fired upon by police in an ensuing chase. A few weeks earlier, he had assaulted his wife with a butcher knife and had chased both her and his 3-year-old daughter out of the home. He had no memory for these incidents. His wife informed him that during an attack he called himself Usoffa Abdulla, Son of Omega. The patient reported that memory lapses had occurred for many years and that others had reported to him that he frequently became violent during the periods for which he was amnesic. Among the incidents in his past of which he was amnesic was an attempt to drown a man in a river and a nocturnal swim of a quarter mile, after which he woke up in the morning in his own bed soaking wet.

During his initial hospitalization, the presence of frequent memory lapse was observed and a diagnosis of psychomotor epilepsy was investigated. Physical findings were negative. Observation and interaction with the patient during periods of which he was later amnesic indicated marked change in personality. Furthermore, during these periods, he would respond to different names. At the time of his first hospitalization, three separate identities, in addition to Jonah, were evident.

By self-report, the first alternate personality to have been formed was that of Sammy. According to Sammy, he emerged when Jonah was 6 years of age, following an incident in which Jonah's mother stabbed Jonah's father. At their first reunion at home, Sammy emerged and, in a detached, rational way, suggested to the parents that they alter their behavior. In general, Sammy, by self-report and by the description of Ludwig et al. (1972), was viewed as rational, calm, and legalistic. He was the personality who claimed the greatest awareness of other personalities and who seemed to know the most about

Jonah. Like the other personalities, Sammy appeared capable of fully occu-
pying conscious awareness and directing behavior. Unlike the other personalities, only Sammy claimed to be capable of awareness of external and internal
(mental) events while the personality of Jonah appeared to be directing behavior. This latter phenomenon of an alter personality aware of the experience of the dominant personality is sometimes termed co-consciousness.

A second additional personality was called King Young. This personality
claimed to be in charge of Jonah's sexual interests. He was pleasure seeking
and particularly interested in heterosexual activities. He is said to have first
emerged soon after Sammy and was first manifest during an incident in which
Jonah was experiencing sex role identity confusion (Jonah's mother would
dress him in girl's clothing). King Young was said to be aware of other personalities "indirectly" and was only moderately knowledgeable about Jonah.

The third additional personality observed during the first hospitalization
was that of Usoffa Abdulla. This entity was described as assaultive, aggressive, and sarcastic. The personality seemed to have intimate knowledge of
Jonah but, like King Young, was only indirectly aware of other personalities.
His avowed role was to protect Jonah, whom he perceived as weak, at times
of danger. Usoffa Abdulla claimed to emerge first when Jonah was 9 or 10
years of age. His first appearance was during an incident in which a group of
white youths were beating up Jonah.

Despite discussions about these personalities, the use of hypnosis in an
attempt to produce a merger or fusion of personalities, and the fact that the
various personalities could at times be called forth by direct inquiry, Jonah
appeared to have no awareness of these entities. Consistently, he appeared
amnesic for the periods in which alter personalities were in control of
behavior.

Although the case described above is a particularly dramatic instance of
multiple personality, the essential features of the case demonstrate a number of the characteristics believed to be general manifestations of this disorder. The diagnosis of multiple personality hinges on the determination
that the same physical being displays two or more distinct personalities,
each of which is internally complex and integrated. The dominant personality, most often the personality that responds to the given name of the
individual, has, at best, only partial awareness of the existence of alter
personalities. Often, this partial awareness may come from reports of outside observers of behavior that appeared out of character during periods for
which the dominant personality is amnesic. At other times, the dominant
personality may become aware of the existence of alter personalities by
the effects of their behavior. For instance, in the "Three Faces of Evelyn"
(Osgood et al., 1976), the dominant personality first learns of the existence
of an alter personality, "Mary Sunshine," by the presence in the morning
of cups containing hot chocolate in the sink; the dominant personality,
"Gina," did not like hot chocolate.

The relations of alter personalities to each other and to the dominant
personality are more varied. As in the case of Sammy, described above, an
alter personality may be fully aware of the dominant personality and have

complete, partial, or no awareness of other alter personalities. The alter personality that is fully aware of the dominant personality may not only be able to report on the subjective experiences of the dominant personality—that is, what the dominant personality was seeing, hearing, or feeling at particular times—but also have decided opinions about the appropriateness of the dominant personality's reactions and behavior. In such a case, the alter personality is co-conscious with the dominant personality. Alter personalities may be companions to each other, bitter enemies, or completely indifferent to each others' existence. They may appear capable of communicating directly with each other without ongoing modification in the behavior of the dominant personality. Such behavior is usually ascertained by later reports of the conversation by one or both alter personalities. They may also communicate more indirectly, through, for instance, automatic writing (Sutcliffe & Jones, 1962; Taylor & Martin, 1944).

The question might be raised as to how, in cases of multiple personality, alter personalities differ from the inconsistent and, at times, contradictory behavior patterns seen in normal individuals. Certainly, most people display different patterns of behavior in varying social contexts, such as at home, work, or leisure. In other psychiatric conditions, such as bipolar disorder, there may be unpredictable phasic changes in behavioral patterns. One might argue that the insistence on being called different names (e.g., Sammy, King Young) and the presence of periodic amnesia might distinguish multiple personality from normal variation in behavioral patterns and from the variations observed in other disorders. It should be noted, however, that neither responsiveness to different names nor amnesia is criteria for the diagnosis of multiple personality. Prince (1906) claimed that multiple personality could occur without amnesia, and Mesulam (1981) described a case of this sort. The diagnosis hinges on the determination that the individual is characterized by two or more distinct personalities or personality states (APA, 1987). In classic cases, there are at least two fully developed personalities. Each personality and personality state has unique memories, behavioral patterns, and social relationships. In adults, the number of personalities or personality states varies from 2 to over 200. Approximately half of recently reported cases have 10 or fewer personalities, and half over 10 (APA, 1987).

Until recently, research on this disorder concentrated mainly on single-case demonstrations of individuals presenting independent personalities that differed markedly in internal organization. In the case of "The Three Faces of Eve" (Thigpen & Cleckley, 1954) and again in the case of Evelyn (Osgood et al., 1976), Osgood and colleagues had the various personalities of each patient evaluate sets of concepts using the semantic differential technique (see Osgood & Luria, 1954). The results of both case studies indicated that the various personalities in each patient differed markedly in the meanings attributed to particular concepts (e.g., My Father, Me, Sex) and in the organization of these meanings in conceptual space. In the more recent case, no one concept had a constant meaning across personalities, although the organization of meanings within each personality seemed largely coherent.

In recent years, there has been a marked increase in reported cases of multiple personality disorder (MPD), with large series relying on questionnaires completed by multiple therapists (Putnam, Guroff, Silberman, Barban, & Post, 1986; Schultz, Braun, & Kluft, 1985). More cases of MPD have been reported in the last decade than in the preceding two centuries (Orne, Dinges, & Orne, 1984). For example, in a survey of 50 psychiatric inpatients and 100 outpatients, 10 percent had MPD, and an additional 5 to 20 percent had amnesia for early traumatic experiences (Bliss & Jeppsen, 1985). Several writers have suggested that the increase is largely spurious, reflecting misdiagnosis and iatrogenesis (Chodoff, 1987; Thigpen & Cleckley, 1984). There are questions as to whether the disorder's prevalence has truly increased, whether diagnostic criteria have changed, whether the diagnosis is now made more astutely, or whether a small number of clinicians are providing most of the cases (Orne et al., 1984).

Despite the great increase in reporting of MPD cases in recent years, few systematic or controlled studies have been conducted. Even in the few studies that have attempted to compare MPD patients with control subjects, reliability of diagnosis has not been independently established (Bliss, 1984). The reliance on multiple therapists from a variety of settings in the largest series (Putnam et al., 1986; Schultz et al., 1985) is not a common practice in research in other areas in the behavioral sciences. Therapists are likely to have differed markedly in level of training, use of DSM-III diagnostic criteria, and bias in favoring a diagnosis of MPD in patients with psychotic, affective, or other personality disorders.

Ludwig et al. (1972) had the dominant and alter personalities in the case of Jonah complete the Minnesota Multiphasic Personality Inventory (MMPI), Adjective Check List, McDougall Scale of Emotion, a self-portrait task, as well as intelligence testing, including some subscales of the Wechsler Adult Intelligence Scale (WAIS). Verbal and Performance IQs on WAIS varied little among the personalities. On the other tests mentioned, however, marked differences among the personalities were obtained. For instance, on the paranoia subscale of the MMPI, Jonah, the dominant personality, scored well within the clinical range. The three alter personalities tested all scored below the normal range. In a recent study, MPD patients did not differ from controls in overall memory performance, but there was indirect evidence that state-dependent learning may play a role in the phenomenology of MPD (Silberman, Putnam, Weingartner, Braun, & Post, 1985).

The fact that, in tests of personality organization, individuals with the diagnosis of MPD may display markedly different profiles that nevertheless are internally coherent or integrated, suggests that such individuals are capable of complex regulation of self-report or self-presentation so as to appear on psychological tests as if they were more than one person. The issue as to whether these results reflect some form of role playing, conscious or otherwise, cannot be resolved on the basis of these data alone. It should be noted that individuals with little or no training may be able to deliberately simulate any of a number of personality profiles. For instance, Kroeger and Turnbull (1975) asked college students to complete the MMPI as if they were an Air Force officer or an artist. Generally, students were capable of producing acceptable profiles without elevated scores on validity scales that would suggest they were simulating.

One way of addressing this issue is to determine whether the alter personalities of the same individual differ consistently in behavior that is thought to be under involuntary control. A hypothetical example may illustrate the usefulness of such a demonstration. A substantial proportion of individuals with endogenous depressive disorder fail to suppress natural production of cortisol in response to dexamethasone (synthetic corticosteroid) challenge, and the dexamethasone suppression test (DST) has been offered as a diagnostic tool in the assessment of depression (Carroll, 1982), although the specificity of these findings is open to question (The APA Task Force on Laboratory Tests, 1987). In the hypothetical case in which a dominant or alter personality presents endogenous depression not seen in other personalities of the same individual, it would be provocative to establish that the depressed personality is positive on the DST while the nondepressed personalities are negative. Such a demonstration would suggest either that the distinct and integrated self-presentations of multiple personality do not reflect some form of role playing, or that the role playing reflected in multiple personality can influence basic neuroendocrinological processes as a function of the role adopted at the moment. By this latter alternative, we would have to revise drastically our conceptualization of role playing.

In a more limited way, some initial attempts have been made to assess differences between alter personalities in psychophysiological behavior assumed to be under involuntary control. Condon, Ogston, and Pacoe (1969) examined frame by frame a film of the patient presented by Thigpen and Cleckley (1954) as "Eve." Frequency of transient microstrabimus (divergence in conjugate lateral movement of the eyes) was determined for the various personalities. Strabimus was observed mostly in "Eve Black" and rarely, if at all, in other personalities. Ludwig et al. (1972) conducted a number of additional studies on Jonah and his alter personalities. They investigated galvanic skin response (GSR) to emotionally laden words; generalization in conditioning of neutral stimuli to electric shock; resting EEG during alert, drowsy, and light sleep states; waveforms of visual evoked potentials; and neurological status (reflexes, coordination, pain sensitivity). A number of differences among the personalities were noted. For instance, each alter personality displayed arousal, as indexed by GSR, to specific emotionally laden words that were unique for each entity, whereas Jonah, the dominant personality, displayed arousal to the words found to be affectively laden for each of the personalities. In line with Usoffa's self-description of being fearless and insensitive to pain, it was found that he conditioned poorly in pairings of a neutral stimulus with electric shock, and, in neurological testing, he was the only personality found to have reduced functioning in regard to touch, two-point discrimination, and pain sensitivity. By no means were all the differences among the personalities in psychophysiological testing readily interpretable. Patterns of generalization found using the conditioning paradigm were complex and did not conform to the personalities' reports of the degree of awareness they had of each other. Nonetheless, the findings of Condon et al. (1969) and Ludwig et al. (1972) raise the possibility that differences among alter personalities extend beyond self-report to behavioral systems that are not under obvious voluntary control. There is evidence of overlap between multiple personality disorder and epilepsy, and temporary personality disintegration may occur as part of postictal confusion or psychosis. Multiple personality may in some cases be related to right temporal lobe dysfunction, and multiple personality may be precipitated or exacerbated by anticonvulsant medication (Drake, Pakalnis, & Denio, 1988).

The issue as to whether the behavior observed in cases of multiple personality reflects some form of role playing is of particular consequence given the setting in which alter personalities are often first observed (e.g., Bliss, 1980). A large number of reported cases were first discovered while patients were undergoing psychotherapy and, in particular, hypnotherapy (Sutcliffe & Jones, 1962). Therefore, it has been suggested that manifestations of multiple personality are in some way a product of psychotherapy or hypnosis, perhaps bizarre attempts to meet demand characteristics imposed by therapy while patients are in an impressionable state. In discussing this issue, Sutcliffe and Jones (1962) noted that,

> although production of multiple personality behaviors in hypnosis inflated the instances of multiple personality, . . . some case arose apart from these conditions, so that the category could not be dissolved away in "hypnosis." At the same time . . . the facility with which multiple personality could be brought about in hypnosis suggested that there was something in common between the two.
>
> *(p. 258)*

The case of Jonah described above (Ludwig et al., 1972) provided ample evidence of the existence of multiple personalities before the patient experienced hypnosis or therapy in a professional setting. This would indicate that at least some cases of the disorder first occur outside the context of professional help. Nonetheless, from clinical reports of the disorder, the degree of hypnotic virtuosity in these cases is striking. Hypnotic susceptibility, like many other skills, is normally distributed in nonpathological populations (Hilgard, 1965). Relatively few people are either completely insusceptible or hypnotic virtuosos. Multiple personality patients appear to be significantly more hypnotizable than normal controls (Bliss, 1984). Bliss (1980) suggested that the emergence of "alter egos" is related to the employment of self-hypnosis in childhood.

Our knowledge about the demographics and clinical features of MPD are based largely on recent studies that have relied on questionnaires completed by multiple therapists. MPD is three to nine times as common in females as in males. The onset is invariably in childhood, although the disorder is rarely diagnosed until late adolescence. Studies indicate that, in most cases, there is a history of abuse, often sexual, or other severe emotional trauma in childhood (Putnam et al., 1986). Incipient MPD in children has been described in 4 cases, characterized by dual identity, trance states, amnesia, and rapid personality change (Fagan & McMahon, 1984).

The course tends to be chronic, although frequency of switching often decreases. Coexistence of mood disorders or other personality disorders is unclear in many cases. A mild to severe degree of social and occupational impairment may be seen. Suicide attempts, externally directed violence, and substance abuse are common. Review of 100 recent cases suggests a core of depressive and dissociative symptoms and a childhood history of significant trauma, primarily child abuse (Putnam et al., 1986). Putnam et al. (1986) found that an average of 6.8 years elapses between the time MPD patients are first seen for symptoms referable to the disorder and the time they receive an accurate diagnosis; during that period they receive an average of 3.6 erroneous diagnoses. There is evidence to support familial transmission in a few cases (Braun, 1985).

The transition from one personality to another is usually sudden, and is often triggered by psychosocial stress or idiosyncratically meaningful social or environmental cues. This transition also tends to occur when there are conflicts among the personalities, and can sometimes be elicited by hypnosis or amobarbital interview. In Putnam et al.'s (1986) series, the meeting of one or more alternate personalities was seen to occur spontaneously in 51 percent of cases, with 23 percent requiring facilitation with hypnosis. In 16 percent of cases, the therapist's request to meet an alternate personality was sufficient to elicit an overt appearance of an alternate. The mean number of personalities was 13.9. The most common alternate personalities were children. Over 90 percent of patients were female (biological sex), and over half of all patients had at least one opposite-gender alternate personality. Suicidal behaviors were the most common expression of psychopathology in these patients, with the majority making serious or nonserious suicide attempts. Most patients appear to hide, deny, or dissimulate their condition rather than dramatize or exploit it, and many experience substantial periods of time when the various personalities do not emerge overtly but appear to coexist in relative harmony (Kluft, 1987).

Most theories of etiology, behavioral and/or psychodynamic, view the emergence of alter personalities as a means of escaping from or avoiding intolerable situations in ways that are outside the normal repertoire of the dominant personality. The disorder is thought to occur most commonly in females of late adolescence and young adulthood. In a review of published cases, the majority were female (Lester, 1977). Of 14 new cases presented by Bliss (1980), all were female. The age of emergence of the first alter personality in each of the 14 cases was believed to be between 4 and 6 years. Of the 100 alter personalities in these 14 cases, 12 had male identities (across 6 patients). Thus, although alter personalities are usually of the same sex as the host, this need not be the case.

Turning to the issue of diagnosis, despite its name, MPD is not classified under personality disorder, but under dissociative states. DSM-III and DSM-III-R provide no explanation for this decision. In an analysis of 33 cases, borderline personality disorder was highly prevalent in patients with MPD, but this was not universal, and the authors suggested that MPD should be considered a separate and distinct disorder (Horevitz & Braun, 1984). There is strong similarity in MMPI profiles as well, and MPD patients display singularly high F (fake bad scale) and Sc (schizophrenia) scores (Bliss, 1984). It remains unclear if some cases of MPD are misdiagnosed as borderline personality disorder, or vice versa.

The main problems in differential diagnosis of multiple personality concern distinguishing the disorder from other dissociative disorders (amnesia and fugue); from schizophrenia and acute psychotic states; from neurological conditions; from other personality disorders, particularly the borderline subtype; and from malingering. Patients who ultimately receive the diagnosis of multiple personality rarely present themselves as characterized by this disorder. Rather, chief complaints may center on amnesia, sleepwalking (somnambulism), depression, or psychophysiological problems such as headaches or fainting. The presenting clinical picture of MPD is often suggestive of an affective disorder with depressed mood, apparent lability of mood, self-destructive and suicidal behavior, insomnia, and sexual dysfunction (Putnam et al., 1986). MPD patients exhibit a plethora of symptoms, including anxiety states, hysteria, obsessions, compulsions, and phobias (Bliss, 1984). In Bliss' series, patients often presented with numerous apparent physical illnesses, experienced unnecessary surgery, and abused medication, suggesting that at least some fit the criteria for Briquet's syndrome (somatization disorder). There are suggestions that MPD patients may have first-rank symptoms, including hallucinations (Bliss, Larson, & Nakashima, 1983; Coons & Milstein, 1986). In a small series, there were indications of overlap between MPD and obsessive–compulsive disorder (Ross & Anderson, 1988).

If chief complaints center on amnesia, clouding of consciousness, or unexplained motor behavior, multiple personality may be confused with other dissociative disorders. A dominant personality is rarely aware of the existence of alter personalities, so a negative report by the patient is not very helpful. Clinicians may find it more useful to interview friends and family members who may report responsiveness to other names, abrupt and seemingly inconsistent changes in behavioral patterns and preferences, and other signs suggestive of multiple personality. Furthermore, the history and course of the disorder may be of aid. It is likely, although not established, that symptoms of multiple personality develop earlier in life than those of other dissociative disorders. Manifestations of psychogenic amnesia and fugue are likely to be less repetitive than those of multiple personality. An individual who reports numerous periods of amnesia during the time span of a week may more likely be presenting multiple personality or a neurological condition (e.g., petit mal or temporal lobe epilepsy) than psychogenic amnesia, which usually involves loss of memory for a specific traumatic event. Also, the prognosis for multiple personality is thought to be less optimistic than that for other dissociative disorders (APA, 1987). Whereas psychogenic amnesia and fugue often remit without intervention, this has not been observed in cases of multiple personality. Suicide attempts, self-mutilation, externally directed violence, and substance abuse are possible complications of this disorder.

Multiple personality may be confused with other behavioral disorders, such as schizophrenia, chiefly because of reports of auditory hallucinations and bizarre behavior. At times, patients with multiple personality report hearing voices, which appear to be those of alter personalities. These voices may be accusatory, as reported in cases of paranoid schizophrenia, or they may appear solicitory, attempting to serve a protective role. Further complicating matters, patients with multiple personality may decompensate into psychotic states. In these cases, the diagnostic decision may rest heavily on the level of adaptation of the dominant personality. The dominant personality, despite memory lapses, auditory hallucinations, and the stress of coping with unexplained, bizarre behavior, may exhibit levels of adaptation not usually seen in schizophrenia. For instance, the patient referred to in "The Three Faces of Evelyn" (Osgood et al., 1976), while presenting the typical symptoms of multiple personality, held a good paying job as a writer for an educational firm and was described as "businesslike, efficient, and productive" (p. 250). It should be noted, however, that while the dominant personality may be nonpsychotic, alter personalities may present a variety of disorders, including psychosis.

Syndromes highly similar to psychogenic amnesia and fugue may occur in the context of neurological disease. Whether this is also the case in multiple personality is of both practical and theoretical importance. Practically, the occurrence of behaviors mimicking multiple personality in neurological conditions raises the problem of differential diagnosis. Theoretically, if the emergence of distinct but internally integrated personalities can be tied to neurological insult, it would raise the question as to whether alter personalities have some neurological representation or whether the pathogenesis that results in the development of multiple personality is related to neurological insult.

A number of published cases of multiple personality concerned individuals who also presented seizures of epileptic and/or hysteric origin (e.g., Horton & Miller, 1972; Prince, 1906; Sutcliffe & Jones, 1962; Taylor & Martin, 1944). Mesulam (1981) and Schenk and Bear (1981) raised the issue of an association between psychomotor epilepsy and disorders of multiple personality and illusions of possession (e.g., demonic possession). Schenk and Bear (1981) presented 3 cases of multiple personality in patients with complex partial seizures. There is little question that these patients met criteria for the psychiatric diagnosis of multiple personality. They displayed distinct personalities with dissociations so divergent that in 2 cases handedness in writing changed as a function of personality. Mesulam (1981) reported further clinical details on this group and on additional patients about whom the diagnosis of multiple personality was not as definite. These cases had undergone examination at the behavioral neurology unit at Beth Israel Hospital in Boston. Of 40 patients with histories of complex partial seizures, confirmed by EEG examination, 13 individuals (33 percent) displayed evidence of recurrent dissociative experiences. This particularly held for female patients; in 12 of 23 females (52 percent) with complex partial seizures, there was evidence of recurrent dissociative episodes. Included in these dissociative episodes were experiences not directly related to multiple personality, such as depersonalization, déjà vu, feelings of demonic possession, and so forth (Schenk & Bear, 1981). Benson, Miller, and Signer (1986) reported 2 individuals with well-defined seizure problems who developed dual personalities, one personality being irritable and hostile, the other placid. Each person was amnesic for the other. The incidence of seizures in patients with multiple personality is higher than expected, and has been reported since the earliest clinical descriptions of this disorder (Charcot & Marie, 1892).

This rate of dissociative disorders, including the rate of multiple personality, appears to be extreme in comparison either to samples of patients with other neurological conditions or to the incidence of these disorders among psychiatric patients generally. Given this, Mesulam (1981) and Schenk and Bear (1981) argued that dissociative disorders may be an outcome of abnormal electrical activity in the temporal lobes. Schenk and Bear (1981) proposed that a consequence of the location of foci in limbic areas was a heightening of affectivity generally and, in particular, a marked tendency to associate fortuitously emotion with sensory experiences. The result is that a wider range of stimuli than would be expected, given the premorbid personality of the individual, come to elicit affective response. In some cases, Schenk and Bear argued that this increased range of reactivity becomes integrated with the personality and may account for the unusual personality characteristics reported in temporal lobe epileptics (e.g., Bear & Fedio, 1977). In other cases, the increased range of affective response is experienced as sufficiently alien, threatening, or ego-dystonic that it is defended against by use of dissociation into alter personalities. Essentially, Schenk and Bear's view accords with behavioral and psychodynamic theories of etiology in positing that the emergence of alter personalities reflects an attempt to escape or avoid stimuli that generate negative affect. In contrast to the latter class of theories, Schenk and Bear claimed that, in at least some cases, the generation of the threatening stimuli is a result of long-term discharge of epileptic foci in limbic areas.

These claims should be examined with caution. As Mesulam (1981) pointed out, he worked in a unit that specialized in epileptic patients presenting psychiatric disorders. The patients discussed above were referred because epilepsy was suspected. It is likely, therefore, that rates of dissociative phenomena may be less striking in other samples of temporal lobe epileptics and that epilepsy and/or EEG abnormalities are generally less frequent in cases of multiple personality. Furthermore, according to the theory offered by Schenk and Bear (1981), personality organization is typically unusual in cases of temporal lobe epilepsy. Although there is some evidence for heightened religiosity, hypergraphia (excessive writing), and other traits in such individuals (Bear & Fedio, 1977), these claims are still quite controversial. Furthermore, although the theory may account for why stress would likely result in shifts in the personality in control of behavior, it would appear hard-pressed to account for the unconfirmed clinical impression that stress early in life, particularly child abuse and rape, are associated with the emergence of alter personalities (e.g., Bliss, 1980). In favor of the view of a particular association between temporal lobe epilepsy and multiple personality is the fact that a number of the ictal subjective experiences of such epileptics are akin to dissociative states. Not infrequently, such individuals report that they experience disturbances of vision, audition, and mood as if they were happening to someone else (Penfield & Jasper, 1954).

The data presented by Mesulam (1981) and Schenk and Bear (1981) are intriguing, and it would behoove any clinician to investigate neurological etiology or concomitants in patients with dissociative disorders. It may be that the association of multiple personality and epilepsy is particularly marked in individuals whose histories do not reveal the type of traumatic events usually thought to be related to the genesis of this disorder. More recent work suggests that at least some MPD patients may be normal on neurophysiological measures. In a case report of multiple personality disorder, no significant changes were apparent on the EEG (Cocores, Bender & McBride, 1984). In another case of MPD, personality change was associated with no significant alterations in cerebral blood flow except right temporal hyperfusion (Mathew, Jack, & West, 1985).

Malingering of multiple personality is rarely observed, and we know of no case to have been reported of an individual diagnosed as presenting multiple personality and subsequently found to be malingering. Of course, the distinction between malingering and multiple personality presupposes that cases of the latter do not involve primarily deliberate attempts to portray distinct personalities, as in role playing, for the sake of secondary gains. Were this issue of differential diagnosis to arise, procedures such as sodium amytal interviewing (e.g., Hall, Le Cann, & Schoolar, 1978) may be helpful.

Depersonalization Disorder

The DSM-III-R criteria for the diagnosis of depersonalization disorder are as follows:

A. Persistent or recurrent experiences of depersonalization as indicated by either
   1. An experience of feeling detached from, and as if one is an outside observer of one's mental processes or body, or
   2. An experience or feeling like an automaton or as if in a dream.
B. During the depersonalization experience, reality testing remains intact.
C. The depersonalization is sufficiently severe and persistent to cause marked distress.
D. The depersonalization experience is the predominant disturbance and is not a symptom of another disorder, such as schizophrenia, panic disorder, or agoraphobia without panic disorder, but with limited symptom attacks of depersonalization, or temporal lobe epilepsy.

The following case description, derived from Blue (1979), meets these criteria:

The patient was a 50-year-old, white, married housewife. She was admitted to a hospital with a chief complaint that "nothing seemed real." She had had a number of previous psychiatric hospitalizations, with a long history of somatic complaints of probable psychogenic origin and also had chronic anxiety. Over the previous 18 years, she had been given therapeutic trials of 16 different medications, including major and minor tranquilizers and antidepressants. She reported some relief with minor tranquilizers, but had developed addiction, which, in turn, required inpatient treatment.

At the time of her most recent hospitalization, she reported "I feel that my legs are moving and I know they are not. I am scared of everything. I feel like my body belongs to someone else. I feel like my body and my mind are detached from each other" (Blue, 1979, p. 904). These feelings of altered bodily experience and of unreality were persistent and of sufficient severity as to interfere with her household duties. They were accompanied by somatic preoccupation, guilt, anger, and hostility and comprised the major symptomatology.

Depersonalization is frequently seen as a component of other behavioral disorders, particularly depression and schizophrenia. Its occurrence as the primary symptomatology with a severity sufficient to interfere with everyday functioning is relatively rare. The forms of altered experience in depersonalization are varied. Individuals may report altered experience of bodily parts. We have seen a young man who felt as though his arm was shrinking and another who believed that his genitalia were changing to those of a female. Other altered bodily experiences include feeling as though one were dead, as though one were a machine, or as though one were captured inside the body of someone else. These altered self-perceptions may be so intense that individuals perform acts of self-mutilation with the avowed aim of proving to themselves that their body is their own or that it is not dead. In such cases, the symptom of depersonalization is usually a component of another primary syndrome (e.g., psychotic depression). By DSM-III-R criteria, depersonalization in such a context should not be categorized separately as depersonalization disorder. Noyes, Kuperman, and Olson (1987) reported a case of depersonalization disorder that was successfully treated with desipramine, which suggests the possibility of a link between depersonalization and depressive or anxiety disorders.

Other forms of depersonalization may not involve necessarily altered perception of physical being, but rather a change in the sense of self. Patients may report that they are no longer themselves, that some or all of the habits, traits, and preferences that made them feel unique or individuated no longer are characteristic. Most commonly, they do not report that they have assumed a new identity or that they are characterized by new or different traits. Rather they claim that a part or all of what is referred to as "personality" is lost.

Feelings of depersonalization are commonly accompanied by feelings of unreality or derealization. Both the sense of self and the sense of the outer world are altered. Typically, these individuals report that the outer world seems like a dream. They sense a haze between the self and the environment. Alternatively, they may report that events in the environment are experienced as theater, with other people seen as stage actors or mannequins. As in the case of feelings of depersonalization, feelings of unreality may be present in a variety of disorders. Indeed, a frequently used inventory for observer assessments of depth of depression includes feelings of unreality as an area to be assessed (Hamilton, 1960).

Other symptomatology that may accompany depersonalization are temporal disintegration and body image diffusion. Freeman and Megles (1977) found in a diverse sample of inpatients that complaints of self-estrangement ("I feel like a stranger to myself") correlated significantly with complaints indicating a confusion about time ("My past and future seem to have collapsed into the present, and it is difficult for me to tell them apart") or goal-directedness and with disturbance in body boundaries ("My body boundaries feel fluid and changing"). Confusion and bewilderment may be prominent. Meares and Grose (1978) pointed out that, when occurring in adolescents, depersonalization disorder may be difficult to distinguish from psychoses with strong reactive components. Dizziness, depression, obsessive rumination, somatic concerns, anxiety, and fear of going insane can be concomitant features.

The dominant clinical impression is that complaints of depersonalization are particularly likely in adolescents and young adults. APA (1987) suggested that mild depersonalization without impairment may be reported at some point in up to 70 percent of young adults. Shimuzu and Sakamoto (1986) reported that depersonalization disorder occurs frequently in Japanese children and hypothesized that the difficulty children have in expressing their feelings may result in underdiagnosis of this disorder. It is also unknown whether there are sex differences or familial patterns in manifestations or incidence.

The course of depersonalization disorder is thought to be less promising than that of psychogenic amnesia and fugue. Although onset may occur rapidly, recovery is often slow. Chronic conditions may develop, with exacerbations related to stress, mild anxiety, or depression. Hypochondriasis and substance abuse are possible complications.

There are two main problems in differential diagnosis of depersonalization disorder. The first pertains to distinguishing the condition from schizophrenia, affective disorder, and anxiety disorder, because symptoms or complaints of depersonalization are not uncharacteristic of these other disorders. The second problem involves differential diagnosis with organic conditions. Depersonalization, like the other dissociative disorders, can be seen in a number of neurological conditions (Penfield & Kriestiensen, 1951; Sedman & Kenna, 1964; Simpson, 1969). It is also common with extreme fatigue and sleep deprivation (Bliss, Clark, & West, 1959). Disorders of the temporal lobe may be particularly likely to result in depersonalization. The experience of déjà vu, taking a novel event as familiar, might be considered the opposite of depersonalization. It, too, is common with neuropathology involving the temporal lobe, particularly in epileptic conditions. In a study of normals, Myers and Grant (1972) found in males an association between reports of déjà vu and of depersonalization. Meares and Grose (1978) suggested that depersonalization and déjà vu both reflect dysfunction of memory in determining whether sensory inputs are novel or familiar.

The residual category in DSM-III-R called dissociative disorder not otherwise specified, includes trance states, derealization unaccompanied by depersonalization, dissociated states in which coercion is involved, and a form frusté of multiple personality disorder. Ganser syndrome, the giving of approximate answers to questions, was given prominence in the past but apparently is not a common syndrome.

THEORIES OF ETIOLOGY

Four general classes of theory have been applied to dissociative disorders to provide conceptual models of etiology. These classes might be termed dissociation and neodissociation theory, psychoanalytic theory, behavioral or learning theory, and neuropsychological theory. Dissociation and neodissociation theory developed out of observations of dissociative disorders and dissociative states in normals. The other three classes of theory were principally developed in other circumstances, but have been used as explanatory models.

Dissociation and Neodissociation Theory

Modern study of dissociative disorders began with Charcot (1890) and was largely advanced by his pupil Janet (1929). Janet introduced the term "subconscious" to characterize sets of ideas and action patterns that were typically not subject to awareness. Borrowing from the conceptualization at the time that the flow of ideas in consciousness was determined by an endless string of associations (or, in latter-day terms, stimulus generalization), Janet argued that some cognitive activity could be disassociated (dissociated) or subconscious. Observation with patients and experiments with hypnosis suggested that the dissociated ideas could, at times, occupy the main consciousness, be the subject of verbal report, and control behavior.

These concepts were mainly descriptive. They suggested that the psyche is characterized by multiple control systems that, at times, may not integrate, and in which one or more systems may not be subject to voluntary control. Janet's (1904) formulation of causes of dissociation was primarily physiological in focus. He assumed that each individual had a genetically determined amount of energy that served to bind psychological elements under the control of the ego. Some individuals are endowed with low levels of this nervous energy. When further depleted by physical or psychological stress, the organization within the ego becomes undone, with elements breaking off or becoming dissociated. Needless to say, this view of mechanism currently has few, if any, adherents.

The legacy of Janet's theory of dissociation lies in its descriptive principles and is best embodied in Hilgard's (1973, 1977) neodissociation theory. In accounting for hypnotic phenomena, as well as types of psychopathology reflected in dissociative disorders, Hilgard presented a neodissociation theory. In essence, the theory holds that consciousness is not unitary (cf. Sackeim & Gur, 1978). The fact that we can, in normal functioning, engage in a primary task, such as talking, while automatically and simultaneously performing a secondary task, such as driving, suggests that there are multiple cognitive control systems that at any one time differ in their access to awareness. In presenting a model of neodissociation, Hilgard claimed that in certain normal conditions (e.g., hypnosis) and in psychopathology, amnesic barriers can exist between independent control systems. While different control systems each may have access to consciousness (e.g., verbal report) or may be manifest less directly (e.g., automatic writing), information need not be shared between dissociated control systems.

An attractive aspect of neodissociation theory is that it appears to conform well with phenomenological descriptions of some types of dissociative disorder. In particular, in multiple personality, there is reason to believe that highly integrated control systems compete with access to consciousness, exert profound influence on behavior, and yet have minimal or no interaction with each other. As discussed below, attempts have been made to test the validity of the theory and to flesh out its theoretical framework in the context of hypnosis research. At present, however, its usefulness in accounting for the genesis of dissociative disorders, as opposed to providing a description of the processes that are disordered, may be questioned. The theory presently has not been elaborated in a way that details the conditions that produce dissociative disorders.

Psychoanalytic Theory

Freud's interest in hysteria was stimulated by his study with Charcot. Freud's formulation of hysteric and dissociative disorders formed the basis for the psychoanalytic view of psychopathology. He shared with Janet a belief that cognitive elements could become cut off from access to awareness. The major difference in perspectives lay in the fact that, to Janet, this process was experienced passively, a result of an ego with inadequate levels of energy. To Freud, however, the relegation of thoughts, wishes, and feelings to the unconscious was more of an expulsion. Mental events that elicited anxiety due to conflict with the demands of reality or conscience were actively defended against. Furthermore, repressed mental contents never directly and fully control behavior, nor are such contents ever fully subject to awareness.

For example, the psychoanalytic viewpoint is that the function of the psychogenic fugue is to mediate between the fantasies and desires of the patient and his or her disapproving superego (Fisher & Joseph, 1949). A fugue may occur with awareness of loss of personal identity, with change of personal identity, or with retrograde amnesia (Fisher, 1945). Luparello (1970) described four main features of "hysterical" fugues: Fugue conditions present an altered state of consciousness with features resembling sleep and dreaming, suicidal wishes are expressed overtly or are only thinly disguised, murderous impulses are expressed, and separation anxiety is a potent motivating force (Geleerd, 1956).

The divergence of psychoanalytic from dissociation theories thus appears to center on two issues. Psychoanalytic theory views dissociative symptoms as motivationally based. Events in life that stimulate conflict may be symbolically disavowed or avoided through psychogenic amnesia. Stress precipitates dissociative disorders, in this perspective, because of its role in intensifying unconscious conflict. Second, psychoanalytic and dissociation theories differ in their claims about the structure of consciousness. Hilgard (1976, 1977) characterized this difference in terms of "horizontal" and "vertical" views of consciousness. In psychoanalytic theory, unconscious mental contents do not have direct access to awareness. Symptoms are expressions of compromise formation between unconscious drives and the demands of reality and conscience. The degree to which unconscious elements are expressed in awareness or behavior depends on the degree to which particular compromise formations are weighted toward gratification or safety (e.g., Fenichel, 1945). This would suggest a horizontal view in that unconscious elements are barred from direct access to awareness. Neodissociation theory posits that, under certain conditions (e.g., dissociative disorders, hypnosis), cognitive control systems that typically may not be represented in awareness can become the center of conscious attention. In neodissociation theory, amnesic barriers are between cognitive control systems. According to either theory, the outcomes of information processing within dissociated control systems may be contradictory. According to psychoanalytic theory, one outcome or decision will be subject to awareness, whereas the other is repressed. The dissociation between control systems is isomorphic with the distinction between ego and unconscious structures. In neodissociation theory, the barrier between dissociated control systems is vertical, with decisions reached within each system capable of being the subject of awareness.

The theoretical power of the psychoanalytic view is that it adds a dynamic perspective to the etiology of dissociative disorders. A common clinical impression is that the onsets of psychogenic amnesia and fugue, and changes in the control of behavior from one alter personality to another in multiple personality, often occur during periods of stress and reflect the influence of events that are motivationally significant. On a descriptive level, a shortcoming of psychoanalytic theory, relative to dissociation theory, particularly concerns the phenomenology of multiple personality. In this disorder, it would appear that differing integrated cognitive and affective systems can assume control of awareness. A typology that assumes a fundamental bifurcation between conscious and unconscious processes would seem to have more difficulty in accounting for such phenomena.

Learning Theory

The characterization of dissociative disorders presented above presents a challenge to contemporary learning theory. It is difficult, if not impossible, to describe these disorders without invoking concepts such as awareness and personality. Indeed, these disorders seem to present pathology of the normally integrative properties of awareness and personality. In the past, learning theorists made few attempts to discuss behavioral disorders other than in reference to observable events—stimuli in the individual's physical environment and behaviors of the individual that produce some change in that environment. Awareness was conceptualized as a portion of an individual's verbal behavior, as much a function of stimulus and reinforcement conditions as any other class of behavior (e.g., Skinner, 1963). It would be fair to say that, like Hume, most learning theorists argued that the notion of an integrated personality is a concept we have been conditioned to impose on the stream of behavior. At any one point, an individual's behavior is determined by past reinforcement history and current conditions. No intervening concept or organizational principle, such as that of personality, was deemed necessary.

In the past, given this perspective, behavioral theories did not differentiate between hysterical or dissociative disorders and malingering. The differential diagnosis of, for instance, psychogenic blindness and malingering depends on a determination of whether the individual subjectively is experiencing a loss of sight, regardless of whether visual stimuli still exert influence on behavior. When there is no place theoretically for considering the nature of subjective experience (as opposed to the report of that experience), there are no grounds for distinguishing between psychogenic blindness and malingering. With this perspective, Ullman and Krasner (1969) claimed that the sensory disturbances reported in conversion disorders are feigned by the patient to achieve secondary gains. Likewise, one could argue that, in psychogenic amnesia and fugue, individuals fake memory loss to achieve an end, for example, to escape from aversive circumstances.

The usefulness of this view depends on one's estimation of the need to distinguish between these disorders and malingering. Theoretically, at least, since the diagnosis of conversion or dissociative disorder is made in the absence of convincing evidence of malingering, it is possible that malingering is involved in all cases, but that it is established in only some.

In recent years, behavioral approaches to psychopathology have shown a greater willingness to incorporate assumptions about unobservable, internal processes, as evidenced by the advent of cognitive–behavioral therapies (e.g., Beck, 1976). Although little attempt has been made to provide a reformulation of the processes involved in dissociative disorder, an outline of a general neobehaviorist view can be offered.

Large classes of behavioral tendencies may be relatively ineffective in securing rewards or in securing the avoidance of aversive circumstances. Individuals have well-developed repertoires of behavior that, in some cases, may prove dysfunctional relative to the opportunities available in the environment. For instance, a person who views himself or herself veridically as passive and inhibited and for whom the arousal of hostile impulses elicits anxiety, may have profound difficulties when faced with situations that generate anger and require aggressive acts. Some individuals may have learned to cope with these circumstances in an unusual way. Instead of modifying their repertoire and learning to become more assertive, they establish a second hierarchy of responses. It may be that during development, strong pressures were exerted on the individual to act in a particular way (passive), and alteration of the dominant hierarchy was associated with perceived and/or realistic aversive consequences. In any event, the second hierarchy may come into play as a function of specific eliciting conditions. In such circumstances, the individual would be seen as acting out of character. This formulation would appear to provide a behavioral account of multiple personality and could be extended to other dissociative disorders.

Behavioral accounts of dissociative disorder share with psychoanalytic theory an emphasis on the role of motivational factors in producing or intensifying symptomatology. Although the two classes of theory may differ in their emphasis on the unconscious conflict related to childhood events, both view dissociative phenomena as reflecting escape or avoidance of anxiety-eliciting stimuli (internal or external). It should be emphasized that, although clinical impressions attest to the role of motivational factors in dissociative disorders, little empirical evidence substantiates this view.

Neurophychological Theories

We have commented that the grouping of dissociative and hysterical conversion disorders in DSM-II referred to psychiatric symptomatology that mimicked neurological disease but appeared to be functional in origin. Furthermore, for each of the four dissociative disorders discussed above, we described vexing problems in differential diagnosis concerned with distinguishing the group from neurological disorders.

Neuropsychological disturbances may be related to the etiology of dissociative disorders in two ways. First, primary neurological disturbance may result in changes in subjective experience, which, in turn, produce the secondary psychological response of dissociative disorder. An example of this view is Schenk and Bear's (1981) hypothesis that, in some cases of temporal lobe epilepsy, a kindling process instills previously neutral sensory input (stimuli) with exaggerated and inappropriate affective tone. This would be an instance of a neurological disturbance producing alteration in subjective experience. To account for an apparently high incidence of dissociation disorder in such epileptics, Schenk and Bear (1981) speculated that the increased inappropriate affectivity was threatening to some individuals, who dealt with the anxiety by containing the altered experience through dissociation. In essence, Schenk and Bear presented a view of etiology that is harmonious with psychoanalytic or behavioral theories to the extent that escape from aversive internal stimuli provides the impetus to dissociation. They differ in positing a neurological underpinning to the conditions that give rise to the aversive state.

A second, perhaps more radical, neuropsychological view is to posit that altered personality functioning observed in dissociative disorders reflects release of neural mechanisms that subserve independent aspects of personality. This view might assume that more than one set of integrated behavioral tendencies or repertoires are neurologically represented. In normal functioning, subdominant repertoires are strongly inhibited. Neurological insult may directly produce release of subdominant repertoires through excitation or disinhibition. Psychological events may also result in their release by functionally mimicking the effects of physical insult.

This type of view has received some support from studies of patients who have undergone corpus callosotomy for the relief of intractable epilepsy. In the weeks immediately following surgery, such patients may display divergent motor behavior on the two sides of the body. Gur (1982) reported observations on 5 such patients. These patients showed this syndrome to varying extents, but the following case was particularly dramatic:

In the first few postsurgery days, a young adult female was interviewed. During the interview, it was observed that when she held a lit cigarette in her left hand, the hand was fully extended out and she did not bring the cigarette to her face. When she was requested to do so, her left hand would not bring the cigarette to her lips; she failed to do so even when her right hand tried to force the left hand over. Subsequently, she found that on several occasions the left side of her body would act in ways that appeared to be against her will. These included incidents when her left hand unbuttoned her blouse (only to be buttoned up immediately by the right hand), when the left side of her body pushed her against a wall while walking down a corridor and would not let her proceed, and when she stole money with her left hand. The frequency of these acts was sufficiently great that the patient referred to that part of herself that was engaging in this bizarre behavior as "Lefty."

Dimond (1979) and Gazzaniga (1970) reported similar observations. For instance, a patient reported to Dimond (1979),

You wouldn't want to hear some of the things this left hand has done—you wouldn't believe it. It acts independently a lot of times. I don't even tell it to—I don't know its going to do anything. Sometimes I go to get something with my right hand and the left hand grabs it and stops it—for some reason. Then one time I was sitting down watching television my left hand just got up and slapped me.

(p. 35)

In the series reported by Gur (1982), reports of the aberrant behavior decreased with increasing time from operation. After a couple of months, the female patient referred to above indicated that she had begun to "live with Lefty" in an amicable way and that the earlier behaviors that had disturbed her were less frequent.

The neuropsychological processes that result in such dissociated behavior following corpus callosotomy are, for the most part, unknown. Equally mysterious is the apparent integrative process that results in a diminution of dissociated acts. These cases are significant simply because they suggest that neurosurgical intervention can produce dissociative behavior. If we assume that the dissociated behavior reflects some splitting in personality organization, then it would seem that the neurosurgical procedure either produced this splitting and/or established the conditions for its emergence. In either case, the supposition in these cases is that the sides of the brain differed in their intentions, wishes, and/or directives for motor behavior during the dissociated acts. This would suggest that, at least in the corpus callosotomy patient, neural representation of intentions, wishes, or motor directives differs in the two sides of the brain. It is conceivable that such differences in neural representation of "personality" exist in the neurologically intact, with subdominant expression typically inhibited. An alternative is that competing tendencies are neurologically represented in the normal individual but are subject to some executive, integrative process so that contradictory behavioral acts are rarely manifest. In either case, the possibility is raised that the dissociated behavior shown by these patients is similar to that observed in some psychiatric dissociative disorders. The physical disconnection of the two hemispheres that produces dissociation postoperatively might be mimicked in psychiatric disorders by functional disconnections of the two hemispheres or of other, more discrete neural systems; by inhibition of neural transmission; or by other means. Neuropsychological theories of the genesis of dissociation may be compatible with purely psychological theories, providing a different level of explanation. For instance, one might inquire about the psychological conditions that could lead to functional disconnection of neural systems subserving divergent aspects of personality.

TREATMENT

A plethora of treatment modalities have been used in cases of dissociative disorder. Although the dominant forms of treatment, in terms of published cases, appear to by psychodynamically oriented psychotherapy and hypnotherapy, successful outcomes also have been reported with other approaches, such as narcoanalysis (e.g., sodium amytal interviews), paradoxical techniques, and pharmacotherapy. A common theme has characterized therapeutic interventions with these various treatment modalities. Most clinicians aim for an integration of disjointed aspects of personality. In psychogenic amnesia and fugue, this may involve helping the individual to recover lost memories and to confront personality alteration during travel. Treatment experience with psychogenic fugue is described in the older literature. Traditionally, hypnosis and short-acting barbiturates have been used to reconstitute repressed memories. Psychodynamic psychotherapy was used during World War II to facilitate resolution of conflicts leading to the fugue state and thus decrease the tendency to dissociate in times of stress, but 20 percent of the men suffered repeated episodes (Parfitt & Carlyle-Gall, 1944). In multiple personality, therapists often report attempts to seek integration among the divergent dominant and alter personalities, usually by bringing the existence of alter personalities into the awareness of the dominant personality. Anecdotal evidence suggests that a characteristic presentation of MPD is nonresponsiveness to psychopharmacological treatment (Kluft, 1987). Some believe that unsuspected MPD is an uncommon source of protracted resistance, interruption, and failure in psychoanalysis (Kluft, 1987). Patients whose MPD remains untreated do not experience remission (Coons, 1986), and those who prematurely leave treatment relapse into, rather than cease, MPD behaviors. Anecdotal evidence indicates that patients may experience a stormy course in therapy but achieve remission of symptoms (Kluft, 1987). Overall, the evidence suggests that the prognosis for MPD is relatively poor.

In the treatment of depersonalization disorder, an attempt is often made to undermine feelings of lost identity and altered physical being by underscoring their irrationality while provoking feelings of "personhood" by encouraging emotional involvement with others, eliciting strong affective reactions, and so on.

Hypnosis and hypnotherapy have been used in the treatment of dissociative disorders with marked frequency. There are several reports of resolutions of psychogenic amnestic episodes during hypnotic interviews and of integrations of multiple personality with the aid of hypnosis. Acknowledgment of successful treatment with hypnosis should be tempered by the view that some manifestations of dissociative disorders may be brought on or exacerbated by the hypnotic state. Although some cases of multiple personality have come to light outside the context of hypnotherapy (e.g., Sutcliffe & Jones, 1962), perhaps the majority of cases that have been reported were first discovered to be instances of multiple personality during hypnotic interactions. A related issue is evident in the reported cases of multiple personality: Patients with this disorder appear to be extraordinarily talented hypnotic subjects. As we noted, standardized testing of hypnotic susceptibility has rarely been conducted on a sample of such patients. From what can be learned from the case studies, however, these individuals appear to fall at the upper range of susceptibility. Were this shown to be the case, it may have implications for understanding both the etiology of multiple personality and the apparent relation between the use of hypnotherapy and the discovery of such cases.

No studies have been reported of the relative efficacy of treatment modalities in cases of dissociative disorder. In line with the natural history of these disorders, psychogenic amnesia and fugue seem to be the most amenable to treatment. In many instances, these conditions may remit without intervention. Multiple personality and depersonalization are believed to be more refractory to treatment. In cases of multiple personality, decompensation to psychosis may occur, with or without therapeutic intervention.

SUMMARY

In this chapter, we have concentrated on pathological and extreme manifestations of dissociation. Dissociative phenomena occur in everyday life. Luborsky et al. (1979) found that experiences of momentary forgetting in the course of psychotherapy shared a number of features with psychogenic amnesia. Using a symptom-context method, they compared the verbal behavior of patients before and after incidents in which patients forgot what they were going to say with control periods, in which no forgetting occurred. They found that, prior to instances of momentary forgetting, patients' speech reflected greater involvement with the therapist, patients evidenced greater anxiety, and the forgotten material was characterized by a theme. This theme typically referred to a core issue in the treatment. Luborsky et al. (1979) speculated that the emergence of this theme, coupled with greater emotional involvement with therapists, precipitated instances of momentary forgetting. This view is similar to the psychodynamic hypothesis that psychogenic amnesia usually pertains to events that are conflict arousing.

Hilgard (1976, 1977) demonstrated a hypnotic phenomenon he referred to as the "hidden observer." When hypnotized and given an analgesia suggestion, normal subjects reported a sharp reduction in the experience of pain, compared with their reports without the analgesia suggestion. Hilgard found that, when hypnotic subjects were instructed that another "part of themselves" could comment on the pain experience, through automatic talking, writing, or key pressing, reported pain was heightened, although it did not reach waking-state levels. The data suggesting that more than one cognitive control center may be capable in the hypnotic subject of providing reports fit well with the subjective experience of many hypnotized individuals. For instance, during suggestions of age regression, many susceptible subjects have reported being aware of being both a child and an adult (e.g., Laurence & Perry, 1981). The experience is as if the adult identity were observing the experience of regression. In a related vein, Sackeim, Nordlie, and Gur (1979) found that subjects in whom total blindness was suggested with hypnosis performed either below chance or well above chance on a visual identification task. Subjects simulating hypnotic blindness were at chance level. The hypnotically blind seemed to present a dissociation between their subjective experience of blindness and the cognitive processing that resulted in nonchance identification of stimulus conditions.

Dissociative experiences in everyday life are not restricted to hypnosis or to events in psychotherapy. It is fair to say that, whenever we lie to ourselves, that is, engage in self-deception, part of ourselves holds a belief that contradicts a belief consciously avowed. Our language acknowledges such dissociation, as it is not uncommon for individuals to claim that "deep inside" or "in their hearts" they knew the truth all along, but could not admit it to themselves. Sackeim and Gur (1978; Gur & Sackeim, 1979; Sackeim, 1983, 1988) provided an experimental analog of self-deception and showed that decisions reached outside of awareness may be accurate and independent of decisional processes represented in awareness. The rarity and elusiveness of pathological forms of dissociation make experimental investigation of analogous processes in normal individuals all the more critical.

At the onset, we raised the age-old problem of the meaning of personal identity. Within psychology, there has been cyclical debate as to whether individuals are, indeed, characterized by a single identity or personality. Taking one side of this argument, Mischel (1968) claimed that the evidence for cross-situational consistency in behavior was so weak that we, like Hume, should question whether the notion of a consistent personality is more a concept we impose on reality than something reflected in human behavior. The phenomenology and overt manifestations of dissociative disorders may provide another perspective on this issue. We have seen that, particularly in cases of multiple personality, the differences between alter personalities are far greater than the inconsistencies within individual personalities. It does seem possible for the same individual to consistently be as different from one time to another as an apple and a watermelon. Furthermore, in cases of depersonalization, people present anxiety and depression that they relate to the subjective experience of having lost their sense of self. These phenomena suggest that the notion of personal identity has value. Without this notion, we would be at a loss in trying to provide a conceptualization of the nature of dissociative disorders.

REFERENCES

Abeles, M., & Schilder, P. (1935). Psychogenic loss of personal identity. *Archives of Neurology and Psychiatry, 34,* 587–604.

Akhtar, S., & Brenner, I. (1979). Differential diagnosis of fugue-like states. *Journal of Clinical Psychiatry, 40,* 381–385.

American Psychiatric Association. (1968). *Diagnostic and statistical manual of mental disorders* (2nd ed.). Washington, DC: Author.

American Psychiatric Association. (1980). *Diagnostic and statistical manual of mental disorders* (3rd ed.). Washington, DC: Author.

American Psychiatric Association. (1987). *Diagnostic and statistical manual of mental disorders* (3rd ed. rev.). Washington, DC: Author.

Bear, D., & Fedio, P. (1977). Quantitative analysis of interictal behavior in temporal lobe epilepsy. *Archives of Neurology, 34,* 434–467.

Beck, A. T. (1976). *Cognitive therapy and the emotional disorders.* New York: International Universities Press.

Benson, D. F., Miller, B. L., & Signer, S. F. (1986). Dual personality associated with epilepsy. *Archives of Neurology, 43,* 471–474.

Berger, D. (1985). Dissociative disorders. In S. Greben, V. Rakoff, & G. Voineskos (Eds.), *A method of psychiatry* (pp. 211–215). Philadelphia: Lea and Febiger.

Bernstein, E. M., & Putnam, F. W. (1986). Development, reliability, and validity of a dissociation scale. *Journal of Nervous and Mental Disease, 174,* 727–735.

Berrington, W., Liddell, D., & Foulds, G. (1956). A re-evaluation of the fugue. *Journal of Mental Science, 102,* 280–286.

Bliss, E. (1980). Multiple personalities: A report of 14 cases with implications for schizophrenia and hysteria. *Archives of General Psychiatry, 37,* 1388–1397.

Bliss, E. L. (1984). A symptom profile of patients with multiple personalities, including MMPI results. *Journal of Nervous and Mental Disease, 1172,* 197–201.

Bliss, E., Clark, L., & West, C. (1959). Studies in sleep deprivation—Relationship to schizophrenia. *Archives of Neurology and Psychiatry, 81,* 348–359.

Bliss, E. L., & Jeppsen, E. A. (1985). Prevalence of multiple personality among inpatients and outpatients. *American Journal of Psychiatry, 142,* 250–251.

Bliss, E. L., Larson, E. M., & Nakashima, S. R. (1983). Auditory hallucinations and schizophrenia. *Journal of Nervous and Mental Disease, 171,* 30–33.

Blue, E. (1979). Use of directive therapy in the treatment of depersonalization neurosis. *Psychological Reports, 45,* 904–906.

Braun, B. G. (1985). The trangenerational incidence of dissociation and multiple personality disorder: A preliminary report. In R. P. Kluft (Ed.), *Childhood antecedents of multiple personality* (pp. 1–28). Washington, DC: American Psychiatric Press.

Carroll, B. (1982). The dexamethasone suppression test for melancholia. *British Journal of Psychiatry, 140,* 292–304.

Charcot, J. (1890). *Oeuvres completes*. Paris: Aux Bureaux du Progres Medical.

Charcot, J., & Marie, P. (1892). On hystero-epilepsy. In D. H. Tuke (Ed.), *A dictionary of psychological medicine* (Vol. 1). Philadelphia: P. Blakiston.

Chodoff, P. (1987). More on multiple personality disorder. *American Journal of Psychiatry, 144,* 124.

Cocores, J. A., Bender, A. L., & McBride, E. (1984). Multiple personality, seizure disorder, and the electroencephalogram. *Journal of Nervous and Mental Disease, 172,* 436–438.

Condon, W., Ogston, W., & Pacoe, L. (1969). Three faces of Eve revisited: A study of transient microstrabismus. *Journal of Abnormal Psychology, 74,* 618–620.

Coons, P. M. (1986). Treatment progress in 20 patients with multiple personality disorder. *Journal of Nervous and Mental Disease, 174,* 715–721.

Coons, P. M., & Milstein, V. (1986). Psychosexual disturbances in multiple personality: Characteristics, etiology, and treatment. *Journal of Clinical Psychiatry, 47,* 106–110.

Daly, D., & Mulder, D. (1957). Gelastic epilepsy, *Neurology, 7,* 189–192.

Dimond, S. (1979). Disconnection and psychopathology. In J. Gruzelier & P. Flor-Henry (Eds.), *Hemisphere asymmetries of function in psychopathology* (pp. 35–46). New York: Elsevier/North Holland.

Dornbusch, R., & Williams, M. (1974). Memory and ECT. In M. Fink, S. Kety, J. McGaugh, & T. Williams (Eds.), *Psychobiology of convulsive therapy* (pp. 199–208). Washington, DC: Winston.

Drake, M. E., Jr., Pakalnis, A., & Denio, L. C. (1988). Differential diagnosis of epilepsy and multiple personality: Clinical and EEG findings in 15 cases. *Neuropsychiatry, Neuropsychology and Behavioral Neurology, 1,* 131–140.

Escueta, A., Boxley, B., Stubbs, N., Waddell, B., & Wilson, W. (1974). Prolonged twilight states and automatisms: A case report. *Neurology, 24,* 331–339.

Fagan, J., & McMahon, P. P. (1984). Incipient multiple personality in children: Four cases. *Journal of Nervous and Mental Diseases, 172,* 26–36.

Feindel, W., & Penfield, W. (1954). Localization of discharge in temporal lobe automatism. *Archives of Neurology and Psychiatry, 72,* 605–630.

Fenichel, O. (1945). *The psychoanalytic theory of neurosis*. New York: Norton.

Fisher, C. (1945). Amnestic states in war neurosis: The psychogenesis of fugues. *Psychoanalytical Quarterly, 14,* 437–468.

Fisher, C., & Adams, R. (1958). Transient global amnesia. *Transactions of the American Neurological Association, 83,* 143–145.

Fisher, C., & Adams, R. (1964). Transient global amnesia. *Acta Neurologica Scandinavica* (Suppl. 9).

Fisher, C., & Joseph, E. (1949). Fugue with awareness of loss of personal identity. *Psychoanalytical Quarterly, 18,* 480–493.

Freeman, A., & Megles, F. (1977). Depersonalization and temporal disintegration in acute mental illness. *American Journal of Psychiatry, 134,* 679–681.

Gazzaniga, M. (1970). *The bisected brain*. New York: Appleton-Century-Crofts.

Geleerd, E. F. (1956). Clinical contributions to the problem of early mother–child relationships. *Psychoanalytic study of the child* (Vol. 11, pp. 336–351). New York: International Universities Press.

Geschwind, N. (1975). The borderland of neurology and psychiatry: Some common misconceptions. In F. Benson & D. Blumer (Eds.), *Psychiatric aspects of neurological disease* (pp. 1–9). New York: Grune and Stratton.

Gillespie, R. (1936, December 12). Amnesia: Component functions in remembering. *British Medical Journal,* (pp. 1179–1182). The APA Task Force on Laboratory Tests in Psychiatry (1987). The Dexamethasone Suppression Test: An overview of its current status in psychiatry. *American Journal of Psychiatry, 144,* 1253–1262.

Goodwin, D., & Guze, S. (1979). *Psychiatric diagnosis.* New York: Oxford University Press.

Gur, R. C., (1982). Measurement and imaging of regional brain function: implications for neuropsychiatry. In J. Gruzelier & P. Flor-Henry (Eds.), *Hemispheric asymmetries of function in psychopathology* (Vol. 2, pp. 589–616). New York: Elsevier/North Holland.

Gur, R., & Sackeim, H. (1979). Self-deception: A concept in search of phenomenon. *Journal of Personality and Social Psychology, 37,* 147–169.

Hall, R., Le Cann, A., & Schoolar, J. (1978). Amobarbital treatment of multiple personality. *Journal of Nervous and Mental Disease, 166,* 666–670.

Haller, W. V. (1957). Das problem der poriomania. *Nervenarzt, 9,* 385–389.

Hamilton, M. (1960). A rating scale for depression. *Journal of Neurology, Neurosurgery and Psychiatry, 23,* 56–62.

Heathfield, K., Croft, P., & Swash, M. (1973). The syndrome of transient global amnesia. *Brain, 96,* 729–736.

Herman, M. (1938). The use of intravenous sodium amytal in psychogenic amnesic states. *Psychiatric Quarterly, 12,* 738–742.

Hilgard, E. (1965). *Hypnotic susceptibility.* New York: Harcourt Brace Jovanovich.

Hilgard, E. (1973). A neodissociation interpretation of pain reduction in hypnosis. *Psychological Review, 80,* 396–411.

Hilgard, E. (1976). Neodissociation theory of multiple cognitive control systems. In G. E. Schwartz & D. Shapiro (Eds.), *Consciousness and self-regulation: Advances in research* (Vol. 1, pp. 137–172). New York: Plenum Press.

Hilgard, E. (1977). *Divided consciousness: Multiple controls in human thought and action.* New York: Wiley.

Horevitz, R. P., & Braun, B. G. (1984). Are multiple personalities borderline? *Psychiatric Clinics of North America, 7,* 9–29.

Horton, P., & Miller, D. (1972). The etiology of multiple personality. *Comprehensive Psychiatry, 13,* 151–159.

Hughlings Jackson, J. (1898). Case of epilepsy with tasting movements and "dreamy states": Very small patch of softening in the left uncinate gyrus. *Brain, 21,* 580–590.

Hume, D. (1911). *A treatise on human understanding.* London: J. M. Dent and Sons. (Original work published 1738)

Janet, P. (1904). *Nervoses et idees fixes* (2nd ed.). Paris: Felix Alcan.

Janet, P. (1929). *The major symptoms of hysteria.* New York: Macmillan.

Kanzer, M. (1939). Amnesia: A statistical study. *American Journal of Psychiatry, 96,* 711.

Kluft, R. P. (1987). An update on multiple personality disorder. *Hospital and Community Psychiatry, 38,* 363–373.

Kraepelin, E. (1909). *Psychiatrie.* Leipzig, East Germany: Verlag.

Kroeger, R., & Turnbull, W. (1975). Invalidity of validity: The case of the MMPI. *Journal of Consulting and Clinical Psychology, 43,* 48–55.

Laurence, J. R., & Perry, C. (1981). The "hidden observer" phenomenon in hypnosis: Some additional findings. *Journal of Abnormal Psychology, 90,* 334–344.

Lester, D. (1977). Multiple personality: A review. *Psychology, 14,* 54–59.

Luborsky, L., Sackeim, H., & Christoph, P. (1979). The state conducive to momentary forgetting. In J. Kihlstrom & F. Evans (Eds.), *Functional disorders of memory*, (pp. 325–354). New York: Wiley.

Ludwig, A., Brandsma, J., Wilbur, C., Bendfeldt, F., & Jameson, D. (1972). The objective study of a multiple personality. *Archives of General Psychiatry, 26,* 298–310.

Luparello, T. J. (1970). Features of fugue: A unified hypothesis of regression. *Journal of the American Psychoanalytical Association, 18,* 379–398.

Mathew, R. J., Jack, R. A., & West, W. S. (1985). Regional blood flow in a patient with multiple personality. *American Journal of Psychiatry, 142,* 504–505.

Mayeux, R., Alexander, M., Benson, F., Brandt, J., & Rosen, J. (1979). Poriomania. *Neurology, 29,* 1616–1619.

McKinney, K. A., & Lange, M. M. (1983). Familial fugue—A case report. *Canadian Journal of Psychiatry, 28,* 654–656.

Meares, R., & Grose, D. (1978). On depersonalization in adolescence: A consideration from the viewpoints of habituation and 'identity.' *British Journal of Medical Psychology, 51,* 335–342.

Mesulam, M. (1981). Dissociative states with abnormal temporal lobe EEG: Multiple personality and the illusion of possession. *Archives of Neurology, 38,* 176–181.

Meyer-Mickeleit, R. (1953). Die dammerattacken als charakteristischer anfallstyp der temporalen epilepsie. *Nervenarzt, 24,* 331–346.

Milner, B. (1966). Amnesia following operation on the temporal lobes. In C. Whitty & O. Zangwill (Eds.), *Amnesia.* (pp. 109–133). London: Butterworths.

Mischel, W. (1968). *Personality and assessment.* New York: Wiley.

Myers, D., & Grant, G. (1972). A study of depersonalization in students. *British Journal of Psychiatry, 121,* 59–65.

Nemiah, J. (1979). Dissociative amnesia: A clinical and theoretical reconsideration. In J. Kihlstrom & F. Evans (Eds.), *Functional disorders of memory* (pp. 303–324). Hillsdale, NJ: Erlbaum.

Noyes, R., Jr., Kuperman, S., & Olson, S. B. (1987). Desipramine: A possible treatment for depersonalization disorder. *Canadian Journal of Psychiatry, 32,* 782–784.

Orne, M. (1979). On the simulating subjects as a quasi-control group in hypnosis research: What, why, and how. In E. Fromm & R. Shor (Eds.), *Hypnosis: Developments in research and new perspectives.* (pp. 519–566). New York: Aldine.

Orne, M. T., Dinges, D. F., & Orne, E. C. (1984). On the differential diagnosis of multiple personality in the forensic context. *International Journal of Clinical and Experimental Hypnosis, 32,* 118–169.

Osgood, C., & Luria, Z. (1954). A blind analysis of a case of multiple personality using the semantic differential. *Journal of Abnormal and Social Psychology, 49,* 579–591.

Osgood, C., Luria, Z., Jeans, R., & Smith, S. (1976). The three faces of Evelyn: A case report. *Journal of Abnormal Psychology, 85,* 247–286.

Parfitt, D., & Carlyle-Gall, C. (1944). Psychogenic amnesia: The refusal to remember. *Journal of Mental Science, 90,* 513–531.

Penfield, W., & Jasper, H. (1954). *Epilepsy and the functional anatomy of the human brain.* Boston: Little, Brown.

Penfield, W., & Kriestiensen, K. (1951). *Epileptic seizure patterns: A study of the localizing value of initial phenomenon in focal cortical seizures.* Springfield, IL: C. Thomas.

Perley, M., & Guze, S. (1962). Hysteria—The stability and usefulness of clinical criteria. *The New England Journal of Medicine, 266,* 421–426.

Pincus, J., & Tucker, G. (1978). *Behavioral neurology* (2nd ed.). New York: Oxford University Press.

Prince, M. (1906). *The dissociation of a personality.* New York: Longman's Green.

Putnam, F. W., Guroff, J. J., Silberman, E. K., Barban, L., & Post, R. M. (1986). The clinical phenomenology of multiple personality disorder: Review of 100 recent cases. *Journal of Clinical Psychiatry, 47,* 285–293.

Rapaport, D. (1967). States of consciousness: A psychopathological and psychodynamic view. In M. Gill (Ed.), *The collected papers of David Rapaport* (pp. 385–404). New York: Basic Books.

Rice, E., & Fisher, C. (1976). Fugue states in sleep and wakefulness: A psychophysiological study. *Journal of Nervous and Mental Disease, 163,* 79–87.

Riether, A. M., & Stoudemire, A. (1988). Psychogenic fugue states: A review. *Southern Medical Journal, 81,* 568–571.

Ross, C. A., & Anderson, G. (1988). Phenomenological overlap of multiple personality disorder and obsessive–compulsive disorder. *Journal of Nervous and Mental Disease, 176,* 295–299.

Russell, E. (1981). The pathology and clinical examination of memory. In S. Filskov & T. Boll (Eds.), *Handbook of clinical neuropsychology* (pp. 287–319). New York: Wiley.

Russell, W., & Nathan, P. (1946). Traumatic amnesia. *Brain, 69,* 280–300.

Sackeim, H. A. (1983). Self-deception, self-esteem, and depression: The adaptive value of lying to oneself. In J. Maisling (Ed.), *Empirical studies of psychoanalytic theory* (pp. 101–158). Hillsdale, NJ: Erlbaum.

Sackeim, H. A. (1988). Self-deception: A synthesis. In J. S. Lockard & D. Paulhus (Eds.), *Self-deception: An adaptive mechanism?* New York: Prentice-Hall, pp. 146–165.

Sackeim, H. A., Greenberg, M., Weiman, A., Gur, R. C., Hungerbuhler, J., & Geschwind, N. (1982). Hemispheric asymmetry in the expression of positive and negative emotions: Neurological evidence. *Archives of Neurology, 39,* 210–218.

Sackeim, H. A., & Gur, R. C. (1978). Self-deception, self-confrontation and consciousness. In G. E. Schwartz & D. Shapiro (Eds.), *Consciousness and self-regulation: Advances in research* (Vol. 2, pp. 139–198). New York: Plenum Press.

Sackeim, H. A., Nordlie, J. W., & Gur, R. C. (1979). A model of hysterical and hypnotic blindness: Cognition, motivation and awareness. *Journal of Abnormal Psychology, 88,* 474–489.

Schenk, L., & Bear, D. (1981). Multiple personality and related dissociative phenomena in patients with temporal lobe epilepsy. *American Journal of Psychiatry, 138,* 1311–1316.

Schultz, R., Braun, B. G., & Kluft, R. P. (1985, October). *Creativity and the imaginary companion phenomenon: Prevalence and phenomenology in MPD.* Paper presented at the Second International Conference on Multiple Personality/Dissociative States, Chicago.

Sedman, G., & Kenna, J. (1964). The occurrence of depersonalization phenomenon under LSD. *Psychiatry et Neurolog (Basel), 147,* 129–137.

Sethi, P. K., & Rao, T. S. (1976). Gelastic, quiritarian and cursive epilepsy. *Journal of Neurology, Neurosurgery and Psychiatry, 39,* 823–828.

Shimuzu, M., & Sakamoto, S. (1986). Depersonalization in early adolescence. *Japan Journal of Psychiatry and Neurology, 40,* 603–608.

Silberman, E. K., Putnam, F. W., Weingartner, H., Braun, B. G., & Post, R. M. (1985). Dissociative states in multiple personality disorder: A quantitative study. *Psychiatry Research, 15,* 253–260.

Simpson, J. (1969). The clinical neurology of temporal lobe disorders. In R. Herrington (Ed.), Current problems in neuropsychiatry. *British Journal of Psychiatry,* Special Publication No. 4.

Skinner, B. F. (1963). Behaviorism at fifty. *Science, 140,* 951–958.

Slater, E., & Glithero, E. (1965). A follow-up of patients diagnosed as suffering from "hysteria." *Journal of Psychosomatic Research, 9,* 9–13.

Stengel, E. (1941). On the etiology of fugue states. *Journal of Mental Science, 87,* 572–599.

Stengel, E. (1943). Further studies on pathological wandering (fugue with impulse to wander). *Journal of Mental Science, 89,* 224–241.

Sugimoto, T., Matsumura, T., Sakamoto, Y., & Taniuchi, K. (1979). Running and laughing fits as the sequelae of neonatal hyperviscosity syndrome. *Brain and Development, 4,* 323–326.

Sutcliffe, J., & Jones, J. (1962). Personal identity, multiple personality and hypnosis. *International Journal of Clinical and Experimental Hypnosis, 10,* 231–269.

Talland, G. (1965). *Deranged memory.* New York: Academic Press.

Taylor, W., & Martin, M. (1944). Multiple personality. *Journal of Abnormal and Social Psychology, 39,* 281–300.

Thigpen, C., & Cleckley, H. (1954). A case of multiple personality. *Journal of Abnormal and Social Psychology, 49,* 135–151.

Thigpen, C., & Cleckley, H. (1984). On the incidence of multiple personality disorder. *International Journal of Clinical and Experimental Hypnosis, 32,* 63–66.

Ullman, L., & Krasner, L. (1969). *A psychological approach to abnormal behavior.* Englewood Cliffs, NJ: Prentice-Hall.

Walton, J. N. (1977). *Brain's diseases of the nervous system* (8th ed.). Oxford: Oxford University Press.

Whitlock, F. (1967). The etiology of hysteria. *Acta Psychiatrica Scandinavica, 43,* 144–162.

Wissfeld, E. (1957). Uber die krankheiten, bei denen poriomane zustande vorkommen. *Nervanarzt, 9,* 389–399.

CHAPTER 11

Sexual Disorders

NATHANIEL McCONAGHY

A number of developments related to the psychopathology and diagnosis of sexual disorders have taken place during the past decade. The term *ego-dystonic homosexuality* was not retained in the revised third edition of the American Psychiatric Association's (APA's) *Diagnostic and Statistical Manual of Mental Disorders* (DSM-III-R; (1987). Gender identity disorders were reclassified in DSM-III-R to disorders usually first evident in infancy, childhood, or adolescence, and expanded to include transvestism in adults as gender identity disorder of adolescence or adulthood, nontranssexual type. The role of biological factors in sexual dysfunctions has been increasingly accepted. A major paradigm shift has occurred with regard to paraphilic behaviors, in that nonsexual urges or mechanisms have been postulated to play a major role in their maintenance.

PARAPHILIAS

DSM-III-R describes the paraphilias as sexual *disorders* characterized by arousal to sexual objects or stimuli that are not part of normative arousal-activity patterns. In other classifications, paraphilias are usually referred to as sexual *deviations,* which are sexual acts or urges considered unacceptable according to current social values. Masturbation, now established as statistically the most normal sexual activity for the majority of males in Western societies for significant periods of their lives, was in the past considered a sexual deviation, as was homosexuality. Sexual activity between adults and children or adolescents is accepted in some areas of the world, as it was in advanced civilizations in the past; however, it is regarded with abhorrence in Western societies and considered evidence of pathology in adults who engage in such practices.

DSM-III-R Criteria, Clinical Presentation, and Course of Individual Paraphilias

Exhibitionism

The DSM-III-R criterion for exhibitionism is that, over a 6-month period, the person has acted on or is markedly distressed by recurrent urges or fantasies involving the exposure of his or her genitals to an unsuspecting stranger. Typically, exhibitionists are males who obtain a high level of excitement from exposing their penis, frequently nonerect, to one or more females, usually strangers at or just past puberty. They may masturbate during or after exposure. The act is usually carried out on quiet streets, in public transport, in secluded areas (e.g., parks or beaches), or from a car. Thirty to 50 percent of women have reported being the victims of exhibitionism (DiVasto et al., 1984; Zverina, Lachman, Pondelickova, & Vanek, 1987). Exhibitionism rarely has been reported in women, and when it has, it appeared to be motivated by attention seeking (Blair & Lanyon, 1981; O'Connor, 1987). Exhibitionism accounts for about a third of the convictions for sexual offenses in England, Germany, the United States, Canada, and Hong Kong, but apparently occurs less frequently in France and Italy. It is rare in South America, the Middle East, Africa, and most Asian countries, including Japan (Rooth, 1973). Recidivism was reported by Murphy, Abel, and Becker (1980) to be greater with exhibitionism than other sexual offenses. Exhibitionists made up 21 of 45 sex offenders consecutively seeking treatment in two studies (McConaghy, Armstrong, & Blaszczynski, 1985; McConaghy, Blaszczynski, & Kidson, 1988). The majority reported they were happily married. Ten of the 21 had carried out additional sexual offenses, mostly sexual assaults or pedophilic acts. With the latter acts, exposure may have been incidental. Onset of exposure usually commenced in adolescence, but subjects were not charged until adulthood.

Voyeurism

The DSM-III-R criterion for voyeurism is that, over a 6-month period, the person has acted on or is markedly distressed by recurrent urges or fantasies involving the act of observing an unsuspecting person who is naked, is in the process of disrobing, or is engaged in sexual activity. R. S. Smith (1976), in his excellent review of the literature on voyeurism, pointed out the lack of uniformity in classification. Gebhard, Gagnon, Pomeroy, and Christenson (1965) used the term *peepers* for males who, for their sexual gratification, looked into a private area or room with the hope of seeing females nude or partially nude without the consent of the females. Commonly, peepers frequent motels, blocks of units, or houses where they peeped successfully in the past, or they may spend hours walking or driving through a neighborhood at night in search of lighted bathrooms or bedrooms. They may enter private property in search of an opportunity to successfully peep, an activity that can lead to their arrest. While peeping, the subject frequently masturbates. This form of voyeurism is the one that commonly leads to criminal charges or requests for therapy rather than the voyeuristic paraphilias of *troilism,* the observation of consenting couples having sexual relations, or *coprophilia,* the observation of a person urinating or defecating. R. S. Smith (1976) referred to a case report of a woman being an eager observer in a troilistic act. Peeping appears to be exclusively carried out by men, and usually commences in adolescence. Treatment is sometimes sought for the rarely reported homosexual voyeurism, which may cause the subject to compulsively spend a considerable amount of time in public lavatories, and for the equally compulsive observation of couples having intercourse in carparks or "lovers' lanes." Occasional episodes of exhibitionism are reported by peepers, and vice versa. Peeping in private property may tempt the subject to sexual assault or theft. Ordinarily, peepers maintain a satisfactory heterosexual relationship.

Pedophilia

The DSM-III-R criterion for pedophilia is that, over a 6-month period, the person has acted upon or been markedly distressed by recurrent urges or fantasies involving sexual activity with a prepubertal child or children. The person is at least 16 years old and at least 5 years older than the child or children. Pedophilia is often acknowledged only when subjects are charged with the offense and is much more common than the frequency of charges indicate. In part depending on how the activity is defined, 8 to 28 percent of women and 5 to 10 percent of men report having had sexual activity with an adult during their childhood (Freund, Heasman, & Roper, 1982; Russell, 1983). Freund et al. (1982) commented on the enormous discrepancy in the percentages of reports of excessive physical force in these offenses, ranging from 5 to 58 percent. A more remarkable discrepancy is in the reported incidence of incestuous pedophilia, the number of victims rising from 1 in a million in the 1950s to 12 percent of women in the 1980s (Russell, 1983). Homosexual attraction of adults to pubertal or immediately postpubertal boys, termed *hebephilia* (Freund et al., 1982), is not specifically classified in DSM-III-R. Such attraction is commonly exclusive and resistant to treatment. To act on the attraction is both illegal and socially condemned, so it is a major problem to its subjects and for society.

Heterosexual and homosexual pedophilia differ markedly. Groth and Birnbaum (1978) investigated 175 men convicted of pedophilia. Of those subjects whose victims were girls, the majority were predominantly attracted to adult women, were married, and showed no evidence of pedophilia interest in adolescence. Their victims were related or well known to them. Of subjects whose victims were boys, the majority were single and had been exclusively attracted to male children since puberty. Their victims were strangers or casual acquaintances. Homosexual pedophiles (and hebephiles) commonly seek victims in pinball parlors or places in which young people congregate. Many homosexual pedophiles are of average or above-average intelligence, yet are totally disinterested in social relations with adults. Their victims may number many hundreds, and the offense is rarely repeated with the same victim. Offenders against girls usually have at most two or three victims who are relatives or family friends. They are commonly primarily attracted to postpubertal women. At the time of the offense, they may have been sexually deprived. They are more likely to be heavy drinkers, of lower socioeconomic class and with little schooling, who have committed other criminal offenses and repeated the offense with the same child recurrently (Lukianowicz, 1972; Swanson, 1968). The association with lower socioeconomic class may not be an artifact of reporting. Of Finkelhor's (1980) sample of college undergraduates, 33 percent of girls from lower income families were sexually victimized, compared with 19 percent of the total sample.

Women rarely commit pedophilic acts. In England, 1 percent of all sex offenses are committed by women. Of 81 women convicted of sex offenses, 39 (48 percent) were convicted of offenses against subjects younger than 16 years old (O'Connor, 1987). O'Connor commented that none of the 39 women noted sexual gratification as a motivation. Nine of the women were the mother or stepmother of their victims. Twenty-five were convicted of indecent acts, half of whom had suffered from psychiatric illness. Fourteen were convicted of involvement in unlawful sexual intercourse. Most of the latter had been aiders and abettors of men, and 2 of them had suffered from psychiatric illness.

Sexual Sadism and Masochism

The criterion for sexual sadism and masochism, which are defined separately in DSM-III-R, is acting on or being distressed for at least 6 months by recurrent intense sexual urges and sexually arousing fantasies of causing or receiving sexually exciting psychological or physical suffering. The victim experiencing the suffering is masochistic, whereas the person inflicting the suffering is sadistic. The sadistic acts listed in the DSM-III-R include dominance by forcing the victim to crawl, or by physically restraining, blindfolding, hurting, raping, mutilating, or killing the victim. Rape or other sexual assault in which the suffering inflicted on the victim is far in excess of that necessary for compliance and in which the visible pain of the victim is sexually arousing, is considered in DSM-III-R to be an expression of sexual sadism. Such acts are carried out by less than 10 percent of rapists. Some rapists are considered to be sexually aroused by forcing a person to engage in intercourse, but not by the victim's suffering. This discrimination between arousal by forcing victims but not by causing their suffering appears unsupported by evidence. It possibly was determined by the ideologically based belief that rape is not sexually motivated.

Koss and Oros (1982) provided data to support the concept that rape represents an extreme behavior on a continuum with normal male behavior. Six percent of 2,016 women university students considered themselves to have been raped, whereas 2.7 percent of 1,846 male students reported that they had used some degree of physical force to have intercourse with a woman against her will. Over 20 percent of the men reported having been so sexually aroused that it was useless for the women to try to stop them, even though the women did not want intercourse. Heilbrun and Loftus (1986) reported that 19 of 50 single undergraduate men reported more than one episode when their dating partners had expressed dissatisfaction because the men had exceeded the sexual limits the partners would have preferred. The men who reported such sexually aggressive behavior were more likely to consider women who displayed fear, anger, disgust, and sadness to be more sexually attractive than women who displayed happiness. Male college students who reported some likelihood of committing rape if they could be sure of not being caught were more aroused by rape depictions, showed greater aggression against women in a laboratory setting (Malamuth, 1981), and reported greater sexual arousal to stories with a sadomasochistic theme (Malamuth, Haber, & Feshback, 1980). Fantasies of tying up or raping a woman are used at times for sexual arousal by a significant proportion of normal men (Crepault & Couture, 1980; D. Smith & Over, 1987). Most of 54 male undergraduates reported pictures of distressed women in bondage to be more sexually stimulating than those of similar women displaying positive affect (Heilbrun & Leif, 1988). These findings support Heilbrun and Loftus's (1986) suggestion that a continuity exists between normal men sexually stimulated by female distress and clinical sadists who introduce physical violence into their sexual aggression. These data cast doubt on the DSM-III-R statement that 90 percent of rapists are not sexually aroused by the victim's suffering.

Sadistic or masochistic subjects rarely seek treatment, so information concerning their behaviors has been gained mainly from questionnaires completed by members of sadomasochistic clubs or advertisers in magazines. Gosselin and Wilson (1980) were able to interview some responders and gained the impression that most sadists had no wish to hurt their partners in their "sex games" any more than was enjoyed or at least accepted by the partners. Many sadists may be aroused by the victims' pleasure or sexual arousal, rather than by their suffering from acts that are painful or humiliating or that render them helpless. In an earlier German study, most sadomasochistic responders were male and predominantly bisexual or homosexual. The few women subjects were paid for their services (Spengler, 1977). In more recent U.S. studies, responders have been 20 to 30 percent female, most of whom were not prostitutes. Sadomasochistic men were predominantly heterosexual, whereas the women were inclined to bisexuality, were more submissive, were less likely to need sadomasochistic activity to have a satisfactory sexual response, and were more likely to feel as if they were having a nervous breakdown at times (Breslow, Evans, & Langley, 1985; Moser & Levitt, 1987). Most responders in the studies were both sadistic and masochistic. Over 50 percent of men and 21 percent of the responding women were aware of sadomasochistic interest by age 14. Most of the men considered it natural from childhood; most women were introduced to it (Breslow et al., 1985). Beating, bondage, and fetishistic practices were common, and more extreme or dangerous practices were rare. Self-bondage and pain infliction during masturbation were reported by a significant minority. Subjects were above average in intelligence and social status, and most wished to continue sadomasochistic activities.

The DSM-III-R description linking bondage and domination with stabbing, strangulation, torture, mutilation, or killing encourages the widespread public acceptance of a strong association between sadomasochism and crimes of violence. Crimes involving aspects of sadism and masochism obtain enormous media attention; however, they are rare compared with homicides occurring in the context of apparently normal sexual relationships (Swigert, Farrell, & Yoels, 1976).

Under masochism, the DSM-III-R includes hypoxphilia, sexual arousal by oxygen deprivation. Oxygen deprivation could be produced by a noose, ligature, plastic bag, mask, or chemical (often a volatile nitrite), or by chest compression. DSM-III-R stated that subjects report the activity to be accompanied by sexual fantasies in which they asphyxiate or harm others, others asphyxiate or harm them, or they escape near brushes with death. Presumably, the former two fantasies, unsupported by published data, were considered justification for classification of the condition under masochism.

The literature on the condition consists mainly of reports of accidental fatalities. The largest series is of 132 cases reported by Hazelwood, Deitz, and Burgess (1983). Thirty-seven of the cases were teenagers, and 5 were female. The authors speculated that the behavior results in 500 to 1,000 deaths in the United States and Canada yearly. It is distinguished from suicide by the characteristic mode of death. The apparatus used to induce oxygen deprivation may show evidence of regular use or of the failsafe procedure that proved ineffective. There are often indications of autoerotic activity, such as the presence of erotic literature, exposure of the genitals, evidence of emission, and sometimes cross-dressing, fetishism, bondage, and/or additional pain-producing devices. Contacts of the subjects were often aware of the activity but ignored it.

Subjects who use nitrites in sexual activities usually state that they use them to enhance sexual excitement or disinhibition and do not consider that they are producing a degree of asphyxia. Most would be surprised to learn of the asphyxia or harmful fantasies attributed to nitrites by DSM-III-R. Classification of use of nitrites or even more extreme forms of sexual asphyxia as masochistic seems open to question.

Fetishism

The DSM-III-R restricts fetishism to a 6-month period of recurrent, intense sexual urges and fantasies involving the use of nonliving objects, usually bras, women's underpants, stockings, shoes, boots, or other wearing apparel. The diagnosis is not made when the fetishes are limited to articles of female clothing used in cross-dressing, as in transvestic fetishism. Fetishism in males that involves the use of female clothes for sexual arousal but minimal desire to dress in them or tendency to feel like a member of the opposite sex when so dressed appears to be on a continuum with transvestic fetishism, as defined in DSM-III-R as intense urges to cross-dress. The older diagnoses that treat fetishism, transvestism, and transsexualism as three separate conditions but with intermediate states, match the clinical data more appropriately than do the DSM-III-R categories. Arousal by some body part, usually the hair, feet, or hands, or a deformity or mutilation of the human body of the preferred sex, disproportionate to the arousal to secondary sexual characteristics, is excluded from fetishism by DSM-III-R and is classified as partialism among the paraphilias otherwise not specified.

Of 48 subjects who sought treatment at a psychiatric hospital over 20 years and were diagnosed as suffering from fetishism (Chalkley & Powell, 1983), 17 reported only one fetish and 22 reported three or more. The most common festishes were for clothing; 28 subjects reported such fetishes, including 10 whose object was men's pants. Seven had fetishes for parts of the body, 7 for footwear, and 7 for rubber, including tubes and enemas. Forty-seven were men; the only woman was a lesbian who reported having a fetish for breasts. Ten subjects stated a homosexual sexual preference. As DSM-III-R points out, the fetishist frequently masturbates while holding, rubbing, or smelling the fetish or may ask the sexual partner to wear it during sexual activity. The fetish-related behaviors listed by Chalkley and Powell in their 48 subjects were wearing clothes or footwear (21 subjects); stealing, mainly clothes (18); observing someone dressed in clothes or rubber items (11); gazing at the fetish (6); inserting it up the rectum (6); hoarding it (6); and, more rarely, fondling, sucking, following, rolling in, burning, and cutting or snipping the fetish. I have also noted the burying and digging up of clothes and the rescuing, cleaning, and preserving in plastic bags of discarded gloves. Chalkley and Powell stated that few of their subjects reported that they were markedly dependent on the fetish for sexual arousal; however, their information was from case notes, and the question may not have been asked. That statement is contrary to DSM-III-R and my experience with patients.

Gosselin and Wilson (1980) found that fetishistic fantasies were common in sadomasochists, and vice versa, and concluded that fetishists and sadomasochists were similar. This conclusion is consistent with the behavior of fetishists who request partners to stand on them in shoes or who use rubber clothes or corsets to produce bodily constriction. Beating, bondage, and fetishistic practices were reported commonly by the sadomasochist responders in the studies reviewed earlier.

Frotteurism

Frotteurism, sexual arousal produced by touching and rubbing against a nonconsenting person, generally in crowded situations, is classified as an individual paraphilia by DSM-III-R. It appears rare that subjects with the condition seek treatment, and the literature concerning it is sparse. The DSM-III-R description claims that frotteurs usually fantasize an exclusive, caring relationship with the victim while engaged in the activity. Forty-eight of 139 paraphiliacs investigated by Freund, Scher, and Hucker (1983) reported toucherism, associated in 38 with other paraphilias, mainly exhibitionism and voyeurism. Fantasies were not reported.

Telephone scatologia (lewdness), necrophilia (corpses), partialism, zoophilia (animals), coprophilia (feces), klismaphilia (enemas), and urophilia (urine) are classified in DSM-III-R as paraphilias not otherwise specified. Since few individuals with these difficulties seek treatment, prevalence rates are unknown. Of 500 women in Albuquerque, 8 percent reported being victims of obscene phone calls, compared with 4 percent who reported being victims of voyeurs and 30 percent victims of exhibitionists (DiVasto et al., 1984).

Diagnosis

Assessment of paraphilias by investigating subjects' penile responses to erotic stimuli relevant to the paraphilia is considered the most valid method in North America (McConaghy, 1989a). The method was introduced following demonstration that men's sexual orientation could be determined from their penile volume responses (PVRs) to brief exposures (10 to 13 seconds) of pictures of nude men and women. Many researchers have employed penile circumference responses (PCRs) instead of PVRs in their work, assuming that PCRs would be equivalent to PVRs. Unlike PVRs, however, PCRs cannot be used to assess the initial stage of penile erection to erotic stimuli. In that stage, some subjects show penile length increases at such a rate that, while penile volume is increasing, circumference is decreasing (Earls & Marshall, 1982; McConaghy, 1974). To diagnose paraphilias by PCRs, stimuli lasting 2 to 5 minutes need to be employed, enabling subjects to have more time to develop sexual fantasies, and thus their responses could be modified (Alford, Wedding, & Jones, 1983). Such modification may have contributed to the failure of replication of earlier studies, which reported successful PCR assessment of rapists and pedophiles. These data are summarized in Table 11.1.

Despite the absence of consistent evidence of the validity of PCR assessment of paraphiliacs as groups, let alone as individuals, Marshall, Earls, Segal, and Darke (1983) recommended routine PCR assessment of individual rapists and child molesters. Marshall and Barbaree (1988) recently reported that reduction in PCRs to deviant stimuli following treatment did not predict child molesters' likelihood to reoffend. In their review of outcome evaluation of paraphiliacs, Kilmann, Sabalis, Gearing, Bukstel, and Scobern (1982) had earlier concluded that PCR assessment was of questionable validity.

PVRs to relevant paraphilic stimuli that could be presented in about 10 seconds should validly assess deviant arousal. Using 14-second movies of nudes of both sexes, aged 6 to 24 years, Freund, Chan, and Coulthard (1979) investigated the PVRs of subjects charged with pedophilia or hebephilia. Eighty-eight subjects admitted attraction to children or adolescents. Only 4 were misclassified as preferring adults; however, 21 pedophiles were misclassified as hebephiles. Eighteen did not admit attraction to children or adolescents. Six were misclassified as preferring adult females, and 6 others as

TABLE 11.1.   Validation of Penile Circumference Response (PCR) Assessment of Paraphilias

Rapists

Mean PCRs of a group of convicted rapists to individualized audiotapes of forced versus consenting intercourse

- were larger (Abel, Barlow, Blanchard, & Guild, 1977; Barbaree, Marshall, & Lanthier, 1979).
- were smaller (in much larger group) (Baxter, Barbaree, & Marshall, 1986).
- did not differ from those of nonrapists (Baxter et al., 1986; Murphy, Krisar, Stalgaitis, & Anderson, 1984).

Rape index

- correctly identified 80 percent of rapists and 73 percent of nonrapists (Abel et al., 1978).
- failed to discriminate rapists from nonrapists (Murphy et al., 1984).

Pedophiles

Mean PCRs of abusers of female children to pictures of nude female children compared with PCRs to pictures of nude males and females of other ages

- were larger (Quinsey, Steinman, Bergersen, & Holmes, 1975).
- were not larger (Baxter, Marshall, Barbaree, Davidson, & Malcolm, 1984; Quinsey, Chaplin, & Carrigan, 1979).

Pedophile aggressive index to 2-minute audiotapes of forced and nonforced sexual activity with children

- differentiated more from less dangerous child abusers (Abel, Becker, Murphy, & Flanagan, 1981).
- did not differentiate more from less dangerous child abusers (Avery-Clark & Laws, 1984).

hebephiles. All offenders misclassified as preferring adults offended against girls. Two of 62 controls were misclassified as erotically preferring male children. The number misclassified as preferring female children was not reported. Freund, McKnight, Langevin, and Cibiri (1972) had earlier reported that normal heterosexual men as a group showed PVR evidence of arousal to pictures of nude female children. As a group, men attracted to male children showed little response to pictures of adult men or women (Freund, Langevin, Wescom, & Zajac, 1975). It is possible that some of the sex offenders (and controls) in Freund et al.'s (1979) study were not misclassified in terms of their erotic preference. Freund had earlier suggested that some men who offend against female children do not erotically prefer them to adult women. Fifteen percent of men (mostly psychology students) expressed some likelihood of engaging in pedophilia if they could be assured of not being caught or punished (Finkelhor & Lewis, 1988).

Fifteen (62.5 percent) of 24 exhibitionists who denied toucherism showed PVRs to 50-second verbal descriptions of exposure as large as or larger than those to descriptions of sexual tactile interactions or intercourse (Freund et al., 1983). Nine (18.4 percent) of 49 controls showed a similar pattern. If the findings were replicated, the test would seem insufficiently sensitive or specific for individual diagnosis.

McConaghy (1988), in a review of methods of diagnosis and assessment of sexual deviations and dysfunctions, concluded that subjects' self-reports as evaluated by clinical interview remain the major source of relevant information. Where possible, such self-reports should be supplemented by reports from the subjects' contacts, including legal and probationary sources in the case of sex offenders. Evidence of the validity of self-reports, at least in the early stage of treatment, has been provided (McConaghy et al., 1988). In sex offenders treated by medroxyprogesterone, strong correlations were found between subjects' reports of the strength of their paraphilic urges and their serum testosterone levels, of which they and the interviewer were unaware.

Etiology

In the 1970s, it seemed accepted without question, at least by behavioral clinicians, that paraphilias were motivated by strong sexual arousal to stimuli that produced little or no arousal in normal subjects. Thus, aversive therapy often was employed in treatment, with the expectation that it would produce conditioned aversions to the relevant stimuli. Such aversions were expected to inhibit the deviant sexual arousal; however, treated subjects were found not to experience aversions to the relevant stimuli, although they reported being able to control the sexual urges they had previously experienced as uncontrollable (McConaghy, 1982). Subjects with compulsive homosexuality who reported such control following treatment continued to show arousal to homosexual stimuli, as evidenced by their PVRs. To account for this paradoxical response of control without reduction in physiological sexual arousal, a behavior-completion hypothesis was advanced (McConaghy, 1980, 1983).

According to the hypothesis, the central nervous system builds up neuronal models of habitual behaviors. Once an habitual behavior is initiated, if incoming stimuli do not match the neuronal model to indicate that the behavior is not being completed, the model for that behavior activates the arousal system. Hence, in subjects who have habitually carried out paraphilic acts, attempts not to complete the acts when they are stimulated to do so will activate the neuronal models for the acts. The resultant increase in arousal causes the subjects to experience high anxiety or tension, which many find sufficiently aversive that they complete the acts even though initially they did not wish to do so. The neuronal models thus act as physiological behavior-completion mechanisms. This hypothesis led to the development of imaginal desensitization as a treatment for compulsive behaviors. The effectiveness of this treatment supported the hypothesis, as did the correlations found between successful response and reduction in tension in the subjects treated (McConaghy et al., 1985; McConaghy et al., 1988). The behavior-completion hypothesis accounted for the ability of treated subjects to control sexual feelings that they continued to experience.

An alternative therapy, based on a conception that some paraphiliacs were not motivated by sexual feelings, was advanced in the 1970s. It attributed the behaviors to males' needs to dominate. The literature supporting the concept in relation to rape was critically reviewed by Palmer (1988); however, he did not examine the evidence from the physiological assessment of sexual arousal.

Marshall et al. (1983) found no difference between the PCRs of rapists and normals listening to descriptions of rape. They concluded that some rapists have deviant sexuality but that most are motivated by needs for power, aggression, and humiliation. This conclusion is incompatible with the findings that most paraphiliacs, including the sexually assaultive, respond to androgen suppression therapy (Gagne, 1981), and that reduction in paraphilic urge correlates with reduction in testosterone level (McConaghy et al., 1988). These data suggest that sexual motivation must play a role in maintaining paraphilic behaviors. When the compulsive element due to behavior-completion mechanisms is removed by treatment, however, the paraphiliac can control or cease the behavior while still experiencing the sexual motivation. Hence, many normals could have a potential for paraphilic arousal but not carry out the paraphilic behavior, because their previous experience had not caused them to develop the relevant behavior-completion mechanisms. Male or female college students reported regular fantasies during masturbation or intercourse of being observed or of observing others in sexual activity, and of forcing others or being forced into sexual activities (Price & Miller, 1984). Evidence of the likelihood of male students engaging in sexual assault and pedophilia was discussed earlier. Moser and Levitt (1987) reviewed reports of sexual arousal of normal men and women to sadomasochistic fantasies and mild behaviors. Twenty percent of normal men showed PVR evidence of strong arousal to descriptions of exhibitionism, similar to those shown by 60 percent of exhibitionists (Freund et al., 1983).

If it could be demonstrated that the increased incidence of paraphilic PVR arousal in the exhibitionists in Freund et al.'s (1983) study was not a consequence of their behavior, the finding would indicate that such arousal predisposes men to exhibitionism. The majority of the 20 percent of men experiencing such arousal do not become exhibitionists, however, so additional factors must be of importance. This is also likely to be true of the other paraphilias in which the paraphilic stimuli produce a degree of sexual interest or arousal in normals.

Apart from the role of deviant arousal in the etiology of paraphilias, personality factors are commonly considered significant. It has been claimed that exhibitionists are shy and unassertive (Langevin et al., 1979), and that child molesters are passive and socially inadequate (Levin & Stava, 1987). Levin and Stava reviewed 36 studies of the personality of sex offenders. Little evidence was provided that the personality of exhibitionists differed from that of normals. Some evidence indicated that rapists and child molesters were guilt-ridden individuals who inhibited aggression, but the studies did not control for the subjects having committed criminal offenses, having been incarcerated in jails, or having expressed feelings of guilt to aid their legal disposition. Sexually assaultive men showed reduced social perception and heterosocial and homosocial skills compared with middle-class men, but not with men of similar socioeconomic background or nonsex offenders (Marshall et al., 1983; Quinsey, 1984).

Adventitious exposure to situations provoking paraphilic behaviors could account for the commencement of such behaviors by subjects falling within the normal range of arousal to those situations. Some exhibitionists and voyeurs reported accidentally seeing a woman naked or being seen naked by a woman as the first occasion of the paraphilia, an incident that they subsequently deliberately repeated. The behavior then became compulsive and was continued after they commenced normal sexual activities. At times, pedophilia is initiated impulsively in relation to an unprovoked opportunity, such as sharing a bed or a bath with a child. Hazelwood et al. (1983) suspected that sexual asphyxia most commonly originated in the fortuitous discovery of its sexually arousing qualities. Breslow et al. (1985) commented that men seemed to discover sadomasochism on their own, whereas women were introduced to it by a sexual partner.

Exhibitionists, voyeurs, and some heterosexual pedophiles and rapists may not experience greater than normal arousal to the relevant paraphilic stimuli, at least initially. This would seem not to be the case with homosexual pedophiles, fetishists, and transvestites. The childhood development of fetishism would appear to negate the theory that fetishism is established in association with sexual arousal at puberty. Rachman (1966) considered the theory supported by his demonstration that penile responses could be conditioned to pictures of women's boots. The presence of loving or hostile feelings to the fetish and the use of diapers as fetishes suggested a possible relationship with transitional objects, involving imprinting (McConaghy, 1984). Evidence that temporal lobe epilepsy predisposed subjects to fetishism, including transvestic fetishism, was not supported by studies of the prevalence of fetishism relative to other paraphilias in epileptics (Kolarsky, Freund, Machek, & Polak, 1967; Shukla, Srivastava, & Katiyar, 1979). The resemblance of transvestism in adult men to female grooming behavior raises the possibility that, like other sex-linked behaviors (McConaghy, 1984), it is established at a critical period in intrauterine development by exposure to opposite sex hormones. No theories appear to have been advanced to explain why, unlike heterosexual pedophiles, homosexual pedophiles (and hebephiles) show minimal attraction to adults of either sex.

Clinical Management

Subjects convicted of paraphilic behavior who minimize or deny it, may come to admit and wish to control it with counseling. Control of compulsive illegal or unacceptable behaviors can be achieved by behavioral methods or androgen-suppressing chemicals. McConaghy et al. (1988) reported that 80 percent of subjects who sought treatment for compulsive paraphilias responded when randomly allocated to a 1-week course of imaginal desensitization or to a 6-month course of medroxyprogesterone. A further 10 percent responded to the addition of the other treatment or to aversive therapy. Ten percent relapsed in the 2 to 5 years following treatment, but responded to further therapy. Resistance to treatment was mainly in adolescents (McConaghy, Blaszczynski, Armstrong, & Kidson, 1989). With imaginal desensitization, subjects are trained to relax. They then visualize being stimulated to carry out the paraphilia, but not doing so and leaving the situation while remaining relaxed. Medroxyprogesterone was given in 150-milligram injections fortnightly four times and monthly four times. Reduction in paraphilic urge correlated with reduction in testosterone level. Both treatments were considered not to permanently modify the subject's sexual interest, but to reduce the compulsive urge, which was maintained by behavior-completion mechanisms. Additional treatment, such as social skills training, is added where it appears appropriate; however, there is no convincing evidence of its value. I have found homosexual pedophiles and hebephiles particularly resistant to developing even social relations with adults of either sex.

Most North American researchers believe it is possible to reduce deviant sexual interest by aversive therapy or satiation techniques and to increase heterosexual arousability by masturbatory reconditioning. Subjects masturbate for extended periods to deviant fantasies with satiation and to heterosexual fantasies with masturbatory reconditioning. Single-case studies using PCRs, which are claimed to demonstrate the efficacy of these therapies, have been criticized (McConaghy, 1982; 1990). Marshall and Barbaree (1988) reported the use of these techniques with child molesters; 5 percent followed up for 1 to 2 years reoffended, as did 25 percent after 4 years. The reoffense rate was significantly less than the 60 percent rate of an untreated nonrandomized control group after 4 years. PCRs did not predict outcome.

SEXUAL DYSFUNCTIONS

Description and DSM-III-R Diagnosis

DSM-III-R provides separate criteria for reduced desire for sexual activity; aversion to sexual activity; lack of physiological or sexual arousal during sexual activity in women; failure to attain or maintain erection or to experience sexual excitement during sexual activity (usually intercourse rather than masturbation) in men, taking age into account; premature ejaculation; dyspareunia, persistent genital pain in relation to sexual intercourse; and vaginismus, spasm of the musculature of the outer third of the vagina that interferes with intercourse.

Many of these dysfunctions are self-explanatory; however, some require further clarification here. Vaginismus may be accompanied by spasm of the adductor muscles of the thighs, preventing their separation when intercourse is attempted. Vaginismus usually results when an attempt is made to penetrate the vagina with any object, including one the patient attempts to insert herself. The patient with vaginismus may experience sexual excitement and pleasure and reach orgasm by activities that do not involve penetration. Vaginismus will inevitably be associated with dyspareunia if intercourse is attempted, the pain being experienced at the entrance to or just within the vagina. It almost always is due to psychological rather than organic factors, unlike deep pelvic pain, the other common form of dyspareunia, which is usually produced or intensified by thrusting after full penetration. DSM-III-R defines premature ejaculation as occurring before, upon, or shortly after penetration and before the person wishes it. Some men seek treatment when they can maintain intercourse for some minutes but not long enough for their partner to reach orgasm. The clinical features of the sexual dysfunctions are sufficiently specific that the only diagnostic problems they present are determining the degree to which organic factors contribute to their etiology and determining whether they are secondary to another DSM-III-R Axis I disorder.

Prevalence

Most subjects with sexual dysfunctions do not present for treatment. Frank, Anderson, and Rubinstein (1978) investigated 100 predominantly white, well-educated, happily married couples. Sixty-three percent of women reported sexual dysfunctions and 77 percent sexual difficulties. The most common dysfunctions were difficulty getting excited (48 percent) and difficulty reaching orgasm (46 percent). The most common difficulties were inability to relax (47 percent), too little foreplay before intercourse (38 percent), disinterest (35 percent), partner choosing an inconvenient time (31 percent), and being "turned off" (28 percent). Forty percent of men reported sexual dysfunctions and 50 percent sexual difficulties. The most common dysfunctions were ejaculating too quickly (36 percent) and difficulty maintaining (9 percent) and getting (7 percent) an erection. Difficulties included attraction to persons other than mate (21 percent), too little foreplay before intercourse (21 percent), too little tenderness after intercourse (17 percent), and disinterest and partner choosing an inconvenient time (16 percent). Despite the high incidence of sexual dysfunctions and difficulties in this apparently normal group, 85 percent of both men and women found their sexual relations very or moderately satisfying. A major finding of interest was that reported sexual difficulties in subjects and their spouses correlated more highly with lack of satisfaction than did dysfunctions in themselves and their spouses. The authors noted the comparable frequency in their normal sample of sexual difficulties and dysfunctions, particularly orgasmic dysfunctions in women, with those of the patient population of Masters and Johnson (1970).

Of a community sample in the United Kingdom of 436 women aged 35 to 59 who were living with partners, 142 reported at least one of four operationally defined dysfunctions: impaired sexual interest (17 percent), vaginal dryness (17 percent), infrequency of orgasm (16 percent), and dyspareunia (8 percent) (Osborn, Hawton, & Gath, 1988). Diagnostic criteria were more stringent than those used by Frank et al. (1978). Only 32 of the 142 women with dysfunctions considered themselves to have sexual problems, as did a further 10 who had no dysfunction. Of all 42, 16 said they wished treatment if it were available, and 1 was receiving it. A significant percentage of women who reported coital orgasm experience it on less than 50 percent of occasions, and many stated that they enjoy intercourse very much although they do not reach orgasm (Butler, 1976; Fisher, 1973; M. Hunt, 1974). Butler further reported that 58 percent of women pretend to reach orgasm on occasion. Most homosexual men do not reach orgasm in the receptor role with anal intercourse, and a number report not reaching orgasm by any method in many of their sexual relationships, which they nevertheless enjoy. The need to reach orgasm may be more a function of role than gender.

Prevalence of dysfunctions in samples of healthy males in Sweden (Nettelbladt & Uddenberg, 1979) and the United Kingdom (Reading & Wiest, 1984) was similar to that found by Frank et al. (1978), except that higher percentages (10 and 16 percent, respectively) reported difficulty achieving climax. These two studies also found no association between premature ejaculation or erectile difficulties and sexual satisfaction in the male and, in the Swedish study, of the female partner also. These findings indicate the limitations of the medical model classificatory approach to sexually related problems of adults. This is even more true of adolescents in whom issues of sexual assault and incest, sexually transmitted diseases, self-identification as homosexual, and pregnancy and its prevention or termination in abortion or motherhood are of major clinical significance (McConaghy, 1989b).

Natural History and Course

Over 50 percent of adolescent unmarried girls rarely or never reach orgasm in heterosexual relations (Sorensen, 1973). This is true of 25 percent of women in their first year of marriage, but of less than 10 percent of women in their twentieth year (M. Hunt, 1974; Kinsey, Pomeroy, Martin, & Gebhard, 1953). Hence, the majority of anorgasmic teenagers will become orgasmic in time without therapy.

The prevalence rates for complete inability to attain erection are approximately 1 percent at 35, 6 percent at 50, 18 percent at 60, 27 percent at 70, and 55 percent at 75 years of age (Kinsey, Pomeroy, & Martin, 1948; Weizman & Hart, 1987). With aging, it takes men longer to reach full erection and to climax, their erection may be less firm, and their ejaculation may be reduced in amount and force. Many men over 50 will not obtain an erection without manual stimulation of the penis. Some find these changes difficult to accept as part of their normal aging process, or fail to discuss them with their partner, and at times attempt intercourse only when they have a nocturnal or morning erection.

Decline in sexual interest and activity and increased dyspareunia in women following menopause has been reported in a number of studies reviewed by Sarrel (1987). Pfeiffer, Verwoerdt, and Davis (1972), from the Duke University Center for the Study of Aging, reported that the percentage of subjects who had ceased intercourse increased in women from 13 percent at age 46 to 50 to 73 percent at age 66 to 71, and in men from 0 to 23 percent at these ages. Bretschneider and McCoy (1988) reported that of 100 white men and 102 white women aged 80 to 102 who were healthy and living in retirement villages, the percentage of women reporting cessation of intercourse (70 percent) was in the same range as that of the younger women in Pfeiffer et al.'s study, but that of men (38 percent) was greater, indicating leveling off in women but a steady increase with age in men. Weizman and Hart (1987) reported that increased frequency of masturbation was associated with decline in frequency of intercourse in elderly men. Presumably, the decline can be attributed to an increased incidence of impotence. Pfeiffer, Verwoerdt, and Wang (1969) reported that among biologically advantaged subjects, 80 percent of men but only 40 percent of women retained sexual interest from 65 to 75. Women's lack of interest appeared related to the absence of a male partner.

Clinical Presentation

Many women with coital anorgasmia see no need for treatment. Indeed, if they did, they would exhaust available treatment facilities. In the 1970s, the majority of women who sought treatment for sexual problems did so for this condition (Kaplan, 1974; Masters & Johnson, 1970); however, of 45 couples presenting with sexual dissatisfaction (Snyder & Berg, 1983), the women's complaints of anorgasmia, difficulty maintaining arousal, and lack of sexual interest were virtually identical in frequency (69, 67, and 67 percent). The most common complaints in the men were low frequency of intercourse (87 percent) and their partner's being nonorgasmic (60 percent). Premature ejaculation (56 percent) and lack of sexual interest (45 percent) were also commonly reported. Complaints of erectile difficulties (25 percent) were not as high as might be expected from their prevalence. As in the studies of normal samples, erectile and ejaculatory dysfunctions in men were unrelated to their or their partners' sexual satisfaction. However, in 28 couples presenting for both marital and sexual problems in the United Kingdom (Rust, Golombok, & Collier, 1988), correlations were reported between both partners' dissatisfaction on an Inventory of Marital State and erectile and ejaculatory dysfunctions, but not with dysfunctions in the women.

Etiology

It seems likely that biological factors, many as yet unidentified, contribute to individual differences in sexual interest. Earlier studies found a positive relationship between level of male sex hormone, testosterone, and frequency of sexual activity within individual men but not between them (Brown, Monti, & Corriveau, 1978; Kraemer et al., 1976). Perhaps because of the improved reliability of hormone assessment, more recent studies have found the relationship to be positive between men also. Udry, Billy, Morris, Groff, and Raj (1985) reported that total sexual outlets in adolescent boys correlated with their serum testosterone levels, consistent with the correspondence of the marked rise of male sexual interest and activity and of testosterone levels at puberty. Testosterone levels correlated with frequency of sexual activity leading to orgasm in men aged 19 to 31 (Knussman, Christiansen, & Couwenbergs, 1986), amount of coital and masturbatory activity in healthy men aged 60 to 79 (Tsitouras, Martin, & Harman, 1982), and sexual interest in impotent men (Segraves, Schoenberg, & Ivanoff, 1983). The correlations were weaker with increase in age of the healthy groups studied, suggesting that factors other than hormone levels, such as relationship aspects and behavior-completion mechanisms, may play an increasing role in determining frequency of sexual activity in men. Knussman et al. considered the possibility that raised testosterone levels could be secondary to the subjects' increased sexual activity. Udry et al. argued that they were primary. The results of manipulation of testosterone levels suggest they are at least in part primary. Testosterone administration increased sexual interest in men with reduced interest, both hypogonadal men with low levels (Skakkebaek, Bancroft, Davidson, & Warner, 1981) and men with normal levels (O'Carroll & Bancroft, 1984). Testosterone reduction by withdrawal in hypogonadal men (Skakkebaek et al., 1981) and by testosterone-reducing chemicals in paraphiliacs with normal testosterone levels (Kraemer et al., 1976) reduced sexual interest.

The role of testosterone in maintaining erectile ability appears less established. Although erectile ability is lost in many men following castration, others have been reported to retain copulatory activity up to 16 years post-surgery (Davidson, Camargo, & Smith, 1979). Of 16 paraphiliacs having regular intercourse who were treated for 6 months with medroxyprogesterone, only 2 whose testosterone levels were reduced to 16 percent or less of pretreatment levels reported erectile difficulties (McConaghy et al., 1988). When testosterone levels of prostate cancer patients were reduced to 5 percent of pretreatment levels, 19 percent were still able to maintain erection with sexual activity (Rousseau, Dupont, Labrie, & Couture, 1988). Raboch and Starka's (1973) suggestion that the level of male sex hormone in healthy men is well beyond the threshold necessary for sexual activity would appear correct as far as erectile ability is concerned.

Data concerning biological factors determining sexual interest and activity in women are conflicting. There is no agreement concerning the frequency of sexual activity in relation to phases of the menstrual cycle (Donovan, 1985). Adams, Gold, and Burt (1978) suggested that the conflicting data could be due to failure to separate female-initiated from male-initiated behaviors. They reported that the former but not the latter behaviors peaked at ovulation in married women using contraceptive devices other than the pill. Adams et al. related this to estrogen rather than androgen levels, because estrogen levels, unlike androgen levels, peak strongly at this time and are markedly reduced by oral contraceptives. Cutler, Garcia, and McCoy (1987) reported reduced sexual activity in both young and menopausal women whose estradiol levels were below 35 to 40 per milliliter. Conflicting results have been reported concerning the relationship between normal midcycle testosterone levels and frequency of intercourse. Raising testosterone to above normal levels at times produce clitoral hypertrophy, increased libido, and sexual activity in premenopausal (Donovan, 1985) and menopausal women (Sherwin & Gelfand, 1987). Hirsute women with raised testosterone levels showed increased masturbation but reduced coital frequency compared with matched controls. Following chemical reduction of testosterone levels and addition of estrogen, the frequencies became equivalent to those of the controls without change in total sexual outlets (Adamopoulos, Kampyli, Georgiacodis, Kapolla, & Abrahamian-Michalakis, 1988). The lack of evidence of a strong relationship between women's levels of sexual activity and normal hormone levels is consistent with the much less clearly defined onset of increase in sexual interest and achievement of orgasm with puberty in girls compared with boys, despite the similar rapid onset of such physiologically determined sexual characteristics as pubic hair development (Kinsey et al., 1953). The fact that most women report having intercourse to show and experience love, whereas most men do so for physical gratification (Carroll, Volk, & Hyde, 1985), is also consistent with a weaker relationship between sexual activity and hormonal determinants in women than in men.

Normal biological variation may be responsible for the fact that some women are coitally anorgasmic. Available data suggest that the biological mechanism for orgasm in females may not be strongly based phylogenetically. Orgasm has been reported to occur in individual female dogs, rabbits, cats of all species, and a variety of female primates; however, the majority of females of these species were considered not to reach orgasm, and no evidence of orgasm has been reported in any females of most infrahuman species (Kinsey et al., 1953). This may, of course, be due to the difficulty the observer experiences in recognizing this response, compared with ejaculation. Some women themselves are uncertain whether they have experienced orgasm.

The gradual increase in incidence of orgasmic experience in women from 15 to 45 years of age suggests that learning plays an important role in their attainment of orgasm. Fear of loss of control due to sexual feelings is considered an important cause of women's failure to become sexually aroused and to achieve orgasm, a concept that has received some experimental support (Bridges, Critelli, & Loos, 1985). Mead (1950) pointed out that adolescent girls are expected to determine the limits of sexual experience and boys to attempt to extend these limits. It would seem inevitable that girls would initially fear and attempt to limit their sexual arousal. Subsequently, when they no longer need to do so, they would require time to lose their fear and relinquish control. At least in Western cultures, there is widespread acceptance that women need to learn from men how to become sexually aroused. In M. Hunt's (1974) study of sexual behavior, the men emphasized the importance of learning to arouse their partners, and the women emphasized the importance of learning from men how to become aroused. Mead (1950) appeared to approve that happy sexual relationships in France and Samoa are based on the man's taking pride and pleasure in arousing the female. The need for women to have a male partner if they are to maintain sexual interest in old age would seem in part a consequence of this attitude. Female liberation ideology may result in women taking more responsibility for their sexual arousal.

Both in psychodynamic and learning theories of personality development, childhood experiences are seen as etiologically important in determining female sexual responsivity. However, in his 1938 study, Terman found the following factors unrelated to regular achievement of orgasm in married women: degree of attachment to mother or father, conflict with mother or father, resemblance of spouse to opposite-sex parent, childhood happiness, type of childhood discipline, or amount of punishment. A premarital attitude of disgust to sex was also unrelated. The results of Terman's 1951 study were in the same direction. In both studies, there was some positive correlation between regular achievement of orgasm and quality of sex instruction. A 1973 study found no correlation between achievement of orgasm and the amount of information given about sex, parental attitudes of permissiveness or repressiveness concerning sex or nudity, openness in displaying affection, reaction to onset of menstruation, or attitude to mother (Morokoff, 1978).

No personality traits have emerged consistently in research studies as related to reduced sexual responsiveness in women. Fisher (1973) reported no correlations with degree of femininity, aggressiveness, passivity, guilt, impulsivity, or narcissism. No correlation with neurotic illness was found by Winokur, Guze, & Pfeiffer (1959) or with a personality measure of neuroticism by Cooper (1969). Biological factors, cultural expectations (McConaghy, 1984), and personal experiences enabling women to learn to experience sexual arousal without anxiety may be the major determinants of female sexual responsivity.

Few studies have investigated the sexual arousability of men, for example, the variables influencing amount of pleasure experienced with orgasm. It seems that learning plays a part in men as well as women. Of Schofield's (1968) representative sample of English teenagers, less than half the boys and a third of the girls said they liked their first experience of intercourse. At follow-up 7 years later (Schofield, 1973), however, the majority had continued to have intercourse and only 5 percent did not enjoy it. It seems that cultural factors play a minimal role in the development of men's sexual arousability.

Currently, the most accepted clinical belief concerning etiology of psychosexual dysfunctions is that they result from inhibition of sexual arousal by anxiety, not due to unconscious presexual conflicts as advanced earlier by psychodynamic theorists, but directly associated with sexual activity. This belief, first advanced by Wolpe (1958), was basic to his direct sexual therapy. Although a number of empirical studies have questioned whether anxiety interferes with sexual arousal, Beggs, Calhoun, and Wolchik (1987) pointed out that in such studies anxiety induced in the subjects was nonsexual in context (e.g., threat of shock).

Wolpe suggested that anxiety could be conditioned to sexual activity by such childhood experiences as being exposed to the belief that sinful behavior would be punished by hellfire or to misinformation (e.g., that masturbation weakens the body and the mind), or by gaining the impression that intercourse was painful when overhearing parental intercourse, which possibly is enhanced by a child's experiences leading to anxiety concerning his or her own aggression. Once conditioned, such anxieties persisted in response to sexual stimuli, although the original beliefs could be forgotten or abandoned. Adult experiences, such as a single episode of impotence or premature ejaculation, due to fatigue, illness, or indulgence in alcohol, also could lead to anxiety concerning future failure, which may become conditioned to sexual activity.

Following Wolpe's (1958) advancing this etiological theory, a substantial literature developed various aspects of his formulations, possibly placing greater emphasis on the concept that faulty learning produces inadequate levels of sexual arousal. Hostility to the partner or fear of loss of emotional control also were considered to inhibit arousal, leading particularly to anorgasmia or failure of ejaculation. Factors considered to result in faulty learning included lack of knowledge about sex, particularly of the need for adequate arousal and clitoral stimulation in women; adopting a spectator attitude; and poor communication between partners about the techniques that arouse them (Hogan, 1978). The nature of the sexual difficulties reported by Frank et al.'s (1978) happily married couples suggest that such poor communication is very common.

The successful use of masturbation in treatment to increase the ability of women to reach orgasm (Riley & Riley, 1978) is compatible with the role of faulty learning or inhibition by anxiety in the etiology of this condition. Its successful use in some middle-aged men who developed impotence when they resumed intercourse after an interval of many months, suggests that disuse might also reduce sexual arousability or erectile competence. Predominant homosexual orientation, at times unconscious, can be responsible for reduced heterosexual interest.

Diagnosis

The first requirement of diagnosis is elicitation of the complaint. Just as most women with dysfunctions do not report them (Osborn et al., 1988), only 6 of 401 men with impotence in a sample of 1,080 male medical clinic outpatients reported the problem. When the topic was broached, they were eager to have their impotence evaluated (Slag et al., 1983). The authors emphasized the importance of questioning all patients as to their sexual function. The major diagnostic problem with psychosexual dysfunctions is exclusion of organic factors, or assessment or their significance when present. Illnesses associated with pain, debility, anxiety, or depression can produce dysfunctions secondarily by reducing sexual interest. Other illnesses, such as diabetes or vascular disease, and medications can produce dysfunctions directly. Alcohol, tobacco smoking, and narcotic drugs reduce sexual functioning, both acutely and chronically. Also, oral contraceptives have been reported to impair sexual responsiveness.

In certain sexual dysfunctions, it is advisable to exclude organic factors unless there is strong evidence that the condition is entirely psychogenic. Vaginismus and dyspareunia necessitate gynecological or urological examination for local pathology. The steady rise in the prevalence of impotence from age 35 suggests that organic factors associated with aging contribute significantly. The belief widely held in the 1970's that most cases of impotence were due to psychological rather than organic factors has been reversed (LoPiccolo, 1982). Impotence that occurs only in psychologically threatening situations, such as when intercourse is possible, is clearly psychogenic. Impotence developing insidiously in middle age, unrelated to precipitating situations, and associated with lack of adequate erections during private masturbation, during sleep, and on wakening, is likely to be secondary, due possibly to depression but usually to organic factors, particularly to disturbance of the penile vascular supply or to unknown factors associated with aging. Physical and endocrine investigations are also indicated in men who complain of minimal sexual interest since puberty in the absence of obvious psychological causes, such as marked religious guilt or indications of strong denial of homosexual feelings. Diagnosable organic factors rarely play a role in diminished sexual feelings in premenopausal women or in premature ejaculation in men. Even when organic factors are of significance in the etiology of sexual dysfunctions, psychological factors frequently are involved as well, at least in the form of anxiety concerning performance.

Questionnaires assessing subjects' sexual behaviors have been developed. If not used in conjunction with a clinical interview, it is important that the questionnaire addresses relevant aspects of the behaviors (Andersen & Broffitt, 1988). Measurement of color change within the vagina by photoplethysmography and labial temperature changes by thermistor seem to provide the most sensitive measures of sexual arousal in women (Hoon, 1979); however, their correlations with individual subjects' subjective awareness of sexual arousal and with presence or response to treatment of dysfunctions have proved remarkably inconsistent (Hatch, 1981). The measurement of penile circumference during sleep, "nocturnal penile tumescence," has been used diagnostically on the questionable basis that subjects who obtain regular sustained erections then but not when awake have impotence of psychogenic rather than organic etiology (e.g., Schiavi, Fisher, White, Beers, & Szechter, 1984; Thase, Reynolds, & Jennings, 1988). In the most comprehensive use of this procedure, on the third night of sleep, patients who showed erections were awakened to have the fullness and rigidity of the erection assessed, the latter by means of a pressure device. There is no evidence of the superiority of this expensive procedure over questioning the patient and his partner concerning the frequency and quality of any erections present during the night or on awakening (Saypol, Peterson, Howards, & Yazel, 1983; Segraves, Schoenberg, & Segraves, 1985).

Clinical Management

Life histories and descriptions of the patient's or couple's sexual difficulties and emotional relationships will enable decisions as to whether the presence of organic factors require investigation, whether personality or relationship difficulties require therapy, or whether the sexual difficulty is psychologically determined in the context of an otherwise satisfactory emotional relationship. In the last case, any faulty beliefs or inappropriate attitudes about sexuality are sought and, if present, cognitively corrected. Evidence of present or past anxiety concerning possible harmful consequences of sexual behavior or the need to reach criteria of performance is sought. In the absence of other causes for the sexual dysfunction, current practice is to assume the presence of anxiety and to target it for treatment, using the method recommended by Wolpe (1958). If the patient is in a relationship, the couple is instructed to regularly cuddle together naked and indulge in foreplay activities, but not attempt intercourse. Only when they are free from anxiety and becoming adequately sexually aroused while cuddling does the therapist give them permission to attempt intercourse. Masters and Johnson (1970) subsequently standardized the treatment into three stages, although without advancing evidence that this increased its efficacy.

For premature ejaculation, Masters and Johnson incorporated a penile squeeze technique to delay ejaculation during masturbation by the partner. To enable the anorgasmic woman to learn to climax, masturbation by herself and/or her partner is commonly recommended. Hawton, Catalan, Martin, and Fagg (1986) were able to follow up 75 percent of couples treated with a Masters and Johnson type program, 1 to 6 years later. Fifty-six percent reported resolution of the problem at the end of treatment. Recurrence or continuing difficulty was reported by 75 percent of those followed-up; this had caused little concern to 34 percent, many of whom were able to cope with the difficulty using the techniques learned. Like DeAmicis, Goldberg, LoPiccolo, Friedman, and Davies (1985), Hawton et al. found that long-term outcome was poor for premature ejaculation in men and impaired sexual interest in women. They recommended that the possibility of relapse and ways of coping be discussed before therapy ended.

When the patient presents without a partner, systematic desensitization to situations of increasing sexual intimacy can be successful with dysfunctional women but, in my experience, less often with men. In this case, however, men are more prepared to be treated by a surrogate therapist partner (McConaghy, 1985).

OTHER SEXUAL DISORDERS

Of the examples of other sexual disorders given in DSM-III-R, the only one that is common in my experience is persistent and marked distress about one's sexual orientation, presenting mainly in adolescent or young adult men concerned about homosexual interest or activities. The nature of their concerns is first investigated, and psychiatric conditions warranting treatment are excluded. Counseling is then initiated by discussing the evidence that the degree to which subjects experience heterosexual or homosexual feelings is established in early life, possibly in utero, and can be measured by subjects' penile volume responses to pictures of male and female nudes.

Sexual orientation in this sense has never been shown to be changed by any treatment (McConaghy, 1984). Evidence is then discussed that about 40 percent of adolescents or young adults are aware of a degree of homosexual feelings, along with predominant heterosexual feelings (McConaghy, 1987). The point is made that, whatever the balance of one's sexual feelings, how one expresses those feelings and identifies as heterosexual or homosexual is largely up to the individual.

Compulsive homosexual or heterosexual behaviors or fantasies that the subject wishes to but cannot control respond to treatment, similar to that for compulsive paraphilic behaviors. In DSM-III-R, these behaviors are described as nonparaphilic sexual addictions, involving a succession of people who exist only as things to be used. The appearance of acquired immune deficiency syndrome (AIDS) has led subjects with compulsive sexual activity to seek treatment to reduce the risk of viral exposure.

GENDER IDENTITY DISORDERS

The development of a sex conversion operation for men wanting to live permanently as women led to increased awareness of those subjects. They were differentiated as transsexual (Benjamin, 1954) from other men who cross-dressed periodically in female attire, for whom the term transvestite was retained. Worden and Marsh (1955) considered transsexuals to have a disorder of sexual identity, that is, the sense of being male or female. Money, Hampson, and Hampson (1955) advanced a separate concept of gender role, stating that incongruities could occur in hermaphrodites or pseudohermaphrodites assigned to be raised in one or the other sex. Gender role was defined as all those things that a person says or does to disclose himself or herself as male or female. Freund, Nagler, Langevin, Zajac, and Steiner (1974) described a gender identity scale to measure this behavior. It assessed sex-dimorphic behaviors shown in childhood; assessed gender preference, the wish to be of the opposite sex; and self-assessed masculinity or femininity of appearance. DSM-III-R followed Green and Money (1969) in restricting gender identity to mean only the sense of knowing to which sex one belongs, and retained the term gender role to mean the public expression of gender identity. DSM-III-R states that gender identity disturbance is rare, but also that mild forms exist and that some are on a continuum, whereas others are discrete. This compromise, understandable as a committee decision, allows acceptance of two conflicting views in the literature. One is that normals have a "core gender identity" that is strongly established in the first few years of life (Stoller, 1968). The supporting clinical impressionistic data were derived from studies of sexually anomalous groups, in particular adult transsexuals. Bradley et al. (1978) noted that children and adolescents with gender identity problems showed a confused rather than a clear-cut cross-sex identity. Also, in opposition to the concept of a core gender identity, evidence was advanced that sexual identity in normal subjects was on a continuum, being weaker and less consistent in subjects who were exclusively heterosexual. Some degree of the wish to belong to and to feel some identity with the opposite sex was not uncommon and correlated with awareness of a homosexual component (McConaghy, 1987; McConaghy & Armstrong, 1983).

Transsexualism

DSM-III-R Criteria and Description

The DSM-III-R criteria for transsexualism are persistent discomfort and sense of inappropriateness about one's assigned sex, with preoccupation for at least 2 years with physical sex conversion, in subjects who have reached puberty. Gender identity disturbance and wish for sex conversion can be part of a schizophrenic delusional system and should be distinguished from the rare condition of transsexualism occurring with schizophrenia.

Because desire for sexual conversion can be met by an operation about which conflicting moral and ethical views exist, polarization of clinical views persist concerning the nature and diagnosis of the condition. Early proponents of the operation for male-to-female subjects considered transsexuals to be essentially normal women trapped in men's bodies by a genetic condition (Benjamin, 1954; Hamburger, Sturup, & Dahl-Iversen, 1953). Opponents saw them as neurotic, with a shallow and immature concept of what women were like, socially, sexually, anatomically, and emotionally. Opponents felt that transsexuals unconsciously distorted their memories of their lives to fit diagnostic criteria, and stated that surgery would leave them neurotic (Ostow, 1953; Worden & Marsh, 1955). Stoller (1971) suggested that the diagnosis be restricted in males to those who had been feminine, not effeminate, since early childhood and who had never shown fetishistic sexual arousal to female attire. Randell (1971) and Person and Ovesey (1974) described many transsexuals who fit neither of these criteria. Many studies exclude from the diagnosis of transsexualism subjects seeking sex conversion who are considered unsuitable for operation, not only on idiosyncratic diagnostic criteria, but also due to psychiatric or social instability. When transsexuals are highly selected in this way, it is not surprising that they show above average intelligence and MMPI scores that provide no evidence of major psychopathology. These findings were reported for 22 transsexuals selected from a pool of 200 (D. D. Hunt, Carr, & Hampson, 1981). Data are rarely provided on the rejected subjects, many of whom would seem to meet DSM-III-R criteria for transsexualism.

Clinical Presentation and Natural History

One study that reported nonpsychotic male subjects accepted for sex conversion found them to differ on a number of characteristics, which justified their division into two groups (Buhrich & McConaghy, 1978b). Most subjects in both groups reported cross-dressing before age 9. Those in the majority, termed *nuclear transsexuals*, continued to cross-dress with increasing frequency in adolescence and early adulthood without ever experiencing sexual arousal to the activity. They sought sex conversion by a mean age of 26 years. They reported predominant or exclusive sexual interest in members of their anatomical sex, consistent with their PVRs to pictures of nude men and women. Most had experienced homosexual contacts to orgasm, about half recently and regularly. Few had experienced heterosexual intercourse. A minority, termed *fetishistic transsexuals,* experienced sexual arousal with cross-dressing at puberty, which gradually diminished in adolescence and early adulthood. They reported a more bisexual orientation, consistent with their PVRs, and were likely to have experienced both heterosexual and homosexual activity and to have married. With increasing age, their desire for sex conversion increased, and they sought conversion at a mean age of 40 years. Fetishistic and nuclear transsexuals did not differ in strength of feminine gender disorder, frequency of cross-dressing, or intensity of desire for sex conversion.

The rarity of fetishism in women was suggested as a possible reason that there were no reports of female fetishistic transsexuals. It also could account for the greater incidence of transsexualism in men than in women (Buhrich & McConaghy, 1978b). Blanchard, Clemmensen, and Steiner (1987) supported this suggestion, reporting that female transsexuals were almost without exception attracted to members of their own anatomical sex and did not experience sexual arousal to cross-dressing. Like male transsexuals, most commenced cross-dressing at around age 9. Mean age of female transsexuals at presentation was 26 years.

Verschoor and Poortinga (1988) compared 55 women and 168 men seeking sex conversion. They found that, unlike 27 percent of the men, no women had married; however, 39 percent had bisexual experience. The women were significantly more likely to be students or employed and in a more stable relationship with a heterosexual partner of the same biological sex. The stability of relationships of female transsexuals has been noted repeatedly and related to the fact that their relationships, unlike those of males, were usually established before sex conversion operations (Kockott & Fahrner, 1988). Blanchard et al. (1987) classified male transsexuals as heterosexual or homosexual, rather than as fetishistic or nuclear. Unlike sexual orientation, which is on a continuum, fetishism is either present or absent, and so would seem the preferable feature to distinguish the two conditions. Estimates of the prevalence of transsexualism have increased gradually from 1 in 100,000 men and 1 in 400,000 women in the 1960s to 1 in 18,000 men and 1 in 54,000 women currently. Eklund, Gooren, and Bezemer (1988) attributed the increase to a lower threshold for applying for and commencing physical sex conversion.

Diagnosis

In discussing transvestic fetishism, DSM-III-R states that no sexual excitement is associated with the cross-dressing in transsexualism, following the earlier U.S. literature (Baker, 1969; Stoller, 1973). Presumably, as Blanchard and Clemmensen (1988) pointed out, fetishistic transsexuals would be classified by DSM-III-R as having gender identity disorder not otherwise specified.

Etiology

Gender identity was considered by Money et al. (1955) to be established in the first few years of life, after which it was unchangeable. Their clinical evidence was disputed by Zuger (1970). Imperato-McGinley, Peterson,

Gautier, and Sturla (1979) described 18 men with genetic alpha-reductase deficiency, which resulted in female-appearing genitalia at birth and male-appearing genitalia and physique at puberty. Almost all of them accepted a male role, having been raised as girls. Herdt and Davidson (1988) reported similar subjects from New Guinea and claimed that the change in role was due to social rather than biological factors, but provided no convincing evidence to support this view. Stoller (1968, 1971) considered transsexualism due to pathological parent–child relationships, but concluded that, in some subjects, desire for sex reassignment could be explained only on the basis of a biological force. Buhrich and McConaghy (1978a), using self-report questionnaire and semantic differential strategies, found no difference in the parent–child relationships of transsexuals, transvestites, and homosexuals. Pomeroy (1967) considered transsexualism to be a defense adopted by subjects who could not accept their homosexuality. Because degree of homosexuality correlates with degree of opposite gender preference, identity, role, and sex-dimorphic behavior (McConaghy, 1987), some exclusive homosexuals at the extremes of the continua for these behaviors could be socially and sexually advantaged by defining themselves as transsexual, particularly those who wish to establish a permanent relationship with an exclusively heterosexual partner. Reports of hormonal differences between transsexual and heterosexual men have not been replicated (Spijkstra, Spinder, & Gooren, 1988).

Clinical Management

The view of earlier researchers (Benjamin, 1954; Hamburger et al., 1953) that no treatment is effective in modifying transsexualism remains widely accepted, so sex conversion is considered the appropriate management. Lothstein (1982) suggested that this acceptance is premature in view of the reported response of transsexuals to psychodynamic or behavioral psychotherapy; however, the number of cases involved was small and their outcome poorly documented (Zucker, 1985). These cases seem unlikely to be typical transsexuals, who rarely consider other forms of therapy if refused sex conversion. Kuiper and Cohen-Kettenis (1988) hoped to use, as controls for 141 transsexuals receiving sex conversion, those who were not considered eligible and those who decided after psychotherapy to refrain from sex conversion. The former subjects refused to cooperate, and there was none of the latter. Most clinics will not accept subjects for sex conversion until they have lived as a member of the sex they wish to join for 1 to 2 years, during which time they must demonstrate stability of employment and lack of psychiatric symptomatology.

Meyer and Reter (1979) compared 15 subjects who received sex conversion operations with 35 who did not because they failed to complete the qualifying period of living and working in the desired role while taking opposite sex hormones for 1 year. Fourteen of the 35 subsequently obtained the operation elsewhere. At follow-up, no operated subjects expressed regret even though they changed little in socioeconomic status, demonstrating no superiority in job or education level to the unoperated. The finding was widely interpreted as indicating that sex conversion was of little value. Fleming, Steinman, and Bocknek (1980) criticized the methodology of the study and, in particular, its failure to assess the emotional lives of the subjects. The importance attached to socioeconomic status seems surprising, particularly as most subjects were males converting to females, who in general are more poorly paid. Certainly, this criterion is not commonly used in regard to outcome of other conditions. Dissatisfaction with having undergone sex conversion appears infrequent (Kuiper & Cohen-Kettenis, 1988), although long-term follow-up of male-to-female transsexuals indicates that only a minority obtain a functioning vagina following vaginal construction (Lindemalm, Korlin, & Uddenberg, 1986). Inadequate data exist to compare the outcome of fetishistic with that of nuclear transsexuals following sex conversion. Kockott and Fahrner (1987) reported that older married men with children who sought sex conversion were more likely to hesitate about accepting it when it was offered.

Transvestism

DSM-III-R Criteria

Transvestism in adolescents is classified in the DSM-III-R as a sexual disorder, fetishism, or transvestic fetishism. In adults, it is classified as a gender identity disorder of adolescence or adulthood, nontranssexual type (GIDAANT). Criteria for the latter are persistent or recurrent discomfort and sense of inappropriateness about one's assigned sex; persistent or recurrent cross-dressing in fantasy or actuality, but not for the purpose of excitement (as in transvestic fetishism); no persistent preoccupation (for at least 2 years) with getting rid of one's primary and secondary sex characteristics; and having reached puberty.

Description and Natural History

Few adult transvestites seek treatment, and their condition is rarely fully described. Buhrich and McConaghy (1977b) compared 35 subjects from a club for transvestites, all members of which were male, with 29 men seeking sex conversion. The mean ages of the self-classified transvestite group (TVG) and of the transsexual group (TSG) were 39 and 29 years, respectively. Twenty-seven of the TVG had married, all had experienced heterosexual intercourse, and 6 had had homosexual contacts to orgasm. Comparable figures for the TSG were 4, 8, and 23. Based on PVRs, all but 1 of the TVG showed predominant heterosexuality, and all but 3 of the TSG showed predominant homosexuality. Five in the TSG and all but 1 in the TVG had experienced fetishistic arousal to women's clothes. Eighteen of the TSG and the nonfetishistic subject of the TVG were cross-dressing permanently. Three of the TVG but 24 of the TSG always sat to pass urine. Three of the TVG but 26 of the TSG felt like women all the time. All these differences were statistically significant, and the researchers concluded that transvestism was a separate condition and not merely a mild form of transsexualism, as some earlier workers believed.

When cross-dressed, 13 of the TVG felt like women all the time and another 13 part of the time. Twenty sat to urinate when cross-dressed. Restricting the TVG to the 34 who had experienced fetishistic arousal to women's clothes, 20 reported satisfaction with intermittent cross-dressing and did not want sex conversion by hormones or surgery, although 9 had considered it, usually in late adolescence (Buhrich & McConaghy, 1977a). All of these cases were considered nuclear transvestites (NTVs). Of the remaining 14, 6 were taking female hormones prior to the study and 7 requested them during it; 11 of the 13 and 1 other subject desired surgical conversion, but were hesitant because of family responsibilities. These 14 were considered marginal transvestites (MTVs), intermediate between nuclear transvestites and transsexuals. Seven of the 14 presented dressed as women, as did 1 of the 20 NTVs. MTVs reported cross-dressing more frequently in the previous 2 years than did NTVs.

Most MTVs commenced cross-dressing by age 9 and NTVs by age 12. NTVs were more likely initially to use only items of female clothes and to fully cross-dress in underwear, dress, and shoes at a significantly later age and less frequently than MTVs. Members of both groups experienced sexual arousal to women's clothes around puberty, the frequency and intensity of which diminished with age. Most reported that, although sexual arousal was an important motivation for cross-dressing in adolescence, currently they did so for feelings of relaxation, relief from stress and masculine responsibility, and feelings of sensuality and elegance; however, about half the subjects in both groups currently heightened sexual arousal during intercourse by fantasizing about wearing women's clothes, and many masturbated with the same fantasy. Most NTVs commenced heterosexual intercourse by age 19 and MTVs by 23. According to self-reports and PVRs, although MTVs were predominantly heterosexual, they showed stronger homosexual interest than did NTVs. The desire to temporarily be accepted as women in company was strong in both groups, but many met this by attending club meetings where they regularly cross-dressed and adopted a woman's name. Although most subjects who seek sex conversion in middle-age are fetishistic transsexuals, some have previously self-identified as transvestites, and give a history more characteristic of MTVs. Nuclear transvestites do not develop a wish for sex conversion in middle age.

Diagnosis

The little research data available concerning transvestism is not easily reconciled with DSM-III-R categories. After initial evasion or denial, adolescent boys reporting fetishistic arousal to female clothes often admit they wear the clothes and, to some extent, fantasize themselves as girls in them. If these statements, often elicited by leading questions, are accepted as true, the diagnosis shifts from fetishism to transvestic fetishism. If, with aging, they cross-dress more fully but no longer for sexual excitement, the diagnosis shifts to GIDAANT, provided they experience discomfort and a sense of inappropriateness about their assigned sex. It is not clear that the majority of transvestites experience these feelings. Many seem quite accepting of their condition. Possibly the intent of the DSM-III-R is that these apparently contented mainly nuclear transvestites not be labeled, and the diagnosis be reserved for the minority of marginal transvestites who desire or seek a degree of sex conversion, mainly by female hormones.

Etiology

Stoller (1968) argued that transvestites are allowed by their mothers to develop a core male gender identity in their early years, but the mothers or other women then attack their masculinity by dressing them in female clothes. He also wrote that incidents of forceful cross-dressing by women were common in case histories of transvestites, but not of transsexuals or effeminate homosexuals. In fact, these incidents are not common in case histories, but in transvestite fiction (Buhrich & McConaghy, 1976). The replacement with aging of sexual arousal by tension relief as the major motivation for cross-dressing is consistent with the hypothesis that sexual behaviors are initiated by sexual drives but, as they become compulsive, are maintained by behavior-completion mechanisms. Commencement of transvestism in childhood and its association with fetishistic arousal in adolescence suggests the involvement of biological factors in its initiation.

Clinical Management

Occasionally, adult transvestites seek treatment to cease cross-dressing due to guilt or because their wives cannot accept it and their marriage is threatened. If, with counseling, they continue to seek cessation of the behavior, it can be treated as a compulsive paraphilia. Like fetishism, it is somewhat resistant and may require a combination of imaginal desensitization and medroxyprogesterone therapy for the subject to attain control.

SUMMARY

In this chapter, diagnosis and clinical features of paraphilias were discussed in relation to DSM-III-R criteria. Rape appears to be on a continuum with the coercive behaviors shown by many men that have a sadistic component. Individual subjects' penile circumference responses to paraphilic stimuli are widely recommended for their assessment, although the technique has been demonstrated to have limited validity. It has been proposed that many paraphilias are not motivated by sexual urges, but by desires for domination, consistent with the much higher incidence in men. The theory seems incompatible with the response of paraphilias to androgen suppression therapy. An alternative hypothesis is that paraphilic impulses are sexual, but that nonsexual behavior-completion mechanisms are responsible for their becoming uncontrollable. Imaginal desensitization therapy developed on the basis of this theory has proved highly effective.

Sexual dysfunctions and sexual difficulties not classified in DSM-III-R are present in a significant percentage of the normal population, but are rarely reported to clinicians. In women, the incidence of anorgasmia with intercourse falls from over 50 percent to about 7 percent from age 15 to age 45, suggesting that learning—probably learning to relinquish control of sexual excitement—is the responsible factor. In men, the incidence of erectile failure rises steadily from age 35, suggesting that organic factors play a major role. Testosterone level appears to determine male sexual interest, but not erectile ability. Relations between hormone levels and sexual behaviors of women appear weak. The complex DSM-III-R classification of transvestism relates poorly to its clinical features.

REFERENCES

Abel, G. G., Barlow, D. H., Blanchard, E. B., & Guild, D. (1977). The components of rapists' sexual arousal. *Archives of General Psychiatry, 34,* 895–903.

Abel, G. G., Becker, J. V., Blanchard, E. B., & Djenderedjiam, A. (1978). Differentiating sexual aggressives with penile measures. *Criminal Justice and Behavior, 5,* 315–332.

Abel, G. G., Becker, J. V., Murphy, W. D., & Flanagan, F. (1981). Identifying dangerous child molesters. In R. B. Stuart (Ed.), *Violent behavior: Social learning approaches to prediction, management and treatment* (pp. 116–137). New York: Brunner/Mazel.

Adamopoulos, D. A., Kampyli, S., Georgiacodis, F., Kapolla, N., & Abrahamian-Michalakis, A. (1988). Effects of antiandrogen–estrogen treatment on sexual and endocrine parameters in hirsute women. *Archives of Sexual Behavior, 17,* 421–429.

Adams, D. B., Gold, A. R., & Burt, A. D. (1978). Rise in female-initiated sexual activity at ovulation and its suppression by oral contraceptives. *The New England Journal of Medicine, 299,* 1145–1150.

Alford, G. S., Wedding, D., & Jones, S. (1983). Faking 'turn-ons' and 'turn-offs.' *Behavior Modification, 7,* 112–125.

American Psychiatric Association. (1987). *Diagnostic and statistical manual of mental disorders* (3rd ed. rev.). Washington, DC: Author.

Andersen, B. L., & Broffitt, B. (1988). Is there a reliable and valid self-report measure of sexual behavior? *Archives of Sexual Behavior, 17,* 509–525.

Avery-Clark, C. A., & Laws, D. R. (1984). Differential erection response patterns of sexual child abusers to stimuli describing activities with children. *Behavior Therapy, 15,* 71–83.

Baker, H. J. (1969). Transsexualism—Problems in treatment. *American Journal of Psychiatry, 125,* 1142–1147.

Barbaree, H. E., Marshall, W. L., & Lanthier, R. D. (1979). Deviant sexual arousal in rapists. *Behaviour Research and Therapy, 17,* 215–222.

Baxter, D. J., Barbaree, H. E., & Marshall, W. L. (1986). Sexual responses to consenting and forced sex in a large sample of rapists and non-rapists. *Behaviour Research and Therapy, 24,* 513–520.

Baxter, D. J., Marshall, W. L., Barbaree, H. E., Davidson, P. R., & Malcolm, P. B. (1984). Deviant sexual behavior: Differentiating sex offenders by criminal and personal history, psychometric measures, and sexual response. *Criminal Justice and Behavior, 11,* 477–501.

Beggs, V. E., Calhoun, K. S., & Wolchik, S. A. (1987). Sexual anxiety and female sexual arousal: A comparison of arousal during sexual anxiety stimuli and sexual pleasure stimuli. *Archives of Sexual Behavior, 16,* 311–319.

Benjamin, H. (1954). Transsexualism and transvestism as psychosomatic and somato-psychic syndromes. *American Journal of Psychotherapy, 8,* 219–230.

Blair, D. C., & Lanyon, R. I. (1981). Exhibitionism: Etiology and treatment. *Psychological Bulletin, 89,* 439–463.

Blanchard, R., & Clemmensen, L. H. (1988). A test of the DSM-III-R's implicit assumption that fetishistic arousal and gender dysphoria are mutually exclusive. *Journal of Sex Research, 25,* 426–432.

Blanchard, N., Clemmensen, L. H., & Steiner, B. W. (1987). Heterosexual and homosexual gender dysphoria. *Archives of Sexual Behavior, 16,* 139–152.

Bradley, S. J., Steiner, B., Zucker, K., Doering, R. W., Sullivan, J., Finegan, J. K., & Richardson, M. (1978). Gender identity problems of children and adolescents. *Canadian Psychiatric Association Journal, 23,* 175–183.

Breslow, N., Evans, L., & Langley, J. (1985). On the prevalence and roles of females in the sadomasochistic subculture: Report of an empirical study. *Archives of Sexual Behavior, 14,* 303–319.

Bretschneider, J. G., & McCoy, N. L. (1988). Sexual interest and behavior in healthy 80- to 102-year-olds. *Archives of Sexual Behavior, 17,* 109–129.

Bridges, C. F., Critelli, J. W., & Loos, V. E. (1985). Hypnotic susceptibility, inhibitory control, and orgasmic consistency. *Archives of Sexual Behavior, 14,* 373–476.

Brown, W. A., Monti, P. M., & Corriveau, D. P. (1978). Serum testosterone and sexual activity and interest in men. *Archives of Sexual Behavior, 7,* 97–104.

Buhrich, N., & McConaghy, N. (1976). Transvestite fiction. *Journal of Nervous and Mental Disease, 163,* 420–427.

Buhrich, N., & McConaghy, N. (1977a). The clinical syndromes of femiphilic transvestism. *Archives of Sexual Behavior, 6,* 397–412.

Buhrich, N., & McConaghy, N. (1977b). The discrete syndromes of transvestism and transsexualism. *Archives of Sexual Behavior, 6,* 483–495.

Buhrich, N., & McConaghy, N. (1978a). Parental relationships during childhood in homosexuality, transvestism and transsexualism. *Australian and New Zealand Journal of Psychiatry, 12,* 103–108.

Buhrich, N., & McConaghy, N. (1978b). Two clinically discrete syndromes of transsexualism. *British Journal of Psychiatry, 133,* 73–76.

Butler, C. A. (1976). New data about female sex response. *Journal of Sex and Marital Therapy, 2,* 40–46.

Carroll, J. L., Volk, K. D., & Hyde, J. S. (1985). Differences between males and females in motives for engaging in sexual intercourse. *Archives of Sexual Behavior, 14,* 131–139.

Chalkley, A. J., & Powell, G. E. (1983). The clinical description of forty-eight cases of sexual fetishism. *British Journal of Psychiatry, 142,* 292–295.

Cooper, A. J. (1969). Some personality factors in frigidity. *Journal of Psychosomatic Research, 13,* 149–155.

Crepault, C., & Couture, M. (1980). Men's erotic fantasies. *Archives of Sexual Behavior, 9,* 565–581.

Cutler, W. B., Garcia, C. R., & McCoy, N. (1987). Premenopausal sexuality. *Archives of Sexual Behavior, 16,* 225–235.

Davidson, J. M., Camargo, C. A., & Smith, E. R. (1979). Effects of androgen on sexual behavior in hypogonadal men. *Journal of Clinical Endocrinology and Metabolism, 48,* 955–958.

DeAmicis, L. A., Goldberg, D. C., LoPiccolo, J., Friedman, J., & Davies, L. (1985). Clinical follow-up of couples treated for sexual dysfunction. *Archives of Sexual Behavior, 14,* 467–489.

DiVasto, P. V., Kaufman, L. R., Jackson, R., Christy, J., Pearson, S., & Burgett, T. (1984). The prevalence of sexually stressful events among females in the general population. *Archives of Sexual Behavior, 13,* 59–67.

Donovan, B. T. (1985). *Hormones and human behaviour.* London: Cambridge University Press.

Earls, C. M., & Marshall, W. L. (1982). The simultaneous and independent measurement of penile circumference and length. *Behavior Research Methods and Instrumentation, 14,* 447–450.

Eklund, P. L. E., Gooren, L. J. G., & Bezemer, P. D. (1988). Prevalence of transsexualism in the Netherlands. *British Journal of Psychiatry, 152,* 638–640.

Finkelhor, D. (1980). Risk factors in the sexual investigation of children. *Child Abuse and Neglect, 4,* 265–273.

Finkelhor, D., & Lewis, I. A. (1988). An epidemiologic approach to the study of child molestation. *Annals of the New York Academy of Sciences, 528,* 64–78.

Fisher, S. (1973). *The female orgasm.* New York: Basic Books.

Fleming, M., Steinman, C., & Bocknek, G. (1980). Methodological problems in assessing sex-reassignment surgery: A reply to Meyer and Reter. *Archives of Sexual Behavior, 9,* 451–456.

Frank, E., Anderson, C., & Rubinstein, D. (1978). Frequency of sexual dysfunction in 'normal' couples. *New England Journal of Medicine, 299,* 111–115.

Freund, K., Chan, S., & Coulthard, R. (1979). Phallometric diagnosis with 'nonadmitters.' *Behaviour Research and Therapy, 17,* 451–457.

Freund, K., Heasman, G. A., & Roper, V. (1982). Results of the main studies on sexual offences against children and pubescents: A review. *Canadian Journal of Criminology, 24,* 387–397.

Freund, K., Langevin, R. M., Wescom, T., & Zajac, Y. (1975). Heterosexual interest in homosexual males. *Archives of Sexual Behavior, 4,* 509–518.

Freund, K., McKnight, C. K., Langevin, R., & Cibiri, S. (1972). The female child as a surrogate object. *Archives of Sexual Behavior, 2,* 119–133.

Freund, K., Nagler, E., Langevin, R., Zajac, A., & Steiner, B. (1974). Measuring feminine gender identity in homosexual males. *Archives of Sexual Behavior, 3,* 249–260.

Freund, K., Scher, H., & Hucker, S. (1983). The courtship disorders. *Archives of Sexual Behavior, 12,* 269–379.

Gagne, P. (1981). Treatment of sex offenders with medroxyprogesterone acetate. *American Journal of Psychiatry, 138,* 644–646.

Gebhard, P. H., Gagnon, J. H., Pomeroy, W. B., & Christenson, C. V. (1965). *Sex offenders: An analysis of types.* London: Heinemann.

Gosselin, C., & Wilson, G. (1980). *Sexual variations.* London: Faber and Faber.

Green, R., & Money, J. (1969). Preface. In R. Green & J. Money (Eds.), *Transsexualism and sex reassignment.* Baltimore: Johns Hopkins University Press.

Groth, A. M., & Birnbaum, H. J. (1978). Adult sexual orientation and attraction to underage persons. *Archives of Sexual Behavior, 7,* 175–181.

Hamburger, C., Sturup, G. K., & Dahl-Iversen, E. (1953). Transvestism. *Journal of the American Medical Association, 152,* 391–396.

Hatch, J. P. (1981). Psychophysiological aspects of sexual dysfunction. *Archives of Sexual Behavior, 10,* 49–64.

Hawton, K., Catalan, J., Martin, P., & Fagg, J. (1986). Long-term outcome of sex therapy. *Behaviour Research and Therapy, 24,* 665–675.

Hazelwood, R., Dietz, P. E., & Burgess, A. W. (1983). *Autoerotic fatalities.* Toronto: Lexington Books.

Heilbrun, A. B., & Leif, D. T. (1988). Erotic value of female distress in sexually explicit photographs. *Journal of Sex Research, 24,* 47–57.

Heilbrun, A. B., & Loftus, M. P. (1986). The role of sadism and peer pressure in the sexual aggression of male college students. *Journal of Sex Research, 22,* 320–332.

Herdt, G. H., & Davidson, J. (1988). The Sambia "turnim-man": sociocultural and clinical aspects of gender formation in male pseudohermaphrodites with 5-alpha-reductase deficiency in Papua New Guinea. *Archives of Sexual Behavior, 17,* 1–31.

Hogan, D. R. (1978). The effectiveness of sex therapy: A review of the literature. In J. LoPiccolo & L. LoPiccolo (Eds.), *Handbook of sex therapy* (pp. 57–84). New York: Plenum Press.

Hoon, P. W. (1979). The assessment of sexual arousal in women. In M. Hersen, R. M. Eisler, & P. M. Miller (Eds.), *Progress in behavior modification* (Vol. 7, pp. 2–61). New York: Academic Press.

Hunt, D. D., Carr, J. E., & Hampson, J. L. (1981). Cognitive correlates of biologic sex and gender identity in transsexualism. *Archives of Sexual Behavior, 10,* 65–77.

Hunt, M. (1974). *Sexual behavior in the 70's.* Chicago: Playboy.

Imperato-McGinley, J., Peterson, R. E., Gautier, T., & Sturla, E. (1979). Androgens and the evolution of male-gender identity among male pseudohermaphrodites with 5 alpha-reductase deficiency. *New England Journal of Medicine, 300,* 1233–1237.

Kaplan, H. S. (1974). *The new sex therapy.* New York: Brunner/Mazel.

Kilmann, P. R., Sabalis, R. F., Gearing, M. L., Bukstel, L. H., & Scobern, A. W. (1982). The treatment of sexual paraphilias: A review of the outcome research. *Journal of Sex Research, 18,* 193–252.

Kinsey, A. C., Pomeroy, W. B., & Martin, C. E. (1948). *Sexual behavior in the human male.* Philadelphia: Saunders.

Kinsey, A. C., Pomeroy, W. B., Martin, C. E., & Gebhard, P. H. (1953). *Sexual behavior in the human female.* Philadelphia: Saunders.

Knussman, R., Christiansen, K., & Couwenbergs, C. (1986). Relations between sex hormone levels and sexual behavior in men. *Archives of Sexual Behavior, 15,* 429–445.

Kockott, G., & Fahrner, E. M. (1987). Transsexuals who have not undergone surgery: A follow-up study. *Archives of Sexual Behavior, 16,* 511–522.

Kockott, G., & Fahrner, E. M. (1988). Male-to-female and female-to-male transsexuals: A comparison. *Archives of Sexual Behavior, 7,* 539–546.

Kolarksy, A., Freund, K., Machek, J., & Polak, O. (1967). Male sexual deviation. *Archives of General Psychiatry, 17,* 735–743.

Koss, M. P., & Oros, C. J. (1982). Sexual experiences survey: A research instrument investigating sexual aggression and victimization. *Journal of Consulting and Clinical Psychology, 50,* 455–457.

Kraemer, H. C., Becker, H. B., Brodie, H. K. H., Doering, C. H., Moos, R. H., & Hamburg, D. A. (1976). Orgasmic frequency and plasma testosterone levels in normal human males. *Archives of Sexual Behavior, 5,* 125–132.

Kuiper, B., & Cohen-Kettenis, P. (1988). Sex reassignment surgery: A study of 141 Dutch transsexuals. *Archives of Sexual Behavior, 17,* 439–457.

Langevin, R., Paitich, D., Ramsay, G., Anderson, C., Kamrad, J., Pope, S., Geller, G., Pearl, L., & Newman, S. (1979). Experimental studies of the etiology of genital exhibitionism. *Archives of Sexual Behavior, 8,* 307–331.

Levin, S. M., & Stava, L. (1987). Personality characteristics of sex offenders: A review. *Archives of Sexual Behavior, 16,* 57–79.

Lindemalm, G., Korlin, D., & Uddenberg, N. (1986). Long-term follow-up of "sex change" in 13 male-to-female transsexuals. *Archives of Sexual Behavior, 15,* 187–210.

LoPiccolo, J. (1982). Book review. Impotence: Physiological, psychological, surgical diagnosis and treatment. *Archives of Sexual Behavior, 11,* 277–279.

Lothstein, L. M. (1982). Sex reassignment surgery: Historical, bioethical, and theoretical issues. *American Journal of Psychiatry, 139,* 417–426.

Lukianowicz, N. (1972). Incest I: Paternal incest. II: Other types of incest. *British Journal of Psychiatry, 120,* 301–313.

Malamuth, N. M. (1981). Rape proclivity among males. *Journal of Social Issues, 37,* 138–157.

Malamuth, N. M., Haber, S., & Feshbach, S. (1980). Testing hypotheses regarding rape: Exposure to sexual violence, sex differences, and the 'normality' of rapists. *Journal of Research in Personality, 14,* 121–137.

Marshall, W. L., & Barbaree, H. E. (1988). The long-term evaluation of a behavioral treatment program for child molesters. *Behaviour Research and Therapy, 26,* 499–511.

Marshall, W. L., Earls, C. M., Segal, Z., & Darke, J. (1983). A behavioral program for the assessment and treatment of sexual aggressors. In K. D. Craig & R. J. McMahon (Eds.), *Advances in clinical behavior therapy* (pp. 148–174). New York: Brunner/Mazel.

Masters, W. H., & Johnson, V. E. (1970). *Human sexual inadequacy.* Boston: Little, Brown.

McConaghy, N. (1974). Measurements of change in penile dimensions. *Archives of Sexual Behavior, 3,* 381–388.

McConaghy, N. (1980). Behavior completion mechanisms rather than primary drives maintain behavioral patterns. *Activitas Nervosa Superior* (Praha), *22,* 138–151.

McConaghy, N. (1982). Sexual deviation. In A. S. Bellack, M. Hersen, & A. E. Kazdin (Eds.), *International handbook of behavior therapy and modification* (pp. 683–712). New York: Plenum Press.

McConaghy, N. (1983). Agoraphobia, compulsive behaviors and behavior completion mechanisms. *Australian and New Zealand Journal of Psychiatry, 17,* 170–179.

McConaghy, N. (1984). Psychosexual disorders. In S. M. Turner & M. Hersen (Eds.), *Adult psychopathology and diagnosis* (pp. 370–405). New York: Wiley.

McConaghy, N. (1985). Psychosexual dysfunctions. In M. Hersen & A. S. Bellack (Eds.), *Handbook of clinical behavior therapy with adults* (pp. 659–692). New York: Plenum Press.

McConaghy, N. (1987). Heterosexuality/homosexuality: Dichotomy or continuum. *Archives of Sexual Behavior, 16,* 411–424.

McConaghy, N. (1988). Assessment of sexual dysfunction and deviation. In M. Hersen & A. S. Bellack (Eds.), *Behavioral assessment: A practical handbook* (3rd ed., pp. 490–541). New York: Pergamon Press.

McConaghy, N. (1989a). Validity and ethics of penile circumference measures of sexual arousal: A critical review. *Archives of Sexual Behavior, 18,* 357–367.

McConaghy, N. (1989b). Psychosexual disorders. In L. K. G. Hsu & M. Hersen (Eds.), *Recent developments in adolescent psychiatry* (pp. 333–366). New York: Wiley.

McConaghy, N. (1990). Sexual deviation. In A. S. Bellack, M. Hersen, & A. E. Kazdin (Eds.), *International handbook of behavior modification and therapy* (2nd ed., pp. 565–580). New York: Plenum Press.

McConaghy, N., & Armstrong, M. S. (1983). Sexual orientation and consistency of sexual identity. *Archives of Sexual Behavior, 12,* 317–327.

McConaghy, N., Armstrong, M. S., & Blaszczynski, A. (1985). Expectancy, covert sensitization and imaginal desensitization in compulsive sexuality. *Acta Psychiatrica Sandinavica, 72,* 176–187.

McConaghy, N., Blaszczynski, A., Armstrong, M. S., & Kidson, W. (1989). Resistance to treatment of adolescent sex offenders. *Archives of Sexual Behavior, 18,* 97–107.

McConaghy, N., Blaszczynski, A., & Kidson, W. (1988). Treatment of sex offenders with imaginal desensitization and/or medroxyprogesterone. *Acta Psychiatrica Scandinavica, 77,* 199–206.

Mead, M. (1950). *Male and female.* London: Gollancz.

Meyer, J., & Reter, D. (1979). Sex reassignment. *Archives of General Psychiatry, 36,* 1010–1015.

Money, J., Hampson, J. G., & Hampson, J. C. (1955). Hermaphroditism: Recommendations concerning assignment of sex, change of sex and psychologic management. *John Hopkins Hospital Bulletin, 97,* 286–300.

Morokoff, P. (1978). Determinants of female orgasm. In J. LoPiccolo & L. LoPiccolo (Eds.), *Handbook of sex therapy* (pp. 147–165). New York: Plenum Press.

Moser, C., & Levitt, E. E. (1987). An exploratory–descriptive study of a sado-masochistically oriented sample. *Journal of Sex Research, 23,* 322–337.

Murphy, W. D., Abel, G. G., & Becker, J. V. (1980). Future research issues. In D. J. Cox & R. J. Daitzman (Eds.), *Exhibitionism: Description, assessment and treatment.* New York: Garland.

Murphy, W. D., Krisar, J., Stalgaitis, S., & Anderson, K. (1984). The use of penile tumescence measures with incarcerated rapists: Further validity issues. *Archives of Sexual Behavior, 13,* 545–554.

Nettelbladt, P., & Uddenberg, N. (1979). Sexual dysfunction and sexual satisfaction in 58 married Swedish men. *Journal of Psychosomatic Research, 23,* 141–147.

O'Carroll, R., & Bancroft, J. (1984). Testosterone therapy for low sexual interest and erectile dysfunction in men: A controlled study. *British Journal of Psychiatry, 145,* 146–151.

O'Connor, A. A. (1987). Female sex offenders. *British Journal of Psychiatry, 150,* 615–620.

Osborn, M., Hawton, K., & Gath, D. (1988). Sexual dysfunction among middle aged women in the community. *British Medical Journal, 296,* 959–962.

Ostow, M. (1953). Transvestism (letter). *Journal of the American Medical Association, 152,* 1553.

Palmer, C. T. (1988). Twelve reasons why rape is not sexually motivated: A skeptical examination. *Journal of Sex Research, 25,* 512–530.

Person, E. S., & Ovesey, L. (1974). The psychodynamics of male transsexualism. In R. C. Friedman & R. M. Richart (Eds.), *Sex differences in behavior* (pp. 315–325). New York: Wiley.

Pfeiffer, E., Verwoerdt, A., & Davis, G. C. (1972). Sexual behavior in middle life. *American Journal of Psychiatry, 128,* 1262–1267.

Pfeiffer, E., Verwoerdt, A., & Wang, H. S. (1969). The natural history of sexual behavior in a biologically advantaged group of aged individuals. *Journal of Gerontology, 24,* 193–197.

Pomeroy, W. B. (1967). A report on the sexual histories of twenty-five transsexuals. *Transactions of the New York Academy of Sciences, 29,* 444–447.

Price, H. J., & Miller, P. A. (1984). Sexual fantasies of black and white college students. *Psychological Reports, 54,* 1007–1014.

Quinsey, V. L. (1984). Sexual aggression: Studies of offenders against women. In D. N. Weisstub (Ed.), *Law and mental health, international perspectives* (Vol. 1, pp. 86–121). New York: Pergamon Press.

Quinsey, V. L., Chaplin, T. C., & Carrigan, W. F. (1979). Sexual preference among incestuous and non-incestuous child molesters. *Behavior Therapy, 10,* 562–565.

Quinsey, V. L., Steinman, C. M., Bergersen, S. G., & Holmes, J. (1975). Penile circumference, skin conductance and ranking responses of child molesters and 'normals' to sexual and non-sexual visual stimuli. *Behavior Therapy, 6,* 213–219.

Raboch, J., & Starka, L. (1973). Reported coital activity of men and levels of plasma testosterone. *Archives of Sexual Behavior, 2,* 309–315.

Rachman, S. (1966). Sexual fetishism: An experimental analogue. *Psychological Record, 16,* 293–296.

Randell, J. B. (1971). Indications for sex re-assignment surgery. *Archives of Sexual Behavior, 1,* 153–161.

Reading, A. E., & Wiest, W. M. (1984). An analysis of self-reported sexual behavior in a sample of normal males. *Archives of Sexual Behavior, 13,* 69–83.

Riley, A. J., & Riley, E. J. (1978). A controlled study to evaluate directed masturbation in the management of primary orgasmic failure in women. *British Journal of Psychiatry, 133,* 404–409.

Rooth, F. G. (1973). Exhibitionism outside Europe and America. *Archives of Sexual Behavior, 2,* 351–363.

Rousseau, L., Dupont, A., Labrie, F., & Couture, M. (1988). Sexuality changes in prostate cancer patients receiving antihormonal therapy combining the antiandrogen Flutamide with medical (LHRH agonist) or surgical castration. *Archives of Sexual Behavior, 17,* 87–98.

Russell, D. E. H. (1983). The incidence and prevalence of intrafamilial and extrafamilial sexual abuse of female children. *Child Abuse and Neglect, 7,* 133–146.

Rust, J., Golombok, S., & Collier, J. (1988). Marital problems and sexual dysfunction: How are they related? *British Journal of Psychiatry, 152,* 629–631.

Sarrel, P. M. (1987). Sexuality in the middle years. *Obstetrics and Gynaecology Clinics of North America, 14,* 49–62.

Saypol, D. C., Peterson, G. A., Howards, S. S., & Yazel, J. J. (1983). Impotence: Are the newer diagnostic methods a necessity? *Journal of Urology, 130,* 260–262.

Schiavi, R. C., Fisher, C., White, D., Beers, P., & Szechter, R. (1984). Pituitary-gonadal function during sleep in men with erectile impotence and normal controls. *Psychosomatic Medicine, 46,* 239–254.

Schofield, M. (1968). *The sexual behavior of young people.* Harmondsworth, England: Penguin.

Schofield, M. (1973). *The sexual behavior of young adults.* London: Allen Lane.

Segraves, R. T., Schoenberg, H. W., & Ivanoff, J. (1983). Serum testosterone and prolactin levels in erectile dysfunction. *Journal of Sex and Marital Therapy, 9,* 19–26.

Segraves, R. T., Schoenberg, H. W., & Segraves, K. A. B. (1985). Evaluation of the etiology of erectile failure. In R. T. Segraves & H. W. Schoenberg (Eds.), *Diagnosis and treatment of erectile disturbances* (pp 165–195). New York: Plenum Press.

Sherwin, B. B., & Gelfand, M. M. (1987). The role of androgen in the maintenance of sexual functioning in oophorectomized women. *Psychosomatic Medicine, 49,* 397–409.

Shukla, G. D., Srivastava, O. N., & Katiyar, B. C. (1979). Sexual disturbances in temporal lobe epilepsy: A controlled study. *British Journal of Psychiatry, 134,* 288–292.

Skakkebaek, N. E., Bancroft, J., Davidson, D. W., & Warner, P. (1981). Androgen replacement with oral testosterone undeconate in hypogonadal men: A double blind controlled study. *Clinical Endocrinology, 14,* 49–61.

Slag, M. F., Morley, J. E., Elson, M. K., Trence, D. L., Nelson, C. J., Nelson, A. E., Kinlaw, W. B., Beyer, S., Nuttall, F. Q., & Shafer, R. B. (1983). Impotence in medical clinical outpatients. *Journal of the American Medical Association, 249,* 1736–1740.

Smith, D., & Over, R. (1987). Correlates of fantasy—Induced and film-induced male sexual arousal. *Archives of Sexual Behavior, 16,* 395–409.

Smith, R. S. (1976). Voyeurism: A review of the literature. *Archives of Sexual Behavior, 5,* 585–608.

Snyder, D. K., & Berg, P. (1983). Determinants of sexual dissatisfaction in sexually distressed couples. *Archives of Sexual Behavior, 12,* 237–246.

Sorensen, R. C. (1973). *Adolescent sexuality in contemporary America.* New York: World Publishing.

Spengler, A. (1977). Manifest sadomasochism of males: Results of an empirical study. *Archives of Sexual Behavior, 6,* 441–456.

Spijkstra, J. J., Spinder, T., & Gooren, L. J. G. (1988). Short-term patterns of pulsatile lutenizing hormone secretion do not differ between male-to-female transsexuals and heterosexual men. *Psychoneuroendocrinology, 13,* 279–283.

Stoller, R. J. (1968). *Sex and gender.* London: Hogarth.

Stoller, R. J. (1971). The term 'transvestism.' *Archives of General Psychiatry, 24,* 230–237.

Stoller, R. J. (1973). Male transsexualism: Uneasiness. *American Journal of Psychiatry, 130,* 536–539.

Swanson, D. W. (1968). Adult sexual abuse of children. *Diseases of the Nervous System, 29,* 677–683.

Swigert, V. L., Farrell, R. A., & Yoels, W. C. (1976). Sexual homicide: Social, psychological and legal aspects. *Archives of Sexual Behavior, 5,* 391–401.

Terman, L. M. (1938). *Psychological factors in marital happiness.* New York: McGraw-Hill.

Terman, L. M. (1951). Correlates of orgasm adequacy in a group of 556 wives. *Journal of Psychology, 32,* 115–172.

Thase, M. E., Reynolds, C. F., III, & Jennings, J. R. (1988). Nocturnal penile tumescence is diminished in depressed men. *Biological Psychiatry, 24,* 33–46.

Tsitouras, P. D., Martin, C. E., & Harman, S. M. (1982). Relationship of serum testosterone to sexual activity in healthy elderly men. *Journal of Gerontology, 37,* 288–293.

Udry, J. R., Billy, J. O. G., Morris, N. M., Groff, T. R., & Raj, H. R. (1985). Serum androgenic hormones motivate sexual behavior in adolescent boys. *Fertility and Sterility, 43,* 90–94.

Verschoor, A. M., & Poortinga, J. (1988). Psychosexual differences between Dutch male and female transsexuals. *Archives of Sexual Behavior, 17,* 173–178.

Weizman, R., & Hart, J. (1987). Sexual behavior in healthy married elderly men. *Archives of Sexual Behavior, 16,* 39–44.

Winokur, G., Guze, S. B., & Pfeiffer, E. (1959). Developmental and sexual factors in women. A comparison between control, neurotic and psychotic groups. *American Journal of Psychiatry, 115,* 1097–1100.

Wolpe, J. (1958). *Psychotherapy by reciprocal inhibition.* Stanford, CA: Stanford University Press.

Worden, F. G., & Marsh, J. T. (1955). Psychological factors in men seeking sex transformation. *Journal of the American Medical Association, 157,* 1292–1298.

Zucker, K. J. (1985). Book review. *Archives of Sexual Behavior, 14,* 377–381.

Zuger, B. (1970). Gender role determination: A critical review of the evidence from hermaphroditism. *Psychosomatic Medicine, 32,* 449–467.

Zverina, J., Lachman, M., Pondelickova, J., & Vanek, J. (1987). The occurrence of atypical sexual experience among various female patient groups. *Archives of Sexual Behavior, 16,* 321–326.

CHAPTER 12

Personality, Impulse Control, and Adjustment Disorders

W.L. MARSHALL and H.E. BARBAREE

In our chapter for the first edition of this book, we (Marshall & Barbaree, 1984) construed all DSM-III (*Diagnostic and Statistical Manual of Mental Disorders,* 3rd ed., American Psychiatric Association [APA], 1980) disorders of personality, impulse control, and adjustment as involving social-interactive problems manifest in action and thought. The modifications apparent in DSM-III-R (APA, 1987) have not altered our perspective. DSM-III-R still regards the personality disorders as arising from enduring patterns of thinking and perceiving that are exhibited in social and personal contexts. Disorders of impulse control involve a failure to resist a temptation to perform an act harmful to the person or to others, whereas adjustment disorders are maladaptive reactions to psychosocial stressors.

According to its authors, DSM-III-R is meant to represent yet one more "still frame in the ongoing process of attempting to better understand mental disorders" (APA, p. xvii, 1987). Because the authors of DSM-III and its revision asserted an atheoretical position with respect to human behavior, they must believe that effective classification is in itself a critical feature of progress toward understanding. In this respect, issues regarding the reliability of the diagnoses, their validity, their distinctiveness, and their overlap become crucial in considering the utility of DSM-III-R in getting us closer to our goal of understanding disordered functioning. Accordingly, we give emphasis to the literature dealing with these issues.

PERSONALITY DISORDERS

DSM-III categorized mental disorders in either Axis I or Axis II, with the latter being reserved primarily for disorders of personality. DSM-III-R retains this feature, and both manuals encourage the clinician to classify a patient under both axes if the person meets the criteria for a disorder in each axis. This reduces the problem presented by those patients who not only appear to be, for example, severely depressed, but also have an enduring personality disorder that is independent of their depression. In an examination of

2,462 patients, Koenigsberg, Kaplan, Gilmore, and Cooper (1985) found that valuable information was contained in Axis II that was not evident in Axis I. An additional advance, included for the first time in DSM-III-R, allows the diagnostician to apply multiple diagnoses that need not be arranged hierarchically, as was required in earlier versions. Establishing that two possible disorders are independent presents serious and sometimes insurmountable problems, however, so that very frequently the decision is left to the clinician's judgment. These problems, as we will see, have given rise to a contentious theme in the literature centering on whether, for example, depression and borderline personality are actually two separate disorders or simply different manifestations of the same problem.

DSM-III-R continues the tradition of DSM-III in maintaining an atheoretical view and offering what is called a descriptive approach. This approach represents a marked improvement over earlier classification systems, and the authors have tried to reduce the level of inference required of the diagnostician by specifying the criteria, as far as possible, in observable terms. With respect to the personality disorders, the DSM-III-R authors admitted that a much higher order of inference is required. The reliability and validity of diagnoses are important not only for clinical purposes, but particularly for investigations that may further our understanding of these problems. The same clinicians must, time after time, be able to make the same diagnosis on the basis of the same information in an unchanged patient. Similarly, different diagnosticians must be able to come to the same decisions regarding specific patients when provided with the same information. Unless these requirements of reliability (inter- and intrarater) are met, the issue of the validity of the diagnoses does not arise. Establishing the validity of diagnoses requires several things, but in a categorical classification system the degree of overlap between disorders must be minimal, or at least it must be possible to reliably discriminate among the different disorders.

Dahl (1986) found that, although DSM-III resulted in an improvement over earlier versions, the reliability of the diagnoses of the personality disorders remained at best moderate. The magnitude of the problem may depend on the information used to make a diagnosis. For example, in one study (Zimmerman, Pfohl, Stangl, & Corenthal, 1986), the diagnosis of personality disorder, which was based initially on observations of the patients, was changed in almost 20 percent of cases after interviews with the families or close friends of the 82 patients.

Livesley and his colleagues in Canada (Livesley, 1986; Livesley, Reiffer, Sheldon, & West, 1987) examined the content validity of DSM-III criteria for personality disorders in relation to a broader set of criteria drawn from the general literature. A panel of 938 psychiatrists rated the trait and behavioral features of each DSM-III personality disorder and also rated the prototypical nature of each of the criteria. Indications were that there were considerable problems with the organization and content of each of the diagnoses. In particular, Livesley pointed out that many of the criteria contained statements describing compound features and that these statements were frequently interpreted differently by different raters. These authors recommended that future descriptions be limited to single statements.

In addition, because Livesley also found that behaviorally defined features were reliably judged by these 938 clinicians, he recommended that criteria for diagnosis be specified in behavioral rather than trait terms. DSM-III-R has moved in both these directions, in hopes that this would improve both reliability and validity. Unfortunately, Morey's (1988) examination of the relationship between personality disorder diagnoses based on DSM-III and those based on DSM-III-R criteria did not encourage optimism on this front. He found that, although DSM-III-R displayed an increase in coverage, it also resulted in greater diagnostic overlap than did DSM-III.

The number and nature of publications appearing in the literature that deal with the personality disorders have apparently been affected by the appearance of DSM-III and DSM-III-R. Prior to DSM-III, considerable attention was given to antisocial disorder and relatively less to the other personality disorders. Since 1980, there has been an increase in the literature dealing with borderline personality, slightly fewer extensive investigations of schizotypal disorder and narcissistic disorder, and still fewer on the other personality disorders. Even the very contentious self-defeating personality disorder (previously called masochistic personality disorder), which has been added over the objections of many (Franklin, 1987) to the DSM-III-R appendix described as "diagnostic categories needing further study," has received little research attention to date. In fact, we found only one recent article dealing with this disorder. Reich (1987) found that 18.3 percent of patients and 5 percent of normals met the criteria for this disorder; however, because the overlap with borderline, avoidant, and dependent disorders was greater than 50 percent, questions are raised concerning the validity and utility of the diagnosis of self-defeating personality disorder.

In this chapter, we highlight the important issues involved in the diagnosis of personality disorders by considering these issues in the context of those disorders for which sufficient research is available. We examine these issues by categorizing the disorders in the clusters identified in DSM-III-R. Insofar as these clusters are meaningful, we might expect greater overlap between the disorders clustered together than between these disorders and those listed under the other clusters, or those listed as Axis I syndromes.

CLUSTER A

Description and Clinical Presentation

According to DSM-III and its revision, patients classified as having paranoid, schizoid, or schizotypal personality disorders evidence clear signs of eccentricity or oddness, and this is certainly consistent with the specified criteria (see Table 12.1).

Patients with paranoid personality disorder tend to interpret what other people say and do as being directed at them. Sometimes this occurs when the behaviors of others are ambiguous, but all too frequently the paranoid personality also sees hidden negative meanings in quite innocent behaviors. The most commonly observed feature of paranoid personalities at clinical

TABLE 12.1. DSM-III-R Criteria for Paranoid, Schizoid, and Schizotypal Personality Disorders

Paranoid Personality Disorder

A. A pervasive and unwarranted tendency, beginning by early adulthood and present in a variety of contexts, to interpret the actions of people as deliberately demeaning or threatening, as indicated by at least four of the following:
  1. Expects, without sufficient basis, to be exploited or harmed by others
  2. Questions, without justification, the loyalty or trustworthiness of friends or associates
  3. Reads hidden demeaning or threatening meanings into benign remarks or events (e.g., suspects that a neighbor put out trash early to annoy him)
  4. Bears grudges or is unforgiving of insults or slights
  5. Is reluctant to confide in others because of unwarranted fear that the information will be used against him or her
  6. Is easily slighted and quick to react with anger or to counterattack
  7. Questions, without justification, fidelity of spouse or sexual partner.
B. Occurrence not exclusively during the course of schizophrenia or a delusional disorder.

Schizoid Personality Disorder

A. A pervasive pattern of indifference to social relationships and a restricted range of emotional experience and expression, beginning by early adulthood and present in a variety of contexts, as indicated by at least four of the following:
  1. Neither desires nor enjoys close relationships, including being part of a family
  2. Almost always chooses solitary activities
  3. Rarely, if ever, claims or appears to experience strong emotions, such as anger and joy
  4. Indicates little if any desire to have sexual experiences with another person (age being taken into account)
  5. Is indifferent to the praise and criticism of others
  6. Has no close friends or confidants (or only one) other than first-degree relatives
  7. Displays constricted affect (e.g., is aloof; is cold; rarely reciprocates gestures or facial expressions, such as smiles or nods).
B. Occurrence not exclusively during the course of schizophrenia or a delusional disorder.

Schizotypal Personality Disorder

A. A pervasive pattern of deficits in interpersonal relatedness and peculiarities of ideation, appearance, and behavior, beginning by early adulthood and present in a variety of contexts, as indicated by at least five of the following:
  1. Ideas of reference (excluding delusions of reference)
  2. Excessive social anxiety (e.g., extreme discomfort in social situations involving unfamiliar people)
  3. Odd beliefs or magical thinking, influencing behavior and inconsistent with subcultural norms (e.g., superstitiousness; belief in clairvoyance, telepathy, or "sixth sense"; belief that "others can feel my feelings") (in children and adolescents, bizarre fantasies or preoccupations)
  4. Unusual perceptual experiences (e.g., illusions, sensing the presence of a force or person not actually present)
  5. Odd or eccentric behavior or appearance (e.g., unkempt appearance, unusual mannerisms, talking to self)
  6. No close friends or confidants (or only one) other than first-degree relatives
  7. Odd speech, without loosening of associations or incoherence (e.g., speech that is impoverished, digressive, vague, or inappropriately abstract)
  8. Inappropriate or constricted affect (e.g., silly; aloof; rarely reciprocates gestures or facial expressions, such as smiles or nods)
  9. Suspiciousness or paranoid ideation.
B. Occurrence not exclusively during the course of schizophrenia or a pervasive developmental disorder.

Reprinted with permission from the *Diagnostic and Statistical Manual of Mental Disorders, Third Edition, Revised.* Copyright 1987 American Psychiatric Association.

evaluation is jealously or a conviction that a partner or close friend is taking advantage of them. These humorless patients appear not to trust anyone and are constantly looking for reasons to distrust others.

Patients with schizoid personality disorder seem not to have any interest in being involved with other people, including their own family. Such indifference extends to all aspects of interpersonal relationships, including sexual behavior. Schizoid patients present as almost devoid of emotions and quite indifferent to feedback from others. These patients seem unable to organize themselves or direct their lives, and are constantly absorbed in their own thoughts.

In the case of schizotypal disorder, the patient has many of the features of schizophrenia (e.g., odd ideas, eccentric behaviors, either odd dress or a disregard for appearance, poor quality relationships), but not of sufficient severity to meet the diagnostic criteria of that disorder. For the schizotypal personality, the major presenting feature is eccentricity of thought. These patients are often extremely superstitious and may emphatically declare the truth of paranormal phenomena. They frequently declare the presence of forces beyond usual human understanding and often speak in an allusory or excessively abstract manner. Their appearance is typically untidy.

Diagnostic Clarity and Differential Diagnosis

Several studies have described considerable overlap between the symptom pictures of schizotypal and borderline disorders (Davis & Akiskal, 1986; Frances, 1985; Resnick et al., 1983). For example, George and Soloff (1986) determined the presence of schizotypal features in patients, defined according to DSM-III criteria, as representing borderline personality disorder. They found the average borderline patient to have seven of the DSM-III criteria for schizotypal disorder, and all met at least one of these criteria. To their credit, the authors of DSM-III-R noted that "frequently, people with Borderline Personality Disorder also meet the criteria for Schizotypal Personality Disorder" (APA, 1987, p. 341), and they wrote that in such cases both diagnoses should be given; such codiagnoses, however, somewhat defeat the idea of a categorical classification system. Obviously, the issue of overlap between Cluster A disorders and those personality disorders assigned by DSM-III-R to other clusters remains problematic, and some modifications are warranted.

Perhaps the most pressing issue with respect to schizotypal disorder is the need to clarify its relationship with schizophrenia. In discussing differential diagnosis, DSM-III-R notes that transient and less severe psychotic symptoms do occur in schizotypal patients, and McGlashan (1987) argued that such transient psychoses characterize these patients. Kendler (1985) suggested that schizotypal disorder presents in subtle form the symptoms of classic schizophrenia, and thus we might expect differential diagnosis to be difficult. Siever (1985) reviewed the literature focusing on the psychobiological functioning of schizotypal patients and noted that the results are consistent with the idea that these patients share common abnormalities with schizophrenics. He encouraged researchers to pursue this line of study, and certainly these and other studies will help resolve this issue.

Considering this literature, we might expect interdiagnostician reliability to be low with respect to schizotypal personality disorder. Contrary to this expectation, Perry, O'Connell, and Drake (1984) found consistency across three raters who evaluated videotaped interviews with 12 patients. Using the schedule for schizotypal personalities developed by Baron, Asnis, and Gruen (1981) and DSM-III criteria, these raters demonstrated the reliability and validity of the schedule, with the single exception that the item dealing with odd speech did not fare well. Six of eight DSM-III criteria were found to be highly specific to schizotypal disorder, but unfortunately these criteria appeared to vary widely in their sensitivities. This study suggests that Baron et al.'s (1981) more structured schedule is worth pursuing as a diagnostic instrument, and its further use may guide improvement in future DSM criteria.

CLUSTER B

Description and Clinical Presentation

According to DSM-III-R, antisocial, borderline, histrionic, and narcissistic personality disorders are characterized by dramatic, emotional, or erratic expressions or behaviors. In fact, this seems to be an odd grouping, and it is somewhat hard to see unifying features to these disorders, except perhaps self-centeredness (see Table 12.2).

Men are four times more likely than women to be judged as having an antisocial personality disorder (Reiger et al., 1984). Such men are characteristically insensitive or indifferent to the needs and rights of others, and they display a rapacious attitude toward the world. They lie, threaten, steal, cheat, or use superficial charm to get their way. Their behavior is often impulsive, irresponsible, or reckless, and they show little regard for future consequences. Except for anger, antisocial patients display little emotional responsiveness, and what they do show is typically shallow and short-lived; however, these men sometimes present with a degree of personal distress when they appear to face a mid-life crisis. At these times, they may be tense, depressed, or convinced that people are hostile to them.

Borderline patients show mood swings and have persistent identity problems. When they are involved in relationships, they regard their partners inconsistently: Sometimes they idealize their partner; sometimes they devalue them. Perhaps the main feature of patients with borderline personality disorders is an instability in various aspects of their lives. Their interpersonal relationships, behaviors, moods, and self-images all fluctuate. They are characteristically unpredictable and impulsive, and this frequently costs them dearly. Borderline patients often complain of feelings of emptiness and boredom.

Flamboyant displays intended to draw attention to themselves are the defining feature of histrionic patients. These patients seem to see themselves as on center stage at all times and cannot tolerate being ignored. Histrionics persistently attempt to draw attention to themselves and are emotionally overresponsive to insignificant events. They seem insincere and shallow as they continually play to an audience. In relationships, they are demanding

TABLE 12.2. DSM-III-R Criteria for Antisocial, Borderline, Histrionic, and Narcissistic Personality Disorders

Antisocial Personality Disorder
A. Current age at least 18.
B. Evidence of conduct disorder with onset before age 15, as indicated by a history of three or more of the following:
   1. Was often truant
   2. Ran away from home overnight at least twice while living in parental or parental surrogate home (or once without returning)
   3. Often initiated physical fights
   4. Used a weapon in more than one fight
   5. Forced someone into sexual activity with him or her
   6. Was physically cruel to animals
   7. Was physically cruel to other people
   8. Deliberately destroyed others' property (other than by fire setting)
   9. Deliberately engaged in fire setting
   10. Often lied (other than to avoid physical or sexual abuse)
   11. Has stolen without confrontation of a victim on more than one occasion (including forgery)
   12. Has stolen with confrontation of a victim (e.g., mugging, purse snatching, extortion, armed robbery).
C. A pattern of irresponsible and antisocial behavior since the age of 15, as indicated by at least four of the following:
   1. Is unable to sustain consistent work behavior, as indicated by any of the following (including similar behavior in academic settings if the person is a student):
      a. Significant unemployment for 6 months or more within 5 years when expected to work and work was available
      b. Repeated absences from work unexplained by illness in self or family
      c. Abandonment of several jobs without realistic plans for others
   2. Fails to conform to social norms with respect to lawful behavior, as indicated by repeatedly performing antisocial acts that are grounds for arrest, whether arrested or not (e.g., destroying property, harassing others, stealing, pursuing an illegal occupation)
   3. Is irritable and aggressive, as indicated by repeated physical fights or assaults (not required by one's job or to defend someone or oneself), including spouse or child beating
   4. Repeatedly fails to honor financial obligations, as indicated by defaulting on debts or failing to provide child support or support for other dependents on a regular basis
   5. Fails to plan ahead, or is impulsive, as indicated by one or both of the following:
      a. Traveling from place to place without a prearranged job or clear goal for the period of travel or a clear idea about when the travel will terminate
      b. Lack of a fixed address for a month or more
   6. Has no regard for the truth, as indicated by repeated lying, use of aliases, or "conning" of others for personal profit or pleasure
   7. Is reckless regarding his or her own or others' personal safety, as indicated by driving while intoxicated, or recurrent speeding
   8. If a parent or guardian, lacks ability to function as a responsible parent, as indicated by one or more of the following:
      a. Malnutrition of child
      b. Child's illness resulting from lack of minimal hygiene
      c. Failure to obtain medical care for a seriously ill child
      d. Child's dependence on neighbors or nonresident relatives for food or shelter
      e. Failure to arrange for a caretaker for young child when parent is away from home
      f. Repeated squandering, on personal items, of money required for household necessities
   9. Has never sustained a totally monogamous relationship for more than a year
   10. Lacks remorse (feels justified in having hurt, mistreated, or stolen from another).
D. Occurrence of antisocial behavior not exclusively during the course of schizophrenia or manic episodes.

366

TABLE 12.2. *(Continued)*

Borderline Personality Disorder

A pervasive pattern of instability of mood, interpersonal relationships, and self-image, beginning by early adulthood and present in a variety of contexts, as indicated by at least five of the following:

1. A pattern of unstable and intense interpersonal relationships characterized by alternating between extremes of overidealization and devaluation
2. Impulsiveness in at least two areas that are potentially self-damaging, other than suicidal or self-mutilating behavior covered in Item 5 (e.g., spending, sex, substance use, shoplifting, reckless driving, binge eating)
3. Affective instability: marked shifts from baseline mood to depression, irritability, or anxiety, usually lasting a few hours and only rarely more than a few days
4. Inappropriate, intense anger or lack of control of anger (e.g., frequent displays of temper, constant anger, recurrent physical fights)
5. Recurrent suicidal threats, gestures, or behavior, or self-mutilating behavior
6. Marked and persistent identity disturbance manifested by uncertainty about at least two of the following: self-image, sexual orientation, long-term goals or career choice, type of friends desired, preferred values
7. Chronic feelings of emptiness or boredom
8. Frantic efforts to avoid real or imagined abandonment, other than suicidal or self-mutilating behavior covered in Item 5.

Histrionic Personality Disorder

A pervasive pattern of excessive emotionality and attention seeking, beginning by early adulthood and present in a variety of contexts, as indicated by at least four of the following:

1. Constantly seeks or demands reassurance, approval, or praise
2. Is inappropriately sexually seductive in appearance or behavior
3. Is overly concerned with physical attractiveness
4. Expresses emotion with inappropriate exaggeration (e.g., embraces casual acquaintances with excessive ardor, uncontrollably sobs on minor sentimental occasions, has temper tantrums)
5. Is uncomfortable in situations in which he or she is not the center of attention
6. Displays rapidly shifting and shallow expression of emotions
7. Is self-centered, actions being directed toward obtaining immediate satisfaction; has no tolerance for the frustration of delayed gratification
8. Has a style of speech that is excessively impressionistic and lacking in detail (e.g., when asked to describe mother, can be no more specific than, "She was a beautiful person").

Narcissistic Personality Disorder

A pervasive pattern of grandiosity (in fantasy or behavior), lack of empathy, and hypersensitivity to the evaluation of others, beginning by early adulthood and present in a variety of contexts, as indicated by at least five of the following:

1. Reacts to criticism with feelings of rage, shame, or humiliation (even if not expressed)
2. Is interpersonally exploitative: takes advantage of others to achieve own ends
3. Has a grandiose sense of self-importance (e.g., exaggerates achievements and talents, expects to be noticed as "special" without appropriate achievement)
4. Believes that his or her problems are unique and can be understood only by other special people
5. Is preoccupied with fantasies of unlimited success, power, brilliance, beauty, or ideal love
6. Has a sense of entitlement: unreasonable expectation of especially favorable treatment (e.g., assumes that he or she does not have to wait in line when others must do so)
7. Requires constant attention and admiration (e.g., keeps fishing for compliments)
8. Lack of empathy: inability to recognize and experience how others feel (e.g., annoyance and surprise when a friend who is seriously ill cancels a date)
9. Is preoccupied with feelings of envy.

and inconsiderate. Although they rarely seem able to fully enjoy sex, they are often flirtatious.

Egocentricity is the central feature of narcissistic patients. They are preoccupied with their own desires and expect others to serve their needs. They are continually self-absorbed and are preoccupied with unrealistic fantasies of personal success. These patients constantly seek admiration and even expect it. Narcissistic patients typically overreact to criticism, which they view as undeserved. They expect others to admire them and bend to their wishes.

Diagnostic Clarity and Differential Diagnosis

Evidence of a link between antisocial personality disorder and somatization has been reported for many years (Cloninger & Guze, 1970; Guze, 1964; Guze, Woodruff, & Clayton, 1971; Robins, Purtell, & Cohen, 1952; Spalt, 1980).

Two recent criticisms of the diagnostic criteria for antisocial personality disorder require noting. Mackay (1986) claimed that this diagnosis is a product of pejorative and judgmental constructs and that the disorder is actually a subcategory of pathological narcissism. Similarly, Bursten (1982) placed antisocial personality within a cluster of narcissistic types, which would also include paranoid, dependent, and avoidant disorders since they all involve intense self-focus. Wulach (1983), on the other hand, declared that criteria for antisocial personality have become too broad and now include the vast majority rather than, as previously, a minority of criminals. Exactly why this is seen as a disadvantage is not made clear, although Modlin (1983) claimed that this diagnosis is fraught with uncertainty and imprecision. Hare's (1983) findings, however, do not agree with these contentions. He found good agreement between independent ratings of psychopathy and DSM-III derived diagnoses, as well as good agreement between DSM-III and his own Behavioral Checklist for Psychopathy (Hare, 1980). This checklist, in fact, seems to be an excellent instrument for research purposes in defining antisocial personality, since Schroeder, Schroeder, and Hare (1983) have, in addition, demonstrated it to have high inter- and intrarater reliability.

Several reports (Abramowitz, Carroll, & Schaffer, 1984; Egan, 1986; Evans, Ruff, Braff, & Cox, 1986; Nurnberg, Feldman, Hurt, & Suh, 1986) suggested considerable heterogeneity within the patient group diagnosed as borderline, and Burkhardt (1984), although agreeing that DSM-III criteria produced improvements, declared that the boundaries that distinguish it from other disorders remain obscure. We have already noted the commonly observed overlap between borderline and schizotypal disorders, but there is suggestive evidence (Clary, Burstin, & Carpenter, 1984; Horevitz & Braun, 1984) that many borderline patients also meet the criteria for multiple personality disorder, a dissociative disorder. Clarkin, Widiger, Frances, Hurt, and Gilmore (1983) similarly observed considerable overlap with various other personality disorders, and Pfohl, Coryell, Zimmerman, and Stangl (1986) and Pope, Jonas, Hudson, Cohen, and Gunderson (1983) found overlap between borderline and histrionic disorders.

One major issue concerning the diagnosis of borderline patients concerns the differential diagnosis with affective disorders. Nakdimen (1986) does not equivocate here; he declared that borderline personality should not be considered a separate disorder, but rather should be classified as a subtype of primary affective disorder. Several authors (Andrulonis & Vogel, 1984; Gunderson & Elliott, 1985; McManus, Lerner, Robbins, & Barbour, 1984; Pope et al., 1983) observed overlap between borderline disorder and affective disorders, and Perry (1985) found that borderline patients had a lifetime history of depression. In agreement with these observations are the findings of neuroendocrine or electroencephalographic studies of the similarities between borderline disordered patients and those with affective disorders (Garbutt, Loosen, Tipermas, & Prange, 1983; Gardner, Lucas, & Cowdry, 1987; Snyder & Pitts, 1984; Sternbach, Fleming, Extein, Pottash, & Gold, 1983; Yerevanian, Schiffer, & Mallon, 1985).

These data on heterogeneity and overlap call into question the reliability of the borderline diagnosis. However, Frances (1985) reported high reliability of the diagnosis, and Davis and Akiskal (1986) found both inter- and intrarater reliability for the borderline diagnosis to be satisfactory.

A procedure that appears to offer hope for improving diagnostic reliability, at least for research purposes, is the Diagnostic Interview for Borderline Disorder, developed by Gunderson and Kolb (1978). In two studies, Hurt and his colleagues (Hurt, Ayler, Frances, Clarkin, & Brent, 1984; Hurt, Clarkin, Koenigsberg, Frances, & Nurnberg, 1986) found that this interview procedure produced reliable diagnoses and readily distinguished borderline disordered patients from those diagnosed as having other personality disorders.

CLUSTER C

Description and Clinical Presentation

Patients who receive a diagnosis of one of the Cluster C disorders, which include avoidant, dependent, obsessive–compulsive, and passive–aggressive personality disorders, are said, by DSM-III-R, to be characterized by anxiety and fearfulness. As with Cluster A, this general description seems to fit the specified criteria (see Table 12.3).

Patients with avoidant personality disorders, as the label suggests, shy away from involvements. They do not enter into relationships unless assured they will not be hurt, although they appear to desire affection. They avoid new experiences and do not like to meet new people, apparently as a result of their low self-esteem, which makes them acutely sensitive to criticism. Consequently, they present as extremely sensitive and untrusting, and it requires patience to win their confidence.

Dependent patients seem afraid of having to rely on themselves, so they consistently avoid making decisions and instead rely on others. Self-denigration is common and seems to be aimed at pointing out their inadequacies so that others will look after them. Dependent personalities

TABLE 12.3. DSM-III-R Criteria for Avoidant, Dependent, Obsessive–Compulsive, and Passive–Aggressive Personality Disorders

Avoidant Personality Disorder

A pervasive pattern of social discomfort, fear of negative evaluation, and timidity, beginning by early adulthood and present in a variety of contexts, as indicated by at least four of the following:

1. Is easily hurt by criticism or disapproval
2. Has no close friends or confidants (or only one) other than first-degree relatives
3. Is unwilling to get involved with people unless certain of being liked
4. Avoids social or occupational activities that involve significant interpersonal contact (e.g., refuses a promotion that will increase social demands)
5. Is reticent in social situations because of a fear of saying something inappropriate or foolish, or of being unable to answer a question
6. Fears being embarrassed by blushing, crying, or showing signs of anxiety in front of other people
7. Exaggerates the potential difficulties, physical dangers, or risks involved in doing something ordinary but outside his or her usual routine (e.g., may cancel social plans because he or she anticipates being exhausted by the effort of getting there).

Dependent Personality Disorder

A pervasive pattern of dependent and submissive behavior, beginning by early adulthood and present in a variety of contexts, as indicated by at least five of the following:

1. Is unable to make everyday decisions without an excessive amount of advice or reassurance from others
2. Allows others to make most of his or her important decisions (e.g., where to live, what job to take)
3. Agrees with people even when he or she believes they are wrong, because of fear of being rejected
4. Has difficulty initiating projects or doing things on his or her own
5. Volunteers to do things that are unpleasant or demeaning in order to get other people to like him or her
6. Feels uncomfortable or helpless when alone, or goes to great lengths to avoid being alone
7. Feels devastated or helpless when close relationships end
8. Is frequently preoccupied with fears of being abandoned
9. Is easily hurt by criticism or disapproval.

Obsessive–Compulsive Personality Disorder

A pervasive pattern of perfectionism and inflexibility, beginning by early adulthood and present in a variety of contexts, as indicated by at least five of the following:

1. Perfectionism that interferes with task completion (e.g., inability to complete a project because own overly strict standards are not met)
2. Preoccupation with details, rules, lists, order, organization, or schedules to the extent that the major point of the activity is lost
3. Unreasonable insistence that others submit to exactly his or her way of doing things, or unreasonable reluctance to allow others to do things because of the conviction that they will not do them correctly
4. Excessive devotion to work and productivity to the exclusion of leisure activities and friendships (not accounted for by obvious economic necessity)
5. Indecisiveness: decision making is either avoided, postponed, or protracted (e.g., the person cannot get assignments done on time because of ruminating about priorities) (do not include if indecisiveness is due to excessive need for advice or reassurance from others)
6. Overconscientiousness, scrupulousness, and inflexibility about matters of morality, ethics, or values (not accounted for by cultural or religious identification)
7. Restricted expression of affection
8. Lack of generosity in giving time, money, or gifts when no personal gain is likely to result

TABLE 12.3.   *(Continued)*

9. Inability to discard worn-out worthless objects even when they have no sentimental value.

Passive–Aggressive Personality Disorder
A pervasive pattern of passive resistance to demands for adequate social and occupational performance, beginning by early adulthood and present in a variety of contexts, as indicated by at least five of the following:
   1. Procrastinates (i.e., puts off things that need to be done so that deadlines are not met)
   2. Becomes sulky, irritable, or argumentative when asked to do something he or she does not want to do
   3. Seems to work deliberately slowly or to do a bad job on tasks that he or she really does not want to do
   4. Protests, without justification, that others make unreasonable demands on him or her
   5. Avoids obligations by claiming to have "forgotten"
   6. Believes that he or she is doing a much better job than others think he or she is doing
   7. Resents useful suggestions from others concerning how he or she could be more productive
   8. Obstructs the efforts of others by failing to do his or her share of the work
   9. Unreasonably criticizes or scorns people in positions of authority.

Reprinted with permission from the *Diagnostic and Statistical Manual of Mental Disorders, Third Edition, Revised.* Copyright 1987 American Psychiatric Association.

present a real problem for clinicians who must constantly be on guard against assuming responsibility for directing the lives of these patients.

An all-encompassing striving for perfection typifies the patient suffering from obsessive–compulsive personality disorder. Of course, since these patients aim so high, their actual performance is disappointing to them. To avoid these disappointments, obsessive–compulsive personalities typically delay or procrastinate and dither about with trivial detail. At clinical presentation, they are neat, formal, stiff, and overly moralistic.

In response to demands by others, passive–aggressive personality disordered patients display indirectly expressed resistance. This resistance is thought to be an expression of covert hostility and is revealed in procrastinating, forgetfulness, and stubbornness. Such behaviors markedly reduce these patients' efficiency, and they consequently frequently fail to reach their potential at work or in their relationships. These patients commonly present all sorts of reasons why they cannot comply with the recommendations or requests made by clinicians.

Diagnostic Clarity and Differential Diagnosis

Because the avoidant patients' fears and anxieties are related to social discomfort and the prospect of being negatively evaluated by others, we might expect a particularly difficult diagnostic problem associated with differentiating these patients from those with social phobia. The description in DSM-III-R makes this very point and indicates that these two disorders may coexist. Turner, Beidel, Dancu, and Keys (1986) compared rather small samples of patients having each of these disorders and found them to be the same in terms of their cognitive content and physiological reactivity, although avoidant patients were more sensitive to interpersonal interactions and had generally poorer social skills. Greenberg and Stravynski (1985) conducted a detailed analysis of 46 patients attending a clinic designed to deal with social dysfunction. Their analyses suggested that the features of these patients more closely match the criteria for avoidant personality disorder than those for social phobia. Reich, Noyes, and Troughton (1987) observed that significantly more phobic patients (88 panic-disordered patients with or without phobic avoidance) than nonphobic patients met DSM-III criteria for one of the Cluster C personality disorders. Again, this issue needs further research attention to clarify the relationship between these Cluster C disorders and the anxiety disorders.

COURSE AND COMPLICATIONS

Personality disorders seem to originate during childhood. A failure to form effective attachment bonds with parents is understood to lead to low self-esteem and adult interpersonal styles that are dysfunctional (Bowlby, 1977a, 1977b). The personality disorders described above can be seen as ways of dealing with, or expressions of, this inadequate sense of the self and the inability to attain, or fear of attaining, close intimate relations with others. Thus, the course of personality disorders seems to extend from childhood through to adulthood.

Once personality disorders become entrenched, they seem to dispose the patients to develop other disorders. As we have seen, there is much overlap within these disorders and between them and other psychiatric problems. Even if these patients do not develop other disorders, however, they will have considerable difficulties in all aspects of their lives. Their social life, work, interpersonal relations, and leisure will all be dysfunctional to some significant degree. Involvement with the law, particularly in the case of antisocial personality disordered patients, will further disrupt their lives. In most cases, these repeated disruptions lead patients to enter treatment, but this does not mean that they will manifest an openness and motivation for change. Quite to the contrary, these patients seem as resistant to the efforts of therapists as they are to the suggestions of friends and relatives.

ETIOLOGY AND NATURAL HISTORY

The etiology of these disorders is not clear, although the diagnostic criteria indicate early adulthood as the time when the problems emerge. In some cases, however, personality disorders in adults are related to disorders evident in childhood. For example, avoidant disorder of childhood or adolescence is described in DSM-III-R as related to avoidant personality disorder, and identity disorder is related to borderline personality disorder. Although DSM-III-R indicates that the personality disorders should be diagnosed in children if the criteria are met, it seems reasonable to assume that these related disorders of childhood are, at least in some cases, precursors of the adult disorders. The suggestion in all these disorders is that there may be a continuity, or growing severity, in the problem behaviors, which, by adulthood, have become full-blown personality disorders.

Although some theorists contend that personality characteristics have a substantial inherited component (Buss & Plomin, 1975; Eysenck, 1977), others (e.g., Smith, 1978) argue that a social learning account can adequately explain the personality disorders. We (Marshall & Barbaree, 1984) described a theory of the etiology of antisocial personality disorder that was meant to be an illustrative application of social learning theory to this general group of disorders. A disruptive or abusive childhood was taken to be related to the later development of antisocial personality disorder.

In more general terms, Rutter (1984), in searching for the childhood antecedents of various psychiatric disorders, found the strongest linkage to be between childhood conduct disorders and adult personality disorders. Similarly, Drake and Vaillant (1985) reinterviewed over 300 of Glueck and Glueck's (1950) original delinquents, and found that 86 of them as adults met the DSM-III criteria for a personality disorder. Because childhood conduct disorders have been found to be products of disruptive family processes (Patterson, 1982; Patterson, Capaldi, & Bank, in press), the linkage with adult personality disorders supports our view that they, too, have their origin in aversive childhood experiences occurring in the context of the family. R.L. Goldberg, Mann, Wise, and Segall (1985) found that borderline personality disordered patients described their parents as less caring and more overprotective than did either other patients or normal control subjects. In the case of patients who as adults meet the criteria for narcissistic personality disorder, Rothstein (1984) claimed that the basic problem for these patients, which he says is fear of humiliation, stems from their parents repeatedly humiliating them. Paris (1985) reported that narcissistic patients are unable to tolerate intimacy in adult relations, and this capacity is understood to result from impaired parental attachments in childhood (R.S. Weiss, 1982).

MANAGEMENT OF THE PERSONALITY DISORDERS

Variations on three quite different conceptualizations of human behavior—psychoanalysis, biological perspectives, and behavioral analysis—have guided thinking about the management of personality disordered patients. In Millon's (1981) landmark book on the personality disorders, he suggested that each disorder requires a unique approach. He advocated behavior therapies for some of these disorders, psychoanalytic approaches for others, and cognitive therapy for yet others; however, he did not expect any treatment to be remarkably effective with such all-encompassing problems.

Whatever support exists for a psychoanalytic approach to these patients is derived from uncontrolled case studies. The only well-controlled long-term outcome study of psychoanalysis with personality disorders was conducted at the Menninger Clinic, and the results were quite discouraging (Stone, 1987).

An extensive body of literature evaluates the effects of pharmacological interventions with various personality disorders, and it seems clear that drug therapies are effective with some of these problems. However, there have been no systematic investigations of the very important issues of refusal rates, treatment dropouts or noncompliance, and relapse rates upon withdrawal of the drugs. These issues, of course, are important for all treatment approaches, but particularly for drug therapies (Marshall & Segal, 1990). Nevertheless, the current evidence contradicts the opinion expressed by Klar and Seiver (1984) that pharmacological interventions for personality disorders rest more on opinion than on demonstrated efficacy.

One early behavioral approach emphasized the operant management of personality disorders (Pieczenik & Birk, 1974), but it overlooked the social deficits that underpin the patients' inadequate ways of seeking reinforcement. Argyle, Trower, and Bryant (1974), on the other hand, proposed a social skills training approach. They offered illustrations of their approach but no controlled evidence.

Borderline Disorder

Otto Kernberg (1975) is considered the leading theoretician in dealing with borderline patients from a psychoanalytic perspective. Although he outlined a treatment program, he did not provide any evidence supporting its value. Classical psychoanalysis has been reported to be effective in individual cases (e.g., Adler, 1981; Cary, 1972; Epstein, 1979; J.J. Weiss, 1974), but a carefully controlled outcome study did not encourage optimism (Stone, 1987).

Most reports of the use of pharmacological agents with borderline patients have been uncontrolled clinical trials (Gunderson, 1986), but there are some recent controlled outcome studies. For example, Soloff, George, Nathan, Schulz, and Perel (1986) conducted a double-blind, placebo-controlled study demonstrating the effectiveness of amitriptyline, and S.C. Goldberg et al. (1986) found that low doses of thiothixene produced a therapeutic effect compared with a placebo control. In fact, studies examining the use of antipsychotics and of antidepressants with borderline patients have suggested differential effects across different subtypes of these patients. S.C. Goldberg et al. (1986) found greater effects for antipsychotics for those patients who displayed predominantly psychotic-like symptoms (e.g., illusions, ideas of reference), and Cole, Saloman, Gunderson, Sunderland, and Simmonds (1984) reported that borderlines who have schizophrenic-like symptoms showed the best response to antipsychotics. Cole et al. also found that borderline patients who also met the criteria for major depression showed maximal improvements when treated with either antipsychotics or antidepressants.

Alprazolam has been suggested as an effective treatment for borderline patients (Faltus, 1984), but Gardner and Cowdry (1985) reported a significant increase in behavioral dyscontrol when these patients were given the drug. Finally, Gardner and Cowdry (1986) found positive effects for carbamazepine (an anticonvulsant) on the behavioral dyscontrol displayed by 16 female outpatients with borderline personality disorder.

Linehan (1987) proposed "dialectical behavior therapy" as an effective approach with these patients. This approach emphasizes the importance of empathy toward borderline patients and an acceptance of their contradictions. Linehan suggested adopting a matter-of-fact way of dealing with the crises (e.g., suicide threats) presented by these patients, and she claimed that they need extensive training in problem solving and social skills. Little evidence is offered, however, for the effectiveness of her approach.

Antisocial Personality Disorders

Earlier reviews of the treatment of antisocial personality disorder came to gloomy conclusions (e.g., Cleckley, 1976; Lipton, Martinson, & Wilks, 1975; McCord & McCord, 1964). Because a majority of the programs considered in these reviews derived their procedures from a psychoanalytic framework, it is not surprising that the reviewers were pessimistic, since such approaches seem ineffective with these clients (Pacht & Strangman, 1980).

Very little effort appears to have been directed at examining the possible value of drug therapy with psychopaths, but two recent studies offered some promise. Kellner (1982) reported that heavy doses of antianxiety agents reduced hostility in psychopathic prisoners, and Stringer and Josef (1983) found that methylphenidate was effective with 2 antisocial patients who had displayed attention deficit disorder as children.

Behavioral interventions with psychopathic patients have ranged from institutionally based token economies (Milan, 1987) to family-focused interventions (Morton & Ewald, 1987), social skills training (Henderson, 1989), and cognitive–behavioral procedures using self-instructions and training in problem solving (Templeman & Wollersheim, 1979). Most of these studies described encouraging outcomes, and Andrews et al. (1990) found that a meta-analysis of treatment outcome with criminal patients, indicated that the behaviorally based programs were maximally effective.

All of the behavioral programs described above targeted a nonspecific group of offenders, many of whom may have met the diagnostic criteria for antisocial personality disorder, but this is not specified. In any case, none of these studies indicated changes on measures of psychopathy as indices of the benefits of treatment. Recently, however, we (Marshall, Turner, & Barbaree, 1989) completed the first stage of an evaluation of a behaviorally oriented "life skills program" conducted in three Canadian penitentiaries. Prior to treatment, all subjects (treated and untreated) scored in the psychopathic range of this measure, whereas after the programs were completed, only the treated subjects showed reductions in psychopathy, and these reductions were statistically significant. This finding and the other results reported above suggest that the behavioral management of antisocial personalities leads to positive changes in both their criminal tendencies and their psychopathic personalities.

Other Personality Disorders

Kernberg (1975) and Kohut (1977) agreed that a modified psychoanalytic view of narcissistic personality disorder is essential if treatment is to be effective, but they disagreed on the basic flaw in these patients. Kernberg believed that a sense of inferiority is basic, whereas Kohut considered the narcissistic person's sense of grandiosity to be the fundamental problem. These differing views led to varying approaches to therapy, but neither author offered a controlled evaluation of the interventions. Single case reports of the psychoanalytic treatment of narcissicism (Ackerman, 1975; Kinston, 1980), however, suggest some possible value. Behavioral and pharmacological approaches with these patients seem to be not at all well developed.

There are numerous uncontrolled reports of psychoanalysis with histrionic patients, but no controlled outcome studies. Likewise, we located no controlled pharmacological studies and only two behavioral reports. Kass, Silvers, and Abrams (1972) successfully treated 5 female histrionic personalities, using contingent punishment and rewards, as well as social skills training.

Just as they had done with borderline patients, S.C. Goldberg et al. (1986) found, in a controlled study, that low doses of thiothixene produced benefits for patients diagnosed as having schizotypal personality disorder, and Schulz (1986) replicated their results.

The remaining personality disorders have been subject to scant systematic investigations of treatment effectiveness.

IMPULSE DISORDERS

One problem presented by incorporating impulse control disorders in DSM-III-R concerns the issue of offenders who wish to avoid convictions on the grounds of being legally not responsible for their crimes. When an offender can claim that he or she suffers from an identified mental disorder and can provide expert testimony in support of this claim, then the question of legal responsibility becomes a problem for the courts to determine. In fact, three state supreme courts (Kansas, Georgia, and Pennsylvania) have called into doubt the constitutionality of an insanity law that does not include impulse control disorders, since these disorders are specified in DSM-III as mental disorders ("Evidentiary and Procedural Questions," 1987). This, of course, is not a problem for routine diagnoses, but will probably persist as a significant issue for those clinicians who work within a forensic service.

Description and Clinical Presentation

All impulse disorders are said to involve a persistent failure to resist temptation or to resist an impulse to act in a way that harms the self or others (see Table 12.4). This inability to resist an impulse is preceded by increasing tension or arousal, and the act brings relief or gratification. Typically, however, the act is followed by guilt or regret.

Patients said to be suffering from intermittent explosive disorder display discrete episodes of assaultive or destructive behavior that is disportionate to any precipitating event. The patients subsequently recognize the inappropriateness of their rage, and they experience remorse. Consequently,

TABLE 12.4. DSM-III-R Criteria for Impulse Disorders

Intermittent Explosive Disorder

A. Several discrete episodes of loss of control of aggressive impulses result in serious assaultive acts or destruction of property.

B. The degree of aggressiveness expressed during the episodes is grossly out of proportion to any precipitating psychosocial stressors.

C. There are no signs of generalized impulsiveness or aggressiveness between the episodes.

D. The episodes of loss of control do not occur during the course of a psychotic disorder, organic personality syndrome, antisocial or borderline personality disorder, conduct disorder, or intoxication with a psychoactive substance.

Kleptomania

A. Recurrent failure to resist impulses to steal objects not needed for personal use or their monetary value.

B. Increasing sense of tension immediately before committing the theft.

C. Pleasure or relief at the time of committing the theft.

D. The stealing is not committed to express anger or vengeance.

E. The stealing is not due to conduct disorder or antisocial personality disorder.

Pathological Gambling

Maladaptive gambling behavior, as indicated by at least four of the following:

1. Frequent preoccupation with gambling or with obtaining money to gamble
2. Frequent gambling of larger amounts of money or over a longer period of time than intended
3. A need to increase the size or frequency of bets to achieve the desired excitement
4. Restlessness or irritability if unable to gamble
5. Repeated loss of money by gambling and returning another day to win back losses ("chasing")
6. Repeated efforts to reduce or stop gambling
7. Frequent gambling when expected to meet social or occupational obligations
8. Sacrifice of some important social, occupational, or recreational activity in order to gamble
9. Continuation of gambling despite inability to pay mounting debts, or despite other significant social, occupational, or legal problems that the person knows to be exacerbated by gambling.

Pyromania

A. Deliberate and purposeful fire setting on more than one occasion.

B. Tension or affective arousal before the act.

C. Fascination with, interest in, curiosity about, or attraction to fire and its situational context or associated characteristics (e.g., paraphernalia, uses, consequences, exposure to fires).

D. Intense pleasure, gratification, or relief when setting fires, or when witnessing or participating in their aftermath.

E. The fire setting is not done for monetary gain, as an expression of sociopolitical ideology, to conceal criminal activity, to express anger or vengeance, to improve one's living circumstances, or in response to a delusion or hallucination.

Trichotillomania

A. Recurrent failure to resist impulses to pull out one's hair, resulting in noticeable hair loss.

B. Increasing sense of tension immediately before pulling out the hair.

C. Gratification or a sense of relief when pulling out the hair.

D. No association with a preexisting inflammation of the skin, and not a response to a delusion or hallucination.

Reprinted with permission from the *Diagnostic and Statistical Manual of Mental Disorders, Third Edition, Revised.* Copyright 1987 American Psychiatric Association.

at clinical presentation, they often appear as despairing and full of self-reproach. Zimbardo (1977) described these patients as unassertive and overcontrolled. Zimbardo saw this behavior as encouraging others to take advantage of these patients, which makes them angry. They do not express this anger, but rather keep it to themselves, ruminate over it, and finally explode in a rage, often at someone or something having little to do with the origins of their anger. Often, it is hard to reconcile knowledge of their explosive rage with their manner at interview.

Kleptomaniacs show a persistent failure to resist temptations to steal. They frequently steal items that are of little value, even when they clearly have the resources available to purchase such items. Often, they either discard the stolen items or surreptitiously return them. Our clinical experience with these patients led us to conclude that kleptomaniacs are unassertive people who experience stress prior to their stealing episodes (Marshall & Barbaree, 1984). Indeed, their unassertiveness often produces the stress or at least allows it to continue. Much like the explosive patients, kleptomaniacs harbor resentment against others that they are unable to express, and this seems directly linked to their stealing, which serves them as a way of indirectly striking back at others.

Pathological gamblers, of course, are chronically unable to resist the lure of gambling, even when it has profoundly disruptive effects on their lives. Again, stress increases the urge to gamble, yet gambling produces stress owing to the financial losses so commonly involved. Gambling is such a central focus in the lives of these patients that everything else (family, job, financial responsibilities, etc.) is neglected. Gamblers seem to attribute control over their lives to luck, and they tend to view their lives as rather dull. Of course, gambling depends on a belief in luck and does serve to increase excitement. We construe this impulse disorder as resulting from social and cognitive deficiencies that do not permit the person to either control, or to perceive the possibility of controlling, his or her life, which the person considers boring.

Repetitive fire setting, which is associated with a sense of pleasure, gratification, or relief, is said by DSM-III-R to be diagnostic of pyromania. Unfortunately, many people who set fires do not meet the diagnostic criteria for pyromania, and this makes it difficult to interpret the literature, since the terms "arsonist," "pyromaniac," and "fire setter" are often used interchangeably. The requirement by DSM-III-R that fire setting be associated with pleasure rather than profit or vengeance means that very few fire setters will be properly called pyromaniacs. Cases in which sexual excitement is involved in fire setting seem rare, and we could find only two reports in which this was clear (Bourget & Bradford, 1987; Lande, 1980). If revenge is permitted as a motive, then the most obvious presenting feature of these patients will be lack of assertiveness, which puts them more in common with the other impulse disorders.

Trichotillomania, a recent addition to the diagnostic manual, has not generated much reported research as yet. These patients persistently pull out their own hair, which produces a reduction in tension or a sense of gratification. In our few contacts with such patients, it was clear that they were very unassertive people who seemed to be under stress and were very anxious.

Diagnostic Clarity and Differential Diagnosis

Although the criteria said to identify kleptomania, pathological gambling, intermittent explosive disorder, and trichotillomania seem clear, the same cannot be said of the criteria for pyromania. Fires set by pyromaniacs are "not done for monetary gain, as an expression of sociopolitical ideology, to conceal criminal activity, to express anger or vengeance, to improve one's living circumstances, or in response to a delusion or hallucination" (APA, 1987, p. 326). Instead, pyromaniacs are said to derive "intense pleasure, gratification, or relief" from setting fires, and they are fascinated with fires.

In an examination of the motives of 50 arsonists, Hurley and Monahan (1989) found that revenge and jealousy were the direct impetus in 30 percent of the cases. Twelve percent reported pleasure or excitement as one of several motives, whereas 28 percent reported experiencing some relief of tension. Similarly, Hill et al. (1982) found that revenge was the most common motive among arsonists, with only 8 percent having clear sexual motives. Bradford (1982) conducted one of the most thorough evaluations of the motives of arsonists, and found attention seeking and revenge to be the most common motives. Bradford found no indication of sexual gratification in any of the cases he examined. Data he obtained from the psychiatric records of the office of the Ontario fire marshal confirmed his own finding that very few arsonists met the DSM-III criteria for pyromania (less than 3 percent in Bradford's sample and less than 0.1 percent in the fire marshal's group).

Perhaps the most serious problem of differential diagnosis for the impulse disorders concerns their relationship to psychopathy (i.e., antisocial personality disorder). This issue is particularly difficult for pathological gambling. Tharp, Maltzman, Syndulko, and Ziskind (1980) found flat arousal patterns in compulsive gamblers in response to aversive events, which matched those shown by sociopaths. Such a response pattern has been shown to distinguish psychopaths from both other offenders and normal subjects. Similarly, Miller (1958) found that gamblers have a strong need for excitement, which is also said to characterize psychopaths (Emmons & Webb, 1974; Skrzypek, 1969). Pathological gamblers also show signs of other personality disorders. Graham and Lowenfeld (1986) found them to have the features of passive-aggressive personality disorder and to be sufficiently unstable as to suggest the possibility of borderline personality disorder. Rosenthal (1986) claimed that pathological gamblers frequently meet the diagnostic criteria for narcissistic personality disorder, and substance abuse is also common among compulsive gamblers (Graham & Lowenfeld, 1986).

Course and Complications

Little or no information is available on the course of these disorders, although the prevalence of fire setting in children and adolescents does suggest the possibility of an early onset of pyromania. Similarly, pathological gambling frequently begins in adolescence, and trichotillomania usually starts in childhood.

In terms of complications, trichotillomania may produce alopecia of the scalp (baldness). The other impulse disorders frequently involve the patient in criminal proceedings or, in the case of gambling, in associations with criminal groups. Gambling also is associated with substance abuse, increases the risk of suicide, and produces impairment in family and work functioning.

Etiology and Natural History

We have construed impulse disorders as stemming from social difficulties, most particularly unassertiveness, and we believe that they originate in childhood or adolescence as a result of poor social training. Certainly, such social deficits can be expected to remain intact while the inadequate responses shown by impulse disordered patients continue to protect them from the need to change. For example, in our understanding of kleptomania (Marshall & Barbaree, 1984), stealing becomes a way of expressing anger generated by people who take advantage of the unassertive kleptomaniac. In a similar fashion, the intermittency of reward in gambling maintains the behavior, as does the pleasure of engaging in an exciting game. The very nature of the impulsive behaviors serves to maintain them. Efforts to seek help seem prompted not so much by a recognition of these deficits as by arrest or family pressure. Indeed, these patients are typically at a loss to understand why they engage in their impulsive behavior.

Management of Impulse Disorders

As we noted, very few fire setters meet the diagnostic criteria for pyromania. Not surprisingly, we found only one treatment study in which the patients were identified as pyromaniacs, although we found numerous reports of the treatment of arsonists or fire setters. Most of these interventions were with juveniles, however, and it is not clear that the same approaches would be effective with adults. With juveniles, a lack of assertiveness seems common and appears to be related to the fire setting (Kolko & Kazdin, 1986; Sakheim, Vigdor, Gordon, & Helprin, 1985). Because revenge is the most common motive for arson committed by adults, then presumably these adults are equally unassertive, which has been confirmed in at least one study (Jackson, Hope, & Glass, 1987). We, therefore, would expect assertiveness training (Gambrill, 1985) or a more broadly based social skills program (Hollin & Trower, 1986) to be an effective approach to the management of arsonists generally. In the single report in which the patients appeared to meet DSM-III-R criteria, Bourget and Bradford (1987) modified their two pyromaniacs' sexual arousal to fires, which eliminated their fire setting propensities.

The same problematic issues concerning the application of diagnostic criteria that are apparent in pyromania also arise in diagnosing kleptomania. We found no recent treatment reports in which the patients were diagnosed as kleptomaniacs, but there were articles describing the treatment of compulsive shoplifters. Glover (1985) employed covert sensitization with a woman who had a 14-year history of daily compulsive shoplifting. During treatment, she imagined stealing and paired this with images of nausea and vomiting. Glover reported that at a 19-month follow-up, she was not only free of the urges to steal, but she was also more self-confident and more socially active. Perhaps social skills training would have been an alternative treatment approach.

Pathological gamblers have apparently been treated within a relapse prevention model derived from the addictions field. In their excellent book on relapse prevention, Marlatt and Gordon (1985) illustrated many aspects of their approach to addictions by the analysis of a man with a serious and long-standing gambling problem. However, we found no controlled studies, or even clinical trials, of this approach to pathological gambling.

Explosive disorder is so obviously related to anger control and ineptitude in social skills that it is quite surprising to find that no one has reported using approaches derived from these fields to treat this disorder. Of course, in the extensive studies of Novaco (Novaco & Welsh, 1987), some patients no doubt would meet DSM-III-R criteria for explosive disorder. Also, Henderson (1989) reported the effective treatment of very violent men with a comprehensive socials skills training program.

In summary, then, impulse disorders are perhaps best construed as the result of social deficits that can be managed by training these patients in social competency. Exactly what aspect of their social functioning should be targeted depends on the problem presented and upon the particular features of the patients.

ADJUSTMENT DISORDER

Description and Clinical Presentation

Adjustment disorder describes the appearance of a relatively short-lived maladaptive reaction to stress. These reactions are understandable but excessive, and are expected to cease upon withdrawal of the stressor. Thus, they are not long-term chronic reactions, but rather transitory (lasting less than 6 months) disruptions to work, school, or social or emotional functioning that are sufficiently severe and maladaptive to warrant attention. Unfortunately, very little research or theoretical literature has dealt with adjustment disorder. This lack appears to be, in part at least, because these problems are, by definition, transitory and not remarkably severe and, therefore, do not appear with any consistency at most clinics.

Because there are various types of adjustment disorder depending on the specific stressor and the individual's characteristic response to stress (e.g., anxiety, depression, social withdrawal, anger, physical complaints), it is difficult to indicate the clinical presentation. The main features seem to be maladaptive expressions in one of a variety of areas that occur in an otherwise competent person. Although the patient sees the problem as certain to endure indefinitely, the characteristic impression they give is of sufficient resourcefulness to inspire confidence that the problem will be overcome with time and a little effort.

Diagnostic Clarity and Differential Diagnosis

The main differential diagnostic problem with the adjustment disorders is to distinguish them, on the one hand, from more severe disorders (e.g., anxiety or mood disorders, personality disorders) and, on the other, from the similarly less severe problems identified in DSM-III-R V code (i.e., conditions not attributable to a mental disorder that are a focus of attention or treatment). Such distinctions rely on the clinician's judgment, and this seems certain to introduce unreliability of diagnosis. The authors of DSM-III-R commented that no absolute guidelines exist to aid in making the fundamental distinction between the V code problems and adjustment disorders, so clinical judgment is often required. As discussed below, such heavy reliance on clinical judgment in the absence of clear guidelines has caused problems.

One criticism of the diagnostic criteria for adjustment disorders is that they tend to divert the clinician's attention away from the possibility that the stressor producing the dysfunction may be the problem rather than the patient's response (Russell, 1986). Also, the heavy reliance on the clinician's judgment as to what constitutes an appropriate or inappropriate response seems likely to reduce the reliability of these diagnoses.

Consistent with requirements, patients diagnosed as adjustment disordered have been found to have milder symptoms of Axis I disorders, particularly depression (Cavanaugh, 1986; de Leo, Pellegrini, & Serraiotto, 1986), or to be physically ill. Those who are depressed, however, do not seem to be at any greater risk for a major depressive disorder than are nonpatients (Kovacs et al., 1986). With respect to physical illnesses, patients with general medical problems (Rodin & Voshart, 1986), liver transplants (Trzepac, Maue, Coffman, & Van-Thiel, 1986–1987), myocardial infarcts (Kaufmann, Pasacreta, Cheney, & Arcuni, 1985–1986), and acquired immune deficiency syndrome (AIDS) have a high likelihood of developing adjustment disorder. Although it is no doubt useful to specify problematic reactions to these very severe stressors in order that the patient can be appropriately helped, the problem remains that, to apply a diagnosis of adjustment disorder to such patients, DSM-III-R requires that their responses be "in excess of a normal and expectable reaction" (APA, 1987, p. 330). Exactly what constitutes a normal reaction to having AIDS is difficult to know, and again the discretion of the diagnostician and all his or her prejudices enter the judgment. With respect to severe or terminal medical disorders, perhaps the diagnosis of adjustment disorder should be set aside and the patients simply offered the best supportive counseling available. Whether the same can be said for all the adjustment disorder diagnoses remains to be seen, but this problem clearly needs to be addressed.

Course and Complications

Given the criteria for diagnosing adjustment disorder, we can expect a brief course, with the complications usually limited to one area of functioning. When the triggering stressor persists, however, a spillover is likely, such that if the initial response involves depressed mood, over time this may begin to cause problems in social functioning, work performance, and conduct in other situations. In fact, coding adjustment disorder by the predominant symptom, as suggested by DSM-III-R, may serve to reduce the clinician's attention to the very real difficulties experienced in other areas of functioning.

Etiology and Natural History

Adjustment disorder may onset at any time in life. It runs a limited course of 3 to 6 months, by which time, even without assistance, the patient usually overcomes his or her problems. If the stressor is of brief duration, the adjustment disorder is usually short-lived, lasting no more than 1 or 2 months. If, however, the stressor persists, then it may take much longer to return to earlier levels of functioning.

Management

There is precious little in the literature that describes treatment of adjustment disorder specifically, but no doubt the same approaches taken to deal with more exaggerated forms of these maladaptive responses would be effective. For instance, when anxiety is the predominant response, then anxiolitic medications or anxiety management techniques seem to be the logical interventions. When social withdrawal predominates, then social skill training, emphasizing an increase in social activities, may be valuable. In all cases, stress management training seems called for.

Whatever specific treatment procedures are involved, encouragement, confidence building, and supportive counseling seem fundamental in dealing with this disorder. In particular, the client should be assured that his or her responses are to be expected in the circumstances and that they do not indicate any underlying flaw in character.

SUMMARY

In this chapter, we considered personality disorders, impulse disorders, and adjustment disorders as defined in DSM-III-R. The personality disorders were subcategorized according to the clusters identified in DSM-III-R. Overall, the diagnostic clarity of these disorders is unsatisfactory. Far more research is needed to properly establish valid criteria for each of the diagnoses if, indeed, the present supposedly distinct diagnoses are supported by research as exemplifying distinct disorders.

Evidently, at the moment, the reliability of the diagnoses of personality disorders is less than adequate, and a good deal of overlap remains in these disorders. "Overlap" here refers to the observation that patients frequently display features of several disorders. Such overlap occurs within the subgroups of these disorders (e.g., many of the personality disorders within each cluster overlap with each other), as well as between these clusters and between these disorders and Axis I syndromes.

Diagnostic clarity seems to be more clearly established for the impulse disorders, with the exception of pyromania. The problem here seems to be that many individuals set fires in a seemingly impulsive way that is not accounted for by the DSM-III-R criteria for pyromania. Because these fire setters present serious social and clinical problems, and because studies have revealed few DSM-III-R categorized pyromaniacs, the authors of DSM-IV may be wise to reconsider the value of such restrictive criteria.

For adjustment disorders, the diagnostic criteria for the various supposedly distinct categories appear to be far too vague to allow reliable diagnosis. The criteria often rely heavily on the clinician's inferences, which, even in skilled persons, seem certain to differ. A creditable feature of the changes in the diagnostic manual, over the past two revisions at least, has been a clear attempt to provide objective criteria that reduce reliance on the inferential skills of diagnosticians. This improvement, unfortunately, is not a feature of the adjustment disorders, and, given the transient nature (by definition) of these disorders, their value (both to therapists and particularly to clients) is questionable.

We have construed the personality and impulse disorders to derive from poor learning experiences in childhood that establish inadequate ways of thinking and behaving. These inadequate processes seem to be exacerbated at times of stress, although usually they represent dysfunctional, if temporarily satisfying, ways of dealing with the world.

Consistent with this perspective, we believe that the most effective management of these disorders involves training the clients to develop more functionally effective behavioral skills and more useful ways of perceiving their world and others. There is clear evidence, however, of the valuable contribution that pharmacological intervention can make to the overall management of these problems. Despite these remarks, treatment of the personality disorders, in particular, remains quite difficult, and more work is needed to refine our approach to these disorders. Certainly, cognitive-behavioral methods have only recently been applied to such problems, and we trust that this represents a beginning to a series of systematic evaluations of this approach.

REFERENCES

Abramowitz, S. I., Carroll, J., & Schaffer, C. B. (1984). Borderline personality disorder and the MMPI. *Journal of Clinical Psychology, 40,* 410–413.

Ackerman, P. H. (1975). Narcissistic personality disorder in an identical twin. *International Journal of Psychoanalytic Psychotherapy, 4,* 389–409.

Adler, G. (1981). The borderline–narcissistic personality disorder continuum. *American Journal of Psychiatry, 138,* 46–50.

American Psychiatric Association. (1980). *Diagnostic and statistical manual of mental disorders* (3rd ed.). Washington, DC: Author.

American Psychiatric Association. (1987). *Diagnostic and statistical manual of mental disorders* (3rd ed. rev.). Washington, DC: Author.

Andrews, D. A., Zinger, I., Hoge, R. D., Bonta, J., Gendreau, P., & Cullen, F. T. (1990). Does correctional treatment work? A clinically relevant and psychologically informed meta analysis. *Criminology, 28,* 369–404.

Andrulonis, P. R., & Vogel, N. G. (1984). Comparison of borderline personality subcentegories to schizophrenic and affective disorders. *British Journal of Psychiatry, 144,* 358–363.

Argyle, M., Trower, P., & Bryant, B. (1974). Explorations in the treatment of personality disorders and neuroses by social skills training. *British Journal of Medical Psychology, 47,* 63–72.

Baron, M., Asnis, L., & Gruen, R. (1981). The Schedule for Schizotypal Personalities (SSP): A diagnostic interview of schizotypal features. *Psychiatric Research, 4,* 213–228.

Bourget, D., & Bradford, J. M. (1987). Fire fetishism, diagnostic and clinical implications: A review of two cases. *Canadian Journal of Psychiatry, 32,* 459–462.

Bowlby, J. (1977a). The making and breaking of affectional bonds: I. Aetiology and psychopathology in the light of attachment theory. *British Journal of Psychiatry, 130,* 201–210.

Bowlby, J. (1977b). The making and breaking of affectional bonds: II. Some principles of psychotherapy. *British Journal of Psychiatry, 130,* 421–431.

Bradford, J. M. W. (1982). Arson: A clinical study. *Canadian Journal of Psychiatry, 27,* 188–193.

Burkhardt, P. E. (1984). A proposed solution to past differences in the classification of borderline personality disorder. *Perceptual and Motor Skills, 59,* 370.

Bursten, B. (1982). Narcissistic personalities in DSM-III: 1. Personality classification. *Comprehensive Psychiatry, 23,* 409–420.

Buss, A. H., & Plomin, R. (1975). *A temperament theory of personality development.* New York: Wiley.

Cary, G. L. (1972). The borderline condition: A structural–dynamic viewpoint. *Psychoanalytic Review, 59,* 33–54.

Cavanaugh, S. V. (1986). Depression in the hospitalized inpatient with various medical illnesses. *Psychotherapy and Psychosomatics, 45,* 97–104.

Clarkin, J. F., Widiger, T. A., Frances, A., Hurt, S. W., & Gilmore, M. (1983). Borderline personality disorder. *Journal of Abnormal Psychology, 92,* 263–275.

Clary, W. F., Burstin, K. J., & Carpenter, J. S. (1984). Multiple personality and borderline personality disorder. *Psychiatric Clinics of North America, 7,* 89–99.

Cleckley, H. (1976). *The mask of sanity* (5th ed.). St. Louis: Mosby.

Cloninger, C. R., & Guze, S. B. (1970). Psychiatric illness and female criminality: The role of sociopathy and hysteria in the antisocial woman. *American Journal of Psychiatry, 127,* 303–311.

Cole, J. O., Saloman, M., Gunderson, J., Sunderland, P., & Simmonds, P. (1984). Drug therapy for borderline patients. *Comprehensive Psychiatry, 25,* 249–254.

Dahl, A. R. (1986). Some aspects of the DSM-III personality disorders illustrated by a consecutive sample of hospitalized patients. *Acta Psychiatrica Scandinavica, 73,* 61–67.

Davis, G. C., & Akiskal, H. S. (1986). Descriptive, biological, and theoretical aspects of borderline personality disorder. *Hospital and Community Psychiatry, 37,* 685–692.

de Leo, D., Pellegrini, C., & Serraiotto, L. (1986). Adjustment disorders and suicidality. *Psychological Reports, 59,* 355–358.

Drake, R. E., & Vaillant, G. E. (1985). A validity study of Axis II of DSM-III. *American Journal of Psychiatry, 142,* 553–558.

Egan, J. (1986). Etiology and treatment of borderline personality disorder in adolescents. *Hospital and Community Psychiatry, 37,* 613–618.

Emmons, T. D., & Webb, W. W. (1974). Subjective correlates of emotional responsivity and stimulation seeking in psychopaths, normals, and acting-out neurotics. *Journal of Consulting and Clinical Psychology, 42,* 620.

Epstein, L. (1979). The therapeutic use of countertransference data with borderline patients. *Contemporary Psychoanalysis, 15,* 2.

Evans, R. W., Ruff, R. M., Braff, D. L., & Cox, D. R. (1986). On the consistency of the MMPI in borderline personality disorder. *Perceptual and Motor Skills, 62,* 579–585.

Evidentiary and procedural questions. (1987). *Mental and Physical Disability Law Reporter, 11,* 166–167.

Eysenck, H. J. (1977). *Crime and personality* (3rd ed.). London: Routledge & Kegan Paul.

Faltus, F. J. (1984). The positive effect of alprazolam in the treatment of three patients with borderline personality disorder. *American Journal of Psychiatry, 141,* 802–803.

Frances, A. (1985). Validating schizotypal personality disorders: Problems with the schizophrenia connection. *Schizophrenia Bulletin, 11,* 595–597.

Franklin, D. (1987, January). The politics of masochism. *Psychology Today, 21,* 52–57.

Gambrill, E. (1985). Assertiveness training. In A. S. Bellack & M. Hersen (Eds.), *Dictionary of behavior therapy techniques* (pp. 7–10). New York: Pergamon Press.

Garbutt, J. C., Loosen, P. T., Tipermas, A., & Prange, A. J. (1983). The TRH test in patients with borderline personality disorder. *Psychiatry Research, 9,* 107–113.

Gardner, D. L., & Cowdry, R. W. (1985). Alprazolam-induced dyscontrol in borderline personality disorder. *American Journal of Psychiatry, 142,* 98–100.

Gardner, D. L., & Cowdry, R. W. (1986). Positive effects of carbamazepine on behavioral dyscontrol in borderline personality disorder. *American Journal of Psychiatry, 143,* 519–522.

Gardner, D. L., Lucas, P. B., & Cowdry, R. W. (1987). Soft sign neurological abnormalities in borderline personality disorder and normal control subjects. *Journal of Nervous and Mental Disease, 175,* 177–180.

George, A., & Soloff, P. M. (1986). Schizotypal symptoms in patients with borderline personality disorders. *American Journal of Psychiatry, 143,* 212–215.

Glover, J. H. (1985). A case of kleptomania treated by covert sensitization. *British Journal of Clinical Psychology, 24,* 213–214.

Goldberg, R. L., Mann, L. S., Wise, T. N., & Segall, E. R. (1985). Parental qualities as perceived by borderline personality disorder. *Hillside Journal of Clinical Psychiatry, 7,* 134–140.

Goldberg, S. C., Schulz, S. C., Schulz, P. M., Resnick, R. J., Hamer, R. M., & Friedel, R. O. (1986). Borderline and schizotypal personality disorders treated with low-dose thiothixene vs placebo. *Archives of General Psychiatry, 43,* 680–686.

Graham, J. R., & Lowenfeld, B. H. (1986). Personality dimensions of the pathological gambler. *Journal of Gambling Behavior, 2,* 58–66.

Greenberg, D., & Stravynski, A. (1985). Patients who complain of social dysfunction as their main problem: 1. Clinical and demographic features. *Canadian Journal of Psychiatry, 30,* 206–211.

Gunderson, J. G. (1986). Pharmacotherapy for patients with borderline personality disorder. *Archives of General Psychiatry, 43,* 698–700.

Gunderson, J. G., & Elliott, G. R. (1985). The interface between borderline personality disorder and affective disorder. *American Journal of Psychiatry, 142,* 277–288.

Gunderson, J. G., & Kolb, J. E. (1978). Discriminating features of borderline patients. *American Journal of Psychiatry, 135,* 792–796.

Guze, S. B. (1964). Conversion symptoms in criminals. *American Journal of Psychiatry, 121,* 580–583.

Guze, S. B., Woodruff, R. A., & Clayton, P. J. (1971). Hysteria and antisocial behavior: Further evidence of an association. *American Journal of Psychiatry, 127,* 957–960.

Hare, R. D. (1980). A research scale for the assessment of psychopathy in criminal populations. *Personality and Individual Differences, 1,* 111–117.

Hare, R. D. (1983). Comparison of procedures for the assessment of psychopathy. *Journal of Consulting and Clinical Psychology, 53,* 7–16.

Henderson, M. (1989). Behavioural approaches to violent crime. In K. Howells & C. R. Hollin (Eds.), *Clinical approaches to violence* (pp. 25–37). New York: Wiley.

Hill, R. W., Langevin, R., Paitich, D., Handy, L., Russon, A., & Wilkinson, L. (1982). Is arson an aggressive act or a property offence? A controlled study of psychiatric referrals. *Canadian Journal of Psychiatry, 27,* 648–654.

Hollin, C. R., & Trower, P. (1986). *Handbook of social skills training: Vol. 1. Applications across the life span.* Oxford: Pergamon.

Horevitz, R. P., & Braun, B. G. (1984). Are multiple personalities borderline? An analysis of 33 cases. *Psychiatric Clinics of North America, 7,* 69–87.

Hurley, W., & Monahan, T. (1989). Arson. *British Journal of Criminology, 90,* 4–21.

Hurt, S. W., Ayler, S. E., Frances, A., Clarkin, J. F., & Brent, R. (1984). Assessing borderline personality disorder with self-report, clinical interview, or semistructured interview. *American Journal of Psychiatry, 141,* 1228–1231.

Hurt, S. W., Clarkin, J. F., Koenigsberg, H. W., Frances, A., & Nurnberg, H. G. (1986). Diagnostic Interview for Borderlines: Psychometric properties and validity. *Journal of Consulting and Clinical Psychology, 54,* 256–260.

Jackson, H. F., Hope, S., & Glass, C. (1987). Why are arsonists not violent offenders? *International Journal of Offender Therapy and Comparative Criminology, 31,* 143–151.

Kass, D. J., Silver, F. M., & Abrams, G. M. (1972). Behavioral group treatment of hysteria. *Archives of General Psychiatry, 26,* 42–50.

Kaufmann, M. W., Pasacreta, J., Cheney, R., & Arcuni, O. (1985–1986). Psychosomatic aspects of myocardial infarction and implications for treatment. *International Journal of Psychiatry in Medicine, 15,* 371–380.

Kendler, K. S. (1985). Diagnostic approaches to schizotypal personality disorder: A historical perspective. *Schizophrenia Bulletin, 11,* 538–553.

Kernberg, O. F. (1975). *Borderline conditions and pathological narcissism.* New York: Jason Aronson.

Kinston, W. (1980). A theoretical and technical approach to narcissistic disturbance. *International Journal of Psychoanalysis, 61,* 383–393.

Klar, H., & Seiver, L. J. (1984). The psychopharmacologic treatment of personality disorders. *Psychiatric Clinics of North America, 7,* 791–801.

Koenigsberg, H. W., Kaplan, R. D., Gilmore, M. M., & Cooper, A. M. (1985). The relationship between syndrome and personality disorder in DSM-III: Experience with 2,462 patients. *American Journal of Psychiatry, 142,* 207–212.

Kohut, H. (1977). *The restoration of the self.* New York: International Universities Press.

Kolko, D. J., & Kazdin, A. E. (1986). A conceptualization of fire setting in children and adolescents. *Journal of Abnormal Child Psychology, 14,* 49–61.

Kovacs, M., Feinberg, T. L., Crouse-Novak, M., Paulauskas, S. L., Pollock, M., & Finkelstein, R. (1986). Depressive disorders in childhood: II. A longitudinal study of the risk for a subsequent major depression. *Annual Progress in Child Psychiatry and Child Development 1985,* 520–541.

Lande, S. D. (1980). A combination of orgasmic reconditioning and covert sensitization in the treatment of a fire fetish. *Journal of Behavior Therapy and Experimental Psychiatry, 11,* 291–296.

Linehan, M. M. (1987). Dialectic behavior therapy for borderline personality disorder: Theory and method. *Bulletin of the Menninger Clinic, 51,* 261–276.

Lipton, D., Martinson, R., & Wilks, J. (1975). *The effectiveness of correctional treatment: A survey of treatment evaluation studies.* New York: Praeger.

Livesley, W. J. (1986). Trait and behavioral prototypes for personality disorder. *American Journal of Psychiatry, 143,* 728–732.

Livesley, W. J., Reiffer, L. I., Sheldon, A. E., & West, M. (1987). Prototypicality ratings of DSM-III criteria for personality disorders. *Journal of Nervous and Mental Disease, 175,* 395–401.

Mackay, J. R. (1986). Psychopathy and pathological narcissism: A descriptive and psychodynamic formulation of the antisocial personality disorder. *Journal of Offender Counselling, Services and Rehabilitation, 11,* 77–93.

Marlatt, G. A., & Gordon, J. R. (1985). *Relapse prevention: Maintenance strategies in addictive behavior change.* New York: Guilford Press.

Marshall, W. L., & Barbaree, H. E. (1984). Disorders of personality, impulse and adjustment. In S. M. Turner & M. Hersen (Eds.), *Adult psychopathology and diagnosis* (pp. 406–449). New York: Wiley.

Marshall, W. L., & Segal, Z. (1990). Drugs combined with behavioral psychotherapy. In A. S. Bellack, M. Hersen, & A. E. Kazdin (Eds.), *International handbook of behavior modification and therapy* (2nd ed.) (pp. 267–279). New York: Plenum Press.

Marshall, W. L., Turner, B. A., & Barbaree, H. E. (1989). An evaluation of Life Skills Training for penitentiary inmates. *Journal of Offender Counselling, Services & Rehabilitation, 14,* 41–59.

McCord, W., & McCord, J. (1964). *The psychopath: An essay on the criminal mind.* Princeton, NJ: Van Nostrand.

McGlashan, T. H. (1987). Testing DSM-III symptoms criteria for schizotypal and borderline personality disorders. *Archives of General Psychiatry, 44,* 143–148.

McManus, M., Lerner, H. D., Robbins, D., & Barbour, C. (1984). Assessment of borderline symptomatology in hospitalized adolescents. *Journal of the American Academy of Child Psychiatry, 23,* 685–694.

Milan, M. A. (1987). Token economy programs in closed institutions. In E. K. Morris & C. J. Braukman (Eds.), *Behavioral approaches to crime and delinquency: A handbook of application, research, and concepts* (pp. 195–222). New York: Plenum Press.

Miller, W. B. (1958). Lower class culture as a generating milieu of gang delinquency. *Journal of Social Issues, 14,* 5–19.

Millon, T. (1981). *Disorders of personality: DSM III. Axis II.* New York: Wiley.

Modlin, H. C. (1983). The antisocial personality. *Bulletin of the Menninger Clinic, 47,* 129–144.

Morey, L. C. (1988). Personality disorders in DSM-III and DSM-III-R: Convergence, coverage, and internal consistency. *American Journal of Psychiatry, 145,* 573–577.

Morton, T. L., & Ewald, L. S. (1987). Family-based interventions for crime and delinquency. In E. K. Morris & C. J. Braukmann (Eds.), *Behavioral approaches to crime and delinquency: A handbook of application, research, and concepts* (pp. 271–303). New York: Plenum Press.

Nakdimen, K. A. (1986). A new formulation for borderline personality disorder? *American Journal of Psychiatry, 143,* 1069.

Novaco, R. W., & Welsh, W. N. (1987). Anger disturbances: Cognitive mediation and clinical prescriptions. In K. Howells & C. R. Hollin (Eds.), *Clinical approaches to violence* (pp. 39–60). New York: Wiley.

Nurnberg, H. G., Feldman, A., Hurt, S., & Suh, R. (1986). Core criteria for diagnosing borderline patients. *Hillside Journal of Clinical Psychiatry, 8,* 111–131.

Pacht, A. R., & Strangman, E. H. (1980). Crime and delinquency. In A. E. Kazdin, A. S. Bellack, & M. Hersen (Eds.), *New perspectives in abnormal psychology* (pp. 353–375). New York: Oxford University Press.

Paris, J. (1985). Boundary and intimacy. *Journal of the American Academy of Psychoanalysis, 13,* 505–510.

Patterson, G. R. (1982). *A social learning approach to family intervention: 3. Coercive family process.* Eugene, OR: Castalia.

Patterson, G. R., Capaldi, D., & Bank, L. (in press). Two paths to delinquency: The paths to delinquency: The early- and late-starter models. In K. B. Rubin & D. Pepler (Eds.), *The development and treatment of childhood aggression.* Hillsdale, NJ: Erlbaum.

Perry, J. C. (1985). Depression in borderline personality disorder: Lifetime prevalence at interview and longitudinal course of symptoms. *American Journal of Psychiatry, 142,* 15–21.

Perry, J. C., O'Connell, M. E., & Drake, R. (1984). An assessment schedule for schizotypal personalities and the DSM-III criteria for diagnosing schizotypal personality disorder. *Journal of Nervous and Mental Disease, 172,* 674–680.

Pfohl, B., Coryell, W., Zimmerman, M., & Stangl, D. (1986). DSM-III personality disorders: Diagnostic overlap and internal consistency of individual DSM-III criteria. *Comprehensive Psychiatry, 27,* 21–34.

Pieczenik, S., & Birk, L. (1974). Behavior therapy of personality disorders. In J. R. Lion (Ed.), *Personality disorders: Diagnosis and management* (pp. 352–367). Baltimore: Williams & Wilkins.

Pope, H. G., Jonas, J. M., Hudson, J. I., Cohen, B. M., & Gunderson, J. G. (1983). Borderline personality disorder: A phenomenologic, family history, treatment response and long-term follow-up study. *Archives of General Psychiatry, 40,* 23–30.

Reich, J. (1987). Prevalence of DSM-III-R self defeating (masochistic) personality disorder in normal and outpatient populations. *Journal of Nervous and Mental Disease, 175,* 52–54.

Reich, J., Noyes, R., & Troughton, E. (1987). Dependent personality disorder associated with phobic avoidance in patients with panic disorder. *American Journal of Psychiatry, 144,* 323–326.

Reiger, D., Myers, J., Kramer, M., Robins, L., Blayer, D., Hough, R., Eaton, W., & Locke, B. (1984). The NIMH Epidemiological Catchment Area Program: Historical context, major objectives, and study population characteristics. *Archives of General Psychiatry, 41,* 934–941.

Resnick, R. J., Schultz, P., Schultz, S. C., Hamer, R. M., Friedel, R. O., & Goldberg, S. C. (1983). Borderline personality disorder: Symptomatology and MMPI characteristics. *Journal of Clinical Psychiatry, 44,* 289–292.

Robins, E., Purtell, J. J., & Cohen, M. E. (1952). "Hysteria" in men. *New England Journal of Medicine, 246,* 667–685.

Rodin, G., & Voshart, K. (1986). Depression in the medically ill: An overview. *American Journal of Psychiatry, 143,* 696–705.

Rosenthal, R. J. (1986). The pathological gambler's system for self-deception. *Journal of Gambling Behavior, 2,* 108–120.

Rothstein, A. (1984). Fear of humiliation. *Journal of the American Psychoanalytic Association, 32,* 99–116.

Russell, D. (1986). Psychiatric diagnosis and the oppression of women. *Women and Therapy, 5,* 83–98.

Rutter, M. (1984). Psychopathology and development: 1. Childhood antecedents of adult psychiatric disorder. *Australian and New Zealand Journal of Psychiatry, 18,* 225–234.

Sakheim, G. A., Vigdor, M. G., Gordon, M., & Helprin, L. M. (1985). A psychological profile of juvenile fire setters in residential treatment. *Child Welfare, 64,* 453–476.

Schroeder, M. L., Schroeder, K. G., & Hare, R. D. (1983). Generalizability of a checklist for assessment of psychopathy. *Journal of Consulting and Clinical Psychology, 51,* 511–516.

Schulz, S. C. (1986). The use of low-dose neuroleptics in the treatment of "schizo-obsessive" patients. *American Journal of Psychiatry, 143,* 1318–1319.

Siever, L. J. (1985). Biological markers in schizotypal personality disorders. *Schizophrenia Bulletin, 11,* 564–575.

Skrzypek, G. J. (1969). The effects of perceptual isolation and arousal on anxiety, complexity preference and novelty preference in psychopathic and neurotic delinquents. *Journal of Abnormal Psychology, 74,* 321–322.

Smith, R. J. (1978). *The psychopath in society.* New York: Academic Press.

Snyder, S., & Pitts, W. M. (1984). Electroencephalography of DSM-III borderline personality disorder. *Acta Psychiatrica Scandinavica, 69,* 129–134.

Soloff, P. H., George, A., Nathan, R. S., Shulz, P. M., & Perel, J. M. (1986). Paradoxical affects of amitriptyline on borderline patients. *American Journal of Psychiatry, 143,* 1603–1605.

Spalt, L. (1980). Hysteria and antisocial personality: A single disorder? *Journal of Nervous and Mental Disease, 168,* 456–464.

Sternbach, H. A., Fleming, J., Extein, I., Pottash, A. L. C., & Gold, M. S. (1983). The dexamethasone suppression and thyrotropin-releasing hormone tests in depressed borderline patients. *Psychoneuroendocrinology, 8,* 459–462.

Stone, M. H. (1987). Psychotherapy of borderline patients in light of long-term follow-up. *Bulletin of the Menninger Clinic, 51,* 231–247.

Stringer, A. Y., & Josef, N. C. (1983). Methylphenidate in the treatment of aggression in two patients with antisocial personality disorder. *American Journal of Psychiatry, 140,* 1365–1366.

Templeman, T. L., & Wollersheim, J. P. (1979). A cognitive–behavioral approach to the treatment of psychopathy. *Psychotherapy: Theory, Research and Practice, 16,* 132–139.

Tharp, V. K., Maltzman, I., Syndulko, K., & Ziskind, E. (1980). Autonomic activity during anticipation of an aversive tone in noninstitutionalized sociopaths. *Psychophysiology, 17,* 123–128.

Trzepac, P. T., Maue, F., Coffman, G., & Van-Thiel, D. H. (1986–1987). Neuropsychiatric assessment of liver transplantation candidates: Delerium and other psychiatric disorders. *International Journal of Psychiatry in Medicine, 16,* 101–111.

Turner, S. M., Beidel, D. C., Dancu, C. V., & Keys, D. J. (1986). Psychopathology of social phobia and comparison to avoidant personality disorder. *Journal of Abnormal Psychology, 95,* 389–394.

Weiss, J. J. (1974). A case example of the borderline personality organization. *Psychotherapy: Theory, Research, and Practice, 11,* 383–386.

Weiss, R. S. (1982). Attachment in adult life. In C. M. Parkes & J. Stevenson-Hine (Eds.), *The place of attachment in human behavior* (pp. 143–165). New York: Basic Books.

Wulach, J. S. (1983). Diagnosing the DSM-III antisocial personality disorder. *Professional Psychology Research and Practice, 14,* 330–340.

Yerevanian, B. I., Schiffer, R. B., & Mallon, P. M. (1985). Electroencephalographic abnormalities in borderline patients. *Journal of Clinical Psychiatry, 46,* 251.

Zimbardo, P. G. (1977, November). Shy murderers. *Psychology Today, 148,* 68–76.

Zimmerman, M., Pfohl, B., Stangl, D., & Corenthal, C. (1986). Assessment of DSM-III personality disorders: The importance of interviewing an informant. *Journal of Clinical Psychiatry, 47,* 261–263.

CHAPTER 13

Eating Disorders (Anorexia Nervosa and Bulimia Nervosa)

BILL N. KINDER

Eating disorders (anorexia nervosa and bulimia nervosa) have received increasing attention in the clinical, scientific, and popular literature in the past decade. Although anorexia nervosa was first described as a clinical entity by Morton in 1694 and bulimia nervosa was identified in 1892 by Osler, these disorders only recently have become a major focus of clinicians and scientists (Shapiro, 1988). The identification of these "new" psychopathological states has posed some basic problems, such as determining what these conditions should be called and what their specific diagnostic characteristics are. For example, various names have been given to bulimia nervosa, including anorexia bulimia nervosa (Esrensing & Weitzman, 1970), subclinical anorexia nervosa (Button & Whitehouse, 1981), binge-eating syndrome (Wardle, 1980), compulsive eating (Ondercin, 1979), and bulimarexia (Baskind-Lodohl & White, 1978).

Specific diagnostic criteria for these disorders have changed significantly in the last decade. In the second edition of the American Psychiatric Association's (APA's) *Diagnostic and Statistical Manual of Mental Disorders* (DSM-II; 1968), anorexia nervosa was coded (with no definition given) under the classification of feeding disturbance. In DSM-III (APA, 1980), more specific criteria were presented, which were then modified in DSM-III-R (APA, 1987) to include, in females, the absence of at least three consecutive menstrual cycles. Bulimia first achieved the status of a separate syndrome in the DSM-III in 1980, and the name was changed to bulimia nervosa in the more recent DSM-III-R, along with changes in the diagnostic criteria.

Because of the recent emergence of interest in these disorders and changes in the diagnostic criteria, the scientific literature is confusing and often contradictory. Making this literature more difficult to interpret is the fact that, in spite of precise diagnostic criteria in DSM-III and DSM-III-R, most researchers have not adhered to these guidelines in the diagnosis of individuals to be included in their studies. For example, Shapiro (1988) reviewed eighteen studies investigating personality correlates of bulimia. It was reported in

Appreciation is expressed to J. Kevin Thompson and Louis A. Penner for their comments on an early version of this chapter.

eleven of these studies that the DSM-III definition of bulimia was used; however, closer examination revealed that this definition was modified in some way in all of these studies. DSM-III criteria state that the bulimic episodes must not be due to anorexia nervosa, yet three studies included individuals with a history of anorexia nervosa. Two other studies operationalized the DSM-III criteria by means of a questionnaire that had not been validated. Shapiro (1988) was able to find only one study of the eighteen that appeared to follow the criteria as stated in DSM-III.

Despite the many methodological problems in this literature, some consistent trends have emerged in the past decade. The remainder of this chapter reviews some of the more important findings.

Anorexia Nervosa

Anorexia nervosa is primarily a disorder of young women. The usual age of onset is during the adolescent period and the early 20s, although the disorder is occasionally seen in prepubescents. Onset after age 30 is rare (APA, 1987). One early attempt at a set of diagnostic criteria for this disorder included that the age of onset must be prior to 25 (Feighner et al., 1972); however, most view this criterion as too restrictive, and no age restrictions are mentioned in DSM-III-R.

Anorexia nervosa occurs predominately in females. Most investigators report that only 4 to 10 percent of reported cases are male (Eckert, 1985). Data concerning the prevalence of this disorder vary greatly. Jones, Fox, Babigian, and Hutton (1980) reviewed data from Monroe County, New York, from 1960 to 1976 and reported 0.35 to 0.64 cases per 100,000 population per year. DSM-III-R notes that the prevalence rate has been reported to be as high as 1 in 100 in females between the ages of 12 to 18. Anorexia nervosa also appears to have become more common in the last two decades, although Eckert (1985) suggested that this may be because of increased case finding due to greater public and medical awareness of the disorder. Nasser (1988) reviewed prevalence data on eating disorders in non-Western cultures and suggested that the reported increases in prevalence were related to recent identification with Western norms in relation to body weight and thinness among females.

Bulimia Nervosa

Similar findings have been reported for bulimia nervosa. Like anorexia nervosa, bulimia nervosa appears to be predominantly a disorder of young females, usually beginning in late adolescence or early adult life. Strangler and Printz (1980) reviewed the records of 500 students seen consecutively for emotional problems at a university student health service and found that 3.8 percent had received a diagnosis of bulimia (5.3 percent of the females). Other studies have suggested even higher prevalence rates. For example, Halmi, Falk, and Schwartz (1981) reported that 19 percent of the females and 6.1 percent of the males in their college sample met all the major symptoms of bulimia as defined by DSM-III. It is reported in DSM-III-R that 4.5 percent of females and 0.4 percent of males in a college freshman sample had a history of bulimia. Pyle, Mitchell, and Eckert (1981) found that the onset of bulimia was associated with a voluntary period of dieting for 88 percent of their sample; a similar percentage reported that the onset of the disorder was associated with some traumatic event usually involving a loss or separation, such as leaving home or rejection by a boyfriend.

J. E. Mitchell and Pyle (1985) suggested that several conclusions may be drawn from the existing epidemiological data. First, binge-eating episodes are relatively common in young college populations, but their presence does not represent a serious eating disorder in most cases. Second, between 8 and 14 percent of young women and between 1 and 10 percent of young men meet DSM-III criteria for bulimia, but lower prevalence rates are reported if more stringent criteria are used. Third, the eating behaviors seen in bulimic patients may represent the extreme end of a spectrum of abnormal eating behaviors. Finally, J. E. Mitchell and Pyle suggested that, like anorexia nervosa, bulimia nervosa may be increasing in the general population and that cultural preoccupations with physical attractiveness and thinness may be related to this phenomenon.

Some of the conclusions of J. E. Mitchell and Pyle (1985) are supported by a more recent study by Drewnowski, Hopkins, and Kessler (1988). These investigators conducted a survey using a national probability sample of 1,007 male and female college students from a stratified sample of fifty-three universities and colleges in the continental United States. Binge eating was found to be relatively common, with 6.1 percent of females and 10.0 percent of males reporting at least two eating binges per week on the average during the preceding 3 months. When the entire DSM-III-R criteria were applied, however, only 1.0 percent of women and 0.2 percent of men in the entire sample were classified as bulimic. The probable diagnosis of bulimia nervosa was most prevalent among undergraduate women (2.2 percent) living in group housing on campus. The results of this well-designed study suggest that previous estimates of bulimia nervosa may in fact be somewhat inflated, at least among college populations.

CLINICAL PRESENTATION

Anorexia Nervosa

The essential feature of anorexia nervosa is a refusal to maintain a body weight over a minimal normal weight for height and age. Earlier criteria required this weight loss to be at least 25 percent below expected weight (APA, 1980), which most investigators found as too restrictive (Eckert, 1985). More recent criteria require the weight to be at least 15 percent below the expected minimal normal (APA, 1987). The term *anorexia* literally means a loss of appetite and thus is somewhat of a misnomer, since actual loss of appetite is relatively rare in anorexic individuals.

Anorexics have an intense, irrational fear of gaining weight or becoming fat, even when they may be quite significantly underweight. Anorexics go to great lengths to lose weight and/or to maintain a low body weight, most often by significantly reducing total food intake. Because there is often family and peer pressure to eat, they may engage in a variety of devious behaviors, such as hiding food in napkins that can later be disposed of in the trash or toilet (Eckert, 1985). The use of laxatives and/or diuretics appears common (Crisp, Hsu, & Harding, 1980), as does extensive exercising (APA, 1987). Self-induced vomiting and binge eating have also been reported in 10 to 47 percent of anorexic patients (Eckert, 1985).

Another central feature of anorexia nervosa is that patients deny their eating disturbance or minimize the severity of their symptoms. They fail to acknowledge their thinness and tend to minimize associated secondary symptoms or problems that occur during the course of the disorder, such as amenorrhea, nutritional deficiencies, and chronic fatigue. Because of this extreme denial, anorexics do not view themselves as psychologically "abnormal" and are thus often quite resistant to therapeutic interventions. There is evidence that the severity of their denial is related to the severity of the disorder and to subsequent treatment outcome. For example, Goldberg et al. (1980) investigated the outcome of a 35-day inpatient treatment program and found a significant inverse relationship between degree of denial and weight gain at the end of treatment.

Another significant aspect of anorexia nervosa is a disturbance in body image. Anorexics claim to "feel fat" even when they may be quite emaciated. A poor self-image, specifically a poor attitude toward the body, is essentially universal among these individuals. These cognitive distortions appear to be accompanied by actual perceptual distortions, as anorexics tend to overestimate their body size. However, the empirical findings in this area have been controversial. The typical research design measuring body size overestimation has individuals estimate the width of their various body parts, usually the chest, waist, hips, and thighs. Body size estimation has been measured by several techniques, including movable calipers, image marking methods, and an adjustable light beam procedure (Thompson & Thompson, 1986).

The consensus is that anorexics significantly overestimate the size of their various body parts. Slade (1985) reviewed the available studies and computed average overestimation ratios, finding that the mean overestimation was 24 percent for anorexics compared with an average of 16 percent for control populations. The specificity and clinical meaning of these results, however, have been challenged on several grounds. Individuals with bulimia nervosa also have been found to overestimate body size (Willmuth, Leitenberg, Rosen, Fondacaro, & Gross, 1985), apparently to an equal or greater extent than anorexics (Thompson, Berland, Linton, & Weinsier, 1986). In developing the adjustable light beam procedure to measure body size estimation, Thompson and Thompson (1986) found that asymptomatic females and males also overestimated the size of four body sites. Several review articles have addressed this lack of specificity of size overestimation in eating disordered patients (e.g., Cash & Brown, 1987; Garner & Garfinkel, 1981); Hsu (1982) questioned the clinical significance in anorexic patients, because the overestimation phenomenon has also been documented in normal adolescents and college students, obese patients, pregnant women, and schizophrenics. Coovert, Thompson, and Kinder (1988) reported that not only do undergraduate female college students overestimate body size, but they also overestimate the size of inanimate objects, in this case "body size" estimates for a mannequin and a ball. Coovert et al. (1988) suggested that body size overestimation may be only a part of a general perceptual process, not specifically related to eating disordered patients. In summary, anorexics overestimate their body sizes; however, this is also the case for many other groups. The exact nature of this phenomenon for anorexics remains to be clarified.

Depression is a common symptom in anorexia nervosa. Eckert (1985) found that the proportion of anorexics reported as clinically depressed in several studies ranged from 35 to 85 percent. These patients often were reported to be depressed before the acute stage of their illness. Biological markers thought to be related to affective disorders, such as dexamethasone nonsuppression and high plasma cortisol levels, have been reported in anorexics (Gerner & Gwirtsman, 1981; Walsh, 1982), although these abnormalities tend to disappear with subsequent weight gain. Finally, a higher than expected frequency of major depression and bipolar disorder has been found in the first-degree relatives of anorexics in several studies (APA, 1987).

It has often been suggested that anorexics are psychosexually immature and that anorexia nervosa may represent a rejection of adult femininity as a refusal to accept the inevitability of becoming a sexually mature woman. In a recent review, however, Scott (1987) found little or no evidence supporting these claims. Similar findings were reported in another review (Coovert, Kinder, & Thompson, 1989); however, these latter investigators did report that two trends are apparent in the studies reviewed. So-called bulimic anorexics (those who binge or purge) tended to be more sexually active than anorexics who controlled their weight by food intake restriction. Also, in spite of the continued appearance in the literature of case studies reporting a high incidence of sexual abuse among eating disordered patients, the empirical data do not support this conclusion.

One recent study, however, provides data counter to the conclusions of these two reviews. Hall, Tice, Beresford, Wooley, and Hall (1989) reported on 158 consecutive first admissions to an eating disorders inpatient facility. Fifty percent of patients diagnosed with anorexia nervosa or bulimia reported some types of sexual abuse, with fathers being the most frequent perpetrators (30 percent of all cases). One-third of the instances occurred prior to adolescence. Furthermore, these researchers identified three specific eating patterns that they suggest may be related to previous sexual assaults. One group reported that their bulimic symptoms were specifically triggered by anger toward male authority figures. Another group of anorexics reported trying to lose so much weight in an attempt to "disgust" the individual who had assaulted them sexually. A third group of obese women reported gaining considerable amounts of weight so that they could become essentially "nonsexual." Although these findings are clearly based upon self-reports and the subjective judgments of the investigators and clearly require replication, the overall high incidence of abuse reported by Hall et al. (1989) suggests that this area clearly needs further empirical investigation.

Bulimia Nervosa

Individuals with bulimia nervosa share some characteristics with anorexics, but there are also some major differences. Like anorexics, bulimics show a marked concern about their weight and make frequent attempts at controlling it. Most bulimics maintain a weight within the average range for their age and height, although frequent fluctuations in weight may be seen due to alternating binges and fasts (APA, 1987).

The essential feature of bulimia nervosa is recurrent episodes of binge eating (consuming large amounts of food in a relatively brief period of time). The food consumed during a binge usually has a high caloric content and is of the type and texture to facilitate rapid eating (APA, 1987). Bulimics can consume a large amount of food during a binge. In an early investigation, Russell (1979) reported that a few of the patients in his study consumed as many as 5,000 to 20,000 calories at a single sitting. J. E. Mitchell, Pyle, and Eckert (1981) had subjects record what was eaten during a binge and found that the average caloric intake per binge was 3,415 calories, with a range of 1,200 to 11,500. These same investigators reported a mean duration of 1.18 hours per binge, with a range of 15 minutes to 8 hours. During binges, food is consumed as inconspicuously as possible or in secret. Many bulimics induce vomiting after a binge. Others try to compensate for the large amount of calories consumed during binges by repeated strict dieting, vigorous exercise, or the use of laxatives or diuretics (APA, 1987). Bulimics also feel a tremendous lack of control over their eating during binges, followed by feelings of low self-worth and depression after a binge.

There have been repeated empirical findings of pervasive depressive symptomatology accompanying bulimia nervosa. Abraham and Beaumont (1982) reported that 70 percent of their subjects reported suicidal ideation following binges. Hatsukami, Eckert, Mitchell, and Pyle (1984) found that 44 percent of their bulimic subjects met the DSM-III criteria for an affective disorder at some time in their lives. Bulimics have also been found to score high on various standardized measures of depression and often obtain abnormal dexamethasone suppression test results (Hinz & Williamson, 1987). A higher than expected frequency of major depression has been found in the first-degree relatives of bulimics in several studies (APA, 1987). These kinds of findings have led some (e.g., Pope & Hudson, 1989) to hypothesize that bulimia nervosa is an affective variant, a form of depression with the same biological basis as affective disorders. In their review, however, Hinz and Williamson (1987) suggested that, based on all the available evidence, it is premature to hypothesize that bulimia nervosa is simply an affective variant. They suggested an alternative hypothesis that bulimia is often accompanied by depression, just as many other disorders, such as alcoholism and chronic pain, are accompanied by affective disturbances. As such, they view the depression that occurs concomitantly with bulimia nervosa as a secondary affective disorder.

It has been reported that bulimics are more likely than normals to engage in impulsive behaviors, such as shoplifting (J. E. Mitchell & Pyle, 1985), and to have a high incidence of substance abuse. Hatsukami, Owen, Pyle, and

Mitchell (1982) suggested there are several commonalities between alcohol abuse and the abuse of food seen in bulimics, including secretiveness and social isolation, preoccupation with the abuse, and the use of the substance (alcohol or food) to deal with stress or negative feelings. Few empirical data exist, however, and this remains an area in which further investigation is needed.

DSM-III-R CRITERIA AND DIFFERENTIAL DIAGNOSIS

Anorexia Nervosa

DSM-III-R provides the following diagnostic criteria for anorexia nervosa:

A. Refusal to maintain body weight over a minimal normal body weight for age and height (e.g., weight loss leading to maintenance of body weight 15 percent below that expected), or failure to make expected weight gain during period of growth, leading to body weight 15 percent below that expected.

B. Intense fear of gaining weight or becoming fat, even though underweight.

C. Disturbance in the way one's body weight, size, or shape is experienced (e.g., the person claims to "feel fat" even when emaciated, believes that one area of the body is "too fat" even when obviously underweight).

D. In females, absence of at least three consecutive menstrual cycles when otherwise expected to occur (primary or secondary amenorrhea). (A woman is considered to have amenorrhea if her periods occur only following hormone, e.g., estrogen administration.)

All of the above criteria must be present for a diagnosis of anorexia nervosa to be made. Although it may appear that Criteria B and C are somewhat subjective, these characteristics are quite pervasive among anorexics and are usually easily elicited during a clinical interview.

In terms of differential diagnosis, significant weight loss may occur with other disorders, most notably depression; however, in these cases, no intense fear of being fat or disturbance in body image is present. Bizarre eating patterns sometimes occur in schizophrenia, but true anorexia nervosa is rare in these individuals; if present, both diagnoses are given. Finally, anorexia nervosa sometimes is present in individuals with bulimia nervosa, and both diagnoses are given in these cases.

Bulimia Nervosa

The criteria in DSM-III-R for bulimia nervosa are:

A. Recurrent episodes of binge eating (rapid consumption of a large amount of food in a discrete period of time).

B. A feeling of lack of control over eating behavior during the eating binges.

C. Regular engagement in either self-induced vomiting, use of laxatives or diuretics, strict dieting or fasting, or vigorous exercise to prevent weight gain.

D. A minimum average of two binge eating episodes a week for at least 3 months.

E. Persistent overconcern with body shape and weight.

Self-induced vomiting is quite common among bulimics; however, this is not required for a diagnosis of bulimia nervosa to be made. What is required is that the individual engage in some extreme behavior(s) to control weight (e.g., *strict* dieting or fasting, *vigorous* exercise).

As with anorexia nervosa, unusual eating patterns are sometimes seen in schizophrenia. If the full syndrome of bulimia nervosa is present in a schizophrenic individual, both diagnoses are given. Several neurological disorders (e.g., central nervous system tumors or Kleine-Levin syndrome) may produce abnormal eating patterns, but the full syndrome of bulimia is rarely present in these cases; if present, both diagnoses are given.

DSM-III-R notes that binge eating is often a feature of borderline personality disorder in females and that both diagnoses should be given if the full criteria for bulimia nervosa are present. Binge eating is one possible criteria for borderline personality disorder (APA, 1987, p. 347), but the true association between these two disorders has been questioned. Pope and Hudson (1989) reviewed the existing studies assessing the prevalence of borderline personality disorder among eating disordered patients and found rates of from 0 to 42 percent across the different samples. These authors noted the high degree of overlap between the symptoms of depression, borderline personality disorder, and bulimia nervosa. They also pointed out that the structured interviews used to assess borderline personality in these studies were for the most part of untested or uncertain specificity and might have produced frequent false–positive diagnoses of borderline personality disorder in patients with eating disorders. Pope and Hudson (1989) concluded that the estimates of borderline personality disorder in these populations may be exaggerated, and they called for extreme caution in making this diagnosis until better data become available.

ETIOLOGY

There are three general classes of theories regarding the etiology of anorexia nervosa. The first, which can be termed the ego-psychological, suggests that anorexia nervosa is a function of impaired mother–child relationships. These theories are best characterized by the work of Hilde Bruch (1973, 1978), who argued that the anorexic individual is often controlled, even exploited as a child by those in the immediate environment. She further suggested that three major types of disturbance characterize the developing anorexic. First, a major problem develops in the anorexic's ability to accurately perceive body image. Second, these individuals have difficulty in perceiving and labeling internal bodily sensations. Finally, there is a sense of personal helplessness and ineffectiveness. In sum, anorexics come to see their behavior as beyond their control but rather under the control of others; anorexia is seen as a desperate effort to gain control over the body as a way of regaining control over the self.

Systems theories suggest that anorexia nervosa develops because of a set of disordered family interactional patterns. For example, Minuchin, Rosman, and Baker (1978) found that the families of anorexics appear to be superficially overly good or nice, but that they are grossly unable to manage conflict situations. These authors suggested that these families are extremely overprotective of family members, are characterized by enmeshment (inappropriate, extreme intermember involvement), and are rigidly resistant to family change. Thus, for the potentially anorexic child, family loyalty and the protection of family members takes precedence over the development of the child's autonomy. Large areas of the child's psychological and physical functioning remain under the control of others long after they should have become autonomous.

A third theory of the etiology of anorexia nervosa is the biological–genetic theory, which proposes that some primary genetic endocrinological defect or trigger precipitates the disorder. Many of the twin and family studies in this area have been limited to isolated case reports. One review indicated that approximately 50 percent of sets of monozygotic twins were concordant for the disorder (Nowlin, 1983). Vandereycken and Pierloot (1981) more critically reviewed the available data and concluded that the notion that genetic factors play a significant role in the etiology of anorexic nervosa has no substantial support.

Few studies have investigated directly opposing theories of the etiology of anorexia nervosa. One notable exception was the study by Harding and Lachenmeyer (1986), which assessed 30 female anorexics and 30 female college students. Three variables suggested by Minuchin et al. (1978)— overprotection, enmeshment, and family rigidity— and one associated with Bruch's (1973) notion of lack of personal control—locus of control—were entered into a multiple regression to predict the severity of anorexic symptomatology. The only variable to contribute significantly to this prediction was locus of control ($R^2 = .37$).

One recent longitudinal study (Attie & Brooks-Gunn, 1989) assessed 193 white females in Grades 7 to 10 and reassessed these same individuals 2 years later. Among the younger subjects, eating problems emerged in response to actual physical changes. It was not until middle to late adolescence that psychosocial and/or personality variables became associated with eating disturbances. At the later ages, abnormal eating behaviors were associated with tendencies toward affective and behavioral overcontrol (specifically depressive symptomatology).

Less theorizing has taken place about the etiology of bulimia nervosa, although several authors (e.g., Bruch, 1978; Minuchin et al., 1978) have extended some of their notions regarding anorexia nervosa to bulimics. Possible genetic–biological factors have been suggested, mostly based upon the close association between depression and bulimia nervosa; however, these data are open to differing interpretations (Hinz & Williamson, 1987). A model proposed by Mizes (1985) suggests that irrational beliefs and significant self-control deficits are central to the pathogenesis of the disorder. Mizes suggested that family factors foster certain irrational beliefs (specifically an excessively high need for approval and high self-expectations), possibly because of parents' distorted overendorsement of the traditional female sex role.

A number of different cognitive distortions have been documented among bulimic populations. For example, Katzman and Wolchik (1984) found bulimics to score significantly higher than controls on scales measuring irrational self-expectations and demand for approval. Schulman, Kinder, Powers, Prange, and Gleghorn (1986) validated a scale to measure cognitive distortions related to automatic eating behaviors and physical appearance. Comparing 55 bulimics with 55 matched controls by a discriminant function analysis, this measure correctly classified 93.6 percent of the subjects.

In summary, various etiologic factors have been proposed for anorexia nervosa and bulimia nervosa, and data support each to varying degrees. These data are open to several interpretations, however, and to date no one factor has emerged as the most significant of these potential etiologic variables.

Natural History

The natural history of anorexia nervosa and bulimia nervosa suggests that these disorders are often unremitting, even after "successful" treatment. Eckert (1985) reviewed a number of follow-up studies of anorexics and found that many patients continued to have body weight below 75 percent of normal and to engage in abnormal eating practices, such as extensive dieting and avoidance of high-calorie food for some time, often many years, after treatment. Vomiting and laxative abuse and psychological difficulties, most notably depression and social phobias, were also relatively common in treated anorexics. Eckert suggested that many chronic anorexics do not live their expected full-term lives, but succumb early to the complications associated with this disorder.

Although less is known about the longitudinal nature of bulimia nervosa, the available data suggest that these individuals also experience significant difficulties over long periods of time. J. E. Mitchell and Pyle (1985) reported that the majority of bulimics have been ill for several years before they are identified and treated. In clinical samples, the disorder is usually chronic and intermittent for many years, with binges and fasting often alternating with periods of normal eating (APA, 1987).

Course and Complications

DSM-III-R states that anorexia nervosa most commonly involves a single episode, although the disorder may be episodic or unremitting until death; mortality rates are said to be between 5 and 18 percent. A recent review (Herzog, Keller, & Lavori, 1988) generally supported these DSM-III-R statements. The studies reporting on relapse found rates ranging from 4 to 9 percent. Mortality rates ranged from 0 to 22 percent, with over half of the studies reporting rates of 4 percent or less; the follow-up periods in these studies ranged from 4 months to 43 years. Of the reported deaths, the cause was anorexia nervosa or its medical complications in 50 percent of the patients, suicide in 24 percent, and other disorders or accidents, lung disease, or unknown causes in the remainder.

The most serious complications in anorexia nervosa are a variety of medical conditions, some of which are potentially fatal if untreated or uncorrected. Most of the symptoms resemble those found in starved or semistarved normals, and most return to normal after a return to more normal eating patterns and subsequent weight gain. The frequency of these symptoms often varies greatly across studies, partially because of the different diagnostic criteria used (J. E. Mitchell, 1985). Amenorrhea is invariably present, and the absence of three consecutive menstrual cycles when otherwise expected is part of the DSM-III-R criteria for females. A variety of hematological and renal complications have been reported (J. E. Mitchell, 1985), as have metabolic problems, including increased serum cholesterol and elevated serum carotene levels. Several coronary abnormalities have been reported in approximately half of anorexic patients (Palossy & Oo, 1977; Webb, Birmingham, & MacDonald, 1988), and several case reports have appeared (e.g., Powers, 1982) that document cardiac failure during treatment. It has been suggested that certain of these coronary irregularities are associated with serum potassium abnormalities, but not with other variables, including admission weight, medications, or the severity of anorexic symptoms (Kay, Hoffman, Boswick, Rockwell, & Ellinwood, 1988). Gastrointestinal problems, including constipation, delayed gastric emptying, and decreased gastric fluid output, have been reported (J. E. Mitchell, 1985), as well as dental pathology, most likely related to high carbohydrate intake and repeated vomiting (Stege, Visco-Dangler, & Rye, 1982).

Much less is known about the possible medical complications associated with bulimia nervosa. Fluid and electrolyte abnormalities and dental problems appear to be relatively common, whereas renal, endocrine, gastrointestinal, and neurological findings occur much less frequently (J. E. Mitchell, 1985).

A variety of psychological symptoms have been reported to occur with anorexia nervosa and bulimia nervosa. In their review, Herzog et al. (1988) reported that twenty-seven of thirty-three articles mentioned psychiatric disorders in anorexic patients at follow-up, the most common of which were depression, obsessive–compulsive characteristics, and schizophrenia. These findings are difficult to interpret, however, due to the generally nonstandardized methods of evaluation; for example, explicit criteria for the diagnosis of a psychiatric disorder were used in only three of the studies reviewed. Among the studies assessing bulimic subjects at follow-up, depression was the most common symptom, being reported in 15 to 36 percent of subjects. None of these studies made diagnoses on the basis of strict, standardized criteria.

Similar findings were reported by Mizes (1985) in his review of symptomatology in bulimics. Negative mood states, most notably depression and anxiety, were often reported. Bulimic subjects were also characterized in some studies as more irritable, passive, weak, and constrained than normal controls. Reviewing the studies that used the Minnesota Multiphasic Personality

Inventory (MMPI), Mizes (1985) reported consistent elevations on the Depression, Psychopathic Deviant, Psychasthenia, and Schizophrenia scales, with relatively low scores on the Masculinity–Feminity scale. He suggested that these findings are representative of significant depression, anxiety, rumination, feelings of alienation, and impulsivity. Mizes (1985) criticized these studies on methodological grounds, citing their often descriptive or correlational nature, lack of appropriate control groups, use of nonstandardized or highly global self-reports, and wide variations in diagnostic criteria.

CLINICAL MANAGEMENT

The major treatment modalities for anorexia nervosa and bulimia nervosa have been pharmacological, psychotherapeutical (usually with a behavioral and/or cognitive emphasis), or some combination of these approaches. Pharmacological approaches have been used most extensively with bulimia nervosa; little work has been done pharmacologically with anorexic subjects.

Most studies with bulimic populations have utilized either tricyclic antidepressants or monoamine oxidase inhibitors. Barlow, Blouin, Blouin, and Perez (1988) administered desipramine in a double-blind cross-over design to 47 normal-weight bulimics. At the end of 16 weeks of treatment, this medication was significantly more effective than a placebo in reducing the weekly frequency of bingeing and vomiting, although the effect was modest and the drug had no effect on depressive symptomatology. In a similar vein, Agras, Dorian, Kirkley, Arnow, and Bachman (1987) administered imipramine to 10 bulimic women and compared them with 10 bulimics receiving a placebo in a double-blind study over a 16-week period. Participants receiving the medication demonstrated a significantly greater reduction in purging (self-induced vomiting and laxative use) compared with participants receiving the placebo; however, only one-third of subjects receiving imipramine had completely stopped purging at the end of 16 weeks. Interestingly, levels of depression, as measured by the Beck Depression Inventory, were not significantly different between the two groups at the end of the study. The antidepressant agent buproprion was found to be superior to a placebo in reducing binge eating and purging in another study by Horne et al. (1988) in a group of nondepressed bulimics.

These three studies are representative of the recent investigations of pharmacological treatments of bulimia nervosa and of the general findings in this area. The results typically favor the drug treatment over placebos; however, the effects are modest at best. Recently, P. B. Mitchell (1988) reviewed the studies addressing pharmacological approaches to the management of bulimia nervosa and concluded that they do offer a promising short-term treatment of the disorder. He questioned the long-term efficacy of these medications, however, since follow-up data are rarely available for periods of more than a few weeks or months. Also, high relapse rates occur upon withdrawal of the drug, frequent changes of medications are required over time, and dropout rates during the active stages of these studies are often very significant (ranging from 18 to 53 percent in the studies reviewed).

Finally, in reviewing many studies of this nature, it is apparent that other treatment modalities are often combined with a pharmacological component. The exact nature of these nonpharmacological treatments is often not well explained, and no attempts are usually made to separate out the potential differential effects of the various treatment modalities.

Psychological treatments for anorexia nervosa most typically are some form of operant conditioning. One of two criteria are generally chosen to be reinforced: specific eating behaviors (e.g., size of portions, number of mouthfuls, caloric contents of foods) or weight gain (usually varying from .1 to .25 kilograms per day or 1.0 to 1.5 kilograms per week) (Bemis, 1987). A fixed-interval schedule is common, with intervals varying from 1 to 7 days. Typical positive reinforcers are freedom of movement within and outside of the hospital, access to various recreational activities, and visiting privileges. Negative consequences have included bed rest, restriction to hospital room or seclusion, and tube feeding.

In reviewing operant approaches to the treatment of anorexia nervosa, Bemis (1987) concluded that the data indicate that operant methods have been found to be "equal or superior to psychotherapy, milieu treatment, intensive nursing regimes, pharmacotherapy, and hyperalimentation in experimental and quasi-experimental comparisons" (p. 445). Long-term follow-up is rarely reported, however, and other questions remain to be answered, such as the effect of these treatments on other variables (e.g., changes in mood and interpersonal behavior). Chiodo (1985) was particularly critical of the reliance upon short-term weight gain as the sole independent variable in many of these studies.

Several different behavioral treatment methods have been used with bulimic patients. Rosen and Leitenberg (1982) used exposure plus response prevention with 6 bulimic patients. The first component exposed subjects to the feared stimulus (e.g., eating certain foods or amounts of foods) in the presence of a therapist. The second component consisted of preventing the escape response, in this case vomiting. Rosen and Leitenberg (1982) reported varying outcomes across subjects: the average reduction in vomiting was 89 percent (1 of the 6 subjects showed no improvement). Similar findings were reported by Giles, Young, and Young (1985), who added a cognitive restructuring component to exposure plus response prevention with 34 bulimics. Fifty-nine percent of subjects attained an 80 percent or greater reduction in vomiting at the end of treatment; 63 percent of the improved subjects were still abstinent from vomiting at follow-up (1 1/4 years).

Rosen (1987) reviewed studies using behavioral treatments of bulimia nervosa and concluded that these are effective techniques for this disorder. Reduction in vomiting ranged from 20 to 96 percent (mean reduction of 70 percent) across studies. Rosen noted, however, a high dropout rate in these studies (mean dropout rate of approximately 15 percent) and concluded that more research is called for before asserting that these modalities are the treatment of choice for bulimic patients.

A variety of cognitive–behavioral approaches aimed at modifying various cognitive distortions have been used in the treatment of bulimia nervosa. In their review of these studies, Garner, Fairburn, and Davis (1987) concluded that, across twenty studies, cognitive–behavioral techniques have had both statistically and clinically significant effects on frequency of bingeing, vomiting, and other symptoms. The median percentage in reduction of bingeing was 79 percent, with a range of 50.7 to 96.5 percent. A similar pattern was found in the reduction of self-induced vomiting across studies. Individually administered treatments appeared somewhat more effective than group methods. Garner et al. (1987) noted, however, that the specific methods used are often poorly defined in these studies, that subject populations have come from several different sources, and that there is a great deal of variation in therapists' experience levels across studies.

Despite these promising results for several treatment modalities with anorexics and bulimics, few definitive data exist regarding prognostic indicators with respect to these disorders. Herzog et al. (1988) concluded that, in the twenty-four studies of anorexia nervosa that reported on predictors of therapeutic outcome, the data were often contradictory. For example, one study found seventeen predictors of outcome, whereas another found no predictors. Across all studies, the variables found to be predictive most consistently were duration of the disorder, presence of associated personality disorders, disturbed parent–child relationships, and presence of vomiting. In the studies of prognostic factors in bulimia nervosa, no one factor was found consistently to predict outcome across studies. Laessle, Zoettl, and Pirke (1987) conducted a meta-analysis of twenty-five outcome studies of bulimia nervosa, considering the relative effectiveness of pharmacological and psychological treatments. Psychological treatments, in general, were superior to drug therapy (mean effect sizes = 1.14 and 0.60, respectively), especially when combined with some form of dietary management (mean effect size = 1.30).

SUMMARY

Clinical and scientific interest in eating disorders has increased greatly in the past decade. An extensive amount of research has appeared in a relatively few years. For example, the review by Hinz and Williamson (1987) of a very limited area of eating disorders research (i.e., of whether bulimia is simply a variant of affective disorders) cited almost 100 references, the vast majority of which were published between 1980 and 1985. Keeping current on the vast amount of literature is complicated by the fact that data appear in a wide variety of psychological, psychiatric, and medical journals. For the most part, there are serious methodological weaknesses across studies. Diagnostic criteria have varied greatly, many studies are based on relatively low numbers of subjects (with case reports abounding), adequate control groups often are not studied, and standardized interview schedules or psychological tests are lacking in many cases. There has been an overreliance on single-outcome measures, such as decrease in purging or weight gain, and follow-up periods are usually only a few weeks to a few months. Long-term or longitudinal data are virtually nonexistent.

In spite of these methodological limitations, some tentative conclusions can be reached. Eating disorders are primarily conditions of adolescence and early adulthood in females, and the medical complications associated with both anorexia nervosa and bulimia nervosa are clearly serious and potentially life threatening without intervention. Both anorexic and bulimic patients evidence significant cognitive distortions about themselves and their body images, and a variety of other psychological symptoms, most notably depression, are frequently noted in both disorders. There are several theories regarding the etiology of eating disorders, and limited support can be found for each in the literature. Similar conclusions can be reached regarding treatment efforts, which have usually been behavioral and/or pharmacological in nature. Laessle et al. (1987) suggested that a behavioral approach combined with some form of dietary management program may be superior to other treatment modalities.

In the past decade, investigators have studied a variety of aspects of eating disorders, and the methodology employed appears to have improved. With continued improvements and refinements in research methodology, the 1990s should lead to a significant increase in our factual knowledge concerning anorexia nervosa and bulimia nervosa.

REFERENCES

Abraham, S. F., & Beaumont, P. J. V. (1982). How patients describe bulimia or binge eating. *Psychological Medicine, 12,* 625–635.

Agras, W. S., Dorian, B., Kirkley, B. G., Arnow, B., & Bachman, J. (1987). Imipramine in the treatment of bulimia: A double-blind controlled study. *International Journal of Eating Disorders, 6,* 29–38.

American Psychiatric Association. (1968). *Diagnostic and statistical manual of mental disorders* (2nd ed.). Washington, DC: Author.

American Psychiatric Association. (1980). *Diagnostic and statistical manual of mental disorders* (3rd ed.). Washington, DC: Author.

American Psychiatric Association. (1987). *Diagnostic and statistical manual of mental disorders* (3rd ed. rev.). Washington, DC: Author.

Attie, I., & Brooks-Gunn, J. (1989). Development of eating problems in adolescent girls: A longitudinal study. *Development Psychology, 25,* 70–79.

Barlow, J., Blouin, J., Blouin, A., & Perez, E. (1988). Treatment of bulimia with desipramine: A double-blind crossover study. *Canadian Journal of Psychiatry, 33,* 129–133.

Bemis, K. M. (1987). The present status of operant conditioning for the treatment of anorexia nervosa. *Behavior Modification, 11,* 432–463.

Boskind-Lodahl, M., & White, W. C. (1978). The definition and treatment of bulimarexia in college women—A pilot study. *Journal of the American College of Health Associations, 27,* 84–97.

Bruch, H. (1973). *Eating disorders: Obesity, anorexia nervosa and the person within.* New York: Basic Books.

Bruch, H. (1978). *The golden cage.* Cambridge: Harvard University Press.

Button, E. J., & Whitehouse, A. (1981). Subclinical anorexia nervosa. *Psychological Medicine, 11,* 509–516.

Cash, T. F., & Brown, T. A. (1987). Body image in anorexia nervosa and bulimia nervosa: A review of the literature. *Behavior Modification, 11,* 487–521.

Chiodo, J. (1985). The assessment of anorexia nervosa and bulimia. *Progress in Behavior Modification, 19,* 255–292.

Coovert, D. L., Kinder, B. N., & Thompson, J. K. (1989). The psychosexual aspects of anorexia nervosa and bulimia nervosa: A review of the literature. *Clinical Psychology Review, 9,* 169–180.

Coovert, D. L., Thompson, J. K., & Kinder, B. N. (1988). Interrelationships among multiple aspects of body image and eating disturbance. *International Journal of Eating Disorders, 7,* 495–502.

Crisp, A. H., Hsu, L. K. G., & Harding, B. (1980). Clinical features of anorexia nervosa: A study of a consecutive series of 102 female patients. *Journal of Psychosomatic Research, 24,* 179–191.

Drewnowski, A., Hopkins, S. A., & Kessler, R. C. (1988). The prevalence of bulimia nervosa in the U.S. college student population. *American Journal of Public Health, 78,* 1322–1325.

Eckert, E. D. (1985). Characteristics of anorexia nervosa. In J. E. Mitchell (Ed.), *Anorexia nervosa and bulimia: Diagnosis and treatment* (pp. 3–28). Minneapolis: University of Minnesota Press.

Ehrensing, R. H., & Weitzman, E. L. (1970). The mother–daughter relationship in anorexia nervosa. *Psychosomatic Medicine, 32,* 201–208.

Feighner, J. P., Robins, E., Guze, S. P., Woodruff, R. A., Winokur, G., & Munoz, R. (1972). Diagnostic criteria for use in psychiatric research. *Archives of General Psychiatry, 26,* 57–63.

Garner, D. M., & Garfinkel, P. E. (1981). Body image in anorexia nervosa: Measurement, theory, and clinical implications. *International Journal of Psychiatry in Medicine, 11,* 263–284.

Garner, D. M., Fairburn, C. G., & Davis, R. (1987). Cognitive–behavioral treatment of bulimia nervosa: A critical appraisal. *Behavior Modification, 11,* 398–431.

Gerner, R. H., & Gwirtsman, H. E. (1981). Abnormalities of dexamethasone suppression test and urinary MHPG in anorexia nervosa. *American Journal of Psychiatry, 138,* 650–653.

Giles, T. R., Young, R. R., & Young, D. E. (1985). Clinical studies and clinical replication series: Behavioral treatment of severe bulimia. *Behavior Therapy, 16,* 393–405.

Goldberg, S. C., Halmi, K. A., Eckert, E. D., Casper, R. C., Davis, J. M., & Roper, M. (1980). Attitudinal dimensions in anorexia nervosa. *Journal of Psychiatric Research, 15,* 239–251.

Hall, R. C., Tice, L., Beresford, T. P., Wooley, B., & Hall, A. K. (1988). Sexual abuse in patients with anorexia nervosa and bulimia. *Psychosomatics, 30,* 73–79.

Halmi, K. A., Falk, J. R., & Schwartz, E. (1981). Binge-eating and vomiting: A survey of a college population. *Psychological Medicine, 11,* 697–706.

Harding, T. P., & Lachenmeyer, J. R. (1986). Family interaction patterns and locus of control as predictors of the presence and severity of anorexia nervosa. *Journal of Clinical Psychology, 42,* 440–448.

Hatsukami, D., Eckert, E., Mitchell, J. E., & Pyle, R. (1984). Affective disorder and substance abuse in women with bulimia. *Psychological Medicine, 23,* 701–704.

Hatsukami, D., Owen, P., Pyle, R., & Mitchell, J. E. (1982). Similarities and differences on the MMPI between women with bulimia and women with alcohol or drug abuse problems. *Addictive Behaviors, 7,* 435–439.

Hinz, L. D., & Williamson, D. A. (1987). Bulimia and depression: A review of the affective variant hypothesis. *Psychological Bulletin, 102,* 150–158.

Herzog, D. B., Keller, M. B., & Lavori, P. W. (1988). Outcome in anorexia nervosa and bulimia nervosa: A review of the literature. *Journal of Nervous and Mental Disease, 176,* 131–143.

Horne, R. L., Ferguson, J. M., Pope, H. G., Hudson, J. I., Lineberry, C. G., Ascher, J., & Cato, A. (1988). Treatment of bulimia with buproprion: A multicenter controlled trial. *Journal of Clinical Psychiatry, 49,* 262–266.

Hsu, L. K. G. (1982). Is there a disturbance in body image in anorexia nervosa? *Journal of Nervous and Mental Disease, 17,* 305–307.

Jones, D. J., Fox, M. M., Babigian, H. M., & Hutton, H. E. (1980). Epidemiology of anorexia nervosa in Monroe County, New York: 1960–1976. *Psychosomatic Medicine, 42,* 551–558.

Katzman, M. A., & Wolchik, S. A. (1984). Bulimia and binge eating in college women: A comparison of personality and behavioral characteristics. *Journal of Consulting and Clinical Psychology, 52,* 423–428.

Kay, G. N., Hoffman, G. W., Boswick, J., Rockwell, K., & Ellenwood, E. H. (1988). The electrocardiogram in anorexia nervosa. *International Journal of Eating Disorders, 7,* 791–795.

Laessle, R. G., Zoettl, C., & Pirke, K. (1987). Metaanalysis of treatment studies for bulimia. *International Journal of Eating Disorders, 6,* 647–653.

Minuchin, S., Rosman, B. L., & Baker, L. (1978). *Psychosomatic families: Anorexia nervosa in context.* Cambridge: Harvard University Press.

Mitchell, J. E. (1985). Medical complications of anorexia nervosa and bulimia. In J. E. Mitchell (Ed.), *Anorexia nervosa and bulimia: Diagnosis and treatment* (pp. 48–77). Minneapolis: University of Minnesota Press.

Mitchell, J. E., & Pyle, R. L. (1985). Characteristics of bulimia. In J. E. Mitchell (Ed.), *Anorexia nervosa and bulimia: Diagnosis and treatment* (pp. 29–47). Minneapolis: University of Minnesota Press.

Mitchell, J. E., Pyle, R. L., & Eckert, E. D. (1981). Frequency and duration of binge eating episodes in patients with bulimia. *American Journal of Psychiatry, 138,* 835–836.

Mitchell, P. B. (1988). The pharmacological management of bulimia nervosa: A critical review. *International Journal of Eating Disorders, 7,* 29–41.

Mizes, J. S. (1985). Bulimia: A review of its symptomatology and treatment. *Advances in Behavioral Research and Therapy, 7,* 91–142.

Nasser, M. (1988). Eating disorders: The cultural dimension. *Social Psychiatry and Psychiatric Epidemiology, 23,* 184–187.

Nowlin, N. S. (1983). Anorexia nervosa in twins: Case report and review. *Journal of Clinical Psychiatry, 44,* 101–105.

Ondercin, P. (1979). Compulsive eating in college women. *Journal of College Student Personnel, 20,* 153–157.

Palossy, B., & Oo, M. (1977). ECG alteration in anorexia nervosa. *Annals of Cardiology, 19,* 280–282.

Pope, H. G., & Hudson, J. I. (1989). Are eating disorders associated with borderline personality disorder? A critical review. *International Journal of Eating Disorders, 8,* 1–9.

Powers, P. S. (1982). Heart failure during treatment of anorexia nervosa. *American Journal of Psychiatry, 139,* 1167–1170.

Pyle, R. L., Mitchell, J. E., & Eckert, E. D. (1981). Bulimia: A report of 34 cases. *Journal of Clinical Psychiatry, 42,* 60–64.

Rosen, J. C. (1987). A review of behavioral treatments for bulimia nervosa. *Behavior Modification, 11,* 464–486.

Rosen, J. C., & Leitenberg, H. (1982). Bulimia nervosa: Treatment with exposure and response prevention. *Behavior Therapy, 13,* 117–124.

Russell, G. (1979). Bulimia nervosa: An ominous variant of anorexia nervosa. *Psychological Medicine, 9,* 429–448.

Schulman, R. G., Kinder, B. N., Powers, P. S., Prange, M., & Gleghorn, A. (1986). The development of a scale to measure cognitive distortions in bulimia. *Journal of Personality Assessment, 50,* 630–639.

Scott, D. W. (1987). The involvement of psychosexual factors in the causation of eating disorders: Time for a reappraisal. *International Journal of Eating Disorders, 6,* 199–213.

Shapiro, S. (1988). Bulimia: An entity in search of definition. *Journal of Clinical Psychology, 44,* 491–498.

Slade, P. D. (1985). A review of body-image studies in anorexia nervosa and bulimia nervosa. *Journal of Psychiatric Research, 19,* 255–265.

Stangler, R. S., & Printz, A. M. (1980). DSM-III: Psychiatric diagnosis in a university population. *American Journal of Psychiatry, 137,* 937–940.

Stege, P., Visco-Dangler, L., & Rye, L. (1982). Anorexia nervosa: Review including oral and dental manifestations. *Journal of the American Dental Association, 104,* 648–652.

Thompson, J. K., Berland, N. W., Linton, P. H., & Weinsier, R. (1986). Assessment of body distortion via a self-adjusting light beam in seven eating disorder groups. *International Journal of Eating Disorders, 5,* 113–120.

Thompson, J. K., & Thompson, C. M. (1986). Body size distortion and self-esteem in asymptomatic, normal weight males and females. *International Journal of Eating Disorders, 5,* 1061–1068.

Vandereycken, W., & Pierloot, R. (1981). Anorexia nervosa in twins. *Psychotherapy and Psychosomatics, 35,* 55–63.

Walsh, B. T. (1982). Endocrine disturbances in anorexia nervosa and depression. *Psychosomatic Medicine, 44,* 85–91.

Wardle, J. (1980). Dietary restraint and binge eating. *Behavioral Analysis and Modification, 4,* 201–209.

Webb, J. G., Birmingham, C. L., & MacDonald, I. L. (1988). Electrocardiographic abnormalities in anorexia nervosa. *International Journal of Eating Disorders, 7,* 785–790.

Willmuth, M. E., Leitenberg, H., Rosen, J. C., Fondacaro, K. M., & Gross, J. (1985). Body size distortion in bulimia nervosa. *International Journal of Eating Disorders, 4,* 71–78.

PART THREE

Special Topics

CHAPTER 14

Motor Activity and DSM-III-R

WARREN W. TRYON

The development of the American Psychiatric Association's (APA's) *Diagnostic and Statistical Manual of Mental Disorders* through its first (APA, 1952), second (APA, 1968), third (APA, 1980), and revised third editions (APA, 1987) has consistently recognized the importance of motor activity and its abnormal states in the diagnosis of mental and behavioral disorders. Table 14.1 below identifies forty-six current, as well as one proposed, DSM-III-R categories in which motor activity plays an explicit diagnostic role. The table does not include differential diagnosis, in which confirming one diagnosis

TABLE 14.1. Activity as an Inclusive Criterion (Diagnosis)

Organic Mental Syndromes and Disorders

1. Delirium (p. 103)
   a. Disturbance of sleep–wake cycle with insomnia.
   b. Increased or decreased psychomotor activity when awake.
2. Organic mood syndrome (pp. 111–112)
   a. Prominent and persistent depressed, elevated, or expansive mood, resembling either a manic episode or a major depressive episode, that is due to a specific organic factor (see diagnostic criteria below).
   b. Prominent and persistent depressed, elevated, or expansive mood. Specify manic, depressed, or mixed.
3. Organic personality syndrome (p. 115)
   a. Marked shifts from normal mood to depression.
   b. Recurrent outbursts of aggression or rage that are grossly out of proportion to any precipitating psychosocial stressors.
4. Organic mental disorders (p. 119)
   a. Primary degenerative dementia of the alzheimer type, senile onset
      1. with delirium (290.30).
      2. with depression (290.21).
   b. Primary degenerative dementia of the alzheimer type, presenile onset
      1. with delirium (290.11).
      2. with depression (290.13).
5. Multi-infarct dementia with depression (290.40) (p. 123)
6. Uncomplicated alcohol withdrawal (291.80) (p. 130)
   a. Depressed mood.
   b. Insomnia.
7. Alcohol withdrawal delirium (291.00) (p. 131)
   a. Delirium (see above criteria).
8. Amphetamine or similarly acting sympathomimetic intoxication (305.70) (p. 135)
   a. Psychomotor agitation.

(continued)

TABLE 14.1. *(Continued)*

9. Amphetamine or similarly acting sympathomimetic withdrawal (292.00) (p. 136)
   a. Fatigue.
   b. Insomnia.
   c. Psychomotor agitation.
10. Amphetamine or similarly acting sympathomimetic delirium (292.81) (p. 137)
   a. Delirium (see above criteria).
11. Caffeine intoxication (305.90) (p. 139)
   a. Excitement.
   b. Insomnia.
   c. Psychomotor agitation.
12. Cocaine intoxication (305.60) (p. 142)
   a. Psychomotor agitation.
13. Cocaine withdrawal (292.00) (pp. 142–143)
   a. Fatigue.
   b. Insomnia or hypersomnia.
   c. Psychomotor agitation.
14. Cocaine delirium (292.81) (p. 143)
   a. Delirium (see above criteria).
15. Hallucinogen hallucinosis (305.30) (p. 145)
   a. Tremors.
   b. Incoordination.
16. Hallucinogen mood disorder (292.84) (p. 147)
   a. Organic mood syndrome developing shortly after hallucinogen use (usually within 1 or 2 weeks), and persisting more than 24 hours after cessation of such use. (See above criteria.)
17. Inhalant intoxication (305.90) (pp. 149–150)
   a. Incoordination.
   b. Psychomotor retardation.
   c. Tremor.
   d. Stupor or coma.
18. Nicotine withdrawal (292.00) (p. 151)
   a. Restlessness.
19. Opioid withdrawal (292.00) (pp. 153–154)
   a. Insomnia.
20. Phencyclidine (PCP) or similarly acting arylcyclohexylamine intoxication (305.90) (p. 155)
   a. Psychomotor agitation.
21. Phencyclidine (PCP) or similarly acting arylcyclohexylamine mood disorder (292.11) (p. 157)
   a. Organic mood syndrome (see above criteria).
   b. Including depression, physical restlessness, difficulty sleeping, decreased need for sleep, and increased activity.
22. Sedative, hypnotic, or anxiolytic intoxication (305.40) (p. 159)
   a. Incoordination.
23. Uncomplicated sedative, hypnotic, or anxiolytic withdrawal (292.00) (p. 160)
   a. Coarse tremor of hands, tongue, and eyelids.
   b. Marked insomnia.
24. Sedative, hypnotic, or anxiolytic withdrawal delirium (292.00) (p. 161)
   a. Delirium (see above criteria).

Schizophrenia

25. Schizophrenia, catatonic type (295.2x) (p. 196)
   a. Catatonic stupor (marked decrease in reactivity to the environment and/or reduction in spontaneous movements and activity) or mutism.
   b. Catatonic excitement (excited motor activity).

414

TABLE 14.1. *(Continued)*

Delusional (Paranoid) Disorder

---

26. Delusional disorder (297.10) (p. 202)
    a. If a major depressive or manic syndrome has been present during the delusional disturbance, the total duration of all episodes of the mood syndrome has been brief relative to the total duration of the delusional disturbance.

Psychotic Disorders Not Elsewhere Classified

---

27. Brief reactive psychosis (298.80) (pp. 206–207)
    a. Catatonic behavior (see above criteria).
28. Schizophreiform disorder (295.40) (p. 208)
    a. Meets Criteria A and C of schizophrenia: on page 194 of manual.
       1. Criteria A includes catatonic behavior.
       2. Criteria C requires that mood disorder be ruled out.
29. Schizoaffective disorder (295.70) (p. 210)
    a. A disturbance during which, at some time, there is either a major depressive or a manic syndrome concurrent with symptoms that meet the criterion of schizophrenia (see Entry 28).
    b. Specify bipolar type (current previous manic syndrome) or depressive type (no current or previous manic syndrome).

Mood Disorders

Manic episode (pp. 217–218)
    a. Decreased need for sleep.
    b. Increase in goal-directed activity or psychomotor agitation.
Major depressive episode
    a. Insomnia or hypersomnia nearly every day.
    b. Psychomotor agitation or retardation nearly every day (observable by others; not merely subjective feelings of restlessness or being slowed down).
    c. Fatigue or loss of energy nearly every day.
30. Major depression, single episode (296.2x) (pp. 229–230)
    a. A single major depressive episode, which includes (p. 222):
       1. Insomnia or hypersomnia nearly every day.
       2. Psychomotor agitation or retardation nearly every day (observable by others; not merely subjective feelings of restlessness or being slowed down).
       3. Fatigue or loss of energy nearly every day.
    b. Has never had a manic episode or an unequivocal hypomanic episode, which includes (p. 217):
       1. Decreased need for sleep.
       2. Increase in goal-directed activity or psychomotor agitation.
31. Major depression, recurrent (296.3x) (p. 230)
    a. Two or more major depressive episodes, each separated by at least 2 months of return to more or less usual functioning.
    b. Has never had a manic episode or an unequivocal hypomanic episode.
    c. Specify if seasonal pattern (p. 224).
32. Bipolar disorder, mixed (296.6x) (p. 225)
    a. Current (or most recent) episode involves the full symptomatic picture of both manic and major depressive episodes (except for the duration requirement of 2 weeks for depressive symptoms), intermixed or rapidly alternating every few days.
    b. Prominent depressive symptoms lasting at least a full day.
    c. Specify if seasonal pattern (p. 224).
33. Bipolar disorder, manic (296.4x) (p. 226)
    a. Currently (or most recently) in a manic episode. (If there has been a previous manic episode, the current episode need not meet the full criteria for a manic episode.)
    b. Specify if seasonal pattern (p. 224).

(continued)

TABLE 14.1. *(Continued)*

34. Bipolar disorder, depressed (296.5x) (p. 226)
    a. Has had one or more manic episodes.
    b. Currently (or most recently) in a major depressive episode. (If there has been a previous major depressive episode, the current episode need not meet the full criteria for a major depressive episode.)
    c. Specify if seasonal pattern (p. 224).
35. Cyclothymia (301.13) (p. 227)
    a. For at least 2 years, presence of numerous hypomanic episodes (all the criteria for a manic episode except marked impairment) and numerous periods with depressed mood or loss of interest that did not meet Criterion A of major depressive episode.
36. Bipolar disorder not otherwise specified (296.70) (p. 228)
    a. Disorders with manic or hypomanic features that do not meet the criteria for any specific bipolar disorder.
37. Dysthymia (300.40) (p. 232)
    a. Insomnia or hypersomnia.
    b. Low energy or fatigue.
    c. Has never had a manic episode.
38. Depressive disorder not otherwise specified (311.00) (p. 233)
    a. Disorders with depressive features that do not meet the criteria for any specific mood disorder or adjustment disorder with depressed mood.
    b. Specify if seasonal pattern (p. 224).

Anxiety Disorders

39. Generalized anxiety disorder (300.02) (pp. 252–253)
    a. Trembling, twitching, or feeling shaky.
    b. Restlessness.
    c. Easy fatigability.
    d. Trouble falling or staying asleep.

Sleep Disorders

40. Insomnia related to another mental disorder (nonorganic) (307.42) (pp. 299–300)
    a. Difficulty in initiating or maintaining sleep.
    b. Occurs at least three times a week for at least 1 month.
    c. Results in daytime fatigue.
    d. Occurrence not exclusively during the course of sleep–wake schedule disorder or parasomnia.
41. Insomnia related to a known organic factor (780.50) (p. 301)
    a. Physical disorders include sleep apnea and arthritis.
    b. Psychoactive substance use disorder.
42. Primary insomnia (307.42) (p. 301)
    a. Not maintained by any other mental disorder or any known organic factor.
43. Sleep-wake schedule disorder (307.45) (p. 307)
    a. Mismatch between the normal sleep-wake schedule for a person's environment and his or her circadian sleep-wake pattern.
    b. Advanced or delayed type: Sleep–wake schedule disorder with onset and offset of sleep considerably advanced or delayed (if sleep–wake schedule is not interfered with by medication or environmental demands) in relation to what the person desires (usually the conventional societal sleep–wake schedule).
    c. Disorganized type: Sleep–wake schedule disorder apparently due to disorganized and variable sleep and waking times, resulting in absence of a daily major sleep period.
    d. Frequently changing type: Sleep–wake schedule disorder apparently due to frequently changing sleep and waking times, such as recurrent changes in work shifts or time zones.
44. Dream anxiety disorder (307.42) (p. 310)
    a. Repeated awakenings from the major sleep period.

TABLE 14.1.   *(Continued)*

45. Sleep terror disorder (307.46) (p. 311)
  a. Recurrent episodes of abrupt awakening from sleep (lasting 1 to 10 minutes), usually occurring during the first third of the major sleep period.
46. Sleepwalking disorder (307.46) (p. 313)
  a. Repeated episodes of arising from bed during sleep and walking about, usually occurring during the first third of the major sleep period.

Proposed Diagnostic Category Needing Further Study

47. Late luteal phase dysphoric disorder (premenstrual syndrome—PMS)
  a. Depressed mood.
  b. Easy fatigability or marked lack of energy.
  c. Hypersomnia or insomnia.

Source: Adapted with permission from the *Diagnostic and Statistical Manual of Mental Disorders* (3rd ed., revised). Copyright 1987 American Psychiatric Association.

requires the exclusion of others for which motor activity plays a defining role. Because Tryon (1986) has reviewed the history of this development in detail, it is not reiterated here. The primary conclusion is that motor activity figures prominently in the clinical manifestation of many disorders and in their differential diagnosis. For example, according to DSM-III-R, the differential diagnosis of attention deficit disorder with and without hyperactivity is accomplished exclusively using objective activity measurements. The central role that activity plays in psychopathology also is evidenced by the relevance of the current discussion to Chapters 3 through 9, 13, and 15 through 17 in this book.

This chapter begins with a discussion of relevant theoretical issues, including the definition of activity and a consideration of its structure. Available instruments and their use in measuring motor activity are then reviewed. Finally, adult DSM-III-R disorders in which motor activity is diagnostically pertinent are reviewed, showing how the previously described instruments can be used to facilitate both diagnosis and differential diagnosis.

THEORETICAL ISSUES

Behavior Is Activity

To behave is to act. When we report having seen a person behave in some fashion, we are generally reporting something he or she has done involving movement or lack of movement. If we report having seen someone walking or a child getting out of a seat during class, we are indirectly reporting limb activity. Busy, active people engage in multiple uses of their limbs during the course of a normal day for various purposes, including personal hygiene, food preparation, work, and recreation. If we report having seen someone sit quietly or sleep, we are indirectly reporting low levels of limb activity.

Behavior is currently understood to involve more than activity. Sensory and cognitive processes are often referred to as behavior; however, information input and processing result in action or inaction, which constitutes the focus of this chapter.

If motor activity is a primary part of normal behavior, it follows that ab-normal behavior may include activity disorder (see Kupfer, Maser, Blehar, & Miller, 1987). Certainly, various neurological disorders result in movement disorders. Neurologists, in fact, are among the most behaviorally oriented clinicians in that they are concerned primarily about a person's ability to move (behave). The major point of the following section is to demonstrate that psychological (psychiatric) disorders are also associated with abnormal motor activity.

Behavioral Measurement

Tryon (1985, 1986) compared behavioral inference, observation, and mea-surement, and then discussed the conceptual shift required by behavioral measurement. In short, measurement is accomplished by instruments, whereas inferences and observations are produced by people. The use of instruments requires the investigator to consider behavioral physics (Tryon, 1985, p. 208) because he or she must think about what the sensor will detect given its physical properties and its location on the person.

Site of Attachment

Activity is commonly referred to as if it were a singular constant aspect of an individual's behavior. The impression that activity is unitary probably stems from trait inferences made by human observers who summarize observations with simple statements about a subject's being hyperactive, normoactive, or hypoactive. In this section, I argue that activity is probably not unitary in nature. In the following two sections, I argue that activity is certainly not a constant feature of any person's behavior.

Presume that we have attached three identical activity sensors on the wrist, waist, and ankle of each of 5 subjects, and each walks 1, 2, 3, 4, or 5 miles. Almost certainly, we would find a strong, if not perfect, linear relationship between miles walked (activity) and wrist, waist, and ankle measurements. The more active subject could be selected regardless of the site of sensor attachment. The person with the most active wrist would also have the most active waist and ankle. Activity would appear to be a unitary phenomenon that could be monitored equally well at all sites of attachment.

Next, we repeat the above experiment, but this time we require all subjects to carry a lightweight box with both hands, thereby immobilizing both wrists. Very likely, the previous linear relationship between miles walked (activity) and wrist measurements would have been obliterated, yet the waist and ankle results would replicate earlier findings.

Consider another example. Psychiatric patients confined to a ward spend most of their time sitting. The more alert patients are perhaps reading or otherwise constructively using their hands. Thus, wrist measurements proba-bly separate patients according to activity level much better than either waist or leg movements.

The conclusion reached from these considerations is that all body parts are not equally active all of the time. Hence, one should not expect high intercorrelations among activity measures taken from different body sites. One must carefully consider placement of the sensor on the subject, probable behaviors to be emitted, and likely situational constraints. Significant statistical relationships may emerge among body sites, given many days of measurements, but this is an empirical matter yet to be studied.

Life-Style

Activity reflects one's life-style. Some people stay up longer and move about more than others; however, no person goes through exactly the same motions day after day. If Wednesday is tennis day, higher activity readings would be expected on Wednesday than other days because of this difference in daily routine. Because weekend and weekday activities often differ, weekend activity measurements may not duplicate weekday values.

The fact that activity measurements reflect life-style can be put to good clinical use. Behaviorally oriented weight control programs often encourage activity increases to help the client both curb appetite and burn excess calories. Waist activity measurements can verify whether increased movements of the person's center of gravity, the most energy-consumptive movements, have occurred. Montoye et al. (1983) reported that vertical acceleration about the waist is correlated ($r = .74$) with oxygen uptake. The therapist's objective is to help the client adopt a more active life-style. Actigraphy can measure the extent to which the therapist has achieved this objective.

Life-style variability sometimes complicates activity measurement. Activity measurements taken from a person throughout the year may show more activity during summer than winter. Such natural variability complicates efforts to measure seasonal affective disorder or cyclothymia.

Scale

The horizontal (x-axis) scale by which activity is reported is time. Activity can be graphed against time measured in seconds, minutes, hours, days, weeks, months, or years. Different impressions are obtained depending upon the horizontal scale employed. The longer the time scale, the more stable the behavior appears to be. Epstein (1979, 1980) persuasively argued that aggregation (over time) enhances psychometric properties of behavioral as well as psychometric data through error reduction. Hence, weekly data points are more stable than daily data points, which in turn are more stable than hourly data points.

Figure 14.1 is a 10-hour activity record taken from my left wrist using an Ambulatory Monitoring, Inc., Motionlogger™ actigraph with a 1-minute epoch. (The actigraph is described in greater detail in the "Available Instruments" section of this chapter.) Activity counts (Redmond & Hegge, 1985) were cumulated over 1-minute periods, and the results written to memory in the solid-state wrist-worn device. Figure 14.1 is a histogram of activity versus time, with one vertical line for each 1-minute epoch from 8:00 A.M. (08:00) until 6:00 P.M. (18:00) on Day 117 (Tuesday, April 26, 1988). Notice how variable the data are at this very small scale: Near-zero values occasionally

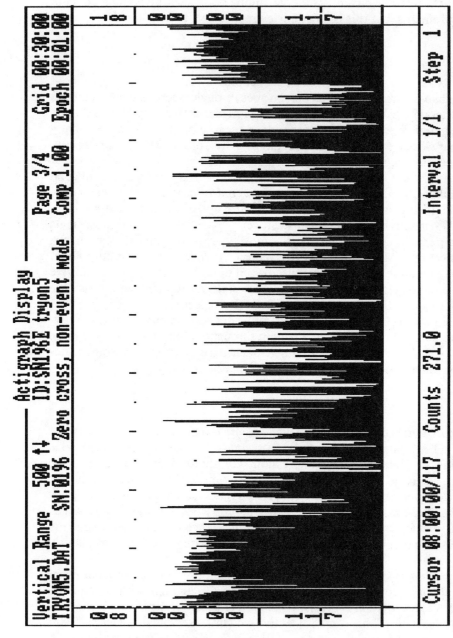

Figure 14.1. Behavioral variability illustrated by sample 10-hour actigraph data taken from my left wrist using a 1-minute recording epoch.

follow epochs of considerable activity. Averaging over ever more epochs will produce more stable, and therefore reproducible, results as discussed by Epstein (1979, 1980).

Different cycles of activity require different time scales. At least two data points are required for every cycle one is attempting to evaluate. In practice, six to ten data points per cycle are recommended. One would have to obtain at least two data points per day to track sleep–wake cycles; however, several data points during both the waking and the sleeping portions of the circadian rhythm are preferred. For example, one may wish to discern whether behavior in the morning differs from behavior in the afternoon and evening. Similarly, one may wish to know if body motility just after sleep onset differs from motility during the middle of the night and just before awakening. Also, one may wish to determine whether monthly or yearly (seasonal) activity cycles exist.

Tremor is a special form of very rapid activity. Normal physiological tremor occurs in everyone at a frequency of 8 to 12 cycles per second (hertz). The amplitude is often too small to be visible with the naked eye, but it is easily measured using either accelerometry (Findley & Gresty, 1984; Gresty, McCarthy, & Findley, 1984; Marsden, Parkes, & Quinn, 1982) or electromyography (EMG) (Matthews & Muir, 1980; Young & Hagbarth, 1980). Lang and Fahn (in press) indicated that accelerometry is currently the most commonly used procedure for tremor measurement. Marshall and Walsh (1956) described several reasons for preferring accelerometry over EMG. First, accelerometers need only be taped to the finger and require no special skin preparation as do EMG electrodes (Gaarder & Montgomery, 1977; Olton & Noonberg, 1980). Second, accelerometer output is less susceptible to electrical interference than is the EMG signal because of its greater amplitude and lower frequency. Third, the considerably lower frequency content of the signal for accelerometry (50 hertz or less) requires far fewer data points to be collected than for EMG (500 hertz or more). Fourth, velocity and displacement values can be calculated from acceleration data.

Neurological disorders, such as Parkinson's disease, both reduce the frequency of this normal tremor and dramatically increase its amplitude. In these cases, the time scale is in milliseconds rather than seconds.

Premorbid Activity Assessment

The wide variation in normal activity strongly argues in favor of comparing the disordered individual with his or her own premorbid condition rather than with a currently unavailable, and probably not very informative, national activity norm (using age, sex, race, socioeconomic class, etc.). This reasoning is the same as for having a reference electrocardiogram (EKG) on file, taken as part of a routine physical examination while healthy, for subsequent comparison should disease arise.

It is therefore highly recommended that activity measurements be incorporated into routine physical examinations. Such assessments may be of interest to cardiologists and other nonpsychiatric care providers because of the relationship between activity and health (wellness). If instruments without an inherent time base are used, then the hours of wearing time per day should be recorded.

AVAILABLE INSTRUMENTS

Activity

Tryon (1985) reviewed the construction, unit of measurement, and reliability of actometers, counters, pedometers, stabilimeters, photoelectric cells, ultrasound devices, electronic accelerometers, and load transducers plus indirect autonomic measures of activity. This section provides new information only.

L. L. Bean, Inc., retails a Digital Electronic Pedometer (catalog number 6052PP; $16.50 postpaid as of August 1988), which is actually a step counter. It measures 2 inches wide × 1.5 inches high × .75 inches deep and weighs 3 ounces. It consists of an eight-digit liquid crystal display electronic calculator that inserts into a base, which clips to the waistband. The base unit contains a vertical displacement sensor that causes the calculator to increment by 1 every time it registers a movement. It can count up to 99,999,999 steps. A slide adjustment changes the threshold setting between walking and running. This device can be programmed with the user's stride length to read out in miles or kilometers if other than step information is required. It requires one G10 battery or equivalent.

Radio Shack retails two types of electronic pedometers. Their less expensive model, the Micronta Walk-Mate™ (catalog number 63-671; $14.95 as of August 1988), measures 1.75 × 1.75 × 0.5 inches. Its five-digit liquid crystal display counts up to 99,999 steps before it must be reset by pressing a button. It has a folding case that conceals the step count and a belt clip. It runs on one RS386A battery.

The second electronic pedometer retailed by Radio Shack, the Jog-Mate™ (catalog number 63-681; $24.95 as of August 1988) has a programmable stride length, has a walk versus jog setting, and records up to 999.9 miles. It runs on one RS386A battery.

Innovative Time also makes a full-feature electronic pedometer ($39.90 + $3 P&H; p. 38 DSK Industries, Inc., Summer 1988 catalog). It calculates distance walked, estimates calories burned (using a table lookup procedure), and beeps when a particular distance has been traversed (specified number of steps taken).

A primary limitation of most activity recording devices is that they lack a time base and automatic recording. Hence, either the participant or someone else must take a reading at specified clock times and record both the activity reading and the clock time. Recording real time allows one to determine wearing time, and therefore activity rate. Sometimes, one must reset the device as part of reading it (cf. actometers). Although this degree of participation is minimal, and can often be accomplished reliably, it sometimes is problematic. For example, Futterman and Tryon (1986) reported that the most depressed outpatient women refused to comply with the self-recording procedures. Undergraduates cooperated with recording instructions for approximately 2 weeks (one daytime and one nighttime recording) before losing motivation. Compliance problems with recording procedures are directly proportional to the number of times per day that one takes activity measurements and the number of steps entailed.

McPartland, Kupfer, and Foster (1976) described a third-generation motor activity recording monitor measuring $4 \times 2 \times 2$ centimeters.[1] Its sensor is a mercury switch that closes whenever it is tilted more than 5 millimeters. An accumulator counts the number of movements over a selectable epoch (1.875, 3.75, 7.5, 15, or 30 minutes) before being written to one of 512 memory locations. Hence, data collection may span from 16 hours to 10.7 days. Data are then downloaded to a computer.

The Vitalog PMS-8 is a portable physiological monitoring system with eight analog-to-digital channels for recording heart rate, respiration, and blood oxygen saturation.[2] A wrist activity sensor can also be purchased.

A particularly convenient, and rather widely used, instrument is the MotionLogger.[3] It was developed from a prototype described by Colburn, Smith, Guarini, and Simons (1976) and has been extensively used by Army basic research with field infantry. The operating characteristics of this device are described by Redmond and Hegge (1985). In brief, the MotionLogger actigraph (so named because it writes activity data to memory) is a solid-state accelerometer-based wrist-worn device measuring $2.5 \times 3.5 \times 0.75$ inches and weighing 3 ounces. It attaches to the wrist or ankle with a Velcro™ wristlet, but can also be worn at the waist. It can be programmed to run in either a zero-crossing or threshold mode. In the zero-crossing mode, it counts the number of times acceleration-related voltages cross zero, when movement changes from being accelerated (+) to being decelerated (−), or vice versa. In threshold mode, a 10-Hertz counter is turned on whenever acceleration exceeds 0.01 gram and the number of counts is recorded. Hence, counts divided by 10 equals time above threshold in 10ths of a second. Both modes employ programmable epochs ranging from 1 second to 99 minutes and 99 seconds. Selecting a 1-minute epoch allows data to be continuously collected 24 hours a day for 8 days. The subject can record the occurrence of an event by pressing a button on the MotionLogger, which records the incident in 1 bit of memory. The MotionLogger is programmed and data are downloaded through an interface attached to the serial port of an IBM or compatible computer running MS-DOS.

As stated above, Figure 14.1 shows sample output from my left wrist for 10 hours using a 1-minute epoch. The grid tics are 30 minutes apart, as indicated. Each histogram bar represents the counts for a 1-minute period; the full scale is 500 counts. The cursor is located on 8:00 A.M., where a count of 271 was recorded. Additional examples of MotionLogger output are presented below for the discussion of sleep disorders.

---

[1] GMM Electronics, Inc., 1200 Riverview Drive, Verona, PA 15147. 412 624-2354.
[2] Vitalog, 643 Bair Island Road, Suite 300, Redwood City, CA 94063. 415 365-1100.
[3] Ambulatory Monitoring, Inc., 731 Saw Mill River Road, Ardsley, NY 10502. 914 693-9240; Outside New York State, 800 341-0066.

Cole, Kripke, Gruen, and Nava (1990) continued development of the MotionLogger under the name Actillume™. This device is preferable to the MotionLogger because the accelerometer output is digitized by an 8-bit analog-to-digital converter, which measures movements on a $2^8 = 256$-point ratio (equal interval + absolute zero) scale. Its microprocessor is fully programmable, whereas the MotionLogger's is not. The primary benefit is that the data are directly proportional to the forcefulness of the behavior being monitored. The Actillume can simultaneously record a second data channel, such as light or temperature.

Tremor

Two approaches are available for measuring tremor: electromyography and accelerometry. EMG begins with the proper preparation and placement of electrodes (Gaarder & Montgomery, 1977; Olton & Noonberg, 1980). Output is amplified and low pass filtered before being digitized by an analog-to-digital board inserted into either an IBM or compatible or a Macintosh SE or II microcomputer. Data collection and analysis are conducted with commercially available software.

Accelerometry begins with a uniaxial, biaxial, or triaxial accelerometer whose output is amplified, low pass filtered, and digitized. Three primary differences exist between accelerometry and EMG; the first two are advantages of the former, and the third is an advantage of the latter. First, accelerometer attachment is much simpler than is proper electrode attachment. Second, many fewer data points are needed for accelerometry than EMG. Third, only EMG is capable of recording the muscle events underlying tremor.

Motor Coordination

Frost (1978) used triaxial accelerometry to measure the extent to which subjects could duplicate simple sinusoidal (periodic) movement between specified targets. Simpler tests of manual dexterity, such as the Purdue Pegboard, are more familiar to psychologists.

Speech

Microphones and uniaxial accelerometers taped to the thyroid process (Adam's apple) can be used to detect speech. The amplification, low pass filtering, and digitizing procedures by microcomputer are the same as previously described.

Alpert, Merewether, Homel, Martz, and Lomask (1986) described their Voxcom system for analyzing speech in terms of fundamental frequency, amplitude, length of utterance, and length of pauses between utterances for up to 15 minutes in real time. The three main components of this system are a stereo cassette tape deck (Nakamichi LX-3), a microcomputer with analog-to-digital converter (Northstar Horizon and Tecmar TM AD212 A/D converter), and a special signal processing unit designed by Buxco Electronics.

Kruger (1987) described an interesting device, called Logoport, that can digitally record ambulatory speech behavior.[4] The device measures $164 \times 108 \times 30$ millimeters, weighs 800 grams, and is worn with a shoulder strap. A small condenser microphone is taped to the subject's throat and connected to one channel of the Logoport. A second channel is capable of recording EKG. Inside is a 512-KB CMOS memory and a 40-MHz quartz clock. Speech is compared with an adjustable threshold every 1 millisecond, thereby establishing an on–off pattern over time. If more than two of eight consecutive samples are classified as on, the entire eight samples are classified as on. The parameters of two and eight are user adjustable. The results of each 8-millisecond analysis (0,1) are written to memory as a 1-byte digit, thereby resulting in 125 samples per second. Total recording time is at least 6.5 hours using these parameters. Two or more Logoports can be synchronized in time to measure dyadic conversations.

MOTOR ACTIVITY IN DSM-III-R

Motor Activity References

Various references to abnormal motor behavior are made within DSM-III-R. The purpose of this section is to review and clarify these references to motor activity.

Psychomotor Agitation

DSM-III-R defines psychomotor agitation as excessive motor activity that is observable. DSM-III-R emphasizes the need for objective measurement by indicating that psychomotor agitation must be "observable by others, not merely subjective feelings of restlessness" (p. 222). Examples include "Inability to sit still, pacing, wringing of hands, (and) pulling at clothes" (p. 404). The term "restless" is sometimes used to describe such purposeless activity. Akathesia is a drug-induced form of this type of psychomotor agitation.

Psychomotor Retardation

DSM-III-R defines psychomotor retardation as "visible generalized slowing down of physical reactions, movements, and speech" (p. 404). DSM-III-R emphasizes the need for objective measurement by indicating that psychomotor retardation must be "observable by others, not merely subjective feelings of . . . being slowed down" (p. 222). Depressed mood is an indirect way of referring to decreased activity. When activity is particularly diminished in the presence of schizophrenic symptoms, the term "catatonic stupor" is used. Further reduction in motor activity is referred to as "semicoma," "coma," or "torpor."

---

[4] Dr. Hans-Peter Kruger, Department of Psychology, University of Wurzburg, Rentgenring 11, D 8700 Wurzburg, Germany.

Mood Shifts

Mood shifts refer to changes from psychomotor retardation to agitation, and vice versa. They are documented by the same criteria as discussed above plus a pattern of alternation. The terms "excitement" and "expansive mood" are also used. The term "hypervigilance" is used less often. If schizophrenic symptoms are present, the term "catatonic excitement" is used. Sometimes increased activity can refer to enhanced purposeful activity, such as increased work or recreational activities, all of which involve higher levels of motor activity.

Speech

Speech reflects emotion (Alpert, 1981), and it may be measured to determine affective disorders. Recent general discussions of such speech assessment are by Kupfer et al. (1987), Rehm (1987), Scherer (1987), and Siegman (1987a, 1987b). Studies by Alpert (1981, 1989), Breznitz and Sherman (1987), Godfrey and Knight (1984), Greden and Carroll (1980), Greden, Albala, Smokler, Gardner, and Carroll (1981), Hinchliffe, Lancashire, and Roberts (1971), Kanfer (1960), Pope, Blass, Siegman, and Raher (1970), Szabadi, Bradshaw, and Besson (1976), Teasdale, Fogarty, and Williams (1980), and Weintraub and Aronson (1967) have all reported reductions in speech rate associated with depression. The only study reporting no relationship between speech rate and depression is that by Rutter (1977). Reduction in speech rate is apparently due to abnormal pauses between words. Greden and Carroll (1980) and Greden et al. (1981) reported that pause times decreased from pretreatment through discharge. The Logoport can be used to obtain clinically relevant speech samples under naturalistic conditions. Speech samples could be taken either at specified intervals or when the person feels particularly depressed, anxious, argumentative, or any other strong emotion.

Vocal prosody refers to the acoustical properties of speech (Monrad-Krohn, 1947, 1963), including tonal variation, emphasis patterns, and timing characteristics. Dysprosody refers to an impaired ability to normally modulate tone and properly emphasize speech. Andreason, Alpert, and Martz (1981) found that mixed-diagnosis psychiatric patients rated as affectively flat have less variability in speech amplitude and pitch (prosodic parameters) than similiar patients rated as nonflat. Alpert (1981) also reported that flatness in schizophrenia is associated with emphasis reduction and that flatness in depression is associated with an increase in pause duration. In a mixed sample of 20 schizophrenic, 17 right brain damaged, 20 Parkinson's disease, 10 unipolar depressed, and 21 normal control subjects, Alpert (1989) reported that "flat affect is associated with shortened utterances and lengthened pauses and with a lower percentage of total time used for talking" (p. 53).

Williams and Stevens (1972, 1981) and Scherer (1981) studied emotional states using spectral analysis of speech. Hargreaves, Starkweather, and Blacker (1965) spectrally analyzed the speech of depressed persons. Spectral speech analysis has also been used to evaluate therapeutic response (Scherer, 1979, 1981). More general discussions of the relationship between speech and emotion are presented by Ostwald (1961) and Siegman (1985, 1987b).

Sleep

Elevated arousal, as described above, can disrupt normal sleep behavior, during which motor activity is remarkably low compared with waking periods. Trouble falling asleep (insomnia) is evidenced by prolonged activity normally associated with sleep onset. Activity is greatly reduced from the waking state but not yet reduced to levels associated with normal sleep. Reported decreased need for sleep is seen as reduced time during which sleep-appropriate activity levels are recorded. Early morning awakening, often associated with depressive disorders, is documented by increases in activity during early morning hours when the individual is normally asleep. Borbely (1986) indicated that ingestion of 0.5 milligrams of Triazolam 30 minutes before bedtime reduces nocturnal activity by prolonging immobility periods. Borbely further reported that narcolepsy increased daytime immobility, due to sleep, and increased nocturnal activity, due to insomnia.

Sometimes people cannot stay asleep; they repeatedly awaken from sleep. Motor (wrist and waist) activity increases at these times, thus allowing their detection. Sleepwalking is an especially energetic form of sleep activity. Its documentation requires that the person ambulate during the sleep period and not remember doing so (APA, 1987, p. 313). Activity measurements obviate the necessity of having a human observer present throughout every night of the assessment period.

Fatigue

Fatigue, sometimes called loss of energy, clinically refers to a cycle alternating between normal and reduced activity levels. The onset of fatigue is presumably correlated with reduced motor activity, as patients often report decreases in daily activities. This relationship has yet to be empirically validated.

Fatigue is of interest to general practitioners (Allan, 1944; Morrison, 1980; Sugarman, & Berg 1984) because it is the seventh most common medical symptom (U.S. Department of Health and Human Services, 1978). A prospective study by Kroenke, Wood, Mangelsdorff, Meier, and Powell (1988) reported that 24 percent of adult patients attending primary-care clinics indicated that fatigue was a major problem for them. Fatigue has been associated with disorders such as multiple sclerosis (Freal, Kraft, & Coryell, 1984; Krupp, Alvarez, LaRocca, & Scheinberg, 1988), chronic dialysis (Cardenas & Kutner, 1982), diabetes (Surridge et al., 1984), postoperative period (Christensen & Kehlet, 1984) and Epstein-Barr virus (Merlin, 1986; Sumaya, 1985). Three paper-and-pencil measures of fatigue have been developed (Cardenas & Kutner, 1982; Kinsman, Weiser, & Stamper, 1973; Montgomery, 1983). Chronic fatigue refers to consistently low activity levels. Sometimes DSM-III-R refers to fatigue as occurring "nearly every day."

Fatigue episodes occurring at least a full day (bipolar disorder mixed, p. 225), nearly every day (major depressive episode, p. 222), every few days (bipolar disorder mixed, p. 225), at least 2 weeks (major depressive episode, p. 218), and at least 2 months duration between episodes (bipolar disorder, recurrent, p. 218), within a 60-day period (seasonal pattern, p. 224), and over 2 consecutive years (seasonal pattern, p. 224) require extended ambulatory (naturalistic) behavioral measurement.

Tremor

Normal tremor (trembling), also called physiologic tremor, refers to a rapid (8 to 12 Hertz) oscillation of the limb, giving the appearance of vibration (Marshall & Walsh, 1956). The origin of this behavior remains controversial (Findley & Capildeo, 1984); however, it is clearly exacerbated by a variety of conditions, including anxiety. Neurological disorders such as Parkinson's disease, cerebellar disease, or mercury poisoning alter normal tremor in specific ways.

Dyskinesia

Dyskinesia refers to a decreased ability to perform voluntary movements, including proper execution of prescribed motor movements of the arms, hands, fingers, and feet.

Stereotypies

Stereotypies, repetitive movements, can currently be well quantified in a laboratory setting, but not in an ambulatory environment. Thus, only brief mention will subsequently be made regarding this class of motor behavior.

Psychomotor versus Ambulatory versus Speech Activity

The DSM-III-R definition of psychomotor agitation clearly involves ambulatory activity. I distinguish between psychomotor activity and ambulatory activity because of possible implications for the factorial structure of activity discussed below.

Psychomotor activity refers to coordinated actions during some form of a specialized task or test in which the subject has to accurately move in space or repeat a task as fast as possible. Examples of coordination tests are the Purdue Pegboard, the Digit Symbol Subtest of the Wechsler Adult Intelligence Scale, and the finger tapping subtest of the Halstead-Reitan Neuropsychological Test Battery. I recommend using accelerometry to measure the complete topography of finger tapping behavior, both for traditional purposes and as a measure of bradykinesia.

Ambulatory activity refers to naturalistic behaviors of locomotion and rest plus the purposeful manipulation of objects. For example, a person gets out of bed, gets dressed, goes outside to collect the morning paper, returns inside, prepares breakfast, and turns pages while reading. Although this person shows purposeful eye–hand coordinated movement during these behaviors, such actions are referred to as ambulatory activity as distinct from psychomotor activity.

DSM-III-R usually refers to psychomotor activity, even though ambulatory activity is strongly implied. It is presently assumed that persons who show psychomotor retardation also show reduced ambulatory activity and possibly slowed speech. Although, as documented above, depression slows speech, studies measuring both speech and other aspects of psychomotor retardation have yet to be conducted. Future research should examine the factorial structure of psychomotor, ambulatory activity and speech measures by obtaining multiple measures. DSM-III-R implies that a single factor will be found across normal and patient populations.

ACTIVITY-RELATED DSM-III-R DIAGNOSTIC CATEGORIES

Because this volume is concerned with adult psychopathology, only adult-relevant DSM-III-R diagnostic categories are discussed here. The order of presentation follows that in DSM-III-R for convenience.

All of the adult diagnostic entities mentioning motor disturbances as part of their diagnostic criteria are listed in Table 14.1. All other adult entities mentioning motor disturbances as part of differential diagnostic criteria are listed in Table 14.2. The reader should note the relevance of Tables 14.1 and 14.2 to several other chapters in this volume. Both tables relate to Chapter 3 on organic mental disorders, Chapter 4 on psychoactive substance use disorder (alcohol), Chapter 5 on psychoactive substance use disorder (drugs), Chapter 6 on schizophrenia, Chapter 7 on mood disorders (unipolar depression), Chapter 8 on mood disorders (bipolar), Chapter 9 on anxiety disorders, and Chapter 13 on eating disorders. Because treatment is directed toward behavioral change, activity measurements are pertinent when treating the

TABLE 14.2.   Activity as an Exclusive Criterion (Differential Diagnosis)

Organic Mental Syndromes and Disorders

1. Delirium versus major depressive episode (p. 106)
2. Withdrawal versus organic mood syndrome (p. 118)
3. Organic mental disorders (p. 119); Elderly people with a major depressive episode (p. 121)

Schizophrenia

4. Schizophrenia, disorganized type (295.1x) (p. 197)
   a. Does not meet the criteria for catatonic type.
5. Schizophrenia, paranoid type (295.3x) (p. 197)
   a. Does not meet criteria for catatonic type.
6. Schizophrenia, undifferentiated type (295.9x) (p. 198)
   a. Does not meet the criteria for catatonic type.

Psychotic Disorders Not Elsewhere Classified

7. Brief reactive psychosis (298.80) (pp. 206–207)
   a. Not due to a psychotic mood disorder (i.e., no full mood syndrome is present).
8. Undifferentiated somatoform disorder (300.70) (p. 267)
   a. Occurrence not exclusively during the course of a mood disorder, anxiety disorder, or sleep disorder.

Source: Adapted with permission from the *Diagnostic and Statistical Manual of Mental Disorders* (3rd ed., revised). Copyright 1987 American Psychiatric Association.

above-mentioned disorders, whether by psychotherapy (Chapter 15), behavior therapy (Chapter 16), or pharmacotherapy (Chapter 17).

Table 14.1 indicates that the behavioral consequences of delirium include disturbance of the sleep–wake cycle with insomnia and increased or decreased psychomotor activity while awake. Hence, these behavioral effects must be documented prior to rendering a definitive diagnosis involving delirium.

Mood disorder can have an organic etiology resulting in manic or depressive symptoms. DSM-III-R clearly indicates that these behavioral effects must first be documented and then attributed to an organic cause to diagnose organic mood syndrome.

Marked activity decreases during depressive episodes and sharp activity increases during recurrent aggressive outbursts require documentation if one is to diagnose organic personality syndrome.

Activity changes associated with delirium and depression can aid in a more precise diagnosis of either the senile or presenile onset of primary degenerative dementia of the alzheimer type.

Multi-infarct dementia sometimes results in depression, which is partly diagnosed by its behavioral effects of reduced daytime and increased nighttime activity. Depression is further revealed by increased interutterance time, as documented above.

Use of or withdrawal from many toxic substances (alcohol, amphetamines, caffeine, cocaine, hallucinogens, inhalants, sedatives, etc.) induces psychomotor disturbances that are part of the formal inclusion criteria for associated diagnoses. Hence, a comprehensive behavioral assessment of these disorders will not neglect relevant activity measurements. Kruger (1987) reported longer phonations and shorter pauses in a young healthy male 5 to 20 minutes after ingesting 200 milligrams of caffeine.

Schizophrenic, catatonic type and schizoaffective, disorders are associated with either marked reduction or augmentation (excitation) of activity. A wide variety of antipsychotic medications (neuroleptics) produce akathesia as a side effect. This term literally means "unable to sit still" and refers to the restless movement sometimes associated with taking antipsychotic medication. The magnitude and temporal course of akathesia is currently unknown, but could easily be studied given present technology. Such information could aid in managing patient medication. A promising research design is to ask that a patient remain seated after being given a dose of neuroleptic medication. Akathesia would likely be revealed through excessive ankle activity.

Mood disorders are unquestionably the most well-studied conditions from the perspective of activity abnormalities (e.g., Godfrey & Knight, 1984; Kupfer & Foster, 1973; McFarlain & Hersen, 1974; Post et al., 1977; Wehr & Goodwin, 1979; Wehr, Muscettola, & Goodwin, 1980; Weiss, Foster, Reynolds, & Kupfer, 1974; Wolff, Putnam, & Post, 1985). Typical findings are that depression is associated with decreased activity, mania is associated with increased activity, circadian rhythms are phase advanced, sleep is fragmented, and early morning awakening occurs.

Diagnosing cyclothymia presents a formidable challenge to behavioral assessment in that it requires from 1 to 2 years of data. The indicated changes take place so gradually that either of two approaches may be used: Daily self-recordings could be made with an inexpensive device, or monthly recordings could be made using more expensive equipment.

Dysthymia is diagnosed partly by fatigue, which is applicable to major depression, cocaine and amphetamine withdrawal, as well as anxiety and sleep disorders. Clinicians regularly indicate that patients report decreased activity during periods of acute fatigue. Hence, it may be possible to track fatigue by repeatedly measuring activity throughout the day. It is most desirable to use a device such as the MotionLogger or Actillume with a built-in time base for such studies so that minute-by-minute activity changes can be evaluated. Periods of acute fatigue can be indicated by the subject using the event recorder button on the MotionLogger or Actillume.

Sleep can be studied behaviorally using a time-based recording system, such as the MotionLogger or Actillume (Borbely, 1986; Webster, Kripke, Messin, Mullaney, & Wyborney, 1982; Kripke, Mullaney, Messin, & Wyborney, 1978; Mullaney, Kripke, & Messin, 1980). Figure 14.2 shows data taken from my left wrist from 10:00 P.M. (22:00) to 8:00 A.M., using a MotionLogger. The grid tics are at 30-minute intervals. The pronounced gap from 11:30 to midnight is associated with showering when the MotionLogger was not worn because it is not waterproof. (Such a distinctive record associated with not wearing the MotionLogger allows one to determine whether the subject was wearing the device as instructed.) The declining activity registered between midnight and 12:30 A.M. is associated with last-minute activities prior to retiring for sleep. The large middle portion of the figure is associated with sleep. The sudden increase in activity is associated with awakening. The brief notch between 6:30 and 7:00 A.M. is again associated with washing, when the MotionLogger was briefly removed.

Figures 14.3 and 14.4 are exploded presentations of the sleep onset and sleep offset portions of Figure 14.2. Each 1-minute epoch is now clearly separated. The primary feature of these data is that activity declines rapidly with sleep onset and increases rapidly upon awakening.

Carskadon and Dement (1982) demonstrated that the amount and quality of sleep partly determines subsequent daytime sleepiness. Levine, Roehrs, Zorick, and Roth (1988) measured sleep efficiency on the basis of minutes of active and inactive time during the entire sleep period, using an algorithm described by Levine, Moyles, Roehrs, Fortier, and Roth (1986). MotionLogger data enable one to compute sleep efficacy in the subject's natural environment (i.e., outside of the sleep laboratory).

Figures 14.2 through 14.4 indicate that it is possible to evaluate one's sleep–wake schedule and the extent to which one has difficulty initiating or maintaining sleep as required by the DSM-III-R criteria listed in Table 14.1. Activity increases associated with dream anxiety disorder, sleep terror disorder, and sleepwalking disorder are easily recorded with instruments such as the MotionLogger or Actillume.

The extent to which women evidence depressed mood and easy fatigability, as indicated by late luteal phase dysphoric disorder, can be assessed by extended motor activity measurements. Perhaps the final decision to include or omit this disorder from future revisions of DSM will be based upon such data.

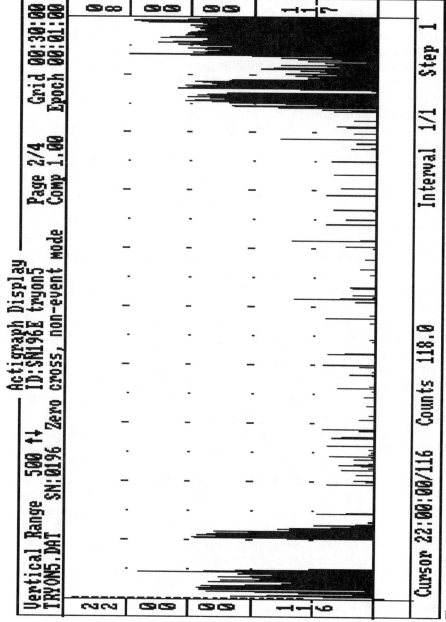

Figure 14.2. Activity during sleep illustrated by actigraph data taken from my left wrist from 10:00 P.M. (22:00) until 8:00 A.M. (08:00) using a 1-minute recording epoch.

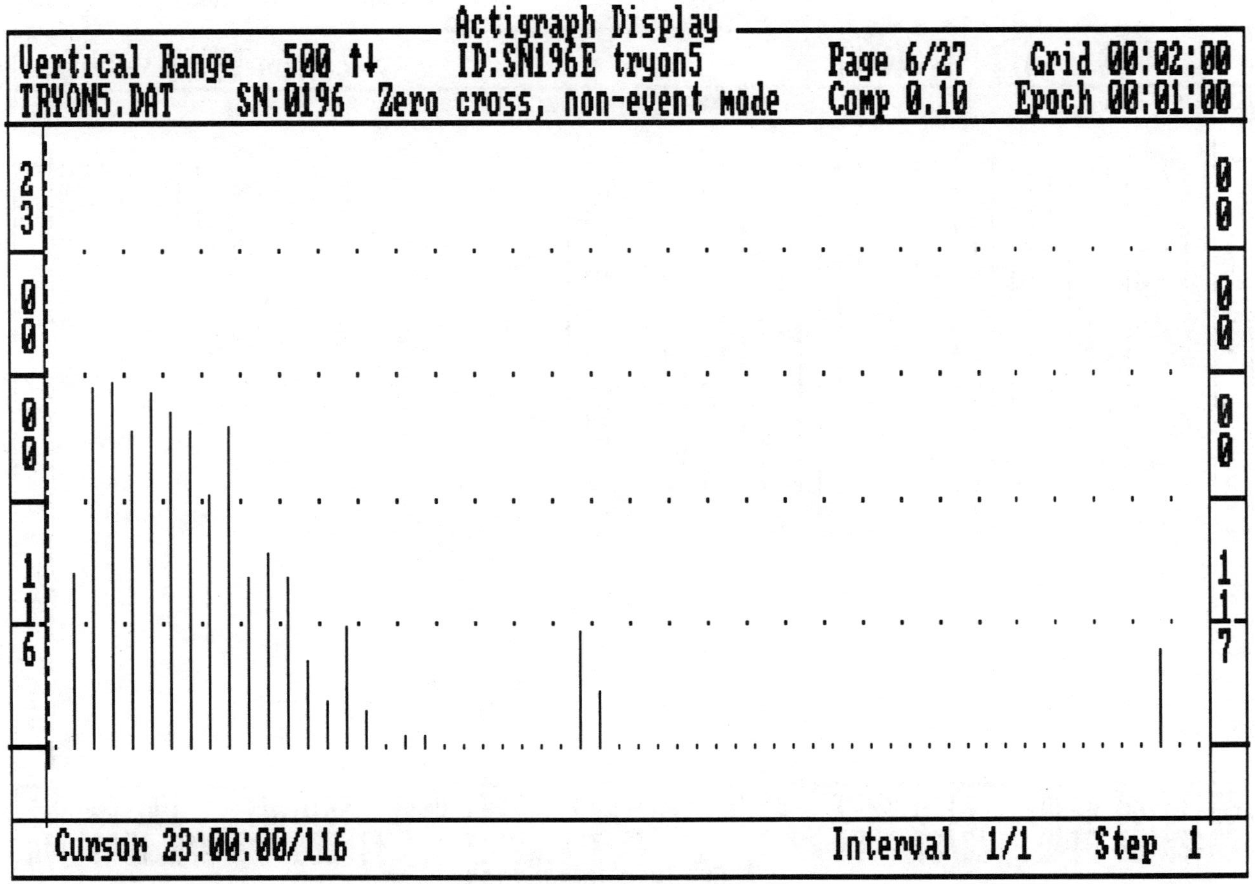

Figure 14.3. An expanded view of the sleep onset portion of Figure 14.2.

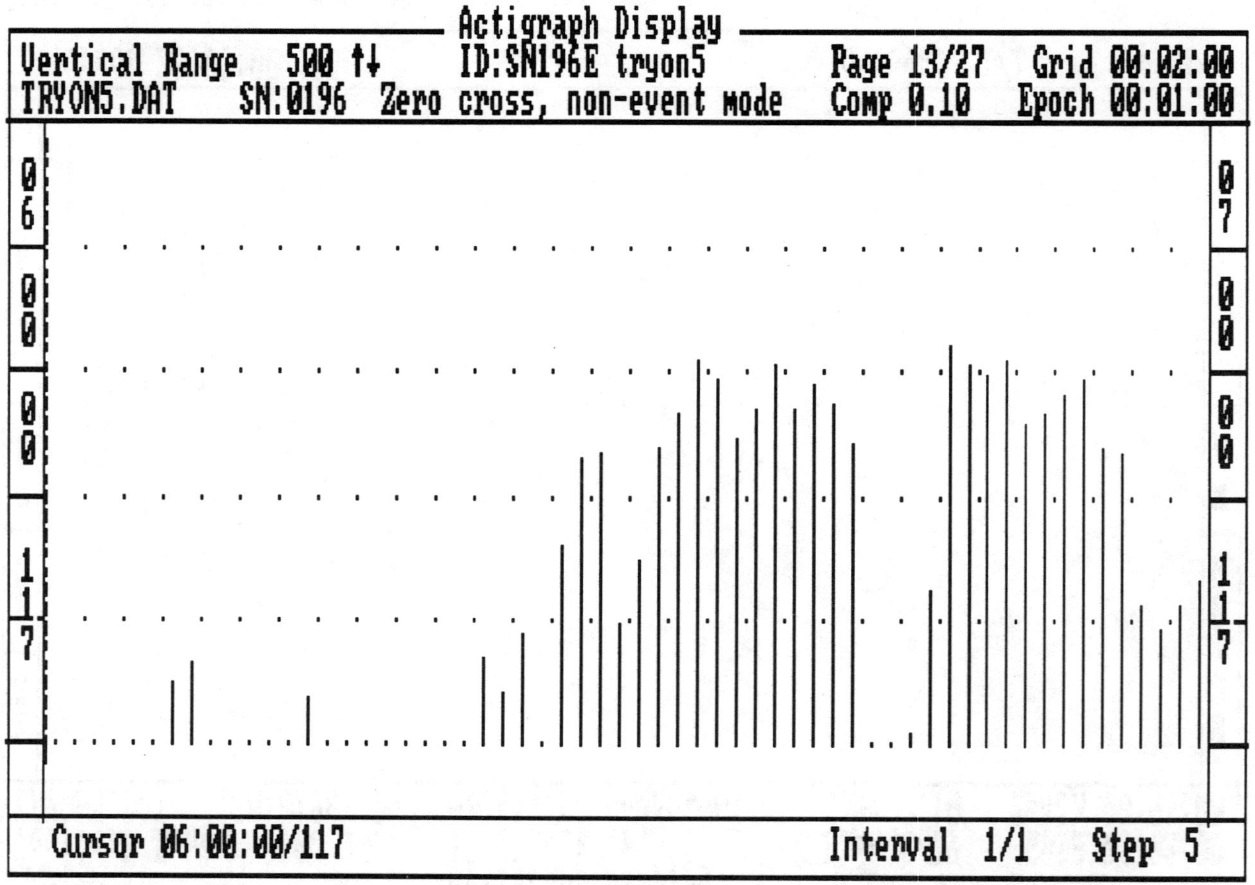

Figure 14.4. An expanded view of the sleep offset portion of Figure 14.2.

DIFFERENTIAL DIAGNOSIS

Table 14.2 lists DSM-III-R diagnoses for which differential diagnosis requires knowledge of motor activity. (Diagnoses for these disorders were described in Table 14.1.) The major point here is that, while trying to definitively establish a diagnosis for which activity is not involved, activity measurements may still be required to exclude relevant alternative diagnoses. For example, diagnosing disorganized type (295.1x), paranoid type (295.3x), and undifferentiated type (295.9x) of schizophrenia does not require activity data, but these diagnoses can be established only if the patient fails to meet criteria for catatonic type (295.2x), which does require activity data. Brief reactive psychosis does not involve activity, but this diagnosis can be established only if the patient fails to meet the criteria for psychotic mood disorder, which does require activity data. Undifferentiated somatoform disorder (300.70) does not require activity data, but this diagnosis can be established only if the patient fails to meet criteria for mood, anxiety, or sleep disorders that do require activity data.

In short, activity measurements have both indirect and direct diagnostic importance, thereby increasing the number of relevant diagnostic entities. It is time that more effort be extended to obtaining a better understanding of normal and abnormal diurnal and nocturnal activity.

SUMMARY

A major conclusion to be drawn from this review is that motor activity measurements pertain directly to the diagnosis of forty-six DSM-III-R entities (plus one proposed category) and to the differential diagnosis of eight disorders. Hence, the behavioral measurement of activity is centrally implicated in a wide variety of psychiatric disorders.

The brief discussion of fatigue pointed to a variety of nonpsychiatric disorders, such as multiple sclerosis, Epstein–Barr syndrome, chronic dialysis, diabetes mellitus, and chronic fatigue syndrome. To this list, we should add Parkinson's disease, which has three prominent motor-related symptoms: resting tremor, bradykinesia, and on–off fluctuations in which the motor system periodically shuts off (Fahn, 1982; Marsden et al., 1982; Yahr, 1975). These disorders are mentioned only briefly here to alert the behavioral medicine reader that the scope of motor activity assessment extends well beyond DSM-III-R to other medical disorders. Also included are the endocrine, collagen, cardiovascular, metabolic, vitamin and mineral disorders, and malignancies, all of which are associated with affective disorders (Klerman, 1987).

Measurement of activity has progressed considerably in recent years. A broad spectrum of devices exist, ranging from inexpensive pedometers and step counters to computerized wrist-worn actigraphs capable of collecting very detailed sleep–wake records. Given the available technology and the broad diagnostic and therapeutic assessment relevance, however, activity research seriously lags behind its clinical relevance.

REFERENCES

Allan, F. N. (1944). The differential diagnosis of weakness and fatigue. *New England Journal of Medicine, 231,* 414–418.

Alpert, M. (1981). Speech and disturbances of affect. In J. K. Darby (Ed.), *Speech evaluation in psychiatry* (pp. 359–367). New York: Grune & Stratton.

Alpert, M. (1989). Vocal acoustic correlates of flat affect in schizophrenia: Similarity to Parkinson's disease and right hemisphere disease and contrast with depression. *British Journal of Psychiatry, 155,* 51–56.

Alpert, M., Merewether, F., Homel, P., Martz, J., & Lomask, M. (1986). Voxcom: A system for analyzing natural speech in real time. *Behavior Research Methods, Instruments, & Computers, 18,* 267–272.

American Psychiatric Association. (1952). *Diagnostic and statistical manual of mental disorders.* Washington, DC: Author.

American Psychiatric Association. (1968). *Diagnostic and statistical manual of mental disorders* (2nd ed.). Washington, DC: Author.

American Psychiatric Association. (1980). *Diagnostic and statistical manual of mental disorders* (3rd ed.). Washington, DC: Author.

American Psychiatric Association. (1987). *Diagnostic and statistical manual of mental disorders* (3rd ed. rev.). Washington, DC: Author.

Andreason, N. C., Alpert, M., & Martz, M. J. (1981). Acoustic analysis: An objective measure of affective flattening. *Archives of General Psychiatry, 38,* 281–285.

Borbely, A. A. (1986). New techniques for the analysis of the human sleep–wake cycle. *Brain and Development, 8,* 482–488.

Breznitz, Z., & Sherman, T. (1987). Speech patterning of natural discourse of well and depressed mothers and their young children. *Child Development, 58,* 395–400.

Cardenas, D. D., & Kutner, N. G. (1982). The problem of fatigue in dialysis patients. *Nephron, 30,* 336–340.

Carskadon, M. A., & Dement, W. C. (1982). Nocturnal determinants of daytime sleepiness. *Sleep, 5,* S73–S81.

Christensen, T., & Kehlet, H. (1984). Postoperative fatigue and changes in nutritional status. *British Journal of Surgery, 71,* 473–476.

Colburn, T. R., Smith, B. M., Guarini, J. J., & Simons, N. N. (1976). *An ambulatory activity monitor with solid state memory.* Paper presented at the 13th annual Rocky Mountain Bioengineering Symposium and the 13th International ISA Biomedical Sciences symposium, Laramie, WY.

Cole, R. J., Kripke, D. F., Gruen, W. & Nave, J. (1990). Ambulatory monitoring of light exposure: Comparison of measurements at forehead and wrist. *Sleep Research, 19,* 364.

Epstein, S. (1979). The stability of behavior: I. On predicting most of the people much of the time. *Journal of Personality and Social Psychology, 37,* 1097–1126.

Epstein, S. (1980). The stability of behavior: II. Implications for psychological research. *American Psychologist, 35,* 790–806.

Fahn, S. (1982). Fluctuations of disability in Parkinson's disease: Pathophysiology. In C. D. Marsden & S. Fahn (Eds.), *Movement disorders* (pp. 123–145). London: Butterworth Scientific.

Findley, L. J., & Capildeo, R. (1984). *Movement disorders: Tremor.* London: Macmillan.

Findley, L. J., & Gresty, M. A. (1984). Tremor and rhythmical involuntary movements in Parkinson's disease (pp. 295–304). In L. J. Findley and R. Capildeo (Eds.), *Movement disorders: Tremor.* London: Macmillan.

Freal, J. E., Kraft, G. H., & Coryell, J. K. (1984). Symptomatic fatigue in multiple sclerosis. *Archives of Physical Medicine and Rehabilitation, 65,* 135–138.

Frost, J. D., Jr. (1978). Triaxial vector accelerometry: A method for quantifying tremor and ataxia. *IEEE Transactions on Biomedical Engineering, BME-25,* 17–27.

Futterman, C. S., & Tryon, W. W. (1986, April). *Preliminary findings of an investigation of motor activity levels in community based depressed psychiatric outpatient sample.* Paper presented at the meeting of the Eastern Psychological Association, New York.

Gaarder, K. R., & Montgomery, M. S. (1977). *Clinical biofeedback: A procedural manual* (pp. 177–191). Baltimore: Williams & Wilkins.

Godfrey, H. P. D., & Knight, R. G. (1984). The validity of actometer and speech activity measures in the assessment of depressed patients. *British Journal of Psychiatry, 145,* 159–163.

Greden, J. F., Albala, A. A., Smokler, I. A., Gardner, R., & Carroll, B. J. (1981). Speech pause time: A marker of psychomotor retardation among endogenous depressives. *Biological Psychiatry, 16,* 851–859.

Greden, J. F., & Carroll, B. J. (1980). Decrease in speech pause times with treatment of endogenous depression. *Biological Psychiatry, 15,* 575–587.

Gresty, M. A., McCarthy, R., & Findley, L. J. (1984). Assessment of resting tremor in Parkinson's disease (pp. 321–330). In L. J. Findley and R. Capildeo (eds.), *Movement disorders: Tremor.* London: Macmillan.

Hargreaves, W. A., Starkweather, J. A., & Blacker, K. H. (1965). Voice quality in depression. *Journal of Abnormal and Social Psychology, 70,* 218–220.

Hinchliffe, M. K., Lancashire, M., & Roberts, F. J. (1971). Depression: Defense mechanisms in speech. *British Journal of Psychiatry, 118,* 471–472.

Kanfer, F. H. (1960). Verbal rate, eye blinks, and content in structured psychiatric interviews. *Journal of Abnormal and Social Psychology, 61,* 341–347.

Kinsman, R. A., Weiser, P. C., & Stamper, D. A. (1973). Multidimensional analysis of subjective symptomatology during prolonged strenuous exercise. *Ergonomics, 16,* 211–226.

Klerman, G. L. (1987). Depression associated with medical and neurological diseases, drugs, and alcohol. In J. D. Maser (Ed.), *Depression and expressive behavior* (pp. 20–29). Hillsdale, NJ: Erlbaum.

Kripke, D. F., Mullaney, D. J., Messin, S., & Wyborney, V. G. (1978). Wrist actigraphic measures of sleep and rhythms. *Electroencephalography and Clinical Neurophysiology, 44,* 674–676.

Kroenke, K., Woods, D. R., Mangelsdorff, A. D., Meier, N. J., & Powell, J. B. (1988). Chronic fatigue in primary care: Prevalence, patient characteristics, and outcome. *Journal of the American Medical Association, 60,* 929–934.

Kruger, H. P. (1987). *A new measurement device for the study of verbal behavior in the open field.* Paper presented at the April meeting of the Eastern Psychological Association, Washington, DC.

Krupp, L. B., Alvarez, L. A., LaRocca, N. G., & Scheinberg, L. C. (1988). Fatigue in multiple sclerosis. *Archives of Neurology, 45,* 435–437.

Kupfer, D. J., & Foster, F. G. (1973). Sleep and activity in a psychotic depression. *Journal of Nervous and Mental Disease, 156,* 341–348.

Kupfer, D. J., Maser, J. D., Blehar, M. C., & Miller, R. (1987). Behavioral assessment in depression. In J. D. Maser (Ed.), *Depression and expressive behavior* (pp. 1–15). Hillsdale, NJ: Erlbaum.

Lang, A. E., & Fahn, S. (1989). Assessment of Parkinson's disease. In T. L. Munsat (Ed.), *Quantification of neurologic deficit* (pp. 285–309). Boston: Butterworths.

Levine, B., Moyles, T., Roehrs, T., Fortier, J., & Roth, T. (1986). Actigraphic monitoring and polygraphic recording in the determination of sleep and wake. *Sleep Research, 15,* 247.

Levine, B., Roehrs, T., Zorick, F., & Roth, T. (1988). Daytime sleepiness in young adults. *Sleep, 11,* 39–46.

Marsden, C. D., Parkes, J. D., & Quinn, N. (1982). Fluctuations of disability in Parkinson's disease—Clinical aspects. In C. D. Marsden & S. Fahn (Eds.), *Movement disorders* (pp. 96–122). London: Butterworth Scientific.

Marshall, J., & Walsh, E. G. (1956). Physiological tremor. *Journal of Neurology, Neurosurgery, and Psychiatry, 19,* 248–256.

Matthews, P. B. C., & Muir, R. B. (1980). Comparison of electromyogram spectra with force spectra during human elbow tremor. *Journal of Physiology, 302,* 427–441.

McFarlain, R. A., & Hersen, M. (1974). Continuous measurement of activity level in psychiatric patients. *Journal of Clinical Psychology, 30,* 37–39.

McPartland, R. J., Kupfer, D., & Foster, F. G. (1976). The movement-activated recording monitor: A third-generation motor-activity monitoring system. *Behavior Research Methods & Instrumentation, 8,* 357–360.

Merlin, T. L. (1986). Chronic mononucleosis: Pitfalls in the laboratory diagnosis. *Human Pathology, 17,* 2–8.

Monrad-Krohn, G. H. (1947). Dysprosody or altered "melody of language." *Brain, 70,* 405–415.

Monrad-Krohn, G. H. (1963). The third element of speech: Prosody and its disorders. In L. Halpern (Ed.), *Problems of dynamic neurology.* Jerusalem: Jerusalem Post Press.

Montgomery, G. K. (1983). Uncommon tiredness among college undergraduates. *Journal of Consulting and Clinical Psychology, 51,* 517–525.

Montoye, H. J., Washburn, R., Servais, S., Ertl, A., Webster, J. C., & Nagle, F. J. (1983). Estimation of energy expenditure by a portable acclerometer. *Medicine and Science in Sports and Exercise, 13,* 403–407.

Morrison, J. D. (1980). Fatigue as a presenting complaint in family practice. *Journal of Family Practice, 10,* 795–801.

Mullaney, D. J., Kripke, D. F., & Messin, S. (1980). Wrist-actigraphic estimation of sleep time. *Sleep, 3,* 83–92.

Olton, D. S., & Noonberg, A. R. (1980). *Biofeedback: Clinical applications in behavioral medicine* (pp. 76–79). Englewood Cliffs, NJ: Prentice-Hall.

Ostwald, P. F. (1961). The sounds of emotional disturbance. *Archives of General Psychiatry, 5,* 587–592.

Pope, B., Blass, T., Siegman, A. W., & Raher, J. (1970). Anxiety and depression in speech. *Journal of Consulting and Clinical Psychology, 35,* 128–133.

Post, R. M., Stoddard, F. J., Gillin, J. C., Buchsbaum, M. S., Runkle, D. C., Black, K. E., & Bunney, W. E., Jr. (1977). Alterations in motor activity, sleep, and biochemistry in a cycling manic–depressive patient. *Archives of General Psychiatry, 34,* 470–477.

Redmond, D. P., & Hegge, F. W. (1985). Observations on the design and specification of a wrist-worn human activity monitoring system. *Behavior Research Methods, Instruments, and Computers, 17,* 659–669.

Rehm, L. P. (1987). The measurement of behavioral aspects of depression. In A. J. Marsella, R. M. A. Hirschfeld, & M. M. Katz (Eds.), *The measurement of depression* (pp. 199–239). New York: Guilford Press.

Rutter, D. R. (1977). Speech patterning in recently admitted and chronic long-stay schizophrenic patients. *British Journal of Social and Clinical Psychology, 16,* 47–55.

Scherer, K. R. (1979). Nonlinguistic vocal indicators of emotion and psychopathology. In C. E. Izard (Ed.), *Emotions in personality and psychopathology* (pp. 493–529). New York: Plenum Press.

Scherer, K. R. (1981). Speech and emotional states. In J. K. Darby (Ed.), *Speech evaluation in psychiatry* (pp. 189–220). New York: Grune & Stratton.

Scherer, K. R. (1987). Vocal assessment of affective disorders. In J. D. Maser (Ed.), *Depression and expressive behavior* (pp. 57–82). Hillsdale, NJ: Erlbaum.

Siegman, A. W. (1985). Expressive correlates of affective states and traits. In A. W. Siegman & S. Feldstein (Eds.), *Multichannel integrations of nonverbal behavior* (pp. 37–68). Hillsdale, NJ: Erlbaum.

Siegman, A. W. (1987a). The pacing of speech in depression. In J. D. Maser (Ed.), *Depression and expressive behavior* (pp. 83–102). Hillsdale, NJ: Erlbaum.

Siegman, A. W. (1987b). The telltale voice: Nonverbal messages of verbal communication. In A. W. Siegman & S. Feldstein (Eds.), *Nonverbal behavior and communication* (pp. 351–434). Hillsdale, NJ: Erlbaum.

Sugarman, J. R., & Berg, A. O. (1984). Evaluation of fatigue in a family practice. *Journal of Family Practice, 19,* 643–647.

Sumaya, C. V. (1985). Serological testing for Epstein-Barr virus: Developments in interpretation. *Journal of Infectious Disease, 151,* 984–987.

Surridge, D. H. C., Williams-Erdahl, D. L. W., Lawson, J. S., Donald, M. W., Monga, T. N., Bird, C. E., & Letemendia, F. J. J. (1984). Psychiatric aspects of diabetes melitus. *British Journal of Psychiatry, 145,* 269–276.

Szabadi, E., Bradshaw, C. M., & Besson, J. A. O. (1976). Elongation of pause-time in speech: A simple, objective measure of motor retardation in depression. *British Journal of Psychiatry, 129,* 592–597.

Teasdale, J. D., Fogarty, S. J., & Williams, J. M. G. (1980). Speech rate as a measure of short-term variation in depression. *British Journal of Social and Clinical Psychology, 19,* 271–278.

Tryon, W. W. (1985). Measurement of human activity. In W. W. Tryon (Ed.), *Behavioral assessment in behavioral medicine* (pp. 200–256). New York: Springer.

Tryon, W. W. (1986). Motor activity measurements and DSM-III. *Progress in Behavior Modification, 20,* 35–66.

U.S. Department of Health and Human Services. (1978). *The National Ambulatory Medical Care Survey: 1975 Summary* (Report No. PHS 78-1784). Washington, DC: Author.

Webster, J. B., Kripke, D. F., Messin, S., Mullaney, D. J., & Wyborney, G. (1982). An activity-based sleep monitor system for ambulatory use. *Sleep, 5,* 389–399.

Wehr, T. A., & Goodwin, F. K. (1979). Rapid cycling in manic–depressives induced by tricyclic antidepressants. *Archives of General Psychiatry, 36,* 555–559.

Wehr, T. A., Muscettola, G., & Goodwin, F. K. (1980). Urinary 3-Methoxy-4-Hydroxyphenylglycol circadian rhythm: Early timing (phase-advance) in manic–depressives compared with normal subjects. *Archives of General Psychiatry, 37,* 257–263.

Weintraub, W., & Aronson, H. (1967). The application of verbal behavior analysis to the study of psychological defense mechanisms: IV. Speech pattern associated with depressive behavior. *Journal of Nervous and Mental Disease, 144,* 22–28.

Weiss, B. L., Foster, G., Reynolds, C. F., III, & Kupfer, D. J. (1974). Psychomotor activity in mania. *Archives of General Psychiatry, 31,* 379–383.

Williams, C. E., & Stevens, K. N. (1972). Emotions and speech: Some acoustical correlates. *Journal of the Acoustical Society of America, 52,* 1238–1250.

Williams, C. E., & Stevens, K. N. (1981). Vocal correlates of emotional states. In J. K. Darby (Ed.), *Speech evaluation in psychiatry,* (pp. 221–240). New York: Grune & Stratton.

Wolff, E. A., III, Putnam, F. W., & Post, R. M. (1985). Motor activity and affective illness: The relationship of amplitude and temporal distribution to changes in affective state. *Archives of General Psychiatry, 42,* 288–294.

Yahr, M. D. (1975). Paralysis agitans (Parkinson's disease). In P. B. Beeson & W. McDermott (Eds.), *Textbook of medicine* (14th ed., p. 636). Philadelphia: W. B. Saunders.

Young, R. R., & Hagbarth, K. E. (1980). Physiological tremor enhanced by maneuvers affecting the segmental stretch reflex. *Journal of Neurology, Neurosurgery, and Psychiatry, 43,* 248–256.

CHAPTER 15

DSM-III-R and Psychotherapy

KENNETH URIAL GUTSCH

The American Psychiatric Association's (APA's) *Diagnostic and Statistical Manual of Mental Disorders* is now in its revised third edition (DSM-III-R; 1987). In some respects, it is an extension of the work introduced in DSM-I (1952), DSM-II (1968), and DSM-III (1980). The original manual may well have served as one of the first steps in the development of a vehicle language (i.e., a common professional language) for American researchers and clinicians who work in psychology-related areas. Because of its practical nature, however, the manual more recently appears to have taken on a universal appeal and now serves psychologists and psychiatrists throughout the world.

Naturally, the American Psychiatric Association, as the publishing organization, deserves much of the credit for the popularity the manual has received. At best, the manual provides a basic classification system by which symptoms of abnormal behavior and emotional disorders can be recognized, defined, and classified; at worst, it provides only limited direction in terms of treatment planning. Thus, although the classification system for abnormal behavior and emotional disorders has become rather standardized, the question of treatment planning is still somewhat of an enigma. The challenges of treatment planning seem further confounded by the idiosyncratic treatment philosophies introduced within the many and varied training settings that exist today. For example, the professional treatment specialists who use the DSM-III-R today include, but are not limited to, psychiatrists, psychologists, psychoanalysts, psychiatric social workers, psychiatric nurses, and community mental health workers. It seems obvious, because of the diversification of training among these professionals, that in practice they are certain to pursue a variety of treatment approaches. Psychiatrists, for example, are prone to use a neuropsychopharmacological approach to treatment, assuming a combination of biochemical, genetic, and environmental causes of emotional disorders. As a result of their medical training and their specific treatment models (e.g., biogenic amine, endocrine, electrolyte, and genetic), they frequently prescribe drugs for their patients.

Psychologists, on the other hand, use a psychotherapeutic approach to treatment based on a psychological rather than a somatic means. Their assumption is that verbal communication applied systematically according to specific psychological principles will result in the acquisition of new

441

skills and/or the acquisition of new understandings (Beck & Shaw, 1977; Mahoney, 1977; Meichenbaum, 1977). Naturally, the literature is replete with research studies that support both of these approaches.

Perhaps the one common denominator among the professionals who practice within these treatment areas is that, when their preferred method of treatment involves a psychological rather than a somatic means, they typically refer to themselves as psychotherapists. Regardless of how they were professionally trained (i.e., as psychoanalysts, psychologists, or psychiatrists), when they use verbal communication rather than organic treatment with their patients, they are, by definition, practicing psychotherapy.

It should be noted, however, that even those who practice as psychotherapists exercise broad differences in their verbal approaches to treatment. Cognitive therapists, for example, believe that emotional disorders are the basic consequence of mood disturbances and that primary disturbances in thinking can cause the development of a disturbed mood state. As a result, their treatment plans are designed to deal with cognitive distortions (i.e., incorrect inferences, erroneous thinking, and/or the inability to distinguish between imagination and reality). Behavior therapists, on the other hand, believe that pathologic behavior is learned and that it develops according to the same laws as those that govern "normal" behavior. Thus, in treatment planning, they rely heavily on modeling, acquisition skills training, and relaxation training.

Perhaps this is simply an eisegesis, but it seems that, regardless of the theory pursued by the therapist, the patient, by virtue of his or her disorder, has a readiness to perceive and/or respond in a given way. This response phenomenon is typically referred to as a "set" (Allport, 1955). Sets for patients with mental disorders are perhaps best identified through the use of DSM-III-R descriptors. For example, when a person experiences depression, the disorder can be identified through an expressed set of cognitive character traits (e.g., despair, futility, rejection, and hopelessness) or an expressed set of behavioral character traits (e.g., nervousness, fatigue, withdrawal, and/or attempts at suicide). Thus, by first understanding the set method by which the patient functions, the psychotherapist can then classify the disorder through the use of DSM-III-R, verify the classification through testing, and then search through the professional literature for studies that have a direct bearing on the disorder (i.e., research studies that support the strength of certain approaches over others).

Because psychotherapists do not presume that treatment by psychological means is always the preferred treatment, they have remained selective in the disorders that they treat. Presently, some of the disorders that, by evidence of research, seem to lend themselves well to treatment through a psychotherapeutic approach include:

1. Anxiety—agoraphobia, social phobia, and simple phobia
2. Depression
3. Personality disorders—paranoid, schizoid, schizotypal, histrionic, narcissistic, antisocial, borderline, avoidant, dependent, obsessive–compulsive, and passive–aggressive

4. Somatoform disorders—hypochondriasis and somatoform pain disorder
5. Eating disorders—anorexia and bulimia

Typically, with each of these disorders, the psychotherapist will probably find that the treatment becomes more effective if he or she first uses DSM-III-R for diagnostic purposes, verifies the diagnosis through testing, and reverts to the professional literature for well-researched treatment studies. By so doing, the psychotherapist can approach treatment planning as described below.

ANXIETY (DSM-III-R, 300.02)

Description

In a disorder such as anxiety, for example, the therapist will find that his or her patient experiences such characteristics as feelings of impending doom, headaches, excessive sweating, rapid heartbeat, tremors, faintness, chest pains, abdominal pains, impaired vision, dizziness, palpitation, vertigo, paresthesia, dyspnea, anticipatory fear, and apprehensiveness.

Diagnosis

Assuming that the patient has already been medically checked for such look-alike syndromes as hyperthyroidism, hyperventilation, chronic kidney disease, heart attack, hypoglycemia, postconcussion syndrome, tuberculosis, or pheochromocytoma, the psychotherapist might hypothesize that the disorder is anxiety. Anxiety is sometimes defined as an irrational fear or persistent uneasiness (tension) that exists without appropriate cause (Kimble, Garmezy, & Zigler, 1984).

Psychotherapeutic Treatment

Because research in the area of psychotherapy has brought about so many treatment changes, it seems essential to go to the professional literature to determine what, if any, treatment approaches have emerged that, by standards of excellence, seem to have a priority over others. In the case of anxiety disorder, the psychotherapist would probably consider Wolpe's (1954, 1969, 1982) *systematic desensitization,* a technique of considerable importance. The technique is built on the principle of stimulus generalization (i.e., the belief that where several stimuli evoke different amounts of anxiety, the inhibiting effect of relaxation on the *least* of the evoking stimuli reduces the level of anxiety on greater anxiety-evoking stimuli). Wolpe's (1982) contention was that counterposing relaxation with anxiety-inducing stimuli can reduce the anxiety; however, it must be recognized that the technique itself is quite sensitive to error, because it necessitates introducing anxiety-evoking items that are weak enough to be easily inhibited by relaxation. Thus, when items are very general in nature and not sufficiently well defined for hierarchical ranking, further questioning of the patient is essential. For example, although a fear of being in public places may, at first glance, appear to be agoraphobic in nature, further questioning may reveal that the person actually experiences an avoidant personality disorder (i.e., a fear of becoming involved with people who will criticize, embarrass, or reject him or her). To miscalculate the cognitive aspects of the disorder may well lead to a false-positive (i.e., a situation in which the psychotherapist feels that the treatment approach is appropriate when, in fact, it is incomplete and inappropriate).

Thus, three preparatory steps seem important in the practice of psychotherapy:

1. Diagnosing the disorder according to the DSM-III-R to determine how broad the base of the disorder is (i.e., how many disorders are actually involved, and which of the disorders seems most dominant)
2. Verifying the DSM-III-R diagnosis through objective testing
3. Going through professional research materials that pertain directly to the disorder(s) to determine how such current information might be used in the best interests of treatment planning.

The challenge of the psychotherapist is to tease out of the patient that information that is necessary for effective treatment. There are, of course, a number of ways to do this. For example, in the *Self-Directed Systematic Desensitization* approach used by Wenrich, Dawley, and General (1976), the patient takes responsibility for much of his or her own treatment. The psychotherapist monitors the treatment and reaffirms for the patient that he or she is on target. In the *Anxiety Management Training* (AMT) approach, however, Suinn (1983) recommended modifying anxiety-induced responses by using relaxation as a coping skill to control anxiety. Patients are trained to identify their anxiety symptoms and to control them through the use of relaxation skills. Interestingly enough, some of these same techniques can be used with agoraphobia (DSM-III-R, 300.21), social phobia (300.23), and simple phobia (300.29).

It should be noted, however, that although some of the trait characteristics are unique to specific DSM-III-R disorders, others overlap one or more of the many disorders and make diagnoses difficult. For example, agoraphobic patients quite typically have a marked fear of being alone, are dominated by avoidance behavior, have recurrent panic attacks, and have a marked fear of public places. Patients experiencing avoidant personality disorder typically have an irrational fear of social situations, are hypersensitive to criticism, have a constant fear of social embarrassment, and have a strong tendency toward withdrawal. Because the differences are not always clear, it is important to use DSM-III-R in classifying the disorder and to use such instruments as the Anxiety Disorders Interview Schedule Revised (Di Nardo et al., 1985) or the Mobility Inventory for Agoraphobia (Chambless, Caputo, Jasin, Gracely, & Williams, 1985) to reaffirm the diagnosis. Without reaffirmation, treatment planning could be hindered by false-positives (i.e., believing that the diagnosis is correct when, in fact, it is incorrect). As Beach, Abramson, and Levine (1981) so aptly pointed out in their suggestions regarding treatment planning for depressives, when cognitive deficits predominate, cognitive treatment is the treatment of choice, whereas when social skills deficits and cognitive deficits appear simultaneously, social skills training is the treatment of choice. The same concept may apply with other disorders. Agoraphobic patients, for example, seem to be dominated by cognitive deficits, whereas patients with avoidant personality disorder seem to have both social skills deficits and cognitive deficits that appear simultaneously. If treatment planning is to be effective, the psychotherapist must recognize such differences.

DEPRESSION (DSM-III-R, 300.40)

Description

Depression is a feeling of despair, loneliness, helplessness, and hopelessness. The source of depression is sometimes difficult to locate because the emotional feelings of the depressed person seem out of proportion to the stimuli involved. Quite typically, the depressed person lacks any real interest in life, is unable to concentrate, experiences feelings of despair and futility, withdraws from relationships, has feelings of remorse, has a poor self-concept, lacks energy, experiences excessive fatigue, and frequently shows signs of a weight disorder, appetite disorder, and/or sleep disorder.

Diagnosis

A DSM-III-R diagnosis of depression can usually be reaffirmed by the use of an instrument such as the Beck Depression Inventory (Beck, 1978). It must be remembered, however, that the etiology of depression remains highly controversial. Some medically oriented psychotherapists believe that depressives have a genetic predisposition to depression and that it is inherited, some believe that depressives experience a disturbance in the monoaminergic function of the brain and that the abnormal hormonal responses that result cause depression, and others believe that depression results when there is a disturbance in the relationship between the biogenic amine activity involved in neural transmission and the functioning of the central nervous system (i.e., that depression results when the availability of one of the catecholamines— epinephrine, norepinephrine, or dopamine—is altered at functionally important sites in the brain). Other psychotherapists (those who are not trained in the use of a somatic means to treatment) typically believe that depression results from events such as chronic illness, death in the family, loss of social status, or financial reversals. The consequences of such feelings are that the depressed person becomes afraid to reach out for new experiences and, as a result, enters into a paradoxical existence. The very action the depressed person takes for protection (withdrawal) is the very thing that nurtures depression (feelings of hopelessness).

Psychotherapeutic Treatment

One of the most widely researched approaches to the treatment of depression is Beck's approach (Beck, 1961, 1978; Shaw & Beck, 1977). Beck's (1976) contention was that depressives have a tendency to perceive things in a negative way and that such distortions in perception are the results of incorrect inferences, incorrect information, erroneous thinking, self-defeating notions, and/or the inability to distinguish between imagination and reality. His treatment plan includes, but is not necessarily limited to, such steps as searching for and defining dysfunctional beliefs, examining the origins of those beliefs, introducing task assignments, and discovering reality.

To implement this approach, Shaw and Beck (1977, p. 315) recommended a technique in which the assessment of a task is written down in three columns. The first column is used to record the event as it actually occurred along with any negative affect experienced from the event. The second column is used to record the cognitions experienced by the patient during the event. The third column is used to deal with the cognitions posited in the second column. This approach helps the therapist to define the basic processes (sets) of thinking and reasoning used by the patient. Once identified, these sets can be dismantled through the use of graduated task assignments.

Perhaps the most unique approach to the treatment of depression was introduced by Lewinsohn, Muñoz, Youngren, and Zeiss (1986). They contended that, although it is normal and natural to feel lonely or sad at times, especially when there is a loss in the family, the person who feels depressed for long periods of time needs to look for help. They further contended that certain types of depression, but not all types, can be reduced by subscribing to their treatment plan. Their treatment protocol is based on a psychoeducational approach in which the depressed person is helped to define his or her problem and what has to be changed, the process by which change can be implemented, the alternative courses of action by which change can be pursued, and the effectiveness of the change once implemented.

To prepare for treatment, according to Lewinsohn et al.'s (1986) plan, the patient reads the booklet, *Coping with Depression* (Beck & Greenberg, 1974). The patient is then introduced to such steps as assessing for depression, analyzing behavior, rating mood changes, developing schedules, and monitoring mood changes. The plan incorporates the use of an activity events schedule, a daily mood schedule, and a relaxation log. The authors provided vivid guidelines for collecting information and explaining how the collected data should be used.

A third approach that seems worthy of consideration when working out treatment plans for depressives is that of Beach et al. (1981). The authors presented an interesting rule of thumb, stating that when cognitive deficits predominate, cognitive treatment is the treatment of choice, and when social skills deficits and cognitive deficits appear simultaneously, social skills training is the treatment of choice. Their approach is based on Seligman's (1975) observation that similarities exist between learned helplessness and symptoms of human depression. Abramson, Seligman, and Teasdale (1978) supported this idea, stating that depressives quite typically lack self-esteem and have motivational, cognitive, and affective deficits.

To reverse the "learned helplessness" syndrome, Beach et al. (1981) contended that the therapist must help the patient to reverse his or her process of thinking from "no control" to "control," convert unrealistic goals to realistic goals, deal with unattainable goals, and overcome the belief that others are inherently more competent.

PERSONALITY DISORDERS

Cluster I
    Paranoid Personality Disorder   DSM-III-R, 301.00
    Schizoid Personality Disorder   DSM-III-R, 301.20
    Schizotypal Personality Disorder   DSM-III-R, 301.22

Cluster II
    Histrionic Personality Disorder   DSM-III-R, 301.50
    Narcissistic Personality Disorder   DSM-III-R, 301.81
    Antisocial Personality Disorder   DSM-III-R, 301.70
    Borderline Personality Disorder   DSM-III-R, 301.83

Cluster III
    Avoidant Personality Disorder   DSM-III-R, 301.82
    Dependent Personality Disorder   DSM-III-R, 301.60
    Obsessive–Compulsive Personality Disorder   DSM-III-R, 301.40
    Passive–Aggressive Personality Disorder   DSM-III-R, 301.84

Personality disorders are behaviors that are characteristic of the person's long-term functioning; they are behaviors that have an early onset in the person's life and continue into adulthood. Quite typically, they reflect serious social skills deficits, impairments in occupational functioning, and subjective distress.

Cluster I
Paranoid Personality Disorder (DSM-III-R, 301.00)

Description

Paranoid-type patients frequently exhibit mistrust, a hypersensitivity to criticism, and restricted affectivity (i.e., a "go-it-alone" attitude toward life). Quite typically, the patient is resentful, embittered, insecure, depersonalized, rigid, suspicious, irritable, critical, sullen, sarcastic, sensitive, conservative, and guarded.

Diagnosis

Confirmation of a tentative DSM-III-R diagnosis can be implemented by using the Paranoia (Pa) Scale on the Minnesota Multiphasic Personality Inventory (MMPI), the Millon Clinical Multiaxial Inventory II (MCMI II; Millon, 1987), or the structured Interview for the DSM-III Personality Disorders (SIDP: Stangl, Pfohl, Zimmerman, Bowers, & Corenthal, 1985).

Psychotherapeutic Treatment

Because gains with patients experiencing paranoid personality disorder come slowly, the therapist will be wiser to sit back and listen to the patient's complaints. When the patient provokes hostility in the therapist, the therapist should acknowledge that hostility, recognizing that such an act of honesty can sometimes be very reassuring to the patient.

Obviously, such patients lack basic trust. This lack creates a fear of intimacy and a low tolerance for ambiguous situations. Arguing is seen as a weakness, and any attempt by the therapist to use techniques that provoke arguments will abort the relationship.

One treatment protocol that seems extremely sensitive to the idiosyncratic tendencies of the patient is that worked out by Edelstein and Eisler (1976) for patients diagnosed as paranoid-type schizophrenics. They use a two-step design in which they monitor for skills deficits, and introduce skills acquisition training to overcome those deficits. It should be noted that, within this treatment protocol, exercises are modeled for the patients and the patients are then instructed to practice what they have learned.

Schizoid Personality Disorder (DSM-III-R, 301.20)

Description

Patients experiencing a schizoid personality disorder frequently exhibit defects in their capacity to form and maintain social relationships. They lack warmth in their relationships with others and are indifferent to praise or criticism by others. They also respond in rigid and depersonalized ways.

Their intricate system of thinking and working seems structured to avoid rejection. In relationships with others, they are awkward and stiff. At best, they seem to have minimal social skills; at worst, they are "aloof" and without friends. Typically, they are shy, unsociable, self-conscious, stubborn, suspicious, quiet, critical, compulsive, rigid, without good manners, without strong emotions, indifferent to praise, and without a sense of humor.

Diagnosis

The schizoid-type person can be identified through the use of DSM-III-R trait characteristics. Identity can be reaffirmed through the use of the MCMI II or the SIDP.

Psychotherapeutic Treatment

Because of the deficits in their capacity to form and maintain relationships, schizoid-type patients are seldom motivated to seek therapy. When they do seek therapy, the treatment protocol by Edelstein and Eisler (1976) should be helpful (see section on paranoia).

Some interesting treatment ideas by Eisler, Blanchard, Fitts, and Williams (1978) include the following:

- Videotaping the social skills of patients prior to therapy to establish a data base for training
- Introducing specific types of problems for the patients to solve
- Introducing a prompt (a support, such as a confederate who forms a relationship with the patients)

- Using monitoring and feedback sessions to help the patients to understand their progress
- Helping patients to acquire social skills through rehearsal, coaching, and modeling.

Schizotypal Personality Disorder (DSM-III-R, 301.22)

Description

Patients experiencing schizotypal personality disorder usually exhibit eccentricities of behavior, perception, thinking, and speech. Their speech patterns are usually digressive, elaborate, and vague. Their use of words is usually idiosyncratic, and they have a tendency to depersonalize their relationships. Typically, they are eccentric in behavior, have odd speech patterns, and exhibit responses that are inappropriate; they also exhibit inappropriate affect, feelings of inferiority, a strong sense of suspiciousness, a hypersensitivity to criticism, a tendency toward magical thinking, a tendency toward social isolation, a sense of loneliness, excessive social anxiety, and paranoid ideation.

Diagnosis

DSM-III-R identification of the schizotypal person can be reaffirmed through the use of the MCMI II or the SIDP.

Psychotherapeutic Treatment

Because the schizotypal patient lacks trust, a therapeutic alliance is extremely difficult. The difference between the schizoid-type patient and the schizotypal-type patient is that the former is preoccupied with unwholesome ruminations, is without tact, is indifferent to praise, and lacks any evidence of personal warmth; the latter exhibits deficits in perception, speech, thoughts, and behavior. Treatment strategies by Edelstein and Eisler (1976) and by Eisler et al. (1978) should be helpful.

Cluster II
Histrionic Personality Disorder (DSM-III-R, 301.50)

Description

Histrionic patients are usually overly dramatic, highly reactive, and intensely expressive. They are excitable, unstable, impulsive, exhibitionistic, deceitful, shallow, emotionally explosive, seductive, fickle, irrational, inconsiderate, demanding, and overly concerned with physical attractiveness. Typically, they seek reassurance, approval, or praise from others, and seem uncomfortable when not the center of attention.

Diagnosis

The disorder appears almost exclusively in women (Halleck, 1967), usually before the age of 20, and seems primarily to reflect a deficiency in the patient's relationship with his or her mother or father. Although diagnosis of the disorder is frequently made on the basis of DSM-III-R descriptors, the MCMI II and SIDP can be used to reaffirm the diagnosis.

Assessment of progress can be made by noting specific changes within the patient, such as a reduction of seductive symptoms, an increase in assertive behavior, an increase in self-esteem, an increase in the ability to deal successfully with negative feelings, and an increase in the ability to distinguish between imagination and reality (Andrews, 1974).

Psychotherapeutic Treatment

Powers (1972) contended that the histrionic patient distorts and manipulates objective reality and that the psychotherapist must establish guidelines (e.g., entering into a contract with the patient regarding the goals of therapy, the number of sessions per week, the cost per session, the length of each session, the need for integrity, the need for reality, the need for not attempting suicide, and the high premium placed on confidentiality). Woolson and Swanson (1972), on the other hand, maintained that, with the help of the patient, the therapist must frame the relationship (i.e., shape the changes and help the patient implement them), help the patient define goals, pinpoint the onset of the problem, establish target objectives, understand the consequences of change, and monitor progress.

Narcissistic Personality Disorder (DSM-III-R, 301.81)

Description

The person exhibiting a narcissistic personality disorder has a grandiose sense of self-importance, a preoccupation with fantasies of success, an exhibitionistic need for constant attention, and a need for constant admiration. Failure to achieve almost always leads to depression. Typically, the patient needs attention, has impaired interpersonal relations, has fantasies of unlimited success, has a tendency toward hypochondriasis, experiences feelings of emptiness, expects special treatment, has a self-centered need for admiration, lacks empathy, has feelings of depression, lacks positive self-regard, and becomes enraged when criticized.

Diagnosis

Assessment through diagnosis is rather basic in that "the arrogance of excellence" attitude of the narcissistic person creates an easy-to-recognize climate of self-importance. To reaffirm the observation, however, the therapist can use the MCMI II or the SIDP.

Psychotherapeutic Treatment

Millon (1981) suggested that the therapist use cognitive reorientation. His contention was that methods of intervention, such as environmental management, psychopharmacological treatment, and behavior modification, appear to have limited value (p. 180). Gutsch (1988) suggested helping the patient to establish a climate of confidence, rehearsing the patient for change, and helping the patient to learn how to generalize from one "change" situation to another.

Antisocial Personality Disorder (DSM-III-R, 301.70)

Description

The patient experiencing antisocial personality disorder frequently acts out against society in amoral, unreliable, and irresponsible ways. As a youngster, the person might exhibit such behaviors as lying, stealing, fighting, truancy, and resisting authority. As an adolescent, behaviors may include excessive drinking, drug abuse, and/or aggressive sexual behavior. As an adult, the person may attempt to impress and/or exploit others. Typically, the antisocial person resists authority, experiences occupational and social impairments, lacks conformity, lacks reliability, shows little compassion, exhibits unstable work patterns, and has an early pattern of alcohol and drug abuse.

Diagnosis

The antisocial personality disorder can usually be detected through the use of DSM-III-R descriptors. The onset of the disorder frequently begins before the age of 15 and continues, without remission, into adult life (Cloninger, 1978). To reaffirm the diagnosis, the therapist can use Lanyon's (1973) Psychological Survey Instrument, the MMPI, the MCMI II, or the SIDP.

Psychotherapeutic Treatment

Cloninger (1978) suggested that the therapist analyze the patient's expressed feelings and determine how he or she is using these feelings to manipulate the therapeutic sessions. Cloninger also recommended firm guidelines (not harsh treatment) in correcting the dynamics of the patient's disorder and cautioned therapists about using drugs in treating the patient because antisocial patients tend to abuse drugs.

Spence and Marzillier (1981) used an approach with adolescent male offenders that might, with some modifications, be appropriate for use with adults. They suggested monitoring behaviors to establish a baseline understanding of the patient's social skills, verifying the disorder through the use of appropriate assessment techniques, identifying deficit skill areas, implementing a skills training orientation through such techniques as modeling, and monitoring the patient–therapist activities through the use of videotape so that areas in which mistakes are being made can be restructured.

Borderline Personality Disorder (DSM-III-R, 301.83)

Description

A patient exhibiting a borderline personality disorder has difficulty in interpersonal behavior and mood stability. Such patients are usually impulsive and unpredictable and do, on occasion, experience transient psychotic episodes (i.e., episodes usually brought on by stress, use of drugs, or use of alcohol).

Typically, they are unpredictable in behavior, unstable in relationships, careless in personal grooming, and often suicidal. They have sharp mood shifts, intense affect (hostility), poor self-images, a tendency toward excessive spending, defects in affectional relationships, brief psychotic episodes, and tendencies toward excessive use of drugs.

Diagnosis

A diagnosis based on DSM-III-R descriptors can be confirmed by using Cattell's (1972) 16 PF, Millon's (1987) MCMI II, or Stangel et al's (1985) SIDP. On the 16 PF, borderline patients usually score low on the Q3 factor, which indicates that they are impetuous, have little regard for social demands, and are not overly considerate of others. They also score low on factors C and H, indicating that they have little tolerance for unsatisfactory conditions, have unpredictable mood shifts, and are extremely shy; on the other hand, they have high scores on factors Q4 and O, which indicate that they are emotionally unstable in their interpersonal relationships and frequently worry about their difficulties (Meyer, 1983).

Psychotherapeutic Treatment

Chessick (1979) suggested that patients who exhibit borderline characteristics be treated by the process of modified psychoanalysis. The therapist needs to be reliable and consistent in treating the patient, give the patient complete attention, be sincere in the relationship, remain calm in his or her approach, work in an area free from distraction, maintain a climate free of moral judgments, and help the patient distinguish between imagination and reality. Adler (1980) suggested creating a climate of support for the patient and developing an awareness of the potential for countertransference.

Dorr, Gard, Barley, and Webb (1983) described the patient's major defense mechanism as "splitting" (i.e., a condition in which contradictory emotional states remain in consciousness but do not influence each other). The "splitting" effect seems to alienate the patient from significant others, perhaps because it is brought on by depression (e.g., feelings of abandonment) and complemented by rage (e.g., anger and hostility toward others for having abandoned the patient). The result is an impulsive driven behavior (i.e., indiscriminate acts of sex, drug abuse, reckless driving, or self-inflicted harm). They suggested that the therapist be direct, use simple reflection when appropriate, maintain a sensitivity to the patient's metaphoric referential link (i.e., what the patient is saying in terms of what the patient is thinking), maintain structure in therapy, respond to the patient's verbal rage with empathy, and challenge transference when it occurs.

Bauer and Sherry (1986), on the other hand, suggested that the therapist define the borderline area in which the patient is functioning, consider the importance of supportive therapy and cognitive reorientation to effective treatment, help the patient develop a sense of security, consider institutionalization as a method of choice should the patient become highly aggressive, and consider medical intervention as the treatment of choice should the patient need prescription drugs to become stable.

Other ideas that seem to have merit in the treatment of borderline patients are Mendelsohn's (1981) use of "active attention" and "focusing" and Glantz's (1981) use of special ways of introducing relaxation.

Cluster III
Avoidant Personality Disorder (DSM-III-R, 301.82)

Description

The patient experiencing an avoidant personality disorder fears rejection and seldom enters into a relationship unless there is some assurance of acceptance. Typically, the patient has few friends, experiences social withdrawal, is hypersensitive to criticism, is in constant fear of personal embarrassment (rejection), and has a strong need for affection, acceptance, and support.

Diagnosis

The therapist can frequently determine the disorder by using DSM-III-R descriptors. Instruments that can be used to reaffirm such assessments are the MCMI II and the SIDP.

Psychotherapeutic Treatment

Although treatment considerations are, at best, both sparse and vague, the following are some considerations for treatment that seem to have merit (Gutsch, 1988, pp. 143–144):

- Help the patient to relax
- Define areas of threat
- Help the patient deal with threat through the use of imagery and relaxation techniques
- Use supportive therapy when appropriate
- Prepare the patient for change
- Identify target objectives through which change strategies can be implemented
- Help the patient establish a backup system (alternative courses of action that can be taken) should the change strategies not work.

Dependent Personality Disorder (DSM-III-R, 301.60)

Description

People experiencing dependent personality disorder lack the ability to make decisions. As a result, both their ability to function occupationally and/or socially become impaired. Typically, they have a desire to cling to others and allow others to make decisions for them; they feel incompetent; they are submissive, compliant, conciliatory, fragile (easily hurt by criticism), afraid of being abandoned, noncompetitive, and timid; and they frequently become devastated by the loss of a close relationship.

Diagnosis

Confirmation of a diagnosis based on DSM-III-R descriptors can be done through the use of the MCMI II or the SIDP. The advantage of reaffirming any tentative diagnosis is that reaffirmation avoids the mistake of misclassifying the dependent person as a "passive" person (i.e., as passive–aggressive).

Psychotherapeutic Treatment

There seem to be varying opinions about treatment. Malinow (1981, p. 7), for example, suggested that the therapist establish a trusting relationship, support efforts on the part of the patient to establish an independent lifestyle, help the patient modulate the anxiety that accompanies decision making, and use supportive therapy when there is any possibility that the patient might be overwhelmed by negative affect.

Hill (1970), a well-known researcher in the area of dependent personality disorder, recognized the need for management programs (i.e., treatment programs) within which all professionals understand and agree on the procedures to be used. She recommended that the therapist, to combat the dependency disorder, establish a close (trusting) relationship with the patient, help the patient explore his or her patterns of living and how they contribute to his or her problems, and encourage the patient to take an active part in scheduling appointment times as therapy reaches a terminal point. By placing some responsibility for scheduling in the hands of the patient, the possibility of having the patient experience separation anxiety is diffused.

Obsessive–Compulsive Personality Disorder (DSM-III-R, 301.40)

Description

People experiencing obsessive–compulsive personality disorders are perfectionists. They insist that others submit to their ways of doing things. They have an excessive devotion to work, a tendency toward indecisiveness, and a great deal of difficulty expressing warm and tender emotions. Typically, they pursue rigidly formulated commitments, exhibit a preoccupation with rules, prefer to work rather than to relate, avoid decision making responsibilities, feel the need to control internal and external events, and are overconscientious about matters of ethics.

Diagnosis

A diagnosis made through use of the DSM-III-R can be reaffirmed through the use of the MMPI, the 16 PF, the MCMI II, or the SIDP.

Psychotherapeutic Treatment

Weintraub (1981) considered the treatment of choice psychoanalytic psychotherapy. He suggested that the therapist establish rapport with the patient, help the patient target those behaviors that are self-defeating, help the patient change ego-syntonic behavior into ego-alien behavior, and inform the patient as to the length of the sessions and the method by which therapy will be implemented.

Turner, Holzman, and Jacob (1983), in a well-researched study, found that patients could overcome compulsions through the use of such techniques as self-monitoring, imagery, thought stopping, fading, self-practice, generalization, and follow-up.

Passive–Aggressive Personality Disorder (DSM-III-R, 301.84)

Description

The person experiencing passive–aggressive personality disorder indirectly expresses resistance to demands for adequate performance. As a result, the person reflects inadequacies in performance, occupational pursuits, and social relationships. Typically, the person is dissatisfied with life, provocative toward figures of authority, resistant to demands for improved performance, unreasonably critical of others, immature, explosive, impulsive, hostile, intolerant, and erratic. The person frequently pouts, dawdles, procrastinates, and protests without justification.

Diagnosis

A DSM-III-R diagnosis can be reaffirmed through the use of the MCMI II or the SIDP.

Psychotherapeutic Treatment

Bandura (1973) suggested that modeling of appropriate behaviors can be used to treat aggressive behaviors. He also recommended that such modeling be accompanied by rehearsals and instructions. Elder, Edelstein, and Narick (1979) recommended a social skills training approach that involves modeling, role playing, instruction, and feedback. Millon and Millon (1974), Malinow (1981), and Bach-y-Rita (1981) suggested forming a trusting relationship.

Malinow (1981) recommended defining the onset of the disorder, training the patient to relax, and using guided imagery; he cautioned the therapist to watch for the hidden effects of depression (potential suicide attempts), which so frequently accompany passive–aggressive behavior. He also noted that the process of moving into relaxation training should not be hurried.

SOMATOFORM DISORDERS

HYPOCHONDRIASIS	DSM-III-R, 300.70
SOMATOFORM PAIN DISORDER	DSM-III-R, 307.80

Hypochondriasis (DSM-III-R, 300.70)

Description

All patients experiencing somatoform disorders exhibit physical symptoms for which there are no demonstrable organic findings. The disorder usually begins before the age of 30 and follows a chronic but desultory pattern of registered complaints. Typically the patient is anxious, dejected, and compulsive, and has the tendency to go "doctor shopping" (i.e., looking for a medical doctor who will support his or her symptoms). Such patients usually have poor social relationships, an impaired ability to function occupationally or socially, and a need to present their medical histories in great detail.

Diagnosis

It is imperative that patients have a good medical examination before proceeding with psychotherapy. One method of assessing the patient objectively is by using the Hypochondriasis (Hs) scale on the MMPI.

Psychotherapeutic Treatment

Kellner (1982a, 1982b, 1985, 1986), who has long researched the area of functional somatic symptoms (somatizers), recommended a treatment approach to hypochondriasis referred to as *Explanatory Therapy.* The approach is based on his evidence from research that patients with somatic preoccupations do not respond well to traditional insight therapy. His approach involves the following contingencies:

- Exploring the patient's attitudes toward disease to differentiate between the patient's fear of acquiring a disease and the patient's fear of having an undiagnosed disease
- Implementing specific treatment strategies, such as gathering accurate medical information, retraining the patient's selective perception, and using deliberate suggestion
- Helping the patient learn cognitive exercises that will influence and alter his or her cognitive structure.

Somatoform (Psychogenic) Pain Disorder (DSM-III-R, 307.80)

Description

As with hypochondriasis, the patient experiencing somatoform disorder complains of pain in the absence of any clear medical evidence of organic origin. The pain, in this case, is usually accompanied by a conflict-producing environmental stimulus. Thus, whenever the stimulus appears, the pain appears. Typically, the patient exhibits an excessive use of analgesics, is constantly doctor shopping, experiences muscle spasms and paresthesia, has a history of conversion symptoms (e.g., blindness), and frequently requests surgery in the absence of medical evidence.

Diagnosis

Pinsky (1978) suggested that an assessment as to whether the disorder is psychological in nature can be made on the basis of specific determinants. If the patient responds in the affirmative to several of the determinants, the person may be experiencing somatoform pain disorder (see Gutsch, 1988, p. 176).

Psychotherapeutic Treatment

One interesting fact about chronic pain is that those who experience it are firmly convinced that they have a physical problem. If the pain persists for more than 6 months, many of these patients will seek surgical intervention. Among the treatment alternatives available for such patients are acupuncture, hypnosis, relaxation techniques, group therapy, behavior modification, nerve blocks, transcutaneous electrical stimulation, and prescribed drugs. Since there seems to be no plausible neurological theory of chronic pain (i.e., beyond a highly hypothetical state), it seems that to view it as a psychological phenomenon rather than as a sensory phenomenon is not without merit.

Blumer and Heilbronn (1982) suggested, for example, that whenever a chronic pain patient complains of pain for which no organic basis can be found, one might expect the presence of an underlying depression (p. 383).

Getto and Ochitill (1982) recommended the use of a team approach to treatment. They suggested that the team include such professionals as neurologists, psychotherapists, and medical specialists. Treatment would include counterposing relaxation skills with pain-inducing experiences, restructuring support systems, reinforcing nonpain behavior, and training family members to reinforce nonpain behavior.

EATING DISORDERS

ANOREXIA NERVOSA	DSM-III-R, 307.10
BULIMIA NERVOSA	DSM-III-R, 307.51

Anorexia Nervosa (DSM-III-R, 307.10)

Description

The person experiencing anorexia nervosa refuses to eat (i.e., enters into a period of voluntary self-starvation). This results in a loss of weight that, when it becomes severe enough, causes the person to look emaciated. Typically, the person exhibits a persistent feeling of "fatness," excessive dependency, introversion, compulsivity, stubbornness, perfectionism, and shyness.

Diagnosis

The physical appearance of the person is one of the first indications that something is wrong. Meyer (1983) suggested that the anorexic person tends to score low on factors A, F, H, and Q1 of the 16 PF and moderately low on factor M. This profile probably occurs after the onset of the disorder, however, and therefore may reflect the anorexic condition only after it has been diagnosed by a physician.

Garner and Garfinkel (1979) designed an Eating Attitude Test, which yields an index of symptoms from which the therapist can identify the anorexic person.

Psychotherapeutic Treatment

Monti, McCrady, and Barlow (1977) recommended establishing a baseline of information about the anorexic habits of the patient; identifying positive reinforcers for use with the patient; and using feedback sessions, relaxation and desensitization techniques, and contingency contracting with the patient.

Brady and Rieger (1975), on the other hand, recommended observing the patient for 5 days before treatment in order to provide a composite of specific information. They recommended that, following the observation period, a case management approach to treatment should be used, which involves establishing a data base, identifying reinforcers that can be used with the patient, and analyzing changes in the condition of the patient.

Bulimia Nervosa (DSM-III-R, 307.51)

Description

The person experiencing bulimia (usually a female) exhibits episodic bingeing followed by self-induced purging. Interestingly enough, bingeing and purging seem to be part of an interlocking pathology, in which the former elicits anxiety (the fear of a weight gain) and the latter reduces it. Typically, the person fears gaining weight, is obsessed with the idea of eating, binges at least once a week, purges by vomiting, is preoccupied with dieting, is secretive, is socially inhibited, and is ashamed of his or her consummatory patterns.

Diagnosis

The bulimic sometimes requests help. If not, the constant bingeing, purging, and obsession with food become apparent to others in the environment.

Psychotherapeutic Treatment

Rosen and Leitenberg (1982) recommended briefing the patient (i.e., helping the patient to understand the nature of the disorder and how it will be treated) and executing change (i.e., helping the patient to understand how to implement change).

Boskind-Lodahl and White (1978) performed extensive research in this area and suggested that the therapist collect information regarding the patient's struggle for independence and use of the binge–purge ritual as a means of avoiding intimacy and responsibility. The therapist should then help the patient develop a greater awareness of what he or she is doing, why he or she is doing it, and how to change. White and Boskind-White (1981) also introduced a day-by-day sequence of steps they initiated in treating a group of 14 bulimarexic women (see Gutsch, 1988).

In another approach, O'Connor (1984) recommended that the therapist direct the patient to obsess about food, to substitute compulsions (e.g., spending time with a friend as a substitute for compulsive eating), to record everything he or she eats, and to binge on purpose. This latter directive establishes therapeutic control. By reversing the process, the patient is instructed to binge, but is denied the conciliatory effects of vomiting.

SUMMARY

Throughout this chapter, my intent has been to reflect on the practice of psychotherapy and the use of DSM-III-R in the development of a practical and defensible basis for treatment planning. Emphasis has been placed on the use of DSM-III-R to identify specific mental disorders, the use of test results to reaffirm the DSM-III-R diagnoses, and the use of well-researched professional literature for treatment planning.

REFERENCES

Abramson, L., Seligman, M., & Teasdale, J. (1978). Learned helplessness in humans: Critique and reformulation. *Journal of Abnormal Psychology, 87,* 49–74.

Adler, G. (1980). A treatment framework for adult patients with borderline and narcissistic personality disorders. *Bulletin of the Menninger Clinic, 44,* 171–180.

Allport, F. H. (1955). *Theories of perception and the concept of structure.* New York: Wiley.

American Psychiatric Association. (1952). *Diagnostic and statistical manual of mental disorders* (1st ed.). Washington, DC: Author.

American Psychiatric Association. (1968). *Diagnostic and statistical manual of mental disorders* (2nd ed.). Washington, DC: Author.

American Psychiatric Association. (1980). *Diagnostic and statistical manual of mental disorders* (3rd ed.). Washington, DC: Author.

American Psychiatric Association. (1987). *Diagnostic and statistical manual of mental disorders* (3rd ed. rev.). Washington, DC: Author.

Andrews, J. (1974). Psychotherapy with the hysterical personality: An interpersonal approach. *Psychiatry, 16,* 750–757.

Bach-y-Rita, G. (1981). Personality disorders in prison. In J. R. Lion (Ed.), *Personality disorders: Diagnosis and management* (2nd edition) (pp. 540–550). Baltimore: Williams & Wilkins.

Bandura, A. (1973). *Aggression: A social learning analysis.* Englewood Cliffs, NJ: Prentice-Hall.

Bauer, G., & Sherry, P. (1986). Understanding and treating borderline personality organization: A reply to Dorr, Gard, Barley, & Webb. *Psychotherapy, 23,* 70–74.

Beach, S., Abramson, L., & Levine, F. (1981). Attributional reformulation of learned helplessness and depression: Therapeutic implications. In J. Clarkin & H. Glazer (Eds.), *Depression: Behavioral and directive intervention strategies* (pp. 131–165). New York: Garland STPM Press.

Beck, A. (1961). A systematic investigation of depression. *Comprehensive Psychiatry, 2,* 162–170.

Beck, A. (1976). *Cognitive therapy and the emotional disorders.* New York: International Universities Press.

Beck, A. (1978). *Beck depression inventory.* Philadelphia, PA: Center for Cognitive Therapy.

Beck, A., & Greenberg, R. (1974). *Coping with depression.* New York: Institute for Rational Living.

Beck, A., & Shaw, B. (1977). Cognitive approaches to depression. In A. Ellis & R. Grieger (Eds.), *Handbook of rational emotive therapy* (pp. 119–134). New York: Springer.

Blumer, D., & Heilbronn, M. (1982). Chronic pain as a variant of depressive disease: The pain-prone disorder. *Journal of Nervous and Mental Disease, 170,* 381–406.

Boskind-Lodahl, M., & White, W. C., Jr. (1978). The definition and treatment of bulimarexia in college women—A pilot study. *Journal of the American College Health Association, 27,* 84–86.

Brady, J., & Rieger, W. (1975). Behavioral treatment of anorexia nervosa. In T. Thompson & W. Dockens, III (Eds.), *Application of behavior modification* (pp. 45–63). New York: Academic Press.

Cattell, R. (1972). *Administrator's manual for the 16 PF* Champaign, IL: Institute for Personality and Ability Testing.

Chambless, D., Caputo, G., Jasin, S., Gracely, E., & Williams, C. (1985). The mobility inventory for agoraphobia. *Behaviour Research and Therapy, 23,* 35–44.

Chessick, R. (1979). A practical approach to the psychotherapy of the borderline patient. *American Journal of Psychiatry, 33,* 531–546.

Cloninger, C. (1978). The antisocial personality. *Hospital Practice, 13,* 97–106.

Di Nardo, P., Barlow, D., Cerny, J., Vermilyea, B., Vermilyea, J., Himadi, W., & Waddell, M. (1985). *Anxiety disorders interview schedule revised* (ADIS-R). Albany, NY: Center for Stress and Anxiety Disorders.

Dorr, D., Gard, B., Barley, W., & Webb, C. (1983). Understanding and treating borderline personality organization. *Psychotherapy: Theory, Research and Practice, 18,* 379–385.

Edelstein, B., & Eisler, R. (1976). Effects of modeling and modeling with instructions and feedback on the behavioral components of social skills. *Behavior Therapy, 7,* 382–389.

Eisler, R., Blanchard, E., Fitts, H., & Williams, J. (1978). Social skills training with and without modeling for schizophrenic and non-psychotic hospitalized psychiatric patients. *Behavior Modification, 2,* 147–172.

Elder, J., Edelstein, B., & Narick, M. (1979). Adolescent psychiatric patients: Modifying aggressive behavior with social skills training. *Behavior Modification, 3,* 161–178.

Garner, D., & Garfinkel, P. (1979). The eating attitude test: An index of the symptoms of anorexia nervosa. *Psychological Medicine, 9,* 273–279.

Getto, C., & Ochitill, H. (1982). Psychogenic pain disorder. In J. Greist, J. Jefferson, & R. Spitzer (Eds.), *Treatment of mental disorders* (pp. 277–286). New York: Oxford.

Glantz, K. (1981). The use of a relaxation exercise in the treatment of borderline personality organization. *Psychotherapy: Theory, Research and Practice, 18,* 379–385.

Gutsch, K. (1988). *Psychotherapeutic approaches to specific DSM-III-R categories: A resource book for treatment planning.* Springfield, IL: Charles C. Thomas.

Halleck, S. (1967). Hysterical personality traits: Psychological, social and iatrogenic determinants. *Archives of General Psychiatry, 16,* 750–757.

Hathaway, S. R., & McKinley, J. C. (1967). *Minnesota Multiphasic Personality Inventory Manual.* New York: Psychological Corporation.

Hill, D. (1970). Outpatient management of passive-dependent women. *Hospital and Community Psychiatry, 21,* 402–405.

Kellner, R. (1982a). Hypochondriasis and atypical somatoform disorders. In J. Greist, J. Jefferson, & R. Spitzer (Eds.), *Treatment of mental disorders* (pp. 286–302). New York: Oxford.

Kellner, R. (1982b). Psychotherapeutic strategies in hypochondriasis: A clinical study. *American Journal of Psychotherapy, 36,* 146–157.

Kellner, R. (1985). Functional somatic symptoms and hypochondriasis. *Archives of General Psychiatry, 42*, 821–833.

Kellner, R. (1986). *Somatization and hypochondriasis.* Praeger-Greenwood.

Kimble, G., Garmezy, N., & Zigler, E. (1984). *Principles of psychology.* New York: Wiley.

Lanyon, R. (1973). *Psychological screening inventory manual.* Goshen, NY: Research Psychologists Press.

Lewinsohn, P., Muñoz, R., Youngren, M., & Zeiss, A. (1986). *Control your depression.* Englewood Cliffs, NJ: Prentice-Hall.

Mahoney, M. (1977). Personal science: A cognitive learning therapy. In A. Ellis & R. Grieger (Eds.), *Handbook of rational emotive therapy* (pp. 352–366). New York: Springer.

Malinow, K. (1981). Dependent personality. In J. R. Lion (Ed.), *Personality disorders: Diagnosis and management* (2nd ed.) (pp. 97–102). Baltimore: Williams & Wilkins.

Meichenbaum, D. (1977). *Cognitive–behavior modifications.* New York: Plenum Press.

Mendelsohn, R. (1981). "Active attention" and "focusing" on the transference countertransference in the psychotherapy of the borderline patient. *Psychotherapy: Theory, Research and Practice, 18*, 386–393.

Meyer, R. (1983). *The clinician's handbook.* Boston: Allyn & Bacon.

Millon, T. (1981). *Disorders of personality DSM-III: Axis II.* New York: Wiley.

Millon, T. (1987). *Millon clinical multiaxial inventory manual II.* Minneapolis, MN: Interpretive Scoring Systems.

Millon, T., & Millon, R. (1974). *Abnormal behavior and personality.* Philadelphia: Saunders.

Monti, P., McCrady, B., & Barlow, D. (1977). Effect of positive reinforcement, information feedback, and contingency contracting on a bulimic anorexic female. *Behavior Therapy, 8*, 258–263.

O'Connor, J. (1984). Strategic individual psychotherapy with bulimic women. *Psychotherapy: Theory, Research and Practice, 21*, 491–499.

Pinsky, K. (1978). Chronic, intractable, benign pain: A syndrome and its treatment with intensive short-term group psychotherapy. *Journal of Human Stress, 4*(3), 17–21.

Powers, H. (1972). Psychotherapy for hysterical individuals. *Social Casework, 53*, 435–440.

Rosen, J., & Leitenberg, H. (1982). Bulimia nervosa: Treatment with exposure and response prevention. *Behavior Therapy, 13*, 117–124.

Seligman, M. (1975). *Helplessness: On depression, development, and death.* San Francisco: Freeman.

Shaw, B., & Beck, A. (1977). The treatment of depression with cognitive therapy. In A. Ellis & R. Grieger (Eds.), *Handbook of rational-emotive therapy* (pp. 309–326). New York: Springer.

Spence, S., & Marzillier, J. (1981). Social skill training with adolescent male offenders: II. Short-term, long-term, and generalized effects. *Behaviour Research and Therapy, 19*, 349–368.

Stangl, D., Pfohl, B., Zimmerman, M., Bowers, W., & Corenthal, C. (1985). A structured interview for the DSM-III personality disorders: A preliminary report. *Archives of General Psychiatry, 42*, 591–596.

Suinn, R. (1983). *Manual: Anxiety management training.* Fort Collins, CO: Rocky Mountain Behavioral Science Institute.

Turner, S., Holzman, A., & Jacob, R. (1983). Treatment of compulsive looking by imaginal thought-stopping. *Behavior Modification, 7,* 576–582.

Wenrich, W., Dawley, H., & General, D. (1976). *Self-directed systematic desensitization.* Kalamazoo, MI: Behaviodelia.

Weintraub, W. (1981). Compulsive and paranoid personalities. In J. R. Lion (Ed.), *Personality disorders: Diagnosis and management* (2nd ed.) (pp. 163–181). Baltimore: Williams & Wilkins.

White, W. C., Jr., & Boskind-White, M. (1981). An experimental-behavior approach to the treatment of bulimarexia. *Psychotherapy: Theory, Research and Practice, 18,* 501–507.

Wolpe, J. (1954). Reciprocal inhibition as the main basis of psychotherapeutic effects. *Archives of Neurological Psychiatry, 72,* 205.

Wolpe, J. (1969). *The practice of behavior therapy.* New York: Pergamon.

Wolpe, J. (1982). *The practice of behavior therapy* (3rd ed.). New York: Pergamon Press.

Woolson, A., & Swanson, M. (1972). The second time around: Psychotherapy with the "hysterical woman." *Psychotherapy: Theory, Research and Practice, 9,* 168–175.

CHAPTER 16

DSM-III, DSM-III-R, and Behavior Therapy

MICHEL HERSEN and SAMUEL M. TURNER

Emergence of DSM-III (APA, 1980a) and the DSM-III-R revision (APA, 1987) have influenced all clinical practitioners, irrespective of theoretical allegiance, including behavior therapists. The impact of these systems of classification on the behavioral area is of some importance. Thus, in this chapter, we examine the relationship between behavior therapy and DSM-III and its successor. We first consider traditional problems of psychiatric diagnosis, citing from the research literature of over three decades. Next, we document improvements in DSM-III and DSM-III-R over the two predecessors: DSM-I and DSM-II. Then, we outline the problems that we see in the current diagnostic scheme. We discuss the philosophy of behavioral assessment and the manner in which it differs from traditional psychological evaluation. Finally, we consider the effects of DSM-III and DSM-III-R on the practice of behavior therapy, and conclude with a discussion of the need for psychiatric diagnosis and classification in general. Throughout the chapter, we stress the ideal in assessment, but we temper this by discussing the pragmatic need for considering and classifying deviant human behavior, given the inherent limitations of the extant nosological schemes.

HISTORICAL PROBLEMS OF PSYCHIATRIC DIAGNOSIS

In considering problems associated with traditional psychiatric diagnosis (e.g., DSM-I and DSM-II), we recognize that any diagnostic system inevitably has limitations. The difficulties, of course, are due to the inherent nature of the task: that is, the imposition of artificial order on naturally occurring phenomena. In that sense, a classification scheme always reflects the biases and oversights of its proponents. DSM-I and DSM-II were considered to have excessive flaws, however, thus defeating the purposes for which they were constructed. Difficulties with these two schemes have been discussed repeatedly in the literature (Frank, 1969, 1975; Hersen, 1976; Spitzer & Fleiss, 1974; Zubin, 1967).

In general, DSM-I and DSM-II may be criticized on the basis of four issues. The first refers to the conceptual cornerstone of the systems. (In our

463

discussion, DSM-I and DSM-II are lumped together inasmuch as DSM-II did not represent a tremendous improvement over DSM-I. As ironically noted by Begelman [1975], they are "twice told tales.") A major difficulty with both systems was that the specific classifications confounded etiology of the disorders with the presenting symptomatology as observed by the clinician; depending on the given disorders or subcategory, greater emphasis might have been given to one aspect or the other. Thus, the diagnosing clinician was hampered in making a judgment. Moreover, in DSM-I and DSM-II, little attention was accorded to the actual duration of symptomatology. An additional problem with these diagnostic schemes was that they only poorly accommodated the complexities of accurate classification when similar life stressors (Eisler, Hersen, Miller, & Wooten, 1973; Eisler & Polak, 1971) led to totally different diagnostic pictures. For example, loss of a loved one might lead to depressive symptoms in one individual but schizophrenic symptoms in another. Moreover, the systems did not generally include precise guidelines for determining how many and which symptoms were required to make a definitive diagnosis.

A second primary flaw with DSM-I and DSM-II involved the relationship of treatment to diagnosis. In most branches of therapeutics, some relationship between diagnosis and treatment is apparent. For example, diagnosis of a cavity in a tooth leads to its being filled, diagnosis of myopia leads to a prescription for corrective lenses, and diagnosis of appendicitis invariably results in recommendation for surgery to remove the infected organ. Strangely enough, however, this relationship was not (and, with the exception of Perry, Frances, & Clarkin, 1990, often still is not) the case in psychiatry. Diagnosis of a specific disorder (e.g., agoraphobia) did not lead to a specific treatment recommendation, especially in psychotherapy. Similar psychotherapeutic approaches might have ensued with diagnoses as varied as agoraphobia, "neurotic" depression, obsessive–compulsive disorder, and a failing marriage. Despite the use of psychological testing to bolster the psychiatrist's diagnostic impression, recommendations for treatment invariably would include statements to the effect that the patient required "a better understanding of his or her dynamics." Psychotherapy (insight-oriented) seemed to be the only antidote. Variations on the theme consistent with the unique character of presenting symptoms were not offered in such ubiquitous solutions. For pharmacological interventions, however, DSM-I and DSM-II recommended somewhat more precise therapies based on the diagnoses. Nevertheless, a one-to-one relationship between diagnosis and treatment was not the norm, even with respect to drug administration.

A third major flaw with DSM-I and DSM-II was its notorious unreliability. As pointed out by Zubin (1967), reliability can refer to three issues when making diagnostic appraisals: (1) agreement between two or more clinicians assessing the same patient, (2) stability of the diagnosis over an extended period of time (e.g., Andreasen et al., 1981), and (3) comparable diagnostic percentages for similar groups of patients. The first definition is of greatest concern to this discussion. As argued by Spitzer and Fleiss (1974),

> There are inherent limitations to the interpretation of the other two uses of the term. For agreement between initial and subsequent diagnosis, one must

consider the possibility that some of the disagreement may be due to changes in the patient's condition and not just to unreliability. The difficulty with interpreting differences in distributions between populations is that one is forced to assume, often without evidence, that the populations do not differ in psychopathology, when in fact they may.

(p. 341)

In light of the above, let us consider a number of studies documenting the weak concordance among diagnosticians using DSM-I and DSM-II categories. In an early study, Ash (1949) used the conference interview method to evaluate the diagnoses made by two or three psychiatrists of 52 male outpatients. For the 35 patients for whom three psychiatrists offered diagnostic appraisals, only 20 percent interrater reliability was found; however, reliability increased to 31.4 to 43.5 percent when two psychiatrists were compared. Interrater agreement for all three psychiatrists was 45.7 percent for the major diagnostic categories; when only two psychiatrists made these evaluations, interrater agreement improved to 57.9 to 67.4 percent. Clearly, then, as one shifts from the major to the minor diagnostic categories and as number of assessors is increased, diagnostic reliability decreases. Even with the major categories, reliability across psychiatrists can best be described as "moderate."

Sandifer, Pettus, and Quade (1964) looked at the diagnostic reliability of 14 senior medical practitioners for 91 patients newly admitted to a psychiatric hospital. Eleven of these practitioners were psychiatrists. The practitioners made their diagnoses while sitting in a group consultation. There was significant variability in interrater agreement from one category to the next, and the likelihood of a second opinion confirming the first averaged only 57 percent.

Nathan, Andberg, Behan, and Patch (1969) had 32 health professionals complete the Boston City Hospital Behavior Check List while attending a case presentation of a 36-year-old male alcoholic who displayed both organic and psychiatric symptoms. Results of the data analyses indicated that more experienced clinicians showed greater likelihood of identifying organic signs, whereas less experienced clinicians focused more on the patient's perceptual symptoms characteristic of depression for schizophrenics.

Cohen, Harbin, and Wright (1975) found that 12 percent (33) of 267 inpatients assessed as psychotic upon admission had their diagnoses changed to neurosis or character disorder upon discharge. Interviews with the diagnosing psychiatric residents indicated that the labels were altered to "protect" the patients from negative environmental reactions to the diagnoses. Thus, Frank's (1969) word of caution with respect to the use of psychiatric diagnosis in research was well taken.

A number of methodological issues may have contributed to the relatively mediocre reliabilities obtained in these early studies (see Grove, Andreasen, McDonald-Scott, Keller, & Shapiro, 1981). Indeed, Grove et al. noted that the more recent studies have yielded higher interrater percentages. This improvement is due, of course, to the better training of raters, the use of standardized interview schedules, and the development of more specific and concrete diagnostic criteria. A number of questions still remain unanswered, however:

Was higher reliability achieved because structured interview schedules were used, because diagnostic criteria were used, or both? Was the intensive training often used to calibrate diagnosticians responsible for the diagnosis? Can less experienced raters also achieve good reliability? Is the good reliability an artifact of less demanding designs for measuring interrater agreement? Would a longer test–retest interval between two interviews in the test–retest studies cause a drastic decrease in agreement?

(Grove et al., 1981, p. 408)

From our perspective, it is important to document high interrater reliability in the psychiatric setting as patients typically are diagnosed. We applaud use of structured rating scales and well-trained diagnosticians. Unfortunately, however,high interrater reliability does not occur in the large majority of clinical settings. Thus, the proponents of the newer studies bear the burden of proof. Either all diagnosticians should be trained or retrained to the level demanded by high-level research designs, or the diagnostic system should be reworked to maximize likelihood of concordance between and among various clinicians.

A fourth problem with DSM-I and DSM-II relates to validity. For example, how well did the diagnostic system discriminate across categories with regard to specific signs and symptoms? Nathan and his colleagues (Nathan, 1969; Nathan, Gould, Zare, & Roth, 1969; Nathan, Robertson, & Andberg, 1969; Nathan, Simpson, & Andberg, 1969; Nathan, Zare, Simpson, & Andberg, 1969) evaluated the symptom–sign notion as it relates to psychiatric diagnosis at the Boston City Hospital. A general research strategy was followed in each study. The researchers evaluated 924 patients using the Boston City Hospital Behavior Check List, a 100-item questionnaire targeting specific symptoms of psychopathology. The following diagnostic entities were contrasted to examine the discriminant validity of these various signs and symptoms (e.g., loss of appetite in depression): psychosis, psychoneurosis, personality disorder, acute brain disorder, and chronic brain disorder. Also, subdivisions of these categories were compared. Findings suggested that there was considerable overlap in the categories, particularly for the subdivisions. In commenting on these results, Nathan, Gould, et al. (1969) concluded that there was "only limited differential diagnostic validity for many of the most common signs and symptoms of psychopathology" (p. 370). Undoubtedly, low diagnostic reliability contributed to the weak differentiation among categories.

IMPROVEMENTS IN DSM-III AND DSM-III-R

Despite the rather considerable criticism of DSM-III and DSM-III-R from both psychiatrists and psychologists (e.g., Cantwell & Baker, 1988; Haynes & O'Brien, 1988; Kendler, Spitzer, & Williams, 1989; McLemore & Benjamin, 1979; McReynolds, 1979; Schacht & Nathan, 1977; Sheehan, Sheehan, & Shaw, 1988), these schemes have some notable improvements over their predecessors (Frances & Cooper, 1981; Spitzer, 1981; Spitzer & Forman, 1979; Spitzer, Forman, & Nee, 1979; Spitzer, Skodol, Gibbon, & Williams, 1980). These improvements are due to a number of factors.

First, the spirit in which DSM-III and DSM-III-R were conceived can be described as more empirical and descriptive than that of their predecessors. Very little emphasis was placed on psychoanalytic theory and considerable emphasis on the findings of research psychiatrists and psychologists. Moreover, much more time and effort were devoted to their construction. As pointed out by Spitzer et al. (1980),

> DSM-III was five years in development, two years more than had initially been anticipated. This extension—granted because of the heated controversy that surrounded the project—was necessary to work out solutions to many of the problematic aspects of drafts of the document.
>
> *(p. 152)*

Many professionals representing different associations (e.g., American Psychiatric Association, American Psychological Association, American Psychoanalytic Association) gave their input.

Second, portions of the draft underwent a series of field tests involving 480 clinicians in institutions and private practice around the country.

Third, a "viable" definition of mental disorder was presented as acceptable to many critics of earlier drafts of DSM-III:

> In DSM-III, a mental disorder is conceptualized as a clinically significant behavioral or psychologic syndrome or pattern that occurs in an individual and that is typically associated with either a painful symptom (distress) or impairment in one or more important areas of functioning (disability). In addition, there is an inference that there is a behavioral, psychologic, or biological dysfunction and that the disturbance is not only in the relationship between the individual and society. When the disturbance is limited to a conflict between an individual and society, this may represent social deviance which may or may not be commendable but is not by itself a mental disorder.
>
> *(Spitzer et al., 1980, p. 153)*

Fourth was the development of relatively clear criteria for each diagnostic category in DSM-III and DSM-III-R. This innovation has led to more precise thinking when the clinician is deciding the correctness of his or her diagnosis. For example, for a patient to qualify for a diagnosis of a major depressive episode, four of the eight listed symptoms should have been present in the patient daily for at least 2 weeks. Also, APA (1980b, 1987b) developed quick references to diagnostic criteria for DSM-III and DSM-III-R. These handbooks have proved to be of immense help to the practicing clinician, as was the case book prepared by Spitzer et al. (1981).

The fifth, and probably most innovative, new feature of DSM-III and DSM-III-R was the development of the multiaxial system to enhance diagnosis. Spitzer et al. (1980) noted that,

> A multiaxial system for psychiatric evaluation provides for the systematic evaluation of an individual's condition in terms of several variables, or axes, that are conceptualized and rated as quasi-independent of each other. The potential advantages of such a system include comprehensiveness and the recording of

nondiagnostic data that are valuable in understanding possible etiological factors and in treatment planning and prognosis.

(p. 154)

Of the five axes in this diagnostic system, the first three make up the *official* diagnosis and the latter two are of psychosocial significance. Axis I involves identification of the clinical syndromes (e.g., bipolar disorder; schizophrenic disorder, paranoid type). Axis II helps identify the personality disorders (e.g., histrionic personality disorder). Under the DSM-III and DSM-III-R systems, it is possible to have a diagnosis under both Axis I and Axis II. Axis III describes the patient's physical condition (e.g., late effects of viral encephalitis). In Axis IV, the severity of psychosocial stressors is rated by the clinician on a 7-point scale from *none* to *catastrophic.* Finally, in Axis V, the diagnostician rates the patient's highest level of adaptive functioning in the past year on a 1 (*superior*) to 5 (*poor*) scale.

Therefore, with the multiaxial system, a more complete biological, psychosocial, and psychiatric picture of the patient emerges than with the earlier systems. Thus, the diagnosing clinician should be helped in identifying appropriate targets for treatment.

Sixth, DSM-III and DSM-III-R provide improved diagnostic reliability (see Spitzer & Forman, 1979; Spitzer et al., 1979). In one study (Spitzer et al., 1979), the kappa reliability coefficient of agreement for 281 adult patients seen in joint interviews was 0.78; however, for separate interviews, the reliability dropped to 0.66. In both instances, reliabilities are for Axis I diagnoses. Reliabilities for Axis II were 0.61 and 0.54 for joint and separate interviews, respectively. In a separate study, Spitzer and Forman (1979) reported joint and separate reliabilities of 0.62 and 0.58, respectively, for Axis IV and of 0.86 and 0.69, respectively for Axis V. The investigators argued, on the basis of these data that,

> Despite greater demand placed on the clinician by the multiaxial system and the difficulties involved in the use of Axis IV, the vast majority of the field trial participants believe that the DSM-III multiaxial system is a useful addition to the traditional diagnostic evaluation. Future studies are necessary to determine the extent to which the multiaxial system and, in particular, Axes IV and V will actually be used in clinical practice and their impact on patient care.
>
> *(p. 820)*

Finally, as noted by Haynes and O'Brien (1988),

> The DSM-III-R, in comparison to its predecessors, more closely approximates an empirically and clinically useful scheme for classifying behavior disorders. This was achieved by explicitly defining components of the system and expanding the number of categories to insure both exhaustive and divergent choices.
>
> *(p. 98)*

For example, DSM-III-R provides greater coverage of child and adolescent disorders (Cantwell & Baker, 1988) and more refined descriptors of adult psychotic disorders (Kendler et al., 1989). Nonetheless, the problems that remain are numerous and significant, and the field is rushing pell-mell to develop DSM-IV before sufficient field trials have been carried out with DSM-III-R. In the next section, we detail many of the problems with DSM-III and DSM-III-R.

HOW SIGNIFICANT ARE THE IMPROVEMENTS IN DSM-III-R OVER DSM-III?

Up to this point, we have focused on some of the changes in DSM-III and DSM-III-R that represent improvement over their predecessors. Despite these improvements, a number of overarching questions need to be addressed regarding some of the basic changes included in DSM-III-R. Furthermore, questions need to be raised about the scientific basis of many of the changes and about the process by which the DSMs are constructed. The basic question is whether the "improvements" in DSM-III-R are significant enough to offset a variety of difficulties brought on by revising diagnostic criteria for a system that had been in place for only 6 years, and whether the changes incorporated in DSM-III-R serve our patients' or our sciences' best interest.

In a stinging critique of DSM-III-R, Rey (1988) provided a compelling discussion that must lead to negative replies to both questions. Although we do not attempt to discuss every specific change here, we note some of the most significant ones. One change was the addition in DSM-III-R of a number of new diagnostic categories, particularly in the child and adolescent areas. According to Rey (1988), the 225 diagnoses in DSM-III-R represent an increase of 10 percent in diagnostic categories; however, the inclusion of the additional diagnostic categories does not appear to be based on empirical research. We have yet to see a rationale for most of these diagnoses that can be supported by scientific inquiry. In fact, we are unaware that any substantive rationale has been offered in many cases. Rather, these categories appear to be the product of group discussions by members of the DSM-III-R task force. In addition to new categories, the names of a number of disorders were changed for reasons that are not entirely clear. For example, the name of the major category "Affective Disorders" was changed to "Mood Disorders."

Several major changes in DSM-III-R concern the hierarchical rules that were a critical part of DSM-III. Except for organic mental disorders and schizophrenia, all hierarchical rules were eliminated (Rey, 1988). The elimination of these rules makes considerable sense in a number of areas, for example, in removing the requirement that depression take precedence over anxiety. Again, however, the rationale for making such major changes was not entirely clear in all instances.

Several perplexing changes were made in Axes III through V of the multiaxial system. For example, Rey (1988; Rey, Stewart, Plapp, Bashir, and Richard, 1988) argued that Axis IV (psychosocial stressors), one of the most criticized axes of DSM-III, was further complicated by DSM-III-R by requiring the clinician to place events within certain time frames. Also, Axis V was completely revised before we were able to determine the usefulness of the scale as it appeared in DSM-III. Having discussed some of the specific pros and cons of DSM-III-R, we now turn to the relationship of DSM-III-R to behavior therapy in particular, and to a scientific approach to understanding psychopathology in general.

BEHAVIORAL ASSESSMENT

From the inception of strategies for the assessment of behavior within a behavioral framework, a core characteristic has been its focus on overt behavior. This is in stark contrast to more traditional methods of assessment in which little concern is given to overt behavioral responses. In a 1972 article in the *Psychological Bulletin,* Goldfried and Kent outlined the differences between behavioral and traditional assessment, and the reader is referred to that source for a comprehensive review. Briefly, traditional assessment has been directed at understanding the characteristics of underlying *personality traits.* A specific type of personality or trait is determined by examining various signs and symptoms. The reliance on signs and symptoms is considered necessary because overt behavior is distorted by the individual's defensive structure. Hence, actual motives are obscured and must be interpreted symbolically as indirect signs (Mischel, 1972). Thus, in the case of the Rorschach, a person's response to a specific inkblot is considered to reveal something about that individual's hidden personality structure. The MMPI and other more objective personality inventories rely on a person's expression of various preferences, which are then contrasted to those of normative populations.

According to Goldfried and Kent (1972), traditional and behavioral approaches to understanding personality also are differentiated at a pragmatic level. Traditional approaches have focused primarily on how to predict behavior, with little emphasis on relating findings to the actual selection of a treatment strategy. Thus, traditional test results often are used to support a psychiatric diagnosis but are not used in the formal treatment planning process. On the other hand, an expert behavior therapist uses behavioral assessment strategies to arrive at a diagnosis, as well as to select a treatment intervention. Some of the ways in which behavioral assessment can be used in diagnosis and treatment, in addition to the growing complexity of the process given the emerging complexity of causative models of behavior, are discussed by Hayes, Nelson, and Jarrett (1988) and Haynes (1988). Finally, the same strategy used for deriving a diagnosis and planning treatment can be used to assess improvement over the course of treatment.

A central feature of behavioral assessment is concern with the precise description of a patient's actions. The behavior therapist needs to ascertain whether behavior occurs, whether it occurs repeatedly, whether it occurs in more than one setting, and whether it is systematically related to the occurrence of other behavior(s) (Cone, 1981, p. 53). In other words, behavioral assessment is criterion referenced, whereas traditional assessment relies on the statistical comparison of one score with a group of scores (Livingston, 1977).

Another useful distinction was that drawn by Goodenough (1949) between the "sign" and "sample" approaches to the interpretation of test responses. The sign approach assumes that the response may best be constructed as an indirect manifestation of some personality characteristic, whereas the sample approach assumes that test behavior constitutes a subset of the actual behavior of interest. Traditional personality tests have typically taken the sign approach to interpretation, but behavioral procedures approach test interpretation with the sample orientation (Goldfried & Kent, 1972, p. 413)

Table 16.1 compares traditional and behavioral assessment. Another difference between the two assessment types of approaches centers around the idea of behavioral consistency. The assumption in traditional assessment is that overt behavior is the function of stable and consistent personality traits. The often cited Hartshorne and May (1928) study on honesty and Mischel's (1968) review of the entire evidence for behavioral consistency have shown that, in many respects, behavior is situationally specific. Although subsequent research has shown consistency in some behavior, particularly abnormal behavior (e.g., Endler, 1973), it remains clear that situational factors are often critical. Thus, Mischel's (1977) statement, "If human behavior is determined by many inactive variables—both in the person and the environment—then a focus on any one of them is likely to lead to limited predictions and generalizations," still appears appropriate today.

Initially, the armamentarium of the behavioral assessor consisted primarily of observational procedures. Over the years, however, we have seen growth in both the number and the complexity of assessment approaches, including sophisticated psychophysiological strategies (e.g., Kallman & Feuerstein, 1986), various analogue assessment devices (Nay, 1986), and, more recently, assessment strategies designed to measure various aspects of cognitive functioning (Parks & Hollon, 1988). In addition, considerable

TABLE 16.1. Comparison of Traditional and Behavioral Assessment Strategies

	Behavioral Assessment	Traditional Assessment
Assumptions		
1. Personality concept	Behavior (f) environment	Behavior (f) underlying causes
2. "Test" interpretation	Behavior as sample	Behavior as sign
3. Situations sampled	Varied and specific	Limited and ambiguous
Primary Functions	Description in behavioral-analytic terms	Description in psycho-dynamic terms
	Treatment selection	Diagnostic labeling
	Treatment evaluation	
Practical aspects		
1. Relation to treatment	Direct	Indirect
2. Time of assessment	Continuous with treatment	Prior to treatment

Source: Reprinted with permission from "Behavioral Assessment: *An overview* by A. Ciminero, in *Handbook of Behavioral Assessment* (2nd ed., pp. 3–11) edited by A. Ciminero, K. S. Calhoun, and H. E. Adams. Copyright 1982 by John Wiley & Sons.

attention has been focused on particular strategies of assessment for specific abnormalities in children and adults (Barlow, 1981; Hersen & Bellack, 1988a; Nelson & Barlow, 1981). For an introduction to the various behavioral assessment strategies, the reader is referred to the *Dictionary of Behavioral Assessment Techniques* (Hersen & Bellack, 1988b).

It can be argued that little advancement has occurred in methods of traditional assessment over the years, whereas considerable advancement and refinement has occurred in behavioral approaches to assessment. Practitioners of behavioral assessment have moved from a period in which they focused on discrete units of behavior (reflecting strict adherence to a situational specific perspective) in rather constricted circumstances, to giving due attention to the interactionist view of behavior (Nelson & Hayes, 1981). Moreover, the field has advanced to the point that concern with more traditional concepts of measurement are now considered. Thus, considerable attention is directed to issues of reliability, validity, and other psychometric concepts (Cone, 1988). In summarizing the differences between behavioral and traditional assessment, it may be said that, although verbal report is considered important in behavioral assessment, the greater focus is on what the individual does as opposed to what he or she says (Nelson & Hayes, 1981).

DSM-III-R AND THE PRACTICE OF BEHAVIOR THERAPY

In the previous version of this chapter, we noted that it was difficult to determine the precise effect of DSM-III on the practice of behavior therapy. DSM-III-R does not differ in structure from DSM-III. The main differences are in the addition of a number of new diagnostic categories, the reliability of various categories, the refinement of a number of the existing diagnoses, and changes in Axes IV and V. Indeed, the DSM systems have drawn numerous criticisms (e.g., Schacht & Nathan, 1977), and we tend to concur with these. Similarly, a number of alternative systems have been proposed (e.g., Adams, Doster, & Calhoun, 1977; Cautela & Upper, 1976), but, as we noted previously, none of them has caught on. We also agree with Nelson and Hayes (1981):

> DSM-III (and its successor, DSM-III-R) holds certain advantages for behavioral assessors as a general classification scheme. For example, adopting the language of the DSM might help behaviorists to communicate with a professional world that is largely nonbehavioral. Such communication is useful in administrative record-keeping, satisfying third-party payers, writing grant proposals, preparing journal articles, referring clients, and as an entry into the psychological and psychiatric literature.
>
> *(pp. 13-14)*

We believe that the widespread use of the DSM terminology by behavior therapists has had a beneficial effect in most of the areas cited above.

It should be clear by now, however, that a diagnostic scheme implies more than a method for classifying psychiatric patients. Only the most naive observer could miss the political (Schacht, 1985; Spitzer, 1985), professional, and financial implications of the DSM systems (Garfield, 1986). Furthermore, the categorical approach to classification of abnormal behavior, upon which DSM is based, also has implications for the scientific study of psychopathology (Garfield, 1986; Zubin, 1978). For example, in some diagnostic categories, significant percentages of patients do not meet many of the core features of those categories. Rather than examining the validity of such categories, discrepancies are often dismissed or new subcategories are created to subsume the variance.

Currently, the DSM nosological system is driving our research efforts in psychopathology, yet the theoretical and empirical basis of that system is in some dispute. This dispute is captured, for example, in the arguments on the validity of categorical versus prototypical approaches to classification. Also, Eysenck (1986) argued that developers of DSM focused on the question of reliability, while the more critical issue was validity. Their attention to reliability was no doubt somewhat a function of previous criticism of the lack of reliability in psychiatric diagnoses. Eysenck is correct, however. The first concern should be validity, because, even though the concepts are related, it is possible to have very high reliability on a given diagnostic category and little validity. This issue is critical: A task force is already busily preparing the draft of DSM-IV in much the same fashion as DSM-III-R was prepared (i.e., without much attention to the issue of validity).

Moreover, the approach to arriving at the various diagnostic categories for DSM-III, DSM-III-R, and DSM-IV has been severely criticized. The basic problem is that decisions regarding which diagnostic categories to include were based on group discussion and consensus rather than empirical data (Garfield, 1986). This method is clearly at variance with the philosophy of behavioral assessment, and it represents a stumbling block to our efforts to develop a science of human behavior. Although the authors of DSM-IV began with the premise that no changes would be made in the system unless empirical data supported the change, the experience of one of us (SMT), who has served on two of the subgroups, indicates that the same political considerations plaguing the previous versions will again be problems in DSM-IV. Criteria for diagnoses are still being made by group "persuasion" rather than by empirical data, and certain individuals are unduly influencing the decision process based on their own idiosyncratic perspectives. Thus, the scientific merit of DSM-IV is not likely to be much better than that of DSM-III-R.

Despite these rather significant shortcomings, and regardless of whether we like it or not, whether we value its scientific credentials, and whether we cherish its political and financial objectives, DSM-III-R and its successor DSM-IV will be with us for the foreseeable future. Thus, it would be advantageous for behavior therapists to work within the system. Indeed, Yates (1981) had noted that a large percentage of individuals writing books on behavior therapy have followed traditional diagnostic lines when organizing their material. It appears that most prefer this over an organizational format that emphasizes techniques, a preference with which we concur.

Keeping in mind the severe limitations noted above, we do not see the DSM system as being totally incompatible with behavioral analysis and modification. First, classification is at the heart of every science. Thus, the current

DSM can provide the needed framework for making more specific behavioral analyses. Second, the notion of specific criteria for reaching a reliable diagnosis is consistent with both the problem-oriented approach to record keeping (Weed, 1968) and the goals of behavioral assessment (Hersen & Bellack, 1988a). Moreover, some of the specific criteria contributing to diagnosis of an overall syndrome may be used as targets for modification (e.g., interrupted sleep, depressed affect). Third, the importance of ruling out and/or establishing a medical component (i.e., Axis IV) to the comprehensive diagnostic picture is warranted (see Hersen, 1981). Fourth, we argue that the path leading to the final diagnosis (i.e., psychosocial stressors) needs greater attention than previously accorded in either traditional or behavioral diagnosis (Axes IV and V). Finally, by working from within the system, behaviorists are more likely to have an impact on future revisions of future DSMs and on the approach to diagnosis in general.

Given the current political realities, it behooves the behavior therapist to be conversant with DSM-III-R terminology. For communicating with psychiatric colleagues, for consistency of diagnoses in research, and for reimbursement from third-party payers, use of the DSM-III-R is a necessity. Furthermore, in view of Nathan's (1981) observation as to equal utility and reliability, perhaps DSM-III-R is as good a system as we have at the moment. Nathan further commented, however, that, "behavioral analysis may be the only categorization system capable of identifying the environment and cognitive variables necessary to change variables which have less to do with 'symptoms' than with the factors on which the symptomatic behaviors are contingent" (p. 9). This latter statement clearly reflects an additional area in which the DSM system is inadequate and suggests how it might be improved. At the individual case level, following DSM-III-R imposes little restraint on the use of further assessment strategies necessary for an adequate assessment and for selecting treatment intervention. Thus, the behavior therapist is free to use the DSM-III-R as well as to conduct other necessary assessment strategies.

PSYCHIATRIC DIAGNOSIS AND CLASSIFICATION IN GENERAL

Why ascribe a diagnostic label at all? This question is particularly relevant in light of the charges that labeling negatively influences the labeled individual for the rest of his or her life (e.g., Klerman, 1977; Tarrier, 1979). Moreover, the use of various diagnoses appears to be associated with such variables as social and cultural factors (Kahn, 1973), socioeconomic factors (Maracek & Kravitz, 1977), and race (Adebimpe, 1982). Szasz (1966) argued that mental illness is a myth and that the assignment of a diagnostic label removes responsibility for various actions from the individual so labeled. Moreover, Rosenhan (1973) poignantly demonstrated that, once the label is affixed, it is virtually impossible to have it removed, regardless of the type of behavior displayed.

Thus, we in the psychiatric arena appear to have a diagnostic system that may negatively influence the lives of patients; is culturally, racially, and sexually biased; and often is unresponsive to the type of overt behavior displayed. These statements are true, DSM-III-R notwithstanding. Despite the difficulties inherent in the current diagnostic scheme, few would recommend abandoning attempts to classify mental disorders. It often has been stated that a classification system is the basis of any science. Thus, Adams et al. (1977) argued:

> The first and fundamental step in the study of behavior, including abnormal behavior, is the grouping of observations into an organized scheme so as to make sense of the bewildering array of response patterns. Classification is the basis of any science because it is the process of identification of a phenomenon so that events can be measured and communication can occur between scientists and professionals.
>
> *(p. 47)*

Indeed, if we are to have a science of human behavior, a system of classification is essential. Moreover, at the practical level, if third-party payers are to reimburse for clinical services, some type of categorization is necessary such that a decision can be made as to which disorders will be covered for reimbursement and which will not. The need for classification exists at the philosophical, scientific, professional, and practical levels.

Although the DSM-III-R system of classification is not the only one available for use, none of the alternatives has caught on. Most of the alternatives have been proposed by psychologists (e.g., Adams et al., 1977; Goldfried & Sprafkin, 1976; Kanfer & Saslow, 1965; McLemore & Benjamin, 1979), and, like the DSM system, little attempt has been made to conduct the requisite psychometric studies of these systems. Therefore, there are no data documenting their possible superiority.

In short, some type of classification system for mental disorders is required if there is to be a science of abnormal behavior. Although DSM-III-R and its predecessors have been severely criticized for their shortcomings, none of the proposed alternatives has been shown to be more reliable or valid, or to be free from the other biases cited above. One area in which a behavioral approach to assessment could bolster the DSM approach is treatment selection. A behavioral approach to assessment can lead directly to treatment intervention, whereas this is typically not the case with a DSM diagnosis. Inclusion of the multiaxial system in DSM-III, DSM-III-R and IV bridges this gap somewhat, but it remains to be seen what influences Axes IV and V actually will have on the selection of treatment procedures (see Perry et al., 1990).

SUMMARY

Although the DSM system was conceived in a relatively nonempirical fashion and represents a traditional approach to assessment, it probably is as effective as any other system of classification available at this time. Most of the improvements in DSM-III were related to its increased interrater reliability and the inclusion of the multiaxial diagnostic system, and this is the case for DSM-III-R as well. Although the philosophies underlying behavioral assessment and the DSM are divergent, following the new diagnostic scheme is essential for the behavior therapist to communicate with his or her nonbehavioral colleagues. In addition, DSM-III-R is the system currently employed to reimburse for clinical services. Moreover, improved aspects of the DSM have led at least one behavior therapist (Nathan, 1981) to argue that systematic assessment and behavioral assessment are now about equal in utility and reliability. Use of DSM-III-R does not preclude application of behavioral methods of assessment, which are necessary for the behavior therapist to select a treatment strategy. At this level, DSM-III-R significantly lags behind the behavioral approach to assessment. Choosing a specific diagnostic category in DSM-III-R does not lead to the empirical use of a specific treatment intervention, psychotic disorders and drug therapy notwithstanding. However, Perry et al. (1990) present clinical data for treatment selection based on DSM-III-R. Although the multiaxial approach introduced with DSM-III, and maintained in DSM-III-R, represents a significant advancement in psychiatric diagnosis, and moves it slightly toward a behavioral perspective, it remains to be seen how reliable Axes IV and V are and how they will influence treatment.

A classification system is essential if progress is to be made in any science; however, to this point, the scientific footing on which the DSM system is based is perhaps its greatest deficiency. Unfortunately, DSM-IV will share this same weakness. Behavioral assessors can play an instrumental role in revealing the nature of these deficiencies and, by doing so, can play an instrumental role in moving the field toward developing a system of classification that is scientifically meritorious.

REFERENCES

Adams, H. E., Doster, J. A., & Calhoun, D. S. (1977). A psychologically based system of response classification. In A. R. Ciminero, K. S. Calhoun, & H. E. Adams (Eds.), *Handbook of behavioral assessment* (pp. 47–78). New York: Wiley.

Adebimpe, V. R. (1982). Psychiatric symptoms in black patients. In S. M. Turner & R. T. Jones (Eds.), *Behavior modification in black populations: Psychosocial issues and empirical findings* (pp. 57–71). New York: Plenum Press.

American Psychiatric Association. (1980a). *Diagnostic and statistical manual of mental disorders* (3rd ed.) Washington, DC: Author.

American Psychiatric Association. (1980b). *Quick reference to diagnostic criteria from DSM-III.* Washington, DC: Author.

American Psychiatric Association. (1987a). *Diagnostic and statistical manual of mental disorders* (3rd ed. rev.). Washington, DC: Author.

American Psychiatric Association. (1987b). *Quick reference to diagnostic criteria from DSM-III-R.* Washington, DC: Author.

Andreasen, N. C., Grove, W. M., Shapiro, R. W., Keller, M. B., Hirschfeld, R. M. A., & McDonald-Scott, P. (1981). Reliability of lifetime diagnosis: A multicenter collaborative perspective. *Archives of General Psychiatry, 38,* 400–405.

Ash, P. (1949). The reliability of psychiatric diagnosis. *Journal of Abnormal and Social Psychology, 44,* 272–276.

Barlow, D. H. (Ed.). (1981). *Behavioral assessment of adult disorders.* New York: Guilford Press.

Begelman, D. A. (1975). Ethical and legal issues in behavior modification. In M. Hersen, R. M. Eisler, & P. M. Miller (Eds.), *Progress in behavior modification* (Vol. 1, pp. 159–189). New York: Academic Press.

Cantwell, D. P., & Baker, L. (1988). Special Article—Issues in the classification of child and adolescent psychopathology. *Journal of the American Academy of Child and Adolescent Psychiatry, 27,* 521–533.

Cautela, J. R., & Upper, D. (1976). The behavioral inventory battery: The use of self-report measures in behavioral analysis and therapy. In M. Hersen & A. S. Bellack (Eds.), *Behavioral assessment: A practical handbook* (pp. 77–109). New York: Pergamon Press.

Ciminero, A. (1982). Behavioral assessment: An overview. In A. Ciminero, K. S. Calhoun, & H. E. Adams (Eds.), *Handbook of behavioral assessment* (2nd ed., pp. 3–11). New York: Wiley.

Cohen, E. S., Harbin, H. T., & Wright, M. J. (1975). Some consideration in the formulation of psychiatric diagnosis. *Journal of Nervous and Mental Disease, 160,* 422–427.

Cone, J. D. (1981). Psychometric considerations. In M. Hersen & A. S. Bellack (Eds.), *Behavioral assessment: A practical handbook* (2nd ed., pp. 38–68). New York: Pergamon Press.

Cone, J. D. (1988). Psychometric considerations and the multiple models of behavioral assessment. In M. Hersen & A. S. Bellack (Eds.), *Behavioral assessment: A practical handbook* (3rd ed., pp. 42–66). New York: Pergamon Press.

Eisler, R. M., Hersen, M., Miller, P. M., & Wooten, L. S. (1973). Treatment expectations of psychiatric inpatients and their relationships to psychiatric diagnosis. *Journal of Clinical Psychology, 29,* 251–253.

Eisler, R. M., & Polak, P. R. (1971). Social stress and psychiatric disorder. *Journal of Nervous and Mental Disease, 53,* 227–233.

Endler, N. S. (1973). The person versus the situation—A pseudo issue? A response to Alka. *Journal of Personality, 41,* 297–303.

Eysenck, H. J. (1986). A critique of contemporary classifications and diagnosis. In T. Millon & G. L. Klerman (Eds.), *Contemporary directions in psychopathology: Toward the DSM-IV* (pp. 73–98). New York: Guilford Press.

Frances, A., & Cooper, A. M. (1981). Descriptive and dynamic psychiatry: A perspective on DSM-III. *American Journal of Psychiatry, 138–139,* 1198–1202.

Frank, G. (1969). Psychiatric diagnosis: A review of research. *Journal of General Psychology, 81,* 157–176.

Frank, G. (1975). *Psychiatric diagnosis: A review of research.* Oxford: Pergamon Press.

Garfield, S. L. (1986). Problems in diagnostic classification. In T. Millon & G. L. Klerman (Eds.), *Contemporary directions in psychopathology: Toward the DSM-IV* (pp. 99–114). New York: Guilford Press.

Goffman, E. (1973). The inmate world. In T. Millon (Ed.), *Theories of psychopathology and personality* (pp. 422–426). Philadelphia: Saunders.

Goldfried, M. R., & Kent, R. N. (1972). Traditional versus behavioral personality assessment: A comparison of methodological and theoretical assumptions. *Psychological Bulletin, 77,* 409–420.

Goldfried, M. R., & Linehan, M. M. (1977). Basic issues in behavioral assessment. In A. Ciminero, K. S. Calhoun, & H. E. Adams (Eds.), *Handbook of behavioral assessment* (pp. 15–46). New York: Wiley.

Goldfried, M. R., & Sprafkin, J. M. (1976). Behavioral personality assessment. In J. T. Spence, R. C. Corron, & J. W. Thibaut (Eds.), *Behavioral approaches to therapy.* Morristown, NJ: General Learning Press.

Goodneough, F. L. (1949). Mental testing. New York: Rinehart.

Grove, M. A., Andreasen, N. C., McDonald-Scott, P., Keller, M. B., & Shapiro, R. W. (1981). Reliability studies of psychiatric diagnosis: Theory and practice. *Archives of General Psychiatry, 38,* 408–413.

Hartshorne, H., & May, A. (1928). *Studies in the nature of character: Vol. 1. Studies in deceit.* New York: Macmillan.

Hayes, S. C., Nelson, R. O., & Jarrett, R. B. (1987). The treatment utility of assessment: A functional approach to evaluating assessment quality. *American Psychologist, 42,* 963–974.

Haynes, S. N. (1988). Causal models and the assessment–treatment relationship in behavior therapy. *Journal of Psychopathology and Behavioral Assessment, 10,* 171–183.

Haynes, S. N., & O'Brien, W. H. (1988). The gordian knot of DSM-III-R use: Integrating principles of behavior classification and complex causal models. *Behavioral Assessment, 10,* 95–105.

Hersen, M. (1976). Historical perspectives in behavioral assessment. In M. Hersen & A. S. Bellack (Eds.), *Behavioral assessment: A practical handbook* (pp. 3–22). New York: Pergamon Press.

Hersen, M. (1981). Complex problems require complex solutions. *Behavior Therapy, 12,* 15–29.

Hersen, M. (1988). Behavioral assessment and psychiatric diagnosis. *Behavioral Assessment, 10,* 107–121.

Hersen, M., & Bellack, A. S. (Eds.). (1976). *Behavioral assessment: A practical handbook* (1st ed.). New York: Pergamon Press.

Hersen, M., & Bellack, A. S. (Eds.). (1981). *Behavioral assessment: A practical handbook* (2nd ed.). New York: Pergamon Press.

Hersen, M., & Bellack, A. S. (Eds.). (1988a). *Behavioral assessment: A practical handbook* (3rd ed.). New York: Pergamon Press.

Hersen, M., & Bellack, A. S. (Eds.). (1988b). *Dictionary of behavioral assessment techniques.* New York: Pergamon Press.

Hollon, S. D., & Bemis, K. M. (1981). Self-report and the assessment of cognitive functions. In M. Hersen & A. S. Bellack (Eds.), *Behavioral assessment: A practical handbook* (2nd ed., pp. 125–174). New York: Pergamon Press.

Kahn, M. L. (1973). Social class and schizophrenia: A critical review and reformulation. *Schizophrenia Bulletin, 1,* 60–79.

Kallman, W. M., & Feurstein, M. J. (1977). Psychophysiological procedures. In A. R. Ciminero, K. S. Calhoun, & H. E. Adams (Eds.), *Handbook of behavioral assessment* (2nd ed., pp. 329–364). New York: Wiley.

Kallman, W. M., & Feuerstein, M. J. (1986). In A. R. Ciminero, K. S. Calhoun, & H. W. Adams (Eds.), Handbook of behavioral assessment (2nd ed., pp. 325–350). New York: Wiley.

Kanfer, F., & Saslow, G. (1965). Behavioral diagnosis. *Archives of General Psychiatry, 12,* 529–538.

Kazdin, A. E. (1981). Behavioral observations. In M. Hersen & A. S. Bellack (Eds.), *Behavioral assessment: A practical handbook* (2nd ed., pp. 101–124). New York: Pergamon Press.

Kendler, K. S., Spitzer, R. L., & Williams, J. B. W. (1989). Psychotic disorders in DSM-III-R. *American Journal of Psychiatry, 146,* 953–962.

Klerman, G. L. (1977). Mental illness, the medical model, and psychiatry. In S. Toulmin (Ed.), Special issue on mental illness. *Journal of Medical Philosophy, 2,* 220–243.

Livingston, S. A. (1977). Psychometric techniques for criterion referenced testing and behavioral assessment. In J. D. Cone & R. P. Hawkins (Eds.), *Behavioral assessment: New directions in clinical psychology* (pp. 308–329). New York: Brunner/Mazel.

Maracek, J., & Kravitz, D. (1977). Women and mental health: A review of feminist change efforts. *Psychiatry, 40,* 323–328.

McLemore, C. W., & Benjamin, L. S. (1979). Whatever happened to interpersonal diagnosis? A psychosocial alternative to DSM-III. *American Psychologist, 34,* 17–33.

McReynolds, W. T. (1979). DSM-III and the future of applied social science. *Professional Psychology, 10,* 123–132.

Mischel, W. (1968). *Personality and assessment.* New York: Wiley.

Mischel, W. (1972). Direct versus indirect personality assessment: Evidence and implications. *Journal of Consulting and Clinical Psychology, 38,* 319–324.

Mischel, W. (1977). On the future of personality measurement. *American Psychologist, 32,* 246–254.

Nathan, P. E. (1969). A systems analytic model of diagnosis: The diagnostic validity of disordered consciousness. *Journal of Clinical Psychology, 25,* 243–246.

Nathan, P. E. (1981). Symptomatic diagnosis and behavioral assessment: A synthesis. In D. H. Barlow (Ed.), *Behavioral assessment of adult disorders* (pp. 1–11). New York: Guilford Press.

Nathan, P. E., Andberg, M., Behan, P. O., & Patch, V. D. (1969). Thirty-two observers and one patient—A study of diagnostic reliability. *Journal of Clinical Psychology, 25,* 9–15.

Nathan, P. E., Gould, C. F., Zare, N. C., & Roth, M. A. (1969). Systems analysis of diagnosis: VI. Improved diagnostic validity from median data. *Journal of Clinical Psychology, 25,* 270–275.

Nathan, P. E., Robertson, P., & Andberg, M. M. (1969). A systems analytic model of diagnosis: IV. The diagnostic validity of abnormal affective behavior. *Journal of Clinical Psychology, 25,* 235–242.

Nathan, P. E., Simpson, H. F., & Andberg, M. M. (1969). A systems analytic model of diagnosis: II. The diagnostic validity of abnormal perceptual behavior. *Journal of Clinical Psychology, 25,* 115–119.

Nathan, P. E., Zare, N. C., Simpson, H. F., & Andberg, M. M. (1969). A systems analytic model of diagnosis: I. The diagnostic validity of abnormal psychomotor behavior. *Journal of Clinical Psychology 25,* 3–9.

Nay, W. R. (1977). Analogue measures. In A. R. Ciminero, K. S. Calhoun, & H. E. Adams (Eds.), *Handbook of behavior assessment* (2nd ed., pp. 233–277). New York: Wiley.

Nay, W. R. (1986). Analogue measures. In A. R. Ciminero, K. S. Calhoun, & H. H. Adams (Eds.), *Handbook of behavioral assessment* (2nd ed., pp. 223–252). New York: Wiley.

Nelson, R. O., & Barlow, D. H. (1981). Behavioral assessment: Basic strategic and initial procedures. In D. H. Barlow (Ed.), *Behavioral assessment of adult disorders* (pp. 13–43). New York: Guilford Press.

Nelson, R. O., & Hayes, S. C. (1981). The nature of behavioral assessment. In M. Hersen & A. S. Bellack (Eds.), *Behavioral assessment: A practical handbook* (2nd ed., pp. 3–37). New York: Pergamon Press.

Parks, C. W., Jr., & Hollon, S. D. (1988). Cognitive assessment. In A. S. Bellack and M. Hersen (Eds.), Behavioral assessment: A practical handbook (3rd ed., pp. 161–212).

Perry, S., Frances, A., & Clarkin, J. (1990). *A DSM-III-R casebook of treatment selection.* New York: Brunner/Mazel.

Ray, N. J., & Raczynski, J. M. (1981). Psychophysiological assessment. In M. Hersen & A. S. Bellack (Eds.), *Behavioral assessment: A practical handbook* (2nd ed., pp. 175–211). New York: Pergamon Press.

Rey, J. M. (1988). DSM-III-R: Too much too soon? *Australian and New Zealand Journal of Psychiatry, 22,* 173–182.

Rey, J. M., Stewart, G. W., Plapp, J. M., Bashir, M. R., & Richard, I. N. (1988). Sources of unreliability of DSM-III Axis IV revisited. *Archives of General Psychiatry, 145,* 286–292.

Rosenhan, D. L. (1973). On being sane in insane places. *Science, 179,* 250–258.

Sandifer, M. G., Pettus, G., & Quade, D. (1964). A study of psychiatric diagnosis. *Journal of Nervous and Mental Disease, 139,* 350–356.

Schacht, T. E. (1985). Reply to Spitzer's "Politics–science dichotomy syndrome." *American Psychologist, 40,* 562–563.

Schacht, T., & Nathan, P. E. (1977). But is it good for the psychologists? Appraisal and status of DSM-III. *American Psychologist, 32,* 1017–1025.

Sheehan, K. H., Sheehan, D. V., & Shaw, K. R. (1988). Diagnosis and treatment of anxiety disorders in children and adolescents. *Psychiatric Annals, 18,* 146–157.

Spitzer, R. L. (1981). Nonmedical myths and the DSM-III. *American Psychological Association Monitor, 12,* 3, 33.

Spitzer, R. (1985). DSM-III and the politics–science dichotomy syndrome: A response to Thomas E. Schacht's "DSM-III and the politics of truth." *American Psychologist, 40,* 522–526.

Spitzer, R. L., & Fleiss, J. L. (1974). A re-analysis of the reliability of psychiatric diagnosis. *British Journal of Psychiatry, 125,* 341–347.

Spitzer, R. L., & Forman, J. B. W. (1979). DSM-III field trials: II. Initial experience with the multiaxial system. *American Journal of Psychiatry, 136,* 818–820.

Spitzer, R. L., Forman, J. B. W., & Nee, J. (1979). DSM-III field trials: I. Initial interrater diagnostic reliability. *American Journal of Psychiatry, 136,* 815–817.

Spitzer, R. L., Skodol, A. E., Gibbon, M., & Williams, J. B. W. (1981). *DSM-III case book: A learning companion to the diagnostic and statistical manual of mental disorders* (3rd ed.). Washington, DC: American Psychiatric Association.

Spitzer, R. L., Williams, J. B. W., & Skodol, A. E. (1980). DSM-III: The major achievements and an overview. *American Journal of Psychiatry, 137,* 151–164.

Szasz, T. S. (1966). The psychiatric classification of behavior: A strategy of personal constraint. In L. D. Eron (Ed.), *The classification of behavior disorders* (pp. 38–41). Chicago: Aldine.

Tarrier, N. (1979). The future of the medical model: A reply to Guse (An editorial). *Journal of Nervous and Mental Disease, 167,* 71–73.

Tasto, D. L. (1977). Self-report schedules and inventories. In A. Ciminero, K. S. Calhoun, & H. E. Adams (Eds.), *Handbook of behavioral assessment* (pp. 153–193). New York: Wiley.

Weed, L. L. (1968). Medical records that guide and teach. *New England Journal of Medicine, 278,* 593–600.

Yates, A. J. (1981). Behavior therapy: Past, present, future: Imperfect? *Clinical Psychology Review, 3,* 269–291.

Zubin, J. (1967). Classification of the behavior disorders. In P. R. Farnsworth & Q. McNemar (Eds.), *Annual review of psychology* (pp. 373–406). Palo Alto, CA: Annual Reviews.

Zubin, J. (1978). But is it good for science? *Clinical Psychologist, 31*(2), 3–7.

CHAPTER 17

DSM-III-R and Pharmacotherapy

DONALD W. GOODWIN, SHELDON H. PRESKORN, and HAROLD M. ERICKSON

The third edition of the American Psychiatric Association's (APA's) *Diagnostic and Statistical Manual of Mental Disorders* (DSM-III) returned the emphasis in American psychiatry to the fine points of making a diagnosis, an emphasis largely absent during the heydey of psychoanalysis. The revised edition of DSM-III was published in 1987 (DSM-III-R). Apart from the addition of some new categories and the changes to criteria for substance abuse, changes were relatively minor. One disconcerting aspect about the development of new criteria every few years is that the Holy Grail of consistency so desirable in research takes second fiddle (to mix some metaphors) to the irresistible urge to invent new criteria.

Although DSM-III and DSM-III-R differed in relatively minor ways, DSM-IV, which is planned for 1994, will likely introduce major changes. One reason is that Robert L. Spitzer, the intrepid commander of the two DSM-III works, is no longer in charge. The DSM-III committees have been dissolved and replaced largely by new members, many with different philosophical views from those of their predecessors. This change in outlook may not make much difference in the world of clinical psychiatry, but research is bound to suffer. Thousands of studies base their diagnoses on DSM-III or DSM-III-R. Changes in diagnostic criteria could easily result in charges that studies based on "old" criteria are no longer valid. Reproducibility, the essence of science, will be even more difficult. When old and new studies disagree, no one will be certain whether the populations or the criteria explain the difference. The new leadership has promised not to make changes for changes' sake, but, given the theoretical shake-up in the committee membership, profound changes seem inevitable.

Meanwhile, the movement in DSM-III toward operational criteria—as precise and nontheoretical as possible—represented a major advance in psychiatric research. Everyone hopes the general principles embraced by DSM-III will not be abandoned in future DSM editions. With psychoanalysis on the wane, diagnosis is "in." The change is still relatively recent, less than a decade old, and we have not had time to answer questions about how the change has affected the practice of psychiatry or how the reemphasis on

---

Dr. Sheldon H. Preskorn's work was supported in part by the Veterans Administration and the Psychiatric Research Institute at St. Francis Regional Medical Center, Wichita, Kansas.

diagnosis, as embodied in DSM-III-R, has affected the way we treat patients and prescribe medications. There is almost no information bearing on these questions.

We have attempted to assemble data relating to one facet of the issue: Are drug studies improved by diagnostic criteria? First, however, some other questions must be asked. Are drug responses diagnostic? If not, why not? Is the problem with the drug or with the diagnosis? These issues are discussed in this chapter, and reasons are given as to why even the best drug studies can produce erroneous results. Following this material, the diagnostic criteria used in DSM-III-R are discussed, as well as the standardized interviews that provide the information to which criteria are applied. Some problems with reliability are involved in the application of criteria and administration of interviews, and these, too, are discussed. Finally, the contribution of DSM-III-R to pharmacotherapy is assessed.

DRUGS AND DIAGNOSES

Are Drugs Diagnostic?

For a long time, it has been recognized that few treatments are specific for psychiatric disorders. Treatment response might support a diagnosis, but never confirm it. For example, if a patient diagnosed as manic improves with lithium, this does not prove that he or she had mania; on the other hand, if he or she does not improve, it does not prove that he or she was not manic. Nevertheless, lithium is widely regarded as *the* most specific of psychiatric treatments. In truth, however, lithium has been reported effective in many disorders, including schizophrenia, alcoholism, migraine, ménière's disease, premenstrual tension, and granulocytopenia (which it also causes) (Bunney & Garland-Bunney, 1989).

It is not surprising that lithium has been tried for many disorders because the common notion in psychiatry is that, if something works for one condition, it probably is good for something else as well. Hence, electroconvulsive therapy (ECT) has at times been successful for epilepsy, phenothiazines for hiccups, and antidepressants for enuresis. Undoubtedly, however, some treatments are better for some conditions than others. For example, lithium is almost certainly better for mania than for premenstrual tension. The point is that, in general, the treatment response is not diagnostic.

Problems in Assessment

For drug therapy, the two reasons for the rather poor fit of treatment to diagnosis both arise from the need for formal studies to assess drug efficacy. The first involves Type I errors; the second involves Type II errors.

A Type I error occurs when a drug appears effective but is not. Although all prescription drugs are compared "blindly" with placebos and found superior before being marketed, even the best studies have defects. For example, active drugs (even if not active for the conditions being treated) may appear superior to a placebo because active drugs often have side effects, such as sleepiness or dry mouth. Patients on active drugs thus *know* they are taking a drug, and this knowledge may increase expectations of improvement, which, in the case of psychological illness, may produce improvement. When the side effects are distressing, another artifact may occur: Patients may *say* they are better to avoid taking the drug.

Another reason for Type I errors relates to the natural history of psychiatric disorders. Many patients undergo spontaneous remission without treatment. When the drug is found only marginally superior to a placebo, this may reflect a higher rate of spontaneous remission in the experimental group than in controls, despite efforts to "match" the groups. In psychotropic drug studies, the test drug may produce improvement in, say, 80 percent of the patients, whereas the placebo produces improvement in 40 percent of patients. Although this difference may be *statistically* significant, it may not be *clinically* significant. Subsequent studies may not show the difference at all, but these studies may appear after the drug has been released. It is also likely that the government and physicians give more credence to positive studies than to negative ones, a tendency not discouraged by the pharmaceutical industry. This tendency would probably occur anyway because of the natural desire by everyone for better treatments.

A Type II error occurs when a treatment is effective but studies do not show it. Perhaps the most common Type II error comes from samples that are too small to show statistically significant differences even if they exist. For example, if Drug A is compared with a placebo in ten studies with 20 subjects each, seven of the ten studies will fail to show a significant difference even if there is one.[1]

Type II errors also result from studies in which drugs that are potentially good are given in the wrong doses, at the wrong times, or by the wrong route.

---

[1] These data came from a computer simulation study performed by Davis, Gibbons, Pandey, and Javard (1981) at the University of Chicago. Davis et al. assumed that

> manifest dichotomous observations [i.e., one if improved, zero if unimproved] actually reflect the crossing of a threshold of an underlying latent continuous dimension. If this assumption is reasonable, then a natural method of simulating such a response process is to simulate a normal distribution with mean zero and variance one and dichotomize the normal deviates at the desired probability points.

In Davis et al.'s study, two populations were simulated. In the first, 100 simulated responses were dichotomized at the 65 percent point on the normal distribution and a second 100 at the 35 percent point. In the second population, the probability points were 75 and 25 percent, respectively.

Given these two simulated populations, ten samples of ten observations in each were drawn from both subsamples within each population. The result was a group of twenty fourfold contingency tables: ten were drawn from a population with proportions 65 versus 35 percent and ten with population proportions 75 versus 25 percent. Only three significant uncorrected and two significant corrected chi-square statistics were obtained from the population in which the actual difference in proportions was 30 percent. Even when the difference in proportions was 75 versus 25 percent, only six of the ten randomly drawn contingency tables yielded significant uncorrected chi-square statistics. Hence, sampling variability and the insensitivity of the chi-square statistic produced a strong negative consensus even when the actual difference in proportions in the population was significant. Even when the population difference was as great as 50 percent, the individual chi-square statistics yielded near-random results.

Many psychotropics were originally tested in a lower dose than was later found optimal. The reverse also happens: Too much may be as ineffective as too little (the "therapeutic window" effect). Long half-lives may mean that a single dose is better than multiple doses, but the design may have omitted this consideration. Some drugs are better absorbed orally than intramuscularly, but this may not be known until after the studies are done (e.g., chlordiazepoxide).

Another source of Type II errors is heterogeneous samples. The phenothiazines, when first studied for schizophrenia, were found ineffective (Gildea, 1958). Later studies showed them to be useful. In the early studies, acute and chronic schizophrenics were unknowingly combined in both drug and placebo groups. Since acute schizophrenia, by definition, spontaneously remits, acute schizophrenics in the placebo group inflated the improvement rate so that it did not differ from that of the drug group. Separating acute from chronic schizophrenia is clinically possible in a high percentage of cases, but for some reason the first investigators did not do so.

Both classical and operant conditioning may contribute to Type I and Type II errors. As Wortis (1989) pointed out, gastric secretion, peristalsis, release of insulin, and hormonal activity are all subject to conditioning:

> Their circadian rhythm itself may well be the product of conditioning with cues, or *Zeitgebers,* derived from light or dark or other attendant circumstances. In isolation chambers or space vehicles these rhythms go awry. Basic physiological mechanisms, to be sure, are released by their appropriate unconditioned stimuli, but in their absence a substitute will do, at least for awhile, until extinction supervenes. If the associated stimulus persists, the pattern of habit will remain more fixed. This also applies to visceral conditioning. After a series of insulin injections, for example, an injection of saline will induce hypoglycemia.
>
> *(p. 371)*

A pill or capsule functions as a conditioned stimulus. When beneficial results are expected, they may occur purely on a conditioned basis; if side effects are feared, these also may occur on a conditioned basis. Such expectations no doubt explain in part the placebo effect, as well as the *failure* of drugs in some cases to exert therapeutic effects.

THE CONTRIBUTIONS OF DSM-III AND DSM-III-R

Diagnostic Criteria

As noted, DSM-III-R included only modest changes from DSM-III. (For the sake of conciseness, the following observations refer to DSM-III with the understanding that they apply equally to DSM-III-R.) In its 5 years of deliberations, the 19-member APA Task Force on Nomenclature and Statistics came up with several innovations in DSM-III that helped produce the ultimate hefty volume of 481 pages (DSM-II had only 119 pages). These included a multiaxial system of diagnosis, a decision tree for differential diagnosis, and field trials. Undoubtedly, the most important innovation was diagnostic criteria.

Each of the 230 diagnostic categories in DSM-III has diagnostic criteria, including both inclusion and exclusion criteria. To receive a diagnosis, a patient must have certain symptoms and lack certain others. Often, the patient must exhibit a particular course. The duration of symptoms is often specified: depending on the category, the patient must be sick for at least 6 months, no longer than 1 week, less than 2 hours, and so forth. Some major categories have subcategories, in which case the patient must fulfill a certain number of subitems to be eligible for the parent category. Because diagnosis consists of choosing items from a number of categories, DSM-III's diagnostic criteria have sometimes been compared to a "Chinese menu approach" to diagnosis.

In early drafts of DSM-III, diagnostic criteria were presented as sacrosanct; that is, patients were expected to fulfill all criteria to qualify for the diagnosis. In the final version, the criteria were called "guides" based on "clinical judgment." According to the authors of DSM-III, although such important correlates as clinical course, outcome, family history, and treatment response had not been fully validated, the diagnostic criteria were expected to enhance interjudge diagnostic reliability. Field trials did show a high degree of reliability, but only of a certain kind; reliability has many facets, as discussed later.

Meanwhile, it is important to know how the diagnostic criteria were derived. They were invented. People sat around a table and discussed their pros and cons, and finally took a vote. Published studies formed the basis for the criteria only as they filtered through the minds of the committee members and consultants. In essence, the criteria are *arbitrary*.

Some would argue that the criteria are not *entirely* arbitrary. Diagnostic criteria had been established for psychiatric diagnosis long before DSM-III. In the early 1960s, clinical investigators at Washington University in St. Louis, The New York State Psychiatric Institute in New York, and the Institute of Psychiatry in London shared the belief that "seat-of-the-pants" diagnosis was inadequate for clinical studies and that criteria not only would improve communication but would yield reproducible studies.

Many members of the DSM-III committee, including its chairman, had experience working with diagnostic criteria. The problem was that criteria-based studies were still relatively few in number, suffered from considerable inconsistencies, and, as said, were introduced into the DSM-III criteria-inventing process only to help influence judgments of the committee members.

Although we agree with the assumption that diagnostic criteria are worthwhile, virtually no evidence supports this assumption. Thus, the question can still be asked: Are diagnostic criteria superior to no criteria? We can address this question as it relates to pharmacotherapy by comparing studies using diagnostic groups having few or no criteria with studies using groups having more elaborate criteria.

We conducted such a study using depression as our model illness and the placebo response as our criterion. Our hypothesis was that diagnoses with explicit, well-developed criteria, compared with those having vaguely defined

TABLE 17.1.   Antidepressant Versus Placebo Improvement Rate in Two
Types of Depression (Mean ± Standard Deviation)

	Endogenous Depression Studies[a] (N = 11)	Neurotic Depression Studies (N = 11)
Improved on antidepressant	56 ± 24%	62 ± 27%
Improved on placebo	17 ± 7%[b]	70 ± 8%

[a]See text for definitions of endogenous and neurotic depression. The data are taken from double-blind placebo versus antidepressant studies listed in the bibliographies of the following review articles: Klerman and Cole (1965); Morris and Beck (1974); Raskin (1974); and Welner, Welner, and Robins (1980).

[b]Different from both "endogenous depression" treated with an antidepressant and "neurotic depression" treated with a placebo ($p < .001$ using Student's t-test).

criteria, would yield a relatively homogeneous group of patients, reflected in a larger difference between drug and placebo response rates.[2]

To test the hypothesis, we compared improvement rates from antidepressant drugs and placebo in two groups of depressions, which we called "endogenous" and "neurotic." Endogenous depression is roughly synonymous with manic–depressive disease, primary affective disorder, and major depressive disorder (the new DSM-III term), whereas neurotic depression is sometimes called reactive depression. Historically, the former category has come to represent a group of explicit psychological and physiologic symptoms that lend themselves to a DSM-III-type structuralization. In contrast, neurotic or reactive depressions tend to be defined in a vague and sketchy manner, sometimes with dysphoria as the single manifestation.

As shown in Table 17.1, studies of endogenous depression found a significantly smaller placebo response than did studies of neurotic depression. The drug response, however, was roughly comparable in the two sets of studies. These results support our thesis that diagnostic entities with explicit, well-developed criteria elicit larger differences between drug and placebo response rates because response within the more explicitly defined group is more homogeneously determined and therefore more sensitive to differences in therapeutic intervention (i.e., specific drug actions vs. the more general placebo effect).

For this specific example, however, another explanation is possible. The spontaneous remission rate in neurotic depressions may be higher than in endogenous depressions. If so, the high placebo rate in neurotic depressives merely reflects the fact that most people with this diagnosis recover without

---

[2]Diagnostic homogeneity implies that patients diagnosed as having a specific condition are identical with regard to certain clinical symptoms, and/or natural history, and/or treatment response. The diagnostic criteria contained in DSM-III increase the likelihood that patients are homogeneous to the extent that the diagnostician adheres to the diagnostic rules, but they do not guarantee homogeneity. Uniformity of signs and symptoms, or laboratory results, does not necessarily reflect a common pathophysiology. For example, glycogen storage diseases can result from several different enzymatic defects with different inheritance patterns; parkinsonism can result from dopaminergic neuronal loss or from treatment with drugs; hyperuricemia may be due to an inborn error of metabolism or to excessive production of nucleic acid from leukemia.

drug intervention. Evidence based on follow-up studies, however, indicates that endogenous depressions actually remit spontaneously more often than neurotic depressions, which, with their diffuse boundaries, tend to persist indefinitely. If this evidence is correct, then the placebo rate presumably would be *lower* in the neurotic group rather than higher. Despite our findings, the assumption that diagnostic criteria indeed produce more homogeneous diagnostic groups remains untested.

Reliability

The introduction to DSM-III does not claim that diagnostic homogeneity results from more specific diagnostic criteria. Rather, diagnostic criteria are promised to improve reliability (interjudge agreement). It is not inevitable that improved reliability will result in purer diagnostic categories with regard to course, outcome, or etiology. Just because two people agree does not mean that both are not wrong. Nevertheless, the value of DSM-III depends almost entirely on whether it does indeed improve reliability, and without reliability it is unlikely that diagnostic homogeneity will be achieved.

Field trials of DSM-III were conducted in more than 200 facilities, using successive drafts of the manual. Perhaps the most important part of the study was the evaluation of diagnostic reliability by having pairs of clinicians make independent diagnostic judgments of the same patient. The clinicians were from all parts of the country and a variety of backgrounds. "Detailed instructions" were given to avoid biases, but only two instructions are mentioned in DSM-III: Do not select easy cases, and do not discuss the patient before filling out the diagnostic forms. The two clinicians were either present at the same interview or did separate evaluations. A total of 384 clinicians interviewed 796 patients.

The results, according to DSM-III's introduction, "generally indicate far greater reliability than had previously been obtained from DSM-II." Since similar studies have not been conducted with DSM-II, the basis for the comparison is unknown. (Previous reliability studies either lacked criteria or failed to describe them.)

Reliability was expressed using the kappa statistic, which corrects for chance agreement. For DSM-III purposes, a high kappa (.70 and above) indicates good agreement between two clinicians as to whether the patient had a disorder within a diagnostic class, even if they disagreed about the specific disorder within the class. For example, a diagnosis of paranoid-type schizophrenia by one clinician and of catatonic-type schizophrenia by another was considered agreement on schizophrenia. Similarly, if one clinician diagnosed borderline personality disorder and the other schizotypal personality disorder, this was considered agreement that a patient had a personality disorder.

The reliability for most classes was considered "quite good," particularly for schizophrenia and major affective disorders. Reliability was low for personality disorders and for adjustment disorders, a diagnostic category applied to one-third of children and adolescents. In general, reliability with children and adolescents was only fair.

A comment about the term reliability is needed here. Diagnostic reliability refers to three different measures: agreement between independent diagnosticians examining the same patients, stability in diagnoses over time, and similarity in diagnostic frequencies for comparable samples. Of the three, interjudge agreement is by far the most important. As noted by Spitzer and Fleiss (1974), there are inherent limitations to the other two uses of the term. For agreement between initial and subsequent diagnoses, one must consider that some of the disagreement may be due to changes in the patient's condition and not only to unreliability. The difficulty with interpreting differences in populations is that one must assume that the populations do not differ in psychopathology, when in fact they may.

In their paper reviewing reliability studies, Spitzer and Fleiss (1974) showed considerable acumen regarding the pitfalls encountered in reliability studies. They reviewed five such studies and found low rates of reliability in all. Because, as they pointed out, some degree of agreement occurs by chance, they designed the kappa statistic, which incorporates a correction for chance.

Spitzer and Fleiss (1974), after reviewing the dismal state of diagnostic reliability in American psychiatry, supported the introduction of explicit diagnostic criteria and the standard interview schedule. "We are confident," Spitzer and Fleiss wrote, "that this merging [of diagnostic criteria and structured interviews] will result not only in improved reliability but in improved validity which is, after all, our ultimate goal." Feighner et al. (1972) published a system of 16 diagnoses, which ultimately became the model for DSM-III (with its 230 diagnoses!). The advantages of structuring interviews became apparent at about the same time; starting with the St. Louis and New York groups, structured interviews began appearing in profusion.

In view of the importance attached to the structured interview, it is surprising that no mention is made in DSM-III of how the information was obtained in the field-trial reliability studies. Was a structured interview used? Was the interview semistructured? Was there *any* interview schedule?

Structured Interview

With the proliferation of structured interviews over the past decade, it has become obvious that the interview is perhaps as important as diagnostic criteria in reliability studies. There are now at least a score of structured diagnostic interview schedules, six of them developed principally by Spitzer and Endicott of the New York State Psychiatric Institute (Hedlund & Vieweg, 1981). (Spitzer, of course, was the admirable chairman and dominant spirit of the DSM-III committee.)

Structured interviews, like criteria, have inherent problems (Goodwin, 1981). Some of the problems are as follows:

1. One never knows whether interviewers asked the questions in the same way.
2. Often, one does not know the experience, training, or biases of the interviewers, who range from moonlighting housewives to venerable academics.

3. One never knows whether the subject understood the question, listened, lied, or had a faulty memory. Regarding memory, the question "How well do people remember life changes?" was raised in a study of 416 normal subjects (Jenkins, Hurst, & Rose, 1979). Life events were assessed at two examinations 8 months apart. At the second examination, subjects were asked to report events during the 6-month period preceding the first examination. At the later examination, subjects "forgot" more than one-third of the events reported at the first examination, including such items as being in an automobile accident or being the victim of a crime.

4. One does not know how interviewers decide to weight answers. If a man was scolded once by a fundamentalist wife for having a beer at a ball game, is the item "Family complains about drinking" scored positive? If he had one blackout at age 19, is he scored positive for blackouts? If he thinks he had a blackout but is not sure, what then? The interviewer's judgment is required, but interviewers differ widely in judgment and in other ways. To a large extent, the content of the interview is dictated by the criteria, but not entirely: Subtle differences in the wording of questions may yield different responses; some interviews "probe," whereas others do not; and some questions are open ended, whereas others are multiple choice with forced responses.

Overall and Hollister (1979a) compared six studies using different interviews and found that diagnoses varied widely depending on the interview. Kendell, Brockington, and Leff (1979) found a low concordance of various diagnostic criteria with clinical diagnoses and also a low concordance between various diagnostic criteria.

In an exchange of letters discussing the merits of diagnostic criteria, Overall and Hollister (1979b) charged that diagnostic criteria are being widely and uncritically adopted without validation. Spitzer, Endicott, and Williams (1979) wrote that the purpose of the Washington University, the New York, and the DSM-III criteria was to improve clinical practice by incorporating into diagnostic criteria distinctions shown by research studies to have validity in terms of course, response to therapy, familial pattern, and so forth. Overall and Hollister (1979b) suggested that there was little documentation for this claim, and cited one study in which "the better of the objective research diagnostic criteria was as good at predicting outcome as were the original clinical criteria," but no better. They also pointed out the critical difference that specific wording of diagnostic criteria can make. They concluded that not only are diagnostic criteria being formulated and published without validation, but continued revision renders existing sets of criteria obsolete before they can be evaluated: "That appears to be one sure way to keep ahead of the scientific community, but it fails to provide evidence that change constitutes improvement."

The DSM-III manual mentions neither interviews nor some other "facts of life" about reliability studies. For example, Sanson-Fisher and Martin (1981) pointed out that disagreements in interview administration may not always reflect scoring disagreements. Interviewers may agree in the scoring of responses, but disagree about the administration of the interview. If this occurs and the reliability of interviewing is not checked, investigators may think reliability has been achieved when in fact it has not. Because reliability depends on the interaction between the interview administration and scoring, both components must be tested.

Implicit in the DSM-III field trials is the assumption that, once agreement has been reached between interviewers, it is thereafter stable and maintained over time. In fact, in those studies in which reliability has been checked over time, the results indicate that agreement does not remain stable. Even when reliability between raters is maintained, "accuracy" may decline, if "accuracy" refers to the extent to which ratings accord with the criteria defined at the inception of the study. Raters may consensually change the manner in which they apply codes and definitions over time. O'Leary and Kanowitz (1975) found that observers who frequently discussed and compared ratings developed their own, rather than using the investigators' interpretations of codes. Although the raters still displayed high agreement, they had as a group "drifted" away from the standards applied at the beginning of the study and were therefore making "inaccurate" but reliable observations.

One reason reliability may not be stable over time is that one or more raters develop an idiosyncratic style of scoring. Also, as found in one study (Reid & Paul, 1976), interrater agreement may fall when observers believe their ratings are no longer being checked for reliability. For these reasons, continuous monitoring of reliability over the period of a study appears advisable. Assessment alone may not reveal consensual drift, with agreement between raters remaining high while accuracy declines, but such drift may be controlled by continually training interviewers together. As noted, if observers know that reliability is being assessed, they apply the rating standards more stringently in an effort to achieve the required level of agreement. Thus, *covert* reliability checks are advisable.

O'Leary and Kanowitz (1975) found that if observers were informed of what to expect in an interview and were given feedback by the investigator in the form of approval or disapproval of the results, observations were found to be biased in the desired direction. Therefore, investigators should give few indications as to the desirability of the obtained results.

Finally, according to Sanson-Fisher and Martin (1981), the "appropriate unit of data on which reliability is calculated should be dependent upon the unit of data used in the analysis." Choice of units can lead to marked differences. The greatest differences appear when disorders requiring a sum of individual scores are compared with ratings of the presence of individual symptoms. Because it is difficult to know in advance what combinations will be desirable in future analyses, some have recommended that reliability calculations be carried out at the level of the individual item and that the full range of the rating scales be utilized—something *not* done in the DSM-III field trials.

Validity

Without reliability (agreement), it is said that there is no hope for validity (truth). This statement is an oversimplification. Although in the parable, the three blind men who described an elephant after touching the elephant at different places—the trunk, the tail, and the leg—were truthful in what they described, the kappa was low. Validity obviously is the ultimate goal. Has DSM-III made the goal more achievable? One must ask what validity is when referring to psychiatric disorders. Just because people agree about something does not mean that what they agree upon is true. How does one know what is true?

In the case of diagnosis, truth equals prediction (Goodwin & Guze, 1988). Information is useful if it predicts accurately. If the diagnostic criteria in DSM-III accurately predict course, treatment response, illness in the family, pathogenesis, and (ultimately) etiology, then these criteria are valuable indeed. The problem is that the criteria are new and are only now being introduced into studies. The easy and fun part was sitting around a table inventing criteria. The hard part follows. Conducting large systematic studies with long follow-ups is tedious and *very* expensive. Without these studies, however, we will never know whether DSM-III criteria actually predict anything. If they do not predict anything, they may be reliable but worthless.

CHILDHOOD DISORDERS

Even more than is true for adult disorders, the psychopharmacological literature is inconsistent and in some cases contradictory in describing children's disorders. Not only is the literature on pharmacotherapeutic approaches to childhood disorders less well developed than for adults, the confusion is compounded by recent changes in DSM nomenclature. Drug studies on disorders such as autism and separation anxiety often yield findings that do not replicate previously published results. For example, although several drugs have been reported to ameliorate the symptoms of autism, negative findings also have been reported that cast doubt on the usefulness of any drug (Campbell & Spencer, 1988).

On the other hand, attention deficit hyperactivity disorder (ADHD) is generally believed to be amenable to pharmacotherapy (Cantwell & Baker, 1988). ADHD is one of the few clinical problems seen by child psychiatrists that often responds quickly and well to small amounts of medication. Although there has been considerable controversy, including extramedical condemnation, about using medication for ADHD, the intensity of these feelings as reflected in lay periodicals and psychological literature has diminished (Henker & Whalen, 1989). It seems unfair to withhold a relatively low-risk drug, such as methylphenidate, which can reverse the downward "behavioral spiral" described by Schulman (1967) and others. Often a child's symptoms lead to scholastic underachievement, punishment, and social opprobrium that damages his or her self-concept and generates anger. Secondary problems of behavioral disorder and/or depression can develop. If the medication is prescribed on school days only, the likelihood of the child's developing drug tolerance is reduced and a positive feedback loop is created analogous to that developed during behavior modification. Instead of being criticized and punished, leading to a sense of failure, the child experiences positive feedback that rewards productivity. The more adaptive behavior tends to be reinforced by the environment. This process can lead to further improvement even after medication is discontinued. Perhaps nowhere else in the DSM-III-R section on child disorders can the connection between a solid diagnosis, based on specific criteria, and therapeutic effects be so demonstrated. A fuzzier syndrome (of which there are many in child psychiatry) surely would have produced the Type I or Type II errors discussed earlier. Clinical investigators should be encouraged to continually refine and redefine diagnostic groups toward progressive improvement in the match of diagnosis with treatment.

The significant changes in the way disruptive behaviors of childhood and adolescence are characterized in DSM-III-R, compared with DSM-III, are perplexing. For instance, although the clinician had the option of diagnosing attention deficit disorder without hyperactivity using DSM-III, DSM-III-R does not offer this option except in a category called undifferentiated attention deficit disorder. This change occurred despite the fact that some highly regarded academic child and adolescent psychiatrists believe that attention deficit disorder without hyperactivity is an actual entity. Fortunately, indications for drug therapy remain the same.

DSM-III coined the term "conduct disorder" (replacing the DSM-II term "socialized aggressive reaction") and divided it into four categories, depending on whether the behavior reflected undersocialization and/or whether it was aggressive in nature. DSM-III-R abandoned the undersocialized and/or aggressive distinction in favor of dividing conduct disorder into three types based on whether the symptoms occurred in a group context or as a solitary aggressive activity. The basis for the change seems arbitrary, based on a perusal of the literature, but in any case the change will add to the difficulties of replication inevitable in replacing older "rules" for newer ones for no apparent reason.

Conduct disorder has a complex etiology and no definitive treatment. Drugs can be helpful, however, for certain target symptoms. For example, a tricyclic antidepressant may improve underlying depressive elements. Haloperidol in low doses can decrease agitation. Beta-blockers or carbamazepine often diminish aggressive, impulsive behavior when organic features are present.

DSM-III-R does, however, take a major step forward in listing the criteria for all three disruptive behavior disorders—attention deficit hyperactivity disorder, conduct disorder, and oppositional defiant disorder—in "descending order of discriminating power based on data from a national field trial," further refining the criteria's diagnostic usefulness. Citing studies is highly unusual in DSM-III-R, a volume largely produced by consensus of experts, who sometimes took votes.

DRUG DEVELOPMENT[3]

Drug development for primarily financial and regulatory reasons is dependent upon research strategies that are based on current conceptualizations of

---

[3] This section has been modified with permission from the publisher from a paper by S. Preskorn (in press).

psychiatric disorders. Our current diagnostic schemes dictate the way we develop new agents. The structure is helpful to the extent that our diagnostic schemes are accurate. To the extent that they are not, progress is retarded. As new agents with novel actions are developed, we must be prepared to modify our diagnostic schemes. We must use such agents to prompt us to better define diagnostic categories and to gain new insights into the pathophysiology of psychiatric disorders.

An unresolved issue in linguistics and anthropology is "whether thought determines language or language determines thought." The parallel issue in psychopharmacology and psychiatry is "whether conceptualization of disease states determines pharmacological discoveries or whether pharmacological discoveries determine conceptualization of disease states." For optimum progress, we must recognize that a reciprocity exists between the disease states and the pharmacological discoveries.

The early years of the modern era of psychopharmacology are replete with examples of serendipity that resulted in a rethinking of psychiatric nosology. An example is lithium carbonate. Although the distinction between manic–depressive illness and schizophrenia had been made years earlier, it tended to be forgotten in the United States until the discovery of the antimanic actions of lithium. Lithium studies were initiated to find an antischizophrenic agent, but lithium instead was found to be useful for a group of affect-laden chronic psychotic patients subsequently rediagnosed as suffering from manic–depressive illness. Similarly, neuroleptics were initially tested as antianxiety agents and tricyclic antidepressants as better antipsychotic agents. Had these compounds not been tested with a broad spectrum of psychiatric disorders, their efficacy may have gone unrecognized.

Today, the highly systematized, regulated, and lockstep approach to drug development reduces researchers' abilities to test compounds in such a wide variety of patients. Costs become prohibitive. Moreover, developing a drug for a new, unrecognized indication is a risky and difficult proposition. There are technical problems: How does the researcher quantitate response? What is the spontaneous remission rate? There are political problems: Will the regulators, the profession, and the public accept the concept of a new disorder so that the drug can be approved and successfully marketed before its patent expires?

Within a phenomenologically similar group of disorders, (e.g., the schizophrenias), it is likely that several etiologically different disorders exist. A strategic question is how to recognize the efficacy of a novel agent that is uniquely effective in a small subsegment of the larger phenotype. Such sensitivity will have both immediate and long-term implications. From an immediate standpoint, such sensitivity will allow the development of drugs for patients refractory to existing agents. In the long term, it can lead to the recognition of a pathophysiologically and/or etiologically distinct subtype of the larger phenotypic disorder. Such information will improve our classificatory system, promote and facilitate further research, and subsequently lead to an improved fundamental understanding of both the subset disorder and the general disorder by removing the noise generated by lumping distinct entities together in syndrome-based research studies.

For example, pharmacological data suggest at least three subtypes of major depressive disorders: melancholia, which responds best to tricyclic antidepressants; an atypical form, which responds to monoamine oxidase inhibitors; and a psychotic form, which requires either electroconvulsive therapy or combination therapy with an antidepressant plus an antipsychotic. This subdivision is further supported by the phenomenological differences in age of onset and family history among the three disorders. Thus, it seems possible that there are similar subtypes of anxiety disorders, schizophrenias, and alcoholism, to name but a few.

With the advent of DSM-III, the predominant view of psychiatric disorders is based on a model in which the "diseases" are defined by a cluster of symptoms. In this regard, we must remember the warning of Thomas Sydenham (1922):

In writing the history of a disease, every philosophical hypothesis whatsoever, that has previously occupied the mind of the author, should lie in abeyance. This being done, the clear and natural phenomena of the disease should be noted—these, and these only. They should be noted accurately, and in all their minuteness; in imitation of the exquisite industry of those painters who represent in their portraits the smallest moles and the faintest spots. No man can state the errors that have been occasioned by these physiological hypotheses. Writers, whose minds have taken a false colour under their influence, have saddled diseases with phenomena which existed in their own brains only; but which would have been clear and visible to the whole world had the assumed hypothesis been true. Add to this, that if by chance some symptoms really coincide accurately with their hypothesis, and occur in the disease whereof they would describe the character, they magnify it beyond all measure and moderation; they make it all and in all; the molehill becomes a mountain; whilst, if it fail to tally with said hypothesis, they pass it over either in perfect silence or with only an incidental mention, unless, by means of some philosophical subtlety, they can enlist it in their service, or else, by fair means or foul, accommodate it in some way or other to their doctrines.

We know that many patients have features of more than one disorder. Does this fact mean that they have multiple disorders or that they have a single disorder that is pathophysiologically and/or etiologically distinct from the disorders with which it shares symptoms?

It is also possible that some neurochemically defined personality traits are independent of any disease state, but interact with several disease states to result in shared features' being apparent. For example, a neurochemically defined dimension from aggressiveness to passiveness conceivably exists that is etiologically independent of several disorders (e.g., alcoholism, schizophrenia, and anxiety disorders) but that modifies the expression of the underlying disease state so that patients with different illnesses share clinical features.

The reason these issues are important is that advances in psychopharmacology may occur ahead of advances in psychiatric nomenclature. With the ability to isolate and define neuronal mechanisms, we can develop agents that influence them before we fully understand the function these mechanisms subsume in human behavior. The development of such drugs may require use of novel strategies, sensitivity to responsiveness in small groups of patients, and recognition that novel agents may work in disorders that are not well defined at the present time.

An example of psychopharmacology preceding psychiatric nomenclature is the development of several classes of drugs that selectively affect the serotonin system. The classes include serotonin-selective reuptake inhibitors, such as fluoxetine and fluvoxamine, and selective serotonin receptor agents, such as 5HTIA agonists, of which buspirone is the prototype. These two types of drugs, through their selective effects on this system (to some extent, opposing or push–pull effects), may both provide useful additions to our therapeutic armamentarium and serve as probes into the behavioral pharmacology of serotonin in man. Considerable evidence from a variety of sources, including anatomy, physiology, chemistry, and pharmacology, indicates that serotonin is an important modulator of the expression of the personality dimension from passiveness to aggressiveness. The development of such agents can simultaneously lead to improved treatment of patients, advance our understanding of the neurochemistry of personality, and provide a means of modifying personality traits independent of disease states, leading to improved resolution of the disease state boundaries by removing the noise caused by the overlap of independent personality traits.

As we learn more about brain function and psychopharmacology, we may have to radically modify our concepts of psychiatric disease. Not only are genetic techniques improving, but our knowledge is progressing in terms of our ability to localize higher cortical functions through a multitude of strategies, including various brain imaging devices (e.g., emission tomography). We are on the threshold of localizing brain regions important in the cortical representation of such higher functions as anxiety, sadness, and vigilance. We know that different pathophysiological processes(e.g., infarction, demyelination, trauma, infection) can produce phenotypically similar neurological presentations by disrupting the functional integrity of the same brain regions. Conversely, the same disease process (e.g., demyelination) can produce phenotypically different clinical syndromes by affecting different brain regions in different patients. With advanced brain imaging techniques, we may well learn more about localization of higher brain functions than we may about disease process.

Advances in psychopharmacology will provide an additional tool in this process, as well as a means of treating more patients. Advances in understanding will come through the development of medications with selective influences on specific neurotransmitter systems. We currently have a number of such medication probes to dissect and test the relationship between serotonin mechanisms and human behavior. Such medications can be used as probes to understand the behavioral neurochemistry of such systems. This knowledge is complementary to that derived from brain imaging studies in psychiatric disorders. With the imaging studies based on metabolic rate markers (e.g., positron emission tomography) or tissue structural integrity (e.g., magnetic resonance imaging), the investigator may not be certain whether the abnormality is in the region of altered function or a system that projects to that region, or whether it involves fibers of passage. Our understanding will be facilitated by knowing what systems are present in those regions and then using medications as probes to dissect the functional integrity of such systems. Eventually, ligand and imaging technology will permit direct testing of whether the behavioral pharmacology of a specific medication probe is due to an abnormality in specific groups of patients.

The current nosology may inhibit rather than promote progress in developing such agents. Current nosology is based on symptom clusters (i.e., syndromes) rather than on pathophysiology. Current diagnostic categories may well represent artificial groups, erroneously including some patients with the different pathophysiologies in the same diagnostic group and erroneously dividing patients with the same pathophysiology into different diagnostic groups because of apparent differences in symptomatology.

The problem is that medications under Food and Drug Administration (FDA) regulations must be developed for specific indications. To the extent that our diagnostic system is in error, the development of highly selective compounds will be hindered. Such compounds may well work only for subgroups within a current diagnostic category and have effects on pathophysiologically related subgroups in another diagnostic category. Given current clinical trial methodology and clinical knowledge, the signal-to-noise ratio may be such that effective compounds are not detected. Conversely, when a compound with a novel mechanism is approved, further work should be done in the clinical setting to better define the medication's spectrum of clinical effects. Knowledge gained through such work may better refine our diagnostic system.

SUMMARY

Has DSM-III or DSM-III-R benefited pharmacotherapy? At this point, the answer obviously is no. Drug trials incorporating DSM-III criteria are just beginning. Despite caveats, however, there is room for optimism. DSM-III is the most explicit definitional system ever created in psychiatry (or, for that matter, in medicine generally). It makes possible a precision of communication not possible in the pre-DSM-III dark ages. Of equal importance, DSM-III is largely agnostic in its philosophy. For the first time, psychiatrists have produced an official nomenclature based on the premise that they do not know the cause of the disorders they describe.

In previous DSM manuals, description and explanation were wedded so intimately that one could not tell them apart. Moreover, the explanations were undiluted and unabashedly psychoanalytical at a time when psychoanalysis was the most popular "school" in American psychiatry, but certainly not the only one. In DSM-II, neurosis is "defined" as anxiety that may be "felt and expressed directly or controlled *unconsciously* and automatically by *conversion, displacement,* and various other *psychological mechanisms*" (emphasis added). One wonders what Rogerians and behaviorists thought of all this.

DSM-III's highly touted reliability studies may not have been as thorough as one might wish. Validity is problematical. Of the 230 categories in the book, perhaps only 12 are based on a clinical literature involving follow-up studies, and therefore have possible predictive value.

With increasing sophistication in drug development, advances in our understanding of brain function and psychopharmacology may occur ahead of advances in psychiatric nomenclature. In time, we may have to modify radically our concepts of psychiatric disease. Indeed, in developing new drugs, the current nosology may inhibit rather than promote progress by including patients with different pathophysiologies in the same diagnostic group. FDA regulations further complicate matters by basing specific indications for a drug on current nosology. When a compound with a novel mechanism is approved, it is important that further clinical work be performed to better define the medication's spectrum of clinical effects. Psychiatrists are becoming increasingly aware of their ignorance and of the complexity of their field. DSM-III both reflects this new spirit and helped bring it about. Over the long run, pharmacotherapy cannot help but benefit.

REFERENCES

American Psychiatric Association (1980). *Diagnostic and statistical manual of mental disorders* (3rd ed.). Washington, DC: Author.

American Psychiatric Association. (1987). *Diagnostic and statistical manual of mental disorders* (3rd ed. rev.). Washington, DC: Author.

Bunney, W. E., & Garland-Bunney, B. L. (1989). Mechanism of action of lithium. In H. Y. Meltzer (Ed.), *Psychopharmacology*. New York: Raven Press.

Campbell, M., & Spencer, E. K. (1988). Psychopharmacology in child and adolescent psychiatry: A review of the past five years. *Journal of the American Academy of Child and Adolescent Psychiatry, 27*, 269–279.

Cantwell, D. P., & Baker, L. (1988). Issues in the classification of child and adolescent psychopathology. *Journal of the American Academy of Child and Adolescent Psychiatry, 27*, 521–533.

Davis, J. M., Gibbons, R. D., Pandey, G. N., & Javard, J. A. (1981). Mechanism: Mathematics and markers of mental disorders. In E. Verden & D. Hamen (Eds.), *Biological markers in psychiatric and neurological disorders*. New York: Pergamon Press.

Feighner, J. P., Robins, E., Guze, S. B., Woodruff, R. A., Winokur, G., & Munoz, R. (1972). Diagnosis criteria for use in psychiatric research. *Archives of General Psychiatry, 26*, 57–63.

Gildea, E. F. (1958, December). Seminar on the brain. Present status of the schizophrenia problem. *American Journal of Medicine*, pp. 942–947.

Goodwin, D. W. (1981). Family studies on alcoholism. *Journal of Studies on Alcohol, 42*, 156–162.

Goodwin, D. W., & Guze, S. B. (1988). *Psychiatric diagnosis* (4th ed.). New York: Oxford University Press.

Hedlund, J. L., & Vieweg, B. W. (1981). Structured psychiatric interviews: A comparative review. *Journal of Operational Psychiatry, 12*, 39–67.

Henker, B., & Whalen, C. K. (1989). Hyperactivity and attention deficits. *American Psychologist, 44*, 216–223.

Jenkins, C. D., Hurst, M. W., & Rose, R. M. (1979). Life changes: Do people really remember? *Archives of General Psychiatry, 36,* 379–384.

Kendall, R. E., Brockington, J. F., & Leff, J. P. (1979). Prognostic implications of six alternative definitions of schizophrenia. *Archives of General Psychiatry, 36,* 25–31.

Klerman, G., & Cole, J. (1965). Clinical pharmacology of imipramine and related antidepressant compounds. *Pharmacology Review, 17,* 101–141.

Morris, J., & Beck, A. (1974). The efficacy of antidepressant drugs. *Archives of General Psychiatry, 30,* 667–674.

O'Leary, C. D., & Kanowitz, J. (1975). Shaping data collection congruent with experimental hypotheses. *Journal of Applied Behavior Analysis, 8,* 43–51.

Overall, J. E., & Hollister, L. E. (1979a). Comparative evaluation of research diagnostic criteria for schizophrenia. *Archives of General Psychiatry, 36,* 1198–1205.

Overall, J. E., & Hollister, L. E. (1979b). In reply to Spitzer et al. "Research diagnostic criteria." *Archives of General Psychiatry, 36,* 1382–1383.

Preskorn, S. (in press). The future of psychopharmacology: The needs and potential. *Psychiatric Annals.*

Raskin, A. (1974). A guide for drug use in depressive disorders. *American Journal of Psychiatry, 131,* 181–185.

Reid, J., & Paul, G. L. (1976). Reliability assessment of observation data: A possible methodological problem. *Child Development, 41,* 1143–1150.

Sanson-Fisher, R. W., & Martin, C. J. (1981). Standardized interviews in psychiatry: Issues of reliability. *British Journal of Psychiatry, 139,* 138–143.

Schulman, J. L. (1967). *Management of emotional disorders in pediatric practice.* Chicago: Year Book Medical Publishers.

Spitzer, R. L., Endicott, J., & Williams, J. B. W. (1979). Research diagnostic criteria [Letter to the editor]. *Archives of General Psychiatry, 36,* 1381–1382.

Spitzer, R. L., & Fleiss, J. L. (1974). A re-analysis of the reliability of psychiatric diagnosis. *British Journal of Psychiatry, 125,* 341–347.

Sydenham, T. (1922). *Selected Works of Thomas Sydenham, M. D.* London: John Bales & Sons.

Welner, A., Welner, Z., & Robins, E. (1980). Effect of tricyclic antidepressants on individual symptoms. *Journal of Clinical Psychiatry, 41,* 306–309.

Wortis, J. (1989). Editorial. *Biological Psychiatry, 25,* 371–373.

Author Index

Subject Index